HISTORY OF NORDIC COMPUTING

IFIP – The International Federation for Information Processing

IFIP was founded in 1960 under the auspices of UNESCO, following the First World Computer Congress held in Paris the previous year. An umbrella organization for societies working in information processing, IFIP's aim is two-fold: to support information processing within its member countries and to encourage technology transfer to developing nations. As its mission statement clearly states,

> *IFIP's mission is to be the leading, truly international, apolitical organization which encourages and assists in the development, exploitation and application of information technology for the benefit of all people.*

IFIP is a non-profitmaking organization, run almost solely by 2500 volunteers. It operates through a number of technical committees, which organize events and publications. IFIP's events range from an international congress to local seminars, but the most important are:

- The IFIP World Computer Congress, held every second year;
- Open conferences;
- Working conferences.

The flagship event is the IFIP World Computer Congress, at which both invited and contributed papers are presented. Contributed papers are rigorously refereed and the rejection rate is high.

As with the Congress, participation in the open conferences is open to all and papers may be invited or submitted. Again, submitted papers are stringently refereed.

The working conferences are structured differently. They are usually run by a working group and attendance is small and by invitation only. Their purpose is to create an atmosphere conducive to innovation and development. Refereeing is less rigorous and papers are subjected to extensive group discussion.

Publications arising from IFIP events vary. The papers presented at the IFIP World Computer Congress and at open conferences are published as conference proceedings, while the results of the working conferences are often published as collections of selected and edited papers.

Any national society whose primary activity is in information may apply to become a full member of IFIP, although full membership is restricted to one society per country. Full members are entitled to vote at the annual General Assembly, National societies preferring a less committed involvement may apply for associate or corresponding membership. Associate members enjoy the same benefits as full members, but without voting rights. Corresponding members are not represented in IFIP bodies. Affiliated membership is open to non-national societies, and individual and honorary membership schemes are also offered.

HISTORY OF NORDIC COMPUTING

IFIP WG9.7 First Working Conference on the History of Nordic Computing (HiNC1), June 16-18, 2003, Trondheim, Norway

Edited by

Janis Bubenko, Jr
Royal Institute of Technology and University of Stockhom
Sweden

John Impagliazzo
Hofstra University
United States

Arne Sølvberg
Norwegian University of Science and Technology
Norway

 Springer

Library of Congress Cataloging-in-Publication Data

A C.I.P. Catalogue record for this book is available from the Library of Congress.

History of Nordic Computing/ Edited by Janis Bubenko, Jr, John Impagliazzo, Arne Sølveberg

p.cm. (The International Federation for Information Processing)

ISBN: (HB) 0-387-24167-1 / (eB00K) 0-387-24168-X   Printed on acid-free paper.

Printed in the United States of America.

9 8 7 6 5 4 3 2 1   SPIN 11369905 (HC) / 11370178 (eBook)
springeronline.com

Dedication

Contents

Preface

Computing in the Nordic countries started in late 1940s mainly as an engineering activity to build computing devices to perform mathematical calculations and assist mathematicians and engineers in scientific problem solving. The early computers of the Nordic countries emerged during the 1950s and had names like BARK, BESK, DASK, SMIL, SARA, ESKO, and NUSSE. Each of them became a nucleus in institutes and centres for mathematical computations programmed and used by highly qualified professionals. However, one should not forget the punched-card machine technology at this time that had existed for several decades. In addition, we have a Nordic name, namely Frederik Rosing Bull, contributing to the fundaments of punched card technology and forming the French company Bull.

Commercial products such as FACIT EDB and SAAB D20-series computers in Sweden, the Danish GIER computer, the Nokia MIKKO computer in Finland, as well as the computers of Norsk Data in Norway followed the early computers. In many cases, however, companies and institutions did not further develop or exploit Nordic computing hardware, even though it exhibited technical advantages. Consequently, in the 1970s, US computers, primarily from IBM, flooded the Nordic market.

Nordic activities in programming, software, and in information systems methodology were, however, more farsighted and more successful. The Nordic countries can claim to host initiative takers to developing and standardising the programming language Algol, the establishment of a theoretical approach to analysis and development of information systems, as well as originators of object-oriented programming and object-oriented development. These are only three examples, and we can find many more in theoretical computer science as well as in practical applications of computing technology.

The Nordic cooperation and exchange was intense during the 1960s, 1970s, and 1980s. The NordSAM conferences, focusing mainly on theoretical aspects, as well as the NordDATA conferences, focusing on a wide range of aspects of computing and applications of computing, drew more than 2000 delegates in annual events, rotating among the Nordic countries. During these years exchange and collaboration between the Nordic countries was remarkably intense. Much of the activities of NordSAM and NordDATA must be attributed to the compassionate work of the different data and information processing professionals and professional societies of the Nordic countries.

There is no question that computers and information technology has had a tremendous effect on the Nordic countries and societies, not only technically but also socially and culturally. The kind of education in information technology, offered in the Nordic countries, differs to a large degree from what appears in other countries, including USA. There seems to be a Nordic consensus that IT, information technology, can and should be used for the benefit of members of the society. This has led to the fact that the Nordic countries are now among the most IT-dense and intense countries in the world. Education in IT in schools and in universities not only focuses on the technical aspects of computers and programming, but also on economical, organisational, human, and social aspects as well. This is supposed to give the students a broader view of IT and the application of IT.

One cannot deal with "Nordic Computing History" without looking inside for the quite interesting "Nordic History of Educational Computing". The process of integrating computing in education on all levels in the educational system goes beyond the technical development of computers and programs. It also incorporates changes in deep traditions, changes in attitudes and policies, reorganising curriculum, and much more. We have seen that this process and the interaction between the political, the educational, and the computer world is, among other themes, were part of the conference and appear in these proceedings.

The general conference topic area includes a wide range of aspects of computing in the Nordic countries, such as programming languages, systems development, education, Nordic co-operation, and the Nordic computer industry. The historical period addressed at the conference covers the time from the early computer age until around 1985. This leads up to the birth of the public networks, but will not cover the merging of data processing and telecommunications.

The Nordic computing started with hardware such as BARK, BESK, and DASK. Why have we come into the position we are now? Could we have done better? What, in the past, did we do well and which decisions were poor? What can we learn from the past? How should we continue in the future?

Consequently, the aim of this conference on Nordic Computing History is to be a first attempt to collect information about its past in order to document our experience and knowledge, which future generations may use in order to make wiser decisions about future endeavours in information technology in the Nordic countries.

The editors would like to stress that the current volume is not to be seen as a comprehensive textbook on Nordic Computing History. The presentations at the conference varied from personal position statements and personal memories to historically well-researched papers. Scholars in the topic in computing history dominantly wrote the latter. Furthermore, the different Nordic countries are not equally well represented in the texts of this book. In particular, the participation of Sweden and Denmark was below expectation. The editors hope this situation will improve at a second conference on the History of Nordic Computing. There is still a considerable wealth of historical knowledge about Nordic Computing in the period 1945–1985 to gather and discuss.

Trondheim, 2004 November

Janis Bubenko, Jr.
John Impagliazzo
Arne Sølvberg

Conference Organization

Arne Sølvberg
Conference Chair, Arne.Solvberg@idi.ntnu.no

Janis Bubenko, Jr.
Program Chair, janis@dsv.su.se

John Impagliazzo
IFIP WG 9.7 Chair, John.Impagliazzo@Hofstra.edu

Gro Gregersen
Conference Coordinator, gro.gregersen@dataforeningen.no

Aud Kvam
Organising Chair, Aud.Kvam@adm.ntnu.no

Program Committee

Acknowledgments

The conference was organised by the International Federation for Information Processing (IFIP) Working Group 9.7 on the History of Computing of its Technical Committee 9 (Relationship between Computers and Society), in cooperation with the IFIP Technical Committee 3 on Education. The Organising Committee of the First Conference on the History of Nordic Computing wishes to extend its appreciation to the following groups:

- The Norwegian University of Science and Technology (Norges teknisk-naturvitenskapelige universitet - NTNU) for hosting the conference and for sponsoring its organization,
- The Norwegian Data Processing Society for its support in sponsoring the conference
- The Special Interest Group on Computer Science Education (SIGCSE) of the Association for Computing Machinery (ACM) for its in-cooperation status and for its donation of 200 copies of its *inroads* Special Issue on Women and Computing
- The IEEE Computer Society for its permission to reprint papers on Nordic computing from its publication *Annals of the History of Computing* and NTNU for printing and distributing this material

We thank the following donors for additional monetary support
- The SISU Foundation of Sweden
- The Danish Society for Information Processing
- The Icelandic Society for Information Processing
- The Finnish Society for Information Processing
- The Department of Computer-and Information Science at NTNU
- NTNU's Computing Centre
- Norsk Regnesentral (The Norwegian Computing Centre)
- Telenor ASA
- SINTEF

REFLECTIONS, THOUGHTS, AND EPISODES
Highlights from the Opening Address

Börje Langefors

Professor emeritus, formerly at the Department of Computer and Systems Science, University of Stockholm and Royal Institute of Technology, Stockholm; borje.langefors@dsv.su.se

My first memory of a congress was when the rebuilt Matematicum in Lund had been finished. A congress of mathematicians celebrated this event. I was amused when professor Riesz, in his opening speech, said, "Congresses are said to be for young strebers and old fools." (The present congress, however, could not be for young strebers, I suppose.)

1.   MISUSE OF STATISTICS

With the advent of computers, a new era was beginning. To make forecasts about it, based upon historic data, should be expected to be misleading. Yet surprisingly, people have made many forecasts on such a basis – without careful thinking.

2.   SAAB

When Saab had begun to develop and apply finite element methods, we experienced a vast increase in need for computations, and our punched-card equipment was not enough. The market for electronic computers was still very scarce and difficult to understand. I visited the Swedish Board for Computing Machinery to ask for advice. I got the answer that they had made a survey (without asking us) of the need for computing and had concluded that when BESC would be finished a year later, it would be able to care for all computing in Sweden, with one third of a shift. (We soon found out that top experts in the USA had made similar estimates). I regarded this as a big mistake. When BESC became operational in 1953, SAAB immediately used one full shift. In 1954, SAAB decided to build the computer SARA. In the 1960s, computer systems enter the market and data systems projects start. They seem to have underestimated systems projects ever since.

3.   LEARN TO MULTIPLY BY TWO

I had always found that my jobs took twice the time I had thought — and had promised. Later I began to realize that I was not alone. Surveys in the USA had found that it was normal that projects took twice the estimated time and cost. Therefore, I formulated the *theorem of underestimation.*

One day when I was to lecture on this, my morning newspaper happened to present big headings, saying that the cost for renovation of the Stockholm Opera Cellar restaurant had run up to twice the estimate and so the name *Opera Cellar theorem* appeared. Later, they had to rename it as the *Huddinge Hospital theorem.*

Multiplication by two is simple, but psychology, it is very, very hard! So, here are some questions?

- What would have happened if decision-makers had been able to multiply?
- Many investments rejected? Slower project development? Delays?
- Or, saved time and avoided backlashes?
- No IT-balloon, or not yet?

4.   FROM DATA TO INFORMATION = KNOWLEDGE

"Everything that can be put in words can be put clearly"
> - *Wittgenstein (famous among philosophers for being impossible to understand)*

"I find it Impossible to express myself in a way that cannot be misunderstood by those who want to misunderstand"
> - *Karl Popper*

5.   THE INFOLOGICAL EQUATION

The Infological Equation (IE)[a] may be shocking, but it does in fact merely combine available knowledge, in a concise way:

> The information I that can be obtained from some data D, depends upon the data <u>and</u> upon the "pre-knowledge" S available to the data user and upon the time t allowed for the interpretation; that is,
> $I = i(D, S, t)$

The basis for the Infological Equation is obvious: To be able to send or receive the information I, one must know the language used to form the message as a minimum.   The point is that once one reflects further, there turns out to be an endless continuation of factors (not all of them of a clearly knowledge character) that influence upon the creation of the data by the sender, and upon the interpretation by the receiver/user.

The time interval t allowed to the interpretation process, is no less important.   It reminds you to be short – and clear – in reporting to a busy CEO (not because he is stupid).   It could also, however, suggest to the decision-maker to involve more people in the decision process (delegate), to gain time and make more pre-knowledge available.

It may take time to recall relevant pre-knowledge, in creative moments it may take away a night's sleep.   Because of the Infological Equation, we have to conclude that the above statement by Wittgenstein is mistaken while we get the intuition that the Infological Equation supports Popper.

The Infological Equation indicates many consequences:
- Perceived, non-linguistic patterns are also data D.
- IE refutes positivistic ambitions.
- Data do not *contain* information.
- Words do not have unique meaning.
- User involvement in data design is necessary.
- The time symbol in IE has important consequences.
- Language translation is impossible to computerize. [b]
- Knowledge atoms do not exist.

5.1   Application of the Infological Equation

In practice, is the IE important?   Does S indeed vary among persons?   It would have been interesting to see empiric studies published on this.

5.2   Lorca Infologico

Strangely enough, the first illustration I found of the IE appeared in a poem by Garcia Lorca called *Canción de Jinete* (Song of the Rider), where he first describes how the man prepares carefully for his ride to Córdoba, and then says:

> *Aunque sepa los caminos*
> *Nunca llegaréa Córdoba*
>
> *Although I know the roads*
> *Never shall I arrive in Córdoba.*

The inherent logical contradiction is resolved if we remember – infologically – that a word can have different meanings: "Córdoba" may refer to the "vision or dream of Córdoba", in addition to referring to the house collection with that name, and to which the roads lead.

5.3   Clarity or time

I often receive books or papers in which people discuss my work. Of course, I always find myself misunderstood in various details. Perhaps I should have been more explicit. This, however, would have taken more time of me but also of my readers. It might well have exceeded the t of the infological equation. However, of course, I may have misunderstood.

6.   CONCLUSION

Now, of course, people will understand or misunderstand what I have said. I finish now with a wish to all of you for a fascinating conference with many creative misunderstandings.

-- *Börje Langefors*

ENDNOTES

a. See Langefors, Börje: *Essays on Infology* (ed Bo Dahlbom), Studentlitteratur, Lund 1995.

b. Failure of machine translation – An example
(Published by Daniel Ryden, daniel.ryden@sydsvenskan.se)

Input:
"God save our gracious Queen,
Long live our noble Queen!
God save the Queen!
Send her victorious,
Happy and glorious,
Long to reign over us;
God save the Queen!"

This text, after several passes through translation programs became:
"Our expensive hour of value Queen
of long of phase our noble God
of the God in good health of the Queen!
In order to save the Queen!
Victoriously you send longer to its lucky
it and him gloreich he,
In order to prevail over us;
God save the Queen!"

AN INTERVIEW WITH BÖRJE LANGEFORS
From SARA to TAIS

Janis Bubenko and Ingemar Dahlstrand

This interview with professor emeritus Börje Langefors (*BL*) was carried
out by his two former co-workers Ingemar Dahlstrand[1] (*ID*) and Janis
Bubenko[2] (*JB*).

JB: Here we are, the three of us: Börje Langefors, Ingemar Dahlstrand and me,
Janis Bubenko, and we are going to talk about Börje's historical times and
memories. Let us start out with the question: How did you actually get into
computing?

BL: I was working at the NAF[3] industries where my boss and I developed a
machine for dynamic balancing of cardan-shafts. We integrated an analog device
into the machine, which gave the necessary correction indications.

JB: When was that?

BL: That was in 1944, because that cardan-shaft was going into the Volvo PV
444 car. After that, I was transferred to NAF-Linköping. In Linköping, I became
acquainted with Torkel Rand, who recruited me for the SAAB aircraft company (in
1949). There I was to work with analog devices for stress calculations for wings.
Rand had done one-dimensional analyses, which worked reasonably well for
straight wings at right angles to the plane's body. However, when we got into
arrow wings and delta wings, we had to analyze in three dimensions, and that was

---

[1] Formerly manager of the Lund University computing centre. Developed Sweden's first Algol compiler
in 1961.
[2] Professor em. at the Department of Computer and Systems Science at the Royal Institute of Technology
(KTH) and Stockholm University.
[3] NAF – Nordiska Armaturfabrikerna (Nordic Armature Factories)

difficult with analog technique. I knew then about the writings of Gabriel Kron, e.g. his Potential Analysis, and had corresponded with him; also, he had published analog networks simulating framed structures. To these I could add elements corresponding to the wing's shell structure. After that, I wanted to leave analogue devices and switch to digital computation. But this called for enormous capacity, it was on a much larger scale than we had imagined.

JB: Did you know about computers then?

BL: I had visited the national computer centre MNA[4] to see if they could help, I think that was when their relay calculator BARK[5] was just ready. I was then planning a study visit to the U.S.A. to Northrop whose Maddida computer I had read about. I asked MNA's director Conny Palm (well known for statistical work on relays) whether there might be a computer suitable for SAAB. Palm said that would not be necessary, because when their electronic computer BESK[6] was ready (it started to work in December 1953) it would handle all of Sweden's computing needs in one third of a shift. How did he know that? We have investigated the need for computing, he said. That can't have been much of an investigation, I said, you have not asked SAAB, I would have known. In 1954, I made that study trip. I found out that many instrument makers built small computers with magnetic tape, and of course I knew about Univac, but I also learned that IBM had built a computer similar to BESK, but with tapes. IBM did not believe in a market for such a computer, but had contracted to build seven of them for the defense industry, as a sort of patriotic gesture.

JB: Was that before the IBM 700 series?

BL: Yes, but perhaps the 700 series developed from it. They called it the Defense Calculator. I wanted to have a look at it, but our Air Force attaché in Washington, Stig Wennerström (later to become famous when caught as a Soviet spy) said that it was impossible. Nevertheless, he did arrange a visit to Douglas Aircraft, Santa Monica. When I thanked him, he said, "Oh you're *welcome*". There, a person received me who had worked with the same problems as me; and *he* got me into the fighter plane factory. However, I concluded that the Defense Calculator could not be exported due to military secrecy, and if it could, it would have been far too expensive. Nevertheless, Univac had working equipment with tapes. The systems of the other, smaller manufacturers did not work.

JB: Would that have been the Univac-I at the Bureau of Census?

BL: Yes, it was. I reported to the SAAB management that the best thing for us to do was to build a BESK copy, but we had to have tapes. I had expected they

---

[4] MNA (Matematikmaskinnämndens Arbetsgrupp) built the computers Bark and BESK and ran BESK on a service bureau basis for more than 10 years.

[5] BARK – Binär Automatisk Reläkalkylator, in operation about 1950 to 1955.

[6] BESK – Binär Elektronisk SekvensKalylator.

would summon me to top management for questioning, but instead I got a free hand to go ahead with the project. Later, computer historian de Geer[7] has claimed that I had a hard time convincing top management about the project, but I do not recall that. However, I did know the task was hard.

JB: What was the problem about the tapes?

BL: There was too much noise, and many bit errors. The tapes had a check bit, but one-bit errors stopped the tape and two-bit errors were not even detected. I thought about this and found that if every character was written twice, we could correct one-bit errors automatically and detect two-bit errors. Double-writing might sound as exaggerated security, but when we gathered flight data it did not matter much whether we discarded wrong data or had a self-correcting code.

I sent two men, one of them was Kurt Widin, to spend a year learning all they could about tapes, and then develop tapes with self-correcting code for our BESK copy, SARA[8]. Widin found a solution in a paper by Hamming, which saved one bit compared to my idea. I gave them the OK to go on with that. We used 9-channel tapes because that was what we could buy in the market.

JB: This must have been about 1955 or 1956.

BL: Yes, Widin probably started work in 1954. Later he went to work for Björn Lind, a remarkable man who had been the chief engineer for the SARA project. They started a control equipment company in Mjölby, financed by multi-millionaire Axel Wenner-Gren.

When the electronics department at SAAB started building D21 computers for sale, they also needed tapes, but they wanted to be clever and do it alone. However, it did not work. After two years, SAAB had to buy back Widin. It is curious how things happen sometimes: Widin had shown his competence and I recommended him, but the D21 group had to try doing it themselves anyway.

SAAB's director of economy had said that "*tapes*" was something Langefors could never make. It amused me, partly because he realized that it was in fact difficult, and partly because I understood who had told him.

ID: I remember that director of finance very well. You, Börje, had asked me to analyze whether SARA, then under construction, could be used for SAAB's administrative data processing. I concluded that SARA was too slow with the primitive sorting methods I knew; that was before quick-sort was generally known. The finance director used this as an argument to drop the SARA option, and then they went ahead and bought a *slower* IBM computer; they wanted IBM at any cost.

JB: When did SARA start working, with tapes and all?

---

[7] Hans de Geer in "På väg till datasamhället", KTH & FA-rådet, 1992.
[8] SARA – SAAB's RäkneAutomat (SAAB's computing machine)

BL: In late 1957, I think. When BESK started in 1953/54, SAAB alone quickly filled one shift.

ID: Yes, when I started running BESK programs for SAAB, in the summer of 1955, I could never get computer time before 10 p.m.

BL: More about those tapes: After we had developed our system on a Potter tape drive, it wore out and we went on with Ampex drives. When Ampex heard about us running three shifts without errors on their drives, they sent a whole delegation to look at it.

ID: In 1956, Stemme[9] and Karlqvist[10] and their group moved from MNA to Facit[11]. It was part of their deal that they would be allowed to keep helping SAAB with building SARA as they had done at MNA. Did that work? Were there problems?

BL: None that I remember. In fact, I tried on three occasions to convince the managements of Facit and SAAB to form a common computer company. Later, when SAAB offered the big Taxes & Census system to the government, we did work together on that.

ID: I remember, and actually still have minutes from 1961–62, when you and I discussed common software as part of a larger cooperation effort that failed because the technical people could not agree. Later, we had a very tangible cooperation when Datasaab[12] stationed Gunnar Ehrling and Göran Engström in Gothenburg to adapt the Facit Algol compiler for the D21. I remember the first time Ehrling appeared; the rain was pouring but he walked calmly over the courtyard in his indoors clothes. Engström lived in Gothenburg for a while but Ehrling was probably only visiting.

BL: He was a very unusual man. I remember we had to remind him now and then to draw his salary.

ID: When did you complete the specification of Algol-Genius? As I remember, Genius was implemented in parallel with D21 Algol.

BL: That should have been roughly when the Taxes & Census deal started in 1960–61.

ID: The European Computer Manufacturers Association (ECMA) had a committee named TC2 that was to develop an "amalgam of Algol and Cobol". It split in three at its first meeting in 1962 and after that, I worked in TC5 Algol. I

---

[9] Erik Stemme, professor em. at Chalmers Technical University (CTH), chief engineer for the building of BESK.

[10] Olle Karlqvist, deceased. Systems manager on MNA and Facit.

[11] Facit Electronics, a daughter company of office equipment manufacturer Facit Åtvidaberg, specialized in computers. Produced some ten BESK copies and later special defense computers.

[12] Datasaab was SAAB's daughter company for computing equipment. It produced the D21-D22-D23 series, some 30 in all, and later specialized in office computers.

wonder why I did not later contact TC2 and present to them Algol-Genius, which was exactly such an "amalgam". Perhaps I did not realize how good it was until I had the opportunity to try it on our D21 in Gothenburg in 1965. Nothing came out of the TC2, but we were evidently not alone in thinking of Algol as a possible language for administrative data processing.

JB: The Taxes & Census deal – What did your cooperation with Facit aim to accomplish?

BL: Perhaps only that Facit should help us with the systems work. However, the deal as such is remarkable and worth telling about. Datasaab almost missed the first deadline to announce its interest! One accountant, Lundin, phoned me on a Wednesday and asked: Is not SAAB going to make an offer? The deadline is on Friday? I had heard nothing but I wrote two letters on my own: one from SAAB and one from SSI, the Swedish Society for Information Processing. Those letters were not offers but rather proposals to have one computer in each administrative region rather than a huge central computer. The SSI letter I could sign myself, being its chair; the other one was signed by SAAB's CEO, Tryggve Holm.

ID: Was that actually the government's initial idea, one computer for all of Sweden?

BL: Yes indeed, and I tried among other things to point out the industrial policy aspect, that small computers could be produced in our country. The SSI letter could be seen as a contribution to the general debate of one large computer versus several small. This was in the early sixties, before I moved to Stockholm.

JB: What was IBM's original proposal?

BL: I think they offered an IBM 707 with IBM 1401 computers in the regions, but those were just to be peripherals. The IBM 1401 was ruled out as insufficient by Datasaab's simulation program, which was run for the 1401 too, at the purchase committee's request.

ID: But that was not the proposal they made later?

BL: No, in 1964, the IBM/360 series was launched and that changed everything. However, the D21 again proved superior, and that was partly due to Algol; thanks to Algol we could use quick-sort! At that time, we heard from a prospective customer of ours that one of the arguments used against the D21 was that it had too large a memory!

JB: *Who* could have said such a thing?

BL: Yes, who indeed? After that, we were careful to explain the advantages of a large memory. The Datasaab proposal was to have D21s in most of the regions.

At that time, I heard that our PR people were to work overtime through Christmas and were grumbling about it, for they had heard that top management themselves did not believe we had a chance. I told them it was 50-50, and in fact,

Datasaab got 50% of the deal; we got the small regions and in the end, we got 100%. MNA early pointed out that the D21 had the larger capacity, but the government's computer selection committee said it was not needed. When the capacity demands were investigated again—that was probably after I moved to Stockholm—they found that D21 should be used throughout, and then fewer computers were needed.

ID: So the D21 computers were first installed in the smaller regions, the committee did not believe the evaluations?

BL: That's right. This is an internationally unique case in that two systems are compared directly in full-scale operation, and that one proves so superior to the other. This should have been brought to the attention of all much more vigorously; it was poor marketing that it was not done. Better marketing is part of the answer to how Sweden might have developed a computer industry. SAAB was notoriously weak at marketing.

ID: Do you recall the final banquet of HiNC-1 in Trondheim last summer? The former director of Norsk Data made a speech claiming that the Scandinavian computer industry never had a chance in view of the massive resources the U.S. poured into computing. However, our problem was not computer techniques; we were usually well advanced there. We lost out on organization and marketing.

JB: Could you explain that 100% again? Did Datasaab get and keep the whole deal, or was that changed again so that IBM got some of the regions?

BL: No, we got the whole deal, but not all the regions got their own computer. The D21 was so powerful that some of the smaller regions could share one between them.

ID: Were you, Börje, the driving force behind the D21 project?

BL: Oh no, not at all. I was called to a talk with our CEO Tryggve Holm, who said the board of directors was skeptical to starting a computer company along with Facit. They had still given Holm a free hand to go on, but only if I and my nearest superior, Hans Löfqvist, made a convincing case for it. However, I would not do that; there were so many economic and company strategic factors I did not know. I knew too little about economics and marketing and I told Holm so. I repeated it at a second talk we had, and we decided to do nothing. Nevertheless, I told Holm—one could be quite frank with Holm, and he appreciated it though his courtiers paled—I said we have to watch the electronics people, lest they go and sell something. "Well, we ought to be able to cope with *that*", Holm thought.

ID: By the way, have you seen that article in Dædalus[13] about the development and plans of Facit Electronics? When the technician left MNA for Facit in 1956, the idea was to build a new and better computer immediately, but they got so many

---

[13]   Dædalus is the annual of the Technical Museum. The article is in the issue for 2003.

inquiries they started to build and sell BESK copies instead. When that market ended abruptly in 1960, it was too late to start a new computer project and catch up; they had split their resources. In the autumn of 1959 when I was newly employed at Facit, we had five offers out and everyone was optimistic, and then all five were rejected and the mood went from top to bottom with a bang.

JB: Who were the competitors?

ID: Mostly IBM.

BL: Regarding cooperation with Facit-Datasaab: I made a first try on Edy Velander's[14] initiative. I met the Facit CEO Carl-Bertil Nyströmer and Stemme and a few others sitting on one side of a large table and myself alone on the other side. I tried to explain to them that Facit did not know about large systems, but I could not make them budge. When I rose to go, they all remained seated; nobody walked me to the door. That was before Facit's move to Solna, I made another try there.

JB: Who was the driving force behind the D21 development, since it was not you?

BL: It was Gunnar Lindström; he was a professor of electrical measurement techniques and came to us from being CEO of Sweden's Atomic Energy Agency. He became engaged in the matter and did sell a computer just two months after my talks with Holm. It had two memories with word length 17 and 20 bits, respectively. I said: "You can't sell that computer; nobody can program it". My office was allowed to make an alternative proposal, my coworkers Magnus Tideman, Sven Yngvell and Bengt Asker took part in those discussions. The electronics people had planned a BESK copy, but not with the D2[15] circuits, they were too expensive. I found that a 20-bit computer with built-in double arithmetic processor would be more efficient than a 40-bit computer. Later we found that 24 bits would be optimal, one reason being that a word could store three 8-bit characters. That proposal became the D21.

ID: At that time, Control Data had 48-bit computers, a word length that seemed sufficient for all reasonable computations.

JB: Changing the subject again, in the early sixties you had started writing the papers that were later to form the TAIS[16] book. How did you get into systems theory?

BL: When we got the order from the insurance company Allmänna Brand, we had some young people working with their system; I followed that work closely. Later when we gave courses at the Rimforsa Homestead I started to think about the problems of administrative data processing. Might matrix techniques and other concepts from stress analysis be useful here?

[14] Edy Velander was then chair of IVA, the Academy of Engineering.
[15] D2 was a special-purpose computer for control of SAAB's fighter planes.
[16] TAIS - Theoretical Analysis of Information Systems

JB: So at that time, you already gave courses in systems development. What did such courses contain?

BL: They contained much of what was to become the first TAIS book in 1964, and then of course, we taught them our software and ordinary project management techniques.

JB: In due time, you were asked to head a research group. Where did that offer come from?

BL: It came from Martin Ferm, Director General of Sweden's defense research agency FOA. I said yes. I was interested, but I did not want a large department, just four to six people. At the first Nordic Symposium on Computers, NordSAM 1959, I had raised this matter on behalf of SSI, as its chair. I urged the establishment of a research council for information processing (IP) and stated that IP was a much larger matter than atomic energy. Many people were against this, but Ferm later invited me to his office. He said he agreed with me and asked if I would be interested in starting IP research at the FOA. "Yes, I would be" was my response, but I wanted to stay in Linköping. However, Ferm wanted to visit us often. I suggested he could not visit us every day and when he wanted to do so, he could still go to Linköping. About that time, interest emerged in Lund at the Department of Business Administration; they wanted courses in IP for administrative use. They asked me to go there and lecture every other week. There, I went on developing optimization and goal theory, among other things.

JB: So the people in Lund were active even before you went to Stockholm in 1965. I was engaged there myself but not until 1967 or so.

BL: In Lund, Kihlstedt and Rehnman were the driving forces. Well, in the end, I had to move to Stockholm, but I went on the condition that I would be stationed at the university, at the Department of Mathematical Statistics, as it turned out.

JB: So your research group was formed in 1965. Who became part of the group and why those particular persons?

BL: At the time when Ferm summoned me, I came somehow to meet Kjell Samuelsson[17] and Björn Tell[18]. My particular interest then was computer-aided problem solving, and we tried to find an interesting name for this activity, like "information research" or "informatology", later to be abbreviated "infology" as proposed by Bo Sundgren[19]. Therefore, the first meeting that started the forming of our group was with those two persons, as far as I remember.

JB: There were others in the group, e.g. Nils Lindecrantz and Lars-Erik Thorelli[20].

---

[17] Later to be professor of Informatics and Systems Science at Stockholm University
[18] Chief librarian at KTH
[19] Later to be adjoint professor at Stockholm Business School
[20] Professor em. of Computer Engineering at KTH

BL: Yes, and somehow Germund Dahlquist[21] was involved too. Maybe he was in the formative meeting. I think Dahlquist proposed Thorelli. How about Lindecrantz?

ID: He worked with us in SAAB-Linköping and then followed Bengt Kredell to ASEA[22], and must have joined your group from there. He died early, did he not?

BL: Yes, it was in the seventies. And you, Janis, do you recall how you entered the group?

JB: I first saw and heard you already in the late fifties at Chalmers, where I worked for Asplund[23]. That was where you were appointed docent in recognition of your computations for airplane wings.

BL: Moreover, I worked with your father[24] on a D21 project. However, I do not think you and I met at that time.

JB: No, it was later, in Linköping when I tried to sell you a Univac computer, probably an 1107. I worked at Univac then as systems and programming manager. So, I had to go to Linköping to tell you what a fine computer the Univac was. In the spring of 1965, I heard about the forming of your research group. I simply called you and asked if I could work for you. You said yes. Your research group started work at Hagagatan. Then the group moved to the clock tower of KTH[25], did it not?

BL: Yes, it was in preparation for applying for the professor's chair. They established the chair position in 1965, but they appointed me in 1967. However, we had started lecturing before that. I remember that you and I were supposed to lecture to the students from the Mining school of KTH. We had expected a crowd, but only a few turned up. They took notes, which they then distributed to the others.

JB: Yes, there we learned how lecturing at KTH is organized! As for the university, we started giving courses already in the spring of 1966. There we enrolled many interested students.

ID: Were you all employed full time?

BL: Yes we were, on FOA grants.

JB: How did they organize our subject area when we moved to KTH? Did we belonged to two different faculties: technical and social science?

---

[21] Professor em. of Numerical Analysis at KTH

[22] ASEA – Allmänna Svenska Elektriska Aktiebolaget, a Swedish company later merged with Brown Boweri, forming ABB.

[23] Sven Olof Asplund, deceased. Professor em. of Structural Mechanics at CTH.

[24] Janis Bubenko Sr, deceased. Professor em. in Electrical Power Systems at KTH.

[25] KTH – Kungl Tekniska Högskolan (the Royal Institute of Technology).

BL: Yes indeed. The Ministry of Education had formed a committee for this. Carl-Eric Fröberg[26] and Kurt Kihlstedt were pushing this matter.

JB: How did it feel being in a technical environment with Germund Dahlquist one flight of stairs up? Did we have good relations with the numerical analysis group then?

BL: Yes, but the pure mathematicians were a problem because they wanted us to be part of their department. I was definitely against that. They clearly stated that administrative data processing was our field. One condition for success was that an economist should be able to study our subject without learning additional mathematics. We were placed under severe pressure. At Hagagatan we sat in the Department of Mathematical Statistics where Ulf Grenander was professor. Grenander cooperated with Zachrisson[27]. When the proposal came up to move us to the Department of Mathematics, Zachrisson was involved and voted for it. Dahlquist, on the contrary, abstained and preferred us to be a separate department.

JB: Getting incorporated into mathematics would have been a problem for numerical analysis, too. They did not belong to mathematics then.

ID: This surprises me in a sort of opposite manner. Dijkstra wrote somewhere that mathematicians and computer scientists do not talk with each other. If they do, they do not discuss their work. However, these KTH mathematicians actually wanted you to do that!

BL: I imagine their interest was based on a hope of spreading interest in mathematics in this way. They seem to have realized that computing would keep growing. But I remember one stay in Lund when we were going to Copenhagen in 1956. There we were trying to make DASK and SARA compatible down to the bit level, also we had a debate on index registers in which you (Ingemar) took part. Magnus Tideman and I stopped over in Lund and talked to a couple of mathematicians. I argued that there would be much in computer science to interest mathematicians. Programming has its roots in logic, which ought to be interesting from a mathematical point of view. However, I got no response at all. As this was not important to me, I let the matter drop.

ID: Today, with functional programming developing, mathematicians would really be in their right element and get a lot out of some cooperation. Moreover, we have something else in common: both mathematics and IP are the "charwomen" of other disciplines.

JB: Around this time, your great work TAIS came into being. It built on several years of work and was first printed in 1966 (by Studentlitteratur, Lund). That book became a sort of bible for our subject. Many things in it still hold. Looking back at TAIS, is there anything you remember with special interest?

---

[26] Professor em. of Numerical Analysis at Lund University.
[27] Lars-Erik Zachrisson, professor em. of Control Theory at KTH.

BL: Oh yes. One of them is what I wrote about executive optimization. One could have developed that further. In addition, what I wrote about processes. I have recently been in contact with a systems analyst at the Taxation Authority. He is interested in what is written about processes. The concepts of process grouping and file consolidation are surely relevant in what is today called "process engineering". In essence, this technique developed in TAIS is not limited to data processing. Another thought I developed in TAIS is that if companies have similar activities, then their basic administrative routines ought to be similar, too. If we cannot easily apply standard software, it is because they have not started by defining their routines at the elementary file level. They always discuss in terms of consolidated files and grouped processes.

JB: In other words, if they had described their routines exactly at the lowest level, one could more easily have found similarities in different enterprises and been able to apply more standard programs.

BL: The reason I talked with the taxation fellow is that they are interested in object orientation. I could show them that much in TAIS gives the basis for what we now call object orientation.

JB: In those days, we made matrix based system descriptions and applied formal methods. Thy do not do that very much now. How do they get the systems to work properly nowadays?

BL: That is a good question, I have been wondering too.

JB: Another interesting passage in TAIS was the "underestimation theorem" – if you do not understand a system, you tend to underestimate its complexity. This fits nicely with your opening speech, where you talk about the difficulty of "learning to multiply (estimates) by two".

BL: There is another thing I still find interesting with TAIS—to develop a formal theory even though I do not handle mathematical objects. I discussed this with a mathematician in Lund who found it interesting, and therefore I went on working with it. I tried to build a formal structure with hypotheses and theorems. This was useful if you wanted to theorize about systems work. I also saw it as a way of organizing your own thoughts, so you could scrutinize them critically. Oh yes, however, there were people who were critical to my way of describing the theory, among them a Russian visiting mathematician at Numerical Analysis Department. Nevertheless, my personal opinion is that this kind of theory formulation must be very interesting and challenging from a mathematical point of view too.

ID: The Russians, being good mathematicians, ought to be interested in TAIS.

BL: Yes, they usually were, I noticed. TAIS was translated, by the way, not into Russian but into the Slovak language.

JB: Have you followed the way the subject originally called "information processing - particularly administrative data processing methods" has developed and spread in Sweden? At most academy sites nowadays, they call it "informatics". This has been confused with what Kjell Samuelsson meant by that word. Some departments call it "computer and systems science" and some "information systems". What do you think is a proper name for the subject?

BL: Kjell Samuelsson persuaded me to let him call his part of the subject "informatics". However, I pointed out to him that they were already calling the subject as a whole "informatique" in French, and thus it was awkward to use the name for a part of the subject. In 1965, I chaired the program committee for IFIP Congress in New York. There I proposed to divide the conference program into five parts, one of them being "Information systems" which could include "Business data processing". This proposal I presented at the opening of the congress. Consequently, the whole world, except for Sweden, now calls "Business data processing" by the name "information systems".

JB: Actually, one department in Sweden does call the subject "information systems", and that is at the university college of Skövde. However, how did that parallel subject "information processing - particularly computer science" ("datalogi" in Swedish) start? Do you recall whether that was in the group of Germund Dahlquist?

BL: I think it is right to say that. We started to discuss the separation of numerical analysis and programming into two subjects. We could have a subject focused on programming that was not tied to numerical analysis too much. I do not quite recall how the word "datalogi" came up.

ID: The Danes launched the word "datamatik" at this time.

BL: Yes, that might have been it. When we discussed the word "informatologi" we naturally also considered "datalogi". I think actually Peter Naur in Copenhagen launched both words: "datamatik" and "datalogi".

JB: At about the time that the "datalogi" subject was formed, our department moved from KTH to the university—to the F house in Frescati. Could you tell us some memories of that process?

BL: What I particularly remember is that we then had an HP (Hewlett Packard) computer, which had the advantage that students could use it online from eight terminals. According to Statskontoret[28] online operation would be too expensive on a big computer and it would be many years before this service could be generally available. My former boss Lars Brising, at that time manager of the government's

---

[28] Statskontoret is the Government's agency for administrative development. It was thus charged with computer purchases and upgrades for all civil government agencies. Statskontoret played a vital role in starting the university computing centers, but its preference for computer families like the IBM/360 series brought it into several conflicts with the university people.

Development Agency, helped me finance the lease of an HP computer and we had HP install it at our place. Statskontoret did not like that, in fact they were vigorously against it. At one time I was summoned to the financial director of KTH, who passed on to me a statement from a university public relations officer that if the computer remained after a certain date, say July 1, that would be a breach of law. I asked him what would happen to me then? The computer stayed, but there was a lot of trouble about it. I think you, Ingemar, must have been involved, since you were in the committee for managers of government computing centres. The committee claimed that such a small computer could not handle eight terminals.

ID: I sat on the board of university computing centres. There were also people from Statskontoret and user representatives on that board. We probably had the matter submitted to us and made a statement.

BL: Anyway, when we were moving to Frescati, we were bringing our eight terminals with us. Then the Numerical Analysis Department said they needed another eight. All of a sudden, they accepted that the HP should handle 16 terminals, and so it did, which I found quite amusing.

JB: That made it one of the first "time-sharing" computers.

BL: Yes, and I remember too that after a week or ten days, fantastic things happened to the students sitting there online. For instance, they had made an interpreter of Cobol programs, written in Basic. I wrote a whole report on what had happened during this brief period.

JB: Yes, interactive programming meant an enormous productivity gain, compared to batch processing, when you had to submit a card deck over the computing centre's counter two or three times a day, at least.

BL: Yes, I know you, Janis, and Tomas Ohlin[29] were very engaged in this matter. Luckily, there was a sensible politician, Hans Löwbeer, who was Chancellor of the Universities at the time. He arranged for the National Computer Fund to buy the HP computer.

ID: Statskontoret opposed anything that did not fit with their ideas. They were against setting up a terminal at the university college in Växjö connected to our computer in Lund, if we had to finance it by a grant for computer time. However, Växjö had checked with the university chancellor, so Statskontoret was steamrollered in this case. Later, we in Lund decided to try reduced night rates for the computer, which was also against Statskontoret's rules. Fröberg promised me that if I went to jail for this, he would bring me sandwiches. We knew then that Statskontoret could be confronted on vital matters. It was Bubenko-Ohlin in

[29] Formerly, professor at the Department of Economic Information Systems, Linköping University.

Stockholm and Fröberg-Ekman in Lund who had taught Statskontoret there was a limit to what they could do[30].

JB: How did you find the physical move to Frescati and the University of Stockholm?

BL: When we got there, we became part of the Social Sciences faculty, where Boalt was the dean. He welcomed me to the faculty and supported our entry in all manners. Among other things, he invited me to lecture at the seminars of the sociologists. Moreover, my lecture made one of students in the audience rewrite his thesis, Boalt told me. I do not recall what I lectured on, but it might have been something from the other book I wrote at that time, "Systems for enterprise management".[31] There I treated matters that might interest sociologists too. Nevertheless, when I told Boalt it would be interesting to see sociologists take part in developing the topic of administrative data processing, Boalt objected. Sociologists could not take sides for the employers against their personnel! I thought if a company could be improved by using computers, that would surely be good for the personnel too.

ID: A researcher like Kristen Nygaard[32] worked at supporting trade union work with computers. There is nothing to say that computers will benefit employers only.

BL: I had an interesting experience in Lund, before 1965, I think. There I had three very obviously left-leaning students. They were very interested in workers' matters, so I suggested they should write their joint bachelor's thesis on how to use IP to support workers' interests and what information might be interesting and useful for employees. However, this seemingly did not interest them enough, for nothing came of it. One of them was German, a very brilliant guy who had been thrown out of Frankfurt on account of a student rebellion. He walked me to the Stockholm train once, and I remember him saying it was so interesting that TAIS reminded him of Mao's Little Red Book. That might be good example of the infological equation.

JB: Speaking of that, Ingemar has gone back and read your opening speech "Reflections on the Past" with great interest. Would you, Ingemar, like to wind up this interview with a few questions?

ID: I have two, really. The one is your saying "The infological equation refutes positivistic ambitions". Could you elaborate on this? What do you mean by positivism, for instance?

BL: There was a lot of discussion and criticism against positivism in our department, e.g. from Kristo Ivanov[33]. Positivism in this sense means to claim that

---

[30] Here *ID* refers to the conflicts about Statskontoret's handling of the procurement of large computers for research and education in Stockholm and Lund, respectively.

[31] "System för företagsstyrning", Studentlitteratur, Lund, 1968

[32] Kristen Nygaard developed the SIMULA language together with Ole-Johan Dahl, both deceased in 2003.

one can define exact atoms of knowledge that correspond exactly to reality. What I want to prove with the equation is that that can't be so. With every token a person uses, his pre-knowledge comes in and influences the result. A word has a different meaning depending on the context in which we use it and the recipient's pre-knowledge and frames of reference.

ID: Okay. Now I understand you better. I have long embraced the opinion that words mean different things depending on the way you use them. However, I count myself as a positivist anyway, in the sense that I think one should be capable of proving or refuting a theory. Otherwise, it is not science but metaphysics. The infological equation should not upset that kind of positivism.

BL: I am not quite sure you are right. What I mean is that I am not sure I could not have objections to that. However, maybe we should not go deeper into that now.

ID: No, let us not. That answers my first question. The second one is this. You write here at the end that maybe you should have been clearer, more explicit in your writings, but it would have taken more of your time and that of the readers. Then you say, "It may have exceeded the "t" of the infological equation". However, I do not think of "t" as a sort of limit, but rather as an independent variable. Do you mean to say it would have "exceeded a reasonable "t" of the infological equation"?

BL: Yes, I am thinking of the time "t" that I expect my reader to have available. That *is* an interesting factor, especially when one considers how explicit one should be. The writer also cannot spend unlimited time on the matter. One must expect the reader to have an "allotted time", to cite an interesting book I recently found in the library.

ID: Okay. I understand that too. I must say I appreciated that poem by Garcia Lorca in your speech. It kept popping up in my head for days.

BL: It could be interesting to confront it with the Wittgenstein quote *"Everything that can be put in words can be put clearly"*. At the HiNC conference, Sandewall[34] extended my quote with the lines *"on that of which we cannot speak clearly, we must be silent"*. He then asked me if that changed my assertion that the infological equation refutes Wittgenstein. However, I do not see why it should.

ID: Isn't it the other way round? Sometimes we have to keep talking even though we are unclear. I do enjoy a piece of the humanities for a change in our very technical environment. Garcia Lorca is a writer known fairly little by us in the North. Do you know Spanish well?

---

[33] Professor em. in Informatics, Umeå University.

[34] Erik Sandewall, professor in Datalogy, Linköping University.

BL: I have read Spanish literature for many years, not just for the sake of learning the language, but also for entering and understanding the cultural environment there.

ID: In terms of the infological equation, you create a larger common "S" (pre-knowledge) with the Spanish person you talk with.

JB: Börje, we thank you for joining us in this very inspiring and informative discussion.

THE PIONEER ERA IN NORWEGIAN SCIENTIFIC COMPUTING (1948 -1962)

Drude Berntsen

Director of the Norwegian Computing Center 1970 – 1989; drudeb@broadpark.no

Abstract: This paper gives a survey of the pioneer era in Norwegian scientific computing. Right after the Second World War research councils and research institutions were established and young scientists got scholarships to study abroad. Many caught interest in the new mathematical machines. In 1950, the Royal Norwegian Council for Scientific and Industrial Research decided to build a Norwegian computer, later called NUSSE, and by 1952 the Norwegian Computing Center for pure and applied research, was organized. The paper describes activities at the universities in Oslo, Bergen, and Trondheim, as well as at the Norwegian Defense Research Establishment at Kjeller. In the late 1950s, both the Central Bureau of Statistics and the Norwegian Meteorological Institute installed their first general-purpose computers. This was before such computers were installed at the University of Oslo and at the NTH, the technical university in Trondheim. The paper closes noting the contract signed in 1962 for the first UNIVAC 1107 to Europe.

Key words: Scientific computing, pioneers, NUSSE, Norwegian

1.   THE PERIOD BEFORE 1949 (BEFORE THE REAL START)

The Central Bureau of Statistics in Norway ordered their first Hollerith tabulator in 1894. Norway used it for the censuses in 1900 and 1910. When the war broke out in 1940, there were 27 punched card installations in the country mostly in public offices, insurance companies, and in industry, but also some in the universities.

Professor Svein Rosseland at the Institute of Theoretical Astrophysics at the University of Oslo (UiO) searched for tools and new methods for solving differential equations. In 1934, he got the permission to build a differential analyzer based on drawings from Vannevar Bush, a professor at the Massachusetts Institute of Technology. This was a mechanical device to solve differential equations. When it was ready for use in 1937-38, it was the most advanced in the world. It occupied about 100 square meters in the basement of the institute.

Early in the war, the Germans asked Rosseland for a meeting to see if they could use the analyzer to calculate ballistic formulas. When they later wanted to use it, Rosseland had gone to the US "on vacation". He became a professor at Princeton University for five years. Professor Brahde who had been present at the meeting could not help the Germans. They soon decided to dismantle important parts of the machine and bury them in the lawn in front of the institute. Without these parts, the machine would be of no use to the Germans. After the war, they reassembled and further developed the analyzer. Ole Amble, who later became a key person in the software development for Norway's first electronic computer, made it possible to multiply on the machine.

However, the economists and the chemists at the University of Oslo, as well as the meteorologists in Oslo and Bergen found interest in punched card calculators as well as desk calculators. So also did the researchers at the newly established Norwegian Defense Research Establishment (FFI). Jan V. Garwick, who had been an assistant to Professor Rosseland, moved to FFI in 1947 and as leader of the mathematical section, he became a key person in the development of scientific computing in Norway in the 1950s. FFI preferred equipment from Frederic Rosing Bull—machines they could modify according to their needs. Bull was a Norwegian inventor who died in 1925, but his patents resulted in the foundation of the French "Compagnie des Machines Bull" in 1933.

2. THE PERIOD 1949–1955
(THE VERY BEGINNING)

The Royal Norwegian Council for Scientific and Industrial Research, called NTNF, was established in 1946. This Council was to promote research and development. Quite a few young scientists received scholarships to the US as part of the Marshall Aid program.

One of those young scientists was Henry Viervoll. In 1948, he wrote home from USA to his professor of physics at the UiO about the modern computers developed during the war. Because of this letter, three professors at UiO proposed to NTNF in November 1948 that they should set up a "Committee for Mathematical Machines". By January 1949, they established the committee. Most of the eight members of the committee were active researchers who themselves were performing heavy computations and therefore were very interested in these new mathematical machines. Viervoll was the secretary for the committee while Professor Halvor Solberg from the Institute of Theoretical Meteorology, UiO, became its chair. The committee had the task of studying the new electronic calculators and estimating their possible use in industrial and scientific applications.

Already in their first year, the committee proposed to NTNF the building of a Norwegian computer and the establishment of a national computing centre for civil use. They proposed to coordinate the use of all available equipment, including punched card equipment at the universities and at FFI. Some funds were also made available, but only just enough to construct an electromechanical machine, estimated to cost NOK 200,000.

In 1950, they engaged Thomas Hysing to be in charge of the construction. First, they planned for a Zuse machine, but after a visit by Professor D.R. Hartree from Cambridge, they discovered that, within budget, they could afford an electronic computer based on components from Dr. Andrew D. Booth who had constructed the APEX C. Construction of the input/output devices could take place in Norway at the Central Institute for Industrial Research (SI) that NTNF had established a year earlier. By this shift in strategy, they extended the time schedule by a year to 1954. They named the computer NUSSE.

The Committee also supported further development of the differential analyzer at the institute of Professor Rosseland, and initiated construction of another differential analyzer in Trondheim at the Norwegian Technical University, NTH. Jens Glad Balchen, who returned in 1951 from a scholarship in the US, constructed DIANA, an analogue computer well suited for his work within the field of automation. He started in 1952; by 1955, this specialized machine was available. They further developed DIANA well into the 1960s.

For the other users NTNF decided, in January 1952, to establish the Norwegian Computing Center for pure and applied research (NCC) as an organization with branches at the university sites and at FFI at Kjeller. The main branch got offices together with SI in Oslo. For the local branches, they appointed contact persons. The NCC had at its disposal various punched card equipment, the differential analyzer at UiO, and later NUSSE and DIANA.

Already by the beginning of 1954, they had installed a new tabulator, reproducer, collator, and sorter at NCC's premises in Oslo. With this equipment, the main branch of NCC could better fulfill its obligations and undertake a variety of jobs for industry and scientific institutions, mostly numerical calculations of mathematical and mathematical-statistical nature.

In those days, IBM rented machines for scientific use at a special discount. Per Gotaas, an insurance mathematician became director of NCC.   He himself worked mainly on these IBM machines.

In Bergen, they wanted to be just as advanced as the Oslo branch.   In 1952, the Institute of Geophysics at the University of Bergen (UiB) rented an IBM 602 A. By mid-1955, they expanded this business to a centre for the whole university. Professor Carl Ludvig Godske was an important person in Bergen.   He was a member of the NTNF Committee for Mathematical Machines, and one of his colleagues was Kåre Fløisand. Already in 1952 Fløisand had published papers in the NCC series on subjects such as "Punched card equipment and their use in scientific computations" and "The mark sensing method and a survey of its accuracy".

The staff at NCC in Oslo also expanded. Ole Amble and Tor Evjen engaged to undertake the mathematical coding and programming of NUSSE, together with Werner Romberg from Trondheim. From 1953, they made routines from scratch for all general functions on the machine, for instance; "subroutines" in machine code on paper tape for calculation of sinus and for square root.   In 1954, the machine was ready for use by others, but the programming was not easy.   Amble was a good mentor; he made documentation and helped new users to get started.

The physicist John Midtdal at UiO was one of the pioneers using NUSSE. When Hysing and his assistant Kjell Kveim went home at night, he started his own work on the machine. He was searching for "the zeroes in the zeta function". He used NUSSE to get within an accuracy of 55 decimal places. Odd Hassel, who in 1969 received the Nobel price for chemistry, worked within crystallography, making a series of two-dimensional Fourier-syntheses for crystal structures. NUSSE could invert matrices and do matrix multiplications.   Amble and Evjen also developed a program for linear programming that could solve 15 equations with 15 unknowns, but Professor Ragnar Frisch, to receive the Nobel Prize for economics in 1969, wanted a program for 100 unknowns.

NUSSE required very stable current. Every day when a big iron foundry, Christiania Spigerverk some 5 km away, turned on or off its ovens, NUSSE failed. Its use needed modification for this and nighttime usage proved best.

Since NUSSE was quite unstable, it was not suitable for commercial jobs at NCC. In 1955, NTNF also put restraints on NCC that they should have users that were willing to pay for their services and especially for programming. NCC had to rely on the punched card equipment for most of its income.

When, in 1956, NCC moved from its premises at UiO to the new institute building for SI, they decided to improve NUSSE. They eliminated many of the weaknesses when it once more became operative in February 1957. By then the scientific community needed more power and they were looking for other possibilities.

3.   THE PERIOD 1955–1961 (IMPORTED COMPUTERS)

The construction of NUSSE had been a research task, but after its completion, SI regarded it as a tool for industrial development. They invented a special purpose device for numerical control, called ESSI. They installed it to control a flame cutter at the Stord shipyard in the autumn of 1960. The Autokon system for the shipyard industry was an important result later on, as addressed by Trygve Reenskaug in this publication.

In 1956, NCC rented a new electronic calculating punch from IBM, an IBM 626. This machine could add, subtract, multiply, and divide and it could execute a program. Being a real mathematical machine, it could automatically do a series of numerical calculations.

They transferred a big job from Bergen to NCC in 1957. The job was to make monthly statistics for the Meteorological Institute. Every month 30,000 punched cards were read and they used a special alphanumerical tabulator with special "weather characters" to present the results.

While NUSSE was under construction, Garwick at the military computing centre at FFI was preparing for an electronic computer. At that time, they used punched card equipment from an improved Bull to solve their special mathematical problems. In 1954, they decided to order a Mercury machine from Ferranti Ltd, a British firm that collaborated with the University of Manchester. As was the norm in the 1950s, it had taken two years from the time of order to the date of delivery. During that time both Garwick and Ernst S. Selmer (who later became professor in mathematics at the UiB) had worked with the development team and influenced the design and instruction set. They therefore knew the machine very well on its arrival. They named the FFI machine FREDERIC and it was one of the biggest at that time.

Few programming tools followed FREDERIC from the supplier and the users became impatient. Among them was Kristen Nygaard who from 1956 was head of a group for operational research. A very active programming group developed at FFI including Svein A. Øvergaard who later became the leader of the next computing centre at Kjeller, and Ole Johan Dahl who developed the language MAC based on Algol. He made an efficient compiler for MAC. FREDERIC was in active use for seven years. The users came from many scientific groups in the Oslo region.

Another impatient user was Professor Godske at the UiB. The University had had support from NTNF for their punch card installation for four years, but this support ceased in 1956, when they joined in with ten firms in Bergen to establish EMMA (Electronic Mathematical Machine A/L) with the intention of renting and operating an IBM 650. They then also experienced that a newly established state committee with the purpose of coordinating government use of computers, did not allow the University to enter into this enterprise. UiB made this a political matter by using the media, and the Ministry of Finance gave in and allowed the use of NOK 130,000. By April 1958, the IBM 650, the only one installed in Norway, had arrived. They advertised it as the first computer suited for both scientific and commercial use.

Hans W. Gullestad who from 1953 had been in charge of the West Coast Punched Card Centre became the Director of EMMA. Later in the 1950s, similar centers appeared in other places. The EMMA became famous by the summer of 1958 when it was used to calculate the taxes for the about one million Norwegians. Punched cards with taxation data for each person were sent to EMMA and after the operation, punched cards with the result per individual were returned. Newspapers all over the country were telling about this "beautiful EMMA with all her attributes, who does everything that has to be done. This wonderful "girl" is an electronic computer that jerks and works and spits out results that are indisputable – maybe?" One of our famous entertainers, Einar Rose, became upset by this talk about his wife and especially when they announced she was available to the whole country.

The staff at the NCC in Oslo also wanted an IBM 650, since IBM offered it on rent at 40% of the normal price for the industry. By 1957, contact had been made between the Central Bureau of Statistics (SSB) and the NTNF. SSB wanted to buy a modern electronic computer. Their choice fell in December 1957 on DEUCE (Digital Electronic Universal Computing Engine) made by English Electric. A committee appointed by the Ministry of Finance was in favor of buying the machine for SSB, if NCC could take over 50% of its capacity for the use of other institutions. The decision was based on a special study of the need for electronic computers in government public service. The director of SSB, P. J. Bjerve was a strong man and he wanted NCC reorganized as an independent research institute under NTNF, an institute that could help run the computer and that could also receive research grants from NTNF. The deal between NTNF and SSB was made and by 1 July 1958, NCC became an institute and the NTNF Committee from 1949 dissolved. In February 1959, DEUCE arrived. SSB was the first statistical bureau in Europe to get an electronic computer, at the cost of 1.1 million NOK. DEUCE had only punched cards as input and output and no line printer at the time of delivery.

NCC moved all its punched card equipment to the premises of SSB in down town Oslo and all together the installation was considerable. They installed DEUCE on the same premises and NCC was the operator and had the responsibility for technical maintenance.   They carried out this responsibility partly by the technicians at SI who had been involved in the construction of NUSSE. There were many problems with the operation of DEUCE, not only in the initial phase, and programming was difficult. The machine was better suited for SSB with their production of statistics based on lots of data and limited calculations than with NCC's more complicated mathematical calculations based on limited input data. The initial contract outlined collaboration for six years, but after two to three years, NCC wanted to cancel the agreement and SSB was looking for additional equipment.   In 1961, SSB itself installed an IBM 1401, the first one in Norway, used for the census of 1960.

NCC's first task on DEUCE was really a struggle.   Ole Amble was responsible. They were to calculate the income for all the forest owners in Østerdalen.   The data about how much timber had been delivered in the winter of 1958-59 was on 60,000 to 70,000 punched cards and they should calculate volume, prices, and income for everybody. The deadline was April 1959 just during the installation period.   Amble and the programmer Svein Bækkevold worked hard through the Easter vacation and succeeded.

In 1959, the Norwegian Meteorological Institute (DNMI) also decided to get a computer that they could use for weather forecasting. They ordered a FACIT from Sweden and it became operative in June 1961. It was then the biggest electronic computer in Norway.   DNMI was the third national weather institute to get a machine of their own.   The cost was 4.5 million NOK.   All input and output was on punched paper tapes or cards. After some time the machine got a very good ALGOL compiler.

By 1959-1960, NTNF was worried because NCC had developed into just a commercial computing centre.   The scientific community had lost their centre, a place for requesting support and getting access to modern technology.   Therefore, they asked Kristen Nygaard at FFI to come to NCC to build up a research group in operational research there.   In May 1960, he left FFI and that summer four other members of his group followed. They did not want to be involved in punched card calculators or DEUCE. Therefore, they kept on using FREDERIC while they were looking for other possibilities.   In the spring of 1961, the ideas for a language that could serve the dual purpose of system description and simulation programming originated at NCC.

At the UiO physicists and chemists continued to use NUSSE, but some of them had moved to FREDERIC.   In 1960, a journalist from the newspaper Aftenposten made a portrait interview with the Swedish financier Axel Wenner-Gren.   By that time, he had given a Swedish made computer

Wegematic to some Swedish universities and he suggested doing the same for Oslo. The UiO was surprised when an offer arrived, but they accepted. In December 1960, the machine arrived. Programming tools were scarce. John Midtdal and Åmund Lunde made a small operating system for it and they made a compendium that they used for teaching programming. Wegematic was at first very unstable, partly due to unstable current. They built a special stabilizer. Ole Amble, from NCC, was in charge of the computing centre that became part of the Institute of Mathematics. Chemists became the main users and after some time, the only users. The machine needed two full-time technicians as the cooling system broke down very often and many tubes needed replacement.

4.   THE PERIOD 1961–62
(EDUCATION EXPLOSION)

In 1962, the University of Oslo rented an IBM 1620 to replace the Wegematic, which they turned over to the chemists. They had many programs running on it and continued to use it for several years.

With the 1620, they used FORTRAN and life became easier for the users. The usage of the machine exploded and two years later, they installed another 1620. This time, the UiO was not offering any courses in computer science, just short programming courses for those who were to use the computer. The offered some courses in numerical analysis as an extension of a technical insurance seminar. Per Gotaas and Ole Amble were the lecturers. The UiB also installed an IBM 1620 and in 1963, they withdrew from EMMA, which became a pure service bureau.

NCC gave a full year course on "programming, system analysis, and quantitative methods" from 1962 and they gave short programming courses in Algol as the lack of skilled programmers was severe.

What about the activities in Trondheim? Svein A. Øvergaard had in 1957-58 been a visiting professor at NTH and he claimed that he gave the first computer science courses there. The year after, seminars started. Lars Monrad Krohn wrote the first master's thesis in digital techniques. He later became one of the founders of Norsk Data. In 1960, he moved to FFI where Yngvar Lundh with strong support from the director of research Karl Holberg, was active in building the electronic computer LYDIA for military use. They completed LYDIA in 1962 when this group undertook to develop SAM, a general-purpose computer.

By 1961, students wrote other theses on programming at NTH. Knut Skog presented his work "Heuristic programming" and they established a group for "Electronic Data Processing" at NTH. They received funds from

NTNF to build a digital computer, but decided instead to enter into collaboration with Regnecentralen in Copenhagen. In March 1962, they signed a contract and in November 1962, a GIER computer was on campus. Knut Skog, Olav B. Brusdal and Nils Michelsen participated in the construction.

NTH discussed whether their computer installation should be linked to the Institute of Applied Mathematics, as was the case in many places or whether it should be a more independent computing centre, that could do jobs also for private industry. They chose the latter and made it part of the foundation SINTEF, that came into being in 1950 just a few months after SI in Oslo.

They hired a British scientist, Norman Sanders, who worked for Boeing, to build up the Centre and persuaded Knut Skog to stay. Together they made the Centre flourish. The first year more than 500 students and employees at NTH had taken programming courses on the GIER. Algol dominated. Data and programs had to be loaded into GIER through paper tape produced on Flexowriters. Output was on paper tape and printed out on the same Flexowriters. Secondary storage was lacking and they had ordered magnetic tapes on a carrousel. They all strongly felt the lack of a line printer. At Easter time, Bech in Copenhagen agreed to supply the line printer and bill them for the carrousel, so that they did not get into trouble with government bureaucracy.

In March 1962, NCC also had entered into an agreement with Regnecentralen in Copenhagen for obtaining a GIER. Scandinavian cooperation was planned connected to this medium size computer. However, the scientists at NCC working on large simulation models felt they needed even more computer power. The possibility for this materialized when in May 1962 Kristen Nygaard was invited to the USA on an "executive tour" by UNIVAC and he was told about the new UNIVAC 1107. On this tour, UNIVAC became interested in the Simula language that Kristen Nygaard and Ole Johan Dahl were defining and in the linear programming work carried out by Sverre Spurkland based on a new method called parametric descent. In June, NCC received a half price offer from UNIVAC. Included in the deal was the delivery of a Simula compiler and a LP package. On 24 October, a contract was signed between NTNF and UNIVAC. NTNF arranged for a loan of 7 million NOK, that NCC should repay over eight years. By doing it this way, NCC did not have to go through normal governmental approval channels and the plans for a new computer to FFI were not disturbed. Consequently, they cancelled the contract for the GIER.

When it arrived in August of 1963, the UNIVAC 1107 was the largest and most modern civil computer installation in Europe. With this very strong tool and a surplus of capacity, a new era for NCC and Norwegian computing started, including the development of Simula and object-oriented programming. You will hear more about that in other presentations in these Proceedings.

REFERENCES

Norsk Regnesentral 1952 - 2002
Ikke bare maskiner. Historien om IBM i Norge 1935 - 1985
DATA gjennom 50 år. Den Norske Dataforenings jubileumsbok 1993
Den forunderlige reisen gjennom datahistorien - Arild Haraldsen 1999
Datahistorien ved Universitetet i Oslo – Fra begynnelsen og til ut i syttiårene
IT historien ved UiO – Per H. Jacobsen. Beta-versjon oktober 2001
Eventyret Norsk Data – En bit av fremtiden. Per Øyvind Heradstveit
RUNIT 25 år – Historisk kavalkade 1952 - 1987
Fra jordas indre til atmosfærens ytre – Oslo Geofysikers Forening 50 år 1949-1999.
    Festskrift.
Norsk datahistorie, Ingeniørforlaget/Teknisk Ukeblad 1989

Abbreviations for mentioned Norwegian institutions

DNMI	Norwegian Meteorological Institute
EMMA	Electronic Mathematical Machine A/L in Bergen
FFI	Norwegian Defense Research Establishment
NR	Norwegian Computing Center (NCC)
NTH	Technical University in Trondheim
NTNF	Royal Norwegian Council for Scientific and Industrial Research
SI	Central Institute for Industrial Research in Oslo
SINTEF	Research foundation linked to NTH in Trondheim
SSB	Central Bureau of Statistics
UiB	University of Bergen
UiO	University of Oslo

THE ROLE OF IBM IN STARTING UP COMPUTING IN THE NORDIC COUNTRIES

Hans E. Andersin

Professor Emeritus, Helsinki University of Technology; hans.andersin@hut.fi

Abstract: This paper explores the role of early IBM strategies such as installing "computing work horses" at various customer and own sites for shared use. It did this by making available a "super computer" at the Northern Europe University Computing Center, by making available programming languages and application programs to the computing community, and, not least, by conducting courses in state-of-the-art equipment and computing methods. The paper covers the time up to the advent of the IBM System 360 in 1964.

Keywords: IBM, scientific computing, data processing, competition, Nordic countries

1. THE UNDISPUTED LEADER IN ADMINISTRATIVE DATA PROCESSING

The US based company International Business Machines (founded in 1911) had achieved by the beginning of the computer era a dominating position worldwide in the field of punched card data processing [1], [3]. IBM punched card equipment was everywhere, in state and local government, in companies, and in military installations. It sometimes utilized the latest developments in electronic circuitry. Competition was only marginal.

The competitive situation changed when electronic computers appeared on the administrative data processing scene. For a short period, the competitors of IBM were in the lead. IBM then tried to win time by making programmable punched card machines and sophisticated electronic calculators available. When it got its first large-scale administrative data processing machines – the IBM 702 followed by the IBM 705 – on the market, the battle against the competition started, soon to be won by IBM, thanks largely to the large and loyal customer base of the company. For smaller customers, the advent of the IBM 650 (announced in 1953, but first installed in the Nordic countries in 1956) and several innovations like the random access method of accounting and control computer RAMAC (first delivery in 1957) paved the way. The real success came with the IBM 1401, announced in 1959, and first installed in the Nordic countries 1960–1961. This data processing machine was priced to capture the small and medium sized customer market. IBM sold 12000 of these 1401 computers worldwide. The IBM 1440, even smaller and cheaper than the 1401, arrived in 1962. Together with the 1440 came exchangeable disk memories, so called 'disk packs'. A larger and more powerful machine than the 1401 was the IBM 1410, announced in 1960. Customers who wanted powerful handling of the peripherals simultaneously with complex data processing ordered systems consisting of interconnected 1410 and 1401 machines.

Simultaneously with introducing new generations of large- and small-scale data processing machines, IBM developed a number of new devices for them such as fast line printers and card readers, magnetic tape stations, and random access storage devices. It also introduced new concepts like independent smart I/O channels. It developed new tools for the user such as operating systems especially suited to data processing needs. IBM implemented the newly developed COBOL programming language for its data processing machines. The announcement of the IBM System 360 in 1964 marked the end of the period of early computing. From that point on, IBM continued to be the undisputed leader in administrative data processing for several years to come.

Why did this happen? Firstly, IBM had by far the largest and most loyal group of punched card equipment customers. These customers felt comfortable in their dealings with IBM because of good assistance in systems engineering, for example, and with maintenance service and the favorable terms of replacing old rental equipment with new. Secondly, the numerous innovations in hardware and software stemming from the vast IBM laboratory organization made most customers believe that IBM would be able to fill their growing needs well into the future. Thirdly, the IBM customer education was the best and the most extensive you could get. Fourthly, IBM had a devoted and well-managed force of sales representatives and systems engineers. All of this was true in the Nordic countries also. In addition to this, IBM was the only data processing machine manufacturer that had a factory in the Nordic Region exporting equipment from the region. Bull, originally a Norwegian company, had long since moved abroad. Nokia was still to come. In addition, the IBM Nordic Laboratories in Sweden rendered IBM a political competitive advantage. In cities in all the Nordic countries, IBM had service bureaus both for getting customers started and for assisting smaller customers who could not afford to have data processing installations themselves. This was the early situation with respect to the administrative data processing market: IBM became the undisputed leader in the Nordic countries.

2.   THE SCIENTIFIC COMPUTING MARKET WAS TOUGHER

When studying the early steps in the field of scientific computing the picture is not as clear and straightforward as in the administrative data processing field. In all the Nordic countries, scientists and engineers had used IBM punched card calculators (e.g. the electronic IBM 604, announced in 1948). The scientific community was aware of the potential of computing machinery. Many of the scientists had either seen with their own eyes or read about how their colleagues in the USA, Britain and other countries had already built themselves more or less powerful computers already in the 1940s. This was to be the case in the Nordic countries also. Here universities and research facilities constructed scientific computers in the 1950s ranging from the very powerful BESK-family to some rather unsophisticated small computers. At that time, nobody was even thinking of IBM as a prospective manufacturer of powerful scientific computers at a price that a Nordic University or a research establishment could afford.

IBM had been participating in the earliest development of computing machinery, the electromechanical Mark I (Automatic Sequence Controlled Calculator) at the Harvard University (1944) and the Selective Sequence Electronic Calculator (1948), a computer utilizing both relays and electron tubes. IBM, however, did not realize that scientific computers could have a market of any significance outside perhaps the defense sector and some universities. Furthermore, the IBM sales force had neither experience nor knowledge of selling to the scientific community.

For the defense market, it designed special computers. When IBM's competitors had shown that the market demanded commercially produced computers, IBM decided in 1952 to announce this special "defense calculator" as the IBM 701, performing 17,000 additions per second. IBM delivered nineteen 701 machines to customers and these were followed by deliveries of the more successful IBM 704 (announced in 1955). These machines used vacuum tubes, CRT's, magnetic tape stations, and magnetic drum memories. We called them "computers" in the present sense of the word. This was a turning point for IBM in USA in the field of scientific computing. Many of the US universities and research establishments jumped onto the IBM bandwagon. IBM announced the 7090 in 1959, one of the first fully transistorized mainframes; it was able to perform 229,000 additions per second. One of the reasons for IBM's success in USA was the generous Educational Allowance Plan introduced by IBM in USA allowing educational institutions to rent IBM equipment for as low as 40% of the list price. Later in the 1950s, it introduced this plan outside USA as well.

What worked in the USA did not work in the academic computing field in the Nordic countries! Here the boom of self-built computers continued far into the 1950s.

2.1   IBM 650 became the work horse for the engineer as well

The engineering users as well as the less sophisticated scientific users, however, were more attracted by large libraries of ready programs and systems software than their academic colleagues who often wanted to make all the programs themselves. For the less sophisticated users the medium size computer IBM 650 (announced in USA 1953) was just right. The 650 started delivery to users in the Nordic countries during the second half of the 1950s. It installed the first 650 in an insurance company (Folksam) in Sweden in 1956. Immediately thereafter, scientific and engineering users, among them the author of this paper, from all the other Nordic countries rushed to Stockholm to use the computer and its large library of ready-made programs that was made available to users free of charge. This model was very much the one in which the 650 became in use in the Nordic countries. The main customer was either a large data processing user such as an insurance company (in Sweden) or a bank (in Finland). Sometimes the main customer was a large scientific user such as a geophysics institute (in Norway), while the secondary users were either one or several smaller engineering or data processing users.

One of the main attractions for the engineering community was the new programming language FORTRAN, developed first for the 704 computer, and then for other computers as well by an IBM group of programmers led by John Backus during 1953–1957. FORTRAN was easy to learn and easy to use and became in practice the most used scientific and engineering language for many decades.

The IBM 1620, a small computer for scientific computing, followed the IBM 650. Some universities in the Nordic countries ordered it. A variant of the 1620, IBM installed the 1710 system for process monitoring and control at a number of plants in the Nordic countries.

2.2 Love versus respect

In the 1950s, a slightly frustrated IBM Applied Science Representative uttered the statement "IBM is not loved but respected". As far as the author remembers, there really existed some animosity between the scientific community and IBM during the early times of computing, at least in the Nordic countries. There were many possible reasons for this. Local IBM sales representatives possessed neither any deep knowledge of scientific computing nor the necessary endurance and motivation to deal with scientist and engineers. In addition, the typical IBM sales representative lacked sufficient insight into computer technology and the theoretical foundations of computing. Some people considered some IBMers arrogant. The IBM company culture that had developed along with the dominance in the punched card business did not please the scientists. The scientific community, who until quite recently had built their own computers, thought that the IBM computers were grossly overpriced. "We do not need all the systems support, software and other 'bells and whistles' that are included in the price" was a common opinion among scientists. When IBM introduced the Educational Allowance Plan for universities, people looked upon it, at least at first, with mistrust because of complicated rules and restrictive clauses. Later the Educational Allowance Plan almost became as an act of unfair competition. IBM's policy of only leasing its systems to the customer was unfamiliar to the scientific community, which was used to the governmental budgeting rules based on outright purchase of equipment.

The respect for IBM came from the fact that many of the Nordic scientists had become acquainted with large-scale 700 and 7000 series IBM machines installed at US universities, research institutions, and industries. Scientists were quite impressed by their visits to IBM plants and laboratories in the USA and Europe. In 1960, IBM unveiled the STRECH computer, the first "super computer". The respect for IBM also originated from IBM's enormous success in administrative data processing. The scientists also envied their US colleagues' apparent abundance of funds allowing for renting large-scale computers while they at home had to get the cheapest available systems. This meant buying mostly non-IBM.

The problems IBM had with its conventional sales force in selling to the scientific community gave rise to a new breed of IBMers, the so-called Applied Science Representatives. The first of the Applied Science Representatives were often people who had taken part in building the first computer in their respective countries. They were, however, seldom skilled and trained in selling to mistrusting academic and engineering customers.

2.3   Algol versus FORTRAN, punched cards versus paper tape

The feud between IBM and its competitors in scientific computing, between IBM and the scientific community, and between practically oriented people such as engineers and computer science oriented people, sometimes took bizarre forms. A part of the scientific community considered FORTRAN, as compared to Algol, a brute force language with insufficient logical structure and complexity. The engineering community and practically oriented scientific computer users did not wait for Algol but started to employ FORTRAN instead and found the language sufficiently usable. IBM continued to support FORTRAN, and their customers continued to use it, for many decades. The universities, however, insisted on teaching Algol and Algol-like languages while continuing to frown upon FORTRAN, even though most of their students were to use FORTRAN in their coming working life.

Another dividing line between the scientific community and IBM was the use of paper tape instead of punched cards as an input and output medium. The paper tape was in some cases more practical and cheaper than punched cards for scientific and engineering applications, but IBM mostly refused to recommend paper tape and forced punched cards upon their customers (with one exception, the electromechanical engineering computer IBM 610). IBM's competitors, on the other hand, did all they could to promote paper tape.

2.4   Success or failure in scientific computing

The success of IBM was indisputable all over the world including the Nordic countries in the field of administrative data processing in terms of sales, market dominance, number of customers, and hardware and software features. Just as indisputable was the failure of IBM to capture the scientific market in the Nordic countries. Towards the end of the period of early computing, some events promised to turn failure into success. The most important was the establishment of IBM Nordic laboratories in Stockholm in 1961. The laboratory employed a relatively large group of scientists from all over the Nordic countries. These scientists received training in other laboratories in Europe and USA and put to work on scientific problems as well as on practical product development. The scientific work included modern control theory and the products were mostly control systems. Many of the laboratory scientists later accepted important positions in Nordic universities in research institutions and in industry, carrying with them deep insights and pleasant memories from their time with IBM.

Another act of IBM that rendered the company a lot of good will was the donation of a large-scale scientific computer to the Technical University of Denmark in Lyngby in 1964. The Northern Europe University Computer Center (NEUCC) grew from this computer to serve the Nordic scientific community, especially university scholars. At the same time, a fund was set up to give financial support to users traveling from their countries to the Center [6].

With regard to computer systems, the announcement of the IBM System 360 in 1964 with deliveries two years later was most significant for the entire market. The 360 offered a product line in which each single product was compatible up- and downward. With the computer came an entirely new operating system. The original intention was to make a computer that they could use for data processing and scientific computing. They did not entirely achieve this intention.

2.5   Summing up scientific computing

Even if IBM were not as successful in the scientific computing market as it was in the administrative data processing market, one might claim that it indirectly influenced the general market for scientific computing in the Nordic countries. One might point to the following influences:

- The vigorous IBM sales efforts, information activities, and publications paved the way for scientific computers of all brands. Many of these activities involved visiting specialists from other, more advanced, IBM establishments.
- Nordic university people and other members of the scientific community learnt computer basics while taking part in early IBM courses.
- Some of the Nordic universities took advantage of the generous rebates that IBM awarded for educational computer rentals.
- The fast growing and well-managed stock of application programs, for the IBM 650, for example, gave many scientific and engineering users a short cut to results instead of developing programs themselves.
- The initial IBM administrative computers were used for scientific and engineering applications by many outside users.
- Typical IBM programming languages such as FORTRAN was the base for more sophisticated programming systems developed in the Nordic countries.
- FORTRAN turned out to be the dominating programming language in the practical engineering market.
- A large number of Nordic scientists had early experience with large-scale IBM scientific computers while studying at, or visiting, US

Universities and research institutions or while using the IBM computing center in Paris or, later, the NEUCC in Lyngby, Denmark.

- The IBM Nordic Laboratories trained a large group of people from all over the Nordic countries to act as systems engineers, teachers, and managers in Nordic universities, institutions, and industries.

- The question: "Was IBM instrumental in wrecking the Nordic national computer industry?" can be answered yes and no. Yes, because IBM was too strong a company to beat by local start-ups. No, because of IBM had a strict and almost paranoid adherence to the restrictions set by anti-trust laws. However, with regard to the IBM sales representatives, one may suspect some hits below the belt. IBM was sometimes accused of "pre-announcing" their new products before they were ready, thereby holding up customers who were about to order from IBM's competitors.

IBM headquarters had specialists who acted when they heard about plans to establish national computer industries in a particular country. They offered cooperation, sub-contractorships, for example, as an alternative to starting a computer industry while warning of the high cost and risk involved in competing with IBM. I was aware of one such (unsuccessful) attempt by IBM in the case of Nokia in the early 1960s.

3.   EARLY COMPUTING IN NORDIC IBM COUNTRY BY COUNTRY

3.1   IBM Denmark

The computer era started in Denmark with the building of an (improved) copy of the Swedish BESK, named DASK [5, 9]. It was ready for use in 1957 and installed at Regnecentralen. The Gier was the second machine built at Regnecentralen in 1960.

The IBM era in data processing began in 1959 when Dansk Folke Forsikrings Anstalt (DFFA) ordered an IBM 7070. DFFA installed a 1410 machine in 1962. The same year, 1962, I/S Datacentralen installed an IBM 7070. The 1401 and its small brother 1440 were, however, the machines that dominated the administrative data processing market in Denmark during the early computing period before the advent of the IBM System 360. Several 305 RAMACs were also installed, one of the first at Toms Fabrikker in 1960.

Just at the end of the era of early computing IBM made a significant contribution to the scientific and educational community. IBM donated an IBM 7090 computer to the Danish Technical University in Lyngby used by scientists in the Nordic countries plus the Netherlands. At the same time, IBM formed an endowment fund for supporting the users of the computer. The new computing center had the name Northern Europe University Computing Center (NEUCC) [6].

3.2   IBM Finland

The national project for building a computer (ESKO at 20 additions per second) in Finland started in 1955, much later than in Norway and Sweden [4]. This was not ready for use until 1960. At that time, the first computer in Finland, the IBM 650, was already installed (1958) at the Postal Savings Bank. The main applications were a number of typical banking data processing tasks, but from the beginning, the scientific community used the available extra computer time. Many of these scientists had started earlier by using the IBM 604 electronic calculator in Finland or the IBM 650 in Stockholm or Paris for their scientific tasks. Finnish universities installed a number of IBM 1620 machines. Regardless, the non-IBM computers outnumbered IBM ones at the Finnish universities. The universities received some of the non-IBM computers gratis. An IBM 1710 process control system was installed in 1963 at the Enso-Gutzeit Kaukopää paper mill. One of the IBM machines used solely for engineering calculations was the IBM 610, based on paper tape, a magnetic drum, and 300 electron tubes plus electromechanical components, which was installed in 1959 at Valmet Rautpohja and Kunnallislaskenta.

In the administrative data processing market, IBM achieved the same dominating position as elsewhere in the world. After the first IBM 650 at the Postal Savings Bank followed a second IBM 650 and two IBM 305 RAMACs (installed at retail company Elanto and wholesale company OTK in 1959), and a horde of IBM 1401s and 1440s. The first 1401 was installed for the tax authorities in 1961. The largest machines installed in Finland before the IBM 360 era were several IBM 1410 systems.

3.3   IBM Iceland

The first computer came to Iceland in 1964 as the Icelandic State and Municipal Data Center obtained an IBM 1401 and the University of Iceland an IBM 1620 (obtained with a 60% educational allowance) [7, 8]. The year before, IBM had arranged for a demonstration of an IBM 1620 at the University. The first courses were held with support from IBM Denmark and gave people the opportunity of using the computer. The state government was of the opinion that these two computers should carry out all data processing and all scientific and engineering computing in Iceland.

FORTRAN courses were offered locally and the IBM Program Library was taken advantage of. This situation lasted until the 1970s and 1980s when the "IBM monopoly" was broken. During the time before 1964, IBM punched card machines were extensively used in Iceland: the first Unit Record equipment came in 1949. The National Register was established in 1952. Some scientists had learned to use IBM computers at universities abroad.

3.4   IBM Norway

First in Norway was the Norwegian built computer NUSSE (500 additions per second). It was ready for use in 1954 [1]. The first and only IBM 650 computer in Norway was installed in Bergen in 1958 as a joint venture between the Bergen University and a group of local industries and the local tax authorities. In 1963, the University of Bergen ordered an IBM 1620. Only one 305 RAMAC was installed in Norway, at Freia Chocolade Fabrik A/S (1960). The 1401 definitely heralded the entry of IBM Norway into the electronic data processing world. In 1961, five 1401 machines were installed in Norway. The insurance company Storebrand installed a large 1410-1401 system with magnetic tapes in 1962. The IBM 1440, announced in 1962, was perfectly priced for the Norwegian market.

In 1963, ten out of twenty-five computer installed in Norway were used for statistical or scientific applications. In 1966, out of a total of 75 computer installations, IBM had installed 43. As to the number of systems on order in 1966, 52 out of 62 were ordered from IBM, most of them IBM System 360.

3.5   IBM Sweden

Scientific computing started in Sweden in 1954 when the first Swedish computer BESK (16 000 additions per second) was inaugurated [2, 3, 5]. It gave rise to a large family of computers at various universities in Sweden, Norway, and Germany. The first IBM 650 customers were Kungliga Flygförvaltningen, Folksam (1956) and Thule. The 650 machines were used in their spare time by scientific and data processing customers throughout the Nordic countries. The Swedish defense research institution (FOA) installed an IBM 7090 in 1961. A few 1620 computers were installed, one of them at the University of Umeå. The first 1710 process control system was installed at the Billerud Paper plant and another at LKAB (mining company in Kiruna) at the beginning of the 1960s. The IBM 1401 was introduced into the Swedish market in 1959 and marks the beginning of the growth period of IBM data processing in Sweden [2]. The Swedish Central Bureau of Statistics installed an IBM 7070 in the early 1960s, and some other 7000-series computer were installed as well. The IBM Nordic Laboratories was founded in 1960.

REFERENCES

1. Nerheim, Gunnar & Nordvik, Helge W.: Ikke bare maskiner, Historien om IBM Norge 1935–1985, Stavanger 1986.
2. Pressmeddelande om IBMs 75 år i Sverige. http://www.ibm.com/news/se/2002/12/10-ibm75.html
3. IBM Archives. http://www-1.ibm.com/ibm/history/
4. Tienari, Martti (ed.): Tietotekniikan alkuvuodet Suomessa (the first years of computing in Finland), Jyväskylä 1993.
5. Bruhn, Erik (ed.): EDB Historik – i nordisk perspektiv, Copenhagen 1991.
6. "Lyngby har fået elektronregnemaskine til 20 mill. kroner", Lyngby-Tårbäck Bladet 28.10.1965.
7. Oddur Benediktsson et al., Computerization of the Icelandic State and Municipalities in the years 1964 to 1985, HINC-1 Abstract.
8. Magnús Magnússon, The advent of the first general purpose computer in Iceland and its impact on science and engineering, HINC-1 Abstract.
9. IBM NYT Bildkavalkade 1950–1975.

ACKNOWLEDGEMENTS

The author was employed by IBM in Finland, in the Nordic Regional Office in Stockholm and in the IBM Nordic Laboratory in various positions during the period 1956–1965 ending up as DP Sales Country Manager in IBM Finland. Many of the thoughts and memories presented above stem from that time. Without the help of present day IBMers who dug for information in the IBM archives, fellow IBMers from my time with the company, and fellow members of the HINC-1 Program Committee who supplied me with helpful information and contacts of various kinds, it would not have been possible to me to write this paper.

COMPUTERISATION OF THE ICELANDIC STATE AND MUNICIPALITIES
From 1964 to 1985

Oddur Benediktsson,
Jóhann Gunnarsson, Egill B. Hreinsson, Jakob Jakobsson,
Örn Kaldalóns, Óttar Kjartansson, Ólafur Rósmundsson,
Helgi Sigvaldason, Gunnar Stefánsson, and Jón Zophoniasson

1. Benediktsson, University of Iceland; oddur@hi.is
2. Gunnarsson, Ministry of Finance; johann.gunnarsson@fjr.stjr.is
3. Hreinsson, University of Iceland; egill@hi.is
4. Jakobsson, Marine Research Institute (retired); jak-mar@xnet.is
5. Kaldalóns, Nýherji; kaldalon@nyherji.is
6. Kjartansson, Skýrr (retired); ottar@heima.is
7. Rósmundsson, Reiknistofa bankanna; Olafur.rosmundsson@rb.is
8. Sigvaldason, Consultant; helgis@hi.is
9. Stefánsson, University of Iceland; gunnar@hi.is
10. Zophoniasson, Internal Revenue Directorate; jon.zophoniasson@rsk.is

Abstract: The paper relates how some key IT applications developed in Iceland following the introduction of the first computers in 1964. The key applications treated are the National Register of Persons, real estate assessment, financial systems, centralised processing of bank checks, fish stock abundance computations, IT in fish processing plants, the control of hydroelectric power stations, and the challenge of adopting the Icelandic alphabet to the use of computers.

Key words: Computers and government, government accounting

1.   INTRODUCTION

The history of electronic data processing in Iceland began in 1949 when Hagstofa Íslands (Statistical Bureau of Iceland) obtained the first numerical Unit Record (punched card) equipment to facilitate the processing of import and export transactions. The government established the National Register of Persons in 1952 based upon the 1950 census and a special nationwide census taken in 1952.

Skýrr (Skýrsluvélar ríkisins og Reykjavíkurborgar - The Icelandic State and Municipal Data Center) was established 1952 by an initiative from Hagstofa Íslands, Rafmagnsveita Reykjavíkur (Reykjavík Electric Power Utility), and the Practitioner General of Iceland. It enhanced the existing data processing equipment to handle alphabetic data and then used it to mechanise the National Register of Persons amongst other applications. IBM Unit Record equipment was in use for the first twelve years (Kjartansson 2002.)

The first electronic computers came to Iceland in 1964 as Skýrr obtained an IBM 1401 computer and the University of Iceland an IBM 1620 computer. In the 1960s, the unofficial policy of the government was that all administrative computation should be centralized at Skýrr and that the scientific, engineering, and educational computing should take place at the newly established Computing Centre of University of Iceland. In the early days, computers were quite costly and difficult to operate and maintain. Furthermore, only few persons had the expertise to develop and maintain computer applications. The advent of "inexpensive" minicomputers in the 1970s changed all this. The monopoly was broken and many larger concerns obtained their own computers such as DEC PDP-8, PDP-11, and IBM System/3. IT system development became common knowledge. In 1980 the University of Iceland acquired a VAX 11/750 system and the usage of interactive system development was realized there. Aside from the equipment already mentioned electronic office equipment or computers from Olivetti, Kienzle, Burroughs, Wang, and others was imported and fierce competition existed amongst the importers.

2.   SKÝRR

Skýrr came into existence in 1952 through a cooperative effort between the Icelandic State and the City of Reykjavík. The main purpose was to share the costs of operating a data centre with IBM Unit Record equipment for administrative data processing applications. They employed Unit Record equipment for the first twelve years. Skýrr obtained an IBM 1401 computer in 1964. It had 4K core memory (see Appendix) and they used punched cards as data media. This system was a direct extension of the Unit Record equipment but with the advent in 1968 of an IBM 360/30 with tape and disk stations Skýrr started to convert from the punched cards to the magnetic tapes and disks as storage and processing media.

2.1   Computers at Skýrr

The number of applications housed at Skýrr grew rapidly in the first years. Some of the applications were based directly on the National Register of Persons such as the voting registers, taxation applications as well as invoicing for the various utilities (i.e. electricity, telephone, thermal water, and state radio). It established a vehicle registration register as well as a real estate register together with real estate assessments, salary systems, and other operations. To meet the processing needs, Skýrr updated progressively its computer configuration. Figure 1 shows an example of a proposed computer configuration at Skýrr in 1974.

By 1985 Skýrr was using two IBM 4382-2 mainframes. The number of employees at Skýrr was five in 1955. It had reached 18 in 1965, 64 in 1975, and 122 in 1985. These figures exemplify the escalating increase in computer usage in the early years.

The software development tools used at Skýrr followed the generations of computers employed. During the IBM 1401 usage (1964-68) programs were written in the 1401 Symbolic Programming System (SPS). With the advent of the IBM 360/30 system, the programming languages Assembler, RPG and PL/I came into use and greatly facilitated the software development. In 1982, the Adabas data base system was in use together with the fourth generation language Natural.

2.2   First attempts at teleprocessing

The year 1973 marked the first steps towards teleprocessing at Skýrr. Then the University of Iceland gained access to Skýrr's IBM 370/135, running the APL programming system over remote terminals. The university APL application was not successful and the university abandoned it after 3 years. The main reason for the failure was limited processing capacity in the 370 computer, which had 96K of memory. A year later the Reykjavík City Hospital installed a terminal for RJE (Remote Job Entry) connected to the IBM computer at Skýrr to facilitate data processing for the clinical laboratory at the hospital. They punched in cards for requests for laboratory tests and the test results and then processed them over night when workload was low at Skýrr. The next morning various working lists and printed reports were ready at the RJE terminal. Subsequently the ever-increasing need for teleprocessing was to have a profound effect on the telephone infrastructure; that is, teleprocessing led to the development of both the connections and equipment inside Iceland as well as the equipment connecting Iceland to other countries.

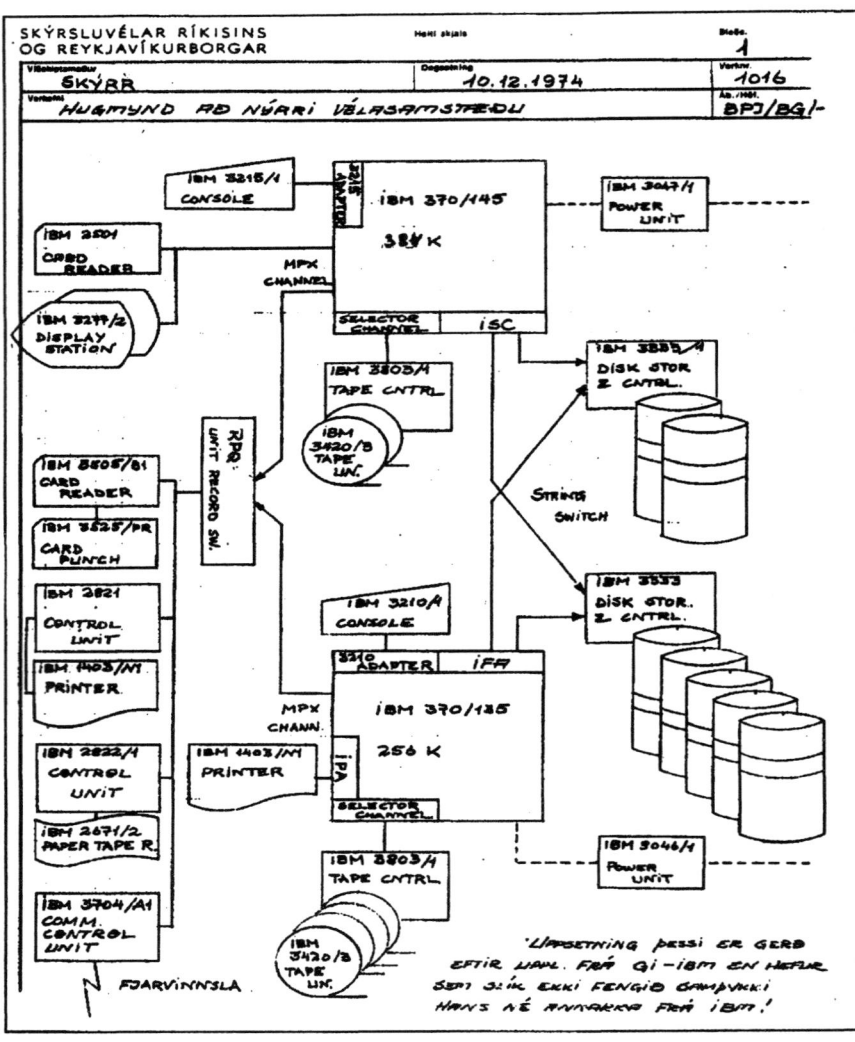

Figure 1. A diagram of proposed computer configuration of Skýrr in 1974

3. COMPUTERS IN THE ICELANDIC ADMINISTRATION

Some of the key computer applications for the Icelandic state in the early days centred on the National Register of Persons, taxation, accounting, budget planning, and real estate assessment.

3.1 The national register of persons

By 1956, the government established the National Register by law for persons and in 1969 for firms. The register evolved from the original punched card system to a computerised system in the 1960s and by 1985, it had become an online system reflecting the status of the population on a daily basis. The first application for the register was to preprint tax returns in the year 1954. The original usage of the register was for population tracking, for use as a voting register, for official administration, for medical research, and for population statistics (Þórhallsson and Zóphaníasson 1985 and Kjartansson 2002). The Personal Identification Number used was composed of the birth date of the person concerned as nine digits DDMMYYNNH (date, month, year, sequential number within the date, and year hundred i.e. 8 and 9). With the advent of the computers, they added a check digit, making the PIN a ten-digit number. This number permeates all data processing in Iceland concerning persons and firms. They use it as identification in official administration, schools, hospitals, pharmacies, banks, on driver licenses, credit cards, and other related areas.

3.2 Computers and the tax authorities

The first task performed by Skýrr for the tax authorities in Reykjavík was printing names and addresses on tax declaration forms in 1954, using the punch card based National Register of Persons as a basis. Later that year, they collected taxes and prepared related documentation for the tax collectors. Within few years, they computerized all other tax districts in this manner. After its establishment in 1962, the Directorate of Taxes assumed responsibility for the development of computerised tax systems.

When the first electronic computers arrived in 1964, the processing methods of the Unit Record era were transferred to the computer with minimal change; the Unit Record was the name given to the punched card. This immediately increased speed, but did little for the part of the process that required deskwork. On the other hand, one of the first labour-saving features in the tax processing system came in 1978 when it became possible to compare automatically employees' tax declarations with employers' statements of paid salaries. As the data-entry devices of those days (i.e. card punches and later diskette recorders) were quite expensive, it was not considered economical to install such devices in the small tax offices in the countryside. The result was that they performed most of the data entry in Reykjavík. In 1982, the tax offices around the county were equipped with inexpensive personal computers (Tandy TRS80 with simple file transfer programs) programmed for data entry and so the workload was distributed out to the local offices.

4.   THE GOVERNMENT ACCOUNTING AND PLANNING SYSTEM

4.1   The expenditure accounting system

The Treasury started using computers in 1978. That year they put to use a simple batch based expenditure accounting system programmed in RPG to run on the Skýrr computer. Output was in the form of printed lists with no possibility for on-screen viewing of data. This was primarily historic accounting with very limited management information. In 1983, they decided to take up online processing. For that purpose, they purchased a complex system for financial accounting called the Management Science of America (MSA). It turned out that the accounting key of MSA, its arrangement, and in fact, various other features did not fit Icelandic requirements; the system proved cumbersome if not impossible to adapt.

In 1985, they discontinued the use of the MSA system. Instead, they decided to develop a new system from scratch. This new system, called BÁR (Bókhalds- og Áætlanakerfi Ríkisins), went into service in 1986 and was considered a success by its users right from the beginning. In the design, they placed a heavy emphasis on error checking and reconciliation of transactions. There were provisions for on-screen management information, both ad hoc summary screens from almost every conceivable view and comparison against budget; this was crucial in the Administration as the State budget dictates what one can spend. This system had built-in teleprocessing possibilities. The BÁR accounting system has undergone considerable changes and has had new features added through the years. The Oracle e-business suite, a new and modern financial system, replaced it during 2003.

4.2   The revenue accounting system

Online data processing had a slow and cautious start in the central administration. They designed a revenue accounting system at Skýrr, which became operative in 1979. This was the first online system used in the administration. This event also marked the beginning of usage of SNA (Systems Network Architecture, the communications protocol developed by IBM in the early seventies) in Iceland. Initially, they installed remote terminals at the Reykjavik Tax Collector's Office (Gjaldheimtan í Reykjavík). At this time, the municipalities owned and operated the tax collector's offices in Reykjavík and five other townships, collecting for both local and central authorities. Elsewhere, these operations were separate. In 1981, four additional tax districts, Akureyri, Kópavogur, Hafnarfjörður, and Keflavík became part of the online system. The remaining tax districts went online during the subsequent years.

4.3   Real estate assessment

In 1966, work began to computerise the real estate assessment process. The availability of computers clearly showed the benefit of automating registration, maintenance, and printing of the description and assessment values. At the same time, the opportunity was seized to automate the process of assessing residential buildings. A model was developed that contained dozens of parameters of an assessment record describing the structure and state of the building and computed an estimated building cost. This value was depreciated according to the age of the building and adjusted it to the estimated market value. The model was developed in FORTRAN II for the IBM 1620 and ran it initially at the University of Iceland Computing Centre in 1970. The city planners also developed initially a unique property reference number (block number) for the City of Reykjavík and its surroundings; the numbers referenced the land and buildings from the first planning stages. A revised model became operative in 1976 based on a set of unit prices collected by the Central Statistical Bureau on a continuous basis in order to compute the "building cost index" and a model built at the Building Research Institute for combining the unit prices into cost of building units. The new assessment model was implemented in FORTRAN IV for a Data General minicomputer. Samples of real estate sales and later registration of all sales became part of the process on ongoing basis and used to compute the relationship between depreciated building costs and market values. These models have served as the basis for the levy of property tax and for planning purposes as well as a registry for real estate properties and their ownership.

4.4   Municipalities in Iceland

In 1970 the municipalities in Iceland (except Reykjavík) were using Burroughs General Ledger machines to account for the local income tax. Each taxpayer had his or her own ledger card where the payments were recorded.   The Skýrr centre (see above) calculated the individual tax assessment and the property rates as computed from the computerised real estate assessment (see above).

The municipalities started to cooperate in the early 70's to find a common solution to their need for improved data processing.   The minicomputers had appeared on the scene, making it feasible to manage the tax collection locally. The solution adopted was based on standard software from IBM, termed the "Taxpayer's Account" system (gjaldendabókhald), running on an IBM System/32. The state taxes and property rates were computed centrally by Skýrr with local taxes and adjustments performed in the Taxpayer's Account system. The Taxpayer's Account systems were in use well into the 1980s the and were then all centralised at Skýrr.

5.   REIKNISTOFA BANKANNA

The larger banks in Iceland started to use punched cards systems for data processing in the 1950s and some had acquired computers by the late 1960s. The growing use of cheques was rapidly becoming an unsolvable task for the banks using traditional methods.

In the year 1970, the public banks in Iceland embarked on cooperation project to find a common solution to their core data processing needs and in particular to the mounting problem of clearing cheques.   Subsequently Reiknistofa bankanna (Icelandic Banks Data Centre) was established and the common processing started in 1975 after an extended period of training and preparation.   The first application involved processing of cheques using Optical Character Reading of numbers imprinted at the bottom edge of the cheques. By 1976, a bank customer could make a cheque transaction in any bank office and the bank would record the transaction into the relevant account with electronic document interchange and with the account balance entered into the account of each Bank at the Central Bank of Iceland. Thus, every evening, RB returned the same results as obtained earlier with the "spot checks" of the Central Bank. The spot checks had taken place three to five times a year at considerable cost and effort. The level of automation achieved by this was unprecedented worldwide as best known. The volume of entries in the cheque system during the first complete operating year was 13.6 million transactions.

By 1981, the electronic booking of transactions and electronic transfer of funds was in effect for all of Iceland. Bank customers could then cash a cheque from any bank at any branch in the country and the clearing was instant. This put an end to the fraudulent practice of covering one bad cheque by the issue of another. The first expedition system went online in 1982, when the cheque system and the main general ledger system developed by the Industrial Bank were incorporated and integrated with other applications at RB. The following year saw negotiations with computer companies for the purchase of online front-desk equipment, and the Icelandic Savings Banks' Association became a full partner. Most of the electronic records of RB became accessible for online queries in 1984. The first online teller system was taken into use in 1985 in the Landsbanki-Breidholt branch and by 1987 paper-free payment exchanges were affected in the Reykjavík metropolitan area.

In the year 1985, the total number of transactions in the common applications of Reiknistofa bankanna was 52.4 million records. The same year the number of employees reached 81. The computer system used was an IBM-4381 mainframe, IBM-DOS operating system, using PL/I as the main programming language. Two years later the IBM-MVS operating system replaced the DOS requiring major updating of all systems and applications. In 1987, central OCR reading of cheques ceased at RB as the online teller terminals recorded all the required data.

6. SCIENTIFIC COMPUTING AND SOFTWARE DEVELOPMENT METHODS

The scientific and engineering community in Iceland started to use the first computer at the University of Iceland in 1964, as soon as it became operative. Some scientists had already learned to use computers at universities in other countries. A steady stream of FORTRAN II courses became available locally. Within a year or two, they wrote or acquired a number of applications from the IBM Program Library or other sources. From the start, they conducted research on software development methodologies (Benediktsson 1967, 1974, 1977.) Meteorologists, astronomers, geophysicists, fish- and livestock researchers, medical researchers, statisticians, and many others brought in their programs and data to execute at the University Computer Centre and to seek expert assistance. On the engineering side, the use of the computer proved particularly advantageous for surveyors and naval architects with their needs for massive computations. They built and simulated a number of operational research models to optimise the control for water reservoirs for hydroelectric power stations and to find the optimum size of a trawler in Icelandic waters. For further information, see Magnusson 2003.

7.   COMPUTING THE HERRING STOCK

The Marine Research Institute started using the punch card system in the late 1950s. Herring tagging was the very first fisheries research data transferred to this system. The most important herring fishery at Iceland traditionally took place during the summer off the north coast, based on the so-called "Norðurlandssíld"; that is, the herring off the north coast of Iceland. When repeated attempts to locate this herring outside the summer season failed, Árni Friðriksson (1935, 1944) suggested that this herring migrated to Norway each autumn to spawn in early spring. According to this theory, it followed that the well-known winter and spring herring fishery off the west coast of Norway was on the same herring stock as the summer fishery off Iceland. In order to test these revolutionary ideas, Icelandic and Norwegian scientists started mass tagging of herring in 1948. By the late 1950s, Iceland had tagged about 100.000 herring and Norway tagged about double that number. The new Automatic Data Processing (ADP) methods greatly facilitated the processing of these data. The system quickly verified Friðriksson´s ideas on trans-oceanic migrations between Norway and Iceland. In addition, they used the tag-returns to assess the abundance of this internationally important herring stock. They presented the results at an ICES Herring Symposium in 1961 and formally published their findings two years later (Dragersund and Jakobsson 1963). Thus, primarily due to tagging and the new ADP methods, it proved possible to elucidate the decline of the stock from the high level of twelve million tons during the early 1950s to five million tons in 1959. Severe scepticism surrounded these results at the time, but later assessments have verified how accurate these first abundance estimates were as shown in Table 1.

Table 1. Abundance estimates of adult Norwegian Spring spawning herring in millions of tons for the years 1953-1959 based on the results from tagging experiments at Iceland and ICES "best estimates" based on the Virtual Population Analysis (VPA) method.

Year	Tagging Results 1961	VPA 1999
1953	12.5	12.0
1954	12.2	9.7
1955	13.9	14.7
1956	12.0	13.5
1957	9.3	10.9
1958	6.6	9.8
1959	5.0	7.6

As mentioned above, the first computers came to Iceland in 1964 when Skýrr obtained an IBM 1401 computer and the University of Iceland an IBM 1620. Prior to this, the landings of the major species of fish had been sampled for several decades with regard to various biological and biometric parameters. When the appropriate programs were in place, the new computers tabulated these accumulated data and combined them to corresponding catches of the fishing fleet the annual catch in numbers of each year class was calculated.

The late 1960s saw the introduction of a new method, the so-called Virtual Population Analysis (VPA), for assessing fish stock abundance. The basic data required for VPA were already available due to the employment of the IBM 1620 and 1401 computers and the new method could be applied such as for the cod and herring stock size estimation at Iceland already for the beginning of the 1970s. Subsequently in the years up to 1980, computer programs routinely estimated the abundance of fish stocks interactively on PDP-11 computers, eventually running Unix variants. In 1984-85, the Icelandic marine scientists obtained access to mail and news feeds when the Marine Research Institute first established a dial-up link to Sweden and subsequently became the first Iceland backbone-link to the predecessor of the internet. This quickly developed into an invaluable link to several key colleagues and sister institutes worldwide.

8.   FISH PROCESSING PLANTS

Fishing and the fish processing industry form the basis of the Icelandic economy. Around the year 1970, fish processing plants started paying a bonus to employees for efficiency in production and utilization of raw material. In the early 1970s, the company Rekstrartækni s/f computerised the bonus calculation for the larger fish processing plants in Iceland. In 1972, Rekstrartækni purchased an IBM System/3 system and IBM Iceland assisted in writing RPG programs for a salary system. They started servicing the processing plant Ísbjörninn (with close to 200 employees), and were so successful that soon they had 16 plants to serve. They arranged monthly meetings with the plant managers to coordinate this new technique. The managers took care not to disclose any critical information about their plants to the competitors with the remarkable exception of the "contribution margin" and the Rekstrarækni staff had to sign a non-disclosure agreement. Based on the operative data obtained in the plants the utilisation of the raw material was computed and measures taken to improve it. As a result the utilisation of the raw material for cod, for example, increased from 36% to

42% in the period 1974 to 1980 resulting in 18% increase in packed products that yielded 5400 ton addition in the total production.

In 1981 Rekstrartækni had four large IBM System/34 computers, when they purchased one IBM System/38 to take over all their data processing. By then they were by far the largest mid-range computer installation in Iceland. Subsequently the fish processing plants began purchasing their own midrange computers and started running their own salary and accounting systems.

9.   LANDSVIRKJUN

One of the earliest minicomputers based on real-time control applications in Iceland became operational in late 1974 in Landsvirkjun (The National Power Authority).   Leeds & Northrup manufactured the "Supervisory Control and Data Acquisition (SCADA) System" for Landsvirkjun and installed it to control and monitor hydroelectric power stations and substations in the power system, which at the time covered the Southwestern part of Iceland.   The system, labelled the Conitel 2050, consisted of a computer based master station and several hardwired remote stations.   The master station was based on a dual configuration of a Lockheed MAC-16 minicomputer.   They installed a similar system at the Reykjavik Municipal Electric Works.   Both these systems were in operation well into the eighties.

10.   COMPUTERS AND THE ICELANDIC ALPHABET

The basic character set for early data processing consisted of the 26 characters in the English alphabet together with the ten decimal numerals. The Icelandic language has ten letters that do not occur in English as shown

Áá Ææ Ðð here. This really means twenty, when one considers both upper and lower case letters. This, together with the tiny **Éé Íí Óó Öö** market, has cost the Icelanders many headaches and **Úú Ýý Þþ** added workload and it took ingenuity to make printed alphanumeric data look reasonable on printed output and display devices.   Throughout the Unit Record period (1952 – 1964), the repertoire was limited to 37 or 38 characters, which meant that people had to make compromises.

Out of the ten additional Icelandic letters, four were considered essential for printing understandable names, namely Ð, Þ, Æ and Ö.   The remaining six are vowels written with acute accents.   In the tight situation, the compromise was to accept the plain unaccented vowels as substitutes as it would normally not cause misunderstanding. It is clear that not everybody was happy, though, to have their names "mutilated" in official documents. By dropping Q, which is not used in the Icelandic alphabet, and using the same glyph for 1 (one) and I as well as the same modified glyph for 2 and Z, this was possible.

The IBM 1401 computer was capable of handling 48 characters, as was the first generation of the IBM 1403 printers. This meant that it was no longer necessary to have the same glyph stand for two different letters/digits. However, there was still only room for two of the accented Icelandic letters and the selection was the characters Á and É. On hindsight, it was of course rather useless to take on only two of the six accented letters.

A revolution can be said to have taken place with the Extended Binary Coded Decimal Interchange Code (EBCDIC), introduced by IBM with its 360 computer line. This was an eight-bit code with 256 different code points and thus plenty of room for letters specific to other languages than English. Therefore, with the IBM 360/30, Iceland obtained the capacity for a full Icelandic alphabet without sacrificing anything else.

It is a remarkable coincidence that at almost the same time the American Standards Association (ASA, which later changed its name to the American National Standards Institute, ANSI) published the first version of it's 7 bit ASCII code (American Standard Code for Information Interchange), which was adapted by all American computer manufacturers except IBM (1). To adapt ASCII to languages using accented letters there were ten open code points for national adaptation. In Iceland, we used a version using a so-called floating accent where the accent was actually stored separately, ahead of the letter on which it was supposed to sit. This solution caused difficulties when sorting. In addition, one needed a special adaptation to most printers to combine the two. This solution was incompatible with EBCDIC.

The 7-bit limitation was a general problem in Europe and many other countries that forced an extension to eight bits. In the seventies, the European Computer Manufacturers Association (ECMA) started working on an 8-bit code table that would address the needs of the various European and other languages for which ASCII was not sufficient. Wilhelm Friedrich Bohn, the IBM representative in the ECMA working group on code tables and keyboards (2), proposed a code table. ECMA released this table, nicknamed the Bohn Code, in 1985 as the ECMA-94 standard. The ISO adopted it and today we know it as ISO 8859-1 or Latin-1 code.

Mr. Bohn was familiar with the requirements of the Icelandic language. Since no other serious contestant for the code points was in question at that time (contrary to what later happened (3)), the complete Icelandic alphabet became part of his proposal, later known as the Latin-1 code page. The

Icelandic government has duly acknowledged Mr. Bohn's contribution to the Icelandic information society.

As far as personal computers, the IBM PC and its clones that were capable of handling eight-bit character sets appeared on the Icelandic market. Each importer created its own version of an Icelandic code table. By 1985 or so, at least four versions were in circulation, plus one for the Apple Macintosh, causing difficulties in exchanging data. Jóhann Gunnarsson, then manager of the University Computing Centre in Reykjavík, called some meetings between the importers and a number of key users. Eventually, he proposed a compromise code table, sometimes named the JG Code; all PC and PC clone importers eventually adopted this code. Jóhann's attempts at persuading the Apple community to adopt the same code points for the Icelandic letters were not successful, however.

In due time, the JG Code was gradually replaced by IBM's Code Page 850, which, as far as placement of the twenty extra Icelandic letters is concerned, is identical to ISO 8859-1.

11. CONCLUSIONS

In this paper, we have discussed the onset of the Information Age in Iceland. The applications that we selected for discussion have been instrumental in transforming Iceland from a rather backward society at the end of the Second World War to a modern society of today. Although Iceland has a very small population (about 230.000 persons in 1980), the degree of administrative computerization in Iceland is comparable with that of many larger Western nations. In a small country, the complexity of application can be brought under control and because of that, development costs are minimal. Stefán Ingólfsson has observed that the cost of developing a system in Iceland can be as small as one fifth or even one tenth of the cost of developing equivalent system in any of the other Scandinavian countries (Kjartansson 2002.)

REFERENCES

1. Benediktsson, O. 1967. "Fortran II málið fyrir IBM 1620 rafreikninn." *Kennslukver, Reiknistofnun Háskólans*, 58 p
2. Benediktsson, O. 1974. "Forritunarmálin ALGOL, FORTRAN og PL/I", Tímarit VFÍ, 86-88.
3. Benediktsson, O. 1977. "Sequential file processing in Fortran IV", *Software Practice and Experience* 7, 655-658.

4. Friðriksson, A. 1935. "Tilraunir til síldveiða við Suðurlandið á varðskipinu Þór vorið 1935" (in the Icelandic.) *Ægir*, vol. 28 pp.125-132.
5. Friðriksson, A. 1944. "Norðurlandssíldin (The Herring off the North Coast of Iceland, in Icelandic with an extended English summary)." *Rit Fiskideildar* no. 1, 388 p.
6. Dragersund, O. and Jakobsson, J. 1963, "Stock Strengths and Rates of Mortality of the Norwegian Spring Spawners as Indicated by Tagging Experiments in Icelandic Waters." *Rapp. Et Proc. Verb.* Vol. 154, pp 83-90.
7. Kjartansson, Ó. 2002. "Upplýsingaiðnaður í hálfa öld." Skýrr hf.
8. Magnússon, M. 2003. "The advent of the first general purpose computer in Iceland and its impact on science and engineering." *History of Nordic Computing*, Trondheim, 2003.
9. Sigvaldason, H. and Tulinius, H. 1980. "Human Health Data from Iceland" *Banbury Report 4*, Cold Spring Harbor Laboratory, 1980.
10. Þórhallson, J.Þ and Zóphoníasson, J. 1985. "Tölvuvinnsla Hagstofunnar." Klemensar bók. Afmælisrit, Félag viðskiptafræðinga og hagfræðinga, Sigurður Snævarr ritstjóri.

ENDNOTES

(1) Steven J. Searle. A Brief History of Character Codes in North America, Europe, and East Asia http://tronweb.super-nova.co.jp/characcodehist.html

(2) TrueType Fonts, http://www.norasoft.de/tt-fonts.html

(3) Turkey, for instance, has tried to persuade the standards community to exchange at least two of the Icelandic letters in ISO 8859-1 with letters from the Turkish alphabet.

APPENDIX

Magnetic Core Memory

The IBM 1401, 1620, and 360/30 computers mentioned earlier were all equipped with magnetic core memory, a much more compact and reliable technology than earlier vacuum tubes and mercury delay lines. Jay Forrester, who was head of the Whirlwind computer project, invented core memory at MIT in the late 1940s. IBM then licensed the technology and core memory became commonplace in much of the first and second-generation of IBM computers. Semiconductor memories largely replaced magnetic cores in the 1970s, but they remained in use for many years in mission-critical and high-reliability applications. The Apollo Guidance Computer, for example used core memory, as did the early versions of the Space Shuttle. (Source: http://web.mit.edu/6.933/www/core.html)

Magnetic core memory had some interesting features. For instance, it did not need constant current to keep its contents. In some cases, after a night's rest it was possible to start with the program and data from the previous day. Also, it emitted electromagnetic waves, which could be detected in the near vicinity of the memory unit. It was discovered that a certain way of programming the IBM 1401 computer made it possible to play some simple melodies that could be heard in a radio receiver put on top of the memory unit. A sequence of NOP (No operation) instructions dictated the pitch of a tone, and the number of times that sequence repeated determined the length of the tone.

Magnetic core memories were expensive to produce, amongst others because it was not possible to automate the production. All the wires had to be threaded by hand.

The illustrations that follow are by the courtesy of F. Doherty, Glasgow.

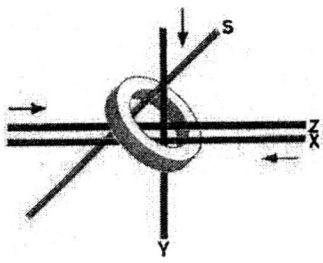   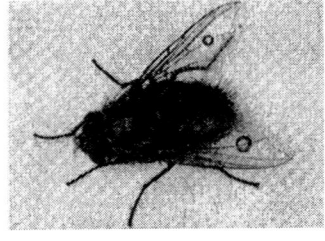

Figure 2. A Magnetic core with its control   *Figure 3.* A 20 mil and 30 mil magnetic core
and sensing wires.   on the wings of a common house fly.

TECHNOLOGY TRANSFER, MODERNIZATION, AND THE WELFARE STATE
Regnecentralen and the Making of Governmental Policy on Computer Technology in Denmark in the 1960s

Per Vingaard Klüver

Institute for History, Aarhus University; hispvk@hum.au.dk

Abstract: This paper will address the mechanisms of computer technology transfer and the perceived role of computers in the modernization project of the Danish society, by analysing the early computer projects in Denmark. Especially it focuses on the similarities between the perception of computer technology and the visions of the welfare state as a modern, science bases and rational society.

Key words: Computers, welfare state, Denmark

1.   INTRODUCTION

In the last decades, the study of the history of technology has increasingly followed the same trends and development as we can find in general history. Social constructivist approaches, actor-network analysis, and discourse analysis are often used techniques, and we can hardly find any historians of technology that does not take the social and/or political context in account in his studies.

The following article has two parts. In the first part, I will outline the transfer of computer technology to Denmark. This resulted in the creation of Regnecentralen, which was responsible for constructing the first Danish computer, DASK, in 1958. After a short description of the emergence of the welfare state in Denmark as a necessary context for the second part, I will look at the first attempt at forming a governmental policy regarding the use of computers in local and national government. This case shows how different conceptions by the various actors of the role and nature of computer technology defined their views on the necessary policies on the computer field.[1]

2.   TECHNOLOGY TRANSFER

In his study on the political reactions to the introduction of computer technology in Sweden, Hans De Geer set up four stages:

1. Information or technology awareness: In this first stage, you get aware of a new technology's existence. Mostly this happens through personal contacts on the scientific-technical level.
2. Technology transfer: A more precise knowledge about the new technology's nature and possibility evolves, and we obtain new information in a systematic manner. We test the technology and gain the first experiences.
3. Technology diffusion: We use the technology more extensively and survey the needs and possibilities. The first official surveys and reports appear.
4. Consequence handling: Consequences for areas such as employment, education, policies, and organizational changes emerge.[2]

The first information of the new computer technology came to Denmark through Sweden. When Stig Ekelöf returned from his fact-finding trip to the USA in 1946 (see Anders Carlsson's article), he gave a report on his findings at a meeting of the interested parties in September 1946. Amongst the participants was Prof. Richard Petersen from the Danish Technical University. On his initiative, the Academy of Technical Sciences (an organization parallel to the Swedish Ingeniörveteneskabsakademien)[3] formed a special committee, Committee on Computing Machinery, which should monitor the international developments on the field of advanced

---

[1]   This article was originally written as a paper for the annual meeting of the Society for the History of Technology in San Jose, CA. 2001. A more detailed narrative can be found in Per V. Küver: From Research Institute to Computer Company. Regnecentralen 1946-1964. *IEEE Annals for the History of Computing._*Vol. 21, no. 2 s. 31-43. In the present article though, theoretical and more general considerations, which had been omitted in the above-mentioned article, will be highlighted.

[2]   Hans De Geer: På väg til datasamhället. Datateknikken i politikken 1946-1963. KTH, Stockholm 1992

[3]   Formed in 1937, its purpose was to promote co-operation between science and industry and the utilisation of applied science. It consisted of various non-commercial laboratories, special working groups etc. It also played a role conducting scientific surveys and offering scientific expertise for government. P.O. Pedersen: *Akademiet for de tekniske Videnskaber*. Copenhagen 1938

computing machinery. The members of this committee were professors from the Technical University and from the faculty of science of the University of Copenhagen, who shared an interest in the use of numerical methods in their special fields.

The minutes from the meetings of that committee clearly indicates, that the members did not have any clear ideas of the possibilities and nature of the new computer technology, and naturally they were exploring all developments, studying reports and publications and obtaining reports from Danish scientists staying primarily in the USA and Britain.[4] A major source of information was the close contacts with Swedish colleagues.

At first, the RMU concentrated its efforts on analogue differential analyzers. We do not know if Ekelöf and Hartree played a role in this decision, but both were experts in that technology. Ekelöf had recommended the procurement of differential analyzers in Sweden before the war.

The Danish Technical-Scientific Research Council (Danmarks Teknisk Videnskabelige Forskningsråd (DTVFR) decided in February 1948 to grant financial support to the construction of a differential analyzer similar to the machines constructed by Vannevar Bush[5] and simultaneously to support experiments in the use of electronic calculators in solving linear equations by Professor Rybner at DTH.

Building an electronic digital computer in Denmark was out of the question at that time. All economic resources where reserved for reconstruction of the Danish economy. Especially US-Dollars were scarce, since most of the Danish exports went to Britain (more on that later). Should they obtain advanced computer technology, it was necessary to find a solution that would put a minimum of strain to the nation's reserves of foreign currencies. This constraint was one of the main reasons why the committee, with some enthusiasm, tried to persuade UNESCO to locate the planned International Computation Centre in Denmark. However, they delayed these plans due to political and commercial conflicts, the committee's interest cooled off.[6]

---

[4] Archive of Akademiet for de tekniske Videnskaber (AtV). Erhvervsarkivet (Archive for Trade and Industry), Aarhus Box 19(B) and Box 6A.

[5.] It was completed around 1956. See Eyvind Frederiksen: Den første danske Differential-Analysator. In *Ingeniøren* nr.17 Copenhagen 1952 pp. 280-290 og M. Fordsmand: Den mekaniske Differential Analysator ved laboratoriet for anvendt matematik, DtH. In *Ingeniøren* nr. 33 Copenhagen 1956 pp. 652-656. AtV box. 76 letter February 3.1947.

[6] The most comprehensive account on the International Computation Centre can be found in Eileen Marie Mahoney: *Negotiating New Information Technology and National Development: The Role of the Intergovernmental Bureau of Informatics.* Ph.D. Temple University 1987, especially pp 54-134. *UNESCO/NS/ICC/1* and UNESCO E/1694/Add. 1

In the first half of the 1950s, it seemed more realistic to obtain funding for acquiring an electronic digital computer. The Korean War had turned the Cold War even colder, and the USA now started to put an increasing pressure on the Danish government to increase DK military expenditures - especially regarding the funds stemming from the Marshall aid. Military expenditures have never been politically popular in Denmark, and the Danish governments of very political color would rather use the funds for long-term scientific and technological research.[7] However, here the Defense Research Council came to the rescue and outlined the need for computers for their research - and like their Swedish counterparts, they emphasized the need for ballistic computations and code breaking.

It was no harm, that some members of the Defense Research Council also where leading members of the Committee of Computing Machinery, especially Richard Petersen. They formed a joint committee and in late 1952, an application was send to the Defense Ministry, requesting funds.[8] A sum of 900.000 Dkr. (at that time approximately $130.000) was granted in 1955 from the counterpart fund of the Marshall aid, making everyone happy. The Danes could start the construction of a computer, and they could tell the USA, that they had used the fund for military purposes!

In the meantime, Richard Petersen had used his influence to give the young engineer Bent Scharøe Petersen the chance to use part of his military service as an assistant in the construction team working on the Swedish computer BESK.[9] Therefore, they decided that the Danish computer should be an improved version of the BESK- machine and hence the name – DAnish version of BeSK – DASK. The military also insisted that it should not be responsible for operating the computer and bearing the financial risk in doing so. The obvious solution was to establish another institution under the auspices of the Academy of Technical Sciences. Therefore, they dissolved the Committee on Computing Machinery and founded Regnecentralen (RC).

---

from the UNESCO-archive at the State Library, Aarhus. Letter to Harald Bohr from R. Petersen 3.6.49, *AtV* Box 19 (B), Erhvervsarkivet Århus

[7]   Leon Dalgas Jensen: *Dansk forsvar og Marshallplanen.* In Historisk Tidsskrift 1991 bd. 91, no 2 p. 459-506

[8]   Letter dated 29. sept. 1952, j. nr. FFR 31/52, *Archive of Forsvarets Forskningsråd. ATV-archive*, op.cit. Box 216.

[9]   Also another young engineer, who came to play a significant role in the construction, Tage Vejlø, was soon involved in another Swedish computer project, SMIL in Lund. Interviews with Tage Vejlø and Bent Scharøre Petersen. See also Bent Scharøe Petersen: *Dasks' første år.* In Poul Svejstrup et. al: *Niles Ivar Bech – en epoke i edb-udviklingen i Danmark.* Copenhagen 1976 pp. 15-20. The book is now available on-line on http://www.datamuseum.dk/rc/NIB/

The reason for constructing a computer instead of buying a commercial computer was partly economical, but it was also because the members of RC were convinced that the operation and maintenance of a computer required a degree of knowledge about its construction that they could only obtain by active participation in the construction of the machine. In addition, research in new scientific methods and techniques utilizing numerical methods and the use of computer technologies they could best obtain by solving practical problems. This would also be the best way to develop courses in coding and planning and identifying possible applications for science and industry. Therefore, it made sense from a research point of view that RC should be directly be involved in running DASK. As we shall see, this hands-on approach would have a direct impact on the views and beliefs of most of the academic milieu on computer technology in the conflict that follows.

They decided not only to copy the Swedish BESK, but also to incorporate a number of improvements that were the result of experiences gained by computer projects around the world. The construction was a shoestring operation. For instance, they applied the magnetic coating of the magnetic drum with the assistance of a modified vacuum cleaner. They assembled core memory on kitchen tables by the wives of the members of the small construction team.[10] After two years, DASK became part of the Danish Defense Ministry on the 13 February 1958, well within the planned time schedule and budget. They presented DASK to the public a couple of months before that, at a big Electricity and Atoms Fair in Copenhagen. They installed a data transmission line and the astonished audience could have their income tax calculated in record time.[11]

DASK was a success and used for technical and scientific computation for Danish industry, mainly shipyards, telephone companies, and machine works, while military computations only played a minor role.[12] RC expanded the activities by creating departments for engineering computations, operations analysis, office automation, mathematical analysis, and electronics engineering in order to develop and promote new numerical methods and computer technology in general. The arranged a number of courses in programming and the application of computers, and RC became very active in developing the Algol-language. The Director, Niels Ivar Bech, was an inspirational and enthusiastic leader, who formed a creative

---

[10] Interviews with Bent Scharøe Petersen and Tage Vejlø.
[11] The presentation at the fair and the inauguration was reported by all national newspapers. They heralded DASK as an important step into the second technological revolution, f.x.: *Danmark i den anden tekniske revolution* Politiken 12.2.1958.
[12] A list dating from early 1960 has 308 different jobs from various companies. Bent Scharøe Petersens private Archive

working climate, where the employees were encouraged to disregard formal structures and co-operate across departmental boundaries.

RC hoped for the possibility to start the construction of a successor in order to explore new developments in electronics (transistors) and architecture - if necessary in co-operation with their Swedish colleagues. However, these plans did not materialize, partly because the Swedish Matematikmaskinnämnden (MMN) did not succeed in creating a permanent institution. Consequently, MMN lost most of his staff to a commercial company.[13] Luckily, the Geodetic Institute came to the rescue. GI had some experience in using calculators for its computations, inspired by Comrie's work in Britain. Its leader, Ejnar Andersen, took the initiative that a small transistorized computer should be constructed in a joint effort by staff from RC and GI. Funding was in place by some creative budgeting by Einar Andersen, and the construction of GIER started.[14]

In the meantime, industrialist Haldor Topsøe made an inquiry into the possibility of purchasing a GIER-machine, since it seems well suited for process-control and calculations. Several more inquiries followed from the universities, and the board of RC reluctantly agreed in starting the production of a small series of 8 machines. It was never the intention that RC should turn out to be a computer manufacturer, its purpose was to promote scientific and practical research into the use of computers and the development of techniques and methods plus training and teaching in the same areas. Nevertheless, as we will see later, things turned out differently.

3.   COMPUTERS AND WELFARE STATE

In order to give the following events a broader perspective, it is necessary to sketch the evolution of the political thinking and the emergence of a new social discourse such as the ideological basis of the Danish welfare state in the 1950s and 1960s.

In his study on the various types of welfare states, Gøsta Esping-Andersen identified three major types – the residual model, the social

---

[13] Hans De Geer op. cit. pp. 36-45. Their plan was to create a Institute for Numerical Analysis.

[14] Descriptions in Christian Gram et. al: GIER – A Danish Computer of Medium Size, in IEEE Trans Electronic Computers. 1963 pp. 629-650. Torben Krarup, "GIER: Den logiske struktur," Ingeniøren 1961 1961, pp. 716-720. H. Isaksson and Bent Scharøe Petersen, " GIER: Systemplanlægning og kredsløb", Ingeniøren 1961, pp 721-728. Einar Andersen, "Hvordan Gier blev født", Svejstrup 1976 op.cit. pp. 45-50. B. S. Petersen, "Gier", NordSam 60. Copenhagen 1960, pp. 13.1-13.7. H. Isaksson, "Kredsløbsteknikken i GIER," NordSam &0, op.cit. pp. 14.1-14.5

insurance model and finally the universal or Nordic model.[15] The latter is characterized by a strong state and that every citizen has the right to obtain social benefits, which guarantees everyone a certain minimal standard of living. Taxes financed this universal system, which also shifts economic resources from the wealthy to the poor, and consequently promotes equality.

The welfare state was not the result of a master plan, but came because of new concepts on the role of the state[16]. During the Nazi occupation, members of the social democratic party and some civil servants had tried to analyze the basic problems of the Danish economy and the lessons learned of the world crisis in the 1930.[17] Mass unemployment and social misery had proved to be a fertile ground for totalitarian political movements. It seemed clear, that a liberalistic, neo-classical capitalist economy could not guarantee adequate investments to guarantee full employment and economic growth. The obvious solution was that the state should play a much more active economic role on the macroeconomic level. Or as Keynes put it: *"I conceive, therefore, that a somewhat more comprehensive socialisation of investment will prove the only means of securing an approximation to full employment; though this need not to exclude all manner of compromises and of devices by which public authority will co-operate with private initiative."[18]*

In addition to this, an analysis of the special problems of Denmark's economic structure supported the need for some sort of planned economy. The main problem was that the Danish economy was very dependent on the agrarian sector. They exchanged agrarian exports mainly to Great Britain for industrial goods, machinery, and energy (coal). Great Britain's post-war economic problems and the dollar crisis in the Western economy emphasized the need for a modernization of the Danish economy in order to make it less vulnerable. Supporting investments in industry should achieve this.

Inspired by Beveridge's program for creation of a social security system and new economic theories by Gunnar Myrdal and John Maynard Keynes especially the Danish Social Democratic Party outlined a reform program

---

[15] Most international scholars have accepted this typology, although with some modifications. Gøsta Esping-Andersen, *The Three Worlds of Welfare Capitalism* Cambridge 1990

[16] K. Petersen and N.F.Christiansen,"The Dynamics of Social Solidarity. The Danish Welfare State 1900-2000," in *Journal of Scandinavian History* vol26 no. 3, 2001 pp. 177-196; E.I. Schmidt, *Red velfærdsstaten* Copenhagen 1997. E. I. Schmidt, "Omkring velfærdsstatens tilblivelse," in *Note. Historielærerforeningen for gymnasiet og HF,* no. 131, 1996 pp. 3-8.

[17] J. O. Krag and P. Gersmann, *Krigsøkonomi og efterkrigsproblemer.* Copenhagen 1944

[18] John Maynard Keynes, *The General Theory of Employment, Interest and Money,* London 1954 (1936) p. 378.

along these lines.[19]   Instead of fighting for state ownership of the means of production, the goal was to guarantee a stable economy by state intervention and economic planning on the macroeconomic level combined with microeconomic liberalization.   In order to create a competitive, export-oriented industry the use of rational, scientific based methods of production and science-based industries should have support, thus creating economic growth and a higher standard of living for everyone.   This meant that the Social Democrats and the allied Labor Unions supported rationalization wholeheartedly.[20]

During the late 1950s, they gradually adopted this line of thinking not only by the Social Democratic party, but also by influential civil servants. The use of experts and scientific analysis on social policy making in the broadest sense was furthered and institutionalized. The general idea was that by applying scientific analysis to economic and social problems, they could identify and prevent by rational measures by the state the causes of these problems.[21]

Because these policies presented themselves to be the result of rational and professional thinking and therefore a-political, the idea of the welfare State became the hegemonic thinking in Denmark during the 1960ies.[22]

---

[19] See for instance the program of the Social Democratic Party 1945 *Fremtidens Danmark. Socialdemokratiets politik,* Copenhagen 1945. In their working program in 1952 it said: "*Danish Export has to develop a greater versatility and our dependency of a single market should be reduced.*" And on effectiveness the Working Program in 1953 stated:"*Capitalistic disorganisation and waste in production and business should be avoided.*" The programs can be found online at http://www.aba.dk/tekst/kilder/ kilderTOC.htm#SD.

[20] N.O. Finnemann, *I Broderskabets Aand. Den socialdemokratiske arbejderbevægelses idéhistorie 1871-1917.* Copenhagen 1985pp. 257-318. M. Rostgaard, "Fagbevægelse og teknologiudviklingen. Rationaliseringer og rationaliseringsdebat i Danmark i 1950erne", in *Årbog for arbejderbevægelsens historie,* 1990, no. 20 pp. 111-134, The same phenomenon can be seen in Sweden. See Anders Carlsson, ""Tekniken - politikens frälsare? Om matematikmaskiner, automation och ingenjörer vid mitten av 50-talet", i *Arbeterhistoria* vol. 92, 1999, pp.

[21] On the view that the welfare model and the idea of the interventionist state represented a new social discourse see N. Bredsdorff, *Embedsmandsstaten under ombrydning – økonomer, keynesianere og rationaliseringseksperter i efterkrigstidens centralforvaltning.* Roskilde   1999.   Available   online   at   http://www.rub.ruc.dk/lib/omrub/ publikationer/skrserie/skr28.pdf

[22] Especially the Conservative Party attacked the Welfare State as simply another form of socialism and called it the Paternalistic State. Klaus Petersen: "Himmel og helvede! Overvejelser om nogle temaer i velfærdsstatens begrebshistorie i efterkrigstidens politiske debat i Danmark" in R. Mariager, M. Mordhorst, K. Petersen (ed.), *Fortællinger i tiden.* Copenhagen 2001 pp. 103-116. The initmate connection between the use of science in

The 1950s saw some major reforms in the social area. One of the most important was the introduction of the Peoples Pension to replace the Old Age Pension in 1956. This reform introduced a tax-financed system with universal flat-rate benefits for everyone, thus being an example of the universal principle, characterizing the Nordic welfare model. The School Reform in 1958, the Rehabilitation Act in 1960, and the Public Assistance Act followed this in 1961. The latter two were notable for two aspects important in this context; Firstly they represented preventive social politics, secondly they removed the last remnants of the old Poor Law, were you could loose certain civil rights if you received social benefits.[23]

4.   FORMING POLICIES

As we have seen above, the formation of the Welfare State called for a more active and a bigger state. It needed more money through various taxes and then they redistributed it along the above-mentioned lines. However, there was a question if national and local administration was up to the task. Did it have enough resources to handle and process the amount of data that would be necessary if they should meet the new tasks of planning and governing?

There were doubts about that. In 1947/48 Viggo Kampmann, at that time head of the Economic Secretariat, which was supposed to analyze the economic consequences of government legislation and co-ordinate the economic policy, suggested to introduce a Pay-As-You-Earn (PAYE) tax in Denmark. It was scarcely possible to turn the tax screw any further within the existing legislation, which also had some other problems, especially if you risked unemployment. If they should solve these problems and more taxes generated and demanded while maintaining a socially just legislation, PAYE was a significant possibility. In contrast to Sweden and Norway, were PAYE was in operation, it was not feasible in Denmark of mainly two reasons. First there was a complicated system of deductions, and secondly because the tax administration was carried out by local government. A central registration would be necessary, if massive tax evasions should be avoided.[24]

---

politics, professionalism and the emergence of the Welfare State see C.-A. Gemzell *Om politikens förvetenskapligande och vetenskapens politisering. Kring välfärdsstatens uppkomst i England. Del I. Teoretisk inledning.* Copenhagen 1989 (available on-line at http://www.hum.ou.dk/projects/histtid/index.htm).

[23] H. Christoffersen, *"Dansk velfærdspolitik efter 1945",* Copenhagen 1984 pp. 49-64

[24] Viggo Kampmann, "Skal vi have skat ved kilden i Danmark" in *Danmarks Kommunalforvaltning* vol.3 no. 3 pp. 32-35. With reference to Sweden he indicates, that

However, the only placed the idea in hibernation; it was not dead. In 1956, the Finance Minister Viggo Kampmann commissioned two reports on the use of data processing equipment (e.g. punched card equipment) in national government administration. The first rapport should survey the various punched card installations in order to rationalize the use of equipment. The second should investigate the feasibility and possible advantages in using electronic data processing (EDP).[25]

The first report examined eleven out of the twelve national government punched card machine installations and they concluded that there was no coordination between them regarding use or procurement. The report suggested, at the largest installations should be combined. It also remarked that 90% of all machines originated from the same supplier, IBM.[26]

It is remarkable, that they entrusted the second report to a consultant from the same supplier, Willy Olsen. The report concluded that there was a basis for creating an EDP centre that could co-operate with the existing national and local government data processing centres.

An the basis of these reports, Viggo Kampmann created a "Supervisory Committee of the Governmental Punched Card and Automation Services", with representatives from the Tax Department, local government, local government data processing and Regnecentralen. This committee immediately ordered a new report that should investigate which they could carry out national and local governmental functions with EDP within the next two to three years. Again, the choice fell on Willy Olsen – with the interesting argument that IBM probably would be willing to let him undertake the task without charge, since the state had indicated the willingness to by a computer! Because of the report, the committee recommended that there should be established a common centre for national and local government or, failing this, for national government alone.

The following discussions on the organization and structure of this centre would turn out to have a decisive impact on the states policies and organizations towards the use of computers. To give some background some

---

the introduction of PAYE at this time in Denmark would require expansion of the tax administration. The same point is made by S. A. Nielsen, "Kildebeskatning og skattefradrag" in *Fagskrift for Bankvæsen*, vol 7. Pp. 75-79.

[25] The various reports and minutes from the commissions meeting can be found in the following archives: *Forvaltningsnævnets Sekretariat – Videnskabeligt Computerudvalg 1946-1965*. Rigsarkivet (National Archive) Copenhagen. *Budgetdepartementet – Tilsynsrådet for Statwns Hulkort og Automatiseringsvæsen*, Box 37/1 and 38, Rigsarkivet, Copenhagen.

[26] *Rapport vedr. gennemgangen af hulkortvirksomheden indenfor statsadministrationen.* Forvaltningsnævnets sekretariat, aug. 1957. *Tilsynsrådet vedrørende Statens Hulkort- og Automatiseringsvæsen 1958-1960* Box 37/1 Part1. Rigsarkivet

short remarks on the relations between national and local government and the evolution of local government data processing appear below.

5. LOCAL GOVERNMENT DATA PROCESSING

Although Denmark has a long tradition for a strong state, the political system is characterized by being rather decentralized. During the political struggles in the late 19th century there was a deep conflict between the civil servants of the central government and the new political and social movements, which had its social basis in the countryside. The civil servants (and academics) were loyal to the ideals of the old elite and to the absolutist state, and were profoundly skeptical to the new political movements – and their counterparts mirrored that. Even after the parliamentary principle finally was introduced in 1901, the then ruling party, Venstre, were still hostile to central government bureaucracies. So this resulted in a political system, where important state functions like collection and administration of taxes, of social welfare, schools etc. was (and is) run by local authorities.[27] Defending its relative autonomy, local authorities therefore are very reluctant to any initiatives that would shift functions and power to national government.

That is why it would have been politically absolutely impossible for instance to create a central governmental data processing institution to handle a centralized PAYE-system, although that from a pure rational and efficiency point of view would have been the logical way to proceed. In the process of creating a central EDP-centre, local government interest therefore had to be taken into consideration.

Local government had indeed established data processing institutions, with IBM in a significant role. In 1947, IBM invited the municipalities of Copenhagen and Frederiksberg to discuss the use of punched card machines for tax calculations. In the following years, systems for that application were developed. At first, the systems were mainly demonstration projects to show the system's viability. Analyzing the process that followed from an actor-network point of view shows that IBM established itself as an obligatory passing point, which resulted in IBM being the only supplier of equipment for the centers established.[28] In 1952, they established the Kommunernes Hulkortcentral (Local Government Punched Card Centre) covering 22 local authorities on the island of Zealand. Gradually similar

---

[27] Tim Knudsen, *Da demokrati blev til folkestyre,* Copenhagen 2001 pp. 96-113
[28] The process parallels the introduction of EDP in Norway as analysed by J. Brosveet, *EDB inn i kommunene! Kommunedatatanken i et aktørnettverksperspektiv.* Trondheim 1996. See especially pp. 87-110.

centers were established as cooperation between local authorities. In 1956, they established a joint centre in Jutland and shortly after a similar centre covered the remaining regional area, the island of Funen.[29]

Having made the principal decision to establish a central EDP-facility, the question remained which organizational structure it should have, especially regarding the local centers, and which guidelines should be outlined for the states policy on that area.

N.I. Bech from RC suggested, that the state should order a large-scale computer immediately, since there would be a long time for delivery. RC's board also put forward a letter of 16 November 1958, which included a detailed suggestion that DASK be utilized promptly for data processing in some of the most obvious areas. RC would assist with the necessary planning and coding work and supply qualified personnel at a reasonable tariff. This meant that the necessary experience could be harvested enabling the organizational and technical questions for the proposed centre to be thoroughly grounded. Simultaneously insufficient usage of the planned large computer installation would be avoided during the start up phase. It gave the possibility of training the necessary personnel for the extensive tasks ahead. The lack of qualified personnel was seen as the major bottleneck hindering the introduction of EDP - education and training was therefore of major importance.[30]

The other members of the committee turned down this proposal. Especially local government representative Kock Nielsen opposed. Bech on the other hand criticized the local government's plans to upgrade their centers with IBM computers without coordinating their plans with the planned national centre. The discussion also revealed different interpretations on the role of RC – while some members saw RC as acting like a commercial company, RC saw itself as a non-profit organization which ultimate aim was to develop professional competence and act as a neutral consultant for state and industry.

The committee then founded a working group to discuss the organizational structure of the national centre. Five different models were part of the discussion:

1. National and local governments establish a combined centre that would handle planning, programming and machine operation.

---

[29] The most comprehensive account on the use of automatic data processing in Denmark can be found in Lars Heide, *Hulkort og EDB i Danmark 1911-1970*. Aarhus 1996. On the use in tax administration see pp. 86-96, 229-233. On local government DP-institutions see A. Laursen, ed. *Historien om en central*. Aalborg 1991 pp. 13-33.

[30] Regrettably the archive of RC was destroyed. Only one copy of the minutes of the meetings of the board of RC survived, rescued by Aage Melbye (hereafter called *Melbye Archive*). The proposal can be found in Letter from the board of RC 11 Nov. 1958, *Melbye Archive*

2.Create a purely national government centre that would handle programming and machine operations.

3.RC to operate machines and handle programming

4.National and local government and RC establish a centre together.

5.Tasks require licensing to tender.

To ensure local and national governments optimal influence over budgeting and work priorities they decided to reject options 3 and 5. Likewise, they rejected the purely national government option, as it would all too easily cause conflict with the proposed local government centre. They concluded that a combined national and local government centre with involvement of RC would be the best solution.

In the following period, there was uncertainty as to what the relationship with local government should be. During summer 1959, Kampmann apparently resolved the situation by offering to ensure finance of the proposed data processing centre. Local government could hardly refuse this offer and during the course of the following months, they negotiated and finalized the arrangement. These negotiations took place in the political sphere and as such, RC took no active part. Finally, Datacentralen (Data Centre – DC) was established in December 1959 and Olsen, much to the surprise of RC, was employed as director. Even more consternation occurred by the fact that a technical working group by DC decided to order an IBM 7070 machine to be delivered two years later. RC had invested considerable effort to collect detailed information on existing computers and projects under way, to find the best technical solution suitable for DC – but RC was not consulted.[31]

The idea behind the establishment of DC was twofold. One was to create a central EDP-institution, which would enable the government to proceed with the plans to create not only a PAYE tax system, but also providing government and administration with the necessary data-processing capabilities needed for the Welfare State. They also considered a centralized institution with a large-scale computer the most efficient,[32] and furthermore should prevent the waste of resources, earlier identified by the reports regarding the use of punched-card machinery. This second goal was represented by §12 of the articles of DC which stipulated, that none of the

---

[31] At that time, B.S. Petersen travelled the USA, collecting information on computers and peripherals (printers, memory etc.) which could be relevant for the planned new large scale computer for RC aas well as for the 'state machine' as he phrased it. He was well aware of the different requirements for the two purposes. N.I.Bech kept him posted about the political developments in Denmark. Luckily these letters have survived. *B.S. Petersen archive*

[32] The so-called Grosch' law – the bigger the computer the cheaper the costs for each operation. H. Grosch, "The Digital Computer as a Research Tool," in *Journal of the Optical Society of America* vol. 43, nr 4 pp. 306-310, 1953, p. 310.

interested parties (local and central authorities) could operate or purchase
EDP-machines without first obtaining permission to do so by DC, but the
result of the political negotiations was, that in practice nothing hindered the
local authorities to do whatever they liked.[33] Also in relation to other state
institutions (for example DSB – Danish State Railways) this paragraph was
largely ineffective, except in one notable case – Regnecentralen and the
introduction of computers in the universities.

In order to secure the function of RC its role in research, education and
development and thereby establishing an independent expertise in the use of
computers, RC created the so-called University Plan in co-operation with the
three universities (Copenhagen, Aarhus and the Technical University, DTH).
The universities agreed in providing buildings for RC, which on their part
offered to provide GIER-machines, which universities could use free for at
least eight hours a day. In addition to that, RC would place their research
and development activities at the universities, and give them access to the
best capacities in the computer area to be utilized in the training of the
students. I addition to that, new methods and tools in areas like numerical
analysis, statistics, and operational analysis could be further developed in
close co-operation with university researchers.[34] This offer was of great
advantage to the universities, given them access to a relatively advanced
computer and new areas of scientific research. For RC, this would guarantee
its survival, and be in accordance with the character of RC as an institution
under the Academy of Technical Science – a non-profit organization that at
the same time would promote the co-operation between science and
industry, train the next generation of experts and solving problems for
industry.

The financial plan was, that the government had to provide loan, that
would be paid back over a couple of years by income generated by RC's
commercial activities as a service bureau and development work for private
and public customers. This would also give students the chance to learn

---

[33] This problem was addressed frequently in the following years. For instance the Board of
DC's comment to the audit report 1963/1964, *Budgetdepartementet – Erik Ib Schmidts
embedsarkiv Box 11*, 21.5.65

[34] This section is primarily based on the following archives: *ATV-archive* Box 216. The
Melbye-archive. Aarhus University Archive, Op.cit. Box : Regnecentralen. 325/60 - NF
22. *Forvaltningsnævnets Sekretariat* op.cit. and *Tilsynsrådet* op.cit.

A good account on the discussions on the University-plan from Aarhus University's
point of view can be found in Svend Bundgaard: *Hvordan EDB kom til Aarhus
Universitet*. DAIMI, Aarhus 1978.

Minutes from meeting between RC og Aarhus University's committee on calculating
machinery 8.6.1961. *Aarhus University archive*. Note on the stablishment of a branch of
RC at Aarhus University 23.6.1961. Op. Cit. More general see Chr. Gram, "Gier på
læreanstalterne," in P. Sveistrup et. al. Op. cit. pp. 51-54

from real life problems, thus giving education and training for the new technology a practice-oriented approach.

They obtained political support by a verbal promise by then Prime Minister Kampmann, who was very eager to promote science and technology and saw the possibilities this plan gave in the efforts to create a modern industrial sector and a rational state.

However, just before parliament's financial committee was to approve the arrangement in the summer of 1962, DC stopped it cold pointing at the infamous paragraph 12. The problem was that the PAYE was delayed, and the newly formed DC already had invested considerable funds in buildings, personnel, and machinery. The board of DC argued, that the scientist should utilize these resources first.

The arguments from DC were understandable giving their conception of the emerging computer technology. Computers were primarily very large and very fast data processing equipment. Their main objective was to prevent waste of resources. To them it all was a question of using the EDP-capacity in the most effective manner, and the position held by RC and their allied scientist was soon seen as just another effort to cultivate own interests, much like every head of department in central administration insisted on having his own DP-department. DC was a big investment and was supposed to pay 3 million DKR lease to IBM that summer, without having any substantial income at that time. The project threatened to turn into a financial and political failure, and they could not allow that to happen.[35]

The scientific milieu on the universities were the primarily supporters of RC. In their eyes, the plan was perfect, since the primary problem for the future was the lack of qualified computer personnel - and the plan exactly addressed that problem. In addition, the plan would boost research and training in various new fields like numerical analysis, operational analysis, electronics etc. The problems DC faced would only be temporary. Soon there would be plenty of work for DC and the biggest problem would be the lack of qualified personnel. Furthermore, the use of DC's equipment would not suit the needs of the universities, since direct access to computers and the combination of research, development and training was of outmost importance.

In this group's frame of mind, DC's resistance to the plan seemed irrational, and they suspected that the real reason for DC's attitude was something else than the official. Soon the suspicion rose, that IBM was behind all this.[36]

---

[35] For details, references to archives etc. see P. Klüver op. cit 1999 pp. See also L. Heide op.cit. pp289-291.

[36] RC had actually had contacts with IBM on the possible involvement in producing GIER. But rumours that IBM had offered a large computer for free to DTH further nourished that

This situation prompted hectic activity especially in the Finance Ministry. The main actor was Erik I. Schmidt one of the most influential civil servants from the 1950s on. Also being a member of ATV's working group on management and business economics, he had good contacts to the scientific community and to the state administration. He was assisted by the before mentioned industrialist Haldør Topsøe, who also was very active as a member of the Atomic Energy Commission and the Danish Technical and Scientific Research Foundation. During the next 1½ years, they tried to work out a compromise. The available documents and notes, especially from E.I. Schmidt indicated that RC was willing to compromise. The application for a state loan was substantially reduced, RC promised not to compete with DC on administrative tasks for the state and so on. However, DC was very reluctant to give in. It was also a matter of principles. If RC were to continue with its plan, it would be difficult to refuse other state institutions desire to get their own computers.

In the meantime, RC's financial situation grew more and more desperate. Trusting that they would accept the University Plan, a department had opened in Aarhus, and the research and educational activities increased. There was only one way to go: Flee forward. So, contrary to the original intend, RC started a series production of GIER and stepped up its commercial activities by installing a large computer, CDC 1604 A, in Valby. All these investments made RC's financial situation even more precarious. It was like riding a tiger, hoping that Parliament eventually would grant RC its much-needed loan. It was finally granted on 16 December 16 1963. However, by then it was too late. On 13 January 1964, RC was reconstructed as a limited company. Its corporate culture would remain to have a distinct academic and non-formal character, and it would continue to carry out activities. That did not make any sense from a business point of view. Nevertheless, it was a commercial company, although a peculiar one, until its next collapse in 1972.

As for DC, RC was right. The need for EDP in state administration grew fast in the next years. DC reached a break-even point in 1964-65, and soon the demand exceeded DC's capacity. PAYE, VAT, and the Central Persons Register were only some of the largest tasks. However, the story was completely different regarding DC's role as the central governing and coordinating organ for the public use of computers. The next years DC had to fight several state institutions (Danish State Railways, Danish Statistical Bureau etc.) wish to get their own computers – with little success.

---

suspicion.. In 1964 IBM actually donated a 7090 to DTH, creating the North Europe University Computing Centre. Letters from N.I. Bech to B.S. Petersen 20 jan. 1960 and 9. March 1960, *B.S. Petersens Archive.* Letter from J.N. Gosselin, IBM, Paris 28.2.1962 to RC's Board, *Melbye Archive.* B. Rosengreen, ed., *NEUCC 1965-1975,* Lyngby 1975

As we have seen, the introduction of computer technology in Denmark follows Hans De Geer's model nicely. The awareness of the new technology actually came mostly through personal contacts on the technical-scientific level. The obtained new information systematically and gained experiences by constructing a machine and techniques are developed by practical experiences. However, this model also tends to underestimate the crucial importance of commercial companies, e.g. IBM, especially if one looks at established bureaucracies. Here there seems to be a more straight line of development, from various filing systems over punched card technology to computers. Nevertheless, as we have seen in the controversy between RC and DC, the latter line of development tends to support an interpretation of computer technology as more a less advanced punched card technology, as a tool for handling large amounts of data only. The line represented by RC supported a broader and more comprehensive view of computer technology. This would later develop to datalogy, as they coined "computer science" in Denmark, which was seen as a new way of analyzing systems and flows of data in general, providing new scientific tools that would proof their worth in planning and governing large systems like society as a whole.[37]

Therefore, the new computer technology with its tools, practices, and theories seems to fit perfectly with the new social and political discourse contained in the idea of the interventionist welfare state. However, they would accept both ideas a few years later.

[37] P. Naur, *Datamaskinerne og samfundet,* Copenhagen 1967.

A FAILURE REVISITED: THE FIRST FINNISH COMPUTER CONSTRUCTION PROJECT
The establishing of a national computing center in Finland

Petri Paju

Cultural History, University of Turku, 20014 Finland; petpaju@utu.fi

Abstract: In this article, the first Finnish computer construction, previously claimed to have produced only an out-dated machine, is studied as an integral part of an attempt to establish a national computer center in Finland. I argue that the aim of the Finnish Committee for Mathematical Machines (1954-1960) was more similar to its Swedish and Danish counterparts than has been recognized, even though the Finnish Committee decided to duplicate a German G1a computer in 1954. The similarity with Sweden and Denmark arises from the aim of the Committee to establish a national computing center, like the ones in Stockholm and Copenhagen, in Helsinki during its first two years. Furthermore, this plan for the national computing center, or the building of a single computer, the ESKO, did not gain the support it needed either from the state nor the former punched card machine users, because of the politically and economically difficult situation in post-war Finnish society. In the uncertain economic year of 1956, the Finnish punched card customers of IBM decided to continue collaborating with IBM alone. Moreover, IBM also benefited by receiving expert work force educated in the Committee's computer construction project. Hopefully this Finnish case, being unsuccessful and therefore unlike other Scandinavian countries, can also assist in further comprehending the preconditions that lead to more successful developments like those in Sweden and Denmark.

Key words: Finnish Computing history, ESKO computer, Scandinavian – German co-operation, punched card use, Rolf Nevanlinna

1.   INTRODUCTION [1]

In Finland, the first, national computer construction project began in 1955 — that is concurrently with the Danish one but years later than the Swedish or the Norwegian construction.[2] Unlike in other Scandinavian countries, in 1954, the Finnish project leaders had chosen to duplicate a German computer. In 1960, the construction work finally concluded with what contemporaries regarded as an out-dated machine, the ESKO.[3] A contributory factor to this judgment was that in 1958, International Business Machines (IBM) imported the first (operational) computer to Finland. By this operation, IBM also claimed to be the initiator of modern computing in the country, thus competing with the national computer construction project. Consequently, IBM dominated the computer market in Finland at the end of the 1950s and in the 1960s.[4]

[1] A draft version of this text has earlier been presented as a paper for the session, "Computers for Scandinavian Modernization", at the annual meeting of the Society for the History of Technology in San Jose, October 2001. The paper and this article are for the most part based on my licentiate dissertation P. Paju, *Ensimmäinen suomalainen tietokone ESKO ja 1950-luvun suunnitelma kansallisesta laskentakeskuksesta*, [The First Finnish Computer ESKO and a 1950's Plan of a National Computing Center, in Finnish]. Licensiate Thesis, Cultural History. University of Turku, Finland 2002. The author is thankful to Anders Carlsson, Lars Heide, Hartmut Petzold, Petri Saarikoski, Hannu Salmi and Jaakko Suominen for valuable comments and suggestions.

[2] H. De Geer, *På väg till datasamhället. Datatekniken i politiken 1946-1963*, [On the way to an information society. Information technology in politics 1946-1963, in Swedish]. Stockholm 1992, p. 17-33; L. Heide, *Hulkort og EDB i Danmark 1911-1970*, [Punched card machines and electronic data processing in Denmark 1911-1970, in Danish]. Århus 1996, p. 250-254; P. V. Klüver, "From Research Institute to Computer Company: Regnecentralen 1946-1964." *IEEE Annals of the History of Computing*, Vol, 21, No. 2, 1999, 31-43 on p. 31, 33-34. It is perhaps worth noting here that in the 1950s there seems to have been practically no interactions with the Finnish computing people and their colleagues in Norway.

[3] ESKO is an acronym from Electronic Serial COmputer (when spelt Finnish way) and it was a popular Finnish male name at that time.

[4] H. Andersin & T. Carlsson, "ESKO – ensimmäinen suomalainen tietokone, [ESKO – The First Finnish Computer, in Finnish]", in M. Tienari, ed., *Tietotekniikan alkuvuodet Suomessa*, [The first years of information technology in Finland, in Finnish.] Helsinki 1993, 11-23 on p. 14-15, 21-22; M. Vehviläinen, "Gender and Computing in Retrospect: The Case of Finland," *IEEE Annals of the History of Computing*, Vol, 21, No. 2, 1999, 44-51, on p. 45; P. Paju, *ESKO – tietokonetta tekemässä. Tietoteknologisen kentän muodostaminen ja nopea muutos Suomessa 1954-60* [ESKO – Making the Computer, Appropriation and Sudden Change of Computer Technology in Finland 1954-60, in Finnish]. Graduate thesis, Cultural History. University of Turku, Finland 1999, on p. 157-163; J. Suominen, *Sähköaivo sinuiksi, tietokone tutuksi. Tietotekniikan kulttuurihistoriaa*, [Getting Familiar with the Electronic Brain, Getting to Know the Computer, in Finnish]. Publications of the Research Center for Contemporary Culture, No. 67. Jyväskylä 2000, 47-51, on p. 55-56.

Some Finnish computing professionals have regarded the first computer construction as an unsuccessful effort – or dismissed it as irrelevant. Retrospectively, computing professionals have criticized the Finnish Committee for Mathematical Machines, *Matematiikkakonekomitea*, (established in 1954) for choosing a German computer to be copied in Finland. These computing professionals have argued that selecting a machine that used punched tape as a storage device for the program was a bad choice because even then more advanced computers had their programs stored in a memory.[5]

Picture 1. The ESKO computer, built in Helsinki 1955-1960 by the Finnish Committee for Mathematical Machines, was based upon a German blueprint of a G1a computer. The G1a in turn was based on a G1 computer designed in the beginning of the 1950s. By the end of that decade, this design was of course almost obsolete. In the ESKO the input medium was paper tape, as the computer had no internal memory for the program but a drum memory from numbers. (Courtesy of the Helsinki University Computing Center.)

So far, the history of computing has mainly been studied by computing professionals in Finland. In this article, my main argument is that their understanding of the ESKO project has been far too machine- and producer-

---

[5] H. Andersin & T. Carlsson, "Tyyntä myrskyn edellä, [Calm Before the Storm, in Finnish]." IBM katsaus 3/1966.

centered. By focusing on the outcome of the ESKO project, the computing professionals have been unable to understand the other motives and plans that the members of the Finnish Committee had, beyond the building of a single computer. Studies from other Scandinavian countries,[6] like Sweden and Denmark, show that the construction of early computers in those countries co-evolved with plans to establish centers for further research and education in the field of computing.[7] These schemes have also been interpreted as national projects against the influence of companies like IBM.[8] If successful, these Scandinavian countries would not have become merely passive adapters of computer technology, but would also have actively tried to shape new technology.

My intention is to analyze the construction of the ESKO computer mainly as a social process.[9] This means I will examine how the Finnish Committee for Mathematical Machines tried to build not only a technological artifact, but also social structures, and show how the interaction that resulted in turn shaped the Committee.[10] I will focus on the first two years (1954-1956) of the Finnish Committee for Mathematical Machines and on the beginning of the construction of the ESKO computer. Drawing on archival material, I will describe how the Finnish group went to

---

[6]   Scandinavian countries include Denmark, Norway, Sweden and Finland.

[7]   H. De Geer, *På väg till datasamhället*, on p. 33-44; L. Heide, *Hulkort og EDB i Danmark 1911-1970*, on p. 211, 250-254; P. V. Klüver, "From Research Institute to Computer Company: Regnecentralen 1946-1964," on p. 31. See also J. Suominen, P. Paju & A. Törn, "Varsinaissuomalainen linja Suomen tietoteknistymisen alkuvaiheissa. Turun laskukeskus ja Wegematic 1000 tietojenkäsittelykone, [Early Computerization in Finland-Proper 1959-1964. A Study of the Beginnings of Computer Center in Turku and Wegematic 1000 Electronic Data Processing Machine, in Finnish]", <u>Tekniikan Waiheita</u> 18(2000): 3, 24-46.

[8]   James M. Nyce and Magnus Johansson in preface to Annals of the History of Computing 2/1999.

[9]   P. N. Edwards, "From 'Impact' to Social Process: Computers in Society and Culture" in *Handbook of Science and Technology Studies*. Eds. Sheila Jasanoff et al. Sage Publications 1995, (ps. 257-285); W. E. Bijker, *Of Bicycles, Bakelites and Bulbs. Toward a Theory of Sociotechnical Change*. Cambridge, Massachusetts, London 1995.

[10] The technical details of the ESKO are therefore not central to this article. Some main features should be noted however. The ESKO was essentially an electron tube computer. It had no internal memory for the program but the program was read from paper tapes (see Picture 1, paper tapes in the background). The paper tapes also served as input media. There was also a drum memory (see Picture 1, in the middle back) for the number data. The operational speed of the ESKO was 20 additions per second. Altogether the ESKO had many special features and solutions that where tried out. For more on these, see H. Andersin & T. Carlsson, *"ESKO – ensimmäinen suomalainen tietokone*, [ESKO – The First Finnish Computer, in Finnish]"; W. Hopmann, "The G1 and the Göttingen Family of Digital Computers" in Raúl Rojas and Ulf Hashagen (eds.): *The First Computers – History and Architectures*. Cambridge 2000, (ps. 295-313).

Germany to acquire a computer and why the decision to copy a German computer was not supposed to be so important a choice.[11]

My argument is that the aim of the Finnish Committee was more similar to its Swedish and Danish counterparts than has been previously acknowledged. I think this is because during its first two years, the Committee, adapting the model of the Swedish computing center, tried to establish a national computing center in Helsinki for the first time.[12] Furthermore, I argue that it was because of the politically and economically difficult situation in post-war Finnish society that this plan for the national computing center (or the building of ESKO) did not gain the support it needed. Finnish society was in a very different situation from Swedish society that had been spared the ravages of the Second World War and was not a neighbor of the Soviet Union. In Finland in the 1950s, the state invested heavily in industrialization that was meant to provide the Finnish people with jobs and to maintain the maximum of economic independence from the Soviet Union. The economic uncertainty seems also to have influenced the punched card machine users who decided not to take risks by supporting the Finnish scientific Committee.

Finally, I argue that, despite its outcome, the ESKO project may have had a strong positive influence as an educational project in an environment not yet devoted to the problems of information technology. Not only were the first computer experts in Finland trained during this construction project, IBM Finland also responded to the competition generated by the Committee and pressure from customers, by offering the "punched card men"[13] courses on new technology. Later, IBM became the largest computer supplier in the country when computers were utilized in modernizing Finnish society towards a welfare state in the 1960s.

---

[11] The construction project in Germany remains a subject for further research. For the German developments, see H. Petzold, *Rechnende Maschinen. Eine historische Untersuchung ihrer Herstellung und Anwendung vom Kaiserreich bis zur Bundesrepublik.* Düsseldorf: VDI-Verlag, 1985; H. Petzold, *Moderne Rechenkünstler. Die Industrialisierung derRechentechnik in Deutschland.* München: Beck 1992; W. Hopmann, "The G1 and the Göttingen Family of Digital Computers"; H. Petzold, "Hardwaretechnologische Alternativen bei Konrad Zuse" in Hans Dieter Hellige (hrsg.): *Geschichten der Informatik. Visionen, Paradigmen und Leitmotive.* Springer Verlag 2003, (ps. 79-140).

[12] In Denmark there also was a computing center created at the same time. See P. V. Klüver, "From Research Institute to Computer Company: Regnecentralen 1946-1964," p. 31, 33-34.

[13] The "punched card men" (reikäkorttimiehet) is what the Finnish punched card organisation managers called themselves.

2.   LIMITED FUNDING IN 1954: WHY NOT A GERMAN COMPUTER?

In the 1940s, Finland was in no position to acquire a computer of its own. Finland, at that time, was a country of four million people, located between Sweden and the USSR. She had suffered heavily from the two wars that she waged against the Soviet Union during the period of the Second World War. After the war ended, Finland was not occupied. However, it had to pay heavy war reparations to the Soviet Union. Those debts were paid off in 1952, which was also the year of the Helsinki Summer Olympic Games. During the Cold War, Finland found itself in a difficult situation, caught between the Western and the Eastern block and, simultaneously, foreign policy relations with the Soviet Union created political battles and uncertainty in the country.[14]

This, often unstable, political, and economic situation and the lack of tradition in science policy, prevented investment in science and technology in Finland, which was then still mostly an agrarian society. The scarce resources for scientific work in Finland led many ambitious Finnish graduates to emigrate, mostly to Sweden and the United States. We can say that there was no science policy in Finland, only the policies of some individual scientists in high positions who belonged to the Academy of Finland – so it was a very different situation from, for example, that in Sweden.[15]

However, at the Helsinki University of Technology, there was a Professor of Engineering Physics, Erkki Laurila (1913-1998), who had conducted research on analogue machines already in the 1930s. He was interested in the new mathematical machines after the Second World War. Despite modest funding, Laurila could observe developments in mathematical machines from journals and, not least, on trips to Sweden. Together with his engineering students, Laurila built an analogue machine in Helsinki in the beginning of the 1950s.[16]

---

[14] For recent history of Finland in English, see O. Jussila, S. Hentilä & J. Nevakivi, *From Grand Duchy to Modern State. A Political History of Finland since 1809.* Translated from Finnish by David and Eva-Kaisa Arter. London Hurst 1999.

[15] The Academy of Finland was created in 1949. K-E. Michelsen, *Valtio, teknologia, tutkimus. VTT ja kansallisen tutkimusjärjestelmän kehitys,* [The State, Technology and Research. The Technical Research Centre of Finland and the Development of the National Research System]. Valtion teknillinen tutkimuskeskus, Espoo, Helsinki 1993, on p. 173-175, 180-186; K. Immonen, *Suomen Akatemia suomalaisessa tiedepolitiikassa 1970-luvulla,* [Academy of Finland in the Finnish Politics of Science in 1970's, in Finnish]. Helsinki, Otava 1995, on p. 18-24. See also Anders Carlsson's article in this volume.

[16] E. Laurila, "Stieltjesplanimetri, suomalainen integroimiskoje, [Stieltjesplanimeter, a Finnish Integration Device, in Finnish]." *Teknillinen Aikakauslehti* 1939; E. Laurila,

Finally, in 1954, Laurila, with the support of the central Finnish scientific authorities in mathematics, made a proposal to the Academy of Finland to establish a committee to investigate the possibilities of having a "mathematical machine"[17] available in Finland. After only a few weeks, the Finnish Committee for Mathematical Machines began its work. To ensure funding, a member of the Academy of Finland and a mathematics professor in the University of Zürich (Switzerland), the. authoritative and internationally well-known Finnish mathematician Rolf Nevanlinna (1895-1980), became chair of the Committee, while Professor Laurila became vice-chairman. The other members of the Committee were mathematicians who represented a wide array of different needs in calculation work, as well as a general who represented the military. The Committee for Mathematical Machines, in 1954, was the first scientific committee to be founded by the Academy of Finland in post-war Finland.[18]

The members of the Committee had many reasons for wanting a computer in the country. The most obvious reason was that a computer would be beneficial for scientific work in Finland. Some members of the Committee had already been able to use the Swedish computers for their calculations, but a computer in Helsinki would be very welcome. Professor Laurila preferred to have his engineers trained in digital computing technology so that they would be able to establish a computing center in Finland. Finally, the military wanted to calculate tables for the Ballistics Office more quickly and cheaply.[19]

"Mekanisoitu ja sähköistetty matematiikka, Tekniikan ja luonnontieteitten matematiikka uusilla urilla, [Mathematics Mechanized and Electrified, Mathematics of Technology and Natural Sciences in a New Direction, in Finnish]." *Teknillinen Aikakauslehti* 1948; P. Paju, *Ensimmäinen suomalainen tietokone ESKO*, pp 38-43. Professor Laurila also received an earlier version of the proposal made by a public investigation group on mathematical machines in Sweden in 1947. *Betänkande med förslag till närmast erförderliga åtgärder för tillgodoseende av Sveriges behov av matematikmaskiner avgivet av matematikmaskinutredningen.* Stockholm den 30 april 1947. Personal Archive of Professor Erkki Laurila. His papers are at present in the National Archives of Finland. Regarding the proposal, see Anders Carlsson's article in this volume.

[17] From now on I will use the term computer for brevity.

[18] A Letter from Erkki Laurila to the State Board for Natural Sciences, 21.3.1954. Archive of the Academy of Finland; The Finnish Committee for Mathematical Machines, minutes of meetings 14.4.1954, founding session. 1954, Archive of the Academy of Finland; Interview with Mr. Erkki Laurila 16.12.1997; Interview with Mr. Hans Andersin 15.5.1998; O. Lehto, *Korkeat maailmat. Rolf Nevanlinnan elämä*, [Higher Worlds. The Life of Rolf Nevanlinna, in Finnish.] Keuruu 2001, on ps. 211-219.

[19] A member of the Finnish Committee, the professor of astronomy at the University of Helsinki, Gustav Järnefelt had had his calculations concerning star models computed already in 1951. Rapport för oktober – december 1951 över arbetet inom Matematikmaskinnämndens arbetsgrupp. Matematikmaskinnämnden's Archive in the

It was the chairperson, Nevanlinna, who was most active in persuading the Committee to choose a German computer. The chairman was offered the design of a computer to copy from Göttingen, Germany.[20] That offer also came as a surprise to Professor Laurila. The Committee had first decided that Laurila should explore alternatives for acquiring a computer, whether to purchase or to build one. While Laurila was making his inquiries, chairperson Nevanlinna visited his old university town in West Germany, Göttingen, in the summer of 1954. Nevanlinna was very excited about the new machines but he was a theoretical mathematician who had defended his doctoral thesis much earlier (1919). It is no exaggeration to state that his knowledge of computer technology was very poor when his friends and colleagues at the Max-Planck Institut für Physik in Göttingen offered him a blueprint of their newly planned, small, scientific, digital computer, the G1a, which people could copy without charge in Finland.[21]

The German computer differed somewhat from what Professor Laurila thought was favorable but he had no better, that is, less expensive, suggestion. An important advantage was that the Germans planned to complete this small machine within one and a half years. It was this tight timetable that helped Laurila content himself with this German project as a learning process for his students, the engineers.[22]

The German alternative was by no means the only one considered, however. Professor Laurila had already sent two of his young engineers, Hans Andersin and Tage Carlsson, who both spoke Swedish as their native language, to study computing in *Matematikmaskinnämnden* in Stockholm. Returning from their short stay in Sweden in autumn 1954, Andersin and Carlsson were able to report to their professor that the Royal Swedish Academy of Engineering Sciences could offer the blueprints of the BESK

National Archives of Sweden, Stockholm; P. Paju, *Ensimmäinen suomalainen tietokone ESKO*, pp. 44-67.

[20] I think Nevanlinna was offered a machine because he was already a famous mathematician in Europe in the 1920s and the German scientists in Göttingen thought this would be another way to win support and legitimate their computer constructions. Nevanlinna had also been a visiting mathematics professor in Göttingen in 1936-1937. At that time, Nevanlinna was a known Nazi-sympathiser. On this topic, see O. Lehto, *Korkeat maailmat,* on p. 139.

[21] A Letter from Ludvig Biermann to H. Piloty, A. Walther and K. Küpfmüller 20.7.1954. Archive of the Max-Planck-Gesellschaft, Berlin; P. Paju, *Ensimmäinen suomalainen tietokone ESKO*, pp. 67-75; Interview with Mr. Erkki Laurila 16.10.1997; Nevanlinna, *Muisteltua*, [From My Memory, in Finnish]. Helsinki Otava 1976, on p. 194.

[22] The Finnish Committee for Mathematical Machines, minutes of meetings 4/1954, 12.10.1954, Archive of the Academy of Finland; Interview with Mr. Erkki Laurila 16.10.1997. See also R. Nevanlinna, *Muisteltua*, [From My Memory, in Finnish], on p. 194.

computer for free to the Finnish Committee.[23] However, the Committee then calculated that to build such a large machine would be too expensive (the German alternative would cost only one fifth of the expense of the BESK). Also, they argued that there would not be enough needs and users for such an efficient computer like BESK in Finland, even in the near future. The young Finnish engineers would have preferred to copy the BESK; for them it was, of course, an up-to-date computer, but after some protests they accepted that they would copy the Göttingen computer G1a. After all, it would only take a year and a half to complete the G1a, they thought.[24]

We can explain in part this selection process by a gap between the generations. For scientists from Nevanlinna's generation in Finland, Germany still represented superiority in technical expertise. For more practical engineers like Professor Laurila, who knew better, this German-mindedness was something from the past that could not be avoided in the Finland of the 1950s.[25] Nevertheless, the Finns must have been impressed by the first Göttingen machine: The G1 – the only such machine operating in Germany – which had already been used successfully for two years by 1954.[26]

A German constructor, Wilhelm Hopmann (1924-2002), planned to build the G1a –computer as a follow-up version to the G1 computer.[27] Hopmann designed the G1a as a "minimal machine"; a construction that would need only a minimal number of parts and would still be of use to scientists from various disciplines.[28] What the Finns, Nevanlinna and Laurila, did not know

---

[23] These were no doubt only preliminary discussions. The Royal Swedish Academy of Engineering Sciences, in Swedish *Ingenjörsvetenskapsakademien* had, according to Anders Carlsson, no formal rights to the BESK drawings. See also Anders Carlsson's article in this volume.

[24] Interview with Mr. Hans Andersin 15.5.1998; P. Paju, *Ensimmäinen suomalainen tietokone ESKO*, pp. 77-81. The Danes accepted an offer to copy the BESK construction for free and their computer DASK was ready in 1957. L. Heide, *Hulkort og EDB i Danmark 1911-1970*, on p. 250-253, passim; P. V. Klüver, "From Research Institute to Computer Company: Regnecentralen 1946-1964.", on p. 33.

[25] H. Andersin & T. Carlsson, "ESKO – ensimmäinen suomalainen tietokone, [ESKO – The First Finnish Computer, in Finnish]", on p. 12-13; Interview with Mr. Erkki Laurila 16.10.1997.

[26] W. Hopmann, "The G1 and the Göttingen Family of Digital Computers," on p. 298-307, 312; H. Petzold, "Hardwaretechnologische Alternativen bei Konrad Zuse". The G1 computer was the first electronic computer to be operated in Germany, starting 1952. It was built in Max-Planck Institut für Physik in Göttingen by a group headed by Heinz Billing.

[27] The G:s are for Göttingen, home town of the institute in which they were built.

[28] W. Hopmann, "Zur Entwiclung der G 1a" in Johannes Wosnik (hrsg): Elektronische Rechenmaschinen und Informationsverarbeitung. *Nachrichtentechnische fachberichte*, Band 4, 1956, ps. 92-96; "W. Hopmann, "The G1 and the Göttingen Family of Digital

when opting to copy the German G1a was that the blueprint was still under development at that time – and it would take much longer than they thought in 1954 to complete this complex minimal construction.

3. THE COMMITTEE'S AIM: A NATIONAL COMPUTING CENTER

The Committee's decision to build a computer in Finland cannot be understood without paying attention to the larger vision of computer use that was developing within the Committee. It seems that, right from the start in 1954, the Committee intended not only to have a computer built but also to create a national computing center in Helsinki, the capital of Finland. Especially for Professor Laurila this computing center was of particular interest. Already when the two engineers who were going to build the computer were still studying computer technology in Göttingen during the winter of 1955, Laurila wrote a letter stating that he would like to appoint one of the scholarship holders, Hans Andersin, as the manager of this future computer center.[29]

This plan to establish a computing center in Finland was elaborated on during the following year, 1955, after engineers began the construction work on the Finnish G1a, the ESKO, in Helsinki. The Committee wanted to take responsibility firstly, for not only the whole scientific calculating work but also for all computer calculation work in Finland, secondly for education in the new field of computing, and thirdly for research and development work in computer machinery. The Committee aimed to have customers including the state, scientists and industrialists.[30] For the scientists, whom the members of the Committee knew best, this center would have meant an enormous improvement in calculating capacity and plenty of new possibilities for research in areas that had been underdeveloped in Finland, such as the atomic research.[31]

The members of the Committee realized that in order to materialize this plan, they needed support from the would-be-customers of the computing center. Perhaps the most important group was the punched card men, the

---

Computers," on p. 298-307, 312; H. Petzold, "Hardwaretechnologische Alternativen bei Konrad Zuse".

[29] A letter from Erkki Laurila to Hans Andersin & Tage Carlsson 28.12.1954. Archive of the University of Helsinki. This choice would leave Tage Carlsson able to fully concentrate on the (more important, at that point) technical side of building this computer and future computing service.

[30] A letter from the Committee secretary Hans Andersin to Rolf Nevanlinna 8.6.1955. Archive of the University of Helsinki.

[31] See K-E. Michelsen, *Valtio, teknologia, tutkimus*, on p. 187-189.

leaders of punched card installations in various organizations, who had formed an association (the Punched Card Association) for themselves in 1953 in order to negotiate with the largest supplier, IBM, better.[32] After constructing the ESKO for half a year in Finland, and anticipating the completion of the machine the following year, the Committee decided to offer to cooperate with the punched card men.

A representative from the Finnish Committee for Mathematical Machines, Dr Kari Karhunen,[33] suggested to the annual meeting of the Punched Card Association in 1955 that there should be a joint effort to create a computing center in the country. This center could then buy a large, general purpose, electronic computer there for all to use.[34] What Dr Karhunen did not specifically mention was that in the beginning this center would probably benefit Finnish scientists most by providing them with modern calculation equipment that the universities could not afford.

For the punched card men, a computing center did not seem such an attractive idea. At least no signs of supporting this suggestion on a large scale are to be found in the journal they published - although they reported on the meeting in question at great length.[35] After studying the punched card machinery they used, one can conclude that this center-like, centralized organization was not a preferred way for them to use new electronic machines – they were more eager to buy computers of their own in order to automate their punched card machine organizations. What they needed was more and faster data processing capacity that was essentially reliable for their businesses.[36] It may be that the punched card men also thought that their needs were very different from those of represented by the scientific members of the Committee. Thus, the punched card men would only marginally benefit from the center. Perhaps also the fact that the ESKO, the first computer used in the computer center, would be a scientific computer

---

[32] Reikäkortti, (Punched Card journal, in Finnish. A journal the Punched Card Association published.) 1/1955; M. Vehviläinen, "Gender and Computing in Retrospect: The Case of Finland," on p. 45; J. Suominen, *Sähköaivo sinuiksi, tietokone tutuksi*, on p. 52-56.

[33] He was a mathematician and a director of a punched card installation in an insurance company.

[34] Uusi Suomi, [a Finnish Newspaper from Helsinki] "A Computing Center and Electronic Calculating Machice are current issues", 28.9.1955.

[35] Reikäkortti, (Punched Card journal, in Finnish) "Events at the Punched Card Association", 2/1955.

[36] P. Paju, *Ensimmäinen suomalainen tietokone ESKO*, pp. 126-140; R. Pukonen, "Automaattisen tietojenkäsittelyn ENSI-askeleet Suomessa, [The First Steps into Automatisation in Finland, in Finnish]", in M. Tienari, ed., *Tietotekniikan alkuvuodet Suomessa*, [The first years of information technology in Finland, in Finnish.] Helsinki 1993,182-188; J. Yates, "Early Interactions Between the Life Insurance and Computer Industries: The Prudential's Edmund C. Berkeley." *IEEE Annals of the History of Computing*, Vol. 19, No. 3, 1997, 60-73.

contributed to this opinion, although most members of the scientific Committee did not want to send that message when building the ESKO. Furthermore, these parties, one mostly of business people and the other of scientists, had no tradition in cooperation.

Picture 2. In summer 1956, the German constructor of the G1a, Wilhelm Hopmann (in the middle) visited Helsinki and also the laboratory where ESKO was built by (from left to right) engineer Hans Andersin, technician Veikko Jormo and engineer Tage Carlsson. At this time, the German project had already been delayed. (Courtesy of Hans Andersin.)

At the same time, IBM Finland presented the punched card men with a future option for a computer of their own, the new middle-sized computer IBM 650. In the summer of 1955, the company had begun marketing their Electronic Data Processing Machines to their punched card customers.[37] The military also did not invest its limited resources in the new and risky computer technology, but instead they purchased a punched card installation (delivered in 1955 or 1956) from IBM.[38]

In addition, the Committee's initiative to establish a computing center suffered a setback in early 1956 when the economic situation in the country deteriorated suddenly and dramatically. In the spring of 1956, the country

---

[37] Reikäkortti (Punched Card journal, in Finnish) "Events at the Punched Card Association", 2/1955. For more on IBM in Norway at the same time, see G. Nerheim & H. W. Nordvik, *Ikke bara maskiner. Historien om IBM i Norge 1935-1985*, [Not just machines. History of IBM Norway 1935-1985, in Norwegian]. Oslo: Universitetsforlaget 1986.

[38] P. Paju, *Ensimmäinen suomalainen tietokone ESKO*, on p. 101. See also J. Suominen, *Sähköaivo sinuiksi, tietokone tutuksi*, on p. 131-132.

faced a general strike. This crisis and the recession that followed made all prospective computer users, that is the large and growing organizations using punched card machinery, postpone their purchases.[39]

Why did this national computing center not receive more support from the state? The fact is that the state in Finland had made heavy investments to industrialize in the 1950s. These investments were supposed to stabilize the economy in order to maintain the country's economical independence from its neighbor, the Soviet Union. In the 1950s and 1960s, Finland was in the process of transformation from an agrarian society into an industrial one – this happened later and faster than in neighboring Sweden and other Western countries.[40] The Prime Minister from the Agrarian party, Urho Kekkonen, who became President of Finland in 1956 and remained so for 25 years, had launched a program for investing in modern industries in order to increase employment among the growing population in the first half of the 1950s. A reliable source of energy was essential for industrialization. The building of large technological projects such as power plants, oil refineries and factories urgently needed public funding, but this left practically no attention or funding for the new computer technology. The ruling politicians did not see computers as helpful in their crucial effort to protect the country from growing Soviet influence, which was the hidden purpose for creating jobs for the Finnish people by industrializing the country in the 1950s.[41]

However, possibly the worst setback for the national computing center plan was that, in 1956, the completion date of the ESKO computer was delayed (for the first time). Building the minimal machine in Göttingen proved to be more demanding and costly than could have been imagined. In Finland, this delay in construction work also led to additional financial difficulties. Consequently, the Computing Center could not start its service. Instead, soon after the first delay, the Committee lost one of its two original employees to IBM.[42]

---

[39] J. Auer, *Hyvinvoinnin rakennuspuita. Postisäästöpankki vuosina 1886-1961*, [Building Basis for the Welfare. Post-Office Bank in years 1886-1961, in Finnish]. Helsinki Postisäästöpankki 1964; Reikäkortti (Punched Card journal, in Finnish) 1/1956.

[40] M. Vehviläinen, "Gender and Computing in Retrospect: The Case of Finland,", 45. A comparable change had taken place in other Scandinavian countries within the previous 50-80 years. Ibid.

[41] M. Kuisma, *Kylmä sota, kuuma öljy. Neste, Suomi ja kaksi Eurooppaa 1948-1979*, [Cold War, Hot Oil. Neste-company, Finland and the Two Europes 1948-1979, in Finnish]. Porvoo, Helsinki, Juva, WSOY 1997, on p. 75-106; O. Jussila, S. Hentilä & J. Nevakivi, *From Grand Duchy to Modern State.*

[42] The Finnish Committee for Mathematical Machines, minutes of meetings 4/1956, 5.10.1956. Archive in the University of Helsinki; H. E. Andersin, "Matematiikkakoneet konttorityössä, [The Mathematical Machines Doing Office Work]." *Teknillinen Aikakauslehti* 19/1956, 463-468; W. Hopmann, "The G1 and the Göttingen Family of Digital Computers"; H. Petzold, "Hardwaretechnologische Alternativen bei Konrad Zuse".

4.   A BENEFICIAL FAILURE, AS AN
          EDUCATIONAL OPPORTUNITY

In recent years, historians of technology have focused attention on failures in technological development work. For example, Graeme Gooday has noted that technological failures – and therefore also successes – have their own interpretative flexibility since technologies in themselves do not fail but are interpreted so by various people.[43] This seems to be the case also with the 'failure' of the ESKO computer. Certainly, the ESKO was not completed according to schedule. It clearly did not fulfill all of the Committee members' and the engineers' expectations. However, in the context of the plans for the national computer center, the ESKO project looks different. What really failed were the Committee's plans for the center and thus their attempt to govern the development of computer technology in Finland. Nevertheless, this major failure had its positive aspects too.

The major impact of building the ESKO computer was educational: during its construction, the first computer specialists were trained in Finland.[44] Furthermore, Finnish IBM offered courses on the new technology to the punched card men from 1955 onwards in a response to the Committee's actions.[45] These responses from IBM also continued in the economically uncertain situation in 1956 and after. This new IBM policy made the future customers for computer suppliers, the punched card men, decide to wait for the electronic data processing machines to go down in price and collaborate with IBM Finland rather than with the Committee of scientists. Under the Committee, the construction work for the ESKO computer seemed to continue for years and years.

Additionally, IBM Finland also hired the two central employees who had been working for the Finnish Committee for Mathematical Machines. These men became the first computer experts in the company and soon advanced to key positions, responsible for computer sales.[46] In summation, IBM Finland, together with certain individuals, benefited most from the unsuccessful academic computer construction project in Finland. In the 1960s, IBM became the largest computer supplier in the market.

---

[43] G. Gooday, "Re-Writing the 'Book of Blots': Critical Reflections on Histories of Technological 'Failure'". *History and Technology*. Vol. 14, 1998, pp. 265-291; W. P. McCray, "What Makes a Failure? Designing a New National Telescope, 1975-1984". *Technology and Culture*. Vol. 42, 2001, pp. 265-291.

[44] H. Andersin & T. Carlsson, "*ESKO – ensimmäinen suomalainen tietokone*, [ESKO – The First Finnish Computer, in Finnish]", on p. 22.

[45] Reikäkortti (Punched Card journal, in Finnish) 1-2/1956; Interview with Mr. Hans Andersin 15.5.1998.

[46] Andersin, "Matematiikkakoneet konttorityössä, [The Mathematical Machines Doing Office Work]", on p. 463; P. Paju, *Ensimmäinen suomalainen tietokone ESKO*, on p. 230.

Another company also received expert work force from the ESKO project. The Finnish constructor of the ESKO moved to a company named Kaapelitehdas, the Finnish Cable Works.[47] The same company had started a similar computing center with the one that the scientific Committee had planned in mid-1950s. This computing center later evolved into the Electronics Department of the Nokia Company.

In sum, we can argue that in important aspects like education on the part of the scientific Committee and increased collaboration with IBM on the part of punched card machinery users, these actors from the 1950s paved the way for computers to enter Finland. This happened first at the end of 1958 (in the state-owned Post-Office Bank) and then in rapidly growing numbers during the 1960s.[48]

5.   CONCLUSION

In this article, I have presented the beginnings of the first computer construction project in Finland by scrutinizing the solutions and proposals made by the Finnish Committee for Mathematical Machines in attempting to shape the new computer technology in Finland in 1954-56. Knowing the limited funds for scientific research, the Committee decided to copy a computer from Germany in 1954. This construction project was to be only the start of establishing a national computing center according to the model provided by the Swedish computing center. The Finnish punched card men, the would-be-customers for the planned computing center, however, preferred to collaborate with IBM in Finland. During the recession that began in 1956, this decision strengthened the resolve to negotiate mainly with IBM. The initiative for the computing center was left unsupported 1956 because, in addition to the above-mentioned points, the state was forced to invest in industrializing the country to maintain independence from Soviet influence. Thus, this article argues that we should not view the first Finnish computer construction only as an engineering project. Instead, we

---

[47] The Finnish constructor of the ESKO was Tage Carlsson. A. Aaltonen, "Nokian elektroniikkateollisuuden synty: nuorten kokeilijoiden ja keksijöiden pajasta huipputeollisuudeksi. [The Birth of Electronics Industry of Nokia, in Finnish]", in M. Tienari, ed., *Tietotekniikan alkuvuodet Suomessa*, [The first years of information technology in Finland, in Finnish.] Helsinki 1993, 108-126, on p. 110-111.

[48] For more on the first computer in Finland, an IBM 650 computer, in the Post-Office Bank, see R. Pukonen, "Automaattisen tietojenkäsittelyn ENSI-askeleet Suomessa, [The First Steps into Automatisation in Finland, in Finnish]", 182-188; P. Paju, *Ensimmäinen suomalainen tietokone ESKO*, pp. 229-231; M. Vehviläinen, "Gender and Computing in Retrospect: The Case of Finland," on p. 45. See also J. Suominen, *Sähköaivo sinuiksi, tietokone tutuksi*, on p. 53, 66-83.

should view it within the context of a social or better socio-technical, effort to establish a national computing center by the Finnish Committee for Mathematical Machines in the mid-1950s. This wider view may help us to understand better the difficulties and outcomes of the ESKO project that ended in 1960 after construction work had faced several delays.

In addition, I suggest that we should not regard this whole ESKO project as a failure but as an important learning process in which a group of Finnish engineers started to learn and study computer technology for the first time. At the same time, it is clear that the Finnish Committee had its weaknesses (like the resources and the material linkage to Germany) and it failed to gain support and to establish a computing center. Overall, the Finnish IBM mastered the change from punched card machines to computer technology far better than the scientific committee did. In this change, as I have demonstrated, the punched card men played a significant role by preferring to collaborate with IBM. Thus, this case reinforces the importance of studying the roles that users play in the process of shaping technology in a society.

Moreover, this view of the social construction of computer technology and the interactions of these different actors in shaping of that technology informs us about the modernization process in post-war Finland. It seems that modernization mostly meant industrialization and it was not until the 1960s that computers became a key element in the modernization of Finnish society and the building of the welfare state structures. Thus, we should analyze the differences in modernization between Finland, on the one hand, and Sweden and Denmark, on the other, by comparing early computer projects in these countries.

ON THE POLITICS OF FAILURE
Perspectives on the "Mathematics Machine" in Sweden, 1945-1948 [1]

Anders Carlsson

Office for History of Science, Uppsala University; Anders.Carlsson@idehist.uu.se

Abstract: This paper departs from the notion that most accounts of the early period of digital computer design and construction in Sweden have had as starting points a business and producer-centered perceptive which has hidden many of those activities that surround all complex technologies. It reinvestigates the ideological foundations underpinning the forming of a State agency in 1947/48, Matematikmaskinnämnden (The Board of Computing Machinery), with the responsibility to monitor all options and, eventually, to construct and manage two digital computers. In doing so, it attempts to understand what kinds of goals that the machines were to accomplish. The argument is that it is perfectly possible to perceive the Swedish computer project as a part of a larger process of change. The paper shows how professionals gathered information in the U.S. and interpreted it locally, and also how the initiative on the whole was a part of a new and progressive post-war agenda favoring basic research and, in particular, the advancement of mathematics for the purpose of modernizing both scientific and technological research and the society at large.

Key words: Computer history, Sweden, BESK, Matematikmaskinnämnden, historiography

1.   INTRODUCTION: AIMS AND SCOPES

This paper is about computer technology ideology and policies in Sweden in the 1940s. It tells a prehistory of two digital computers, designed and

---

[1] Based on research which is still ongoing, this paper should be read as work in progress. The contents form a part of my forthcoming PhD thesis, *Elektronvalsen: Studier i svensk datorteknik under 1950-talet* (The Electron Waltz: Studies in Swedish Computer Technology in the 1950s).

constructed in Sweden 1948–1953: one relay machine called BARK, operational from mid-1950s and one full-scale electronic machine in the so-called IAS-class, named BESK, operational from early 1954.[2] The basic question is simple, yet broad: Why did politicians in a small country like Sweden, with just over 6,500,000 inhabitants at the time, fund such a complicated and comparatively costly project with such a tremendously uncertain outcome?[3]

In order to provide an answer I will make a close reading of a public investigation presented in 1947, the first proposal made in order to raise funds for the introduction of digital computer technology into Sweden, and try to sort out issues that they have previously neglected. The investigation text is rich in claims and references and has the advantage of being an intermediary inscription, linking the aims and scopes of different actors.[4] My argument is that computers became useful assets not the least since they could relate to other proposed changes regarding scientists' and, in particular, engineers' skills. This paper will not describe the BARK and the BESK.[5] It will rather be about expectations, hopes, and attempts to relate the very first experiences, however elusive, to a larger ambition concerning technical and social renewal in Sweden in the years immediately after World War II.

Furthermore, I wish to contribute to the historiography of Swedish computing by revisiting the discussion about the outcome of the BARK and BESK computer project. The two machines were highly successful by

[2] BARK: *Binär Aritmetisk/Automatisk Relä-Kalylator*. BESK: *Binär Elektronisk Sekvens-Kalkylator*. Concerning the IAS-class of computers, see William Aspray, *John von Neumann and the Origins of Modern Computing* (Cambridge/MA, 1990), pp. 86-94.

[3] The Swedish project was early in comparison with, for instance, the corresponding ones in Denmark and Finland. Cf. Petri Paju, *Ensimmäinen suomalainen tietokone ESKO ja 1950-luvun suunnitelma kansallisesta laskentakeskuksesta*, lic. thesis in Cultural History, University of Turku (2002), and P. V. Klüver, "From Research Institute to Computer Company: Regnecentralen 1946-1964", *IEEE Annals of the History of Computing*, vol. 21 (1999). However, one other point of reference would be the Netherlands, where, "in the second half of the 1940s, scientists and engineers took several initiatives to develop digital computers", according to Jan van den Ende, *The Turn of the Tide: Computerization in Dutch Society* (Delft, 1994), p. 92.

[4] [Josef Weijne], *Kungl. Maj:ts proposition till riksdagen angående närmast erforderliga åtgärder för tillgodoseende av Sveriges behov av matematikmaskiner; given Stockholms slott den 9 maj 1947*, below referred to as "Prop. 1947:275".

[5] For close descriptions, see Göran Kjellberg and Gösta Neovius, "The BARK: A Swedish General Purpose Relay Computer", *Mathematical Tables and other Aids to Computation*, January 1951, and Erik Stemme, "Den svenska automatiska räknemaskinen BESK", *Teknisk Tidskrift*, vol. 85 (1955). The BESK lay the foundation to other computer projects in Sweden, among these the SARA at Saab's aircraft industries (1956–57), the SMIL at the University of Lund (1956–57) and the Facit EDB, a commercial version from Åtvidaberg Industries (1957–63), and also the DASK in Denmark.

contemporary standards since they were useful in solving problems identified as relevant ones. By attracting visitors and observers such as journalists and foreign researchers, they also helped sharpening the image of Sweden as a scientifically and technologically advanced and "modern" nation. Influential historical accounts, however, have maintained that the project, at least on the grand scale, was a failure. Due to decision-makers' hesitancy no persistent State computer industry or no large-scale cooperation between industry and the State, as had been the case in the electrical power and telecommunications sectors, was established. Instead, the country became a victim of market forces as IBM in the mid-1950s started to sell and rent digital computing machinery, dominating the market from 1960 onward by means of its hegemonic practices – so the story goes.[6] Although such accounts certainly recognize the importance of understanding technological change as a social process, they do focus on *construction* and *production* of computers in restricted senses of the concepts and they imply that a successful State-funded research or development initiative almost by definition should result in an industrial program that is beneficial for the nation. The furthest-reaching aim of this paper is thus to discuss "failure" and "success" against the backdrop of the first attempts to define what the BARK and BESK machines were in fact meant to accomplish.

2.   SCIENCE AND TECHNOLOGY IN THE "STRONG" SOCIETY

Two contexts are important to this paper. The first one is a self-image about Sweden being an outsider, a unique nation, yet open to influences. Historians and political scientists have derived its mixed identity from its mix of capitalism and socialism. Decisive components in the construction of such a "middle way" came from ideological negotiations – although never explicit – between the isolationist conservatism of the early 20th century and the emerging Social Democrat movement. Nationalistic ideals and labor

---

[6] I am particularily referring to Jan Annerstedt, *Staten och datorerna: En studie av den officiella datorutvecklings- och datorforskningspolitiken*, FEK-meddelande nr 41, Kommittén för forskningsorganisation och forskningsekonomi (Stockholm, 1969). The one major opponent of the views expressed there is Hans De Geer, *På väg till datasamhället: Datatekniken i politiken 1946–63* (Stockholm, 1992), an account focusing on the computers as potential aids toward a rationalization of the governmental administration. Cf. Sten Henriksson, "Den svenska utvecklingen", in Peter Naur, *Datamaskinerna och samhället* (Lund, 1969). There is no history of IBM Sweden although the company had had a Swedish office since the late 1920s. For "national" cooperation between industry and the State, see Mats Fridlund, *Den gemensamma utvecklingen: Staten, storföretaget och samarbetet kring den svenska elkrafttekniken* (Stockholm, 1999).

solidarity merged into one, and seen from the opposite shore of the Atlantic, the Swedish nation increasingly appeared like an interventionist, corporate State and a highly successful techno-economic regime. However, the image of America had been central to this small grand-scale national project and a local interpretation of the combination of American production ideals and work ethics became part of what we sometimes refer to as "the social democrat synthesis".[7] Engineers and leading industrialists highlighted themes like corporate research and scientific management in their proposed programs for domestic industry. This in part explains why scientists and engineers already during the decades before World War II steered their interests towards the U.S., extending and strengthening their already wide-ranging international networks. Notably two of those mentioned below, Stig Ekelöf and Edy Velander, established durable contacts with American colleagues, and as the war ended in 1945, these were to be exploited again.

The second context more explicitly addresses political power in relation to science and technology. Terms like *change* and *progress* have been truisms in the political debate ever since the early 1900s and have often been loaded with scientific-technological connotations. This is a result of both the labor movement's interest in finding means to growth and social security and professional claims. Early on, technological research was described as a strategic resource for communication, control, administration and policy – functions defined by representatives of the increasingly strong engineering profession, most of whom to be members of the new *Ingenjörsvetenskapsakademien* (The Royal Swedish Academy of Engineering Sciences, IVA) in 1919.[8] This Academy became a key actor in spreading the message of rationalization during the interwar years, bringing a new set of engineering norms into the pedagogy of industrial planning practices, based on professional ideals.[9] In addition, its members had a great influence in shaping the national research policy agenda. Edy Velander of the Academy was an important individual in the preparations preceding the establishment of *Tekniska Forskningsrådet* (Technical Research Council,

[7] Aant Elzinga, Andrew Jamison and Conny Mithander, "Swedish Grandeur: Contending Reformulations of the Great-Power Project", in Mikael Hård and Andrew Jamison (eds.), *The Intellectual Appropriation of Technology: Discourses on Modernity, 1900-1939* (Cambridge/MA, 1998), p. 130.

[8]   Bo   Sundin,   *Ingenjörsvetenskapens   tidevarv: Ingenjörsvetenskapsakademin, Pappersmassekontoret, Metallografiska institutet och den teknologiska forskningen i början av 1900-talet* (Umeå, 1981), pp. 195-206.

[9] See Hans De Geer, *Rationaliseringsrörelsen i Sverige: Effektivitetsidéer och samhällsansvar under mellankrigstiden* (Stockholm, 1978), passim, ch. 6-8.

TFR) in 1942, referring to the then widespread idea about technology's essential function in reaching national economic goals.[10]

All this is crucial in the understanding of the mid and late 1940s. We should also note that, in spite of political instability and expectations of a post-war recession, an unexpected and unprecedented economic growth period was emerging. Consequently, after World War II, scientific and technological research received portions of the national budget so large that they have been considered extreme in international comparison.[11] Because the country had been rather neutral during World War II the institutional landscape was relatively untouched. They could be revisited and exploited further to implement a strongly felt need for social renewal and draw level with recent changes in scientific and technological research. In the years prior to the emergence of the digital computer research project TFR was complemented with several other research councils, notably one for medicine in 1945 and one for science in 1946. Prime Minister Tage Erlander, who took office in 1946, regarded these councils, along with other political "tools", as instrumental innovations in the creation of the "strong" society.[12]

3. DEFINING COMPUTERS

The first indications about large calculating machines reached Sweden in fall 1943, the receiver being the recently established *Försvarets radioanstalt* (the Defence "radio institute", FRA). According to FRA's own accounts of the knowledge about computers in the years 1943-45, the lack of details had not prevented its engineers and mathematicians to theorize about what kinds of problems the machines were used for and thereby, by rudimentary reverse-engineering, assume the basics of their potentials and functions.[13] In any case the very scale of this technology, both in terms of labor division

---

[10] TFR and its successors are scrutinized in Hans Weinberger, *Nätverksentreprenören: En historia om teknisk forskning och industriellt utvecklingsarbete från den Malmska utredningen till Styrelsen för teknisk utveckling* (Stockholm, 1997).

[11] Sven Widmalm, "Inledning", in idem (ed.), *Vetenskapsbärarna: Naturvetenskapen i det svenska samhället 1880–1950* (Hedemora, 1999), p. 9.

[12] Tage Erlander, *Tage Erlander: 1955–60* (Stockholm, 1976), pp. 15, 26-32. For a useful survey of all research councils, see Gösta Funcke, *[Introduktion till] Naturvetenskaplig forskning i Sverige* (Stockholm, 1963).

[13] Anonymous, "PM i matematikmaskinfrågan", Försvarets radioanstalt, archive, Databehandlingsfrågor, F IV:4. This document was most likely put together in March, April or possibly May 1946 in response to a proposal about the organization of a "mathematical laboratory" in Stockholm. See also Carl-Gösta Borelius, "Databearbetningens historia vid FRA", unpublished manuscript, Försvarets Radioanstalt, p. 1, and De Geer, *På väg till datasamhället*, p. 30, n. 13.

and hardware complexities, could be estimated by following the Harvard MARK I machine, which was inaugurated openly in 1944.[14]   Further information about these machines, the centerpiece probably being the ENIAC, was analyzed at various Swedish defense organizations in January 1946 as U.S. authorities a few months earlier had declassified some relevant accounts and descriptions.   The response was immediate in the sense that FRA presented the issue to the Government and pushed for a thorough evaluation in addition to its own disappearance from all necessary future investigations.

More useful knowledge about and reports from concrete experiences of big-scale computing reached the country as Swedish researchers reestablished their exchange with American colleagues, beginning in 1946. One of them was Stig Ekelöf, a professor in electrical engineering at Chalmers Institute of Technology in Gothenburg, who traveled in the U.S. that year.   One of his purposes was to buy instruments.   However, by agreement with IVA, *Kungl. Vetenskapsakademien* (The Royal Swedish Academy of Sciences), *Marinförvaltningen* (the Navy authorities), *Försvarets forskningsanstalt* (the Defense's research institute, FOA) and also indirectly with FRA and various academic departments, he also observed installations that he called "super calculators".[15]   Ekelöf was an important actor, in particular with regard to how they described these calculators.   He had already communicated the prospect of calculations carried out with the help of various analyzers to the engineering society in the latter part of the 1930s.[16]   Among his new reports – apart from those given at lectures and other presentations – was an extensive non-printed survey of American machines and computer research institutions and, in more digestible form, the paper "Matematikmaskiner" in *Teknisk Tidskrift* (Journal of Technology) in 1949, including a rich bibliography.[17]   Equally importantly, he was appointed as a member of the 1947 group funded by the

---

[14] See I. Bernard Cohen, *Howard Aiken: A Portrait of a Computer Pioneer* (Cambridge/MA, 1999), p. 121.

[15] Cf. De Geer, *På väg till datasamhället*, pp. 19 f.

[16] Stig Ekelöf, "Matematiska maskiner i U.S.A.", *Teknisk tidskrift*, vol. 69 (1939). See also Enar Eskilsson, "Maskinell lösning av differentialekvationer", *Teknisk tidskrift*, vol. 65 (1935).

[17] Stig Ekelöf, "Matematikmaskiner" in *Teknisk Tidskrift*, vol. 79 (1949). At Chalmers, partly under Ekelöf's supervision, analog computers were constructed and used successfully in the 1950s. For an account of analog machines, see Magnus Johansson, "Early Analog Computers in Sweden: With Examples from Chalmers University of Technology and the Swedish Aerospace Industry", *IEEE Annals of the History of Computing*, vol. 18 (1996). The question about "digital" vs. "analog" problems is treated briefly in "Från Flinta till Ada", *Minnesbubblor och datavisioner: Svenska samfundet för informationsbehandling 25 år* (Malmö, 1984), by Elsa-Karin Boestad-Nilsson, who was a prime programmer in the early 1950s.

Government that investigated how to introduce this new technology into the country. This group, apparently following Douglas Hartree who was a consultant on organizational issues to the group, coined the Swedish term for *computer* that was used throughout the late 1940s and 1950s, namely *matematikmaskin*, or "mathematics machine".

The motives were numerous, apparent at the so-called computer conferences held in 1947 and in the constitution of the investigating group, reflecting the assumed functions and uses of the machines by calling one representative each from key academic disciplines: electrical engineering (Ekelöf), physics and mathematics apart from one from IVA (Velander) and the Ministry of Defense respectively.[18] The military needs were expressed openly. In the text that later that year became the Government's proposal to the parliament, we can read about the urgent demand of producing a new ballistic "lexicon" but also about signal intelligence and about the fact that all potential research on rocketry seemed to imply a mathematics machine.[19] Input like this came typically from FRA, *Marinförvaltningen* and FOA.

However, in my view, we must not exaggerate the military influence. True, the speedy process that advanced the emerging computer project from merely being a suggestion to becoming a State-sanctioned investigation must be explained by the urgent needs of the military.[20] (The formal proposal came on 13 January 1947 and was followed only ten days later by a complimentary recommendation by *Naturvetenskapliga Forskningsrådet*, the Scientific Research Council. This resulted in the appointment of the investigating group on January 31.) Nevertheless, applications such as ballistics and code breaking were regarded as provisional and not enough for the financial venture that they seemed to need and it was stated quite clearly in the proposal that the ballistic calculations could be negotiated with a smaller custom-made machine. Others should also use computers; therefore, the passages about the need for a *general-purpose* machine, meaning they would not design a computer for a particular user or algorithm but rather for a general customer group of scientists and engineers from private and public sectors. Stellar statistics, nuclear physics, aero- and hydrodynamics, electrodynamics, mechanics, mathematical statistics (here incorporating meteorology, economics, forestry, sugar and textile research) and hydropower construction – all these were regarded as fields of inquiry that would prosper from a fast calculating machine. In fact, the first formal

---

[18] The members were: Nils Rosén (chairman, Ministry of Defence), Stig Ekelöf (electrical engineering, Chalmers Institute of Technology, Göteborg), Edy Velander (The Royal Swedish Academy of Engineering Sciences), Ivar Waller (physics, Uppsala University), Nils Zeilon (mathematics, University of Lund).

[19] Prop. 1947:275, pp. 7 f.

[20] Prop. 1947:275, pp. 2, 7.

proposal to investigate this new calculating technology, the one on January 13, had come not from military quarters but from representatives of the engineering profession.

4.   PROFESSIONAL MOVES

Edy Velander, then executive director of IVA, was a strong proponent of cooperation and exchange with other nations and the Academy did support a number of trips to other countries in order to collect information about recent advances.[21] In this regard, computer technology was only one in the row studied by professionals traveling overseas. Yet computers drew special attention and the Academy, as a complimentary contribution to the Parliament's appropriation of a very large sum (SEK 2,000,000) for *carte blanche* use, functioned as a promoter and coordinator of a one-year scholarship program. This allowed six young mathematicians, physicists, and engineers to work and conduct extensive investigations at the Observatory in Oslo, IBM in New York, Harvard, MIT, the Radio Corporation of America, and the Institute of Advanced Study in Princeton. The Academy also engaged its technical attaché – a post established and once held by Velander – at the Swedish consulate in New York as an observer.[22]

The scholarship holders in the U.S. traveled widely and received access to many, if not most, of the ongoing computer projects. They did so not the least by following in the footsteps of an older generation of Swedish engineers who had gone overseas for short study periods to places like Harvard and MIT. The commitment of the IVA thus expressed a wish to sustain existing professional networks by giving them new contents; it is a striking fact that Ekelöf and, in particular, Velander knew several of – or, by pointing at earlier acquaintances, had very little trouble getting to know – the visitors' supervisors. However, it also exemplifies the Academy's preparedness to support a State initiative in a mutual agreement about the necessary procedures. The Government and the Academy were actors on equal foot, although with different resources at hand, and they defined a common goal. The following actions were therefore seen not as part of a

---

[21] Edy Velander, "Intensifiering av våra utlandsförbindelser inom teknisk och vetenskaplig forskning", *Teknisk tidskrift*, vol. 76 (1946).

[22] See correspondence in IVA's archive, vol. 439, at Riksarkivet, Stockholm. Four of the stipendiater are mentioned in Herman Goldstine, *The Computer: From Pascal to von Neumann* (Cambridge/MA, 1972), p. 350: Gösta Neovius, Göran Kjellberg, Erik Stemme, Carl-Erik Fröberg. However, a fifth one, Arne Lindberger, shared his time between IBM and Harvard and a sixth one, Bengt Holmberg, made the shorter study trip to the differential analyzer in Oslo.

simple fact-finding mission to bring the technology over the Atlantic but, typically, as a mixture of research and finance, demanding the involvement of the ministries of defense, trade and education and recognizing the continuous surveillance by the Academy.

One argument in the investigators' work had clearly stressed the importance of a wider perception of the contents of computer technology in the late 1940s than being merely useful hardware and it provided a common rationale for the Academy and the Government. In discussing the needs and motives for a launch of the project, a term that was by no means commonplace now proved meaningful: *industrimatematiker*, or "industrial mathematician".[23] On a general policy level, they related this term to the question about national independence in the sense that Swedish engineers were regarded as falling short in mathematics compared to colleagues in other countries. Consequently, the industry was considered to be too dependent on foreign skills and results and thus mathematics should have an emphasis at the universities and institutes of technology, preferably by appointing professors in applied mathematics.[24]

This argument was, in a way, a translation of the present political situation: these were tense times in international politics and Sweden had no plans to abandon its neutral profile, at least not in writing.[25] Indeed, although statistics already formed an integral part of the vision of *social ingenjörskonst* (social engineering), mathematics in a more general meaning had recently become a strategic resource of a significantly high order. Having been mostly unaffected by industrial ambitions in the interwar years, the mathematical field in the U.S. was altered substantially by the industrial power of the war, forming new ideals and practices. "The 'purest' mathematicians, or those most attached to basic research [...] changed their fields, or reoriented their goals, their work habits, and their criteria of rigor", according to Amy Dahan Dalmedico.[26] Previously non-applied

---

[23] Prop. 1947:275, pp. 8 f.

[24] Cf. Arne Kaijser and Joar Tiberg, "From Operations Research to Future Studies: The Establishment, Diffusion, and Transformation of the Systems Approach in Sweden, 1945-1980", in Agatha C. Hughes and Thomas P. Hughes (eds.), *Systems, Experts, and Computers: The Systems Approach in Management and Engineering, World War II and After* (Cambridge/MA, 2000), p. 396.

[25] The question about Sweden's "neutrality" during the Cold War is far from settled. "Technological cooperation was far-reaching", according to Hans Weinberger, "'På sidan av de stora kraftlinjerna'? Teknik, vetenskap och det kalla kriget", in Widmalm (ed.), *Vetenskapsbärarna*, p. 363 (my translation). See also Karl Grandin, "Naturlig neutralitet? Tage Erlander, Torsten Gustafson och den svenska atompolitiken, 1945-53", in the same volume.

[26] Amy Dahan Dalmedico, "Mathematics in the Twentieth Century", in John Krige and Dominique Pestre (eds.), *Science in the Twentieth Century* (Amsterdam, 1997), p. 657. Cf.

mathematicians had been involved in goal-oriented missions like the atomic bomb, missile guidance, and computers, bringing them closer to professionals of other disciplines. New mathematical sub-disciplines and activities emerged, operations research being one and the new set of analytical tools (such as Monte Carlo) within probability and statistics another. Calculations became increasingly legitimate in areas where little or no attention was given to advanced mathematical practices. Referring to this situation, the investigators presented mathematics as a key element, not to say an emblematic quality, for the needs to renew the engineering profession and the overall industrial performance in Sweden in the years immediately following World War II.

The question had been touched upon in *Teknisk Tidskrift*, an important debate ground and source of information for the engineering society, most likely with some reminiscences of the debate about the "terror of mathematics" in schools in the early 1930s.[27] The opinions about the use of mathematics were not uniform. In some quarters, mathematics, construed as synonymous to "theory", were discharged towards the background of a claimed need for more *practical* engineers. Here, the crossover between mathematics and the already established engineering disciplines seemed confusing if necessary at all.[28] However, others welcomed a potential overthrow regarding the role of mathematics: "If the habit of calculation has not been accomplished through academic studies it will hardly be accomplished [at all] later on [...]. [Calculations] might often give unexpected results which corrects irrational misapprehensions and, thereby, offers a new view of things".[29]

In the Government's proposition to the Parliament, the investigators expressed similar ideas in a more coherent manner and they related them to the new material resource. The military motive was clear since there was a "need for a mathematical machine for Swedish use, which is supposed to facilitate and hasten scientific and technical research [...] and make new areas available for research of this kind, all this besides the fact that the need is particularly well documented within the defense organization". Simultaneously the former part of this quotation is interesting also because it demonstrates a kind of activism. By "facilitating" and "hastening" through

---

Peter Galison, *Image and Logic: A Material Culture of Microphysics* (Chicago, 1997), ch. 4.

[27] See Daniel Lövheim, "Kampen om läroplanen: Synen på naturvetenskap och matematik i läroplansdiskussion och läroplansformering 1922-1937", unpublished manuscript, Dept. of History of Science and Ideas, Uppsala University, September 2002.

[28] P Eg. Gummeson, "Den svenska ingenjören och vårt lands framtid", *Teknisk tidskrift*, vol. 76 (1946).

[29] Jarl Salin, "De tekniska högskolornas pedagogiska problem", *Teknisk tidskrift*, vol. 76 (1946) (my translation).

the means of a computer project, the State should not only support research but also actively step in and expedite the emergence of new methods.

The investigators reinforced this view by repeating expressions about "pushing", "pressing", and "forcing" research. It is imperative to note that they made the argument by drawing boundaries between apparent hardware options. Indeed, punched card machines seemed to belong to the rather disparate group of calculating devices presented in a general background in the investigators' plan. Likewise, we should note that, according to a survey made by the investigators, those who favored the acquisition of new machinery *the most* had in fact been users of punched cards. The general view was nevertheless that of a disturbing lack of experience from any automatic calculating machinery among industrial actors; that is, among those who believed to have the most critical need for mathematics in terms of obtaining the tools that, in the end, should generate general societal change. Punched card machines were not construed to be "modern" whereas the new machines should – and this is decisive – "in a near future create completely new possibilities for utilization of mathematics within science and technology".[30]

The "need for a mathematical machine for Swedish use" was ultimately responded to by *Matematikmaskinnämnden* (The Board of Computing Machinery, MMN), a State agency created in 1948 to plan, design, and eventually manage the Swedish-built BARK and BESK machines. In an earlier attempt to formulate a solution, in fact as early as 1946, the idea had been to establish a national "laboratory" of mathematics. Although such an institution never opened MMN in many ways functioned as a more independent institute for numerical analysis. Retrospectively, one commentator has even regarded it as a research council meaning that it did not confine itself to support research but actually contributed to shaping new research areas.[31] By differentiating the costs for computer time, the Board disposed a tool for profiling its own enterprise and supporting such assignments or orders considered as relevant.[32]

---

[30] Prop. 1947:275, pp. 3-8, 12; quotations on p. 3 and 4 respectively (my translations).

[31] Funcke, *Naturvetenskaplig forskning i Sverige*, pp. 61 f. The English translation of Matematikmaskinnämnden (MMN), "The Board for Computing Machinery", is somewhat misleading since MMN was not a board in the strict sence of the word but rather a calculating service unit with its own administration and workshops. A distinction should be made between MMN's actual board and its working group, the latter being its mathematicians, engineers, technicians and administrators. The English name is used here since it was the official translation in the 1950s.

[32] The pricing for computational services is touched upon, although not analyzed, in De Geer, *På väg till datasamhället*, ch. 2. The choices made are subject to further investigations.

5. CONCLUDING REMARKS: BETWEEN FAILURE AND SUCCESS

The narrative of failure enrolls a few dramatic developments in the history of the BARK and BESK computer project. During 1956, it became clear that MMN would not be able to counter-bid for a number of those engineers, mathematicians, and technicians who had been the most involved in the design and construction of the BESK computer. The result: a "flee" of MMN employees to AB Åtvidabergs Industrier – two mathematicians already having taken up posts at LM Ericsson – where they would be instrumental in establishing the company as the first industrial producer of computers in Sweden, prospering as such by the privilege of using the BESK design commercially.[33] Furthermore, in spite of an attempt to renew the BESK design into a "Super-BESK" machine in the early 1960s, they transferred MMN's duties and resources to *Statskontoret*, an agency for public management, in 1963, thereby mostly serving the mission of rationalizing the State administration. At that time the BESK, altered in several ways, was still running whereas BARK had been dismantled already in 1955 as the military calculations had been completed. Due to these transitions, there was no way for the State to fulfill any possible industrial ambitions.

However, as for instance historian of technology Thomas Kaiserfeld has pointed out concerning a much more recent "failed" Swedish computer project, the notion of failure is not self-evident but rather subject to perspectives and perceptions about technological change.[34] The narrative of failure often depends on a linear logic regarding the relation between technological "qualities" and market potential – a logic that cannot be taken for granted due to the multiple meanings that most technologies have. In this paper, I have revisited the social landscape in which politicians met other powerful groups to examine how they *represented* computers as the very first measures were taken to investigate this new technology. As a result, I wish to stress the importance of seeing the computers as tools for the renewal of the engineering profession and of scientific research and the society as a whole in the years immediately after World War II, rather than techno-scientific ends in themselves or, for that matter, as purely military tools. Several motives, two of which were military requirements and the

---

[33] Cf. Henriksson, "Den svenska utvecklingen", 88. It should be noted that the "flee" arose a much more vibrant media discussion than the one Henriksson refers to.

[34] Thomas Kaiserfeld, "Computerizing the Swedish Welfare State: The Middle Way of Technological Success and Failure", *Technology and Culture*, vol. 37 (1996), pp. 277 ff. Kaiserfeld focuses on the school computer Compis (Computer in School), launched in 1984.

prospect of advancing scientific research and technology and engineering skills, formed the same agenda. The Swedish Government was indeed willing to support learning about computers by funding a major research program, regarding science and technology as essential to building a modern, post-war, "strong" and independent welfare society. At the same time, representatives for the engineering elite supported the formulation (or construction) of a renewed engineering identity in which mathematics would encourage experimenting as well as guarantee a higher degree of confidence and also independence from "external" influences. The computers were supposed to materialize and intensify such a transition.

This is not to say that the State *could not* have established a successful computer industry. Nevertheless, I do claim that the financial support to MMN from the Government and the Parliament was never assigned for the creation of a computer industry. Historian Hans De Geer has rightly emphasized that the creation of a national industry is not an obvious task for a government.[35] This is especially the case, one may add, in a technological field surrounded by political uncertainties, as was the case in the mid 1950s when computers, apart from being scientific instruments, were construed as industrial tools with a possible potential to drive workers within industrial production and administration out of competition.[36] Given the mixed complex of professional and political motives framing the practices of translating available information and knowledge from a U.S. to a Swedish context and shaping the organization of MMN, it seems imbalanced to judge the Swedish computer project in the 1950s solely from an industry or production-focused point of view.

Such an argument has historiographical implications. In his book *The Computer: From Pascal to von Neumann* (1973), Herman Goldstine, who supervised one visiting Swedish mathematician at IAS in Princeton 1947-48, noted that "the computing people in Sweden have turned their attention [...] to numerical analysis and the computer sciences away from machine construction."[37] Indeed, a look at the BARK and BESK computers as "mathematics machines" points at other possible outcomes of the computer project than merely to establish a State-owned computer industry. In the later part of the 1950s, *coding* was the one major skill that the modern engineer – the "electron-engineer" – should master.[38] However, already in

[35] De Geer, *På väg till datasamhället*, p. 15.
[36] Cf. Anders Carlsson, "Tekniken – politikens frälsare? Om matematikmaskiner, automation och ingenjörer vid mitten av 50-talet", *Arbetarhistoria: Meddelande från Arbetarrörelsens Arkiv och Bibliotek*, 4/1999. For a substantially longer version, see "Elektroniska hjärnor: Debatten om datorer, automation och ingenjörer 1955-58", in Sven Widmalm (ed.), *Artefakter*, to be published in 2004.
[37] Goldstine, *The Computer*, p. 350.
[38] Carlsson, "Tekniken – politikens frälsare?", p. 29.

the late 1940s and early 50s, in the process of translating the need for mathematics into an educational effort, coding turned out to be what needed to be supplied for. Here, it is interesting to note that the spread of coding practices took place through courses arranged in collaboration between MMN and the Department of Meteorology at the then University College of Stockholm, where Carl-Gustaf Rossby launched a research project to develop numerical methods for weather forecasting in the late 1940s.[39] Early on, the use of the BESK was a key element in this project, and by taking the courses, meteorologists as well as other potential users learned how to use the BESK computer some two years prior to its dedication. Through the interaction between the mathematicians at MMN and the course participants – and parallel to the mounting of vacuum tubes, cathode-ray tubes and memory drums – essential experiences were made regarding how to program and, in general terms, how to arrange an operative center of calculation.[40]

This is where the notions of "producers" and "users", being separate categories, become unacceptably simplified. Computers in the 1940s and 50s, seen not as machines but as *practices*, were collective undertakings involving various forms of skills and knowledge. Mathematics in the form of coding or programming was the common ground where negotiations about design and needs led to practical functioning.

REFERENCES

Annerstedt, Jan, *Staten och datorerna: En studie av den officiella datorutvecklings- och datorforskningspolitiken*, FEK-meddelande nr 41, Kommittén för forskningsorganisation och forskningsekonomi (Stockholm, 1969).

Aspray, William, *John von Neumann and the Origins of Modern Computing* (Cambridge/MA, 1990).

Boestad-Nilsson, Elsa-Karin, "Från Flinta till Ada", *Minnesbubblor och datavisioner: Svenska samfundet för informationsbehandling 25 år* (Malmö, 1984).

Carlsson, Anders, "Tekniken – politikens frälsare? Om matematikmaskiner, automation och ingenjörer vid mitten av 50-talet", *Arbetarhistoria: Meddelande från Arbetarrörelsens Arkiv och Bibliotek*, 4/1999.

- - -, "Elektroniska hjärnor: Debatten om datorer, automation och ingenjörer 1955-58", in Sven Widmalm (ed.), *Artefakter*, to be published in 2004.

---

[39] This theme will be developed in a forthcoming thesis chapter on the collaboration between MMN and the Department of Meteorology. The forecasting program was in turn a collaborative effort involving IAS in Princeton and, to some extent, the University of Chicago. Cf. Frederik Nebeker, Calculating the Weather: Meteorology in the 20th Century (San Diego, 1995), pp. 158-162.

[40] The issue was discussed in some detail in the correspondence between the heads of the two institutions. See for instance Stig Comét to Carl-Gustaf Rossby, 1953-08-27, Department/Institute of Meteorology at Stockholm University, archives, E1A:2.

- - -, "Elektroniska hjärnor: Debatten om datorer, automation och ingenjörer 1955-58", in Sven Widmalm (ed.), *Artefakter*, to be published in 2004.

Cohen, I. Bernard, *Howard Aiken: A Portrait of a Computer Pioneer* (Cambridge/MA, 1999).

Dalmedico, Amy Dahan, "Mathematics in the Twentieth Century", in John Krige and Dominique Pestre (eds.), *Science in the Twentieth Century* (Amsterdam, 1997).

De Geer, Hans, *Rationaliseringsrörelsen i Sverige: Effektivitetsidéer och samhällsansvar under mellankrigstiden* (Stockholm, 1978).

- - -, *På väg till datasamhället: Datatekniken i politiken 1946–63* (Stockholm, 1992).

Ekelöf, Stig, "Matematiska maskiner i U.S.A.", *Teknisk tidskrift*, vol. 69 (1939).

- - -, "Matematikmaskiner", *Teknisk Tidskrift*, vol. 79 (1949).

Elzinga, Aant, Andrew Jamison and Conny Mithander, "Swedish Grandeur: Contending Reformulations of the Great-Power Project", in Mikael Hård and Andrew Jamison (eds.), *The Intellectual Appropriation of Technology: Discourses on Modernity, 1900-1939* (Cambridge/MA, 1998).

Erlander, Tage, *Tage Erlander: 1955–60* (Stockholm, 1976).

Eskilsson, Enar, "Maskinell lösning av differentialekvationer", *Teknisk tidskrift*, vol. 65 (1935).

Fridlund, Mats, *Den gemensamma utvecklingen: Staten, storföretaget och samarbetet kring den svenska elkrafttekniken* (Stockholm, 1999).

Funcke, Gösta, *[Introduktion till] Naturvetenskaplig forskning i Sverige* (Stockholm, 1963).

Galison, Peter, *Image and Logic: A Material Culture of Microphysics* (Chicago, 1997).

Goldstine, Herman, *The Computer: From Pascal to von Neumann* (Cambridge/MA, 1972).

Grandin, Karl, "Naturlig neutralitet? Tage Erlander, Torsten Gustafson och den svenska atompolitiken, 1945-53", in Widmalm (ed.), *Vetenskapsbärarna*.

Gummeson, P Eg., "Den svenska ingenjören och vårt lands framtid", *Teknisk tidskrift*, vol. 76 (1946).

Henriksson, Sten, "Den svenska utvecklingen", in Peter Naur, *Datamaskinerna och samhället* (Lund, 1969).

Johansson, Magnus, "Early Analog Computers in Sweden: With Examples from Chalmers University of Technology and the Swedish Aerospace Industry", *IEEE Annals of the History of Computing*, vol. 18 (1996).

Kaijser, Arne and Joar Tiberg, "From Operations Research to Future Studies: The Establishment, Diffusion, and Transformation of the Systems Approach in Sweden, 1945-1980", in Agatha C. Hughes and Thomas P. Hughes (eds.), *Systems, Experts, and Computers: The Systems Approach in Management and Engineering, World War II and After* (Cambridge/MA, 2000).

Kaiserfeld, Thomas, "Computerizing the Swedish Welfare State: The Middle Way of Technological Success and Failure", *Technology and Culture*, vol. 37 (1996).

Kjellberg, Göran and Gösta Neovius, "The BARK: A Swedish General Purpose Relay Computer", *Mathematical Tables and other Aids to Computation*, January 1951.

Klüver, P. V., "From Research Institute to Computer Company: Regnecentralen 1946-1964", *IEEE Annals of the History of Computing*, vol. 21 (1999).

Lövheim, Daniel, "Kampen om läroplanen: Synen på naturvetenskap och matematik i läroplansdiskussion och läroplansformering 1922-1937", unpublished manuscript, Dept. of History of Science and Ideas, Uppsala University, September 2002.

Nebeker, Frederik, *Calculating the Weather: Meteorology in the 20th Century* (San Diego, 1995).

Paju, Petri, *Ensimmäinen suomalainen tietokone ESKO ja 1950-luvun suunnitelma kansallisesta laskentakeskuksesta*, lic. thesis in Cultural History, University of Turku (2002).

Salin, Jarl, "De tekniska högskolornas pedagogiska problem", *Teknisk tidskrift*, vol. 76 (1946).

Stemme, Erik, "Den svenska automatiska räknemaskinen BESK", *Teknisk Tidskrift*, vol. 85 (1955).

Sundin, Bo, *Ingenjörsvetenskapens tidevarv: Ingenjörsvetenskapsakademin, Pappersmassekontoret, Metallografiska institutet och den teknologiska forskningen i början av 1900-talet* (Umeå, 1981).

van den Ende, Jan, *The Turn of the Tide: Computerization in Dutch Society* (Delft, 1994).

Velander, Edy, "Intensifiering av våra utlandsförbindelser inom teknisk och vetenskaplig forskning", *Teknisk tidskrift*, vol. 76 (1946).

[Weijne, Josef], Kungl. *Maj:ts proposition till riksdagen angående närmast erforderliga åtgärder för tillgodoseende av Sveriges behov av matematikmaskiner; given Stockholms slott den 9 maj 1947.*

Weinberger, Hans, *Nätverksentreprenören: En historia om teknisk forskning och industriellt utvecklingsarbete från den Malmska utredningen till Styrelsen för teknisk utveckling* (Stockholm, 1997).

- - -, "'På sidan av de stora kraftlinjerna'? Teknik, vetenskap och det kalla kriget", in Widmalm (ed.), *Vetenskapsbärarna*.

Widmalm, Sven, "Inledning", in idem (ed.), *Vetenskapsbärarna*.

- - - (ed.), *Vetenskapsbärarna: Naturvetenskapen i det svenska samhället 1880–1950* (Hedemora, 1999).

ARCHIVAL MATERIAL

Försvarets radioanstalt; Matematikmaskinnämnden (Riksarkivet, Stockholm); Ingenjörsvetenskapsakademien (Riksarkivet, Stockholm); Meteorologiska institutionen, Stockholm University.

BIRTH OF COMPUTER SCIENCE EDUCATION AND RESEARCH IN FINLAND

Reino Kurki-Suonio

Tampere University of Technology, Finland; reino.kurki-suonio@ut.fi

Abstract: Several Finnish universities established chairs in computer science/information processing in 1965–68. Rather than reflecting natural evolution within universities, external needs motivated this. The first professors came from computing practice but had also academic ambitions. This paper is a recollection on how the new discipline developed in an atmosphere of conflicting goals

Key words: Academic education, information processing, Finland

1. INTRODUCTION

As in many other countries, the first computer was built also in Finland at a university.[1] During this project (1955–60), the leading position in computing expertise and education had shifted from universities to companies that imported computers. This was mainly due to the meager resources available to universities in post-war Finland. As a result, computer science did not evolve naturally within universities, as happened in many other countries. This led to a situation where the new discipline came to them from outside of the scientific community.

In 1960, Finnish Cable Works (FCW) started a Computing and Electronics Division (one of the roots of today's Nokia), which competed

---

[1] ESKO, a pre-von Neumann computer, was built at Helsinki University of Technology in a project of the Mathematical Machines Committee. When completed, it was moved to the newly established computing center of the University of Helsinki, where it served as their first computer.

with IBM in computer sales and computing center services. A key person in this initiative was Olli Lehto, professor of mathematics at the University of Helsinki, whose person also strongly influenced the working atmosphere in the newly established group. Several of the key employees had fresh Master of Science degrees and had ambitions for doctoral studies. Although competition with IBM turned out to be difficult, the goal of being number one in computing expertise made the environment to what was sometimes referred to as "Salmisaari[2] University". Ambitions in understanding the new field both theoretically and in practice bore fruit for the society, when serious computing education began. Several members of the FCW group then moved to universities and became professors of computer science and related disciplines.

We can argue, whether "computer science" is a correct term to use here. A more literal translation of the Finnish name "tietojenkäsittelyoppi" would be "discipline of information processing". The word "science" was intentionally not yet used in this context, to avoid pretending that the scientific basis of the emerging discipline were well understood, and to allow inclusion of topics that a strictly scientific attitude might exclude. We use the abbreviation IP of this discipline in what follows.

We should mention that there was also a notable exception from the above pattern of introducing IP to Finnish universities. In Turku, the University of Turku (UTu) and the Åbo Akademi University (Swedish university in Turku) had in 1960 established a joint computing center, which was the first academic computing center in Finland, and which received a first-generation Wegematic 1000 computer as a donation from Sweden. Instead of introducing IP as an academic discipline at an early stage, UTu followed a more conventional line of progress. Olavi Hellman introduced a strong computing component in the applied mathematics curriculum in mid-1960s and Arto Salomaa's work on automata and formal languages soon developed the mathematics department into a well-known center of theoretical computer science.

Another interesting path was taken in computer engineering research at Helsinki University of Technology, where they designed and built an architecturally innovative computer (REFLAC) in mid-1960s. The idea was Teuvo Kohonen's, and this research project gave him a concrete basis from which he started to develop his theory of associative memories and neural nets towards the end of the decade.

So far, documentation on the early development of computing in Finland is available mainly in Finnish. The most complete reference is a compendium edited by Martti Tienari and mentioned in the end of this paper. Much of the material in this paper appeared also there in Finnish, and

---

[2]   The offices and the computing center were located in Salmisaari, Helsinki.

one can find there references to original sources. Because of my personal perspective, the reader should not take this as a balanced and total picture of the origins of IP education and research in Finland.

2. SOME MORE BACKGROUND

As we already mentioned, only meager resources were available to academic institutions in post-war Finland. In spite of this, applied mathematicians were eager to promote computer use, and courses in programming and numerical computing were included in several engineering and applied mathematics curricula in early 1960s. Some vague ideas arose then also about the need for more serious IP education. Inspired by the ideas with which I had come in contact in my work at FCW, I wrote in 1962 about academic IP education:[3] "Soon it will not be sufficient for universities to give courses in computer appreciation and programming techniques only. The field itself is a rich area of research and closely connected to topical research in other fields. Therefore it is soon time for universities to start research and special education in it."

At that time, we had both state and private universities, but also the latter depended mostly on state money. University budgets required approval by the ministries of education and finance, and each contained a relatively stable list of unfilled wishes, from which only the topmost could be satisfied each year. As a result, it was not in the interest of existing departments to propose new ones, which would have reduced their own chances to get anything.

The need for well-educated computing professionals grew, however, rapidly in practice. One of the institutes in which this was strongly experienced was the State Computing Center (SCC). Its director, Otto Karttunen, had also much power in the ministry of finance and his support was influential in establishing the first chairs in IP. Knowing that it would obtain such a chair, if a university proposed it, certainly helped in getting a proposal on a university's priority list.

Through the 1960s and 1970s, the position of SCC was also such that no state office could acquire computing equipment without their permission, which gave Mr. Karttunen the nickname "Data Czar". This rule applied also to private universities, including the use of their own funds on computing. Since SCC offered computing services that competed· with other plans to satisfy computing needs, the situation was bound to lead to difficulties in getting suitable computers to universities.

---

[3] Free translation from Arkhimedes, a journal of Finnish mathematicians and physicists.

As for the structure of degree curricula in universities, they divided studies in each discipline into three stages for which they used traditional Latin names.[4] Students could pass the first stage, *approbatur*, in one year. The second stage, *cum laude (approbatur)*, required one to two additional years, and the highest level, *laudatur*, one could achieve (in practice) after a total of four to five years.[5] An MSc degree in mathematics and natural sciences, for instance, required the *laudatur* level and the MSc thesis in the major discipline, and *cum laude* and *approbatur* levels in two minor disciplines, respectively. The choice of minors was relatively free.

3.   A SURPRISE MOVE

Tampere was (and still is) a progressive industrial city, but its wish to have university-level education in technology and/or business studies had not been fulfilled. However, the School of Social Sciences – a private university-level institution – had moved there from Helsinki in 1960. In the new environment, and with active support from the city, it soon started to develop towards a full-fledged university. As a surprise to the major universities, IP was first started there as an independent academic discipline in 1965.

By then this school had faculties only in social sciences and humanities, under the charismatic leadership of a visionary rector, Paavo Koli. Close contacts began with FCW in using their computing services and expertise in statistical methods. In fact, Dr. Seppo Mustonen[6] from FCW then worked there as an acting professor, and the development of computing in the school was included in his responsibilities.

In February 1965, Koli presented a plan to establish a new faculty of economics and administration, in which Mustonen's proposal for a chair in IP was included. As a motivation for this chair, the estimate was given that Finland would need some 200 academically educated IP professionals (system analysts and programmers) within the next five years. The mundane needs in the practice of computing were not, however, what Koli mainly had in mind. When the new faculty started in fall 1965, he expressed his visions in public, speaking forcefully about the society's need for well-educated analysts and decision makers with profound knowledge of quantitative and computational methods. In today's perspective, this seems like an early vision of educating leaders for the information society.

---

[4] In engineering studies, the system was different, and will not be discussed here.
[5] In the absence of strict timetables, studies often lasted much longer; some universities exercised an upper limit of ten years.
[6] Now professor emeritus of statistics, University of Helsinki.

How could Koli force his ideas through, when money for universities was so scarce? The school was small, and he was a charismatic leader who could persuade his colleagues to support his visionary ideas. Secondly, as a wartime hero he used a tactic of surprise, which was not far from blackmailing for state money. Having established permanent chairs with temporary funding, he threatened the ministries with bankruptcy of the school, unless they granted the required money. Of course, this tactic could not work long, and he had to abandon it when the school received permission to have a name change to the University of Tampere (Uta) in 1966. Therefore, they never fully implemented the ideas of Mustonen and Koli, but this sequence of events is the way IP began as an academic discipline in Finland.

4.   STARTING IP IN TAMPERE

When the above plans were prepared in Tampere, I was a fresh PhD on leave of absence from FCW, spending a year as visiting scientist at Carnegie Institute of Technology, now called Carnegie-Mellon University (CMU). My first contact with computers had been with DASK at Regnecentralen in Copenhagen, where FCW sent me in 1960. My advisor there had been Dr. Peter Naur[7], from whom I had also received a fresh copy of the Algol 60 report. After overcoming initial difficulties in reading it, it had inspired me to doctoral work on formal languages and syntax analysis of programming languages.

When asked to come to Tampere to start IP education as an acting professor, I did not feel competent for the challenge, of course. The first computer science departments had emerged only quite recently – even CMU was then just starting one – and no generally accepted recommendations or textbooks were available. On the other hand, I was afraid that another choice might lead the new discipline in Finland into a direction that would be divergent from what I had learned during that year from Alan J. Perlis, Allen Newell, Donald Knuth, and others. To ease my responsibility, I first accepted only half of the position, and continued part-time at FCW. For the other half, we hired Miikka Jahnukainen, who had experience in teaching IP system analysis and who had been involved in the design of a prototype curriculum for such education.

At that time, a severe split existed in computing practice according to two main application areas. In *business data processing,* the focus was in system analysis and design, whereas the emphasis of *scientific computing* was on

---

[7] Now professor emeritus of computer science, University of Copenhagen.

numerical analysis and "scientific" programming languages. My experience at FCW had convinced me that an application-oriented approach would not be appropriate for IP education, even though this was what people in practice seemed to be expecting.   Instead, I wanted to emphasize application-independent topics like data structures and associated algorithms, and expressing complex IP processes in algorithmic languages. Additionally, to satisfy the urgent needs in business data processing, we complemented this computer science oriented core with courses that prepared students for the system analysis practices of the time. This resulted in a clear division of labor between Jahnukainen and me.

The new discipline gathered immediately a large number of students. Although many seemed to come to our courses just for curiosity, my first courses had still 150 students by Christmas time, and some 100 of them passed the *approbatur* level within the first two years.   In our innocent enthusiasm, we extended IP into a full-scale discipline as soon as it was possible. We even started *laudatur* courses in 1967 with the aid of only two more vacancies, an associate professor, and a lecturer.

In addition to an introductory course, the *approbatur* level required two one-semester courses that reflected the dual character of the curriculum. The *cum laude* level initially contained four required courses.   They included "Programming II" (data structures and algorithms), "Introduction to systems thinking" (introduction to a theory of systems, formal models of systems, models and design of IP systems), "Programming III" (a mixture of principles of programming languages and operating systems), and "Boolean algebra" (theory and applications of Boolean algebra, normal forms and simplification of logical functions, logical structure of a simplified computer).   In addition, two elective courses were required, for which we tried to offer different kinds of alternatives.

The initial requirements for *laudatur* contained a "maturity examination" for which no course was given and which therefore turned out to be a higher obstacle than intended. In it, we expected students to demonstrate ability to apply the ideas that they already learned and to show general familiarity of such programming languages that we did not teach them. The only required *laudatur* course was "Programming IV", which emphasized the importance of different language paradigms.   In winter 1967–68, Simula, Comit (predecessor of Snobol), and Lisp were used in this course, although only pen and paper were available for exercises. In addition, three elective *laudatur* courses were required; the selection included an advanced course in system analysis and design, and a course in theory of computing.

As for initial experiences, the "programming" and "system analysis" courses remained more separated than I had been hoping. Only few students appreciated both, and many of those who preferred system analysis had severe difficulties in data structures and algorithms. One reason probably was in lack of motivation, since at that time, such knowledge was not much appreciated or used in the practice of business data processing.   After all, they still considered programming in these circles as a lower-level technical activity.   With a heavy heart, I eventually agreed that "system analysts" could pass the *cum laude* level also without such knowledge.   In each case, in the 1970s this development led Pertti Järvinen, Jahnukainen's follower as associate professor, to start a specialization of IP in the Scandinavian spirit of "systemeering".

5.   SPREADING OF IP TO OTHER UNIVERSITIES

The increasing need of IP professionals soon made also other universities prepare plans for IP education.   Without further surprise moves, the universities of Helsinki (UH) and Jyväskylä (UJ) established IP chairs in 1967, and Helsinki University of Technology (HUT) and the University of Oulu (UO) followed a year after.

The first professor at UH was Martti Tienari, who also came from FCW. His PhD was in pure mathematics, and at FCW, his responsibilities included scientific computing.   Before starting at UH, he spent the winter 1966–67 at the Computer Science Department of Stanford University, where the main emphasis was on numerical analysis at that time.   HUT's first professor, Hans Andersin, had been involved already in the ESKO project, and had gained broad experience of industrial and business computing at IBM and SCC.

As "remote" universities, UO and UJ had more temporary arrangements with acting professors, until Pentti Kerola and Eero Peltola, respectively, stabilized their situations.   Kerola's background was in IBM and industry, and before UO, he worked as an associate professor at HUT.   Peltola had started with Wegematic and FCW had hired him.   He had also worked for many years in the IP department of UH.

Although they could have used the curriculum at UTa as a point of reference and there was frequent contact between all IP professors, each university introduced some of its own flavor in its IP education.   Between UTa and UH especially, there was much affinity; the major difference was that the latter also had numerical computing in its curriculum.   Once stabilized, IP at UO differed mostly from the other universities.   There Kerola started to develop his "systemeering" approach in a form where computer science topics had less emphasis.   We could see similar trends at UJ, where they did not group IP among natural sciences and mathematics, but among social sciences and economics.

All first-generation IP professors came from IP practice, not from established academic departments, and they felt strongly the responsibility to educate people for practical needs. This, together with continued contact with practice, obviously affected the development of curricula. They constantly sought compromises with representatives of practice, so that students would get both a theoretical basis of IP – which the people in practice did not yet possess and often did not appreciate – and obtain sufficient knowledge of the tools and practices of the time. Of course, the balance between the two was (and still is) an endless topic for debate. What they appreciated most in practice was the knowledge of using IBM S/360 Assembler and OS/360 operating system.

The situation is also reflected in Karttunen's memoirs, written in 1985, where he expresses disappointment with "theoretical comparison of programming languages and theory of system analysis" that was taught in universities, and tells how students with *cum laude* or *laudatur* levels in IP often refused to be hired for the trivial work offered at SCC.

6.   COMPUTERS IN IP EDUCATION

In early 1960s, there were small computers like Elliott 803 and IBM 1620 in universities, and computing services by IBM, FCW and SCC were used in addition. (At UTa, they started IP education using FCW services in Helsinki, since a computer of their own arrived only during the spring term 1966.) For IP education, it was, of course, intolerable that they would use a single small computer – with only paper tape and/or punched card input – for all computing needs in a university. Therefore, plans to obtain facilities that are more convenient were an immediate initiation by the new IP professors.

There were several problems in this. First, computers were expensive. Secondly, IP had yet to receive recognition as a discipline that needed computers as laboratory equipment; universities acquired computers primarily for other purposes. Thirdly, as already mentioned, they also needed approval by SCC, which offered competing services in university cities. Of SCC attitudes, it is revealing to read from Karttunen's memoirs that he considered computers to be only "toys" and "status symbols" for universities. Thanks to its special legal position, UH succeeded, however, relatively soon in getting a solution that served them well for a long time (Burroughs B 6500/8500).

At UTa, a more modest proposal for a modern time-sharing computer (PDP-10, predecessor of DEC 20) appeared in 1968. In a carefully formulated statement, SCC suggested to investigate cooperation with them instead, in order to find a more economical solution that would satisfy the local needs of SCC, UTa, and the newly started Tampere University of Technology (TUT). Such an investigation showed, however, that the needs of the three parties – business computing services, IP education and research, and scientific computing – were so much incompatible that a single IBM S/360 system to meet them would cost more than three computers that are more specialized. The final word of SCC was, however, that, since their IBM S360/30 still had unused capacity in Tampere, also IP education at UTa should be satisfied with using it.

In December 1969, this deadlock was resolved by the decision of SITRA[8] to buy a centralized Univac 1108 to satisfy the computing needs of Finnish universities and research institutes. According to the plan, Tampere would get a single card reader/line printer terminal for UTa and TUT. Since it was clear that we could not expect anything else for years, they negotiated this terminal as exchangeable into a general-purpose time-sharing computer (Honeywell H1640), which they extended at UTa to give remote batch services on Univac concurrently with local time-sharing. This solution turned out to serve well for several years.

Struggling for suitable computers was not, however, over. In 1975, a centralized computer acquisition process was started for several universities. Although DEC System 20 was unanimously preferred, universities outside Helsinki were in the end forced to accept Univac computers, which were not good for time-sharing – not to speak of use as laboratory equipment for experimental system software. They have never disclosed the details of why it was so important for high-level political forces to manipulate the process to this end.

UTa was especially frustrated of this overruling of university expertise, and of not getting a computer that would suit the line of development chosen for its IP education and research. This led to a colorful chapter in the history of computing in Finnish universities, a long arbitration court process (the "great computer war") in which the main question was, whether Univac satisfied the promises made of its time-sharing use. This "war", which ended in 1980, perhaps sped up the process in which state control on university computers was gradually relaxed.

7.   BEGINNINGS OF IP RESEARCH

When the first generation of IP professors entered universities, their research merits were relatively weak and often not central to IP. In most

---

[8] A fund established to celebrate the 50 years of Finland's independence in 1967.

cases, they started as acting professors, trying to achieve qualification by individual research in their own computing-related fields.   The large numbers of students and a pressure to develop textbooks and other teaching material left, however, only little time for this.

As already mentioned, a notable exception to this pattern was UTu, in which a strong research group in theoretical computer science arose quite early.   Within IP departments – and more so in IP practice – this research was considered as pure mathematics rather than IP.   Contacts between IP and Kohonen's research at HUT were also minimal at that time.

The first to succeed in starting a solid research group in IP was Tienari at UH. The first area that he chose for himself and his students was the theory of rounding errors in numerical algorithms.   With the decreasing international emphasis on numerical analysis, he moved, however, in the 1970s to compiler techniques and associated theoretical research – the most classical area of computer science – in which his group soon became internationally known.

At HUT, Andersin started a group that worked on graphical computing. The engineering goals of this group resulted in topical expertise in this area, and in a spin-off company, which was successful for a number of years.

At UTa, my idea of IP research was that it should arise from practical motivation and should aid in the design and construction of complex systems.   Since compilers and operating systems were prime examples of such systems, I wanted to connect the research with practical work on them. The Honeywell 1640 system mentioned above offered the first real opportunity for such work.   When industrial development of computers started in Finland in late 1960s (Strömberg 1000, soon followed by Nokia's Mikko series, and then by Nokia MPS 10 in the 1980s), more opportunities arose.   This also led to starting of a software house (Oy Softplan Ab), through which IP at UTa – and later at TUT – had close connections to industry. For universities one of the benefits of this was cooperation in the development of software engineering education.

Another important component of Finnish IP research that they started in the 1970s was the "systemeering" or information systems research. Pentti Kerola at UO and Pertti Järvinen at UTa were then its main proponents.

8.   CONCLUDING REMARKS

As described, they introduced IP in Finland as an independent academic discipline at an early stage. In an atmosphere of conflicting goals, they sought compromises between computer science, which was getting its shape internationally at the time, and the practical needs of the society. Although

IP practice was not completely satisfied with us, we developed a solid basis in the 1960s and 1970s for today's capabilities to build the information society, and for the wide discipline of IP, ranging from theoretical computer science and algorithmics to software engineering and information systems research. Close contacts between IP education and industry also date from these early years.

REFERENCE

Martti Tienari (ed.), *Early Years of Information Technology in Finland.* Suomen Atk-kustannus Oy 1993 (in Finnish).

THE ADVENT OF THE FIRST GENERAL-PURPOSE COMPUTER IN ICELAND
Its impact on science and engineering

Magnús Magnússon

Professor emeritus and first Head of the Computing Centre, University of Iceland; magmag@hi.is

Abstract: This paper first tells the rather unusual story of the acquisition of the first scientific computer by the University of Iceland. It then goes on to describe the efforts by the staff of the University Computing Centre to introduce key persons to the use of computers and to teach selected groups of people programming and assist them in using the computer. Finally, it lists several applications in widely different areas that ensued during the first six years of the computer's operation.

Key words: IBM 1620, education, applications, record linkage

1. THE ADVENT OF THE IBM 1620 - PERSONAL REMINISCENCES

This is a story of how the University of Iceland came to acquire the first general-purpose computer in Iceland. In 1960, a few Icelandic students had encountered electronic computers during their university studies abroad. I had actually started using the EDSAC I computer in Cambridge in England already in 1950, using machine language. At the instigation of the Icelandic Mathematical Society, two engineering students in Denmark spent 3 months in 1960 working on the DASK computer at Regnecentralen, using machine language. One of them went on to work on the GIER computer using Algol a couple of years later. One student in England had begun to use the Mercury computer in 1960, using Autocode. Two students in the United States started work on IBM 650 and 704 computers around 1960, using machine language and later FORTRAN and MAD (Michigan Algorithm Decoder). These people, with different computing backgrounds, were the human resources available to initiate scientific computing in Iceland.

Thus, in the beginning of the 1960's a few scientists and engineers in Iceland had used computers in their studies abroad but no computer was available in Iceland. The possibility of acquiring a computer had been looked into, e.g. acquiring a Mercury computer, but that possibility was not realistic. An Icelandic engineer visited Regnecentralen in Copenhagen in 1959 and its director, Niels Bech, came to Iceland in the summer of 1960. He even broached the idea of setting up a branch of Regnecentralen in Reykjavík with a GIER computer, but that was not a realistic idea and the matter did not go further.

In September 1960 the representative of IBM in Iceland, Ottó A. Michelsen, wrote to the Faculty of Engineering at the University of Iceland, and to the National Research Council, offering a 60% Educational Allowance on the purchase or rent of an IBM 1620 Model I computer that had been launched in October 1959. Neither the University nor the Council felt able to accept the offer at the time.

In a proposal from 1961 for the establishment of a Science Institute at the University of Iceland, a recommendation was made to acquire an electronic computer for the institute.

In 1963, an Icelandic electrical engineer spent several months at Regnecentralen in Denmark studying the GIER computer. The idea was to obtain components and assemble a GIER computer in Iceland. That plan did not materialize.

In October 1963, the IBM representative arranged for an IBM 1620 Model I computer to make a "stop-over" in Iceland en route from Canada to Finland,. Courses in FORTRAN programming were held with support from IBM in Denmark and people were given the opportunity to use the computer. This aroused great interest, primarily among scientists and engineers. IBM followed that up by again offering the University of Iceland a 60% Educational Allowance on the rent or purchase of an IBM 1620 computer and now the University responded positively.

The Rector of the University entrusted me, the only professor with computer experience, with the task to obtain funds to rent a computer and to set up a computing centre. This involved obtaining financial support from the Government and Parliament and possibly other sources. I discussed this matter with the Minister of Education, dr. Gylfi Þ. Gíslason, who showed an interest but stressed that the running costs of the computing centre be covered, at least partly, by income derived from the use of the computer. I approached the directors of governmental and municipal institutions and private firms and convinced most of them of the potential benefit of the use of the computer. I thus managed to obtain from several institutes "subscriptions" to 1-3 hours of computer time per month. The next step was to write a proposal to the Budget Committee of the Parliament for funds to rent the computer.

As I was writing the proposal, the Minister of Education called me and asked about the purchase price of the computer. Although I had been preoccupied with the rental costs, I could give the Minister an approximate price in Icelandic krónur. About ten minutes later, he called me again and said that the Icelandic Development Bank had decided to donate to the University the purchase price of the computer on the occasion of its 10th anniversary! It turned out that the Minister was actually at a meeting of the Board of Directors of the bank where the directors were discussing how the bank should celebrate the anniversary. An agreement for the purchase of an IBM 1620 Model II computer, that had been announced in December 1962 and was a significant improvement on Model I, was signed in December 1963 for delivery in December 1964. That is how the University of Iceland came to acquire the first general-purpose computer in Iceland.

The University Computing Centre was set up in December 1964 with an IBM 1620 Model II computer with a memory of 40,000 binary coded decimals (BCD) and a card read/punch unit. Later we purchased two magnetic disk drives, each removable disk holding 2 million digits, with funds from the US Atomic Energy Commission. We also acquired a line printer on loan from IBM. Scientific computing was introduced in Iceland with this equipment.

In the preparation for the setting up of the computing centre, I had the invaluable assistance of Dr. Oddur Bendiktsson, who had just returned from the United States. He later became the first professor of computer science at the University. Helgi Sigvaldason, who was one of the Icelandic engineers at Regnecentralen in 1960 and who had worked on GIER in Copenhagen from 1962 to 1964, came to the Computing Centre at the start. Both of them have contributed to this conference. The third member of the initial staff was Dr. Ragnar Ingimarsson. These three came from different computing backgrounds, having used FORTRAN, Algol, and MAD respectively. Figure 1 shows the principal people involved with the project.

Figure 1. The IBM 1620-II computer in the University Computing Centre in 1964. On the picture from left: Þórhallur M. Einarsson (IBM), Ragnar Ingimarsson, Helgi Sigvaldason, Oddur Benediktsson, and Magnús Magnússon

2. INTRODUCTORY COURSES IN THE USE OF COMPUTERS AND IN PROGRAMMING

Initially, we held courses for directors and senior staff of institutes and private firms to introduce them to the use of computers and their potential usefulness, but not to make them proficient programmers. That was the aim with courses for the junior staff and students. In some cases, this worked out differently. For example, we held courses for staff and students of the Medical Faculty at the University. The senior staff reacted and started planning the use of the computer in their research, whereas the students did not. The Business Administration faculty and students showed little interest.

We held intensive Fortran II programming courses for the junior staff of research institutes and engineering firms. Many of them became enthusiastic users of the computer. We also introduced them to various programming packages relevant for their work. Most importantly, courses were held for engineering students at the University. The first courses were optional but in 1965-66, they became a compulsory part of the curriculum. The University of Iceland was one of the first universities in the Nordic countries to introduce compulsory programming courses in university curricula. These students became key persons in the development of the use of computers in science and engineering in Iceland.

3.   SOME EXAMPLES OF PROJECTS UNDERTAKEN USING THE COMPUTER

Many and varied projects emerged that required use of a computer. Some of them were quite successful, others not. In addition to holding FORTRAN programming courses, we placed an emphasis on encouraging and assisting people in the use of the computer in their own work.

At the University, the first project was to computerize the calculation of the Almanac for Iceland, which had been calculated by hand and by the use of electric calculators. This led to a great improvement in the form and scope of the Almanac. Data from the Magnetic Observatory in Reykjavik were processed and analyzed on the computer. Other applications followed.

Engineers were introduced to program packages such as COGO (Coordinate Geometry), a civil engineering software package, and CPM (Critical Path Method) or PERT (Program Evaluation and Review Technique). The staff of the City Engineering Department used COGO extensively in their surveying and planning work. CPM/PERT was not much used. The business administration software package COBOL (Common Business Oriented Language) did not catch on, due to lack of interest by business administration people. The Public Roads Administration and the staff of the Computing Centre worked out the layout of the first major road in Iceland, between Reykjavík and Keflavík Airport, using the 1620. The staff of the State Electricity Authority began using the computer in their geodetic survey work. A major long-term project on the simulation of electrical power systems was undertaken in cooperation with the National Power Company. This involved the optimization of the use of reservoirs and thermal resources. (Sigvaldason 1967) Several engineering firms started using the computer. This revolutionized their work in many ways.

In 1965, the Genetics Committee of the University of Iceland initiated, in cooperation with the Computing Centre, a research project in human genetics, which was supported by the US Atomic Energy Commission. This involved an extensive record linkage program, at least by the standards of the time, covering persons in the Icelandic National Census of 1910 and those born since. The census records were linked, using the Symbolic Programming System (SPS), to the National Register of living persons or to death records, recording inter alia the cause of death. Similarly, the birth records from 1910 onwards were linked to the National Register or to death records. Thus a database of the 85,000 in the Census and the 165,000 born since, about 250,000 persons, was set up. Blood group records of 27,000 persons were linked to the database. This unique database was used in various human genetics studies. The record linkage project aroused considerable international interest and was presented at meetings in the US and UK (Magnússon 1968). It was for this project that we acquired two magnetic disk drives, each removable disk holding 2 million digits.

An operational analysis of the herring industry was planned in 1965. This was to involve collecting and analyzing data on the location and catching of the herring, the landing ports, the landing facilities, and capacity of the processing plants as well as distances from the fishing grounds. The idea was to optimize the whole system taking into account the overall economy and to be able to direct the fishing boats to the most advantageous landing ports from the point of view of distance to the ports, time for landing the catch and distance to the next fishing grounds. The owners of the fishing vessels and processing plants showed little interest, however, choosing to rely on the judgment of their skippers and, perhaps, to guard their interests as owners of the plants. The project was abandoned.

An operational analysis project to optimize the use of trawlers for supplying fish for freezing plants in North Iceland was undertaken in 1969 by the staff of the Computing Centre in cooperation with the Fisheries Association. This involved assembling and analyzing large amounts of data on the Icelandic fishing fleet, the number and sizes of trawlers, their catch on each trawl, the fishing grounds and so on. Comparison was made between the profitability of trawlers of different sizes. The conclusion was that the most economical size of trawlers was 400 to 500 tonnes. However, the authorities and the fishing industry ignored this conclusion and larger and less economical trawlers were built. (Benediktsson et al. 1969)

Due to the rapid changes in sea conditions around Iceland and the danger it entails for small fishing boats, an attempt was made to forecast the wave conditions around the coast of Iceland. This was actually prompted by the loss of a fishing boat due to unforeseen sea conditions. A program was developed for this purpose. The idea was to obtain data from the Meteorological Office in the afternoon, feed the data into the computer, run the program, and broadcast the forecast at midnight. The program worked well in hindcasting but the problem was that it took the IBM 1620 24 hours to make a 3 hour forecast!

Already in 1965, I had the idea that we should attempt to make a computer model of the Icelandic economy. In discussions with Professor Koopmanns, later a Nobel Prize winner in Economics, at a meeting in Iceland in 1965, I pointed out that the Icelandic economy was dominated by the fishing industry and it should therefore be relatively simple to model. Professor Koopmanns agreed and encouraged us to make the attempt. An economic modeling program package was obtained from the University of Vienna for this purpose. However, little progress was made at the time, largely due to lack of interest by economists who were not ready to embark upon such an undertaking.

The computerization of the real estate assessment process was started in 1966 and became a long-term project. (See the paper by Oddur Benediktsson et. al. at this conference).

In medicine, there was interest in using the computer right from the beginning. The Cancer Register, i.e. a register of all known cancer cases in Iceland, was processed and analyzed on the 1620. The Heart Association put all the records from the extensive epidemiological studies undertaken by the Association on the computer for processing and statistical analysis.

Several institutes and companies started long-term projects in applied statistics using the computer. Of these the Agricultural Research Institute, the Marine Research Institute, and the Meteorological Office were particularly active. Furthermore, actuaries from insurance companies used the computer to analyze the car insurance business among other things.

In the humanities, a very interesting pioneering project was initiated on the IBM 1620. The project involved the frequency analysis of the words occurring in an Icelandic novel and led to a concordance project. Later similar analyses were made of several Icelandic sagas.

4.   CONCLUSION

As seen from these examples, it is clear that the staff of the Computing Centre succeeded in introducing computer applications in very diverse fields by their dedicated work. Although the IBM 1620 computer was extremely modest by modern standards, it had a profound impact on the use of computers in science, engineering and other fields in Iceland. It played a decisive role in the introduction to the computer age in Iceland.

REFERENCES

Bendiktsson, O., Sigvaldason, H., Hafsteinsson, J. og Jóhannsson, K., Bráðabirgðaskýrsla um aðgerðarannsóknir á útgerð togskipa með tilliti til hráefnisöflunar fyrir frystihús á Norðurlandi. Fiskifélag Íslands og Reiknistofnun Háskólans, 1969.

Magnússon, M., Medical Record Linkage in a Self-Contained Community, Oxford 1968. Unpublished manuscript.

Sigvaldason, H., Decision rules in operating hydro and thermal power systems. In Economy of Water Resources, NATO Advanced Study Institute, Bifröst, Iceland, June 1965. University of Iceland Computing Centre, 1967.

EARLY CURRICULA IN COMPUTER SCIENCE AT THE UNIVERSITY OF ICELAND

Oddur Benediktsson

University of Iceland, oddur@hi.is

Abstract: With the acquisition of the first computer in 1964, the University of Iceland introduced programming into the engineering curriculum. Subsequently it introduced an applied mathematics curriculum in the Mathematics Department with some emphasis on computer science. In 1976, it offered a separate computer science programme that rather closely matched the recommendations of the ACM Curriculum 78.

Key words: Computing curricula, computer science, applied mathematics

1.   INTRODUCTION

This paper treats the development of curricula in computer science at the University of Iceland leading to the establishment of a programme in computer science. The early development took place within the School of Engineering and Science during the period 1965 – 1985. The teaching of information technology in other subject areas at the university such as business administration, library studies, social sciences, and linguistics is outside of the scope of this paper.

The government established the University of Iceland in 1911. The initial lines of studies were theology, medicine, law, and studies of Old Icelandic. During the Second World War, a programme in engineering developed as the customary access to the Technical University in Copenhagen had become impossible due to the German occupation of Denmark. The majority of Icelandic engineers and scientists had studied in Copenhagen until that time. After 1945, an undergraduate programme in engineering (three years) became a permanent feature of the university curricula and in the late 1960s, the University added BA programmes in mathematics, physics, biology, geography, and geology. The School of Engineering offered these programmes. The early 1970s saw the establishment of the School of Engineering and Natural Science and the awarding of BS degrees in engineering, mathematics, and the natural sciences.

Graduate studies in engineering, mathematics, and the natural sciences started later. In the 1990s, new colleges and universities emerged in Iceland. The University of Reykjavík, a private university sponsored by the Chamber of Commerce, places an emphasis on computer science.

2. FIRST PROGRAMMING COURSE

The University of Iceland acquired its first computer, an IBM 1620, in 1964 (Magnússon 2003). In the academic year 1965-66, FORTRAN II programming became a required part of an "applied mathematics" course in the engineering curriculum. Students of mathematics and physics could also take the FORTRAN course. Figure 1 depicts the description of the course for the academic year 1968-69 (Háskóli Íslands 1968). This course offering for engineers remained unchanged as an introduction to computer programming for the next two decades although the programming language used gradually changed from Fortran II to Fortran 77 and later to C++.

---

12. HAGNÝTT STÆRÐFRÆÐI

12.21 Fortrannámskeið, B, V, R, (S2)   1968 -69

        Umsjón :   Próf. Magnús Magnússon
        Kennari :   Dr. Oddur Benediktsson

        3. misseri   1 F + 1 Æ   samt. um 13 + 13 h

Forskriftagerð á Fortran II máli miðuð við rafreikni Háskólans, IBM 1620. Æft eru dæmi úr fylkjareikningi og nemendur skulu skila sjálfstæðum loka- dæmum úr öðrum kennslugreinum, svo sem landmælingu o. fl. Almenn kynn- ing á tölvum og þeim grundvallarhugtökum, sem reikningur með þeim bygg- ist á.

Figure 1. Fortran course description academic year 1968-69

3.   APPLIED MATHEMATICS

In the academic year 1972-73, a new three-year sequence of study, the BS in Applied Mathematics, became a curriculum in the Mathematics Department at the University of Iceland. The core curriculum consisted of mathematical analysis, algebra, and statistics in addition to computer science, numerical analysis, and operations research. A similar degree programme currently exists in that department.

4.   COMPUTER SCIENCE

Computer science became a separate three-year BS degree programme at the University of Iceland in 1976. Institutionally, it began in the Mathematics Department and continued there for ten years before becoming an independent department. Figure 2 depicts the initial curriculum in computer science (Háskóli Íslands 1976.)

BS-NÁM Í TÖLVUNARFRÆÐI (T), 1. - 6. MISSERI   1976-77 13

Grein nr.	heiti	Náms-ein.	Meðalfjöldi stunda í viku Misseri					
			1.	2.	3.	4.	5.	6.
11.11	Stærðfræðigreining I	4	4/3					
11.12	Línuleg algebra og rúmfræði	3	3/2					
11.16	Forritun og tölvur	2	2/1					
11.21	Stærðfræðigreining II	4		4/3				
11.23	Töluleg greining	2		2/1				
11.28	Forritunarmál	3		3/1				
11.31	Stærðfræðigreining III	3			3/2			
11.32	Líkindareikningur og tölfræði	2					3/2	
11.34	Bestunarfræði	3			3/2			
11.36	Tölvunotkun	3			3/1			
11.46	Rafreiknifræði	3				3/1		
11.49	Gagnavinnsla	3				3/1		
11.56	Gagnasafnsfræði	3					3/1	
11.57	Kerfisgreining	3					2/4	
11.66	Kerfisforritun	3						3/1
11.67	Kerfishönnun	3						2/4
Í viðskiptadeild:								
	Rekstrarhagfræði	6	4/2	4/2				
	Bókfærsla	3	4/2					
	Reikningshald I	3		2/2				
	Samtals Einingar	59	15	15	9	6	8	6

Figure 2. Computer science core courses academic year 1976-77

Of the 90 credit units required for the BS degree, 59 were mandatory while 31 were electives. Of the 59 obligatory units, 12 were part of the

School of Business Administration (SBA) at University of Iceland. Students commonly selected electives from the engineering course or those offered at the SBA.

Of the core requirement for the three years (six semesters) BS degree in computer science (CS), approximately two semesters were proper to CS, one semester to mathematics, and one semester to business administration, forming a total of about two years of study.

It is instructive to compare the core course to the ACM Curriculum 78 and the ACM Master's Level Recommendations (ACM 1979, 1981) worked out in curriculum committees of the Association for Computing Machinery. In Table 1, the first two columns correspond to the first two of Figure 2. The third column shows the closest possible equivalent to the ACM designation.

Table 1: The 1976-77 computer science course plan compared to the ACM curricula

	Course name	ACM
11.11	Mathematical Analysis I	MA 2
11.12	Linear Algebra and Geometry	MA 3
11.16	Programming and Computers	CS 1
11.21	Mathematical Analysis II	MA 5
11.23	Numerical Analysis	CS 17
11.28	Programming Languages	CS 8
11.31	Mathematical Analysis III	MA
11.32	Probability and Statistics	MA 6
11.34	Optimisation	MA
11.36	Computer Usage	CS 5
11.46	Computer Systems	CS 3
11.49	Data Processing	CS 22
11.56	Database Theory	CS 11
11.57	Systems Analysis	CS 14
11.66	Systems Programming	CS 6
11.67	Systems Design	CS 14
SBA	Economics	
SBA	Bookkeeping	
SBA	Accounting I	

Of the eight designated CS core courses in the ACM Curriculum 78 (1), only CS 7 was not explicitly covered by a core course at the University of Iceland. Courses equivalent to CS 11, CS 14, and CS 17 in the ACM 78 were CS elective courses and CS 22 from a master's level (see above) course named Performance Evaluation.

The 1976-77 core curriculum changed considerably in the subsequent years and the offering of elective courses was increased. By the mid-1980s, discrete mathematics, data structures, algorithms, and distributed processing replaced the SBA courses in the core curriculum, whereas the mathematics was roughly the same and the time for electives remained unchanged.

5.　LATER DEVELOPMENTS

In 1985, the School of Engineering and Natural Science split into two separate entities: the School of Engineering and the School of Natural Science. In 1988, an independent Department of Computer Science emerged in the School of Natural Science and a decade later in 1999 it moved to the School of Engineering. The Department initiated a degree programme in software engineering in 2001. In the period from 1968 to 2003, more than 500 hundred students have graduated with the BS degree in computer science from the University of Iceland.

ACKNOWLEDGEMENTS

Many thanks are due to Skúli Sigurdsson for reviewing the paper thoroughly and suggesting many improvements.

REFERENCES

1. ACM Curriculum Committee on Computer Science, 1968. "Curriculum 68: Recommendations for the Undergraduate Program in Computer Science," *Communications of the ACM*, March 1968, vol 11, No 3, 151-197.
2. ACM Curriculum Committee on Computer Science, 1979. "Curriculum 78: Recommendations for the Undergraduate Program in Computer Science," *Communications of the ACM*, March 1979, vol 22, No 3, 147-166.
3. ACM Curriculum Committee on Computer Science, 1981. "Recommendations for Master's Level Programs in Computer Science," *Communications of the ACM*, March 1981, vol 24, No 3.
4. ACM Committees on Computer Curricula, 1981. "ACM Recommended Curricula for Computer Science and Information Processing Programs in Colleges and Universities, 1968-1981." Report, ACM 1981. (Note: this report includes the three above listed ACM papers.)
5. Háskóli Íslands. 1968. Kennsluskrá 1968 – '69 reglugerð o.fl. Verkfræðideild.
6. Háskóli Íslands. 1976. Kennsluskrá 1976 – 1977.Verkfræði- og raunvísindadeild.

7. Magnússon, Magnús 2003. "The Advent of the first General Purpose Computer in Iceland and its Impact on Science and Engineering." History of Nordic Computing, Trondheim, 2003.

ENDNOTE

(1) The core courses were: CS 1 - Computer Programming I, CS 2 - Computer Programming II, CS 3 - Introduction to Computer Systems, CS 4 - Introduction to Computer Organisations, CS 5 - Introduction to File Processing, CS 6 - Operating Systems and Computer Architecture I, CS 7 - Data Structures and Algorithmic Analysis, and CS 8 - Organizations of Programming Languages.

RESEARCH AND CURRICULA DEVELOPMENT AT NORWEGIAN UNIVERSITIES
From the early years to the mid-1970s

Terje O. Espelid, Arne Maus, Svein Nordbotten,
Knut Skog, Arne Sølvberg

*1. Espelid, University of Bergen, Dept. Informatics ,HIB - Thormøhlensgt. 55, N-5020
Bergen; terje@ii.uib.no*
*2. Maus, University of Oslo, Dept. Informatics, P.O.Box 1080 | N-0316 Blindern, Oslo,
Norway; arnem@ifi.uio.no*
*3. Nordbotten, Professor Emeritus, University of Bergen, Dept. Information Science;
Svein.Nordbotten@infomedia.uib.no*
*4. Skog, Professor Emeritus, NORUT Information Technologies, Science Park Tromsø;
Knut.Skog@itek.norut.no*
*5 .Sølvberg, The Norwegian University of Science and Technology (NTNU), Dept. Computer
and Information Science, Sem Sælands v. 7, N-7491 Trondheim, Norway;
Arne.Soelvberg@idi.ntnu.no*

Abstract: Early computing curricula in Norway were based on training courses in
              programming that were developed as computers were made available for
              research at universities and research institutes during the 1950's.   These
              developed into formal curricula starting from the mid-1960s. This developed
              differently at the different universities, which account for in the sequel.   It
              describes the main points in the development of research profile and curricula
              for the four Norwegian universities.

Key words: Norwegian universities, history, curriculum, research

1.   INTRODUCTION

All four Norwegian universities introduced formal computer curricula
during the period 1963-73. They started differently at the four universities
and developed different research profiles. A common feature was heavy

emphasis on software, software engineering and on computer applications. The universities are in Bergen, Oslo, Trondheim, and Tromsø. The University of Oslo is the oldest of the four, and is a classical university, which at the time had approximately 15-20.000 students. The University of Bergen is also of a classical profile but had considerably fewer students, approximately 5-7000. The University of Trondheim was a loose federation of two professional schools, one technical university (NTH – Norges Tekniske Høgskole) with approximately 3000 students, and one school of a more classical profile, which had grown out of a teachers' seminar, and had a similar number of students. They just established the world's most northern University of Tromsø and had only few students and a young, enthusiastic academic staff. From 1960 to 1975, the Norwegian universities increased their student numbers by 10.000 every fifth year, from 10.000 in 1960 to 40.000 in 1975. During this considerable expansion, it was possible to absorb a very rapid building up also of Computer Science education.

At the University of Oslo, the first professor was Ole Johan Dahl. In 1968 he moved to the University from the Norwegian Computing Center (Norsk Regnesentral) were he had been inventing the first object oriented programming language Simula together with Kristen Nygaard. For this, they shared the John von Neumann medal in 2002 and the A. M. Turing award in 2001. Dahl joined the numerical mathematics group of the University's Department of Mathematics, and after ten years his group in computer science and the numerical analysis group together with the cybernetics section of the Department of Physics, formed in 1977 a separate Department of Informatics at the University of Oslo. Dahl's work on programming and compiler technology was very influential in forming the scientific profile of the curriculum, and on teaching of computer science as a whole in Norway. Programming, programming languages, non-numerical algorithms but also several courses in numerical methods was at the core of the curriculum.

In Bergen, the Faculty of Natural Sciences and Mathematics organized the first curriculum with emphasis on numerical analysis and programming in 1963. Kjell J. Overholt of the Department of Mathematics was primus motor and a master degree in applied mathematics with specialty in numerical analysis and programming was established in 1964. Both the research and the curriculum reflect a strong mathematical influence in the first decade. Today the Department of Informatics has six strong research groups with emphasis on theoretical computer science. The Faculty of Social Sciences organized its' first curriculum in 1972 which placed heavy emphasis on computer applications. The first professor was Svein Nordbotten who moved to Bergen from the Norwegian Bureau of Census, where he had been responsible for the Bureau's computer operations. He established a scientific profile of Information Systems at the new Department of Information Sciences. The Norwegian Business School is also situated in Bergen, and organized a separate line of Information System specializations in the mid-70's, with Professor Leif Methlie, who later developed research and teaching in expert systems, financial systems and recently in e-commerce.

In Trondheim, there were several parallel developments at NTH (the technical university). They organized a University Computing Center in 1962 and immediately started to teach large number of students in programming. Research and teaching grew up during the 1960s at the departments of Engineering Cybernetics (Professors Balchen, Pettersen and Landsverk), Telecommunication (Professor Sørbye), and Industrial Engineering (Professor Bjørke), where computer courses were offered during the last year of engineering studies. Other important application departments were Structural Engineering (Professor Holand), Ship Design (Professor Moe) and Chemical Engineering (Professors Borgen and Cyvin). In 1967, the first distinct computer science education of one year and a half became an elective at the study of Technical Physics. In 1972, this resulted in the establishment of a Department of Data Processing at the Faculty of Mathematics, Physics, and Economics, which took over the teaching obligations of the University Computing Center, and some of its staff such as Professor Arne Sølvberg who became the first department chair. The computing center heritage formed the research profile and the teaching profile in Trondheim largely, with heavy emphasis on computer applications in general, and in software engineering.

In 1972, the first students enrolled at the northernmost university in the world, the University of Tromsø. A geophysical research laboratory in Tromsø already existed in 1928 for the study of Aurora Borealis, atmospheric electricity, terrestrial magnetism, and allied phenomena. This activity became the starting point of the Department of Physics at the university, and included a dedicated computing laboratory. The laboratory had the responsibility of providing computer services to the entire new university and allocated seven scientific positions. This organized mixture of computer services and science was based on experience from medicine where on the job training was and still is a fundamental aspect of education and research. In 1973, Knut Skog, who had been instrumental in setting up the Computing Center in Trondheim, became professor at Tromsø's computer laboratory. After two years of internal debate, the laboratory and a Department of Computer Science separated into two separate departments. Skog had spent time in 1962 with Peter Naur's group at Regnecentralen in Copenhagen when a GIER computer with its Algol compiler arrived at NTNU as its first computer. His interest for computer applications and computer operations from his Computer Center years in Trondheim blended with his expertise in programming languages and influenced the Tromsø curriculum to have heavy emphasis on software engineering.

Therefore, we see that the roots were different for computer research and education at the four universities. Trondheim and Tromsø had a heavy influence by an engineering culture that came out of NTH – the Norwegian Technical University. In Oslo, the early co-habitation of computing and mathematics influenced the research profile into a more theoretical strand. In Bergen, the activity remained organizationally divided, and refined their respective research profiles to a more application-oriented strand at the Faculty of Social Sciences, and a profile of theoretical computer science at the Department of Informatics. The sequel that follows gives a more detailed account of the historic development at the four universities.

2. THE UNIVERSITY OF BERGEN

At the University of Bergen the first computer, an IBM 650 (nicknamed Emma), were installed at the Department of Geophysics in April 1958. This was the result of an initiative by Professor Carl L. Godske and a consortium, EMMA A/S (acronym for Elektronisk Matematikk MAskin), consisting of the university and private companies in the Bergen region were behind the investment. The plan was to use Emma both for commercial and scientific tasks. This marks the start of both the Computing Center and the use of computers in science at the University of Bergen. Emma soon became out of date and was followed in the first decade by IBM 1620 I (1962/63), IBM 1620 II (1964) and IBM 360/50H (1967) with Kåre Fløysand as the head of the Computing Center, [UIB96]. Godske's scientific interests were in meteorology, climate, and hydrodynamic models. They illustrated the fact that in the initial period, the computers' ability to do number crunching was the focus. It was therefore quite natural that the Department of Mathematics in 1963 offered the first two Computer science courses for students: one in numerical analysis and one in programming. In 1964, a new graduate program (cand. real.) in applied mathematics with particular emphasis on numerical analysis and programming was established with Kjell J. Overholt as primus motor.

2.1 Informatics at Bergen's Faculty of Natural Sciences and Mathematics

In the spring of 1963, university lecturer Kjell J. Overholt at the Department of Mathematics gave the first formal course in numerical analysis (5 credits out of 10 credits totally per semester) for approximately ten students. A student laboratory based on electromechanical calculators (twelve machines) was available to help students do the practical computations. In the autumn 1963, Professor Ernst S. Selmer, Department of Mathematics, and Kåre Fløysand, The Computing Center, gave the first programming course (5 credits) for approximately ten students, [UIB96]. Three different programming languages were taught: an assembly language and Bell's interpretative language (Emma) and FORTRAN (IBM 1620 I). The students got practical programming experience through exercises in searching, sorting, number theory, and numerical methods (the spring course was a prerequisite). Both teachers and students gathered around the computers once a week in order to run their punched cards programs giving a 'hands on experience' and creating a strong feeling among the students of being part of a pioneer era.

In 1964, the Department of Mathematics established a new master degree within applied mathematics with emphasis on numerical analysis and programming and in the autumn of 1966, the first group of four students graduated with this specialty. Overholt consulted Carl Erik Fröberg, the first editor of BIT, who gave advice concerning which topics to include in this education. Among the topics were Algol, numerical linear algebra and numerical solution of differential equations.

The 60-ties represents a pioneering time for education in 'informatikk', a term inspired by French and coined as the Norwegian name of a field including 'numerisk analyse' and 'databehandling' in the last half of the seventies. The number of students studying the introductory programming course steadily increased and counted 120-150 in the early seventies. In the exercises, the focus on numerical methods was weakened and emphasis on other application areas of computers strengthened. The curriculum for undergraduate studies were restructured and in 1973, ten years after the start, these students were offered three different courses in 'databehandling', 9 credits totally, including one course in data-structures in addition to an introductory programming course and a course focusing on assembly languages and computer architectures. The Department of mathematics had at this time, 1969, bought its' first computer, NORD-1, and this was used both in teaching and for master projects.

Introducing a new master degree, cand. scient., in Norway in 1979 implied a total revision of the curriculum and 'informatikk' appeared for the first time independent of the curriculum in mathematics in Bergen. The curriculum contained 40 credits of informatics subjects offering both themes relevant in other fields in science as well as complete master studies in 'Informatikk'. The number of students exploded in the early 1980s with the result that access both to the introductory programming course (maximum 260) and the master program became regulated.

The 1960s was a golden age for the Norwegian universities and at the Faculty of Natural Sciences and Mathematics in Bergen, they used this to strengthen the activities in mathematics, chemistry and physics recruiting new faculty members. In 1968, the first position dedicated to this new field was advertised and Kjell J. Overholt was appointed as the first docent in this field. By 1973 the faculty had increased to three members and ten years later, 1 January 1984, they established the Department of Informatics by moving the informatics group from the Department of Mathematics and the group counted at that time six faculty members. The Faculty of Natural Sciences and Mathematics developed a plan in 1983 [IIPlan83] for strengthening of the field Informatics and in the next ten-year period, the staff grew from six to fourteen members. In this period the Department expanded the curriculum especially on the master level and in addition established a formal research education through a Dr. scient. program, [IIUIB97].

Today the Department of Informatics has 24 faculty members divided into six research groups that varied in size from three to five members. These groups were in algorithms, bioinformatics, coding theory and cryptography, numerical analysis, optimization, and finally a programming technology group. Bioinformatics is an activity dating back to 1992, while the other five themes goes back at least twenty years, numerical analysis, algorithms and optimization being the oldest. The department has a theoretical orientation and in a recent international evaluation of ICT in Norway initiated by the Norwegian Research Council, all groups received a very good grade, [ICT02].

A natural question to ask today is: Why did the department establish these particular research fields? Looking back at the first twenty years or so the staff constantly had a high teaching burden taking into account both undergraduate and graduates. In this phase the group preferred open job-descriptions while announcing vacancies, rather than to restrict the research area to a specific field. This way one was able to attract well-qualified applicants. At some point it was time for consolidation: in order to create strong research groups vacancies were used to strengthen the ongoing activities rather than to spread a small staff too thinly on the enormous informatics field, [IIUIB97].

2.2   Information Science at Bergen's Faculty of Arts

In the humanities and social sciences, some disciplines started early to use computers in their research. In the natural sciences, extensive and complex computations were dominating, while in humanities and social sciences the organization, storage, processing, and retrieval of large numerical and textual data sets became the more important tasks.

The pioneers outside the natural sciences were Professors Stein Rokkan and Ludvig Holm-Olsen at the Faculty of Arts who about 1965 started work on the idea of developing an academic training for researchers in social sciences and humanities to use modern computer equipment in their research. In 1970, their initiative resulted in funding for one professor and two associate professors in the discipline, which they named *informasjonsvitenskap* (information science). They appointed a professor from the beginning of 1972 and shortly after the appointed two associate professors. The following year, the *informasjonsvitenskap* organized as a separate department, *Institutt for informasjonsvitenskap*, in the newly established Faculty of Social Sciences, with responsibilities for serving both the Faculty of Arts and the Faculty of Social Sciences.

The course structure was four sets of courses with a four-level progression, each level corresponding to a semester. The four areas were system theory and development, program tools and programming, data organization, storage and retrieval, and hardware related topics. After the two years of coursework, the students had the possibility of preparing a dissertation corresponding to three semester's full-time work. This course structure has remained with a few modifications for about 25 years. Exams from *informasjonsvitenskap* were accepted, with exams from other disciplines, as components in the degrees Cand.mag., Cand.philol, Cand.polit. and to a more limit extent, in the degrees Cand. real. and Cand.scient., as well as in degrees from Norges Handelshøyskole.

From half a dozen students starting in 1972, the number of students at the department grew rapidly. Candidates with degrees in information science were well received in public administration and private industry. The number of students exploded in the early 1980s with the result that they had to regulate access to the department.

Research at the *Institutt for informasjonsvitenskap* was from the first years focused on problems and tasks in large computer based information systems and the organization of large data sets associated with such systems. When work on administrative information systems started at NHH, their group became a close cooperation partner.

On the national arena, *Institutt for informasjonsvitenskap*, was one of the founders in 1976 of the original *Norsk Informatikkråd* in which the department found other partners at other universities and schools. Within the other Nordic countries, many contacts happened among which the impulses received from Professors Børje Langefors and Peter Naur were particularly important.

3.   THE UNIVERSITY OF OSLO

The use of electronic computers at the University of Oslo predates any organized teaching by many years. The first computer (Nusse, 1954) was a homemade version built at the Physics Department by the new Center of Industrial Research (SI) after a British model, APEXC. They soon moved that computer from the university campus. The first computer for general use by researchers and administrative staff was the Wegamatic 1000 (1960), followed by an IBM 1620-I (1962) and IBM 1620 –II (1964). It was not until the CDC 3300(1967-76) with its multitasking operating system made it practical to have a large number of students running their exercises mixed with much heavier physicists or chemist calculations and the payroll and other administrative tasks by the university administration. The infrastructure was then ready for teaching computer courses, as we now know them [Jacobsen01, NR02]. We must note that teaching of computer courses and the running of the computer itself was for many years (1964-1972) organized in the same administrative unit – at the numerical analysis section of the department of mathematics.

Typical for that early period was the fascination by the computer itself. One saw the establishment of national computer centers ("every country should have one") - in Norway in 1952. Later, central computers appeared at various research organizations including every university and in every bank and major public administrative organization. The purchase of any publicly owned computer or computer equipment became a strategic decision in Norway that required approval by the State Council for Data Processing.

Typical for the 1960s was then a short user courses in how to program, operate, and run your own program on a specific computer. At and around the University of Oslo, the preferred programming language was Algol 60. Several short courses were available in the early 1960s, especially at the NR – the Norwegian Computing Center.

3.1   The 1970 curriculum at the University of Oslo

Even though the Department of Physics had courses in cybernetics and electronics, they did not develop a full computer related curriculum. That task was the responsibility given to the section for numerical analysis of the Department of Mathematics. From the first recorded courses, we find one pure computer course using Algol 60 in 1964 called "Introduction to programming of electronic computers" and a numerical analysis course entitled, "Analysis and execution of calculating tasks on electronic computers". Later on in 1969, that last course expanded into two courses,

"Numerical Analysis I" and "Numerical Analysis II". In 1969, courses had also started at the Department of Physics where we find "Information theory I", "Signal statistics", "Regulation technology" and "Computer technology". Until 1970, we find, however, no coherent curriculum.

In 1968 Ole Johan Dahl, one of the two inventors of Simula (the first object oriented programming language), was appointed professor at the Department of Mathematics in numerical analyses (that professorship was almost ten years later converted to one in computer science). He very soon designed three courses at the undergraduate level in addition to a number of graduate courses. The first undergraduate course titled "Non-numerical methods" – which is the all-familiar course in "algorithms and data structures" – also some years later writing a very good textbook for that course together with Dag Belsnes [DahlBelsnes73]. The title of the course drew some wry remarks from a fellow professor at the Department of Mathematics that it was strange for their first full professor in numerical analysis to entitle his course on "Non-numerical methods". Dahl also designed undergraduate courses in "Machine language and operating systems" and "Programming languages". The entire undergraduate curriculum from 1970 [Jonassen74] on was then (with percentage of a semesters work in parenthesis) as follows.

    DB0 – Basic course in the use of computers. (with FORTRAN) (20%)
    DB1 – Numerical Methods I. (50 %)
    DB2 – Machine language and operating systems.(30 %)
    DB3 - Non-numerical methods (algorithms and data structures).(40 %)
    DB4 – File-systems (administrative systems) (30 %)
    DB10 - Programming languages (grammars and compilation) (30 %)
    DB11 – Automata theory. (30 %)
    DB20 – Numerical Methods II. (40 %)
    DB21 – Numerical solutions of partial differential equations. (40 %)
    DB30 – Mathematical optimization. (60 %)

This curriculum was then permanent for almost six years, when the numerical section of the Department of Mathematics became the Department of Informatics in 1977 by also joining with the section for cybernetics at the Physics Department. The Faculty of Mathematical and Natural Sciences dictated the use of FORTRAN in the beginners course DB0. However, after some years this changed to a more substantial course using Simula (50% of a semester). If one should characterize this curriculum, one could use the two terms "Computer Science" and "Numerical Analysis".

3.2   A note on early curriculum related research at the University of Oslo

One might think that the inventors of object orientation, Ole-Johan Dahl and Kristen Nygaard would continue their research in that direction, but only partly so. First, the term "object-orientation" did not yet exist and secondly, they thought Simula was only one among many new promising programming languages at that time. Dahl was however eager to demonstrate to his students the ability of the class concept to model lists, trees and graphs. He also organized graduate courses in discrete simulation using Simula. However, only after Allen Kay had designed Smalltalk (heavily influenced by Simula) did the term "object-orientation" appear. Ole-Johan Dahl, after having successfully assisted the implementation on Simula on the CDC 33000, and introduced Simula into his courses, went on to formal specification and verification of programs, which he by and large continued with for the rest of his life. The proof system Abel and the book "Verifiable programming" are here the main results. Kristen Nygaard designed two new languages, Delta for the specification of systems (not machine compilable) and Beta, intended to be a more well structured, clean, orthogonal, object oriented language. In addition, Nygaard started the systems development group at the department where he, among other aspects, introduced the workers right to participate in systems design. The early work of the numerical section of the department, headed by Tom Lyche, made them well known for their work on splines (the Oslo algorithm) and for their continued work on partial differential equations.

4.   THE NORWEGIAN UNIVERSITY OF SCIENCE AND TECHNOLOGY

The University of Trondheim went through a major reorganization in 1995 and changed its name to Norges Teknisk-Naturvitenskapelige Universitet (NTNU) – the Norwegian University of Science and Technology. Another reorganization in 2001 led to a formation of the departments of computer and information sciences, telematics, telecommunications, electronics, engineering cybernetics and mathematics into one new Faculty of Information Technology, Mathematics, and Electrical Engineering. All of the basic computer science and telecommunication disciplines were by this organized under one leadership. The faculty is of considerable size. Approximately 400 MSc's and 30 PhD's in ICT received education in 2002 and a substantial number of students who major in other subjects receive supportive IT-education. The road to this situation has been long and bumpy. The sequel covers the first years of the travel towards the current organizational harmony.

NTH – The Technical University of Norway – was rather late in introducing computers in research and teaching. When they completed it on a broad scale starting in 1963, the pace forward was remarkable. In a couple of years, the number of students in introductory courses went from zero to a thousand. By 1964, almost every department of NTH had substantial research activities that needed computers, and introductory courses in computer programming became a common part of the education of most engineering students.

At the department of Engineering Cybernetics, Jens Glad Balchen (now Professor Emeritus) initiated in 1952 the construction of the electronic differential analyzer DIANA. Digital control elements appeared around 1955. Applications initiated for numerical control in industrial engineering in cooperation with Norwegian industry and the Department of Industrial Engineering at NTH. Digital computer capacity for research and development came from others, mostly from the Norwegian Defense Research Institute at Kjeller who had the then large FREDERIC computer.

4.1   "Out-sourcing" to SINTEF: The service bureau approach

By 1958, it became clear for the NTH leadership that the university had to find better solutions for satisfying both the scientific needs for computing power, and the needs of the university administration. The Rector had a meeting with IBM during the autumn of 1959, but decided to delay the starting of internal proceedings until they filled the vacant professorship in numerical mathematics. NTH's "Computer Committee" appeared in early 1961 and recommended the alternatives of buying either an IBM 7074 or a GIER computer from Regnecentralen in Denmark. Indications from the Government were that there would be no room for the more expensive IBM solution in NTH's next budgets. NTH's response was to develop the GIER solution.

While everybody agreed on the need for a digital computer, it was difficult to find good solutions within the university organization for operating the computer, and for establishing a solid economic base for future expansions. The chosen solution was an early form of "outsourcing". In 1950 NTH had been instrumental in establishing the contract research organization SINTEF, which in cooperation with NTH conducted externally funded research. SINTEF had the organizational flexibility needed for the task. They negotiated an arrangement between the two during 1961, and in

February 1962, NTH formally asked SINTEF to take the responsibility for operating a computing center at NTH.

The main idea was that NTH should provide computers and office space, while SINTEF provided staff. SINTEF paid all computer services and SINTEF would have some free computer capacity, and be permitted sell this to industry, in order to use the income to pay for staff and additional equipment. A new organizational unit, Regnesenteret NTH, became a SINTEF department during the autumn of 1962. The young research assistant Knut Skog had been in Denmark over the winter working on the GIER computer, and became the temporary leader for the effort until they found a permanent manager. The arrangement was very successful. The essential elements of the chosen organizational structure lasted for more than twenty years until a major reorganization took place in 1984.

This "outsourcing" arrangement had deep and lasting consequences for computer science teaching and research at NTH. Not only did they outsource the computer operations, but they outsourced teaching to SINTEF as well, until they established a university Department of Data Processing ten years later. Implicit in the organizational arrangement was that they should finance operations by income from selling computer power and associated services in the NTH-external market. NTH had in effect created a service bureau to provide for its computer needs. Education of future users soon became an important priority for Regnesenteret, in order to be able to sell more computer power and services. Students and university staff provided the central customer group. The training courses developed during the first years provided the kernel of later curricula. The service bureau background of the first curricula has had a lasting effect on choosing priorities and directions of computer science teaching at NTNU until this day.

The first manager of Regnesenteret NTH was Norman Sanders. He came late 1962 from Boeing's Computing Center, and set up shop in a very short time. By 1965, the staff had expanded to 25 persons. There were four groups for computer operations, administrative data processing, technical computing, and education. SINTEF's contract research profile influenced the priorities of research and development that they did. The attitude was pragmatic and oriented towards application of computers. Theoretical computer science had meager conditions. Norman Sanders returned to Boeing in 1965 and Nils Høeg, who also came from Boeing's computing operations, succeeded him. Karl Georg Schjetne took over as leader of Regnesenteret in 1971and stayed on well into the 1980s.

Regnesenteret NTH became involved in a number of development projects. Some of them led to systems that have lived on until this day, for 30-40 years, the original system solutions surviving scores of modifications, and the many major changes in computer technology of the last 30 years.

Examples are SAPO (development started 1966 by Bjørn Nagel), which is SINTEF's project management system, and BIBSYS (development started 1970 by Ingeborg Torvik Sølvberg), which is the Norwegian national library automation system for research- and university libraries. A third example is a class scheduling system for schools (development started in 1964, Harald Michaelsen), which is still in use. Another example is UNINETT (development started 1976), which originally was a data net for Norwegian universities and research institutes but which later on has become an even more central part of the Norwegian data net infrastructure. We can trace the roots of UNINETT to 1964 when Regnesentret started to experiment with remote computing over the telephone net.

During the first year of operation of Regnesentret more than one thousand students and staff were given introductory courses in programming. Over the next few years, the introductory programming course found it way into the curricula of the various engineering studies. In 1967, around 750 students took the course as part of their normal studies. NTH admitted 730 new students that year. After only five years since the arrival of the first computer at NTH, almost all of the engineering students had a mandatory introductory course in programming.

NTH had a heavy bias towards Algol from the start. The GIER computer, which arrived to NTH in November 1962, was an Algol computer. Peter Naur's GIER Algol compiler was the second realization of Algol 60, a couple of months the junior of Dijkstra's compiler. Because of the high quality of its software, GIER was a remarkably attractive computer, in spite of its modest hardware capabilities. When the UNIVAC 1107 replaced the GIER in 1965 as the major "work-horse", FORTRAN emerged as a major contender to Algol. Even if UNIVAC had an Algol compiler, the language gradually gave way to FORTRAN, COBOL, Simula, and Pascal. Nevertheless, the Algol roots of NTNU's teaching are still easily spotted.

4.2   Computer science became part of the academic structure at NTH in 1972

In 1968, the education group at Regnesentret gave eight different courses for a total of 1400 students, which expanded to 12-15 courses and 2500 students at the end of the decade. There were some additional courses at the Electrical Engineering departments, particularly at Engineering Cybernetics and the Telecommunication department, and several user-oriented courses were available elsewhere, but for limited numbers of students. The teaching volume at Regnesenteret was outgrowing the "outsourcing" arrangement. It was time to organize computer education as an academic discipline.

There was a beginning discussion about whether NTH should organize specialist education in computer science. There were two opposing views. One view was that we should teach programming as support subjects in existing engineering curricula. According to this view, computing was not a "real" discipline that could stand by itself, but was a support discipline in a similar role as mathematics. Specialization in computing should occur in the context of studies of "real" disciplines, like physics, mathematics, and electrical engineering. The other view was that the future would see the emerging of a large information technology sector that had its own knowledge needs, and that specialist education at the universities had to support this emerging sector.

The support discipline view won the first battles. One-year specialization curricula occurred in physics and in electrical engineering. It soon turned out that each specialization comprised the same basic computer courses in, for example, in programming and databases. NTH's teaching tradition was to organize specialized departments to teach courses of common interest to many of the other disciplines, e.g., the mathematics department teaches all of the common mathematics courses for the engineering students. Therefore, they decided to establish a Department of Data Processing, and place this together with other "service teaching" departments like mathematics and economics. It is well worth noting the choice of name for the new department. While other universities chose names like informatics, computer science, and information science, NTH chose the mundane name of "data processing" for its new academic discipline. This choice reflects the service bureau roots of the computer education of NTNU. The Norwegian name was "Institutt for Databehandling", abbreviated to IDB, in the best of the three-letter abbreviation tradition of the computer industry.

As a concession to the "specialist education" view, they decided to give the new department a quota for an intake of twenty students a year to a master track in "data processing" of 2½ years. This started in 1972. The computer science track in physics became the new "data processing" track, but continued at electrical engineering. The Department of Engineering Cybernetics hired Olav Landsverk as their computer engineering professor who offered specialization in computer architecture, and also offered a real-time computer system specialization with Odd Pettersen. The Department of Telecommunication likewise continued to offer education in digital technique for telecommunication systems with Professor Håkon Sørbye and colleagues.

The first of a series of university reorganizations took place in 1970 when the University of Trondheim (UNIT) established with NTH as a major part. Regnesentret NTH expanded its activities to all parts of the university and changed name to Regnesentret ved Universitetet i Trondheim, or RUNIT for short. There were intentions of having IDB to serve all parts of the UNIT, but organizational structure of the new university could not easily accommodate this, and IDB served NTH first, and rest of the University on an ad hoc basis. All of the courses were open for all of UNIT's students, but only NTH offered organized curricula in computing.

The "data processing" IDB-department grew out of the education group at Regnesentret. Key persons who have been with IDB from the start are Kjell Bratbergsengen, Reidar Conradi, Arne Halaas, and Arne Sølvberg, who where youngsters at the time, and still are active professors at the department. By more recent student generations, they were known as "the gang of four". Olav B. Brusdal, who had been with Regnesentret from the start after spending time in Copenhagen where he participated in building NTH's GIER computer, joined IDB in 1975, and stayed until he retired in 2000. Tore Amble was in the original group, but went elsewhere for many years until he returned to the department in 1990.

There were three possible specializations in the master track program in "data processing", in programming, in information systems, and in numerical mathematics. There was no requirement of prerequisite computer courses except of the introductory course in programming. The first year of the 2½-year master track in data processing consequently had to be filled with elementary computer science material. This became less than desirable by IDB's scientific staff, and a potential danger for the students' chances to compete effectively in the job market. Therefore, IDB started a lobbying campaign for persuading the university leadership of the need for a full 4½-year curriculum in data processing. The campaign succeeded. The first students for a full 4½ -year engineering study started in 1978.

The major point in the new arrangement was that students could apply directly for a full 4½-year master study in data processing on equal footing with electrical engineering, industrial engineering, and all of the others. The intake was only twenty students a year. The number of applicants was overwhelming. The young ones had already sensed that change was in the air, and that the IT-age was emerging. The intellectual quality of the student intake was amazing. The curriculum changed by moving courses that are more elementary to the first two years. The low number of students did not permit a wider specialization than in the original three tracks. They retained the "data processing" attitude to the teaching of the subject. Emphasis on project-oriented teaching was heavy. Industry well received the resulting knowledge profile of the students. Our students became very attractive in the job market.

In 1962 computer technology was unknown territory at NTH, except for a very few. It took fifteen years to reach full recognition for the new discipline at NTH, through the decision in 1977 to establish a full engineering curriculum, on equal footing with the already established engineering disciplines.

4.3   Continuous reorganizations and growth has led to NTNU's Faculty of Information Technology, Mathematics and Electrical Engineering

The characterization for the next 25 years included frequent reorganizations and steady growth in students and staff. The student increases have always come prior to staff increases. The teaching load has consequently always been high. This has been the case almost everywhere in our discipline, and we are no exception.

In most cases, reorganizations have reflected changes in the technology. During the late 1970s, it became quite clear that the telecommunication industry was changing its technological basis from electronics to software. In 1983, this perceived development led to the merging of IDB, the Telematics group of the Telecommunication Department, and the Computer Architecture group of Engineering Cybernetics. The new department changed name to the "Institutt for Datateknikk og Telematikk", abbreviated to IDT, and moved to the Electrical Engineering Department, which in the process, changed its name to Electrical Engineering and Data Technique, abbreviated to ED!! The reorganization coincided with a major expansion of the IT education in Norway, which took place between 1986 and 1990. The number of computer science majors doubled and NTH took the lion's share. The new IDT department consequently got a flying start. It is always easier to reorganize during expansion than during contraction!!

IDB was always engineering oriented. The non-engineering part of the University of Trondheim decided to establish its own Department of Information Science (IFI – Institutt for Informasjonsvitenskap) in the beginning of the 1980's. The scientific profile was somewhat "softer" than IDB's, in particular after IDB became IDT. During the major reorganization of the University of Trondheim in 1995 the IDT-department, which had been formed only 10 years earlier, was broken up. The Telematics-part of IDI formed a new department at Electrical Engineering, while the old IDB together with Computer Architecture was moved to a new Faculty for Physics, Informatics and Mathematics, and in this process merged with IFI. The new department got was named "Institutt for Dateknikk og Informasjonsvitenskap", abbreviated to IDI. Once more, the reorganization coincided with a major expansion of computer science education in Norway, of which NTNU again got the lion's share. The new faculty lasted only for 6 years, when IDI and the Mathematics department in 2002 merged with electrical engineering to form the current Faculty of Information Technology, Mathematics, and Electrical Engineering.

A long and bumpy road it has been. Who says that universities can't change???

5. THE UNIVERSITY OF TROMSØ

The computing environment got a flying start by being attractive as an exiting location for young pioneering scientists from the University of Oslo and by attracting 8-10 graduate students mostly from the northern part of the country, having their undergraduate background from both Oslo and Bergen. During a very short time, we were a group of 15 to 20 people trying to form a research profile of our own. In particular, the rapidly growing capacities of the "processors on a chip" and the microcomputer (the earliest PC) caught the attention of this young faculty from the very beginning.

An attempt to turn the department into a graduate school did not receive approval. The teaching burden of the undergraduate curriculum in addition to the teaching of some 20 graduate students was growing fare above the young department's most flexible limits. The department was the youngest and smallest of the four departments of the Faculty of Mathematical and Physical Sciences. As a result, it was constantly in the minority when the voting for more lecturing capacity had taken place. Bridging the gap between demand and supply of teaching capacity obviously took time that otherwise should be spent on research.

REFERENCES

[DahlBelsnes73] – Ole-Johan Dahl og Dag Belsnes: *Algoritmer og datastrukturer.* Studentlitteratur, Lund 1973

[ICT02]-Research in Information and Communication Technology in Norwegian Universities and Colleges, A Review, NFR 2002.

[IIPlan83]- Plan for utbygging av Informatikk-faget, Det matematisk-naturvitenskaplige fakultet, UiB, 1983.

[IIUiB97]- Oppsummering av perioden 1984-1996 og langtidsplaner, Institutt for informatikk, UiB, 1997.

[Jonassen74] – Arne Jonassen: *Gjøkungen, databehandling og numerisk analyse,* Mat. inst. avd. D, Univ. i Oslo 1974.

[Noodt97] – Aud Veen Noodt: *:Datahistorien ved Universitetet i Oslo, Institutt for informatikk 1977-1997,* Inst for Informatikk, 1997.

[Jacobsen01] – Per H. Jacobsen*: IT-historien@UiO,* USIT 2001

[NR02] – Lars Holden og Håvard Hegna: *Norsk Regnesentral 1952 – 2002,* NR, 2002

[UIB96]- Nils Roll-Hansen et al.: Universitetet i Bergens historie, Bind II, UiB, 1996.

INTRODUCING INFORMATION TECHNOLOGY AT NORWEGIAN REGIONAL COLLEGES
Distiktshøgskoler og Ingeniørhøgskoler

Per Ofstad

Norges Landbrukshøgskole; per.ofstad@imf.nlh.no

Abstract: Information technology was introduced in the curricula at the Norwegian Regional Colleges in years 1965-1975. New Regional Colleges were established all over the country. In this period, we experienced the rapid development of minicomputers and the Norwegian company, Norse Data AS, played an important role in supplying suitable equipment for the educational market. This development was very well supported by the governmental policy in the fields of education and IT.

Key words: Information technology, education, regional colleges, Norsk Data AS

1. INTRODUCTION

The 1960s were The Golden Years for the Norwegian universities. The period of reconstruction after the war was over and it was time to secure a bright future for the nation. Education and research became the focus. In addition to the expansion and modernization the existing universities, the University of Tromsø was established in 1968 under strong protests from the old institutions. The number of students grew rapidly.

There was a strong political push to develop a regional system for higher education. The government appointed a high-level committee in August 1965. The committee, called The Ottosen Committee after its chair Kristoffer Ottosen, was given the task to develop proposals for the structure and contents of the new system. Again, the existing institutions protested, this time including the new university in Tromsø. The second report from the Ottosen committee came in June 1967. The recommendation was to build a set of regional colleges (distriktshøgskoler).

It was obvious that the fast growing field of data processing (DP) had to be a major discipline at the regional colleges. The Ottosen committee appointed a subcommittee in 1968 to come up with proposals for how this field should be included in the regional colleges. This committee, called "Barca komiteen" after its chair Eivind Barca. Prognoses, made by the committee, showed a rapid growing demand for personnel with a solid educational background in data processing disciplines. The committee delivered its report in 1970, the same year as the colleges in Kristiansand, Stavanger and Molde started as pilot institutions. All of them had a curriculum in data processing and related fields. In 1972-73 there were six regional colleges if operation. In the years to come another six colleges emerged.

The staff in the new institutions enjoyed a great freedom in developing their teaching and research activities. They used this freedom to find a profile that was appropriate for their own background and that also could take care of the important interaction with activities in the region. The regional colleges developed soon into very useful regional centers of competence in the fast growing and changing field of information technology. This was one of the main goals of the Ottosen Committee.

2.   TECHNICAL COLLEGES

Another regional system of colleges was the technical colleges. These institutions, some of them had been in operation for many years, were partly at the high school level and partly at the post-gymnasium level. In the late 1960s, the time was ripe for a revision of the curriculum in the technical colleges to incorporate the new field of information technology. Created in 1968, a committee looked into this. The Harloff committee, named after its chair Albert Harloff, delivered the report in 1971. The technical colleges needed computers and suitable software. The government provided the necessary funding. Some of the colleges had the privilege to have important and useful neighbours. Tinius Olsens Tekniske Skole and Kongsberg Våpenfabrikk had long traditions of good cooperation in several areas. In the 1960s, Bergen Tekniske Skole had moved close to the University of Bergen and could benefit of assistance from the university when the information technology entered the curriculum. Kåre Fløysand at the university played a very important role in this cooperation. Trondheim Tekniske Skole had a close and natural contact with the Norges Tekniske Høgskole (The Technical University of Norway). Arne Lyse at TTS was the driving force to build up the new department for information technology at TTS.

Because of the Harloff committee, several technical colleges were in process of buying computers in the spring of 1972. Norsk Data saw the opportunity and wanted to dominate the educational market and ND delivered bids to several technical colleges. Einar Krokeide, director at Gjøvik Technical School, saw the advantages by coordinating the procurement process. Together with Knut Brautaset they took initiative to a meeting in Grimstad at Sørlandets Tekniske Skole to coordinate the purchasing of equipment for six institutions. Only two Norwegian companies, Kongsberg Våpenfabrik (KV) and ND, competed for this large contract.

KV had delivered a system, SM 4, to Tinius Olsens Skole and KV had a great reputation in the Norway. KV was a big company with long industrial traditions and a heavy political influence. ND had one trump card to meet this formidable opponent, working relevant software.

The computers, SM 4 and Nord 1, were almost identical since they had the same origin at the Defense Research Institute at Kjeller. KV made a small modification to make the two computers incompatible.

At ND Bo Lewendahl and Jørgen Håberg had worked day and night to finish the prototype system for Nord TSS and the Basic compiler. They had finished the work on the prototype system a few days before the critical meeting in Grimstad. The meeting, 20-21 April 1972, specified the software and hardware requirements, questions concerning the bids and for discussion of further cooperation between the institutions. ND and KV were each given a two-hour presentation of their bids, demonstrating their systems and responding to the requirements. Per Hovde represented KV and I was representing ND in this fight for this important contract. KV had very little relevant operating software to demonstrate. We could demonstrate the prototype of the NORD TSS with the new Basic compiler. Our system worked perfectly with a Teletype and a modem connection to the data centre at ND office in Oslo. Kåre Trøym assisted me in Grimstad. The next day we got the first order. It was from Gjøvik, signed by Krokeide. Very soon, ND had gained a dominating position in this important market.

Several technical colleges bought timesharing service from the company TeamCo AS in the first period. This solution proved useful for the introductory programming courses in Basic in the very first period. It was an expensive and not very reliable solution. The institutions had to have control over their own computing facilities.

3.   REFLECTIONS

The following is an illustrating story from the early days. It happened when Agder Regional College was to buy its first computer system. My friend, Tor Brattvåg, was the head of the department of data processing and I was marketing director at Norsk Data (ND), then a small and newly started company. ND had submitted a bid, based on Nord-1 and the timesharing system Nord TSS. We knew that Hewlett-Packard (HP) was our main opponent. For ND it was critical to keep HP out of the Norwegian market and it was important to win the regional college market for ND computers.

In the critical days before Agder should decide, I called Brattvåg. He informed me that the President of HP Europe should arrive in Kristiansand the next day. I responded directly "Just a moment; you can talk to the World President of Norsk Data, Mr. Lars Monrad-Krohn". Brattvåg laughed and told me that they would get a very favorable bid from HP. HP wanted to enter the Norwegian market with their computers. I then asked if HP would give the same offer to the other regional colleges. Brattvåg answered that this was a special offer to Agder and they were in favour of this offer. After this conversation, it was obvious that HP was trying to enter the market with a dumping offer, and we started a political action. Øivind Fjell, working in the marketing department at ND, was a schoolmate of the Minister of Industry. Øivind called him and asked for a meeting. One hour later Øivind and I met him in the Parliament and explained the situation. The minister took swift action and when we returned to ND, the message came from Agder informing us that HP was out and ND was in.

This was the first, but not the last, time that ND used political manoeuvring to get a contract. After a short period, ND dominated the market for computers in the regional colleges. Only Møre & Romsdal Regional College in Molde was lost to DEC. Since the Nord Time Sharing System included the Basic compiler, it was so decisive in winning the education market for ND in the early 1970s.

4.   CONCLUSION

I will include some comments about the development of the previously mentioned systems. Rolf Skår met Bo Lewendahl in the U.S. and Bo came to ND in 1971. Bo had worked for a company in California as a member of a team that developed a very advanced timesharing system in the mid 1960s. This was an excellent school for the young and very talented Bo. The company went broke after just one delivery, a system to the University of Hawaii. At ND Bo quickly implemented the editor QED, a copy of the

Californian system, on Nord 1 and embarked on the task of designing and implementing a timesharing system for Nord. After a few months, the first version of the system was in operation.

At the same time, Jørgen Haaberg worked on a Basic compiler for Nord 1. He was then a student at the University of Oslo and made his thesis work at ND under supervision of Monrad-Krohn. The prototype of his Basic compiler was ready in the spring 1972, about the same time as Bo's TSS. ND had a system that functioned well and was very well suited for educational purposes.

NORDIC COOPERATION WITHIN THE FIELD OF COMPUTING

Erik Bruhn

Cofounder of Danish Data Society and Nordic Data Union - Chiefeditor of the nordic magasin DATA –administrator of BIT 1970-2002; ebru@ddf.dk

Abstract: Already in 1959, active users started the Nordic co-operation organizing the first joint symposium in the use of computers with 270 participants. The cooperation enlarged rapidly and developed into well-organized forms. This paper concentrates on the cooperation between the Nordic user federations and especially on the joint journal projects, DATA, and BIT.

Key words: Nordic computers – NordDATA - BIT

1.   INTRODUCTION

In 1948, the Swedish government established an organization called "Matematikmaskinnämnden" that would investigate the possibilities for building a number-machine (mathematics-machine) in Sweden. One of the leading people in that committee was Professor Carl-Erik Fröberg, who for the last fifty years has influenced the computing society, especially in the Nordic countries.

The first machine was ready in February 1950 and had its inauguration in April in Stockholm. They named the machine BARK and it was a 32-bit machine capable of performing an addition operation in 150 ms and a multiplication operation in 250 ms. BARK consisted of 5,000 telephone-relays.

Work continued to improve BARK and one person meant very much in that connection – Erik Stemme – who after a study tour to the USA headed the work leading to the building of BESK (Binär Elektronisk Sekvens

Kalkylator). With a 40-bit machine, it was now possible to perform an addition operation in 56µs and a multiplication in 350µs. The memory-capacity was 512 words. The length of instruction was 20 bits and thus every word could contain two instructions. BESK was ready in 1953.

When BESK was build, Finns, Norwegians, and Danes started looking at what was going on in Sweden. They wanted to have *a machine* as well. Thomas Hysing was heading a project under "Utvalget for Matematikk-maskiner", that lead to the building of NUSSE (Norsk Universal Siffermaskin Selvstyrt Elektronisk). NUSSE was ready end 1954.

From 1954 to 1960, Finland developed and built ESKO (Elektronisk Serie-KOmputator) through the governmental organization "Matematikmaskinkommision" headed by the well-known mathematician Rolf Nevanlinnas. Together with university rector P.J. Myrberg, the role of Professor Nevanlinnas in that connection was considerable. Hans Andersin and Tage Carlsson headed the actual work. Unlike other Nordic initiatives from that period, ESKO did not use the BESK design; rather, they based it on the German machine G1a from Göttingen. That machine was not ready, though, and it took much more time and money to get ESKO ready than originally planned. When ESKO was finally ready, the general development had gone a much further. The primary function of ESKO ended up being educating pioneers within the computing field.

Denmark was the last of the Nordic countries to get started. The Danes followed the work with BESK closely but did not have enough resources of their own to get started before end 1955, when "Regnecentralen" (Dansk Institut for Matematikmaskiner) was established under the management of "Akademiet for de tekniske Videnskaber" and started building DASK.

The building and use of computers in the four Nordic countries brought constructors and scientists together and a need for exchange of experience emerged. Again, "Matematikmaskinnämnden" took the initiative by an invitation to a "*Nord*isk *S*ymposium over *A*nvänding av *M*atematikmaskiner" (NordSAM) in Karlskrona together with "Kungl. Orlogsmannasälskabet". Soon a need for Nordic cooperation emerged and again the Norwegians took the initiative by inviting representatives from all the four Nordic computer societies. Ironically enough the information societies were not invited and the continuation of NordSAM became one of the three "important legs" that built upon the Nordic cooperation; the two others were the publications of magazines and the Nordic conferences (NordDATA).

2. NORDDATA

NordDATA soon became a great success and continued to exist until 1995. Through the years, NordDATA contributed considerably to the economic wellbeing of the Nordic computer societies by producing a good profit to every society every four years. The number of participants kept raising and in 1985 NordDATA had 2,450 participants. A long array of politicians and international experts contributed. One of those in the 1970s and 80s was Phil Dorn, who was a permanent writer in DATA.

NordDATA usually took place in June and therefore the conference gave many participants a good opportunity to see new places in the Nordic countries - even outside their capitals. The conference venues included places as Tammerfors, Åbo, Göteborg, Stavanger, Bergen, and Trondheim. The many participants who often brought their spouses and the guests often marked the city.

NordDATA did not take place in 1974 because the Swedish societies had accepted to arrange the IFIP Congress in Stockholm - with great success and nice weather. During the conference DATA, which had started in 1971, did a publication every day bringing news from the conference, interviews with the many international experts, and tips on tourism around Stockholm.

One specific peace of news was especially interesting. DATA was the first news media in Europe to inform us about Nixon resigning as president of the USA. We were working with dataCONGRESSnews at 4 o'clock in the morning; during that time, we were listening to the radio. When hearing about Nixon resigning, a few pictures were eliminated go give place to this great peace of news. DATA had an editorial staff of twelve people especially put together for the occasion and Nordic IT-suppliers who paid for publishing it.

Many companies used NordDATA in the continued professional education of their employees. They were partly presented for "state of the art" technology presentations and NordDATA partly became the place were you got your thoughts confirmed or were given ideas as to how you could solve the problems you were facing. Moreover, off course NordDATA provided good opportunities for networking and thus getting worthwhile contact. Finally yet importantly many good friendships have started during NordDATA conferences.

The aim of the NDU seminars was to bring together data-professionals, politicians, scientists, and administrators to discuss the problems arising in the wake of the new technology emerging and thus contributing to reasonable laws and guidelines within the area. Many highly skilled participants often succeeded in getting relevant problems on the agenda and ensuring that discussions remained focused.

Ten seminars had taken place in eight Nordic cities. The first one was "Persondata og integritet" (personal data and integrity) in 1975 in Oslo and it is probably the seminar that had the greatest impact. When the seminar took place, they had a law on data protection in Sweden and a similar law was being prepared in Denmark and Norway. The discussions taking place at the first NDU seminar in which amongst others all the members of the Danish Parliament committee on legal affairs participated. It did in fact influence these laws considerably. At the same time, contacts occurred between politicians, IT-professionals, and civil servants.

Another seminar on "Edb og skolepolitik" (IT and schools) took place in Reykjavik in 1983 and many of the influential school-people of the time participated. With certainty, they moved more than commas in the reports on school-policy written that winter. Other issues discussed were society's vulnerability, the need for a data policy, data policy and working life, data-science, development of technology, the conditions of people, freedom of speech, freedom of communication, IT and intellectual property rights, and data technology and culture.

3.   PUBLICATIONS OF JOURNALS

The "third leg" was the publication of journals under the management of NDU. Amongst the Danes, Finns, and Norwegians they had already agreed in 1965 that this activity should have high priority. The Swedish society had an agreement with Sven Hed, who published "Automatisk Databehandling", after having closed the society's own journal, DATA. In January 1966, Denmark and Norway started to cooperate on publishing the Norwegian journal "Moderne Databehandling". The Finns considered it easier to read a Swedish journal than a Danish/Norwegian one and they therefore went into an agreement with Sven Hed as well.

During all meetings in NDU discussion ensued on the way to publish a common Nordic journal without considering any commercial interests. Actually, not allowing companies like IBM, Bull, and ICT to have too much influence in the Nordic computer societies was an important detail. They had their own user-groups where they could scamper about.

After the NDU general assembly in 1970, they established a committee consisting of Hans Rällfors (Sweden), Eivind Barca (Norway), Jussi Tuori (Finland), and me from Denmark. The committee looked into the possibilities of publishing a Nordic journal either by cooperating with an existing publishing house or by buying one. The committee soon decided that NDU should have its own journal, but also that professional publishing expertise should participate in the work herewith. The committee chose Lars

Wickmann from Bonniers Affärsforlag; he was to contribute his broad knowledge from one of the biggest Nordic publishing houses and he was a great support as editor.

In December 1970, an extraordinary NDU general assembly meeting decided to establish a limited company with each of the Nordic societies contributing DKK 17,500 in share capital and Bonniers contributed DKK 30,000. However, the societies bought Bonniers share in 1977. In this way, it was possible to establish a secretariat where the manager was to both promote Nordic cooperation and establish a common Nordic journal.

Publishing professionals did not give the new company any chance to survive because of a mix of articles, written in different languages. Nevertheless, it soon turned out that where there is a will, there is a way. I created a possibility for reading the neighbor-languages (Finnish not included). It may take a little more time, but as long as the information is valuable, it was all right.

The market for computer journals turned out to be profitable and our journal had good years, during which the societies did not have to contribute. We only had to pay the variable printing costs in connection with the group subscriptions. We paid the rest by selling ads.

The journal soon established contacts with the professionals and experts who were capable of influencing the development of thing both technically and society wise. In that way, the journal – together with the NDU seminars and NordDATA – definitely contributed to the use of computing in the Nordic countries being at a very high level and according to many, the highest in the world. This was probably also an effect of no one specific group having the ability to decide on developments. A long range of specialists, scientists, and opinion formers regularly had articles in DATA, like also international feature writers like Phil Dorn (USA) and Nancy Foy (UK).

When the market turned out to be profitable and the journal had good years, many other PC and computing journals and magazines became competitors. The competition became tough, but DATA ended up living for 18 years ending with a book "EDB historik - I nordisk perspektiv".

The Nordic cooperation had many good years with a permanent secretariat and regular meetings four times a year. I hope that the future will bring us someone who sees it as his or her mission to re-establish an effective and positive coordination of the Nordic society activities and have the Nordic cooperation flourish again.

4.   *BIT*

The earlier mentioned NordSAM conference in Copenhagen in 1960 also was the beginning of the journal *BIT*, now in publication for 43 years. In the founding meeting, the participants included Bech and Fröberg (Sweden), Peter Naur (Denmark) Jan Garwick (Norway), and Olli Lokki (Finland). They agreed that the journal should contain articles on computer technology, numeric analysis, operational analysis, programming, and data processing.

From the beginning, it was crucial that articles in *BIT* should be on a very high professional level. Many international scientists have published their scientific articles in *BIT* and the journal has contributed to establishing contacts between Nordic and international scientific communities.

BIT soon became a great success technically and with regard to the number of subscribers (688 subscribers after one year). *BIT*'s finances were a problem, though. During the first ten years, we had to get support from a variety of organizations, especially "Regnecentralen" (Denmark), but also "Matematikmaskinnämnden" (Sverige) and "Norges Forskningsråd". Later on the Publishing Board supported *BIT* financially until 1983. In 1983, we saw a strong raise in income because of the fact that all subscribers outside the Nordic area received subscription rates in US dollars. The dollar started rising in 1983 and *BIT* has been financially independent since then.

"Regnecentralen" was unable to host *BIT* in 1971 and we needed a new setup. Therefore, Svenska Samfundet för Informationsbehandling, Norsk Selskab for Elektronisk Informationsbehandling, Dansk Selskab for Datalogi, and Finska Dataföreningen founded *Stiftelsen BIT* with its own articles.

The close contact with NDU was natural, bearing in mind that the field of activity of *BIT* and the NDU members were identical. NDU had established a secretariat in Copenhagen that same year and it therefore was natural to place the administration of *BIT* in Copenhagen as well.

In 1993, a discussion came up on whether it was opportune to have "computer science" and "numerical mathematics" in the same journal. It ended up with a group of Finns starting a new journal called the *Nordic Journal of Computing* with Esko Ukkonen as its editor in chief.

At the same time, BIT changed its name to *BIT Numerical Mathematics* with Åke Björck as its editor in chief. Since the fields of activity of *BIT* and the NDU members were no longer identical, they decided in 2003 – in connection with a change of secretariat – to form a new foundation. According to the articles of the existing *BIT* foundation, this decision requires confirmation at two general assemblies. From 2004, the board of the new *BIT* foundation will consist of representatives from the four Nordic academies: DNVA, STA, ATV, and IVA.

As of 2004, the Institut Mittag-Leffler, a Nordic science institute under the management of The Royal Swedish Academy of Sciences administers *BIT*. The institute works closely with universities in all the Nordic countries. Institut Mittag-Leffler also publishes *Acta Metematica*, one of the world's most well respected journals. I hope that BIT can benefit from that fact and thus expect a raise in the number of subscribers. *BIT*'s good financial situation since the mid 1980s has made it possible to award several Carl-Erik Fröberg-prizes. Last year, the prize went to Stig Faltinsen from Oslo.

COOPERATION AS A DRIVING FORCE IN NORDIC IT

Jussi Tuori

President of the Finnish Computer Society 1970-1972, DP Director of Kansallis-Osake-Pankki 1973-1980; jussi.tuori@pp.inet.fi

Abstract: The paper describes the early user cooperation and states that it was an essential prerequisite of high level of IT in Nordic countries. It describes the cooperation in the domestic, Nordic and international level. It gives many examples but is not comprehensive by any means. It gives a very pessimistic view of the future.

Key words: Cooperation between users, users and research, users and manufacturers, domestic level, Nordic level, international level

1.   INTRODUCTION

Even in the call for contributions to this conference, cooperation is mentioned as one of the essential factors for the success of Nordic IT. I am prepared to go even further, I believe that the Nordic countries never would have reached the high level of IT they now have, had it not been for the good user cooperation in the early days. We can be proud of always having been very advanced, compared to other countries, in using the latest technology and the most effective working methods, as well as in creating applications tailored to help users in their internal and external operations.

My point of view is a user point of view. In this paper, I wish to describe how the cooperation between different users, between users and suppliers, and between users and research institutions was organized. I will also try to analyze some of the results of this cooperation. I will not describe the scientific or technical cooperation. In that area, sharing the results and experiences has always been – and still is – a normal and natural practice. In the business world this is not the case.

Despite the fact that the practice of sharing results and experiences is not very usual in the business world, we were, for several reasons, able to achieve remarkable results with cooperation in the early years of IT we were. In business, IT was not considered as a competitive factor, and in fact, the top management of most companies was not particularly concerned with it. In most cases, it was a tool for rationalization; it could improve the profitability, but it did not have any direct impact on business itself before sometime in the middle of the nineteen seventies. It was not until then that many realized what an effective tool IT is for building up the competitive edges. From that time on, we really started to use IT to improve business processes and moved from internal to external processes.

It is also true to say that it was only in the late seventies that we could give top and middle management some tools they could actually use. We can all remember how we tried to sell what our top management knew as MIS systems. The truth was that those systems were nothing else than enormous accounting systems, which could only help our top management very slightly. We who were in IT actually knew very little about the working processes and needs for information within the management.

In all the Nordic countries, the business environment was local and quite closed. The big waves of internationalisation were still ahead. The countries are small, and one can say that everybody knew everybody. The people working in IT were young and inexperienced, and so it was natural for them to try to find colleagues and cooperation partners.

2.   DOMESTIC COOPERATION

I shall start with the local and *domestic* cooperation within the countries. My natural example is Finland, which is the country I know best. The representatives of other Nordic countries might feel somehow offended by the fact that I am not going to recapitulate the development in their countries as well. However, our countries have been so similar that such a full recapitulation would result in very much repetition, and unfortunately, there is not enough time for that in this context.

A main forum for cooperation was the Finnish Computer Society, founded in 1953 as a society for punched card professionals. They changed the name in 1961 and it became the Computer Society. It was quite exceptional that companies joined the society as company members and even paid the membership fees for their employees right from the beginning. Thus, the cooperation was approved and even favoured by the companies.

All the people active in IT management, systems and operations, etc., attended the meetings of the society. The society was a little like a club. A typical feature was the joint dinners after the meetings. Even a newcomer could meet all the pioneers and the top managers of IT during those meetings. The discussions were open and vivid. This is not possible anymore.

The need for cooperation was very big in the beginning of the sixties. As it was a totally new technology that was being introduced, everything had to be created from scratch. In fact, only the elementary computers and programming languages existed. There were no methods and practices in system work. We can all remember how we were drawing elementary flowcharts with those small green drawing sheets. There were no practices for organizing the IT- or DP-work or the project management. Finally yet importantly, there were neither experienced people nor any kind of training available. The suppliers were offering courses in programming, but that was all. The only way to solve these problems was cooperation.

The State Computer Centre led the development of the system work processes and created a model for system work in close cooperation with other users. The big users solved the training together. The first two courses were organised by the Research Foundation for Applied Mathematics and Data Processing residing in Turku and chaired by prof. K.V. Laurikainen. Already at that time the IT managers of the big users took the actual responsibility for the courses. The driving force was Eero Kostamo. Another foundation to continue the activities was under planning. However, it could not be realised. The Computer Society did not have resources enough for training activities at that time, so the IT managers founded a training company, Tietojenkäsittelyneuvonta Oy in 1963. The system work model developed at the State Computer Centre was the basis of the training courses. The training material was written jointly by the EDP-managers of the biggest users, and all the case studies came from these same big users. These system courses were the basis of the training of system professionals until the late seventies.

Training was one of the most important subjects discussed by the users also later on. The Society and the people active in the Society had a decisive role in founding the ADP Institute in 1970. An association was formed to support the new institute financially, and to give the training a strong user point of view. That institute was the basic training centre for new system professionals and programmers in Finland all through the following twenty years. Now the institute is part of the Finnish standard educational system.

However, we must not forget the invaluable role played by the universities and colleges in the training activities within IT. They rapidly and effectively expanded their activities from the beginning of the seventies.

In 1971, the Computer Society transformed into a federation with independent local and even countrywide problem-oriented associations as its members. The new structure made it possible for the Federation to expand both its membership and its activities significantly, and so it happened. Now the Federation has 27 member associations, which have about 800 company members and about 23,000 personal members.

Training and education – not the basic, but complementary training – was one of the main activities of the Federation throughout the years. For instance, the Federation organized large annual conferences, and still does. The Federation has also had an important role in creating teaching chairs in IT at several universities. Other important activities include publication of books and journals, as well as research and other kinds of development, among which are standards and IT terminology (which is still under development). Last, but not least, the Federation has played a part in working with government, authorities, legislation, media, etc., in order to improve the basis for developing IT. As for international activities, I shall return to them later on.

The founding of the Development Centre for Information Technology (TIEKE) in 1981 is one major project of national importance. The need for more resources in the research about and the development of IT outside the universities was enormous. Many people felt that the scientific work at the universities was so theoretical that the users needed more practical research work. The Finnish State, the Federation, and the ADP Institute founded the Development Centre. It took over all the research and standardisation projects that the Federation had had. Very soon, it played a very active role in data transmission projects. The Centre has been very successful. It has now changed its name and is called the Finnish Information Society Development Centre.

Already in the seventies, telecommunication was a very good example of user cooperation. It was at the same stage of development as the system work had been a decade earlier. There was no standard and procedures required agreement. The only thing that was certain was that there existed an enormous need for telecommunication. The international EDI-work could not give solutions for the specific Finnish problems. Therefore, a joint organisation for operators and users was founded in 1981, in order to create standards and procedures for data transmission between organisations (OVT). The first structure was ready in 1986. (The history after that would need at least a half-day session to be properly rendered.)

The banks had their own project for the data transmission between themselves and that between banks and their customers (POLM). This was a big and successful project. It started as early as 1969, and it developed in different stages up to eighties. It was organised within the Finnish Bankers Association. We can proudly say that the result has been one of the most advanced and efficient payment systems in the world. One explanation for that is that we only had seven banks or banking groups with their own computer centres and systems. The situation is much worse in bigger countries with thousands of banks. The other Nordic countries had similar projects, for instance SIBOL in Sweden.

The users were equally active to create a new operator for data transmission. They were not happy with the possible monopoly of the PTT, so they founded a new company, Datatie ("Dataway"), together with the private local operators. We can say that this was an important starting point in opening the competition within data communication in Finland. These are only a few examples of the user cooperation.

The computer manufacturers already created their user groups in the sixties. Some of those have been extremely successful. Many of them operated both domestically and internationally. The one that was best-known in Finland was Compus, the association for Nokia users, such as Siemens, GE, Honeywell, and Bull. Especially during the 1970s, its activities were versatile and wide, starting from conferences that had a few hundred delegates, included domestic and international excursions, comprised tens of simultaneous working groups, and published the reports of the groups as a book.

Additionally, the big IBM users founded an unofficial association to defend their interests against IBM already in the sixties. In those days, we really needed that kind of user interest watchdog. Even if the task of this association was mainly to defend the interests of users against the computer manufacturer, it also spun off several joint projects to improve both the system work and the effective operations with IBM computers.

The situation with specific user organisations according to computer manufacturer was, naturally, often problematic. The manufacturers used the organisations as marketing tools, and the users tried to defend their interests against the manufacturer. It was very difficult to achieve some balance between the two parties.

There have also been several groups within or outside the Computer Society or associations with joint interests for instance in programming techniques, privacy, auditing, social matters, etc.

I want to end the domestic part by mentioning the club for IT-directors of large users and university professors. The goal was to update the knowledge in the latest developments in a very confidential atmosphere, no protocols, no papers, only high-level presentations and afterwards some social programme, for instance sauna. The membership has been limited to 25, and new members can join only by invitation. The club was founded in 1978 and is still going strong.

Just as a curiosity, some years ago some people within the Computer Society at last realized that IT is already a mature field with people of mature age.   They started a club for retired people called "the Grey Panthers".   Using the idea from the "Senior Club" organised in Denmark by Erik Bruhn, the model was modified for the Finnish context and is now running with success.

3.   NORDIC COOPERATION

I will start the *Nordic* level with the cooperation within different industries.   In the sixties and seventies, Nordic companies were mainly domestic companies.   They might have had some alliances with companies from other Nordic countries.   Actually, there were no truly global or even international company.   In most cases, there was not so much competition between countries.   Often, we preferred cooperation instead of competition. The cooperation was either *bilateral* or *multilateral*.

This was true for instance in my industry, banking.   The commercial banks were grouped in two chains, the Nordic group and the Scandinavian group.   It was, however, very natural to exchange IT experiences within the whole industry.   The commercial banks in the Nordic countries had started their biannual organisational conferences already in 1948.   They were two-day conferences with state-of-the-art presentations and many working groups.   From the seventies onwards, the main emphasis was on IT.   The competition between banks and the bank crisis ended this cooperation.   The last conference was held in 1988 on Bornholm.

Apart from the professional programme, the conferences offered the possibility to create even life-long friendships in very pleasant surroundings. Here I must stress that one of the most important prerequisites for a successful cooperation is a good and working personal relationship.   The conferences also led to interesting joint projects.   The eighties and internationalisation changed everything.   Those conferences died in the mid-eighties, the friendships, however, are still going strong.   Similar type of cooperation was created also in many other industries, but I'm not going to mention them simply because I don't know them that well.

The *multilateral Nordic* cooperation has been very active.   At the end of the fifties and the beginning of the sixties, there were many mainly bilateral contacts between Nordic countries.   In most cases, they were of a technical or scientific nature.   Building the first computers, for instance, aroused many active contacts.   From 1959 on, there had been NordSAM conferences. They were very technical and scientific, discussing the different features of the early computers and the theory behind them.

However, there was an enormous need for an organised cooperation also in economic life and between users there.   On 23 May 1966, the Nordic Data

Union (NDU) was established in Helsinki by the Nordic Computer Societies, and an important part of the joint activities was channelled through it.

The NordSAM conferences transformed into the annual NordDATA conferences. Their nature changed and they became user dominated. The main part of the papers was state-of-the-art-type papers. I personally think that it was very important to keep the active interaction between users and scientists alive. All that resulted in a huge success. At the largest NordDATAs there were between two and three thousand participants. The conferences circulated between the four Nordic countries (Iceland was not included as organiser). NordDATA also became the Nordic computer societies' main source of income. However, this product died step by step in the early nineties.

The Norwegian-Danish joint journal Moderne Databehandling is an example of early bilateral cooperation. The Norwegians had published the journal for ten years in 1966 when the Danes joined in. The journal was published until 1971, when the Nordic journal was established.

The other big project was a joint professional journal DATA which was created in 1971. Erik Bruhn will describe the birth, life, and death of DATA more closely in his paper. However, in spite of the success at the start, the journal did not have resources to compete with the big commercial journals, and the last issue appeared in December 1988. There still is a scientific Nordic journal, BIT. It is a highly valued journal and the resources needed are much smaller than in commercial journals. Through an initiative taken within the BIT cooperation, two other scientific journals in the Nordic countries have also been founded.

The third significant line of activities was the NDU seminars. The main purpose of these seminars was to gather IT people, politicians, top management from business and scientists together to discuss social, economic, educational, etc., problems related to the introduction of this new technology. These seminars were well attended, each having between fifty and a hundred delegates. Altogether ten seminars were organised in the years 1975–1985. Among the topics discussed were "personal data and integrity", "the vulnerability of the society", "he need for an IT policy in the society", "IT and educational policies". We can say that some of the seminars had a quite far-reaching impact in the Nordic countries. Especially the topics on integrity and education set off a lively discussion in some countries, which then led even to new legislation.

One cannot overemphasize the role of Erik Bruhn when talking about the Nordic cooperation. He was Mr. NDU since the late sixties. He made the journal DATA on his own. The NDU seminars were his idea, and they were totally managed by him. He deserves our warmest applause.

As the last example of Nordic cooperation, I want to mention the joint excursions, which the Swedes initiated. The target country was USA, and the excursions could last for as long as three weeks and would have about sixty participants forming different groups, each with their own programme, according to their line of business. The excursions were organised during ten years, starting in mid-sixties. They considerably helped the users to have a state-of-the-art knowledge – about what was happening on the biggest world market – and to see what new ideas we could bring home, if any. In this connection, one must mention another pioneer, and that is Kjell Hultman, who, on top of his other domestic and international activities, organised these excursions.

4.   INTERNATIONAL COOPERATION

Some words will also have to be said about the *international* cooperation. The main channel was the International Federation for Information Processing (IFIP), founded as early as 1959 in Paris. The Nordic contribution to IFIP has been remarkable both in the organisation and within its technical committees and working groups. The Scandi-mafia has always held high positions, from the IFIP Presidency to the TC Chairmanships. They have been fulfilling their duties in an outstanding way. We Nordic people can be proud of being reliable; we do what we have promised to do. Also technically and professionally, we have always been advanced.

IFIP has grown into a large organisation over the years. It has always organised a great number of congresses, conferences, symposia, seminars and working meetings. IFIP is not developing new programming languages anymore, like Algol in the early sixties, but is dealing with a great variety of important topics on everything from a highly technical to a social and cultural nature. IFIP has organised large world congresses, at first every three years, and then every two years. Their development closely resembles the history of the NordDATA conferences. In the sixties, seventies and early eighties they had thousands of delegates, even more than four thousand. The number of delegates has since been decreasing, and is now around a thousand. The IFIP world congress was held in Stockholm in 1974. That was a big success but required a huge effort from the hosts. A special feature during that congress was that a newsletter was given out every day. This was the responsibility of our Nordic journal DATA.

The time span treated by this conference is up to the year 1985. Yet, it must be mentioned that new platforms for cooperation have turned up. An important one is the Council of European Professional Informatics Societies (CEPIS). One very interesting topic there has been the PC driving licence. This is a Finnish innovation, and it has been highly successful in many countries.

I have previously described the Nordic cooperation between banks, so I must mention also the international cooperation to develop the payment systems, SWIFT. It started already in 1979, and the Nordic banks were very active there. There have also been similar projects in many other industries, such as aviation, travel agencies, etc.

The importance in the Nordic countries of the EU as a platform for cooperation within IT has increased considerably since Sweden and Finland joined the EU. One can say that the European platform is already the main platform instead of the Nordic.

The nature of IT is so international, that it is impossible even to try to describe comprehensively the international cooperation of the Nordic countries on various levels in a paper like this one. However, I happen to have personally been actively involved in a very specific cooperation, which might be mentioned here, perhaps as a curiosity. For fifteen years, I was the Finnish chairperson of the working group in Cybernetics of the Scientific-Technical Cooperation Committee between Finland and the Soviet Union. The Committee was a State Committee, so it had a strong political backing. The first agreement in Cybernetics was signed in my sauna in 1970 between the Finnish Computer Society and the Soviet Academy of Sciences. The cooperation was surprisingly active. We had annual symposia. We exchanged delegates for longer periods – sometimes as long as nine months; the total annual number of exchange days was around four hundred. We had joint development projects mainly of scientific nature. However, something collapsed and so did these activities.

5.   CONCLUSION

What, then, will the future be like? Unfortunately, from the cooperation point of view it does not look very good. The economical environment has changed totally. Even the Nordic companies are in many cases multinational. IT is now one of the most important competitive factors for the companies. One can also say that IT is already everywhere in our society, in the companies, in working life, and in our homes. The World Wide Web has changed the world. The old centralised IT organisations in the companies are gone. The IT people cannot form a club anymore. There are so many people and players that the old familiar feeling is missing. The good old days are gone forever.

HISTORY OF THE NORDIC COMPUTER INDUSTRY
Panel Discussion

Christian Gram, Tero Laaksonen, Tomas Ohlin, Harold (Bud) Lawson, Rolf Skår, and Ole Stangegaard

1. *Gram, Panel Chair, Bondehavevej 135, DK-2880 Bagsvaerd, Denmark; chr.gram@ddf.dk*
2. *Laaksonen, Comptel, Finland; tero.laaksonen@comptel.fi*
3. *Ohlin, Linköping University, Sweden; tomas.ohlin@telo.se*
4. *Lawson, Lawson Konsult AB, Stockholm, Sweden; bud@lawson.se*
5. *Skår, Norwegian Spacecenter, Norway; rolf.skaar@spacecentre.no*
6. *Stangegaard, Milestone Systems, SPSS, Denmark; ole@spss.com*

Abstract: In this panel session, people from the four countries – Finland, Sweden, Norway, and Denmark – who participated in the early development of computers and computer industry discuss how the computer industry started and what happened 30 to 40 years ago. We will try to answer questions as follows. How and why did the computer development and industry start in each country? How did it manage the change from research/development into industry? How and why did some of the early companies not succeed? What were main achievements and successes?

Key words: Nordic, computer, industry

1.   INTRODUCTION
by Christian Gram

In the Nordic countries several initiatives were taken to develop computers, and some of them led to production and marketing of computers from the early 1960s. Many of the companies ran into financial difficulties, went through a number of painful transitions of ownership, and finally stopped or absorbed by larger foreign companies. The following sections shed light on what happened to the attempts to create a Nordic computer industry. Each co-author describes important events in his country and reasons for why things developed as they did 30 to 40 years ago.

In Finland, the ESKO-project at Helsinki University developed a small computer around 1960, but the lead was soon taken by NOKIA. Tero Laaksonen, now executive officer in COMPTEL, had managed NOKIA's computer operations and he discusses it from a NOKIA point of view.

In Sweden, early players were FACIT and DataSAAB, and through the 1960s and 1970s they manufactured computers and related equipment with some success. Harold Lawson, who was a consultant to DataSAAB and CPU architect of their last mainframe, mentions some key points in their development process, while Tomas Ohlin discusses whether a better IT policy in Sweden could have led to a viable computer industry.

In Norway, some defense researchers started a computer development already in the late 1950s. Out of this grew the computer company Norsk Data, where Rolf Skår was among the founders and became the general manager.

In Denmark, the story starts with the research institute Regnecentralen, which transformed into a commercial company producing computers and operating as a service bureau. Ole Stangegaard, who worked for the government's service bureau, describes what he sees as lost and gained opportunities. Christian Gram adds a few remarks on two other Danish computer companies.

2.   FINNISH COMPUTER INDUSTRY
   by Tero Laaksonen

My experience begins in the early 1970s and mainly in Nokia's computer division, later Nokia Data, and then ICL. Overall, I think that there was a lot pioneering in the Nordic countries not only in application software, but also in hardware, operating system design, and other research. This applies also in Finland. There were a few initiatives in the country that resulted in industrial scale production, the foremost being Nokia.

The results of the local R&D were quite good and attained quite a success, though mainly locally. What went right was perhaps the swift execution of ideas, true entrepreneurship, and good quality of products. In Finland's case, even commercial results were quite good as long as a preference for "Made in Finland" existed. However, as soon as de facto standards emerged along with the IBM PC, difficulties started to accumulate. Standards invited to mass-production, and the players with risk taking capability could swiftly gain strong market position.

Nokia introduced some wonderful examples of early technologies such as local area network long before Ethernet became commercially accepted, black and white screen on the PC, and others. Specialized solutions for retail POS as well as for retail banking were extremely successful as long as more "standard" products could not erode the prices.

In the aftermath, one could say that Finland created products as good as any other country did; even in the era of de facto standards there existed swift adaptation to the technology. However, the sales and delivery networks were lacking. Even if this was clearly understood, there was not enough willingness and daring to invest in this. In Finland, the thinking was that the country could not expect to excel in such high technologies. A prominent Finnish industrialist put this into words saying, "In Finland it is possible to make products that are at least of the size of a horse". There was common agreement with this sentiment.

The government tried to create a strategy that would consolidate the industry. In this way, the consolidation would make it stronger. However, the initiative never materialized into a working model, and one could say in hindsight that failure in this trial was lucky for the country because in all aspects it would have resulted in a subsidized, bureaucratic, and inefficient structure. On the other hand, Finland did successfully develop education. With current skills in hi-tech engineering, even marketing areas have experienced a true turn around, thanks to the pioneering work and the accumulated knowledge from those times.

What would happen if history had taken alternative paths? From the Finnish industry point of view, there were only very weak opportunities to manufacture large volumes of commodity products and to distribute them. The sources of the key technologies were elsewhere and the accessible market was simply too small. On the software side, there was ground for development and they grasped that. Much depends on credibility and since the country as part of the Nordic community can boast of many achievements, the world-class paper industry for example; even other competencies such as the Finnish IT development have attained a greater degree of respect.

3. EARLY DREAMS ABOUT A SWEDISH MAINFRAME COMPUTER INDUSTRY
by Tomas Ohlin

The Swedish ICT market appearance in the sixties was very different from that of today. IBM was an extremely dominant market part, and Televerket was the only telecom provider. The market was biased.

It seemed impossible to introduce competition on the computer market. The dependence on one provider was almost total back up. It unified and streamlined systems service to a degree that would show to be unhealthy, at least in a crisis. The thought of national technological dependence was a view considered unhealthy for a country like Sweden.

Could a small country develop market alternatives by itself? What type of ICT policy would then be relevant? A natural thought was to ask for state support of some kind.

What type of systems would then be of concern? Would hardware and software services have application? At the time, computer systems for many analysers conceptually were hardware oriented. They considered relevant to count and compare speed and memory sizes. Telecommunication connectiveness was also relevant, but not crucial. We should remember that the 1960s was the era before time-sharing and multiprogramming. The systems structures were star shaped, software systems were block oriented, with fixed-type operating systems, well-defined compilers, and application packages that were only beginning to show structural similarities. With regard to developing computer services, these were relevant for ICT policy making only to an astonishingly limited extent.

So, what was Sweden's capacity as a computer developer and provider? Moreover, which was its market strength? It was relevant to develop further the position of SAAB. Its computer division, DataSAAB, had been successful with model D21, and D23 was in the mind of some planners. FACIT was developing certain types of office systems. On the software side, many Nordic computer users accepted Algol as an able competitor to FORTRAN and COBOL; DataSAAB had active software development in this domain. Algol Genius was a Swedish invention, with the impressive Norwegian Simula development nearby (1967). What could Sweden do to support all this?

Swedish public ICT policy just came into being, but there was already a strong tradition of state support to other industrial branches. It was not difficult for leading industrial politicians to extrapolate into the computer field. They formed a broad public committee, *Dataindustriutredningen*, in 1971. Harry Brynielsson was the chair and this author took part in the work.

The committee mapped the computer system development and market situations, and asked itself about possible public measures. Naturally, they expected some type of DataSAAB support, but how would they formulate this? Moreover, what would this look like as seen from a political perspective? Certain general public reforms were suggested, with educational measures, general research expansion, usage related measures, standardization and structural support. They invented a new form called the "national projects". This would include large projects of social importance, with national equipment and software suppliers. The added additional research support aimed directly toward the Swedish computer manufacturers by certain committee members.

Government showed thoughtfulness when it received these proposals for public support proposals in 1974. Would such measures be effective? IBM was eager to ensure that they would not. After public consideration, only few of the proposals materialized. In retrospect, those proposals for public ICT support now seem fair and relevant. However, it turned out to be a difficult task to develop a national alternative to the computer market situation of that time. The international forces turned out to be much stronger than expected.

Yet, the almost total IBM market dominance of that time later met with successful challenges. IBM abandoned the de facto monopoly strategy with its dependence. Did this relate to certain measures outside of the market? Did public policy play a role? To some extent, it is true. We must remember, though, that IBM made a mistake by not realizing the phenomenal force in the expansion of the personal computer. Nevertheless, this was fifteen years later. The Swedish public ICT measures of the1970s were not directly successful. However, they did establish a foundation. Can we do all this again? Perhaps we can.

4.   COMPUTER ARCHITECTURE DEVELOPMENT IN DATASAAB
by Harold (Bud) Lawson

Note: A more comprehensive presentation on this point appears in a separate paper in the proceedings; namely, Panel contribution: The Datasaab FCPU (Flexible central processing unit).

The goal is to place into perspective of general computer industry developments some computer architecture developments around the late 1960s and early 1970s, in particular, the DataSAAB FCPU. I have written several articles that are relevant in this regard. See the references.

The announcement of the IBM 360 was a critical turning point in the computer industry. Here we saw a mismatch between processor architecture and system software, see the *Mythical Man Month*, and the *March into the Black Hole of Complexity*. This resulted in unstable platforms of hardware and software. The source of these problems is function distribution in computer system architectures where a model from 1976 showed the dramatic affects of complexity. The DataSAAB Flexible Central Processing Unit (FCPU), building upon ideas from the Standard Computer MLP-900, was a 64 bit asynchronously controlled microprogammable processor. It included the ability to implement multiple instruction repertoires and raised the semantic level and can be compared to the Burroughs B5000, 5500, 6500 and some of the Soviet Machines.

Many things could have happened. For instance, cooperation with Regnecentralen – RC4000 was a possibility. Others include cooperation with Burroughs, cooperation with Motorola, and the Styrelsen för Tekniska Utveckling (Project P). What did happen was something different. First, the arrival of microprocessors changed hardware economics and in the end, as well now observed, has proved to be a catastrophe for software economics. What could happen in the future? We can expect further catastrophes, more stable and secure platforms, and would probably reinvent what others have already done. There is a big market out there for the right products that include platforms and applications.

References
"*Function Distribution in Computer Systems Architectures*", Proc. 3rd Annual Symposium on Computer Architecture, 1976.
"*Salvation from System Complexity*", IEEE Computer, Vol. 31, No. 2, Feb 1998, pp 118-120.
"*Infrastructure Risk Reduction*", Communications of the ACM, Vol. 40, No. 6, June 1998, pp120.
"*From Busyware to Stableware*", IEEE Computer, Vol. 31, No. 10, Oct 1998, pp117-119.
"*Rebirth of the Computer Industry*", Communications of the ACM, Vol. 4, No. 6, June, 2002, pp 25-29.

5. HISTORY OF NORDIC COMPUTER INDUSTRY AS SEEN FROM NORWAY
by Rolf Skår

NDRE (FFI, Forsvarets Forskningsinstitutt) scientists visiting MIT in the period 1957-1969 developed the knowledge to design state-of-the-art computer systems in Norway. The pioneer was Yngvar Lundh visiting MIT during the TX-0 period. MIT developed the TX-0 by a team led by Ken Olsen, founder of Digital Equipment. Many regard the TX-0 as the "mother" of all modern computer architectures leading the way to today's microprocessors.

5.1 Choices

Computer design architecture included several choices. The first of these included the choice of word length (24, 16, or 32 bit), electronics (germanium or silicon, TTL), and memory technology (ferrite core and the switching to solid state RAM). Choices in architecture also involve the inclusion of virtual memory (paging) in hardware or not, the use of hardwired or microprogrammed logic, floating point arithmetic and its speed, and whether to use RISC or CISC instruction sets.

Software choices also played a part - principally the choice of operating system. Options include real time processing, time-sharing, transaction processing, multi-mode processing, combination processing, and network access. For languages, we needed to choose FORTRAN and/or COBOL, ALGOL, Pascal, SIMULA, and proprietary system language development. We even had choices of applications process control such as scientific general purpose for universities and research institutes, commercial transactions, and other processing applications.

5.2   Rivalries

Of course, rivalries existed. The rivalry between Norsk Data and Digital Equipment (PDP-8, PDP-11, and the VAX) as seen from a Norwegian perspective is interesting. The complete split between the IBM total dominance in commercial computing and the modern minicomputer as seen from the mini- or the supermini-computer side is interesting. It included the almost total lack of communication and transfer of people between these two dominant camps. IBM was still selling and promoting punched cards when Norsk Data was working from online display terminals. Later, IBM was promoting word processing running from central mainframes. The financial challenges faced Norsk Data. It became a public company through listings on London Stock Exchange and NASDAQ in New York. Finally, we have witnessed the long historic trends from the TX-0 to WINTEL (Windows and Intel microprocessors) machines and with it the downfall and disappearance of both mainframe and minicomputer architecture.

6.   EARLY DEVELOPMENTS IN DENMARK
by Ole Stangegaard

6.1   Personal background

Trained as line officer in the Danish Army, Ole Stangegaard received a leave of absence in August 1960 to join the first ten employees at 'I/S Datacentralen af 1959' (DC). Initially responsible for computer operations and later for computer programming, he became vice president in April 1964 with direct reference to the Board of Directors of DC. On leave from this position, he transferred to the Ministry of Finance in 1966 serving as head of the department responsible for the Danish government's computer planning and acquisitions, maintaining responsibility for computer acquisitions at DC.

Stangegaard left the Danish governmental area of computing in October 1967 and founded the computing subsidiary ØK Data of the East Asiatic Company (EAC), then a major Danish shipping, trading and industrial conglomerate with activities on all five continents. ØK Data did not only provide computing resources to the EAC companies in Denmark and abroad, but also actively pursued business with Danish and international customers outside the EAC group. In 1979, ØK Data acquired the service bureau activities of Regnecentralen (RC). In 1985, Stangegaard joined Price Waterhouse (PW) as partner in their at that time infant consultancy practice in Denmark. When he eventually retired in 1994, that practice had grown to more than two hundred consultants. Today he serves as chair of a small number of Danish IT and telecom businesses.

6.2   Historical background

Two organizations, Regnecentralen (RC) and DC, dominated the Danish computing scene in the early 1960s. RC came into existence in October 1956 under the auspices of the Danish Academy for Technical Science (ATV). It had built the first Danish computer, the DASK, in 1957. RC's business ideas were two-fold: To develop, produce, and market computers (GIER, RC 4000), and to operate a computer service bureau initially based on RC produced equipment but eventually using mainframe computers from CDC. The dichotomy between these two business ideas proved to be fatal for RC forcing a division of the two activities into separate companies in 1979.

For better and worse, the academic origin dominated RC creating an innovative environment with respect to both hardware, software, and application development, but failing to establish commercial skills e.g. in marketing and strategic partnering and RC suffered from a chronic lack of working capital. The Danish government and the Danish municipalities in December 1959 had founded DC and funded it handsomely through the Ministry of Finance with the specific objective of improving efficiency of the public administration through computerization. DC's virtual monopoly in the public sector and IBM's role as preferred vendor to DC created a rapid growth and certain technically innovative applications (OCR, telex based remote access to databases) but also a bureaucratic and self-sufficient approach to the Danish computing scene. Subsequent to privatization in 1990, they sold DC to CSC Inc in 1995. Today, it remains one of the largest computer service organizations in Denmark.

6.3   Opportunities lost

It seems evident that the scenario with two important and early players as RC and DC in spite of – or because of – different backgrounds, both financed by public funds, if properly managed could have become a dominating IT enterprise in Denmark or even on a Nordic scale. Clearly, this did not happen. RC and DC have now both disappeared and/or been acquired by international IT enterprises.

So, what was the reason for this opportunity missed? In my view, it was as often as many times before and after, the lack of true management talent and political foresight. It would have taken a major management effort to bridge the gap between the mainly academic origin and atmosphere at RC and the public sector origin and attitude at DC. The charismatic manager of RC, Niels Ivar Bech, viewed with disdain the IBM trained and overcautious managing director of DC, Willy Olsen. With deep mutual suspicion, they actively discouraged attempts to establish contacts or cooperation by the staff of the two enterprises, which gradually developed into direct competition. In this way, one great opportunity for harvesting the benefits of the early start of computing in Denmark was lost. Had the management talents and personalities been different, the outcome might have developed in the creation of a productive 'centre of gravity' for the early IT development in Denmark.

6.4   Opportunities gained

The rationale in 1959 for establishing a central government data processing facility, DC, was the political decision to change the Danish income tax system from paying in arrears to a 'pay as you earn' system (kildeskat). This required a central registration of all income earners. They consequently decided to centralize the up-till-then municipal population registers established in 1924 into a nationwide central population register (CPR) and simultaneously to computerize it. In the process, all Danes received a ten-digit personal identification number (CPR-nummer). This created much political apprehension about the potential for a 'Big Brother watches you' society. However, common sense prevailed and since then the wide usage of precise personal identification has changed the way – both the public and the private sector – of running the Danish society.

Following the successful and universally accepted implementation of the CPR, DC centralized and computerized other decentralized registers. Administrative registers like the Central Motor Vehicle Register (CMR), the Register of Housing (BBR) are good examples of important computer applications during the early 1960s in Denmark. In each case, the introduction had to overcome much political and organizational resistance; but in each case, they reaped considerable advantages – primary as well as secondary ones.

6.5   Summary

In summary, it is fair to say that during those years, the pioneers built the infrastructure of the 'information society' as we know it today. Those of us who were then active in this process may not have been aware of the full impact of our efforts. However, in retrospect, we were instrumental in changing the way our society functions. It has been a privilege to take an active part in such a revolutionary undertaking.

7.   THREE DANISH COMPUTER COMPANIES
by Christian Gram

7.1   Personal Background

From 1958 to 1973, Christian Gram was employed by the Danish company Regnecentralen, first part-time and later full-time. Because of his mathematical background, he mainly worked with software development, consulting, and teaching. However, he also participated a little in hardware development. Since 1973, he has taught computer science at the Technical University of Denmark, from which he retired in 2000.

7.2   Regnecentralen

At Regnecentralen (RC), established 1955 by the Danish Academy of Technical Sciences, a group of clever people worked enthusiastically to develop, produce, and sell computers and computer services. From 1957 up through the 1980s, they developed several computers and peripheral units and sold them with some success in Denmark and in Europe. In 1988 – after several financial crises – the British ICL bought RC resulting in a loss of its independent status.

The technological standard of both hardware and software was high, with several unique contributions in different areas such as paper tape readers, memory   addressing,   storage   allocation,   compiler   structure, multiprogramming operating system, process control, and standard systems for bookkeeping. Nevertheless, RC failed to manage the change from a pioneer company, with emphasis on technical development, into an industrial oriented company driven by the hard reality of marketing factors.

7.3 A/S Chr. Rovsing

In 1963, Christian Rovsing (CR) started his company, and CR quickly grew into a successful computer industry until its financial collapse in 1984. CR specialized in process control for airplane and space technology and developed a 16-bit minicomputer used in several advanced communication systems.

The failure in 1984 seems related to the fact that the company expanded very rapidly and continued to invest in new development projects paid by expected sales – sales that never came to fruition.

7.4 Dansk Data Elektronik

In the early 1970s at the Technical University of Denmark, a group of electronic engineers worked with the new concept of microprocessors. In 1975, they decided to start a new company, Dansk Data Elektronik (DDE) where they developed several smaller and larger computers, the most successful of which were Unix-servers with multiple processors. DDE also developed design automation systems and advanced real-time application systems for industry such as for newspaper production. Through the 1980s, DDE expanded considerably and established subsidiaries in several European countries. Later DDE stopped computer production and development because of hard competition internationally. DDE tried to survive as a software company, but after financial difficulties around 2000 the company was sold and totally reorganized in 2001.

7.5 Failure or Success

At least three times, technically very capable people have started computer development and production and run it successfully for some twenty years. However, the rapid technical international development and the rapid growth of the international computer industry never left the Danish companies the time to consolidate. Therefore, they failed to establish a firm platform and a steady market from which they could finance further development.

The Danish computer industry has had at least two major impacts in Denmark. First, a large number of young people developed deep insight into computer technology and computer science. Later, many of them taught computing at universities and other schools where they helped educate the next generation. Secondly, the Danish society and Danish business life has benefited from early stimuli to introduce and use computers, often in advanced applications.

8.   CONTRIBUTIONS FROM THE AUDIENCE
by Christian Gram

Below is a short list of statements from the audience about the importance of the early Nordic computer industry.

Military significance: "The computer development had success in many military and quasi-military applications, in Sweden through DataSAAB, in Norway through NorskDATA, and in Denmark through A/S Rovsing."

Programming languages: "Scandinavian software developers have contributed very significantly.   There were very early works on compilers for Algol (RC in Denmark and Facit in Sweden).   Norsk Regnecentral developed Simula, the forerunner of all object-oriented programming."

Scientific cooperation: "The Nordic computer congresses started already in 1959, the internationally recognized scientific journal BIT was founded in 1960, and in 1971 the Nordic IT societies started the journal DATA. All in all we had fine opportunities for exchanging ideas."

Process control: "In all the four countries we were pretty early using computers for process control and in embedded systems."

Last words: "All the good ideas were around – and they *could* have led to a much better IT-world!"

THE DATASAAB FLEXIBLE CENTRAL PROCESSING UNIT

Harold (Bud) Lawson

Lawson Konsult AB, Lidingö, Sweden; bud@lawson.se

Abstract: This panel presentation described some computer architecture developments around the late 1960s and early 1970s. In particular, it placed the Datasaab Flexible Central Processing Unit (FCPU) in perspective to computer industry developments in general. The presentation consisted of several articles as noted in the reference section. It identified papers specifically published about the FCPU as well as other papers related to fundamental aspects of the computer industry. In this paper, I present some further background to the presentation and discussion at the panel session.

Key words: Computer architecture, microprogramming, hardware-software tradeoffs, computer history

1.   A CRITICAL TURNING POINT IN THE COMPUTER INDUSTRY

This article reflects my panel presentation given at the HiNC1 conference. Perhaps the most critical turning point in the computer industry occurred in 1963 when IBM introduced in System/360 series. As the suite of system software developed and led to Operating System/360, it became clear that it required significant amounts of machine code to implement basic computing tasks. This lead to enormous trade-off problems in decision making at the individual programmer level, for the projects related to major software components (compilers, utilities, and so on) as well as for those responsible for the entire product and its release to customers. Thus, a mismatch between the hardware architecture and the software systems caused fundamental problems.

As Operating System/360 unfolded, it turned out to be the most complex suite of software ever written. In this era Dr. Fred Brooks, co-architect of the hardware inherited the task of managing OS/360. It is in this era that he wrote his classic book "The Mythical Man Month". The descent deeper and deeper into decaying software architecture marked the beginning of what I have called, "The March into the Black Hole of Complexity". One can compare this decay with the notion of Entropy in thermodynamics. All initial energy dissipated and the system collapsed. Further, all attempts to improve it made it even more complex and subject to further decay.

For the first time, the world was more or less forced (by the clever marketing of IBM 360 products) into accepting unstable platforms of hardware and software upon which they were to build their critical "value added" software applications. Reflecting the decayed state of the software, a new phenomenon evolved; namely, as bug reports appeared and bugs corrected in OS/360, the new releases introduced new bugs. It stared a new mental attitude on the part of user communities that gradually accepted poor product quality. A move toward accepting software instability from which the world has never recovered. (The source of many current computer security and reliability related problems).

2.   THE DATASAAB FLEXIBLE CENTRAL PROCESSING UNIT

During the late 1960s and early 1970s, a few companies where involved in developing alternative solutions to the IBM computer system architecture. Some of these machines could implement multiple instruction repertoires via flexible microprogrammable architectures. Harold Lawson participated in the design of the Standard Computer MLP-900 in the late 1960s and was the architect of the Datasaab Flexible Central Processing Unit (FCPU) in the early 1970s. The purpose of the FCPU was to emulate the previous D22 instruction repertoire thus providing a D23 identity. There were several innovative features of the 64-bit machine and in particular, an asynchronous approach to the execution of microinstructions. This led to significant gains in simplifying the development of microprogram logic. An important aspect since they believed that they would develop a significant quantity of microprgrams. Plans were made to implement higher-level language and system software oriented instruction repertoires, thus simplifying the production of future software. This would have provided a new profile for Datasaab as a supplier of computer systems. The approaches used machines like the Burroughs B5000, 5500, 6500 provided inspiration as to what high-level architectures could accomplish.

3.   WHAT HAPPENED?

The introduction of the microprocessor technology in the mid-1970s and its rapid growth changed hardware economics. This, in retrospect has led to a false view of the economics of the entire suite of hardware and software. The microprocessors of today still reflect the primitive instruction repertoires of the 1970s. While the microprocessors of the 1970s were quite okay for simpler applications, today they are used as the platforms for systems of enormous unprecedented complexity. They were not designed for this purpose. An absurd situation that is just accepted!!! The world pays the price repeatedly for the costs of poor software quality partially resulting from the fact that the software runs on a low-level machine where complex trade-offs must be made. We can contrast this to a high-level machine architecture where there is typically only one or only a small number of best ways of accomplishing a particular computing task. That makes decision making much simpler.

4.   WHAT COULD HAVE HAPPENED?

Had the microprocessor not made an entry, it is interesting to speculate what could have happened in respect to the FCPU. The FCPU stirred up significant interest in the Nordic countries as well as some places in the USA and England. There were discussions between Datasaab and Regnecentralen concerning cooperation in using their high quality operating system RC-4000 as a basis for exploiting the flexibility in the FCPU – that is, tailored instruction sets to support the OS. At a later stage, some meetings with Burroughs occurred to discuss cooperation. There was also discussion with Motorola about cooperating on specially designed integrated circuits for the future. None of these business opportunities came to fruition.

5.   WHAT HAPPENED TO THE FCPU?

The Styrelsen för Tekniska Utveckling created Project P about 1973 and managed to get several researchers interested in the FCPU. Amongst other activities, Jaak Urmi did work on a LISP machine at Uppsala and Sven Tavelin at Chalmers performed work on operating systems.

Commercially, I believe there were nine processors built. Several were delivered to customers and ran as D23s, some into the late 1970s. The FCPU resulted in significant interest in the US and at several universities in the USA and Europe where the FCPU concepts were taught as a part of computer architecture courses. As noted in the reference list, several scientific paper contributions were made. In particular, the paper on the FCPU by Lawson and Magnhagen was selected for the Best Paper Award at the Second Annual International Symposium on Computer Architecture. Some work was done on providing higher-level instructions; in particular, vector arithmetic instructions were implemented via microprograms that resulted in significant performance improvements. However, the FCPU was not further commercially developed according to original plans to support the implementation of higher-level languages and operating system functions. Very unfortunate!!

In the late 1970s, the LYSATOR computer club at Linköping University installed one of the few remaining FCPUs. Some experimental work, including a Forth language interpreter became operational on the machine. LYSATOR members had fun and learned a lot in experimenting with the novel features of the machine. That FCPU hardware eventually wound up in a barn in Östergötland county and is, as far as I know, the only remaining machine. Hopefully, it will become part of the Linköping Computer Museum.

6.   PATENT CASES

The FCPU has been referenced in two patent infringement cases. One involving infringement upon byte instruction logic of the Intel 386/486 microprocessors. While much more primitive then the general concepts of the FCPU, the byte instructions of the Intel processors operated asynchronously, like the FCPU. Thus prior art existed and was published, thus Intel should not have received a patent. In another case, a smaller computer manufacturer in the US used many FCPU concepts in developing a computer in the late 1970s and later claimed that a very large manufacturer (who also remains unnamed) had copied these architectural concepts.

7.   CONCLUSION

A permanent documentation of the concepts and ideas behind this innovative asynchronously controlled 64-bit microprogrammable processor is provided in the papers produced. A modern version would be a good instrument for improving function distribution between hardware and software and lead the way toward more stable and secure platforms—just waiting for someone to reinvent the wheel!!! I would imagine that this would happen sometime, perhaps not in my lifetime.

REFERENCES

FCPU Related References

Harold Lawson and Bengt Malm , A Flexible Asynchronous Microprocessor, The Scandinavian Computer Journal BIT, Volume 13, Number 2, June 1973.

Harold Lawson and Lars Blomberg. The Datasaab FCPU Microprogramming Language, Proceedings of the SIGPLAN/SIGMICRO Interface Meeting, May 1973. Also published as Saab Scania Report GM-72:296, November 1972.

Lars Blomberg and Harold Lawson, SILL Specification (A System Implementation Language Proposal), Internal Saab Scania Document, May 1974.

Harold Lawson and Bengt Magnhagen, Advantages of Structured Hardware, Proceedings of the Second Annual Symposium on Computer Architecture, Houston, Texas, January 1975. [Selected as the best paper at the Symposium.]

Harold Lawson and Bengt Malm, The Datasaab Flexible Central Processing Unit, A chapter appearing in the Infotek State of the Art Series Report 17 on Computer Design, 1974.

Harold Lawson, An Asynchronous Approach to Microprogramming, A chapter appearing in Microprogramming and Firmware Engineering Methods (editor: Prof. Stanley Habib), Van Nostrand-Reinhold, 1988.

Other References

The following references relate to papers where the fundamental problems of the computer industry are discussed.

Harold Lawson, Function Distribution in Computer Systems Architectures, Proc. 3rd Annual Symposium on Computer Architecture, 1976.

Harold Lawson, Salvation from System Complexity, IEEE Computer, Vol. 31, No. 2, Feb 1998, pp 118-120.

Harold Lawson, Infrastructure Risk Reduction, Communications of the ACM, Vol. 40, No. 6, June 1998, pp120.

Harold Lawson, From Busyware to Stableware, IEEE Computer, Vol. 31, No. 10, Oct 1998, pp117-119.

Harold Lawson, Rebirth of the Computer Industry, Communications of the ACM, Vol. 45, No. 6, June, 2002, pp 25-29.

INTRODUCTION OF COMPUTERS IN NORWEGIAN SCHOOL MATHEMATICS

Herman Ruge

Formerly of The Central Institute for Industrial Research, and Forsøksgymnaset Oslo, Daas gate 16, 0259 Oslo; mruge@online.no

Abstract: "Forsøksgymnaset in Oslo" was an experiment in School Democracy that started classes in automatic data processing in the fall of 1968 as a part of school mathematics in the 11th year.   We started simple programming in FORTRAN on punched cards, off line. Later we had a teletype terminal with paper tape, changed to the BASIC language, and ran programs online by telephone to a distant computer.   We also designed the logic simulator "Benjamin", with four "And", "Or", and "Not" elements, battery and lamps, which could be connected in logical networks to be studied.   In 1970, we arranged two two-day seminars for teachers during the Christmas and the summer holidays and presented the whole course.   We did this eight times and helped to qualify many teachers.   The first Examen Artium in Data was organised in June 1970.

Key words: Mathematics, logic, Boole, forsøksgymnaset, Norway

1.   INTRODUCTION

In the fall of 1967 Forsøksgymnaset i Oslo started by young students who wanted to create a democratic and experimenting secondary school. The school lacked a teacher in mathematics, and I applied because I liked their plans.   In addition, I had worked with technical cybernetics for ten years, and wanted to try automatic data processing (ADP) as a school subject.   In April 1968, we applied for permission to use this in the mathematics curriculum at the humanistic and science classes, arguing: "In ten years, when our students have entered the work force, they will need this." The Ministry of Education declined the application, but we wanted to go on, and so the Ministry made a committee.

What should be the contents of this new school subject? In 1968, the students knew almost nothing about computers. So we started with simple historic calculators—the Abacus (counting frame), Pascal's addition machine (as in the kilometer counter in a car), Leibniz' multiplicator (as in the cash register in the shops), and Hollerith's punch card machine with electric switch logics, designed for the US Census in 1890. We discussed automata and their programs, like music boxes and gramophones. The traditional chocolate vendor machines also had to ask questions and receive answers: "Is there a coin in the slit? Is it of the correct type? Is there any chocolate in the machine?"

These programs were illustrated with flow-charts. We also discussed artificial languages, as in traffic control, with red, green, and yellow lights. This language has an alphabet with a number of symbols with accepted meaning (semantics) and rules for sequences (syntax). How could we improve this? Another discussion was the use of binary numbers, and other bases.

2.   PROGRAMMING IN FORTRAN

We planned the data subject as a part of school mathematics. We felt that "Modern mathematics" was a mistake, which made mathematics less relevant. Programming in a high-level language like FORTRAN could refresh the traditional mathematics, enabling the students to see it in a new perspective. For example, a variable is a quantity with a name such as x, y, A, $A2$ and an address in the computers memory. The number in the memory cell is the current value of the variable. As another example, in the hierarchy of arithmetic such as $1+2\times3 = 7$ or $(1+2)\times3 = 9$, classical school mathematics suggest to dissolve parentheses; however, the parenthesis demands "do me first."

FORTRAN 1968 was somewhat cumbersome, like the distinction between integers and fractions. Input/output-operations were also intricate. The problems had to be simple. Indicated variables such as $A(x)$ were considered an upper limit. Our method to illustrate and check a simple FORTRAN program was to draw a square on a paper for each of the variables as pictures of the memory cells, and draw a bigger square for the printout. Students should pretend to be the computer and follow the program strictly. They should write numbers into the memory cells and produce the output according to the program. A new number would wipe out the old.

"Playing the computer" helped the students to program and it was a good method for faultfinding. Correcting pupils' programs can be a heavy burden for the teacher so we had to teach them to help themselves. Some typical exercises are as follows:

Write a program that

- Prints out a function table for $y = 2x$ with x varying from 0 to 5
- Reads in ten numbers and prints out the highest
- Prints out the numbers in a sequence, starting with the lowest
- Reads in the numbers A, B, and C and prints out the solution to the equation $Ax^2 + Bx + C = 0$

Few traditional math problems were suited for our course. However, we had to find and make new ones that could justify the use of a big computer while being understandable and interesting.

We found such a type in the stepwise "simulation of processes". The simplest was the "dog curve" that stated: A dog plays in a field while its owner walks along the x-axis. Suddenly he calls the dog, which starts to run towards him. The dog is a little foolish; it looks at him each second and runs in his direction for the next second. Compute the curves that the dog and the man will follow! This is a classical problem in differential equations. In a digital computer, we could approximate it by finite differences: Define the direction of the dog towards the man, move the dog one second forward, move the man one second forward, and so on. Other examples were the Volterra's interaction between rabbits and foxes on a desert island, and the development of a contagious epidemic, or a news item - the logistic curve. The elementary course in FORTRAN, Algol, or BASIC gave the students a new understanding of traditional algebra. The University gave us access to their large computer CDC 3300. A couple of students went there, punched the programs on cards, and received – often the next day – the printouts on large sheets. We named the first textbook *ADB for NFG* 1968.

3.   BENJAMIN

We also wanted to teach the students something about how electronic computers worked. Statements such as "It is not necessary to know how the TV works to watch a TV program!" often criticized this thought. However, process knowledge was an important part of school curricula. Therefore, we designed an elementary electronic computer to illustrate some principles. In the language classes, we used a mathematics book with some classical logics, about statements and syllogisms: "According to Aristotle, a syllogism is a sequence of thoughts where certain things are stated and other things follow with necessity from the first ones" (implications). Then followed more advanced logic, such as two statements joined together, some set theory, and the use of different notation systems emphasizing binary numbers. It was an engaging book, but difficult to teach. However, each Tuesday I taught much of the same theory to university physics students. The textbook we used there was Brusdal's *Electronic Computers*. We could use this simple mathematics for very different purposes.

In the 1850s, the Irish mathematician George Boole developed a method for computing logical conclusions – a "calculation of statements" – on rational thinking. The statements could have only two values, True or False, and the operations were Or, And, and Not. This "Boolean algebra" remained for a long time pure theory. However, in 1938 the American student Claude Shannon discovered that one could use it for electric switch networks, as in telephone exchanges and computers. Two switches coupled in a series constituted an And, and in parallel an Or. Boole's algebra thus became a basic theory for digital computers. Circuit networks of And, Or, and Not made it possible to calculate with numbers and sort data written in binary systems.

In 1969, logical circuits were mass-produced as cheap microelectronics. We used many of them at SI. So we soldered together each of the three circuit types: And, Or, and Not on a A4 sized sheet, four of each type. We could couple these twelve circuits in a network, with separate conductors, contact pegs, switches, and signal lamps. This resulted in a simple electronic computer for school use. We called it a "logical simulator" and named it "Benjamin". We developed a number of training exercises and started to use Benjamin in the teaching of mathematics and computer science. Some friends had established an electronic workshop and we gave them the production rights. They gave Benjamin an attractive design, with gold plugs on a white sheet in a frame of oak tree. They produced several hundred Benjamin simulators for secondary and vocational schools.

Benjamin realized basic mathematics of different origins, applications, and names: Boolean algebra, Statement calculus or Mathematical logics, Set theory, Binary mathematics. The technical terms used varied accordingly: The functions And and Or were also called "Boolean multiplication and addition"; in logic, they are "conjunction and disjunction" and in set theory they are "cut and union". The symbols varied accordingly.

In the summer of 1970, we wrote the textbook *Exercises in electronic logics*, with networks for statements like "If you wish, and I have the time, and it is not raining, then we will go for a walk." These exercises included alarm circuits, Boolean algebra, set theory and binary computing, flip-flop memory, all elements in computers. We designed the book for teaching with laboratory work, with exercises both in the mathematics lessons and humanistic classes and in computer science in the science classes. They also used it in junior high schools and vocational schools. Some students discovered for the first time how coupling of conductors could make lamps light up. For others, Benjamin served as an introduction to advanced electronics. Anne was a student who later became an electrician at Spigerverket in Oslo. She told me about a machine which should become automated, with conductors leading to a mysterious box. "But suddenly I understood that this was only a large Benjamin, and then everything became clear."

In the fall of 1969, we bought a Teletype teleprinter (which we named "Katja") and a modem. It became a terminal for a Bull computer based in Stockholm. We changed the language from FORTRAN to BASIC. BASIC was a time-sharing computing language developed by the teachers Kemeny and Kurtz in 1964 and was better suited for school use. Now the students could write their programs on paper tape, ring up the computer, and read in the program at high speed. This was a big pedagogical improvement. Students became less dependent on the teacher. Programming and computing increased. However, the price per second was high. We made a new textbook called *Programming Course in Basic: Language elements and program structures*, Oslo 1971. The length of the course was 70 school-hours. The first official school examination in this subject took place in June 1970.

4.   COMPUTER SEMINAR FOR TEACHERS

Around Christmas of 1969, we invited mathematic teachers from all over Norway to a computer seminar 2-3 January 1970 with the same curriculum as for the students, in a compressed version. Jan Wibe from Trondheim and Kjell Bjarne Henden from Sogndal were the first two to register. They were active teachers in their respective regions and contributed much to the further development. Seminaret was a success. It was repeated in June and then every six months, in all eight seminars. Over a hundred teachers participated. Many of them had computer experience, but needed the discussions for the school-oriented subjects. We made the seminars as a "dugnad", a voluntary effort by teachers, students, and participants. They were stimulating for us all and actually started this subject in many schools in Norway.

In March 1970, we presented our plans and experiences to the OECD-conference on Computer Education in Paris, and later to the Inter-Nordic seminar in Helsinki. FGO was the only Nordic school with this kind of education. The French had ambitious plans, and showed a great interest in our ideas.

In Norway, strong local interest prevailed in the gymnasiums, but also a lack of funding. In 1984, fourteen years later, the School Ministry made an all-out effort to introduce computer education in all schools. At that time, over 30,000 students had already acquired a basic data competence at school and had become part of a work force that needed just that knowledge of computers.

REFERENCES

Ruge, Herman, "Automatisk databehandling i skolen" *Den høgre skolen*, No 3, 1969
Ruge, Herman, *Øvinger i elektronisk logikk*, Forsøksgymnaset, Oslo 1970
Ruge, Herman, *Programmeringskurs i Basic*, Forsøksgymnaset, Oslo 1971

Author's Note
See also: Steinar Thorvaldsen and Jan Wibe, "The First IT-Course in Norwegian Upper Secondary Education", *Proceedings from the HINC1 conference.*

FROM PROGRAMMING TO SYSTEM DESIGN
The First Twenty-five Years of Vocational Information Technique Education in Finland

Lauri Fontell

ATK-instituutti, lauri.fontell@atk-instituutti.fi

Abstract: The article outlines the evolution of vocational education from one-week programming courses to the two and a half year degree program. It focuses on how the contents of education have changed with the expansion of the use of information technique and with the development of computers. One of the more important questions addressed in this article is whether the employers in the field have considered the quantity and quality of instruction to be sufficient with respect to the demand of labor force in the country.

Key words: Vocational education, programming, system design.

1.   THE BEGINNING AND DEVELOPMENT OF TRAINING OF ADP PROFESSIONALS

The training of ADP professionals in Finland began in the early 1960s when hardware importers started to organize basic courses in ADP and programming languages.   In Finland, the most important companies involved in these activities were IBM and *Suomen Kaapelitehdas*, now known internationally as Nokia.   The courses often consisted of only one week of instruction in the basics of ADP, followed by one week of instruction in programming languages.   In government and business institutions that had to process large amounts of data, such as banks, insurance companies, and wholesale businesses, a need soon emerged for more extensive and longer instruction in ADP and in the designing of data systems for comprehensive processing of data.   There was significant mobility in the labor force at the time, and thus these companies and public institutions continuously found themselves faced with a need to train new personnel.

To address this need for ADP instruction, they developed an information system design course. They offered the first course in November 1962 and it was four weeks long. A group of private individuals then founded a company called *Tietojenkäsittelyneuvonta Oy*, 'ADP Consulting Ltd.', which took over the responsibility for these courses and began to develop their contents. People who in their work were involved in information systems design processes participated in these courses almost as a rule.

The first Finnish systems design model emerged from the course materials of the above mentioned courses and from the various research groups of an association called *Tietokoneyhdistys* — The Finnish Data Processing Association (FDPA). They used this model at many businesses and public institutions when they designed their systems; they also used it at different schools and at the universities in their instruction.

The need for professional training of programmers and ADP designers in the public sphere became ever more acute as the use of computers became more and more widespread. Various business corporations contacted the FDPA, asking it to lobby with the government in order that formal and government sponsored ADP instruction could begin in Finland. In 1967, the FDPA put together a committee, which would then elaborate and articulate suggestions on how they could do it.

The committee decided they would recommend the founding of a special vocational school that would give training in ADP skills. A new committee emerged with the task of developing this concept further. The new committee submitted its memorandum to the FDPA at the end of 1968. The FDPA then invited its member organizations to discuss the contents of this memorandum. The result of these discussions was that the founding of such an institution was necessary and thus another committee assembled to plan the execution of the decision to found such a school and to obtain any permission from the government that would be necessary for this purpose.

Some of the members of this third committee participated in a Scandinavian meeting in Bergen, Norway, in the spring of 1969, and they also visited Sweden in order to acquaint themselves with the one year long training of programmers that was available in that country. Because of the work of this committee, the *ATK-instituutti*, 'The ADP Institute', was founded in Finland in February 1970 for the purpose of training programmers and ADP designers.

At first, the institute offered three-month courses, but as of the autumn of 1971, these courses became extended so that they lasted a complete year. The required basic education for these courses was a high school or vocational school diploma. From 1974 on, the institute also began to offer further training for those persons who already had acquired a basic education in the field. This further training was three semesters of instruction, which was not required to follow immediately one after the other. As of 1978, the basic course that the institute offered would last for 2 1/2 years. Those who had completed this basic course received a datanome's diploma, the name for the degree borrowed from Denmark. From time to time, the faculty of the institute would compare the instruction it offered with the corresponding instruction given in Denmark. They did the comparison in conjunction with Allan Dresling's visits in Finland and later through the Finnish faculty's visits to Denmark.

Parallel to this line of instruction, the training offered by business colleges in ADP also became more extensive. In the autumn of 1969, the Riihimäki Business College started to offer a one-year course in ADP as supplementary education for business college graduates. This was the first course of its kind in Finland.

In their curricula, the ADP Institute and the business colleges in Finland focused on commercial and administrational ADP applications. These institutions did not address the training of maintenance personnel and programmers for technical tasks. At the end of 1970, the Ministry of Education formed a committee to investigate the need for instruction in this neglected area. The committee recommended that they establish a technical college. By chance, at the same time, some school facilities had become available in the town of Raahe in the Oulu Province. The committee found the premises in Raahe more than satisfactory, and thus they established a new technical college in Raahe in 1971. The graduates of the college would become ADP engineers and technicians. In the beginning, the college also offered half a year courses, and later one-year courses in programming.

In addition to these three institutions, three vocational education centers for adults began to offer instruction in the field, training programmers, computer operators, and keyboard operators. In addition, the Vocational School for the Visually Impaired, the present Arla Institute (Vocational Training and Development Center) in Espoo, near Helsinki, began to train visually handicapped persons as programmers.

Only around the mid-1980s was there a significant change in this situation. As the need for ADP professionals grew exponentially, the Ministry of Education had to appoint a committee to find a solution to the problem of how to address this need. The committee recommended that instruction in the field take place on a much wider scale than before. Fifteen business colleges and institutes now began to offer studies leading to the degree of datanome. Similar studies leading to the degree of computer engineers and technicians appeared in virtually all the forty schools of technical education in Finland.

The Ministry of Education initiated a public discussion on the possibilities of raising the quality of vocational education in the early 1990s, and this discussion lead to the plans to develop higher vocational schools into polytechnics. The scope of these plans included ADP instruction, too, with virtually all polytechnics having degree programs in ADP, beginning from 1992.

2.   THE VOLUME OF EDUCATION VS. THE NEED FOR EDUCATION

2.1   The number of computers in Finland

In 1966, they estimated that there were approximately 5,000 ADP professionals in Finland. They also estimated that in the next few years, this number would grow by about 200 new professionals every year, because the number of computers was growing fast. By the time they established the first vocational school offering training in ADP 1970, the need for professionals in this field had become even more urgent, since no training in this field had existed in Finland between 1966 and 1970. The table below shows the trend of the number of computers.

Year	1958	1961	1964	1967	1970	1973	1976
The number of computers	1	12	65	155	206	317	5500

2.2   ADP Professionals in Finland

In 1977, the Finnish National Data Delegation and the FDPA published a study on the need for ADP professionals and the educational programs that could produce such professionals. In 1974, 167-trained programmers graduated from vocational schools, and three years later, the number had increased to 235, while there were also 58 persons who completed the advanced training course. This means that not until 1977 was the Finnish educational system able to reach the level that had been considered necessary a decade earlier. Now there were 86 ADP engineers and technicians graduating from the Raahe Technical School every year. In the 1977 study, it showed the need that the educational system should be able to produce 318 graduates from the vocational schools each year. However, towards the end of the 1970s, the economic recession caused a decrease in the investments in the business sector of the country, and thus the demand for ADP professionals did not grow as had been expected.

As microcomputers became more common in the early 1980's, the demand for ADP professionals increased dramatically. As the length of the basic program that the ADP Institute had offered had extended, the institute had reduced the number of new students it had accepted. Now however, they decided to increase the number of new students to the level originally planned, that is, to 120 students per year.

In the spring of 1984, the Ministry of Education appointed a committee to survey the situation. The committee recommended that the number of new students to be admitted to the program for the datanome degree be increased from the then current 120 to 350 new students, and that 700 new students be admitted to the basic program for ADP technicians. The training of ADP technicians had already spread from Raahe to several other technical schools. The Ministry of Education immediately granted permission to accept 426 new students for the datanome programs in various business schools everywhere in the country. Thus, the ministry's actions clearly exceeded the recommendations of the committee, and this was actually more adequate as far as the needs in the labor market were concerned, since it turned out that the number of people working in the field grew by 20% every year around that time. However, this increasing trend slowed down for a few years when a severe economic recession hit Finland in the early 1990s, its effects being here much worse than elsewhere in the world.

The committee had also recommended that basic training be available to graduates of business and technical schools. The committee estimated that it would be necessary to admit 600 to 700 students per year to this supplementary training program, but in 1985, only 110 students attended to it, which meant that proposal of the committee did not become reality as the number of new students did not really increase. This led to a situation in which non-ADP professionals persons who had to make use of ADP in their work did not have a chance to acquire the necessary knowledge on ADP that would have enabled them, for example, to discuss their problems and needs with the ADP professionals. The following table shows the growth of the number of the ADP professionals.

Year	1963	1965	1971	1974	1976
Total	1950	3050	7109	8581	9926
Designers	150	370	1006	1768	2178
Programmers	200	340	928	1095	1138

3.   FROM PROGRAMMING TO SYSTEMS DESIGN

As mentioned earlier, the hardware importers were giving training to ADP professionals in the first phase. The main emphasis was on the basics of ADP and on programming languages. The programming courses arranged by the importers focused mainly on teaching the programming language used by the hardware that the importers had in their stock. The courses were one week long, that is, they consisted of about 30 to 36 hours of instruction. The designer course in 1962 was four weeks long, consisting of 140 hours of instruction. Out of this, 7% were devoted to basics, 9% to programming, 32% to systems design, and 37% to descriptions of implemented systems.

When the degree programs began, the amount of time used for instruction had increased manifold. At the same time, there was also a change in the required basic education for these programs. In the early days, many of those coming to this field had a university level degree or a diploma from a college level institution. Now the majority of those studying in these programs were high school graduates. The one-year courses focused mainly on programming and tasks related to programming. The total amount of instruction offered was 1,200 hours. Out of this, programming took 40–45%, while information systems design received only 10% of the instruction hours. In addition to this, instruction was offered in the basics of ADP, business management, English, verbal and written communication skills and mathematics.

Judging from the results of a questionnaire directed at employers and at those graduates who had worked in the field for at least two years, the instruction offered at this point met its objectives to the following degree: The employers gave a rating of 3.3 and the graduates a rating of 3.8 — the maximum rating would have been 5. To the question of whether the offered subjects were relevant to the skilled needed in work situations, the rating given by both groups was 4.1. The employers voiced an opinion according to which more emphasis should take place to the methods and tools of information systems design.

As I mentioned above, systems design played only a minor role in the training of programmers. The reason for this was the fact that they considered systems design was something for which there were two important preconditions to satisfy if one were to pursue it successfully: a university degree *and* a good knowledge of the field for which one would be designing the systems. In spite of this general prejudice in the field, the ADP Institute began to offer an advanced degree program for programmers containing 53% of systems design, 7% of programming and general information on the field, and 9% of communication and language studies.

The aim of the degree program was to produce technical ADP designers, not designers who would work on entire information systems.

Towards the late 1970s, everyone in the ADP field realized that the era of pigeonholes was over. Teams were designing ADP systems and the members of the teams participated both in planning and in implementation. It was now necessary to widen the scope of the instruction. The answer to this challenge was the program for the degree of datanome.

The amount of instruction offered in this program was 3,100 hours, out of which work practice as an intern took 22%. In the early stages of this program, the systems design was given 14% of the instruction hours and programming was allotted 24 %. As the program evolved, the allotted amount of instruction changed so that systems design increased its share to 16% and the share of programming decreased to 20%. A final project became part of the program and they estimated that it accounted for 7% of the work needed for the degree. As the time needed to complete the program increased, the number of instruction hours allotted to both programming and systems design increased significantly. The following table shows this progress.

Education	2 week course	Design Course	Programmer 1 year	Adp-designer 1,5 years	Datanome 2,5 years
Year	1960s	1962	1970s	1974 -	1978 -
Duration, hours	80	140	1210	1330	3135
Content*					
Basics	50	7	10	4	7
Programming	50	9	41	3	20
System design		32	5	23	15
Business		37	8		10
Language			8	9	10
Mathematics		8	5	4	4
Practice			17	53	22
Final Project					7
Others		7	6	4	5
	100	100	100	100	100

* The content of education in percent

4. THE DEVELOPMENT OF THE CONTENTS OF INSTRUCTION

On the basic level, programming techniques were dependent on the available hardware and the programming language it used. It was already in the 1960s when they discovered the problems relating to the management of programs. They realized that the program they used had a logical organization and they could divide its functions into modules. The various businesses involved developed program libraries, into which they collected the modules that they needed in more than one system. There was a development toward universally applicable modules using parameters. An upper limit to the size of a module could be given as a maximum number of commands allowed. The intention behind this was to make the programs more transparent and to increase the potential to test them.

As the ADP Institute began its operation in the early 1970s, it was necessary to offer a new subject that would be partly independent of whatever programming language the students were studying. This new subject was called programming techniques. The idea was to investigate the implemented data systems and look for functions that most systems utilize. Standard program algorithms began part of these functions. Among these functions were, for example, punch card input, reporting, processing of tables, processing of sequential files, and verification of the social security number. The basic functions of the modules were performed by the most important sentences of the programming language being used. These functions were data input, data writing, data transfer, comparison of data, and arithmetic functions. The programs were documented either with flowcharts or by semi-programming. There were also attempts to teach decision table technique, but this did not gain much ground. Methods for designing programs began to appear around the world in the 1970s and among these methods, JSP gradually became the most important one. This mode of thinking, developed by Jackson, was widely adopted in the 1980s.

To reduce the amount of time needed for programming, there were efforts in various parts of the world to develop computer-aided software engineering (CASE tools). This meant, among other things, that computer systems should be able to produce programming code based on the documentation of the system analyst. Thus, the focus in ADP training was shifting towards analyzing and designing systems.

The preconditions for the evolution of the systems development training were the creation of suitable teaching materials and the description of well functioning implemented systems. The first systems design course, held in 1962, had in fact consisted of the sharing of personal experiences that people involved in the field had accumulated. This was the basis of the development of system design methods in Finland and the sphere of the FDPA largely carried out this development work.

The starting point for this work was a book by Eero Kostamo called *Atk-systeemien suunnittelun perusteista*, 'On the Foundations of Information Systems Design', published 1965. This book begins from the general systems theory and covers the entire systems design field, ending with software engineering phasing. Indeed, from this book on, phasing became the dominant mode of approach in the field in Finland.

It became important to be able to work methodically. Miikka Jahnukainen collected into his book *Atk-systeemien dokumentointi ja standardointi*, 'The Documentation and Standardization of ADP Systems', published 1966, the procedures and rules of documentation used by business enterprises and government institutions in Finland.

A working group appointed by the FDPA produced in 1968 a book describing the model of systems design adopted in Finland in more detail than Mr. Kostamo had done in his book. This book was called *ATK-systeemityön rakenne ja sisältö*, 'The structure and contents of ADP systems design', and the model it described came to be called the *hålkaka* or *hålbröd* model, if one were to use its Swedish name, from the traditional Finnish kind of rye bread that is round in its shape and has a hole in the middle. This name for the model reflected the recurring cycles one would go through, as the system would evolve.

In this model, the main phases of systems design were research, designing, implementation, and maintenance. The model emphasized the fact that this kind of work consisted essentially of tasks that were iterative in their nature. During the life span of an ADP system, these phases would repeat as the applications become more and more expanded and the methods of data processing evolve further and further. The main phases divided into subphases, and these they described by spelling out the aims, contents, and tasks of the systems and the results they expected to produce. This publication would then be useful for years and years by the students of the field.

The next textbook that shaped the evolution of systems design appeared in 1974. The ADP Institute had appointed a working group in which people from the business and government spheres participated. The basis for the work of this working group came mostly from Sweden, from the publications on the theoretical framework for systems design and the methods that had been developed in this area in that country.

The working group produced a booklet called *Tietosysteemin rakentaminen*, 'Constructing ADP Systems', 1974, and the booklet was nicknamed "hammer and nail", the expression having been derived from its cover illustration. The booklet presented a basic vocabulary that the working group had adopted, beginning from the functions and management of institutions or businesses all the way to the operation of ADP systems. They placed more emphasis than before on the importance of ADP systems when they were integrated into the basic functions of the institutions or businesses.

The structure of an ADP system appeared into four areas; that is, (1) its functions, (2) data, (3) design of manual tasks, and (4) computerized tasks. A total of 38 different system design tasks were identified, and depending on their nature, these were assigned to one of the four areas mentioned above. They found that designing an ADP system is always a project, and that is why they gave the planning and the management of the designing process special emphasis. In the guiding the process of system design, phasing was used as a guiding principle. In the process, those of the 38 tasks that they found to be necessary in the designing of a particular system were divided into different phases. The idea was that in the designing work it would be possible to make use of the various phasing models found in the literature.

All the way until the early 1980s, the instruction in the ADP field in Finland centered on the designing and maintenance of centralized data systems. As microcomputers became more common and they evolved into more and more intelligent data terminals, the ways of constructing data systems began to change. This development also made it possible to experiment with prototyping with the microcomputers. In addition, the maintenance and updating of old ADP systems became important aspects of developing ADP systems. Using these needs as its starting point, the working group strove to improve the model for systems design. The product of this work was a book called *Tietojenkäsittelyn kehittämismalli*, 'The developing model of data processing', published in 1987. It was nicknamed "The Windmill", as it had on its cover a picture of a windmill with six vanes and an axle, illustrating the seven different vantage points used in the book. These were: (1) the development of the functional unit in question as a whole, (2) the development of the functions in the target area, (3) improving the human input in the unit, (4) the development of data banks, (5) the development of data communication channels, (6) the development of the contents of computerized tasks, and (7) the development of ADP solutions.

In addition to the model itself, the methods of design also developed. It was common to use conceptual analysis, that is the "entity-relation" method, and as well as the normalizing in the development of data banks. The wall posting technique, or the SSA Structured Systems Analysis, or YSM Yourdon Structured Method or the Finnish TISMA methods also guided the process of system design and its documentation. Either these methods came from the literature or they were the results of internal planning and management practices of various institutions or businesses.

5.   SUMMARY

Vocational training in the ADP field in Finland evolved in close cooperation with institutions and businesses that were using ADP. Thus, a person trained in ADP skills always had the preparation for the tasks that would await him or her in the future job. However, there was always a shortage of skilled workers in this field. The output of the educational system never met the demand for work force that the employers in the field had. Nevertheless, it has been true that the quality of ADP in Finland in the spheres of commerce, administration, and technology has always ranked among the best in the world.

THE BIRTH OF IT IN UPPER SECONDARY EDUCATION IN NORWAY

Steinar Thorvaldsen and Jan Wibe

1. Thorvaldsen, Section for Informatics, Tromsø University College; steinar@hitos.no
2. Wibe, Norwegian University of Science and Technology; jan.wibe@plu.ntnu.no

Abstract: The first course in computer science started at "Forsøksgymnaset" (The Experimental High School) in Oslo in 1969. In 1970, it spread to three upper secondary schools (Drammen, Sogndal and Trondheim). The subject was close to mathematics, and the focus was on programming and electronic logic. FORTRAN was the programming language and the programs ran on a large computer, the Univac 1108, located at the technical university (NTH). No relevant subject-related software was available at that time, but the class developed some powerful cases in mathematics and physics. In electronic logic, we used an electronic machine called *Benjamin* to do binary operations in the classroom. We can call *Benjamin* the first "processor" in upper secondary education in Norway. In this paper, we will show that many of the long lasting trends in the subject can be observed in the initial period itself

Key words: ICT, High School, logic simulator, Univac, Fortran

1. SOME BACKGROUND

The period 1960-70 was in the prime time of the space age, with the first man in space in 1961 and the first man on moon in 1969. Technology was developing very rapidly, and science and technology was in the headlines of the news and media.

In the same period, the teaching of mathematics started to change with the introduction of modern mathematics that included set theory, logic, and Boolean algebra. Some scientists even considered programming and the use of computers to become a kind of "second literacy". This was to enhance the intellectual power of humanity. A significant role in the future education would be the ability to write computer programs and reason on them. Combined with mathematical and linguistic concepts, this was to provide an important foundation for future generations. The computer would be more than just a technical tool in the learning process. It could possibly bring about a renovated intellectual background, a new operational setting where a child in its development could exploit organically and naturally this new machine. In this optimistic setting, computer science was to have an ability to create in the pupils an organizational, algorithmic, and operational attitude.

In Norway, "Forsøksgymnaset" applied for permission to test "Mathematics with computer science and statistics" in April 1968, and the first school committee to deal with computer science in the Norwegian Upper secondary education was established by "Gymnasrådet" on the 25th of November 1968 with the principal, Alf Gudbrandsen as chair. Other members were the economist Eivind Barca, Aage Vestøl from "Norsk regnesentral", Alf Baltzersen from Drammen Gymnas, Arvid Amundsen from "Institutt for alkoholforskning", Jan Gram from "Forsvarets forskningsinstitutt", Herman Ruge from "Forsøksgymnaset" in Oslo and Ragnar Solvang (Ruge 2003).

The new subject should be part of mathematics and they planned the curriculum according to that perspective. Programming was a continuation of the traditional algebra that one could teach with the same goal and motivation. A practical solution was to exchange the new course in computer science with the old course in projective geometry (projeksjonstegning). The old course had two lesson-hours a week and became part of the curriculum around 1870.

The school committee presented its first report in June 1969. This was just in time for starting up at Forsøksgymnaset with Ruge as teacher. The first class had their exams in June 1970. The final proposal from the school committee was presented in February 1972 and had the title: "Innstilling om databehandling i gymnasundervisningen". In the meantime, several other schools had started with courses in computer science. The first three were Drammen, Strinda (in Trondheim) and Sogndal upper secondary schools (gymnas). The Univac 1108 as shown in Figure 1 was the computer they used in Trondheim.

Figure 1: Univac 1108. Students in upper secondary education in Trondheim had access to such a computer at the technical university in 1970.

Very few teachers knew about computer science and programming. Because of this, Ruge arranged a seminar for teachers on the 2nd and 3rd of January 1970. As far as we know, this was the first course of its kind in Norway and Norwegian television even broadcasted it. The seminar was on computers and cybernetics, with practical exercises in electronic logic. The material developed during the seminar was later used by the schools. Among the participants in the seminar were Kjell Henden from Sogndal, Jan Wibe from Trondheim, Jan Ommundsen from Ris, and Per Arnstedt from Drammen. They were later to play a leading role in the further development of the curriculum. The seminar in January 1971 had also participants from Sweden (Åke Anderson from the Swedish "Skolöverstyrelsen", and Lars Bengtson from the department of physics at Stockholm University). In the summer of 1971, Ruge gave a lecture at the Nordic congress for mathematics and science teachers ("LMFK-kongressen") in Bergen.

2. THE CURRICULUM

The school committee appointed by "Gymasrådet" had a long discussion about the content of the course. Was it necessary for the students to learn programming, or could they use standard software? The conclusion was in favour of programming. The whole process of developing and testing a program would give basic skills, both in computer science and in problem solving. The committee agreed upon this.

However, what programming language should we use? There was a lot of software discussion at the time: Algol, Fortran, Basic, or the Norwegian Simula? In practice, it was not much to discuss, one had to take the one that the computer was running.

The course should also include some of the computers own type of mathematics, some coding theory and electronic switch logic. Main items in the course content:

- About computers – classroom teaching
- Electronic logic – with exercises done on a simulator
- Programming (Fortran, Basic or Algol) – as standard mathematical teaching
- Programs with problems from some of the school subjects – mostly as group work.

The programs should be punched on cards and run on a real computer! At Strinda gymnas, Fortran was used the first year. Later, they used Basic and the programs ran on PDP-11 at Trondheim engineering college. They did this by communication and a modem on both sides. Basic was a language actually designed for schools by teachers.

3.   BENJAMIN: THE LOGIC SIMULATOR

An important element in the plan was to learn something about how a computer was working. In 1969, transistor circuits were mass-produced as cheap microelectronics. Herman Ruge had used them in his job at the Central Institute for Industrial Research (SI). The three basic types of logical ports (AND, OR, NOT) were mounted on a small box, together with contacts, switches and signal lamps. All parts linked together with flexible cables as shown in Figure 2. It was a "Logic Simulator" and they gave it the name "Benjamin", (Ruge 1970, 2003). Herman Ruge produced a book with exercises. A small electronic company "Nortronic" put the simulator in production, with oak on the desktop and gold on the contacts. The selling price was around 500 Norwegian kroner. At Strinda gymnas, the son of the principal (Berntsen) produced a local version of Benjamin. Benjamin made its debut at the first OECD "Seminar on Computer Science in Secondary Education" in Paris, March 1970. The "Centre for Educational Research and Innovation" (CERI) arranged the seminar.

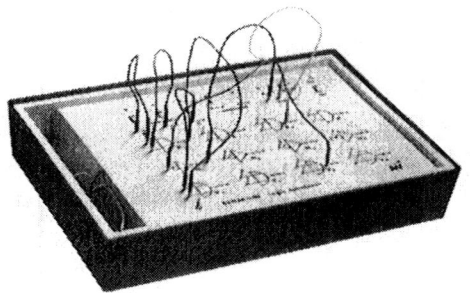

Figure 2. The logic simulator "Benjamin"

By using Benjamin, we were able to implement basic mathematics such as Boolean algebra, mathematical logic, set theory, and binary arithmetic with addition circuits. Statements of the type "If you are interested and I have time, then we may go for a walk" could be an implementation on Benjamin. The circuits also functioned as a 1-bit memory (or-element with feedback). For advanced projects, two or more machines could be linked together. It was a perfect application of modern mathematics. However, in the spring of 1972, a big debate on modern mathematics started, and as a result, most of the mathematical logic was taken out from the textbooks.

Logic simulators were not a new invention (Gardner 1968), and it probably could not be patented. Nevertheless, the Norwegian version had a very simple design and some had plans for selling many thousands of them to England using a plastic version. However, it was too expensive, so England produced its own version instead. "Nortronic" manufactured some 400 of them and even a more advanced model with shift registers, adders, and a clock. Today there are PC-programs that can simulate the logical circuits on the screen.

4. PROGRAMMING

At Strinda gymnas, we used the following procedure when we worked with exercises in programming, analyzed the problem using flowcharts and wrote a program on paper. Then, we handed over the written program to punch operators at the technical university and they punched out the program on special cards, one statement per card. The punching machine was expensive and very noisy. Then the cards were fed into the computer. In the next day or so, we received the results (or an error report from the compiler!). Finally, the finished program ran with different sets of data produced by the students, like lab-data from experiments in physics.

We used the same textbook in Fortran (Sølvberg 1970) as the students at the university. The next year, Strinda changed to programming in Basic. They used a terminal (teletype) and the programs ran at the technical college.

Among the examples implemented in the class at Strinda gymnas, were computations of quantities from experiments in physics, of the type we today would use a spreadsheet. We also computed the value of the number *e* using a convergent process. One of the more ambitious projects we had was plotting of mathematical functions. There was no graphical screen, we did the drawing using printers with space and dots as in Figure 3. The final version of this program consisted of six subroutines and a total of 350 lines Fortran code. It could solve nearly all the exercises on functions in our textbooks, drawing graphs and determining all maxima, minima, zeros, and inflection points!

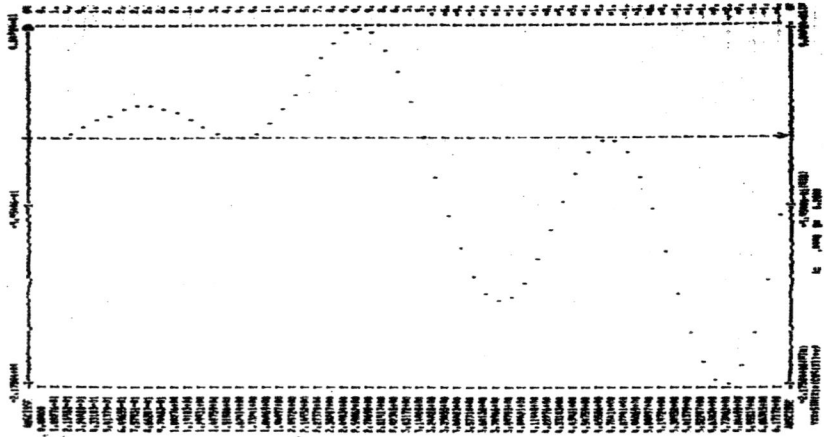

Figure 3. A programming project in function analysis was used to solve real exercises in mathematics, here a plot of the function $f(x) = \sin(x) \cdot \cos^2(x)$

5.   CONCLUSIONS

The new subject in computer science which started at "Forsøksgymnaset" in Oslo in 1969, spread rapidly to schools all over the country. In 1975, the number of students was around 1000. In the autumn of 1977, students studied computer science in 162 of the 417 upper secondary schools in Norway, close to 40%. In 1983, it was close to 250 schools and 6750 students (Ruge 2003).

Computer science was in some items linked with *modern mathematics*, especially logic and set theory. However, it was also part of the science paradigm *"learning by doing"*. We always taught the subject with some kind of local equipment in the local classroom.

In 1969, Herman Ruge designed the first digital "processor" used in the classroom. It was a logic simulator called "Benjamin" and illustrated with hands-on experience how a digital computer functioned. In 1972, a debate on modern mathematics started in the media and as a result, they eliminated most of the mathematical logic from the textbooks; hence, also "Benjamin".

At the initial stage, some *universities sponsored* the schools with runtime on their computers. Students were at this initial stage capable of developing far-reaching programs to meet their own educational needs, products that would have been well worth a study by the school reformers. Early in the 70s, the students could conduct their exercises on the computers from their classrooms via terminals. Standard programming stayed part of the school curriculum for many years.

This is all part of a general trend. To do their work, students and teachers want to have an entrance to computers at the *simplest possible access level*. The paradox in this rule is that computers gets more and more like boxes for the users—like black boxes. In old days, cars were also quite seldom and the function of the motor was part of the curriculum. Today, we all have cars and the physics of the motor is absent from the standard curriculum. As A.N. Whitehead said, "Civilization advances by extending the number of important operations which we can perform without thinking about them".

REFERENCES

1. Gardner, Martin: Logic Machines, Diagrams and Boolean Algebra. Dover 1968.
2. Ommundsen, Jan B. & Wibe, Jan: Eksamensoppgaver i databehandling for den videregående skole. J.W. Cappelens forlag 1983.
3. Ruge, Herman: Automatisk databehandling i gymnaset, Den høgre skolen, nr.3, 1969.
4. Ruge, Herman: Øvinger i elektronisk logikk. Førsøksgymnaset i Oslo, 1970.
5. Ruge, Herman: Utvikling og reform av videregående skolematematikk. Manuscript, 2003.
6. Sølvberg, Arne: Fortran. Tapir forlag 1970.
7. Whitehead, Alfred N: An Introduction to Mathematics. Williams and Norgate 1911.

IT FOR LEARNING: A NEED FOR A NEW APPROACH?

Anita Kollerbaur

Department of Computer and Systems Sciences (DSV), Stockholm University/Royal Institute of Technology; anita@dsv.su.se

Abstract: This paper presents the development and use of IT for learning in Sweden during the period 1966–1986. An overview of the major activities and course of events has two phases of categorization: 1966-1973 as the orientation period and 1973-1986 as the research period. This paper describes the research project PRINCESS in some detail. PRINCESS adopted a cognitive approach to the use of IT for learning, applied an interdisciplinary, and a systems thinking approach to research. A holistic model was developed and studied empirically in several stages. The results presented 1983 are summarized, most of them are still sustainable. The impact of PRINCESS in schools and in academia is briefly discussed. Based on the experiences from more than 20 years of own research in the area, some possible explanations are elaborated on why we still after some 40 years and despite the technical development, not seem to be able to utilize the real prospects of IT for learning. The conclusion is that we probably need a new approach to IT and learning and sketch a vision for a future learning environment.

Key words: IT for learning, interaction, iterative design methods, object orientation

1.   INTRODUCTION

It is often believed that e-learning (or the use of IT for learning) is an application introduced during the 1990s. However, the first steps were already in place in 1959 in the US and in the mid 1960s in Sweden.

There are many interpretations of the meaning of e-learning; a common one seems to be the use of Internet in education. Lately, significant investments in e-learning have occurred; many have failed while some were successful. Nevertheless, the boom for IT for learning has still not appeared.

Reflections in this paper are mainly based on the research in the PRINCESS project[23] (Project for Research on Interactive Computer-based Education Systems) and in the research group CLEA (Computer-based Learning Environments, 1973–1986.[27,29] To facilitate for the interested reader the reference list includes other material.

2.   AN OVERVIEW OF THE DEVELOPMENT IN SWEDEN 1966-1986

2.1   1966-1973 – orientation period

We characterize the period 1966-1973 as an orientation period including a number of investigations and study trips. It began 1966 with a Swedish delegation studying the use of computers in education in the US. Experiences and recommendations were presented in the report "Datamaskinförmedlad undervisning".[2] The first initiative was then taken to start experiments in Sweden using a dedicated systems for Computer-Assisted-Instruction(CAI), the IBM 1500 system; however, the idea was turned down.

Nils Lindecrantz[3], started a course at the Department of Computer and Systems Sciences (DSV) in 1968 and published a textbook in the area. The course planted the seed that later grew to the PRINCESS project. In 1969, this author received funding for the first field trip to study the Plato-system[10] at the University of Illinois, at that time the most advanced complete system for computer-based education.

A throughout investigation of the situation in the US up to 1972 was presented by Stiernborg[5]. Funds for a six-month scholarship to study CAI in the US were through the donation of Dir. Arne Berglund, Mercator International Group, to the Sweden-American Association. As holder of the scholarship, this author did in depth studies of the main systems used in the US 1972–73,[8] resulting in a licentiate thesis in the area 1973.[9] The thesis included the research plan for the PRINCESS-project.

2.2   Research period 1973-1986

Beginning in 1972, the authorities changed approach concerning the use of computer-assisted instruction. The Ministry of Education and Science took the initiative to start new investigations. The school authorities of Linköping did a pilot study reported 1973.[7] This study led to the DIS project[19] (Computer in the School project) within the Swedish National Board of Education (NBE). The goal for the project was to develop an action program for education about computers and their use in Swedish schools. DIS defined three areas for action:

- Education about computers and their use in society
- The use of computers in schools to modernize teaching content in various subjects
- The use of computers as an aid to learning

Lars- Erik Björk, a dedicated mathematics teacher at Sunnerboskolan, played a leading role practically in modernizing math teaching and learning in Sweden and thus strongly influencing the work in DIS.

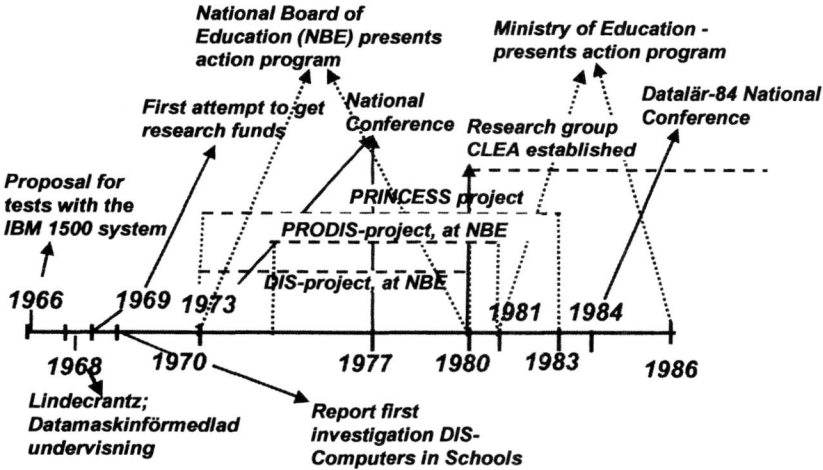

Figure 1. IT-for learning in Sweden 1966-1986.
Major activities and courses of events.

Another project, PRODIS 1979-1981,[22] also within NBE, studied the requirements for software to be used within the first two areas. DIS and PRODIS led to compulsory introductory modules about computers and their use in society from the 9th grade and the use of computers in schools to modernize teaching content in various subjects within upper secondary school. State funds were available for purchasing software and hardware. It was also stressed that the use of computers as an aid to learning required research, which lead to the start of the PRINCESS project, Project for Research on INteractive Computer-based Education SystemS in 1973.

PRINCESS formed the base for establishing CLEA (Center for research on interactive Computer-based LEArning environments) 1980-1987 as one of the first national centers within a program for strengthening the research in data processing financed by the Swedish National Board for Technical Development (STU). Within CLEA and its successors, they engaged in a number of projects extending the research in PRINCESS to other areas and perspectives. For instance, research on communicative aspects of interactive systems, the use of the KOM-system for computer supported communication in Swedish communities and studies of visuals for information, such as the use of colors. Research in CLEA was yearly reviewed by international researchers, headed by Professor Arne Sölvberg, NTU, Norway. Review judgments were "excellent". The research is summarized in CLEA progress reports 1980-1987.[27,29]

One mission in PRINCESS and CLEA was to watch the international frontlines in the area in Europe, the US,[17] and also in Japan[18]. We made extensive efforts into activities for disseminating information. In 1973, we arranged the first conference in the Parliament Building in Stockholm, presenting the state of the art in the area in Sweden and internationally[10]. The minister of education, Ingvar Carlsson, later prime minister of Sweden, opened the conference. For this time Professor Bitzer, Computer-based Education Research Laboratory (CERL) University of Illinois made a spectacular demonstration of the PLATO IV system by interactively working with the computer system at CERL in the US via the telephone network. The data communicated included advanced graphics.

The 1973 conference led to the national conferences in 1977,[15] 1984,[25] and 1987.[30,31] The proceedings of these conferences also give overviews of other Swedish activities than within PRINCESS and CLEA. Further PRINCESS took the responsibility of disseminating the results to a broad public audience. A brochure, in English and in Swedish was produced and distributed to all Swedish schools, politicians, decision-makers and parties interested in the use of computer-aids in education[23].

3.   PRINCESS PROJECT 1973-1983

3.1   Background and general information

The PRINCESS-project started after four years of funding efforts. By then the group already had substantial knowledge in the area from internal projects at DSV[11] as well as from a series of studies of the situation in the US[8] and a licentiate thesis.[9] Since this was the first research project in Sweden in the area and a female researcher led it, the project received significant recognition.

The attitude in Sweden to the use of computers for learning was at that time extremely negative. A common perception was that computers should replace the teachers. Pedagogic theories based on behaviorism resulted in the use of programmed instruction where the students' paths were predefined; where the computer was mainly used for checking the progress of students and neither teachers nor students could influence the content or the methodology.

Projects demonstrating early uses of computers as cognitive tools strongly influenced PRINCESS. The most important ones were the work at Xerox with Allan Kay and Adele Goldberg (for instance Smalltalk, Dynabook, and its use[6]), at BBN with John Seely Brown, Allan Collins, and Wallace Feurzeig (for instance AI in CAI and use of a database system in geography[4]), and the Plato system at the Computer-based Education Research Laboratory (CERL) at University of Illinois headed by Donald Bitzer.[10]

When PRINCESS started, the hardware and software environments were very primitive; interactive systems were rare, terminals were primitive, personal computers were not available yet, communication was extremely expensive and most software lacked any signs of user-orientation.

3.2 Goal, method and organization

PRINCESS research should answer the questions if and how it could improve education by the use of computer aids. A model of a system for computer-based education (see Figure 2) was iteratively developed and evaluated. The research approach was interdisciplinary, emphasizing information processing and pedagogic. Activities included both basic and applied research. Furthermore, the research used a systems thinking with a holistic perspective, the conception that pedagogic requirements should influence the techniques and that people involved should participate in systems development. Development of methods and systems were interleaved with empirical studies.

Figure 2 presents our model of IT for learning. Normally only hard-, soft- and courseware were considered but we also took into account other aspects; methods for documentation, criteria for when we should use interactive systems, the environment in which to integrate IT for learning including both aspects that we had to influence and aspects we knew were impossible to change. Among these were changed roles of teachers and students, the interplay between IT and other media, and analysis of requirements on curricula and school development.

The model was developed in cooperation with users throughout the research. We implemented and studied situations as close as possible to regular use of IT for learning in schools. Four major stages of design, development, empirical tests, and evaluation were performed. The final period included almost all students, half of the teachers and many subject areas in Tibbleskolan outside Stockholm.   Tibbleskolan is an upper secondary school with study programs in human and social sciences; the experimental period included around 1000 students and 80 teachers.

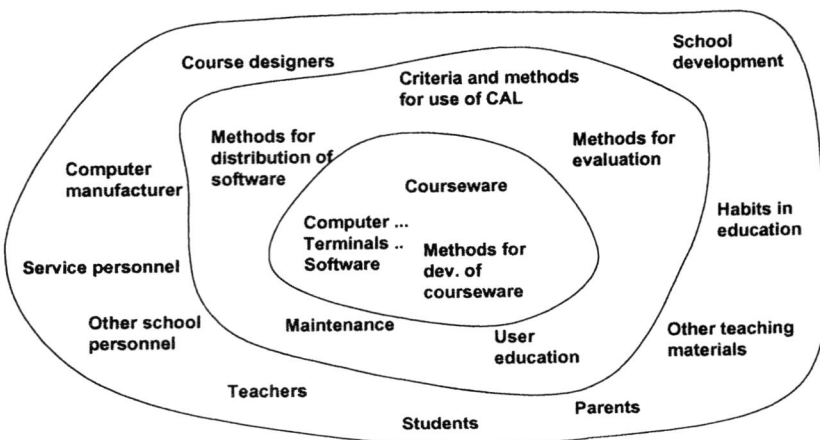

Figure 2. PRINCESS model in the frames and its surroundings

We analyzed existing methods of system development and found that they were not usable within PRINCESS and CLEA environments. Therefore, a special method (PUSUM) evolved, which received presentation in a doctoral thesis.[21] We chose a DEC10–SIMULA environment for the development of courseware, thereby fulfilling the requirements of supporting realization of complex models.   In this object-oriented environment, PRINCESS also created new tools for development of courseware, forming the program library PRINCIP including:

- DESIGN a tool to support development of the interactive parts
- Primitive tools for subject modeling in PRINCIP
- MAGIC a tool for development of computer assisted games for educational purposes.

PRINCESS used various terminal/workstations—teletypes, STANSAAB Graphics terminal, and Plato IV-Plasma-terminals. From this basis, the GLAS (Graphic Low cost Advanced System) concept evolved. GLAS allowed graphic presentation and we could use it as a terminal and as a high performance personal computer. The system was put together 1981 from components imported from the US. CLEA further developed GLAS to handle 16 million colors and to include the possibility to digitalize video signals.

The main financiers of the project were the Swedish National Board for Technical Development (STU) and the Swedish National Board of Education SÖ. The total funding corresponding to 40 years of full-time work was extremely favorable. However, it should be taken into consideration that PRINCESS consisted of several sub-projects. The core research group included Anita Kollerbaur (project leader), Carl Gustaf Jansson, Hans Köhler, Louise Yngström, and Jerzy Hollenberg. The size of the group varied through the years.

The financiers appointed scientific advisors and a reference group to the project. Scientific advisors were Professor Börje Langefors of DSV and Professor Bengt-Olof Ljung from Pedagogics at the Stockholm Institute of Education. The reference group included financiers and representatives from different areas and organizations. The most important were Dir Arne Berglund of Mercator International Group, Professor Germund Dahlqvist of KTH, Nils-Erik Svensson of the Bank of Sweden Tercentenary Foundation, Lennart Levin of the National Swedish Board of Universities and Colleges, Thomas Ohlin of STU, Bengt Dahlbom and Esse Lövgren of NBE, and Stig Fägerborn and Peter Bagge of the Swedish Agency for Public Management.

3.3 IT for learning – the PRINCESS approach

PRINCESS applied the cognitive tool approach, implying that knowledge derives from the experience gained while performing meaningful activities, including analysis, reflection, and discussions. The students should be in the center and in control of the learning process. We regarded IT as one tool among other tools and materials. The tools enabled the students and the teachers to plan the learning situations and environments. Further the tools were designed to support students working in groups as we regard interactions among the learners of equal importance as individual interactions with the applications.

The use of computer aids was appropriate according to the PRINCESS approach when:

- The quality of teaching could be improved, for example to concretize and give better opportunities for project work and interdisciplinary studies
- Existing methods and other aids were insufficient, for instance by simulation of complex or dangerous realities
- It provided students and teachers with additional resources and offering more freedom
- Providing access to the special qualities of computers as means for handling and presenting information.

Furthermore, an interactive program should make operations on nontrivial models available such as work with analytical models, information retrieval and simulation. It should also be easy to use, be flexible, easy to modify and develop. Figure 3 illustrates this approach.

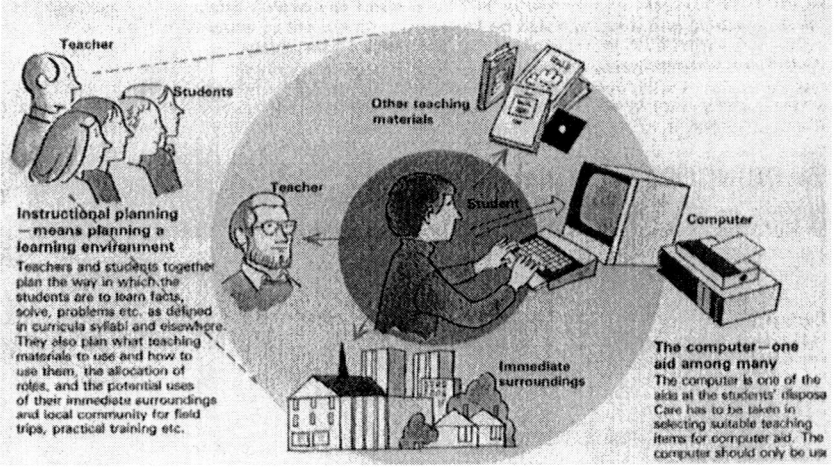

Figure 3: The popularized presentation of the PRINCESS approach to IT for learning[23]

4.   SAMPLE OF APPLICATIONS

One important goal for PRINCESS was to demonstrate the possibilities of IT for learning through applications within various subjects and learning situations.

4.1   Traffic education

One of the problems for primary education is to teach students safe traffic behavior. For that purpose a primitive simulator for riding a bike in a roundabout was developed in cooperation with STANSAAB, a Swedish Computer Company, and The National Road Safety Office.

The "bike" consisted of pedals (for speed) and handles (for maneuvering). Despite more like a moped, students perceived it as a real bike. Their task was to ride the bike trough the roundabout. Cars and other bikes, followed normal traffic rules and occasionally even randomly generated rule breaking rules occurred so students confronted different situations each time. Limited computer capacity did not allow repeated studies of how the use of the simulator changed the students' traffic behavior. Nevertheless, the few studies we made showed positive effects.

Figure 4: A simulator for riding a bike through a roundabout

4.2 Mathematics

Interactive graphics were used for heuristic mathematics teaching with a type of math lab, POLY. The computer aid made it possible for the students to study polynomial expressions and their graphic representations by constructing their own problems. POLY made it possible to study advanced problems in shorter time and was applicable with a number of methodological approaches and levels of study. It also proved to be useful in the teaching of arts and social sciences. In many cases, it transformed the students' attitudes and understanding of mathematics. A normal attitude towards math seemed to be that it should be boring and since students had fun working with the program, they themselves did not consider this learning mathematics.

4.3 Application based on databases

We made two major demonstrations of the use of databases: One in history and one in food sciences. We put extensive work into developing database-handling tools in SIMULA and user-friendly editors for the content of databases used by teachers themselves.

In both cases, we utilized professional, extensive sets of data from a demographic database, with data from the Swedish parishes of two communities 1821-1899. The researchers used the same data. In natural science, the database included data from a printed table published by Livsmedelsverket (National Food Administration) and from other expert bodies. Models of the subject area and functions for retrieving and presenting data were iteratively developed and tested. We used both programs for problem- and project-oriented learning.

In history, we could study individuals, families, and entire "clans". For each individual it was possible to retrieve a lifeline, setting out major events in his or her life. It was also possible to find persons in a particular family, their occupations, and other points of interest. Within a "clan", it was possible to retrieve the ancestors and descendants and get statistics about them. By combining these items, the students could find out a great deal about conditions in the 19th century, doing their own research in history based on real data. This would have been impossible without computer aid.

In food science, a model of nutritional requirement together with the database, made it possible for the students to calculate nutritional requirements the nutritional balance - both allowing and disregarding individual activity - for individual meals, for an entire day, for a as well as the nutrient content of dishes and foodstuffs. The program, called KOST, also allowed searches for foodstuffs containing particular nutrients, development of nutritionally balanced recipes etc. With KOST, the students were able to use more advanced data than normally, they could also study their own problems. Functions for saving and retrieving data from students' projects made comparisons possible both for individual students, but also for collaborative learning. Diet surveys before and after the experiment showed that the students had grown more serious of the food they ate and that they had altered their eating habits. For the first time in school, students could do numerous experiments based on their own data, which was a strong motivating factor.

5.   STILL SUSTAINABLE RESULTS FROM PRINCESS

It is striking that most of the main approaches and results from PRINCESS seem accurate also today. We were thirty years ahead or far too early. Some persons considered us as dreamers, our ideas would never be realizable on a broad scale.

The main results available in 1983 were:

- The use of the cognitive approach to IT for learning was possible, resulting in improved learning. Examples of courseware used the advantages of the technology, demonstrated numerous pedagogical use of each application including situated and collaborative learning.

- Introducing computers as tools for learning was regarded as a process of change applying a holistic perspective; roles and processes were affected, mainly those of teachers and students.
- We perceived the difficulties to liberate our thinking on new lines, methods for stimulating creativity have to be applied, where teams covering different competencies cooperate; teachers, students, systems experts, interface experts and programmers.
- We stressed the communicative aspects of interactive systems; meaningful processes for learning demands support for communication of what we then called the subject model, support for navigation, orientation and for performing actions. Explicit presentation of the assumptions behind a subject model is required for appropriate learning. These are examples of early results in the area of Human-Machine-Interaction, HMI.
- PRINCESS developed and used iterative methods for systems design and development with user participation, teamwork, repeated steps of design, development, and evaluation of prototypes. Combinations of evaluation methods from different disciplines were used depending on the stage of design, for instance participant observation and interviews at early stages. PRINCESS approach for design of interactive systems design is widely applied today.
- The object-programming environment with tools for different levels of a system to fulfill requirements on flexibility and maintenance, and the approach to represent systems to support both communication with users as well as implementation. However, programming competence was still required for developing courseware of the type PRINCESS aimed at. These were early demonstrations of modern software architecture, and tools.
- Finally, we demonstrated the importance of influencing the hardware and software environment from the user and use perspective.

6.   THE IMPACT OF PRINCESS

6.1   In schools

The PRINCESS approach to the use of computers as pedagogical tools was fully agreed upon by the Swedish National Board for Education, and also influenced further activities in the area. Already in 1986, extensive financial support for courseware development was available and in addition, a group at the Ministry of Education and Science for coordination was established. Later, even more extensive support for the area was made available both from the ministry and from the Knowledge Foundation in Sweden.

The functional requirements applying to GLAS provided the base for a technical procurement project for a school computer, initiated by the National Board for Technical Development, resulting in the school computer COMPIS: (English for PAL). COMPIS went to market in 1985. However, the effort failed, partly due to the reason schools not accepting a dedicated system, partly due to the fast growing Mac- and PC-markets.

6.2   Within academia

Being a young group in a young department more oriented towards influencing the educational system rather than making academic careers, we made the mistake of publishing very few articles internationally before 1987. In total we produced three academic theses,[9,21,29] four papers in English but a wealth of material, tools, methods, demos, software and articles in Swedish. The final documentation of the project appeared as a book in Swedish.[23]

However, the influence on research and education within our own department is substantial. Courses in computer-based education and human-computer-interaction emerged in the mid 1970s. In 1993 the area grow into one of DSV's specializations for its master's program. The laboratory for Knowledge and Communication, K2lab, has its roots in PRINCESS and CLEA and is today the largest research laboratory at DSV. K2lab is led by one of the PRINCESS researchers, Carl Gustaf Jansson, now a professor at DSV.

7.   A NEED FOR A NEW APPROACH?

Since 1986, the research and applications of IT for learning have grown, particularly during the late 1990s, when the concept of e-learning became widely used often assuming the use of internet. Today, most of the obstacles perceived in PRINCESS - lack of computer power, limited multimedia facilities, problems with efficient communication, and high costs - are eliminated. New possibilities are available for distribution of education via Internet, technologies for computer-based cooperation, etc. Furthermore attitudes about the usefulness of computers in education are mainly positive nowadays.

Independent of all efforts put into to the area, the great breakthrough has not yet appeared in Sweden, at least not within the state financed educational system. An exception might be the Swedish Net University established in

2002, planned to be a strong brand name for Swedish distance education provided by Swedish Universities.

There are certainly no simple explanations to why IT for learning is still in its infancy. The main forces behind the evolution of IT for learning are complex; interplay of many factors exists such as educational policies, attitudes, the economics involved and of course the technical developments. The large amount of perspectives and actors is partly illustrated in the PRINCESS model of Figure 2.

Could the main problem be that IT requires changed roles and processes that in turn requires time that is not available? Another reason could be costs; in schools it is difficult to find money for regular upgrading of equipment and teachers knowledge. A fact is that it is still too costly to develop high quality courseware. Is the reason that IT-tools are still not adapted to a widespread use? My personal view is that this requires tools available and usable analogous to paper and pencil. Another plausible explanation may be that the main approach has to be changed. Still today, established methods, content, and organization within education have only been transferred to a new medium.

Experiences from development, introduction, and use of IT in other areas have shown that the goal and content of activities within an organization, the working processes, and the relations are examples of aspects that should receive consideration in new perspectives. Very simply, this could also be expressed as IT applied to an existing organization neither saves costs nor increase quality, to make impact re-thinking is required.

The question then becomes, is our educational system properly organized for the society of today and tomorrow? Is there a need for a new approach? In addition, what would be a vision of a future educational system?

In 1994 such a vision was presented. It was based on the early experiences of IT for learning. The vision got its final form during a workshop with participants representing research within different academic areas, different educational areas and levels as well as industry and government. The goal was to create an environment for a lifelong, free and border-less learning. Figure 5 summarizes these ideas. The vision is documented in Swedish.[32] In the following a few comments to the vision is presented. The main idea was that in the future we will have an individually controlled pedagogic, where basic knowledge, mentors, knowledge banks, and usable technology are available for all with the aim of supporting lifelong learning.

Centers of Knowledge are the meeting points for lifelong learning, a mixture of library, common meeting point, and schools. In the center all groups will meet, independent of age, interest, and country. It includes learners of all ages and study forms; compulsory school, adult education, enterprise courses and courses on university level. The Centers of

Knowledge are nodes in a national and international net, thus establishing borderless learning environments making occasional study group possible. Completely new programs for education ought to be established and integrated: interdisciplinary studies are a reality. The view of classes and stages will to a large extent be changed; the classroom has become a virtual one. Groups will assemble according to interests, not on age. Individual study-plans completely organize education and lifelong CVs document the studies.

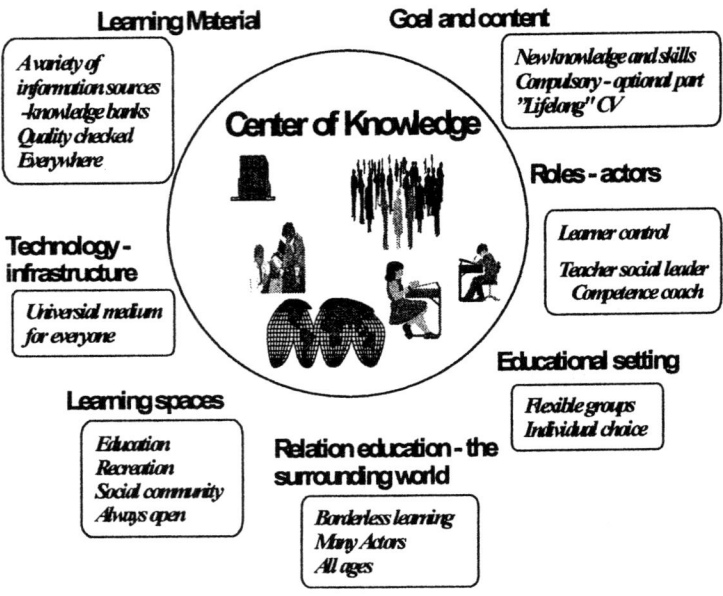

Figure 5: The 1994 vision for IT for learning

Goal and content for the curriculum has been revised, new knowledge and skills are defined to fulfill requirements of the future IT-based society. Roles are changed, the learner is in control; the teacher becomes a social leader and a competence coach. New actors appear, sometimes the learner becomes the coach for other learners, and seniors have become new important actors. Finally, the learning materials are to a large extent available everywhere via a variety of information sources. All materials used for learning have to be quality checked. IT is of course a prerequisite for realizing the vision and a universal medium adaptable for each use and individual is used.

As this vision is almost 10 years by now it is time for a re-vision. Based on a new vision, research and development for future environments for learning, covering all aspects applying holistic approaches would guide us towards new thrilling experiences.

REFERENCES AND BIBLIOGRAPHY

The list is mainly chronologically ordered. For documents in Swedish, the headlines are translated.

[1] Teaching Machines and Programmed Study Material, NBE-document, 1962 (In Swedish).

[2] Computer mediated Education, Ministry of Education, 1966:8, 1966 (In Swedish).

[3] Lindecrantz N.: Computer-mediated Education, Studentlitteratur, 1968.

[4] Carbonell J.: AI in CAI, An Artificial Intelligence Approach to Computer-Assisted Instruction, IEEE Transactions on Man-Machine System, Dec. 1970.

[5] Stiernborg M.: The computer for Use in Education,– an Overview of Computer-Assisted Instruction and Computer Managed Instruction, Rep. from Dept. of Education, Stockholm Univ., 1972 (In Swedish).

[6] Kay A., Goldberg A.: Personal Dynamic Media, Computer, vol 10, no 3, March 1972.

[7] The Computer in the School Community, (DISK), Pilot Study performed by Linköping Board for Education, Commission from NBE, NBE 1973 (In Swedish).

[8] IVA Special report USA, author A. Kollerbaur, IVA 1973:8 (In Swedish).

[9] Kollerbaur A.: Analysis of Systems for Computer-based Education, and Hypothesis for Future Research, Licentiate thesis, DSV, 1973 (In Swedish).

[10] Computers as Tools in Education, Conf. Proceedings 1973-10-02—03, STU information nr 19-1974 (In Swedish).

[11] Kollerbaur A., Köhler H., Yngström L.: Computers in Education, Data Processing Technology, TRITA- EDU-010, March 1975 (in Swedish).

[12] Collins A. et al: Reasoning from incomplete knowledge, Research and Understanding, Studies in Cogn. science, Academic Press 1975

[13] Yngström L.: A method for analysis and construction of interactive computer-based teaching programs, in Lecam, Lewis, (eds) Proceedings of IFIP Computers in Education, North-Holland/American Elsevier, 1975, pp 37-40.

[14] Kollerbaur A.: PRINCESS – a Project with User-Oriented, Interdisciplinary Approach to Computer-Based Education, Paper presented on a Sperry-Univac seminar i Rome 1976.

[15] PRINCESS; Document from a Conference on Computer-based Education 1977, TRITA-IBADB-5003, DSV, 1977 (In Swedish).

[16] Brown J.S.: A paradigmatic example of Artificial Intelligent Instructional system, Proc of the First Int. Conf. on Applied General Systems Res. Resent Dev. and Trends, June 1977.

[17] Kollerbaur A, Jansson C-G J.: Computer-based Education – the State of the Art and Trends, Report from a Studies in the US and Canada 1978, PRINCESS activity report (In Swedish).

[18] Report from Swedish Delegation on Future Education & Technology to Japan, Sweden-Japan Foundation for Research and Development, April 1979.

[19] The Computer in the School (DIS), NBE's Action Program and Final Report, NBE Project 628, NBE 1980 (In Swedish).

[20] Yngström L.: Interactive Computer Based Education, A General Description, in Lewis, Tagg (eds) Computer Assisted Learning, Scope, Progress and Limits, North-Holland, Amsterdam, N.Y., Oxford 1980, pp 173-183.

[21] Köhler H.: Methods for Systems Analysis and Development of Computer based Educational Systems, PhD thesis 1981, Dep. of Information Processing, Stockholm University/KTH, 1981, ISBN 97-7146-121-3 (In Swedish).

[22] Software and Hardware for the Swedish Schools (PRODIS-Project), Final report NBE Project 6205, NBE 1981(In Swedish).

[23] Kollerbaur A., Jansson C-G., Köhler H., Yngström L.: Computer Aids in Education – PRINCESS Final Report, ISBN 91-970520-0-0, 1983 (in Swedish). A popular abstract in English, Computer Aids in education, Presenting the PRINCESS-project, DSV 1983.

[24] Kollerbaur, A.: Computers in Swedish Schools, report from Educational Research Workshop in Frascati, nov 1982, Council of Europe, Strasbourg 1983

[25] Datalär-84, Proceedings from a Conference about IT for learning for Teachers about Research, Development and Methods, ISBN 91-970520-1-9, Stockholm 1984 (In Swedish).

[26] Action Program för Education about Computers for Schools and for Adult Education, Ministry of Education, DsU 1986:10, Stockholm 1986 (In Swedish).

[27] CLEA progress reports 1980/81, 1981/82, 1982/83, 1983/84, 1984,/85, CLEA reports to STU, Dep. of Computer and Systems Sciences, DSV, Stockholm University/KTH.

[28] Jansson C-G.: Taxonomic Representations PhD Thesis, DSV 1985, ISBN 91-7170-991-6

[29] Kollerbaur A.: Summary of research in CLEA 1985/87, CLEA report to STU.

[30] Kollerbaur A.: (ed) Datalär-87 Proceedings, part I from a Conference about IT for learning for Teachers about Research, Development and Methods, ISBN 91-970520-2-7 (In Swedish).

[31] Kollerbaur A.: (ed) Datalär-87 Proceedings part II from a Conference about IT for learning for Teachers about Research, Development and Methods, ISBN 91-970520-3-5 (In Swedish).

[32] Kollerbaur A., Brunell M, et al: Learn with IT, Proposal for Research and Development for Change within Swedish Education, Electrumstiftelsen in Kista Science City, Dec 1994, (In Swedish).

THE EARLY NORDIC SOFTWARE EFFORT

Ingemar Dahlstrand

Formerly at the Department of Computer Science, University of Lund, Sweden;
Paragrafgränden 26, SE-22647 Lund, Sweden

Abstract: Early Nordic cooperation comprised ideas, programs, even computer blueprints and resulted in rapid progress. Regnecentralen contributed importantly in developing Algol 60. Algol for Facit EDB was used at many sites. Further advances were Datasaab's Algol Genius and the Norwegian Simula project. Regrettably, failure of our compiler companies led to software setbacks. We revisit the Algol debates considering later advances like functional programming. For example, provability of programs depends on recursion and absence of side effects. Computer progress forced cooperation between people from different environments. Too little was done consciously to avoid the ensuing cultural clashes, which impeded progress.

Key words: Software, compilers, Algol 60, Nordic historical efforts

1.   EARLY NORDIC PROJECTS AND COOPERATION

1.1   Background

When I started working for the SAAB aircraft company in June 1955, the computer BESK at Matematikmaskinnämnden (MMN) had been in operation for one and a half year and was already running three shifts. The SAAB aircraft company, the University of Lund, and Regnecentralen in Copenhagen had started constructing modified BESK copies, based on blueprints generously supplied by MMN. These went into operation within the next two or three years. The move of the original BESK group from

MMN to Facit Electronics in 1956 started a commercial production of BESK copies called Facit EDB, ten of them altogether. This gradually widened our circle of cooperation.

Software was extremely primitive in 1955 limited to a small library of standard procedures. We heard about a formula translating language FORTRAN, but for us that seemed far beyond reach. In 1956, we received, for the first time, access to an assembler for symbolic addressing. Our group at SAAB translated these tools to the machine code of our BESK copy so we had something to start with. Already then, we discussed software with the people at Regnecentralen, but as long as we worked at assembly language level, slight incompatibilities were enough to block actual program exchange.

1.2   The NordSAM conferences

In 1959 the first Nordic computing symposium, NordSAM, had taken place in the marine base town of Karlskrona. For the next 10 or 12 years, these yearly symposia were the important events of Nordic computer world, the place where ideas were hatched and results reported. (Later they became rather too big and too commercial to fill this role). In Karlskrona we first heard of the ongoing work on Algol, centered in Copenhagen; Regnecentralen administered the Algol Bulletin in which the international discussion about Algol 58 took place. With the publishing of Algol 60, writing an Algol compiler had high priority at Facit Electronics, where I was now working, and they placed me in charge of the project.

1.3   Algol implementation

Our goal was essentially to replace machine coding with Algol programming on all of the ten Facit EDBs. Our company sold some of them and ran some of them on a service bureau basis. It meant that the compiler had to be user friendly; a lot of thought went into identifying source code errors and producing readable decimal memory dumps. We assembled a network of contact persons to handle teaching, counseling, and reporting of compiler errors. The compiler had to produce efficient machine code. To achieve this we sacrificed recursion, and we were prepared to give up other features like expressions called by name ("Jensen's device"), switches and Boolean variables, as long as we could get the compiler to work and handle straight, everyday coding fast and well.

We were two persons full time on the project, Sture Laryd and myself. We divided the work into (1) a preprocessor that caught source code errors and built up an identifier dictionary, (2) a formula translator proper and (3) a postprocessor that linked intermediate code with standard procedures to produce executable code. Laryd took upon himself the formula translator, which was the most difficult part since we had no experience whatever in this area. He completed the work on time, by and by including almost all of the features that had seemed so difficult at the start.

Given our lack of experience, cooperation with other groups was important, indeed crucial, to success. Via Regnecentralen a journal article from the German ALCOR Group came inte our hands and provided a first foundation. Our visits to Copenhagen and discussions with the people there were invaluable. We learned not only how to implement but also how to interpret the sometimes quite difficult Algol 60 Report. In particular, the procedure part gave us headaches. The final Paris conference in January 1960 had accepted contradictory changes to it, so Peter Naur had to straighten out the whole procedure concept and have it accepted by correspondence. Right away people started to note unexpected effects of the new version; for instance, Jensen discovered his famous device at this time [1].

Our first compiler was ready in October 1961, and was gradually improved up to 1964, taking into account new I/O hardware, slight computer modifications to improve procedure handling, and, of course, the experience gained – and errors found! – through operation. And, we gained a lot of experience indeed. Once Facit-Algol was available, use of assembler languages withered in a couple of years, except for maintenance of existing projects and a few large projects where time or space were of overriding importance [2].

1.4   Failure of hardware project

The hardware program of Facit Electronics was put to test in 1960 when competition with U.S. suppliers became a threatening, and finally overwhelming, reality. A number of important deals were lost to the Americans, and our company ceased building general-purpose hardware in 1964. The existing computing centers of Facit Electronics were reorganized into a service bureau Industridata, with the business idea of selling leftover time on the computers of the owner companies. In spite of this inauspicious start, Industridata continued in business for 20 years and made a place for itself both in technical and administrative ADP.

1.5   Algol-Genius at DataSaab

The Algol group at Facit Electronics took part for a couple of years in compiler work for SAAB, which had gone into commercial computer building around 1960, and was implementing an amalgam of Algol and Cobol, called Algol-Genius. This computer effort went on until 1976 and scored a number of well-earned successes, including supplying the computers for the Swedish taxation and census authority. Eventually, however, this company, too, failed in the face of stiff international competition.

1.6   Hardware failure sets back software

I think it is safe to claim that our software effort was a success. Modern tools were made available at an early stage and certainly contributed to our countries becoming advanced computer users from that time on. Unhappily, much of the momentum gained was lost through the failure of our hardware effort. The entry of powerful American computers with software in the FORTRAN and COBOL tradition in many places swamped the Algol-using groups. Indeed, they dutifully implemented Algol on many computers sold in Scandinavia; but unless these compilers allowed the user to call FORTRAN procedures, they could not compete with FORTRAN.

It is perhaps not obvious today why that should be so. However, in those days software in general and compilers in particular were not portable and thus closely tied to the associated computer. Computer suppliers developed compilers to sell hardware, computer and software being offered as a package. A famous U.S. court decision in 1964 started the slow "unbundling" process. Suppliers dutifully put separate price tags on hardware and software, but the software tag sometimes seemed more of a hint about the possible bargaining range. It was quite some time before separate software houses became big business.

1.7   Use of the Norwegian Algol successors

In the university world (where I have been since 1968, in Lund) we were lucky to have good Algol compilers at Control Data and Univac. Especially the NU-Algol compiler for the Univac 1100 series, written in Norway as part of the SIMULA project, was reliable, efficient and contained a string extension. This made it one of the most practical programming tools I have come across in my computing life. Simula gradually gained ground and has been used at our Computer Science Department for object-oriented programming and real-time at least until 1997 (when I went into retirement). Our pupils sometimes criticized us for using such an old language, but we could not really find anything newer that was better.

2. ALGOL DEBATES REVISITED

What were, then, the points we discussed in the Algol Bulletin and at our meetings? There are three points I would like to mention; they are typing, side effects, and recursion.

2.1 Typing

In pure Algol 60, it is optional whether to specify the types of formal parameters or not. But we cannot compile a procedure without specifications without following all possible calls of the procedure from the main program. If the actual parameters of these calls happen to conflict it may be necessary to compile several instances of the procedure; compiling it separately from the main program of course is not possible at all. A closely related problem was the existence of procedure parameters that were themselves procedures. This made the tracing of procedure calls very difficult. Since Algol 60 allowed integer labels, it might happen that an actual parameter like the number 3 might end up as a label at the end of one chain of calls and as an integer somewhere else. All this seemed overwhelmingly difficult at the time.

We patched these problems by making specifications mandatory and forbidding integer labels altogether. However, a real problem remained, namely the insufficient typing of procedures and functions. Today we know that the type of a procedure is in fact a composite type, including the types of all its parameters and the type of its function value if it has one. This insight forced itself on the FORTRAN people handling very large programs, where separate compilation is a necessary evil. A Fortran 90 main program has to contain a complete specification of any separately compiled procedure that it calls. In Pascal, a formal parameter that is a procedure always has a composite type specification, even when there is no separate compilation.

Making specification of parameters mandatory deprived us of the possibility of writing generic procedures. There is a legitimate need for generic procedures: for instance, one should only have to write one quicksort procedure and then be able to use this for any type for which we define the relational operators. Put in another way, there should be a way of defining and working with a supertype "sortable". Another such supertype would be "arithmetic", allowing us to write generic matrix procedures.

For other reasons, *explicit* specifications are mostly unnecessary. In a functional programming language like Miranda, we can compute the types of all entities in the program at compile time from the operations used and the calling sequences that are inherent in the program structure. The compiler finds all typing errors in this process, so the typing is strict, or rather, as strict as necessary. Type specifications may be added to ease understanding, but the only place they may actually be needed are for the input files.

All of this we could not possibly have foreseen in 1960. We did what we had to do just to push through those first implementations. What we perhaps did wrong was that we did not question Algol enough; we did not draw a line between design weaknesses in Algol and our own implementation problems. Algol seemed so brilliant it was almost sacrilege in our environment to criticize it. However much we admire our brain products, we must see their faults and get on with progress – or someone else will.

2.2   Side effects

Let us now turn to the side effects issue and begin by having a look at the famous function Sneaky that Mike Woodger presented to the Algol community in December 1960 [3].

```
real procedure Sneaky (z); real z; value z;
begin Sneaky := z + (z - 2)↑2; W := z + 1 end Sneaky;
...
P := Sneaky(k) * W;
```

It was reasonable to assume that W would enter into this expression with its new value k+1, as a side effect of Sneaky. Suppose we changed the order of the factors? Would W * Sneaky(k) return a different result, based on some previous value of W?

There were three ways of tackling this problem. The computer scientists among us wanted to prescribe the exact order of evaluation of primaries. They wanted every well-formed program to have a defined result. The mathematicians threw up their hands in horror at this. If two expressions were mathematically equivalent, they ought to produce the same result. Therefore, they wanted to forbid a function to change global variables at all. The rest of us we ready to leave the case undefined, thus discouraging sneaky coding. The dispute took on a religious fervor and almost split the Algol community in two.

The computer science side won the day, in the sense that they established evaluation from left to right. However, the mathematicians won the public relations battle, one might say. For tens of years afterwards, new programming languages would prohibit "undesirable side effects" – even in command languages that did not contain functions at all.

It is interesting to see that in Miranda side effects can not take place (since there is no way of changing an entity once bound to a value) and this is one of the features which make it possible to transform and prove Miranda programs [4]. It is also interesting to note how strict one must be to achieve this freedom from side effects; for instance random numbers in Miranda conceptually form an infinite array, the elements of which are unknown at start and computed as needed. So instead of

    `square(random) ≠ random*random`

which is a paradox, we have

    `square(random[i]) = random[i]*random[i]`

whereas

    `square(random[i]) ≠ random[i]*random[i+1]`

Simple and logical!

2.3   Recursion

Recursion, or more precisely whether to implement it, was a third topic discussed intensely. At Facit we decided not to, which probably gave us a faster executing code, which again probably contributed to the rapid spread of Algol among our customers. However, I do admit I did not realize the importance of recursion for a "clean" implementation. (Ours had a persistent bug or two that propagated to SAAB's Algol-Genius compiler.) Nor did I see that applications in linguistics (including compiling) require recursion; nor did I foresee that recursion is another one of the bases for program proving in the sense of Miranda.

2.4   Input/Output

Input/output was not a topic of strife between the Algol groups, since they left it explicitly to the implementer. The lack of string facility made it difficult to do much more than a few ad hoc procedures in this area. Donald Knuth's I/O scheme, which came later, ingeniously circumvented the formal problems of I/O by list procedures. It was a very difficult scheme to implement; I spent a summer trying and failing. When General Electric did implement it for ASEA's new GE-625 it made the printer slower than the one running on their old Facit EDB. Moreover, of course, behind the scenes it required just the character variables and string handling we were so reluctant to add explicitly to the language.

Looking back, I regret the time we spent on polishing, standardizing, and subsetting Algol. Algol had played out its role, once they had implemented it in a number of sites and sown the seeds that were to give such a rich harvest of new languages. Making extensions where we deemed them necessary would have given us more benefit, in the short run and the long run.

2.5   Is there a *sens moral*?

With the benefit of hindsight, I can see that I took the wrong view in most of these discussions. I can only hope I did not seem too fanatic. Fanaticism clouds the vision and creates opposition; what one rams through in this way is seldom good enough and rejection will be its eventual outcome.

A more positive formulation of the same *sens moral* would be "Think, travel, and talk". One of the bad things about today's world is the impediments to travel such as expensive fuel, humiliating security controls, companies saving money the wrong way. Most trips pay for themselves in terms of knowledge gained and new ideas. Now and then, a single trip gives so much benefit that it pays for a decade of travel budgets. Cutting the travel budget in a crisis is a bit like throwing away map and compass when you are lost in the woods: it may lighten your burden but does not help you get out.

2.6   Why did our hardware efforts fail?

Why did our hardware efforts fail? Too little is known about what went on behind the scenes in government and in the companies involved. The easy way out is to say that it was inevitable. Much larger actors (Charles de Gaulle comes to mind here) failed, at much greater cost. Nevertheless, the fact remains that the Swedish government through MMN stumbled to the forefront of an extremely interesting field and let slip this chance, only to pump much more money into SAAB when it was too late. There cannot have been an ideological block or fear of technique in general: hundreds and thousands of millions went into nuclear power and even steel, and Sweden has a long history of making its living by innovation.

3.   CULTURAL DIFFERENCES AS A CAUSE OF FAILURE

Perhaps we who worked in the field spent too little time talking to politicians, managers and the like. A few of us did, but most of us were so engrossed in making things work that we had little energy left for this long-range work. There was certainly no lack of conviction among us that this new gadget, the computer, would revolutionize the world. However, talking across cultural barriers is difficult. It takes a lot of experience to realize that we have to do it anyway, as the following examples try to show.

3.1 Technicians vs. administrators

In the early days, even elementary knowledge of computing was lacking outside our little band of specialists. For instance, when our managing director was going to inaugurate our compiler, he thought it was a piece of hardware and wondered whether it was transistorized. Not unreasonable – nowadays such special hardware is actually built – but at that time a serious lack of knowledge for one who had to make strategic decisions for our company. My point here is that we, who knew, did nothing about it. This was an awful mistake and one of the causes of failure. We might not have gotten through to our manager, but there is no excuse for us not trying. This kind of mistake – young experts looking down on their elders instead of sharing knowledge with them – is repeated daily with equally sad effects.

It is interesting to note that the company did not apply its strict routines for industrial secrecy to software development; we could cooperate freely with other institutions. On the other hand, they kept us out of hardware development; to this day I do not know what plans might have existed beyond building BESK copies and I/O equipment for them.

We had another very concrete problem in that the company wanted to use computers for office work, whereas we, their computer people, had received training in scientific and technical work. Few of us knew what an administrative office was like let alone how it worked. We never bridged this gap; we remained strangers in our company and were eventually pushed out to do what we knew best, as a service bureau. Our mother company never really found its place in this strange new world and foundered tragically some ten years later, after having been in business for some 500 years.

3.2 Professors vs. Computing centers

Yet another example of cultural differences, in this case between people of the same background and education. In 1964, the Swedish government's agency for administrative development, Statskontoret, decided it was time to organize computer resources for the universities. A scheme was set up which included fresh money earmarked for computer time, which the respective universities shared out to departments, which in turn passed it on to teachers and researchers. They could use the money to pay for computer services from any of the computing centers set up at the same time. The scheme also allowed the centers to earn money from external sources and use this money for extra computing equipment. To the rational people at Statskontoret this seemed a generous and flexible scheme of things. So, it seemed to me, coming from the service bureau world to head the Lund center in 1968. It turned out otherwise.

The money allotted to the universities was for a one-shift operation of the centers. The idea was that the departments should find more money from other sources if the earmarked money was not enough – and very soon, it was in fact not enough. This went completely against the grain of university life. University people would not use hard-earned money intended for salaries to pay for computer time. Finding money for the computing center was the task of the head of the center, just as finding money for books was the job of the library director. The centers remained at one shift. A storm of protest ensued that finally forced Statskontoret to accept radically lowered night rates, after which our university customers rapidly filled three shifts. Meanwhile we had managed to find quite a lot of external customers, at some centers almost 50%. Now criticism took the opposite direction; they accused us of neglecting the university customers for the external ones. Eventually the centers decentralized as the advent of PCs made the old organizations obsolete. (After a dozen years as a teacher at the Computer Science Department, I now understand the academicians' side of the debate much better!)

The list of examples of cultural clashes could be long. Think of the lawyers who tried for decades to use copyright to protect program owners against unauthorized *use* of programs. Consider the standards institutes, organized on national lines, trying to cope with computing where the only national issues are character sets. Surely cultural differences of all sorts are so very important to success in a new branch that working place culture ought to be a subject in its own right at technical universities.

4.   CONCLUSIONS

I would to like to conclude by giving my personal answers to two questions maybe all of us should ask ourselves at the end of the day: What is my greatest error of judgment in working life? I have to choose between two – equally embarrassing – alternatives: underestimating the impact of networks and the impact of the PC wave. Not that I did not expect the future to contain networks, but I expected a network to offer a much more standardized set of services and terminals, much like the telephone service used to be. I did not dream of people tinkering with their own computers on the present scale. A terminal, yes, and a printer, yes, and a friendly service man from the national computer service coming home on call to exchange non-working or too slow equipment. I dislike being told that my computer is ready for the scrap heap and that I have to go through all the cost and trouble of switching to a new one, though the old one is sufficient for my needs. In other words, I expected (and wished for) a sort of computer service bureau on a national or global scale.

Does work remain undone? Yes, we still lack a standard, convenient, safe programming language in general use and a teaching and help service to go with it. Too much interest has come to focus on ready-made programs, which may be fine for the general user, but is far too restrictive in a research environment. It is as if we had invented printing and writing, but failed to educate people beyond the ability to read comic strips. The full potential of the computer will not be realized until the direct use of it is in every man's hands, a parallel to the alphabetization of the common man that took place in the 1800s. That is the challenge I would like to pass on to the next generation.

REFERENCES

In this paper:

[1] Peter Naur: *The European side of the last phase of the development of Algol 60;* pp 110-113 in Richard L. Wexelblat (ed.): *History of Programming Languages*, Academic Press, 1981, ISBN 0-12-745040-8

[2] Ingemar Dahlstrand: *A half year's experience of the Facit-Algol 1 compiler*; in BIT (Nordisk tidskrift for informationsbehandling), Regnecentralen, Copenhagen, Vol. 2 (1962), pp 137-142.

[3] M. Woodger: *Comment on a function designator changing the value of a formal variable*; Algol Bulletin 11.4, P. Naur (ed.), Regnecentralen, Copenhagen 1960.

[4] R. Bird & Ph. Wadler, *Introduction to Functional Programming*, Prentice Hall, 1988, ISBN 0-13-484197-2

Other books concerning Nordic computer history:

[5] Poul Sveistrup, Peter Naur, H. B. Hansen, Chr. Gram: *Niels Ivar Bech - en epoke i edb-udviklingen i Danmark* (Niels Ivar Bech - an epoch in the EDP development in Denmark), Copenhagen 1976, ISBN 87-980512-0-2.

[6] Jan Annerstedt et al.: *Datorer och politik - Studier i en ny tekniks politiska effekter på det svenska samhället* (Computers and politics - Studies on the political effects of a new technique on Swedish society); Zenith/Bo Cavefors förlag, 1970.

ALGOL-GENIUS
An Early Success for High-level Languages

Bengt Asker

Formerly employee of Datasaab and Ericsson; Bengt.Asker@comhem.se

Abstract: Algol-Genius, an Algol 60 implementation with features from COBOL, was
the brainchild of Börje Langefors.   In 1964, assembler was the dominant
programming language, but Algol-Genius broke that trend among Datasaab
D21 customers.   Algol-Genius programs were still in production in the late
nineties.

Key words: Algol, Datasaab computers, programming languages

1.   INTRODUCTION

The main topic of this paper is the programming language Algol-Genius.
Since the history of the first Datasaab computers, D21 and D22 had little
representation at this conference, I will place Algol-Genius in the context of
Datasaab's early history.

2.   HOW DATASAAB WAS BORN

Saab was one of the first organizations in Sweden to use computers on a
large scale. Aircraft design required extensive computing. Initially, women
did this on desk calculators. Börje Langefors pioneered the of use punch
card machines for matrix calculations. When Besk became available, Saab
was one of the heavy users and soon built a copy, called Sara. These efforts
meant that Saab early on acquired competence in software development. On
a parallel line, in other parts of Saab, Viggo Wentzel designed a
transistorized digital computer, aiming at an airborne version. The result

was a prototype, one of the first transistorized computers in the world, called D2, which he demonstrated to the Swedish air force in 1960. It was a desktop computer; in fact, it covered the entire desktop. See Figure 1.

Figure 1. The D2 desktop computer

Saab had attempted to diversify from a total dependence on military products. Now it could use this unique combined expertise in hardware and software to launch a commercial computer, the D21. Gunnar Lindström was the typical entrepreneur heading the division. Quite naturally, Viggo Wentzel took care of the hardware and Börje Langefors the software. Saab's CEO Tryggve Holm, one the last patriarchs, said in a speech to prospective customers: "We woke up one day at Saab and found that we made computers"

The first customer was Skandinaviska Elverk, not surprising since Gunnar Lindström came to Saab from the power utility sector. The first order, shown in Figure 2, has become quite famous. It is a three-line letter, dated 14 December 1960, ordering a computer according to the offer so and so.

3.   DATASAAB D21

3.1   Hardware

The first delivery of the D21 occurred in 1962. It was a very competitive computer for its time. Maximum primary storage was 32K words (96KB) with a cycle time of 4.8 μs. The addition of two 24-bit integers took 9.6 μs. Secondary storage was tape, an inventive construction that originally was developed for Sara with the appropriate name Saraband. Based on a suggestion from Börje Langefors, the designer Kurt Widin invented a coding, which he later found out was called a Hamming code, that corrected one bit and detected two-bit errors. Searching for a block, reading, and writing occurred in parallel with processes in the CPU. This was a novelty in that price class and contributed strongly to the excellent performance of D21. Basic input and output was, in conformance with the Nordic tradition, punched tape, with a very fast tape reader from Regnesentralen. Since they designed the D2 for process control, it had an interrupt function that carried over to D21.

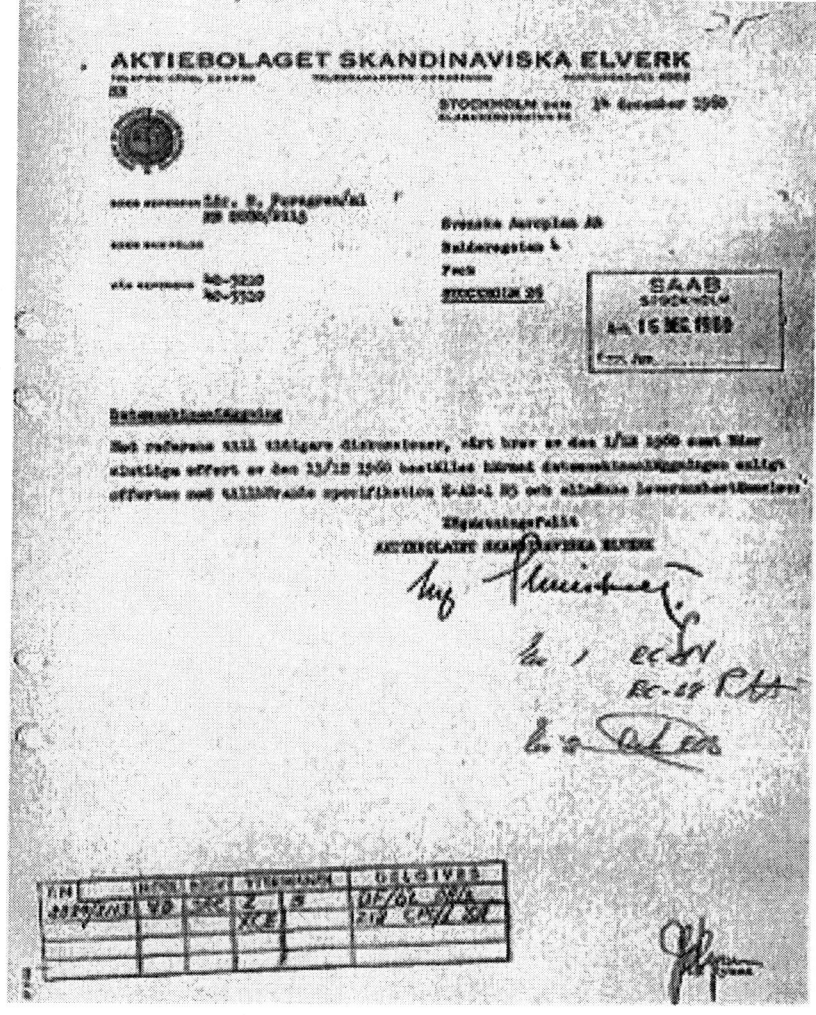

Figure 2. The first D21 contract

3.2   Market

The computer was a reasonable success. In all, they manufactured 32 computers, mostly sold in Scandinavia, a few also in Czechoslovakia and Hungary. Some early customers after Skandinaviska Elverk were Gothenburg University, Slakteriförbundet, Kockums shipyard, Volvo Flygmotor, Allmänna Brand (insurance), Saab and SMHI (weather forecasts). This was an interesting mixture and shows that the D21 was a truly general computer. With the exception of SMHI and Gothenburg University that had extremely demanding computations, they all used Algol-Genius extensively.

The biggest order came from the county governments (Länsstyrelserna). At first, orders for some twenty computers went to IBM and its 360/30. After heavy lobbying, they changed the decision so that IBM received only half of the orders and Datasaab the other half. Since the two computer brands were incompatible in every respect, this meant that two parallel software development efforts had taken place for the Länsstyrelserna. Today, this would be unthinkable; at that time, however, it was not a unique compromise. The companies delivered the computers between 1963 and 1966. However, in 1969 the parliament decided that the counties should replace the IBM computers with D21s, because of their superior performance, mainly in sorting. In the end, they delivered eight D21 and seven D220. The Länsstyrelserna did not use Algol-Genius for two reasons: Application development started before the compiler was available and the computers had a much-squeezed memory.

3.3   Other software than Algol-Genius

The interrupts in D21 were never used for true multiprocessing, only to run I/O in parallel with computing. Therefore, the "operating system" occupied a tiny 1024 words in primary memory. In addition, "Dirigenten" (the conductor) translated job control statements into a very compact representation and proved to be very efficient and flexible.

The name of the assembler was DAC. As a protest against the very stereotyped punched card tradition, it sported special features such as a free format, use of capital and small letters, the use of + instead of ADD, the use of C+ for LOAD.

The D21 excelled in sorting. The tape system with parallelism and the comparatively big memory contributed of course, but also the advanced sorting algorithms used. At this time, Donald Knuth and others had just published their pioneering research and Åke Fager did a great job in implementing the results for D21.

4.   ALGOL-GENIUS

4.1   4.1   Accidental problems

Fred Brooks' first published *The Mythical Man-month* in 1975. He based the book on his experience as a project manager for IBM's OS/360. *The Mythical Man-month* is mandatory reading for anyone interested in computer history and is now available in a new edition, which also contains *No Silver Bullet*. In this essay, Brooks divides the difficulties in software design in essential and accidental. His point is that we will never find the silver bullet that kills the essential difficulties but that we have made great progress eliminating the accidental. One example of essential problems is the inherent complexity that "software entities are more complex for their size than perhaps any other human construct, because no two parts are alike." Another is the necessity to conform to and implement rules and regulations "forced without rhyme and reason by the many human institutions and systems to which his interfaces must conform." Accidental problems are those that are inherent in the "machine programs concerned with bits, registers, conditions...." The first step to eliminate the accidental problems was assemblers; then came the problem-oriented languages with FORTRAN leading the way. Algol and of course Algol-Genius came soon after. I would claim that Algol-Genius went as far as you could reasonably go to eliminate the accidental problems with the machine resources then available. Today's software world with so many complexities such as the web and distributed components requires much more powerful tools. That is another story to which I will return. The essential problems we still have to live with!

4.2   The first version

In 1962, the dominating language for business data processing was assembler, in particular in the IBM world. Börje Langefors was convinced that we could and should use high-level languages. Algol 60 was already well established at that time and they defined the first version of COBOL. Since D21 had no decimal arithmetic, it was judged that performance in a COBOL implementation would not be acceptable. The decision to choose Algol was because early COBOL was not a good programming language. It had a very primitive procedure concept with no parameters; all variables were global and it featured some dangerous constructs like COMPUTED GO TO and ALTER. A syntax that prescribed "ADD A TO B GIVING C" instead of "C := A + B;" did not make things better. (COBOL has evolved since then!) However, COBOL had a feature that was missing in Algol—it could handle records. So, Langefors suggested that we add a record and input/output part to Algol, modeled after COBOL. The addition was called Genius (Generellt in ut system).

Ingemar Dahlstrand had then implemented Algol for the BESK and the Facit EDB in a pioneering work. We used the experience from that implementation and engaged one the designers Sture Laryd. He worked together with Gunnar Ehrling, a pioneer from Matematikmaskinnämnden and so we were able to get a good, efficient, and reliable implementation of the Algol part. The specification was compatible with Algol 60 with few exceptions. Consult Ingemar Dahlstrand's paper on the implementation of Algol 60 for further details on that subject.

Based on the ideas from Börje Langefors, Gunnar Hellström and the author made the detailed specification and supervised the implementation of the Genius part. Data declared in Genius were globally accessible. The syntax was rather faithful to COBOL except that it used underlining, like in Algol, instead of reserved words. Looking back, at that time, the fact that in Algol you could use any names for your variables was a great advantage in the view of many. However, all modern languages use reserved words and no one is complaining. The record concept was mostly used to model and format data on peripheral equipment; it was not as flexible as in later languages like Pascal.

Procedure calls replaced the verbs in COBOL since they were part of the Algol program. One could perform operations such as open and close files and read, search, and write records as one would expect.

4.3   Applications

The first version of Algol-Genius was released in 1964 and it soon became evident that the language, as well as its implementation, was well suited for a wide range of applications. Algol-Genius became the preferred programming language for most of our customers. This was true both for technical and administrative applications. It turned out that for specific cases, only assembler could substantially improve performance. Let me just mention one example. Kockums shipyard was then the leading builder of huge tankers in the world. Under the leadership of Kai Holmgren, it introduced CAD/CAM methods early on. With Algol-Genius as a base, the developed a language and a system called Styrbjörn/Stearbear for the entire design process. Kockums shipyard is long gone, but Stearbear still lives on, now under the name of Tribon. The software it uses had its beginnings from D21 and Algol-Genius way back, of course. Nevertheless, Tribon is still a very successful, although not a very well known Swedish software company.

4.4   Extensions

Datasaab had a very active user club and one favorite subject of that club was extensions to Algol-Genius. Since we owned the language, the formalities were minimal. If enough customers wanted an addition and we deemed it reasonable, we would implement it. One feature, which I still have bad feelings about, concerned the use of punched tape. Algol-Genius already had very powerful procedures for that. However, we got a request for further automation from Industridata, who used D21s and later D22s in their service bureaus. They had to accept and process tapes coming from machines such as cash registers with many different formats. Together with them, we designed a table driven method to handle this, but it was not very successful and surely not worth the effort. Nevertheless, it is a good example of the close cooperation we had with the customers.

5.   DATASAAB D22

5.1   Hardware

1968 marked the launching of the D22. It was a much more advanced computer with protected mode for the operating system, ability to address 256K word (768KB) of memory with a cycle of 1.6µs. Floating-point arithmetic was part of the hardware. Professor Germund Dahlquist was a consultant on the project and did pioneering work in specifying a new arithmetic with a minimum of rounding errors. The D22 could manage character handling and decimal arithmetic to obtain efficient execution of COBOL programs. Quite an effort went into making the decimal hardware as COBOL-compatible as possible. We could have all of these improvements without breaking the compatibility with D21. Existing binary D21 programs could run on the D22 without problems.

The D22 could support modern and extended peripherals. The most important addition was the inclusion of disk memories with removable disk packs. The tape standard changed to be compatible with the market (read IBM) at that time, while still being program compatible with the D21. A front-end computer handled the D22's communication with the outside world; it was Datasaab's own 2100. That same computer also played a role the ATM described by Viggo Wentzel; consult his paper on the topic in these Proceedings.

5.2   Market

D22 was of course the natural choice for the D21 customers. But sales were not limited to those, all in all some 70 systems were delivered up and until 1975. However 70 was a way to small number to create any interest in the independent software vendors that begun to emerge at this time. They picked of course IBM machines as their target. For this reason, the first IBM-compatible machines, exemplified by Amdahl, made their entrance at this time. Datasaab D23 was an attempt to build a computer that could emulate D22 as well as IBM/360. But time run out for this project, it was in fact doomed from the beginning.

5.3   Other software than Algol-Genius

The major software effort for D22 was an operating system. It inherited the name Dirigenten, but was on a very different scale, with true multiprocessing facilities. The work was lead by Jan Nordling. Dirigenten was optimized for batch processing and was extended for time-sharing later on. Jan Nordling and his colleagues had taken part in the design of the hardware that consequently was well suited to multiprocessing, but there was still a lot of new ground to be covered.

As indicated above, D22 could handle a COBOL as well as a FORTRAN implementation. Good and efficient but not widely used, Algol-Genius continued to be the preferred language.

Datasaab developed applications in some targeted areas, mainly health care and logistics. They appropriately named the logistic system "Lagom." It was quite successful and survived the D22 by being converted to Univac 1100 and to Unix.

5.4   Algol-Genius

Since D22 was compatible with D21, conversion was no problem. The Algol-Genius language required a few additions, the major one being indexed-sequential files for the disk memories. Still, substantial work had taken place on the compiler to take advantage of the new features in the hardware.

6.   UNIVAC 1100

6.1   Background

The small number of computers we managed to sell and the consequent lack of interest from software vendors killed Datasaab's mainframe line (tunga linjen in Swedish).   A deal was made with Sperry Rand, who acquired the D21, D22 and D23 lines, resulting in a joint venture, called Saab-Univac, formed in 1975 The goal was to convert as much as possible of the customer base to Univac computers, specifically Univac 1100.

6.2   Algol-Genius

We soon decided that the best way to move the existing customers to the Univac 1100 was to implement Algol-Genius for that computer. Once more, we had an Algol implementation that we could use, this time already running on 1100. It came from the University of Trondheim (sic!) and required very few changes and additions. We had to build the Genius part from scratch. Since it was quite dependent on the operating system and the file system, we implemented it in close cooperation with Univac. For that purpose, Hans and Christel Ljungren spent a winter in Minneapolis/St Paul.

It was not possible to achieve 100% compatibility because of differences in the hardware as well as in the operating system, but it turned out that the conversion was painless, compared to other alternatives.   Algol-Genius contributed no doubt to the fact that Saab Univac lost only few Datasaab customers to other vendors.

Saab-Univac did not commit itself to develop Algol-Genius and furthermore, it was after all a proprietary language. The customers thus gradually converted to other languages. Even so, Algol-Genius enjoyed a long life. Even at the end of the nineties, some companies were using Algol-Genius programs in their production efforts; the subject of necessary ongoing maintenance contributed to its final extinction. As far as the author knows, none has survived the millennium.

6.3   What can we learn?

Software is expensive to develop but cheap to produce, copy, and distribute. This means that volume is crucial for economic well being. With large volume, a vendor has a great freedom in setting prices on his software. Maybe even more important than the price advantage is the fact the large volume attracts other players. It generates interest to do other creative things such as developing add on products and specializing in consulting and training for that software, which in turn makes it even more attractive to customers. Consequently, in each specific software area, there will always be a gorilla and a few chimpanzees [Moore]. Datasaab not only tried to build and sell software, it did so with software that could only run on its own, very proprietary, platform. Moreover, this was in a language area and a geographic market that was minimal. In hindsight, the result was inevitable.

If it were difficult then, today it would be almost impossible. Operating systems, middleware, and development environments run to millions and millions lines of code. The corresponding D22 software was tiny! So now, we have one gorilla (Microsoft) and a few chimpanzees (the Unix/Linux companies). By using one of these platforms and specializing in a specific software area, it is possible to succeed. In other words, let others solve the accidental problems and focus on the essential ones. I have already mentioned Tribon; another example is Opera from Norway and doubtless, there are many others, unknown to me. (Linux, by the way, solves the accidental problems. The invention is a fascinating and novel business idea. Can you, by the way, call "giving away for free" a business idea?)

The area of embedded systems is also very interesting. Whether it is mobile phones, process control, or car and engine control, it starts out as a very proprietary product. Only the hardware vendor has access to the interface specifications and is interested in developing the software. But gradually, as the applications grow, the need for other sources arises, as well as the interest from software vendors to contribute. Standards evolve that make this possible. So far, we in Scandinavia have been quite successful in embedded systems but the fight is not over yet. We hope that Symbian, backed by Nokia and Ericsson-Sony, will become a force in the mobile phone market.

REFERENCES

[Brooks] Fredrick Brooks, *The mythical man-month*, Addison Wesley 1995
[Mooore] Geoffrey Moore *Inside the tornado*, HarperBusiness 1995
[Wentzel, et al] Tema D21, *Datasaabs vänner*, 1994
[Yngvell, et al] Tema D22-D23, *Datasaabs vänner*, 1997

THE BIRTH OF SIMULA

Stein Krogdahl

Department of Informatics, University of Oslo, Norway; steinkr@ifi.uio.no

Abstract: When designing Simula, Ole-Johan Dahl and Kristen Nygaard introduced the
              basic concepts of what later became object-orientation, which still, 35 years
              later, has a profound impact on computing.   This paper looks at the
              background for the Simula project, the way it developed over time, and the
              reason it could became so successful.

Key words: Computing history, programming languages, Simula

1.   INTRODUCTION

On many occasions, people have told the history of how the programming language Simula came into being. Perhaps the foremost of these was the paper on Simula at the "History of Programming Languages" conference in 1978 [5] by Ole-Johan Dahl (OJD) and Kristen Nygaard (KN) themselves. However, people have given many other accounts, e.g. one by J.R. Holmevik [9] in 1994 and one by OJD [2] in 2001.

Most of these papers provided chronological accounts of what happened during the years when OJD and KN developed the two Simula languages, first the special purpose simulation language Simula (now usually referred to as Simula 1) and then the general-purpose language Simula 67. The latter is now officially renamed "Simula", but to make a clear distinction, we shall refer to it here as Simula 67.

This paper will take a slightly different view in that it will first give a rather short chronological overview of what happened when they developed the Simula languages during the years 1961 to 1967. After that, we will look at different aspects of Simula 67, and try to find where they originated, when they came into the development of the Simula languages, and how and why they got their final form in the language. The papers [5] and [9] contain much more extensive lists of references than this paper does.

2.   A CHRONOLOGICAL OVERVIEW

This section gives an overview of the development of the Simula languages during the years 1961 to 1967. Four phases define this development.

2.1   The early design phase (1961-August 1962)

The start of the Simula story is, as most such stories, not clearly defined. Sometime around 1960/61 KN started working on ideas for a language that could naturally describe complex dynamic systems. The background was that he had worked with so-called "Monte Carlo simulations" while at Norwegian Defense Research Establishment (NDRE). People performed these simulations both "by hand" and on early computers. KN felt a strong need for a language or a notation in which he could describe such systems at a much higher level than was usual at the time. From the nature of the problems he had worked with, his main interests were discrete event models, where they modeled a dynamic system as a set of variables operated upon by a sequence of instantaneous events.

In January 1962, we find the first written account of this effort. In a letter to a French operations research specialist, Charles Saltzmann, KN writes:

"The status on the Simulation Language (Monte Carlo Compiler) is that I have rather clear ideas on how to describe queuing systems, and have developed concepts which I feel allow a reasonably easy description of large classes of situations. [...] The work on the compiler could not start before the language was fairly well developed, but this stage seems now to have been reached. The expert programmer who is interested in this part of the job will meet me tomorrow. He has been rather optimistic during our previous meetings."

The expert programmer was OJD, whom KN knew very well from NDRE (from where KN had left in 1960, to work at the Norwegian Computing Center (NCC)). From then on, KN and OJD were working together to obtain a draft of the language, and in May 1962 they had a first specification. By then they had also coined the name SIMULA (SIMUlation LAnguage) for the language, and their idea was to implement it as a preprocessor to a general Algol compiler. They presented their ideas for this language at the IFIP 62 World Conference in Munich, in August 1962 [11].

In this early version of Simula, they modeled a system by a (fixed) number of "stations", each with a queue of "customers". The stations were the active parts, and each was controlled by a program that could "input" a customer from the station's queue, update variables (global, local in station, and local in customer), and transfer the customer to the queue of another station. Stations could discard customers by not transferring them to another queue, and could generate new customers. They could also wait a given period (in simulated time) before starting the next action. Custom types were declared as data records, without any actions (or procedures) of their own.

We shall refer to this language as "Simula 0", but it probably never had a stable definition and never had an implementation.

2.2 The Simula 1 design phase (Autumn 62 - March 64)

After the presentation of the ideas for Simula 0 in Munich, KN occupied himself with organizational and financial matters. This resulted in the purchase of a UNIVAC 1107 to NCC for a discount price, and, in the same contract, in funding for the implementation of Simula on UNIVAC 1107.

OJD went on working with the language, and in May 1963, he joined the NCC as a full time employee. However, it became more and more apparent that implementing the new language as a preprocessor to Algol was not the right way to go. The LIFO (stack) nature of the Algol procedure calls turned out to be too restrictive for implementing the "stations" and "customers" of Simula 0.

Thus, still determined to build upon an Algol compiler, they had to dig deeper into it, and replace the simple LIFO allocation mechanism with what today we would call a heap. For this purpose, OJD designed a scheme for automatically regaining unused memory (which did not compact the retained objects).

Inspired by the new freedom obtained from this allocation scheme, they also saw that a generalization of the language was possible. In Simula 0, stations were the active parts and customers the passive ones. They now replaced these with *one* concept that could describe all the different "objects" that should participate in a simulation. This concept was called a "process" (declared with the keyword "activity"), and could play both an active and a passive role in simulations. They kept track of the processes by (un-typed) pointers, and they did not restrict their lifetime by any LIFO discipline. The whole system had a built-in notion of simulated time that controlled the execution of the processes when they were active.

In March 1964, they had a well-defined language. It resembled Algol, with the addition of the process concept and the accompanying apparatus for simulation programming.

2.3 Implementation of Simula 1 (April 1964 - January 1965)

The implementation started immediately. Since they already understood much of the complexities surrounding the garbage collector, the whole task of reworking the UNIVAC 1107 Algol compiler to a Simula 1 compiler was finished already in January 1965. OJD led the work and to large degree carried it out. However, Bjørn Myhrhaug and Sigurd Kubosch from NCC (both of which were central in later Simula 67 implementations) also participated. They had occasional help from the team around the UNIVAC 1107 Algol compiler (Joseph Speroni, Ken Walter, and Nicholas Hobacker).

2.4 The design phase of Simula 67 (January 1965 - summer 1967)

When OJD and KN started using Simula 1 in various projects, they soon observed that people could profitably use it for other programming tasks than simulation. Thus, they started to explore what a more generalized version of Simula 1 should look like. However, the spark that really made the development of a new general-purpose language take off was probably a paper on record handling by C.A.R. Hoare [8]. It proposed to describe records by record classes and to introduce "record subclasses", described as extensions of other classes. It also argued that with such a scheme one could type pointers without losing too much flexibility.

Even if OJD and KN saw that Hoare's proposal had ideas that fitted well with a generalized version of Simula 1, it also had aspects that were difficult to combine with other ideas they had for the new language. A breakthrough came late in 1966, when they saw that they could declare classes and subclasses syntactically, independent of each other, instead of in one closed construct as in Hoare's proposal.

With this insight, other aspects of the new language (which they now had named Simula 67) naturally found their place, and they worked intensively the first months of 1967 to finish a paper for the IFIP TC 2 conference to be held in May at Lysebu in Oslo (chaired by OJD). The theme here was Simulation languages, and their paper [6] was finished in March, just in time for submission to the conference. Towards the conference they still worked with new ideas, and after much discussion, they came up with the (now well-known) concept of "virtual quantities".

In May 1967, they signed a contract with Control Data to implement the (still unfinished) language Simula 67. The implementation should be carried out at KCIN (the "Kjeller Computer Installation" serving NDRE) for CDC 3600, at the University of Oslo for CDC 3300, and in Paris (by Control Data itself) for the CDC 6000 series. To establish a first basic definition of Simula 67, a meeting (called the "Simula 67 Common Base Conference") took place at NCC in June, where people from Control Data, KCIN, University of Oslo, and NCC met, together with a few invited specialists.

Also at this conference KN and OJD proposed new additions to the language, notably a proposal that would make it possible to define named "inline objects", that is, to use classes as types in traditional variable declarations. However, as they did not fully work through this proposal, either conceptually or implementationally, the implementers voted it down. Probably they must have felt that the implementation task was large enough as it was.

This conference also set up a body called "Simula Standardization Group" (SSG), with representatives from NCC and the different implementers. Its first task was to establish a formal language definition. The main remaining issues were text handling and mechanisms for input/output and in the definition of these Bjørn Myhrhaug from NCC played a central role. They formally froze the language in the "Simula 67 Common Base Language" report, accepted by SSG on February 10, 1968 [4]. Bjørn Myhrhaug also, together with OJD, wrote an implementation guide for Simula 67 [3], which was important for later implementations of the language.

All the Control Data compilers were finished during the spring of 1969. In 1969, they also decided that NCC itself should complete a compiler for the UNIVAC 1100 series and implement Simula 67 for IBM 360/370. These implementations were finished in March 1971 and May 1972 respectively.

3.   THE DIFFERENT ASPECTS OF SIMULA 67

The previous section gave a brief chronological overview of the development of the Simula languages. In this section, we shall take an orthogonal view, look at different aspects of Simula 67, and try to find their roots and the way they developed throughout the design process of Simula 1 and Simula 67.

Most of the interesting aspects of Simula 67 are associated with the class concept and the way one can generate objects of classes. When defined in 1967, the class concept represented a revolutionary new combination of properties. Some of these came from the long development of the Simula 1 language, some came from other researchers, and some were developed by OJD and KN in the last months before they defined the language.

3.1   The object as a process

We shall first look at an aspect of Simula 67 which is not well known, and which is taken over by very few of its successors. This aspect is the ability of objects to act as processes that can execute in a "quasi-parallel" fashion. This special type of parallelism is in fact a form of sequential execution, but a form where you can get some of the benefits obtained by organizing the program as a set of "independent" processes. The idea is that classes in Simula 67 (and processes in Simula 1) have statements of their own (like procedures), and that these start executing as soon as an object of that class is generated. However, unlike procedures, objects may choose to temporarily stop their execution and transfer the control to another process. If one returns control back to the object, it will resume execution where the control last left off. A process will always retain the execution control until it explicitly gives it away. When the execution of an object reaches the end of its statements, it will become "terminated", and can no longer resume (but one can still access local data and call local procedures from outside the object).

The quasi-parallel sequencing is essential for the simulation mechanism in Simula 1. Roughly speaking, it works as follows: When a process has finished the actions it should perform at a certain point in simulated time, it decides when (in simulated time) it wants the control back, and stores this in a local "next-event-time" variable. It then gives the control to a central "time-manager", which finds the process that is to execute next (the one with the smallest next-event-time), updates the global time variable accordingly, and gives the control to that process.

The idea of this mechanism was to invite the programmer of a simulation program to model the underlying system by a set of processes, each describing some natural sequence of events in that system (e.g. the sequence of events experienced by one car in a traffic simulation).

Note that a process may transfer control to another process even if it is currently inside one or more procedure calls. Thus, each quasi-parallel process will have its own stack of procedure calls, and if it is not executing, its "reactivation point" will reside in the innermost of these calls. This means that not only processes and other objects, but also procedure calls must be stored on "the heap". (With the memory sizes of 60ies, they did not consider the later practice of allocating a large continuous chunk of memory to the stack of each process/thread). Thus, the traditional stack of procedure calls disappeared in implementations of both Simula 1 and Simula 67, everything was on the heap (even if we could optimize this to some extent for specific programs).

Quasi-parallel sequencing is analogous to the notion of coroutines described by Conway in 1963 [1]. In papers on Simula 1 or Simula 67, OJD and KN always refer to this paper when discussing quasi-parallelism, usually by saying something like "a set of quasi-parallel processes will function as coroutines in the sense of [1]". However, Simula 0, designed in 1962, also had some traces of quasi-parallel execution, even if they did not fully develop the process concept until February 1964. It is therefore not clear to the current author whether OJD and KN developed this concept themselves, or got it from Conway.

Many of the uses OJD and KN found for Simula 1 in other areas than simulation used the quasi-parallel sequencing for some other purpose (e.g. to traverse two search trees "in parallel"). Thus, there was no doubt that Simula 67 should retain this mechanism. Another reason for this was that they wanted the simulation aspect of Simula 1 to be expressible within Simula 67, as a separate package. However, the concept of simulated time then naturally belonged in this package, while a more basic mechanism for quasi-parallel sequencing was included in the Simula 67 language.

3.2   Dynamic generation of objects

A ubiquitous property of today's object-oriented languages is the ability to generate objects dynamically. This was also a basic mechanism in Simula 1 and indeed in Simula 67. However, the decision to allow this, taken in the transition from Simula 0 to Simula 1 was probably not quite straightforward. When they designed Simula 0 in 1962, the idea was to implement the language as a preprocessor to an Algol compiler, thus having to stick to the LIFO allocation discipline of procedures and blocks of that language.

This hampered the design of Simula 0 so that, for example, the number of "stations" (the active components) had to be fully determined at compile time, while the number of "customers" (the passive elements) had to be given at the start of each execution. Thus, when they saw that even this scheme was cumbersome to implement as planned, they looked for other solutions. Moreover, when forced to go deeper into the Algol compiler, they sought a solution that gave full freedom to generate objects at run time.

To obtain this they had to abandon the simple LIFO scheme for allocating procedure calls in Algol. This meant digging into the Algol compiler and its run time system, and implement a scheme where both objects and procedure calls could come and go (that is, become inaccessible) in any order. For security reasons, they also wanted the system itself to find which objects and procedure call instances it could delete. For this purpose, OJD designed a garbage collector scheme based on reference counts and free-lists, and with a last resort search mechanism that could also find loops of objects that it could delete. It never moved any objects. This scheme was part of the Simula 1 implementation.

Later, when the Simula 1 implementation was finished, they learned (through their NDRE mentor Jan V. Garwick, once he returned from USA) about a four-phase compacting garbage collector that could do away with all the fragmentation they experienced with the Simula 1 implementation. They used this algorithm in the first Simula 67 implementations and it has since been a reliable element in most Simula 67 implementations.

3.3   Objects as "records", and access from outside

The decision that one single concept, the process concept of Simula 1, should cover all needs from quasi-parallel processes to simple data records was probably one of the most important ones in the history of the Simula project. As seen in the previous section, this decision was made possible by another important decision: to abandon the simple stack allocation scheme of Algol.

The significance of the "single concept decision" lies in the following:

- From this decision, it follows that also the need for simple data records (with no actions of their own) should be covered by the process concept. Thus we obviously have to be able to access such records from outside (e.g. by "dot access") to utilize their local data at all. Then, again by the single concept decision, one should allow access from outside also for processes in general.
- The process concept of Simula 1 is modeled after the Algol block. Therefore, it allows local procedures in addition to local variables and actions of the process itself. Thus, records with procedures and variables, but with *no* actions of their own, follow as a natural special case. Then again, to use such procedures we obviously have to be able to call them from outside the record. Thus, one should also allow calls to local procedures from outside processes in general.

We now recognize the latter point as one of the basic characteristics of object-orientation. The former point was very important for obtaining flexible communication between the processes in a simulation.

For reasons of flexibility and simplicity, they decided that processes should only be accessible through pointers. In Simula 1 there were no concept of subclasses, and the pointers were therefore not typed (typed pointers would have led to problems e.g. when processes of different kinds should be kept on a linked list). To keep the language type-safe, Simula 1 therefore had a rather cumbersome way of accessing the "inside" of a process referenced by a pointer 'pntr':

inspect pntr **when** P1 **do begin** ... **end when** P2 **do begin** ... **end** ...;

Here P1, P2, ... must be names of process declarations ("process types"). The effect of the above statement is first to determine the actual type of the process referenced by 'pntr', and then to enter the corresponding block, where the attributes of this process can be accessed directly.

When they introduced subclasses in Simula 67, the absolute need for such a construction disappeared (see below). However, the inspect statement could still be convenient in many situations, and they included it in Simula 67 (in a slightly different form).

3.4   Classes and subclasses

OJD and KN saw a number of cases where processes had many common properties when programming in Simula 1. However, because there were also differences, two fully separate processes had to be described. They had no way of utilizing the similarity. This all changed when C.A.R. Hoare published a paper on record handling [8], where he proposed classes and subclasses of records, but in a scheme where a class and all its subclasses were described in one closed syntactic unit.

He also proposed to type pointer variables with record classes (or subclasses) and only to allow them to point to records of the typing class and to records of all its subclasses. This gave full access security when allowing, for example, "pointer.attribute" only when the attribute is defined in the class typing the pointer. Hoare wrote "attribute(pointer)", as was common at the time, but Simula 67 turned to the now ubiquitous "dot-notation" (which was probably first used for this purpose in PL/1).

Equally important, with this scheme typing of pointers was almost not felt a nuisance at all. All records that should enter lists could be "subrecords" of a suitable record class "element", but otherwise be different.

However, even if this seemed promising, it did not really fit in with all the requirements they had for the new Simula 67. Hoare's records had no actions of their own, and, most importantly, the closed syntax did not fit in with other ideas they had. Nevertheless, late in 1966 they finally found a principle that made all the pieces fit together. The main idea was to allow the declaration of subclasses of a class C independently of where one declared C. That is, we can declare a new subclass D of C wherever the declaration of C is visible (with certain block level restrictions). The syntax chosen was to write C as a "prefix" to the declaration of D: "C **class** D (...); **begin** ... **end**" (which is why, in Simula literature, we often find the notion "prefix class" instead of the now more usual "superclass" or "base class").

The great advantage of this scheme is that we could write general-purpose classes separately and, for example, place them in public libraries (in textual or compiled form). Later, different users could fetch these classes, and could write subclasses to satisfy their own specific needs. This scheme was essential when they later wanted to program the simulation properties of Simula 1 as a package in Simula 67.

3.5   Virtual procedures

Virtual procedures are now an integral part of object orientation, even to the degree that in some languages, *all* procedures are virtual (e.g. in Java). However, the story of virtuals started with a very specific problem that OJD and KN wanted to solve. It was only after submission of the Lysebu paper in March 1967 that they had time to look at the following problem:

As with procedures, classes in Simula 67 may have formal parameters to which actual values must be given when an object is generated. However, for technical reasons they did not allow procedures as parameters to classes, even if they saw that this could be very useful when one wanted the "same statements" to have slightly different effect in different objects.

After much work and discussion, they finally found a mechanism they agreed could regain much of the lost flexibility. By declaring a procedure in a class C as "virtual", it could be redefined (overridden) in a subclass D, and in objects of class D this redefinition should have effect also when the procedure is called in the code of class C (and when the procedure is called in a D-object by dot access through a C-typed pointer). Thus, the same procedure call could activate different "versions" of the procedure, at least in objects of different subclasses. As we know today, this mechanism turned out to be very useful.

The proposal for virtuals just reached the Lysebu conference, and was included in the final version of the paper [6].

3.6   Classes as packages

A basic idea with Simula 67 was that we could implement the simulation aspects of Simula 1 as a separate "package" in Simula 67. OJD and KN saw that implementing a variety of specially tailored library packages for different application areas would be important for the usability of the new language. As implementing the simulation aspects of Simula 1 was no simple task, the ability of Simula 67 to describe such a package became an important yardstick for its quality.

They immediately saw that such packages often would contain more than one class, and they therefore needed some sort of container to keep these classes together. Their solution was to use classes also for this purpose and this worked fine because they had retained the full block structure of Algol in Simula 67. They could therefore have classes within classes, and could use the outermost class as a container representing the package as such. The innermost classes would then be those offered for normal use (either for direct object generation or for making subclasses that are more specific).

With this scheme, they could also make one package build upon another by simply making one "package class" a subclass of the other. To bring packages into the user's program Simula 67 uses "block prefixing". By prefixing a normal block with the name of a package class, the content of that class became visible in the block, just as if the block was the body of a subclass of the package class (also so that virtual procedures of the package class could be redefined in the prefixed block). Thus, e.g. for a simulation package, where the processes should be able to enter linked lists, they could have a scheme like this (where "!...;" is a comment, and the classes are slightly simplified):

```
class LinkedList; ! A package class implementing list handling ;
begin
    class Head; begin <a first-pointer, and suitable procedures>; end;
    class Elem; begin <a next-pointer, and suitable procedures>;   end;
end;
```

Using this package, one can define the simulation package as follows:

```
LinkedList class Simulation; ! This package uses package LinkedList ;
begin
    Elem class Process; ! All processes can be elements in lists ;
    begin <initial statements>;
        inner;     ! See explanation below ;
        <terminating statements>;
    end;
    <Further classes (or other declarations)>;
end;
```

We can then use such a package as follows:

```
Simulation begin
    Process class Car; begin ... end;
    Process class Bus; begin ... end;
    ...
end;
```

Note that package classes are totally normal classes, except that a class referring to "this" (the current object) is not legal as a block prefix.

One mechanism they saw the need for through examples like the one above, is the "inner" mechanism used in the class Process in the Simulation package class. This keyword has the effect that statements of subclasses of Process are positioned where the "inner" is, which means that the Process class gets control before and after the statements of a subclass. Thus, we can properly initialize and terminate any object of a subclass of Process (e.g. Car or Bus) by statements given in the prewritten class Process.

One may notice that the inner mechanism has similarities with the virtual mechanism, as the keyword "inner" represents the *statement part* of the actual subclass (if any), while the virtual mechanism correspondingly picks the *procedure redefinition* of the actual subclass. These mechanisms entered the Simula project for quite different purposes, and one may wonder whether a unifying mechanism had been found if the project had proceeded (as indicated earlier, the virtual mechanism came very late). However, it is interesting to note that in the language Beta (designed by KN and three Danish colleagues as a further development of the Simula ideas, see e.g. [10]) both the inner and the virtual concepts are retained as separate mechanisms.

It is impressive that OJD and KN saw the need for a package concept already in 1967. It is told (but not confirmed) that they discussed if a special concept like "package" or "module" should be introduced (instead of package classes), but the chosen solution has a pleasant economy of concepts, which might have decided the matter. However, it has the disadvantage that you can only bring in one package in each block. As multiple prefixing for classes (which later became known as "multiple inheritance") was not included in Simula 67, it followed naturally that also multiple *block* prefixing was excluded. With a separate concept for packages (for which you were *not* allowed to dynamically create new "package objects") it would have been easier both implementationally and conceptually to allow more than one package to be brought into a given block.

4.   CONCLUDING REMARKS

In this final section, we shall look at the following question: How could a small project with (for most of the time) only two participants produce a language and a set of concepts so powerful and pervasive that they today, 35 years later, underlie most software development? Obviously, it is impossible to give a complete answer to this, but we shall look at some key circumstances around the Simula project that the current author thinks were important for its success.

- First and foremost, both KN and OJD were extraordinary talented researchers in the field of language design. They were well oriented in the relevant literature of the time and had contact with a number of other researchers during the design of the Simula languages. They were persistent in their work, and never stopped looking for more general and elegant solutions. Last but not least: they had an excellent judgment concerning the balance between efficiency and elegance when they had to make a choice, but they always strove to obtain both.

- Even if OJD and KN were similar in the sense that they both had the qualities described above, they were quite different in other respects, and could thereby complement each other during the work. KN had the idea to start with, and even if OJD indeed participated in developing the concepts, KN probably remained the one that most naturally expressed the high-level dreams and hopes for the project. On the other hand, OJD was the one who immediately saw the implementational consequences of the different proposals, and could thereby mould them into a form that, to the largest possible extent, took care of both implementational and conceptual aspects.

- Both KN and OJD were robust personalities, and critique of new ideas did not at all drown in politeness. In [5] they wrote, "In some research teams a new idea is treated with loving care: How interesting! Beautiful!" This was not the case in the Simula development. When one of us announced that he had a new idea, the other would brighten up and do his best to kill it off." In such an environment, they accepted no new concept without deep and lengthy discussions.

- They were part of a European tradition in language design that strongly emphasized concepts such as economy, orthogonality, and simplicity. The first and foremost result of this proud tradition was the Algol language, and also, as described above, the elements of that language had a direct and profound influence on the Simula project.

- If we consider the object-oriented concepts as the main outcome of the Simula project, we can see that starting the project by designing a language for simulation was of utmost importance for that outcome. A central aspect of simulation programming is to represent the part of the world that we want to simulate by a suitable data structure inside the machine. Thus, KN and OJD saw that advanced and flexible mechanisms for describing and setting up data structures were of vital importance for a successful simulation language, and they worked hard to obtain such mechanisms. Through this they were led to a language design for Simula 1 that invited the programmer to first choose the data structure, and then tie the actions (or action sequences) of the model to the part of that structure where they most naturally belong (and not the other way around, as was natural in "procedural languages" like Algol). We can view this change of programming strategy as the main paradigm shift towards object-orientation. It naturally first appeared in the world of simulation, but OJD and KN could later take their experience with this principle from the simulation world to the design of the general-purpose language Simula 67 (and here it paved the way for the later concept of abstract data types, see [7]).

- It was very fortunate that Hoare's ideas on records and subrecords in [8] appeared exactly at the time when KN and OJD were working on generalizing the ideas of Simula 1 to fit in a general-purpose setting. Thus, they could immediately recognize the potentials of Hoare's ideas, and after intense work, combine them very successfully with the ideas they already had. This merge of ideas was probably the most important event in the development of the object-oriented concepts.

- It was probably also important that the Simula project spanned such a long period. If it had been a project with full funding from the start and a strict time limit, it would probably have ended up with an implementation of the Simula 0 concepts. Instead, the funding was not at all clear, and KN had occupied much of the time with other matters (which to some extent resulted in funding for the Simula project). However, OJD could keep the project going, having discussions with KN whenever possible. Thus, the ideas developed over many years and run through many phases. It was probably also vital for the outcome that they implemented a full-fledged language (Simula 1) along the way, so they could study its potentials and shortcomings in real use.

- Finally, with the shift from the special purpose simulation language Simula 1 to forming a general-purpose language they got the problem of designing Simula 67 so they could naturally express the simulation aspects of Simula 1 as a separate package in Simula 67. As these simulation aspects relate to many different mechanisms in the language (e.g. the coroutine mechanism) this was no easy task. Thus, the ability of Simula 67 to describe such a package in a simple and direct way became an important yardstick for measuring the quality of different proposals.

ACKNOWLEDGMENTS

While preparing this paper I have been in contact with a number of people, and in particular, I would like to thank the following persons for help and advice: Karel Babcicky, Håvard Hegna, Donald E. Knuth, Dag F. Langmyhr, Arne Maus, Bjørn Myhrhaug, Birger Møller-Pedersen, Olaf Owe, Jo Piene, and Wilfried Rupflin.

REFERENCES

[1] M.E. Conway. Design of a separable transition-diagram compiler. *Comm. ACM*, 6, 1963.

[2] Ole-Johan Dahl. The Roots of Object Orientation: The Simula Language. *Software Pioneers' Conference, Bonn, June 2001. In "Software Pioneers", Springer, 2002.*

[3] Ole-Johan Dahl and Bjørn Myhrhaug. *SIMULA 67 Implementation Guide.* Norwegian Computing Center, Oslo, Norway, Publ. S-9, June, 1969.

[4] Ole-Johan Dahl, Bjørn Myhrhaug, and Kristen Nygaard. *SIMULA 67 Common Base Language.* Norwegian Computing Center, 1968.

[5] Ole-Johan Dahl and Kristen Nygaard. The development of the Simula language. In Wexelblat, editor, *History of Programming Languages*, pages 439-493, 1981.

[6] Ole-Johan Dahl and Kristen Nygaard. Class and subclass declarations. In *Proceedings from IFIP TC2 Conference on Simulation Programming Languages, Lysebu, Oslo, ed.: J. N. Buxton*, pages 158-174. North Holland, May 1967.

[7] C.A.R. Hoare. Proof of correctness of data representations. *Acta Informatica, Vol 1, no 4*, pages 271-281, 1972.

[8] C.A.R. Hoare. Record handling. *Algol Bulletin No. 21*, November 1965.

[9] Jan Rune Holmevik. Compiling SIMULA: A Historical Study of Technological Genesis. *IEEE Annals of the History of Computing*, Vol 16, No. 4, 1994.

[10] B.B. Kristiansen, O.L. Madsen, B. Møller-Pedersen, and K. Nygaard. *Object-Oriented Programming in the BETA Programming Language.* Addison-Wesley, 1993.

[11] Kristen Nygaard. SIMULA: An Extension of ALGOL to the Description of Discrete-Event Networks. *Proceedings of the IFIP congress 62, Munich, Aug 1962*. North-Holland Publ., pages 520-522.

CLUB ACTIVITY IN THE EARLY PHASES OF MICROCOMPUTING IN FINLAND

Petri Saarikoski

Lecturer, Digital Culture, Degree Programme in Cultural Production and Landscape Studies, Unviersity of Turku, Siltapuistokatu 2, PL 124, 28101 Pori. Formerly Researcher, Deparment of History, University of Turku; petsaari@utu.fi

Abstract: History has ignored several aspects concerning the early phases of Finland's computerization activities. This article concentrates on the early history of microcomputing in Finland, in the light of three computer clubs.   An interactive relationship between paid work and private hobbies was typical in the early phases of microcomputing.   The educational and do-it-yourself aspects of about computers enhanced learning.

Key words: History of microcomputing, computer hobby, computer clubs, Finland

1.   INTRODUCTION

Research on the history of Finnish information technology is still in its early stages.   There is remarkable little research available on the early history of microcomputing in the 1970s. In some memoirs, there has been a tendency to underline the importance of computer hobbyists as pioneers and actors of personal computing.[1]   In other countries, especially in the United States, long traditions in this research field already existed. Some writers, for example Steven Levy, have described computer hobbyists or computer hackers as dedicated and idealistic technological crusaders.   Levy has

---

[1] For example, Mikrojen 20 vuotta ("The First 20 Years of Microcomputers") in Mikrotietokone Suomessa 1973-1993 ("Microcomputers in Finland 1973-1993"), Risto Linturi, Martti Tala (eds.). Helsinki 1993.

pointed out that the early users of microcomputers were actually users of the first PCs and they created a PC culture in societies of their own.[2]

In my research work, I have concentrated on the history of the home computer culture in Finland from the 1980s to the 1990s.[3] Jörgen Nissen and Tove Håpnes have also examined this phenomenon in the Nordic region.[4] In this paper, I will concentrate on the early microcomputing during the 1970s and the 1980s. I will explore certain important social and cultural aspects of early personal computing. How important was the role of computer hobbyists in the development of microcomputing? What kind of new activities did early microcomputing provide? What was the interaction between work and hobby? We approach these questions by studying the activity of three computer clubs: The *1800 Users' Club Association*, the *Mikrofan–Computer Club Association of Pirkanmaa*, and the *Microprosessor Club of Salora Ltd.* There are still only few detailed studies available in Finland on the history of computer clubs.[5] The lack of documented historical research on the early stages of microcomputer clubs presents a need for basic research.

2.   THE MICROPROCESSOR AND FINLAND: THE EARLY STAGES OF THE 1970S

In research on the history of computing, we generally regard the invention of microprocessor as the beginning of "microcomputer revolution". The development of microprocessors was still only a small – albeit important – turning point in the history of computing industry. The most important feature was the technical advancement in the semiconductor industry. The development of integrated circuits, semiconductor memory, and other inventions resulted computers were more effective although their physical size was reduced. Historians of information technology have usually called this technical progress the "Revolution in Miniature". One of

---

[2] Levy 1994.

[3] Pioneerien leluista kulutuselektroniikaksi. Suomalainen kotimikroharrastus tietotekniikan murroksessa 1980-luvun alusta 1990-luvun puoliväliin. ("From the Toys of Pioneers to Consumer Electronics. The Cultural History of Home Computing as Hobby in Finland from the 1980s to 1990s."). Turku 2001.

[4] Håpnes 1996, Nissen 1993.

[5] This article is an updated version of article published in Tekniikan Waiheita, periodical published by Finnish Society for the History of Technology. Saarikoski 2002. The doctoral thesis of Jörgen Nissen provides further insight into this field within the Nordic countries. Nissen 1993.

the major features of this "revolution" was the development of minicomputers.[6]

Researchers have usually emphasised the importance of the social activity of young students who used minicomputers as personal working stations. In Finland, the sales of mainframe and minicomputers increased during the 1960s. According to some sources, there were some 210 mainframe computers and about 700 minicomputers in the spring of 1971.[7] The teaching of data processing began in the Finnish universities during the 1960s, and some basic courses were available in some schools and institutes in late 1960s and early 1970s. The very first courses were probably those offered in Tapiola co-educational school in 1965, arranged by IBM Finland and Helsinki University of Technology.[8]

In the late 1960s, the construction plans for personal computers appeared in special interest magazines.[9] The availability of cheap and advantageous microcomponents increased in the beginning of the 1970s. The culmination of this process was the introduction of first microprocessors in 1971-1972.[10] After this point, the mass production of microcomputers was technically possible although not profitable. The Altair 8800 (introduced in the spring the 1975) is often mentioned as the first successful microcomputer. The computer hobbyists mainly used the Altair, which was a kit computer.[11]

Finnish computer experts and professionals were fully aware of the importance of microprocessor industry. When the first microprocessors were introduced, Finnish research and development (R&D) work began almost immediately. For example, the import of Intel 8008 -type microprocessor began already in 1973. In Finland, early adopters of microcomputing had already some experience, particularly of electronic circuits, kits, and electronic hobbies. Some of the enthusiasts were already professionals or students of data processing. Professionals and/or students of information technology who started their activities in 1973-1974 conducted the first microcomputer clubs.[12]

Finland imported microcomputers almost as soon as they were available in Europe. Although memoirs and surveys have often mentioned that microcomputers that were popular in the United States, for example Texas

---

[6] Campbell-Kelly, Aspray 1996, 222-226, 240-241, Ceruzzi 2000, 182-189, 207-211. Jaakko Suominen has concluded that in Finland the term "miniature" was already in use during the 1960s. Suominen 2000, 167, 305.

[7] Jokela, Korkala, Sarso 1972 chapter 1. pages 6-10.

[8] Tietokonekerho Tapiolassa, IBM Katsaus 2/1965, 20, Pantzar 2000, 84.

[9] Wiio 1993, 152.

[10] Ceruzzi 2000, 211-224, Campbell-Kelly, Aspray 1996, 236-237.

[11] Freiberger-Swaine 2000, 43, Campbell-Kelly, Aspray 1996, 240-244. For the reception of Altair kit computer among the computer hobbyists, see Levy 1994, 191-197.

[12] Bell, Linturi, Tala 1993, 9-10.

Instruments, Imsai, and TSR-80 did not sell very well in Finland. Interestingly several important computer models were not even imported to the country. High customs duty was one of the main reasons for this. During the period 1975-1980, serial produced microcomputers were considered particularly expensive tools for computer professionals. According to some sources, in Finland the Commodore PET and the Apple II were the best-known serial produced microcomputers in the late 1970s.[13]

To conclude, the above factors resulted in the long-term popularity of kit computers in Finland. However, in the early stages, the availability of kit computers was limited. Some of the importers of microprocessors provided only "evaluation kit" -type assembly kits that contained a hexadecimal keyboard, LED display, and primitive operating system. Between 1974 and 1977, there was virtually no company providing domestic kit computers for the Finnish market. When Telmac 1800 was introduced in October 1977, the shortage of equipment supply was partly relieved. This kit computer was designed by Osmo Kainulainen and it was based on the RCA Cosmac CDP 1802 -microprocessor. Osmo Kainulainen has mentioned that they invented the Telmac after some professional experimentation with Cosmac-microprosessor. Nevertheless, the demand for Telmac was so extensive that he and his co-workers founded a manufacturing and marketing company.[14]

Telmac was the most popular microcomputer in Finland in late 1970s. Computer hobbyists were particularly keen to buy the Telmac assembly kit as their first microcomputer. Approximately 2000 units were sold in four years and according to some statistics, the market share of Telmac was about 60-70 percent.[15] Simultaneously, demand for kit computers increased as schools and other institutions providing education in data processing needed suitable, cheap microcomputers. The most important kit computers produced by educational institutes of data processing and/or electronics were TAM (Tampere University of Technology), Innocomp (Helsinki University of Technology), and Ninekit (Helsinki Polytechnic).[16]

---

[13] Bell, Linturi, Tala 1993, 12.
[14] Telmacin synty, Osmo Kainulainen, Tieturi 3/1983, 8-9.
[15] Mikrouutisia läheltä ja kaukaa, Vesa Valtonen, Prosessori 1/1979, 18.
[16] For more information, see some Finnish articles. Oma tietokone jokaiselle kurssilaiselle, Prosessori 1/1979, 7, Huippunopea ohjelmointijärjestelmä Z80-mikroille - ZBASIC, Timo Koivunen, Prosessori 6-7/1980, 54-55, Ninekit - vahva kotimainen harrastajamikro, Johan Helsingius, Prosessori 12/1981, 75.

3. THE COMPUTER CLUB ACTIVITY OF TELMAC USERS

For beginners, assembling a kit computer was a difficult task. The range of use for kit computers was also very limited. Computer hobbyists were pleased if they managed to turn a microcomputer on. This was quite general problem caused by the lack of knowledge and education. For the average computer hobbyist, the foundation of a computer club offered the easiest solution. Therefore, the popularity of Telmac-computer clubs was high especially in the late 1970s and the early 1980s. Osmo Kainulainen founded the *1800 Users' Club Association*, the biggest Telmac computer club, in the spring of 1978. This club was mainly a national support association for all Telmac users,[17] consisting of some 450 members in 1980. The *1800 Users' Club Association* was not considered as a marketing channel for Telmac and Osmo Kainulainen had no official status in club.[18]

The *1800 Users' Club Association* worked actively during the late 1970s and the early 1980s, the forms of activity included assembling computer equipment, programming and general studying of computer technology. Moreover, many Telmac-users provided useful knowledge on computer science and electronics. In addition, the clubs provided possibilities for program exchange and equipment supply. The club published its own magazine called *Tieturi*, where for example, the published instruction plans for different kinds of circuit boards, converters and other peripheral devices. Different kinds of programming tips accompanied these plans. Members also organised meetings between Telmac-hobbyists.[19]

With the growing popularity of Telmac-microcomputers, some other computer clubs were also born in late 1970s. For instance, *Mikrofan– Computer Club Association of Pirkanmaa*, founded in 1979, and is still running today. The most important goals and plans for this club were defined as "watching the development of microcomputer field, providing educational courses for programming and electronics, and supporting equipment trade". It is noteworthy that in planning their club activity, *Mikrofan* had same kinds of principles as the *1800 Users' Club Association*. In addition, local identity was of course an important

---

[17] Telmacin synty, Osmo Kainulainen, Tieturi 3/1983, 11.
[18] Vilkas toimintavuosi 1800 Users' Clubilla, Prosessori 3/1980, 34-35.
[19] For articles, see Analogi-digitaalimuunnin ADC 0809 -piiristä, Hannu Pulkkinen, Tieturi 4/1982, 9-13, Epromin (2716) ohjelmointi Sairasen muistikortille, Pertti Juvonen, Tieturi 5/1982, 12-17, Kerhokoneen käyttöjärjestelmä, Heikki Levanto, Tieturi 1/1983, 8-11, Seikkailu muistiavaruudessa, Pertti Juvonen, Tieturi 4/1983, 18-22.

driving force. Almost all of the members came from the city of Tampere and its environs.[20]

Assembling peripheral devices was popular, presumably due to the limited availability of devices and the high price levels. Computer clubs also aimed to create devices for commercial purposes. The members built different kinds of professional devices, some of which were quite impressive. For example, in the early 1980s, *Mikrofan* constructed a LED-panel for the Tampere Theatre; the size was 7 meters wide and 2 meters high. A Commodore 64 home computer operated this advertisement panel and it was in use until 1999.[21]

Experimental activity also had its less serious side. This was particularly evident when Telmac-users "played" with their machines and, as a result, created fun, playful inventions. The miniature railways operated by microprocessors offer a good example.[22] Interestingly, miniature railways were popular among electronic hobbyists and early computer hackers.[23] Similar features characterised software creation too. Hobbyists programmed not only applications but computer games too. However, the status of entertainment software was always ambivalent, a point worth of further attention. Computer gaming was often regarded as a childish hobby and the programming of games as an activity for the younger generation. On the other hand, games and the playful use of computers also served useful purposes. For instance, members of the *1800 Users' Club Association* willingly admitted that in the beginning, computer hobbyists were always "just playing".[24]

Electronic hobbyists and radio amateurs were among the first to take up microcomputers as a hobby. Consequently, quite many of the founding members of computer clubs had also been members in electronics clubs and associations of radio amateurs. Some of the computer hobbyist also had a professional background, which explains why the average age of a typical computer hobbyist was well above 20 years. There are several remarkable similarities between the hobby users of early microcomputers and those of electronics and radio technology. For example, the interaction between work and hobby, the importance of clubs and associations, and the experimental ways of dealing with new

---

[20] Kokouskutsu. Perustavan kokouksen jatkokokous. Mikrofan 20 vuotta ("Mikrofan 20 years") -CD-ROM, Mikrofanin piirissä jo 100 nuorta. Innostus riittää mikrokerhon jäsenyyteen, Mikko Hamunen, Tietoviikko 17.11.1983.

[21] Pekka Ritamäki, interview December 13. 2001.

[22] See, for example, instructions for building such kinds of miniature railways. Pienoisrautatie ja 1802, Hannu Peiponen, Tieturi 5/1982, 18-21.

[23] Levy 1994, 17-38.

[24] These are Pekka Ritamäki interview December 13. 2001. Vuoden vaihtuessa, Lauri Levanto, Tieturi 1/1983, 7.

technology form similarities. In addition, these actors also shared the solid community spirit between the hobbyist and general "pioneer spirit". There was also tendency to regard these hobbies as an adventurous, masculine free time activity.[25]

When new, inexpensive 8-bit serial produced home computers like Vic-20, Commodore 64, and Sinclair Spectrum came onto to market in the early 1980s, the popularity of kit computers in computer clubs began to decrease. The marketing of IBM PCs started in 1983 and strengthened belief in the success of commercial produced microcomputers. At the same time, microcomputers guided youngsters into the future of information society. The latter idea was based mainly on the popular discourse, but it was also backed by the Finnish government's well-known plan for an information society.[26] Of course, other factors also influenced the microcomputers first major breakthrough onto the consumer markets, economic reasons are amongst the most important. In 1982-1984, Finland's economy was booming and families had extra money to spend. Consequently, the sale of consumer electronics increased substantially. Families bought, for example, video recorders, and extra televisions and, for the first time, microcomputers.[27]

The new home computers and the whole expansion of the computer markets created a younger "home computer generation". The hobby of working with home computers established and continued old masculine habits and traditions of technologically oriented hobbies. Computer games and programming became popular especially among the young men and boys.[28] The importance of home computers began to gain recognition when new clubs and associations were founded. Again, professionals and students of data processing and electronics had some role in establishing these new clubs. In addition, youth workers, teachers, and other people interested in association activity established more and more computer clubs.

Courses on microcomputers started to become more common, which stimulated the activity of more professionally oriented computer clubs. In many cases, the assembling of kit computers, electronics, and peripheral devices was thus considered an activity defined by professionals and experts largely than before. Some suggested reasons for this are as follows.

---

[25] Spigel 1992, 26-30, Boddy 1995, 59-60, 66, Salmi 1996, 162-163.

[26] This was based on the discussion in mass media. I have followed this discussion mainly through writings published in popular computer magazines such as *Prosessori* and *Tietokone* which has been mentioned above and in popular technical magazines such as *Tekniikan Maailma*.

[27] For more information of this development, see Saarikoski 2001, 33.

[28] Saarikoski 2001, 32-33, 64.

1. The price level of serial produced microcomputers came down.
2. The construction of microcomputers became increasingly complicated.
3. Programming and using the new applications became more rewarding for the users.

This also presented certain problems and challenges for the older computer clubs. For example, in the early 1980s some members of the *1800 Users' Club Association* still believed that there was a future in the teaching of computer electronics. For example, Reijo Toivanen–the chief editor of *Tieturi* club magazine–noticed already in 1982 that "nowadays commercial manufacturing of kit computers has virtually ceased. This kind of independent activity is almost the only way to encourage new hobbyists who are interested in kit computers and electronics".[29] The *1800 Users' Club Association* was still functioning in the late 1980s, but after this time, there was no sign of activity.[30] Some computer clubs solved the problem by making reforms in their way of acting. *Mikrofan*, for instance, started to use serial produced microcomputers and consequently programming applications gained more popularity.[31]

4.   INTERACTIONS BETWEEN PAID WORK AND PRIVATE HOBBIES

Expertise gained in computer clubs could be usefulin working life. The interaction between paid work and private hobbies was more obvious in computer clubs established in electronics industry. *The Microprosessor Club of Salora Ltd* is a good example.[32] Salora Ltd was the largest manufacturer of television sets in Scandinavia. The use of microprocessors in television sets grew steadily in the 1970s.[33] Competition in the television industry, the rapid development of microprocessors and the lack of education were the main reasons for the foundation of this particular computer club in 1979.[34] According to Petri Paju, in the Finnish electronics industry, the linkage between work and hobby had a strong connection to production values and culture—this

[29] Ideoita ilmassa, Reijo Toivanen, Tieturi 5/1982, 7.
[30] Kymmenen vuotta Telmacin kerhotoimintaa, Uutiset, MikroBitti 8/1988, 6.
[31] Interview Ritamäki 13.12.2001
[32] Saloran mikrokerho, Jorma Lindell, Saloran mikrokerhon paperit 30.12.1988.
[33] Åke Nyholm interview October 20. 2000. See also, Mikroprosessori televisiossa, Pekka Valjus, Prosessori 6-7/1980, 8-10.
[34] Mikroprosessorikerho Salora Oy:ssä, Jorma Lindell, Papers of the Microprosessor Club of Salora Ltd 27.12.1982, 1-2.

view was particularly pointed out by the engineers of Salora Ltd.[35] Once again, most of the members – usually electronics engineers – had earlier been interested in radio amateur activity and electronic hobbies.[36] When members were making plans for club activity, they presented an idea that club could provide some basic education on microcomputing for the other workers in Salora Ltd. To support the plan, the computer club arranged some evening courses in Basic-programming and application management.[37]

For the Salora company, the microcomputer hobby was of course a useful activity and worth supporting. Club members could arrange their own microcomputer education and create some new applications and equipments, which could not be created and tested during working hours.[38] The computer club had the indirect impact of creating the necessary expertise for educating company engineers on the latest information technology. Demand for this kind of activity decreased during the 1980s due to increasing education on microcomputing in schools and universities.

5. CONCLUSION: THE MICROCOMPUTER HOBBYISTS AS PLAYERS AND INVENTORS

Microcomputer hobbies as a whole were clearly a major stimulator for personal computing. The major conclusion to be drawn from this study is that computer club activity was actually a continuation of the old social and cultural features of technically oriented hobbies. Electronic hobbies and radio amateur activity played a decisive role in this development. It is also important to notice that association activity had influential traditions in Finland.

We can view the early microcomputer hobby and club activity as side product of research work dealing with microprocessor technology. All three computer clubs mentioned here had this kind of connection. A particularly strong interaction between work and hobby was established in *The Microprocessor Club of Salora Ltd*. One can say that, for the engineers of Salora Ltd, work was actually a well-developed hobby. We can see the advancements in microcomputer technology as a major reason why this kind of activity changed during 1980s. We can say that work, education, and hobby were all blended together. Computer hobbyists

---

[35] Paju 2003.
[36] Jouko Happonen and Arto Vihtosen men's interview December 19. 2000.
[37] Mikrokerhon historia, Jorma Lindell, Papers of the Microprosessor Club of Salora Ltd 30.12.1988, 2.
[38] Jouko Happonen, Arto Vihtosen interview December 19. 2000.

engaged in computer hobby thereby playing a key role in the first users' exploration of the possibilities of microcomputers. The history of these computer clubs also gives us a clear vision of how the research work and hobby use of microcomputers altered during the 1970s and the 1980s.

SOURCES

Archive sources
Papers of the Microprosessor Club of Salora Ltd. Collected by Jorma Lindell 31.12.1988. Electronic Museum of Salo -project collections

Interviews (Collected by Petri Saarikoski and Jaakko Suominen)
Åke Nyholm 20.10.2000 (Nokia Display Products, Salo)
Jouko Happonen, Arto Vihtonen 19.12.2000 (Nokia Display Products, Salo)
Pekka Ritamäki 13.12.2001 (Mikrofan, Tampere)

Literature
Bell, Clas von, LINTURI, Risto, TALA, Martti. Mikrojen 20-vuotta. ("The First 20 years of Microcomputers") Mikrotietokone Suomessa 1973-1993 ("Microcomputers in Finland 1973-1993") (9-34).Risto Linturi, Martti Tala (eds.). Yritysmikrot Oy: Helsinki 1993.
Boddy, William. Elektrovisio: Sukupuita ja sukupuolia. ("Archaeologies of Electronic Vision and the Gendered Spectator") Sähköiho, kone\media\ruumis (53-82). Erkki Huhtamo, Martti Lehti (eds.). Vastapaino: Tampere 1995.
Campbell-Kelly, Martin, Aspray, William. Computer. A History of the Information Machine. Basic Books: New York 1996.
Ceruzzi, Paul E.. A History of Modern Computing. The MIT Press: Cambridge, London 2000.
Freiberger, Paul, Swaine, Michael. Fire in the Valley. The Making of the Personal Computer. McGraw-Hill: New York 2000 (1984).
Håpnes, Tove. Not in Their Machines: How Hackers Transform Computers into Subcultural Artefacts. Making Technology Our Own? Domesticating Technology into Everyday Life (121-150). Merete Lie, Knut H. Sørensen (eds.). Scandinavian University Press Oslo 1996.
Jokela, Esko, Korkala, Jussi, Sarso, Pekka. Tietojenkäsittelyoppi. Osa 1. Laitteisto ("The Basics of Data Processing, Part 1: Hardware"). Tampere 1972.
Levy, Stephen. Hackers. Heroes of the Computer Revolution. Penguin Books New York 1994 (1984).
Nissen, Jörgen. Pojkarna vid Datorn. Unga entusiaster i Datateknikens värld. ("Boys in front of Computers. Young Enthusiasts in the World of Computer Technology"). Linköping Studies in Arts and Science no. 89. Department of Technology and Social Change. University of Linköping 1993.
Paju, Petri. Huvia hyödyn avuksi jo 1950-luvulla. Nim-pelin rakentaminen ja käyttö Suomessa. ("Interactions between work and entertainment in the 1950s. The Construction and usage of the Nim-game in Finland") Wider Screen 2-3/2003. http://www.film-o-holic.com/widerscreen/. 11.9.2003.
Pantzar, Mika. Tulevaisuuden koti: arjen tarpeita keksimässä. ("The Home of the Future. Domestication of Everyday Life") Otava: Helsinki 2000.

Saarikoski, Petri. Pioneerien leluista kulutuselektroniikaksi. Suomalainen kotimikroharrastus tietotekniikan murroksessa 1980-luvun alusta 1990-luvun puoliväliin. ("From the Toys of Pioneers to Consumer Electronics. The Cultural History of Home Computing as Hobby in Finland from the 1980s to 1990s.") Licentiate thesis, General History, University of Turku. Turku 2001.

Saarikoski, Petri. Juottelua ja heksakoodia. Kerhotoiminnan asema ja merkitys suomalaisen mikrotietokoneharrastuksen varhaiskaudella. ("Solder alloy and Hexadecimal code. The History of Finnish computer club activity in the early phases of microcomputing"). Tekniikan Waiheita 3/2003. Finnish Society for the History of Technology. 2002.

Salmi, Hannu. "Atoomipommilla kuuhun!" Tekniikan mentaalihistoriaa. ("The History of Mentality and Technology") Helsinki 1996. Edita: Helsinki 1996.

Spigel, Lynn. Make Room for TV. Television and the Family Ideal in Postwar America. University of Chicago Press: Chicago 1992.

Suominen, Jaakko. Sähköaivot sinuiksi, tietokone tutuksi. Tietotekniikan kulttuurihistoriaa. ("Getting Familiar with the Electric Brain, getting to know the Computer") Research Centre for Contemporary Culture, publication no. 67. University of Jyväskylä. Jyväskylä 2000.

Wiio, Osmo A. Mikrotietokoneet. ("Microcomputers") Mikrotietokone Suomessa 1973-1993 ("Microcomputers in Finland 1973-1993") (152-158). Martti Tienari. Suomen Atk-kustannus: Helsinki, Jyväskylä 1993.

Maganizes

IBM Katsaus 2/1965.
Prosessori 1/1979, 3/1980, 6-7/1980, 12/1981.
Tieturi 4/1982, 5/1982, 1/1983, 3/1983, 4/1983.
Tietoviikko 17.11.1983.
MikroBitti 8/1988.

CD-ROMs

Pirkanmaan mikrotietokone Mikrofan 20 vuotta ("Mikrofan - Microcomputer Club of Pirkanmaa, 20 years of activity") -CD-ROM.

MIPROC
A fast 16-bit microprocessor

Harald Yndestad

Aalesund University College; Harald.Yndestad@hials.no

Abstract: The Norwegian Defense Research Establishment was an important innovator
              of new computers, software, technology, and instrumentation in 1960s and
              1970s. One of the innovation projects was the MIPROC microprocessor.
              MIPROC had 16-bit architecture and a separated program memory to gain
              more speed. The control was based on a ROM to reduce the TTL chips
              numbers. The CPU had 75 instructions where each instruction executed in
              250 ns. The technology was an important innovation by it self. The chips
              were implemented thin-film technology. By this technology, the data
              processor was reduced to four thin-film capsules.

Key words: Microprocessors, computer hardware, MIPROC

1.   INTRODUCTION

In the period 1960 to 1980, the Norwegian Defense Research
Establishment (NDRE) was an important innovator of computers, software,
technology, and instrumentation. The most important project was the
Penguin missile. This project forced the innovation of other smaller projects
to solve instrumentation problems. One of these projects was the MIPROC
microprocessor.

Analog electronics formed the basis for the electronics used in
instrumentation. Analog electronics had fast signal processing, but at the
same time, there were some basic limitations. Hard-wired analog electronics
had no room for flexibility and the signal was influenced by noise and
temperature drift. In this period, there was a paradigm shift from analog to
digital electronics. Texas Instruments introduced the 74-series of TTL chips,

National Semiconductor introduced the 3-state bus, and Intel introduced digital RAM and ROM. These digital chips opened the possibility of making programmable electronics for signal processing. Programmable electronics solved the fundamental problems of analog electronics. It opened the possibility of storing data in a memory. From stored data in a memory, it was possible to introduce a new generation of smart signal processing, smart control, and smart decisions.

The paradigm shift to digital programmable electronics opened a new set of challenges. Signal processing in real time needed a fast processor. The CPU architecture then had to be a simple design made for fast sequential operations. In 1970 computers still needed much space and the processor had to be reduces to a small card in a Penguin missile. Implementing the computer by thin film technology solved this problem. A third problem was the software needed for special dedicated computers. To solve the software problem, it was necessary to develop an assembler, a simulator, and a high-level language. The fourth problem was making a robust mechanic realization that was able to match military specifications.

The 16-bit MIPROC (MicroPROCessor) prototype was developed in 1972. The initial project group was Harald Schiøtz (project leader), Harald Yndestad, Sigurd Myklebust, and Ole Tormod Kristiansen. The LOGSIM CAD program tested the CPU design implemented on TTL chips. MIPROC had 16-bit architecture and separate program memory to increase the speed. Most of the control was ROM based to reduce the number of TTL chips. The CPU had 80 instructions where each instruction executed in 250 ns. The technology was an important innovation by it self. Thin-film technology implemented the CPU to reduce volume and weight.

A/S Infomasjonskontroll developed an assembler and a simulator in 1973. The following year, the Norwegian Computing Center at Blindern developed the high-level language PL/MIPROC. PL/MIPROC was an Algol-like programming language connected to the CPU registers. A/S Aker Electronics in Horten produced the MIPROC microprocessor for the Norwegian market and Plessey Microsystems in England produced it for the international marked.

2.   THE MIPROC CPU ARCHITECTURE

The design of the MIPROC CPU architecture had three main targets. The first target was to implement a mini-computer instruction set which was able to handle signal processing. The second problem was developing as high speed as possible to handle fast signal processing. At the same time the power consumption had to be as low as possible.

The problem was solved by a simple 16-bit parallel CPU architecture. The CPU architecture had four basic units connected to a data bus and a control bus. This simple architecture made it possible to have simple, fast, and parallel operations. Figure 1 shows the simple 16-bit CPU architecture. The Arithmetic Unit had a 16-bit AC register and a 16-bit MQ register. Both registers connect to the 16-bit data bus. A 16-bit MAR register addresses the data memory. In this module, the RAM memory and the MAR address register connect to the CPU data bus. The control unit had a PC program counter, a RAM program memory, and a set of ROM. The ROM decoded the program code and produced the Control bus. We implemented a ROM feedback state machine to increase the multiplication speed. The In/Out unit had a control of the A/D-converters, the D/A-converters and digital in/out signals (Schiøtz, 1972; Yndestad, 1972; Schiøtz and Myklebust, 1976).

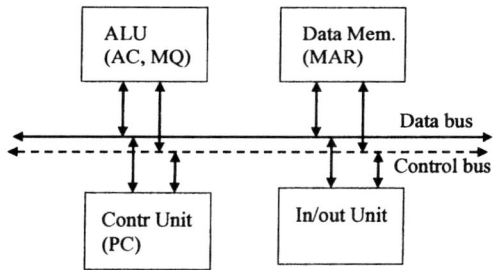

Figure 1. The MIPROC CPU Architecture.

Figure 2 shows the simple Arithmetic Unit. All logical and arithmetic operations executed in a 16-bit ALU (74181). Storage of the computed result was in the 16-bit accumulator register AC. The MQ register was a temporary register.

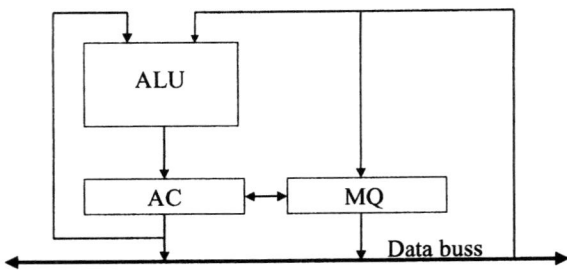

Figure 2. The Arithmetic Unit

The Arithmetic Control Unit (Figure 3) was the most complex part of the CPU. A 5 MHz oscillator clock was driving the 16-bit program counter (PC). The PC-state had a direct address control to the program memory. A set of ROM decoded the program memory code, which supported all control code to the common control bus. The CPU had separated program memory and data memory to gain speed. A separated program memory increased the speed 100%. All arithmetic operations were able to execute in a cycle time of 250 ns. A connection between the control code and the data Bus opened for a direct jump and set operations. The control unit had a micro controller to control multiplication, division, and conditional operations. The micro controller had a feedback control implementation between a register and a ROM. We designed this micro controller to gain fast multiplication and divisions. Table 1 shows the general specifications for the CPU.

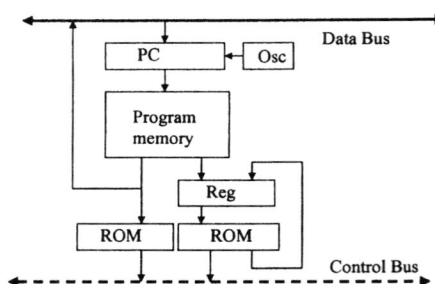

Figure 3. The Arithmetic Control Unit

Table 1: General specifications for the CPU

a) Word length	a) 16 bits
b) Maximum data memory	b) 64 K words
c) Maximum program memory	c) 64 K words
d) Maximum number inputs	d) 192
e) Maximum number outputs	e) 192
f) Basic execution time	f) 250 ns
g) Time for multiplication	g) 3.2-6.4 us
h) Time for division	h) 3.2-6.4 us
i) Number of instructions	i) 80
j) Direct data address	j) 256 words
k) Indirect data address	k) 64 K words
l) Dynamic address	l) 64 K words
m) Power supply	m) 5 v, 2 amp
n) Number TTL chips in the CPU	n) 18

3. THE MIPROC SOFTWARE

A/S Informationskontroll in Asker developed the basic MIPROC software for application development and software debugging in 1973. The MIPROC software had four main modules as shown in Figure 4. The MIPROC Assembler was the software package to transform the user software into the MIPROC instruction code. The BITSIM Simulator was a simulator of the MIPROC CPU architecture. The simulator was written in FORTRAN IV and the software was a model of the MIPROC CPU down to the bit level. This MIPROC model thus simulated all instructions and all basic CPU functions. The BITSIM Simulator linked to a WORLD Generator. The WORLD Generator was a simulation model of the external environmental that produced input signals to the MIPROC processor. The simulation model thus tested the application software on sampled real input data. USER Debug was a software package to debug application software. By special instructions in BITSIM Simulator the programmer was able to trace the state of the CPU in time periods (Risberg, 1973).

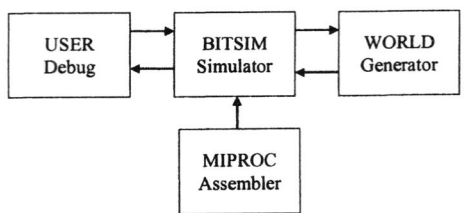

Figure 4. Simulator system

3.1   The PL/MIPROC language

The MIPROC microprocessor was designed for signal processing, which needs complex mathematical algorithms. To handle the complex algorithms, it was necessary to have a high-level language. At the same time, it was necessary to have real time control operations on the register level. The solution was an Algol-like pseudo high-level language to replace the assembly language.

PL/MIPROC was a programming language designed specifically for MIPROC. The language resembles Algol in structure, but contains data types and primitive operations, which allow the user full access to the basic functions of the MIPROC CPU. The basic structure in PL/MIPROC was the compound BEGIN...END, COMMENTS, the assignment A:=I+10, logic expressions as A:= B OR C; conditionals IF-THEN-ELSE and CASE IF; loop structures such as FOR-DO, WHILE-DO, REPEAT-UNTIL, functional PROCEDURES, and operation on memory arrays. The language was developed by Norwegian Computing Center in Oslo and was an important contribution to do programs readable, efficient and reliable (Wynn, 1974).

4.   THE HARDWARE IMPLANTATION

We implemented and produced MIPROC in a thin-film version and as a standard TTL version. The thin-film version of MIPROC was for applications where volume and weight were the ultimate problem. A complete processor had four thin-film capsules on a custom-made card (Figure 5). The arithmetic unit and the data memory were implemented on a 5 x 5 cm capsule. This capsule was probably the biggest thin film capsule ever produced. The control unit and the I/O unit were implemented on a 2.5 x 5 cm capsule.

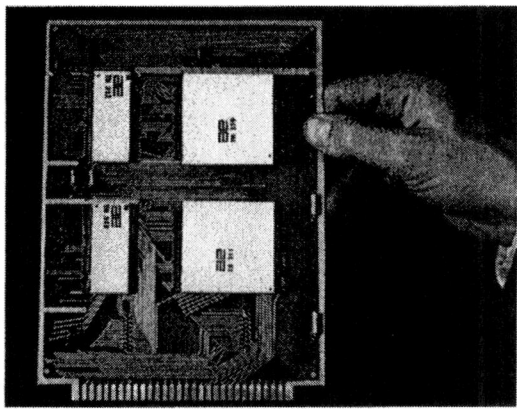

Figure 5. The MIPROC thin film version

Figure 6 shows the Standard MIPROC on a double Europe card. A Standard MIPROC was part of a number signal processing applications. Typical applications were Fast Fourier spectrum analysis, Kalman filters, and control applications. If one processor was too slow, additional processors were connected to increase the speed. NDRE at Kjeller developed the prototype and A/S Akers Electronics in Horten produced it.

Figure 6. Standard MIPROC on a double Europe card

In 1974, the Norwegian Defense sold the international production rights to Plessey Microsystems in England for one million pounds. Plessey Microsystems constructed a factory in Towcester that employed about 300 people to produce the microprocessor, software, and specialized hardware applications. The processor was produced as a standard MIPROC. The most known specialized hardware was a Fast Fourier processor. Late at the 1980s, the MIPROC 16 was advertised in American journals under the headline "The fastest microcomputer known to man."

5.   DISCUSSION

The simple parallel CPU architecture opened the possibility of making a simple, small, and powerful processor for fast signal processing in specialized instrumentation early at the 1970s. This opened the possibility of developing a new generation of electronic equipment. After the prototype period, we analyzed a new MIPROC concept to meet the next generation signal processing. This was a multi-processing systems and a processor based on ECL-technology (Yndestad, 1973; Yndestad, 1974).

The MIPROC microprocessor opened a possibility of a new export industry. In an early phase, industrial partners were interesting in producing MIPROC for the international marked. In this period, Intel and others were starting to make microprocessors with greater integration. It was clear that eventually this technology would be smaller, faster, cheaper, and more reliable. The result was that the production rights were sold to Plessey Microsystems in England and consequently never produced the next MIPROC generation. MIPROC made it possible to develop the first new generation of programmable electronics for signal processing in real time. The microprocessor thus contributed to a new generation of intelligent instrumentation before it was possible by the microprocessors from Intel and others. The new generation of digital instrumentation thus came earlier to the market.   About five to ten years later, the more integrated microprocessors replaced the MIPROC.

REFERENCES

1. Risberg, Hans: Brukerbeskrivelse MIPROC's simulatorsystem. A/S Informasjons-kontroll. Asker. 11.april 1973.
2. Schiøtz, Harald: Programmering av MIPROC. Teknisk Notat E-458. FFI. Kjeller. 1972.
3. Schiøtz, Harald and Myklebust, Sigurd: Analysis and evaluation of a revised MIPROC design. Teknisk Notat E-768. FFI. Kjeller. January 1976.
4. Wynn, Paul: PL/MIPROC. User's Guide. Norwegian Computing Center. Oslo. Publication No. 492. November 1974.
5. Yndestad, Harald: MIPROC Dataprosessor, Kretsteknisk beskrivelse. Teknisk Notat E-497. FFI. Kjeller. 15. desember 1972.
6. Yndestad, Harald: MULT_MIPROC, Et system for parallell prosessering av data. Teknisk Notat E-538. FFI. Kjeller. 12. juni 1973.
7. Yndestad, Harald: Forslag til en hurtigere versjon av MIPROC. Teknisk Notat E-600. FFI. Kjeller. 28. januar 1974.

FROM BINARY STRINGS TO VISUAL PROGRAMMING
A Nordic perspective on history of programming and programming languages

Knut Skog

NORUT Information Technologies, Science Park, Tromsø. Knut.Skog@itek.norut.no

Abstract: Starting with the events around the first von Neumann machine in 1945, this paper presents the some of the main steps in the development of programming and high level languages for instructing machinery to perform according need, ideas, or any form of stated requirements. The main emphasis is on Nordic contributions. The paper leads up to present time with the marked influence of the network and its web technology, a technology offering programming light for millions of computer owners and users. Some concern is raised as to the latest trend of regarding documents and programs as being the same notion.

Key words: Computer programming, Nordic history

1.   PROGRAMMING AND LANGUAGE

Keeping in touch with the art of computer programming for more than four decades is like standing up against an intellectual hurricane - the most forceful and rapid changing technology ever in the history of humanity. Still there is more to come. The computer is a device instructed by man to perform operations according to his will. Mostly these operations have an immaterial effect but connected to mechanical devices the operations can also cause material effects. Let us not forget that when the device is a missile the effects of the programs are potentially highly devastating.

The instructions to a computer appear in lexical forms of some artificial, formally and carefully constructed language, a language never spoken, only written by a programmer, and read by him and the computer.

Strangely enough, it is my experience that reading other peoples programs is not at all appealing. In some cases, it feels like passing the border of privacy. We write to a computer using a programming language.

The focus of this paper is on programming languages during the last forty years, and an attempt to extract what may be an essence with lasting value. Making an evaluation of the close to 150 different recognised programming languages of this period is impossible. At this occasion, I narrow my focus to the Nordic scenes and its pioneers. The field of programming is so large that I can only ask forgiveness if the reader feels that I have ignored important events.

People have a natural talent for creating languages that reflects his environment. This became apparent when they tried to build a tower in Babel, reaching Heaven. We read in Genesis (11:1-9.) "But God confounded their tongue, so that they did not understand one another's speech". Like the people of Babel, computer programmers do not always understand each other. However, as long as computers do, a language is valuable. Some will say that all these languages have enriched the computer industry whereas other will claim it has been a curse.

The history of computing and computer languages is prevalent. A link to thumbnails of the history of programming languages appears in [CompHist].

2.   IN THE BEGINNING

Instructing mechanical counting machinery to perform their data processing task happened long before World War II. Lady Lovelace's program for calculating Bernoulli numbers on Babbage's Analytical Engine is a well-known example. Ten years before the first electronic computer with modifiable stored program was running, Allan Turing [Turing] presented many of the theoretical aspects of computing in his description of a universal finite state transition machine. However, the focus on programming - as we know it today - starts with von Neumann's work on the EDVAC (Electronic Discrete Variable Automatic Calculator) in 1945. We stress the word *variable* since it denotes the flexibility of this electronic device. It is also a reflection of the modern notion of a computer that in von Neumann's mind, *in itself should be able to modify its program*. His idea of heuristic aspects of computers appears in many of his later papers. (See his lectures on "Theory of self-reproducing automata" in [Burks], Chapter 11.)

[Burks] has well-documented von Neumann's contributions to computer programming. This reference also contains a remarkable paper, "von Neumann's first computer program", written by Donald E. Knuth

[Burks, chapter 2]. Von Neumann wrote this sorting and merging programs in 1945 as part of design of the EDVAC computer, a machine that at that stage had an auxiliary memory of 8192 words of 32 bits. Note however that it was not possible to access randomly the memory of EDVAC. The kind of programming challenges von Neumann was facing we know today as micro coding. Despite many low-level type of operations, his work for the first time introduced the basic programming notion of a subroutine using relative addresses and symbolic coding with mnemonic names of variables and instructions. He was a frequent user of flow diagrams in planning the structure of his programs.

Deeply rooted in the world of mathematics his systems analysis was in mathematical notation and the resulting program in a form that we call *assembly coding* as can be seen in the extract below from Donald E. Knuth's paper.

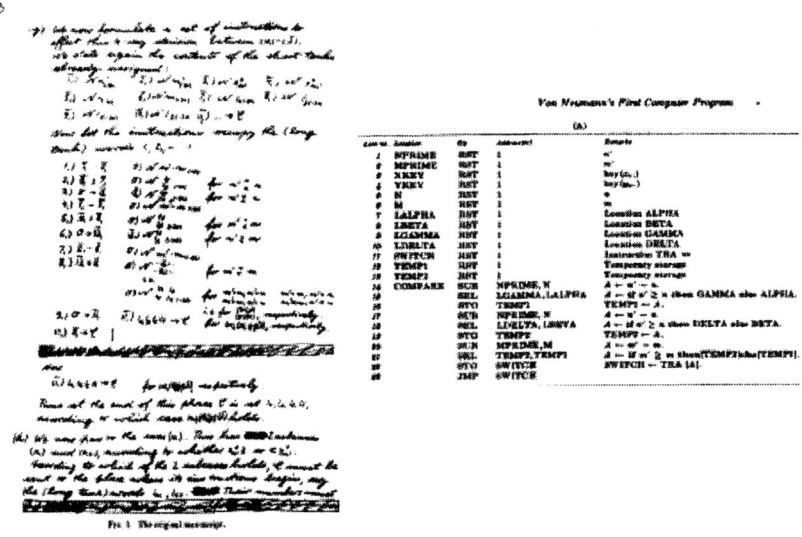

It is fair to say that programming at this stage was regarded as a type of work requiring deep insight in the architecture and behaviour of the computer and its binary nature. People considered it a craft for a person trained in logic and mathematics. Von Neumann himself was, however, one of the first that suggested key board shortcuts for denoting patterns in the binary string of a instruction instead of writing sequences of 1 and 0. He started the era of programming in the form of *assembly coding*.

3.   THE FIRST PROGRAMMING LANGUAGES

In the middle of the fifties, IBM had made its Naval Ordnance Research Calculator (NORC), the most powerful computer in existence at the time. It was a vacuum tube machine with 3600 words of main memory and binary coded decimal arithmetic operations. This machine was part of the environment in which John Backus and his team of programmers invented FORTRAN (FORmula TRANslator), the first programming language in which the human or problem domain was the prime focus and where the computer itself translated the scripts of the language into binary instructions and numbers. This translation required a program of a new kind, compilers as they where called. The FORTRAN compiler was able to produce code almost as efficient as assembly code and they reduced programming time considerably. People say that when John Backus presented the idea of a compiled programming language to von Neumann, his reaction was not at all enthusiastic. In his mind, a computer should do calculations and not such clerical tasks as compiling.

The FORTRAN was targeted for scientific and numeric calculations and loved by scientists who could write formulas the way they where used to. It offered two name scopes (local and global) for variables, familiar mathematical ways of writing expressions and intuitively natural statements for loops and conditional branching. Later separately compiled subroutines were added. The extensive growth in the programmer population in the sixties and the seventies is mainly due to FORTRAN. As member of the committee that created ALGOL a few years later, John Backus introduced the syntax notation that, slightly modified by Naur, to day is known as Backus Naur Form (BNF).

It is symptomatic that John Backus and his work did not come out of a university research environment. His own background was highly irregular. IBM management of his time deserves credit for supporting his diverse and eclectic bunch of people that was outsiders to the academic establishments and hackers of its time. John Backus and his team of programmers new from hard work what was needed and created the first and for a long time the most used higher level programming language.

The need for programming tools closer to the problem domain was generally acknowledge in the late fifties and in 1958, the first version of the Algorithmic Language ALGOL was borne. Two years later the language was the target of international cooperation and an agreement on ALGOL60 was a fact much due to the work at Dansk Regnecentral and with Peter Naur as the supreme editor putting all pieces together. ALGOL was the first programming language of a scientific flavour. It was an orthogonal language, meaning it has a relatively small number of basic constructs and a set of rules for combining those constructs. It introduced nested (block-structured) scopes of names, strongly typed variables, procedure parameters by name or reference, and recursive procedures and dynamic arrays. In close cooperation with the Dutch ALGOL group (Dijkstra, van der Pool, van Wijngaarden), Naur, Jørn Jensen and the Danish group pioneered the stack for dynamic memory management and its addressing schema for recursive execution.

Although ALGOL never reached the level of commercial popularity of FORTRAN, it is considered the most important language in terms of its influence on later language development. ALGOL's lexical and syntactic structures became so popular that virtually all languages designed since have been referred to as "ALGOL-like". On the Nordic scene, Peter Naur and Jørn Jensen (in the compiler team of 1962, they where called the Doctor and the Master) made substantial contribution to our conception of high level programming languages and the associated compiling techniques.

Automated data processing was an established industry of its own at the time the first variable (stored program) automatic calculator was born, made for numeric calculations, not for data processing. However, when they connected the calculator to punched card equipment and magnetic tapes, the "calculator" was ready for *data processing*. For this task, the quest for non-mathematical programming tools came at the end of the fifties.

From the home page of COBOL we quote:

> In 1959, an industry-wide team was assembled to formulate a common business programming language. The Conference on Data System Languages (CODASYL) developed a new language, and created the first standardized business computer programming language. COBOL (Common Business Oriented Language) was developed under the auspices of the U.S. Department of Defence in cooperation with computer manufactures, users, and universities. The initial specifications for COBOL were presented in a report of the executive committee of CODASYL committee in April of 1960. It was designed to be a business problem oriented, machine independent and capable of continuous change and development.

COBOL with its highly verbose lexical style was the first effort in creating exact computer programs with statements that intuitively could be understood by humans. The idea of instructing the computer the same way you instruct people is ill founded. However, as with native languages, people who once have learned them tend to love them and COBOL is still a living programming language in many commercial applications with roots back to the late sixties and the seventies.

4.   OBJECT ORIENTATION

With SIMULA 67, a new dimension – the dimension of object orientation (OO) – was added to the art of programming. SIMULA was originally designed as a language for discrete event simulation, but was soon regarded as a general purpose programming language. ALGOL like and like ALOGOL SIMULA never became widely used, however the language has been highly influential on programming methodology and modern systems engineering. It implemented the mechanics of OO and paved the way for a new systems design philosophy. It invented the notion and mechanics of the class concept with inheritance and polymorphism, object instantiations and dynamic heap allocation. In this it broke the traditional sequential way of reasoning on how the computer programs should be organized and demonstrated how to "think and write" in terms of parallel event-driven tasks. It formed what to day is the foundation for modelling of computer applications at large.

[Holmvik] thoroughly documents the history of the work of Kristen Nygaard and Ole Johan Dahl and their colleagues at Norsk Regnesentral on SIMULA 67. Being myself affiliated with the activity in the period from the fall of 1965 to 1968, I feel inclined to present some of my recollections. One is that Bjørn Myrhaug, a junior member of the SIMULA team, deserves recognition for his pioneering implementation work on heap allocation and "garbage" collection.

In the fall of 1965, I was working at the Computer Laboratory at the Technical University of Norway in Trondheim. At that time, like Norsk Regnesentral, their mainframe compute was a UNIVAC machine. That machine replaced the GIER ALGOL computer that left a large community of scientists and students, trained as ALGOL programmers, in the FORTRAN desert. Based upon a strong request for an ALGOL service, my own scientific interests and experience in compiler writing from Dansk Regnesentral and Control Data Corp., an implementation of ALGOL on the UNIVAC machine started in early 1966. Since SIMULA was ALGOL++, it was agreed that our compiler should be expanded in due time to include the SIMULA capabilities.

As it turned out this effort was like shooting at a moving target. The SIMULA specifications were constantly changing and not ready when we had to make important decisions on the compiler side. However, the compiler was organized in a very open table driven manner in order to cope with the not yet seen capabilities, hoping that whatever the requirements where, they could be handled by adding new entries to the tables. In Trondheim, we completed the regular ALGOL implementation and shipped the compiler source code to the SIMULA team for additions. That this created some pain is rather obvious. The date for the completion of the SIMULA 67 implementation on the UNIVAC computer is not quite clear but my guess is late 1970 early 1971.

Alan Kay first recognized the real substance and importance of the new model and associated programming concepts that SIMULA brought in the outside world (US). The history of science is full of cases where the implication of scientific research is not fully recognized in its time. I dear say that even Kristen Nygaard, who was a man not known for muting his opinions, did not realize the importance and impact of their work at the time it was done.

Alan Kay took the SIMULA concepts into his Smalltalk language at XEROX Park and this again had a substantial influence on the development in programming and programming languages in the states. James Gosling at SUN picked up many of Smalltalk's capabilities when he developed the NeWS (network-extensible window system) in the late 1980s. This work was the foundation for the JAVA language in the early 1990s.

Bjarne Stroustrup at BELL Labs, an exiled Dane, created C++ by adding the object oriented language elements of SIMULA to the C language of the UNIX world, very much a creation of Kernighan and Ritchie. C was born early in the 1970s and was probably the most used systems programming language in the early 1980s. By extending it, Bjarne Stroustrup brought object-orientation to systems programming. C++ is by far the most used low-level systems programming language of to day. Being an unsafe language with many low level characteristics like loose typing and dynamic memory allocation in the hand of the programmer with the risk of creating memory leaks, the cost of risky programming is no longer justified in terms of faster code. One may wonder why maturity sometimes comes slowly as we see the newly born C#, an offspring of Microsoft, finally offer automatic garbage collection and strong typing to its users.

Bjarne Stroustrup's achievement was to give systems programmer an object-oriented tool within their "native language" framework C. It was an effort right in time and on the right spot. It is difficult to envision modern commercial software without C++.

There is a straight line from SIMULA to the unified modelling language (UML) of today. However, probably the most fundamental effect of the language is realizing that it led us to the most fundamental notion of computer science *Abstract Data Types* (ADT), the basic building block of computer programming. The SIMULA class is the concrete implementation of ADT and the truest reflection of the formal definition of the word data. The Object Management Group is now the most vivid forum of the SIMULA heritage.

A breakthrough of a philosophical nature – how to reason and how to support this reasoning with programming constructs – is not or will never be recognized by commercial measures. The conceptual and philosophical contribution to computer science made by Nygaard and Dahl in the middle of the 1960s is in my opinion equally important as von Neumann's in the middle of the 1940s.

5. MODERN TIMES

A new area in computing started when Transmission Control Protocol/Internet Protocol (TCP/IP) became the de-facto standard for networked computing. From local area computing to world wide web (www) computing is a mayor brake from closely related development steps starting with von Neumann "variable calculator" ending with timeshared mainframe computers in the late 1980s. With hundreds of millions of computers on the net, reaching into schools, offices, homes, cars, almost anywhere within reach of even modest communication services, computers are effecting the population of the world in ways no one could imagine ten to fifteen years ago. Before approaching the network impacts on programming, let us split the notion of programming in non-professional programming and commercial professional programming.

The use of modern devices like mobile telephones, television sets, kitchen stoves, etc. require people without training to perform simple programming in operating these computerized gadgets. The combination of complexity and flexibility of things spread in quantities of hundreds of millions throughout the world is unparalleled in our history. Closest comes the car costing 100 times more with a much simpler task (move from here to there) to perform. In its simplest form, millions of people unconsciously do non-professional programming simply by operating menus and setting options.

The trend of reaching out to the novice programmer with lightweight programming tools like Basic, Visual Basic, and XBasic continues and is a consequence of a highly flexible device being a mass-market commodity. There are simply not enough highly trained people for adapting computer technology to applications. Providing tools for adaptation in so-called user-friendly programming manners is not to be underestimated. For certain applications, tailored light programming environments has proven to be extremely successful.

Turning our attention to professional programming, the role of the programming language as such is becoming more and more integrated with its environment. It is simply not enough to type and edit statements in your favourite plain text editor and turn it to its compiler. The reason is that we can hardly make any application without extensive use of components.

Managing these component libraries in the development process is necessary for a reliable and cost effective development. Component based application frequently involves very large quantities of code and requires tools for maneuvering, displaying, and versioning as important mechanics of the programming environment.

6. PROGRAMMING OF OUR TIME

To navigate within all of the source code of a modern application the code itself must be kept in html like document format in which links to components and modules is the prime navigation tool. The transition from plain program text to an html-formatted form is far more than "pretty printing". It is an indispensable function of program manipulation and reading. Of the total effort spent in applications programming, 80% goes into maintenance, frequently handled by other persons than those who initially wrote the programs. The readability of a program frequently depends on comments in the code itself. The problem of keeping commentaries consistent with the code is well known. The best remedy here is to stay away from low level programming styles letting the code speak for itself.

It is my opinion that the programming language issue of our time gives us only to alternatives for commercial developers: Java and C#. To my knowledge, these are the only fully commercially supported languages and environments for professional development. C# is the latest on the arena, though not the forerunner. Major developments on the environment side of these systems are likely to come. This change all relates to managing component growth and integration by sharing concentrated and distributed resources through the network.

6.1 Document program and data

Keeping track of the latest trends in network application development is an interesting challenge. There is a tendency to regard document and program as equivalent notions. The simple reasoning seems to be that a program is data, document is data, and therefore, a program is a document. This seems very harmless, but it has some serious consequences.

First, let us recall that data is a "representation of ideas or facts in a manner suitable for some process" (IFIP definition). For a document, the process for which the representation shall be suitable is ultimately a human reader, or listener for that sake, where as for the program the suitable representation is ultimately for the computer to execute. However, the matter becomes complicated by the fact that humans also read a program and for that purpose, it should be well documented. Here the computer is an assistant.

The same is true for a modern digital document that a computer reads, or rather processes, to make it neatly readable and easy maneuverable. The only problem with our equation is that it makes a computer and a human identical in terms of representational requirements for their processing needs. This is in my opinion fundamentally wrong. So where does this philosophical reasoning bring us. What impact does it make and where?

Librarians are professional document workers. In the early 1970s, they introduced the Standard Generalized Markup Language (SGML), the first markup language, now an ISO 8879 standard. They developed it for adding computer detectable content structures to a document.

The development of web servers and network readers/browsers adapted the markup method to apply to documents that are typeset and linked. The Markup Language (ML) of what we call e-documents is HTML where HT stands for Hyper Text. Together with the *Multipurpose Internet Mail Extensions* (MIME) standard, HTML and TCP/IP (with domain name services) are the cornerstones of the Web and its grate success. Hypertext is a multimedia network integration facility that offers interactive (active server pages) capabilities in which the reader may deliver (write) data for processing. This e-document is far more potent than ordinary paper documents. No wonder a blur exists between program and document distinctions.

To follow up this success the www Consortium (W3C) has generalised html into eXtendable Markup Language (XML). In this language the low-level extensions occurs in a document type definition (DTD) notation and at higher level by XMLSchemas. The XMLSchemas offer a data structuring capability in which primitive built-in data types such as date, time, string, decimal, integer, and float become building blocks for composed data structures. There is no means for defining operations. The basic idea is that a XML document is data structured by markups. We do not state the processing aspect of this data, however; the marks receive mnemonic names to indicate intuitively the meaning for a human reader. By lookup in name-servers at URLs, we can inspect and interpret the XMLSchema for tags.

6.2   Reflections

XML is the promised new way of exchanging data among web processes using the hypertext transport protocol (http). It is a character-encoded vehicle for interoperability and is a working well for small volumes of data. However, we should not take its scalability for granted.

There are three reasons for my deeply founded skepticisms. First, methods for the computer process itself are left out. By that, we are defining a document primarily for human interpretation. This human is faced with the task of using his tag interpretation in order to make the exchange understood. Second, with increasing volume and complexity, the XML exchange will hardly be looked at with a bare eye. The reader will most likely use a tag interpretational service anyway. Third, the volume of the verbose XML format, even when compressed, is substantially larger than for anything seen so far. Even with constantly increasing transmission speeds, there will always be bottlenecks, in particular in mobile communication.

Hence, the rapidly growing and extremely potent web community does not seem to recognise the basic difference between document and program. In particular, they do not adhere to the object-oriented philosophy. Consequently, the golden rule of striving for orthogonal design and conceptual economy seems to be dropped. In addition, the tendency of modelling by defining exchange formats seems to be the new trend. A most striking example is the vocabulary for the exchange of geo spatial data define in the XML dialect called Geography Markup Language (GML3.0). The number of tags introduced for this application has passed 1000. The appendix of this paper gives an example of part of a GML exchange packet.

7. VISUAL PROGRAMMING

At the end of this jumpy tour through the first fifty years of computer programming, I would like to return to the "programming light" issue. The volume of new code created by non-professional programmers today by far out-weights that of the professionals. In my notion of programming, I include the craft of "html blacksmiths" – also called web-masters and web-typographers. Tools available for web publishing in multimedia forms, with active animated and interactive page areas, offer a kind of visual select and paste type of programming by which they build many networked applications. They may even give the reader (or should we say the client) means of data input (menu selection, radio button, text-fields, etc.) which when sent to application servers, interacts with databases and depositories of various kinds, and returns requested information to the client.

Obviously, there will never be enough professionals to create all the home pages on the net. It is a fact that people trained as web designers, with no programming education, are capable of producing impressive active documents, in which some kind of interpretative programming (scripting) activated through the common gateway interface (CGI) is giving great flexibility on the client side. Hence, for the new generation of light programmers, the time when programming was writing compiled code is gone. The masses of light programmers claim their rights and they will most likely grow in capabilities with the advancements of supporting development environments. These environments are as themselves visual.

8.   FROM UML TO EXECUTABLES

To deal with the server side challenges with interfaces to databases which themselves could be part of a networked service, the developer are still required to master a complete general purpose heavy duty programming language as the integration method for components used.   More than anything else, the network technology has created a major change in our conception and understanding of the notion of both programs and documents and even the computer itself. "The network is the computer" was a saying at SUN late in the 1980s. Today it is reality. We may call it by different names, but system design and implementation of today is network oriented. Adding this dimension to the object-oriented approach making what we could call networked object orientation and tying it to our overall modelling work, is the requirements of heavy-duty programming of our time.

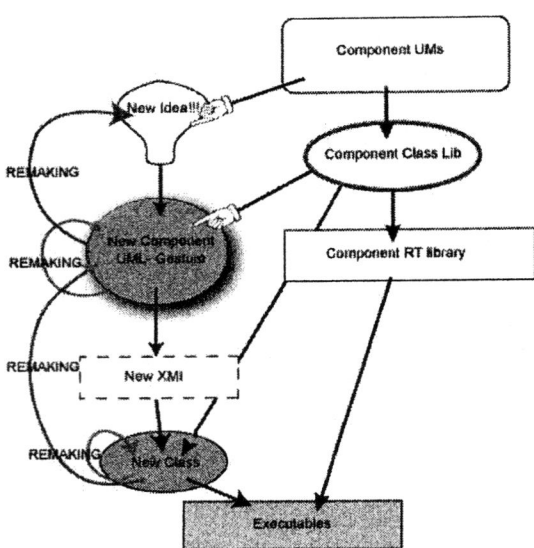

The previous diagram is just to stress that programming as the task of creating executable code for applications is confined to input from a modelling activity and from component libraries. To implement any new idea of real substance, the developer must make his selection of supporting component libraries that at the final stage merge with his own programs. From gestures or diagrams for which the current gospel is named Unified Modelling Language (UML), formalized specifications are transferred to the programming stage through the XML Metadata Interchange (XMI) format. However, the process remains to be a chain of iterations and remaking. Maintaining these iterations by the environments of system development is another great challenge of our trade.

REFERENCES

[CompHist] http://www.levenez.com/lang/
[Turing] "On computable numbers, with an application to the Entscheidungsproblem", Allan Turing, London Mathematical Society, ser. 2. vol. 42 (1936-7), pp.230-265.
[Burks]: W. Aspray and A. Burks (ed): *Papers of John von Neumann on computing and computer theory*, Charles Babbage Institute, reprint series for the history of computing, volume 12. The MIT Press, Cambridge Massachusetts, London.
[Holmvik]: http://java.sun.com/people/jag/SimulaHistory.html

APPENDIX

The following is an example of geographic data represented in the Geography ML format, an application of XML with application specific data structures define as XMLSchemas at specific name server URLs. The genuine data values represented in this packet is given in bold for ease of readability. Colon prefixed names refer to namespace assigned to the prefix (gml) in the head of this package extending the XML namespace (xmlns:gml="http://www.opengis.net/gml").

```
<gml:featureMember>
  <SchoolDistrict>
    <gml:name>District 28</gml:name>
    <gml:boundedBy>
      <gml:Box srsName="http://www.opengis.net/gml/srs/epsg.xml#4326">
        <gml:coord><gml:X>0</gml:X><gml:Y>0</gml:Y></gml:coord>
        <gml:coord><gml:X>50</gml:X><gml:Y>40</gml:Y></gml:coord>
      </gml:Box>
    </gml:boundedBy>

    <schoolMember>
      <School>
        <gml:name>Alpha</gml:name>
        <address>100 Cypress Ave.</address>
        <gml:location>
          <gml:Point srsName="http://www.opengis.net/gml/srs/epsg.xml#4326">
            <gml:coord><gml:X>20.0</gml:X><gml:Y>5.0</gml:Y></gml:coord>
          </gml:Point>
        </gml:location>
      </School>
    </schoolMember>

    <gml:extentOf>
      <gml:Polygon srsName="http://www.opengis.net/gml/srs/epsg.xml#4326">
        <gml:outerBoundaryIs>
          <gml:LinearRing>
            <gml:coord><gml:X>0</gml:X><gml:Y>0</gml:Y></gml:coord>
            <gml:coord><gml:X>50</gml:X><gml:Y>0</gml:Y></gml:coord>
            <gml:coord><gml:X>50</gml:X><gml:Y>40</gml:Y></gml:coord>
            <gml:coord><gml:X>0</gml:X><gml:Y>0</gml:Y></gml:coord>
          </gml:LinearRing>
        </gml:outerBoundaryIs>
      </gml:Polygon>
    </gml:extentOf>
  </SchoolDistrict>
</gml:featureMember>
```

FERRANTI MERCURY AT THE NORWEGIAN DEFENCE RESEARCH ESTABLISHMENT

T. William Olle

T. William Olle Associates, 2 Ashley Park Road, Walton on Thames, Surrey KT12 1JU, England; BillOlle@aol.com

Abstract: This paper presents the author's experience in using what was probably the first commercially available stored program electronic digital computer used in the Nordic countries, namely the Ferranti Mercury installed at NDRE in August 1957. It describes the computer hardware and what came much later to be called the system software.

Key words: Ferranti Mercury, Norwegian Defence Research Establishment, machine language programming, Jan Garwick, SHAPE Air Defence Technical Centre

1.   PERSONAL BACKGROUND

I started work at the SHAPE Air Defence Technical Centre (SADTC) in The Hague in The Netherlands in July 1957. The advertisement for the post in the well-known monthly magazine "Nature" in February 1957 stipulated a requirement for a postgraduate degree and experience in programming a digital computer. There were not too many people around at thee time who could meet that requirement.

Dr. Jan V. Garwick conducted the interview for this post. Garwick was on loan to SADTC from the Norwegian Defence Research Establishment (NDRE) and spending six months with SADTC, prior to the delivery to NDRE of the Ferranti Mercury. By the time I started at SADTC, Jan Garwick had returned to NDRE in order to be there when they delivered the Ferranti Mercury. Although Ferranti had promised delivery much earlier, delays in those days were very typical.

My four years of programming experience had taken place at Manchester University using the Ferranti Mark 1 computer, which was a forerunner of the Ferranti Mercury and which claimed to be the first commercially available computer delivered in the world when it was installed at the University in 1951. Only two Mark 1 computers were made (the other went to the University of Toronto in Canada, which I also used in connection with a summer vacation job in 1955). The upgrade, referred to as the Mark 1*, was in fact sold to seven customers, two of which were exported from the UK.

SADTC did not have its own computer in 1957, or indeed until 1959. The first two programming jobs, which I undertook after joining SADTC, used the Ferranti Mark 1 at Manchester University. When Jan Garwick returned for another period in The Hague starting some time during 1958, it was for two years. I remember that he and I did an informal evaluation of computer resources in the Netherlands, which could be used for SADTC's scientific work that was often highly classified. The results of this evaluation turned out to be disappointing. There were indeed computers in use in the Netherlands, but these were mainly commercial machines. (In those days, there was a very clear distinction between scientific and commercial computers. This lasted until the seminal announcement of the IBM360 series in March 1964.)

Against the background of this informal evaluation, Jan Garwick did no difficulty in convincing the SADTC management that any computing work that we did should be done on the Ferranti Mercury at Kjeller, near Lillestrpm about 25 kilometers east of Oslo. Even though Kjeller was a difficult journey from The Hague, the machine was obviously superior and machine time was readily available. NDRE was anxious to sell time and the all-important security facilities were well in place.

2.   MERCURY HARDWARE

Manchester University and Ferranti Ltd (which were also based in Manchester) built on their experience with the Mark 1 and Mark 1*. As described by Simon Lavington in his excellent book on *Early British Computers* written in 1980, development started at Manchester University in 1951 on a prototype called MEG (megacycle engine). We should note that the MEG used cathode ray tube storage (widely known as the Williams tube after the inventor). The MEG ran its first program in May 1954.

The Ferranti Mercury was announced in late 1954. It had a number of significant improvements over its two predecessors, namely the Mark 1 and Mark 1*, the most important of which was floating-point arithmetic. It has frequently been asserted in Manchester that the Mercury was the first machine in the world to provide floating-point arithmetic. Having personally struggled for four years with the fixed-point arithmetic of the Mark 1, floating-point arithmetic was much appreciated.

The high speed memory was based on magnetic core technology rather than the cathode ray tube based technology of the Mark 1, Mark 1* and MEG. The Mercury had a very much-increased speed. It was generally claimed to be 20 times faster than the Mark 1 and consumed half as much electrical power, even though it was still a "valve" machine.

Jan Garwick had taken the bold step in 1954 of persuading NDRE to order a Ferranti Mercury based on its paper specifications. This was what came to be known subsequently as a "paper machine". The machine that Garwick ordered was to be the first machine off the production line. It is not clear what the delivery date promised for the machine was at the time it was ordered, but it was not delivered until August 1957.

To get some indication of the development between 1951 and 1957, it is interesting to compare some of the technical specifications of the Ferranti Mercury with those of its predecessor the Mark 1. [1, 5] Both had a 40-bit word length. However, the Mercury 40-bit word was divided into a 10-bit exponent and a 30-bit mantissa.

Both used a 5-bit character code that went with the five-channel paper tape input that many computers of the time inherited from the telex code and equipment. Both used a magnetic drum as what was then called "backing store". (In those days, the English used the word "store" and Americans used "memory").

Both had cathode ray tubes on the console. Both provided a paper tape punch as well as a character printer for output. These devices were inherited from the world of telex communications. Another significant similarity was that both had index registers (referred to as B-registers on the Mark 1) which were used to modify the address to which an instruction referred. The Mark 1 was the first machine to provide this capability. In early 1950, the Cambridge EDSAC was the first machine in the world to provide a regular computing service and it did not have B-registers.

The two fundamental advances from the Mark 1 to the Mercury were the use of core storage and the floating-point arithmetic. The Mercury instruction set provided facilities for both fixed-point arithmetic and floating-point arithmetic. The average time for a fixed-point addition and multiplication on the Mark 1 were 0.67 and 6.00 milliseconds respectively. The corresponding times for the Mercury were 60 and 210 microseconds respectively. The Mercury's time for floating point addition was 180 microseconds and for multiplication 360 microseconds.

Before leaving the topic of hardware, it is useful to note that the physical size of the Mercury was about one-third the size of the Mark 1. This, of course, was an important consideration for the amount of floor space that was needed and also the amount of air conditioning. Mercury consumed 12 kW of power compared with 25 kW for the Mark 1.

3.   MERCURY SYSTEM SOFTWARE

The term "software" had not yet quite made it across the Atlantic by 1957. Concepts such as batch processing, supervisor programs, and operating systems had yet to evolve. Even the term "symbolic assembly language" had not quite arrived.

The term used in those days to refer to what was needed to input a program was "input routine". The established practice with Ferranti computers (such as the Mark 1 and Mark 1*) was for the organization purchasing the machine to develop its own input routine. For instance, Manchester University had its own input routine. The Ferranti Mark 1 at the University of Toronto in Canada had a different input routine. To run a Manchester program on the Toronto machine (as I did in the summer of 1955), it was necessary first to feed in the Manchester input routine and store in on the magnetic drum storage and then "booting" this input routine before feeding in the tapes containing the Manchester programs.

The term "bootstrap" was used for the few lines of code necessary to read the input routine from the drum into fast storage, so that it in turn could input other programs. "Bootstrap" and hence "booting" must be the oldest in computer terminology as it was always necessary to boot up the machine, which meant entering the input routine.

At Manchester University, the input routine for the Mark 1 did very little apart from reading the tapes into the machine and storing the blocks of code on to the drum. The fast store addresses to which an instruction referred would be machine addresses as used by the machine itself. However, the availability of B-registers meant that we could modify these addresses prior to execution by adding the content of the B-register to the address that was being referenced.

The task, which occupied Jan Garwick before the delivery of the Mercury to NDRE, was to develop an input routine, bearing in mind that this was the first Mercury delivered anywhere. Ole Johann Dahl ably assisted Garwick in this work and together they designed and implemented a system and wrote a handbook [2]

Since the NDRE Mercury was as indicated the first machine, he suggested to Ferranti's that the subsequent Mercury's could use the same input routine. For whatever reason, Ferranti did not accept this suggestion and they produced an input routine [3] that was used on the remainder of the production line [4].

I personally never used the Ferranti input routine and am not in a position to compare the merits of the two. Garwick was certainly upset that Ferranti had not used the development by Dahl and himself. However, sometime later possibly around 1960 after Garwick had returned to NDRE from SADTC, SADTC discovered that there was more machine time available on the Ferranti Mercury at the University of London. I ran application programs there that had been developed in Norway using the Garwick and Dahl's input routine without any difficulty on the London machine. This was an early example of what we now call "portability"!

I had to learn how to use the so-called Norwegian input routine by studying (in The Hague) the handbook [2] written by Jan Garwick and Ole-Johan Dahl. The principles learned in over four years of experience with the machine code of the Mark 1 helped, but there were significant differences. For what was usually highly complex computation work, the floating-point arithmetic was a tremendous help.

Furthermore, it was no longer necessary to refer to machine level addresses in a program, as it was possible to create symbolic variables that the input routine would subsequently assign to a physical address. The programming was by no means equivalent to an Autocode or higher-level language, but it was much easier than working with physical addresses in the high-speed memory.

4. COMMERCIAL SUCCESS OF MERCURY

As previously indicated, the NDRE Mercury was the very first to be delivered. Even Manchester University, who had been responsible for the design of the prototype MEG, did not get their machine until three months later. One of the major scientific applications of the era was atomic energy work and indeed, one of the main users of the BDRE machine was the Norwegian Atomic Energy organization.

However, according to reference [4], atomic energy authorities in UK, France, Switzerland (CERN), Sweden, Belgium, and Venezuela followed the pioneering path of Norway by installing a Ferranti Mercury. In all, nineteen Ferranti Mercury machines were installed around the world. Reference [4] indicates that four of these (all outside the UK) were still in use as late as 1970. Reference [5] indicates that the Manchester University Mercury was in use until 1963. Reference [6] suggests that the motivation to develop Simula on a machine that was more widely used (namely the Univac 1100 series) lead to the acquisition of such a machine and possibly the end of the NDRE Ferranti Mercury.

REFERENCES

[1] "Early British Computers" by Simon H. Lavington. 1980   Published by Manchester University Press. ISBN 0-7190-0810-7

[2] "Programmer's Handbook for the Ferranti Mercury Computer Frederic at the Norwegian Defence Research Establishment" by Ole-Johann Dahl and Jan V. Garwick. 1958. Published by   Norwegian Defence Research Establishment.

[3] "An input routine for the Ferranti Mercury computer" by J.A. Fotheringham and M. de V Roberts. Published in The Computer Journal Volume 1 Issue 3, pp 128-131.

[4] "Sales of Ferranti Mercury computers"   Extract   from   "The   Ferranti   Computer Department -   an informal history"   by B.B. Swann 1975. See National Archive for History of Computing, catalogue NAHC/FER/C30.

[5] "MEG/Mercury".   University of Manchester   Department of Computer Science. <http://www.com[uter50.org/kgill/mercury/mercury.html>

[6] "Historia om det norske progammeringssprΔket Simula." Jan Rune Holmvik.   1994 <www.nifu.no/Fpol/4-95/art7.html>

MAKING COMPUTING AVAILABLE

Norman Sanders

*Formerly at the Computing Centre, The Norwegian Technical University, Trondheim,
Norway; Norman_Sanders@compuserve.com*

Abstract: The Computing Centre of the Norwegian Technical University was established
               in January 1963, with a staff of 1.5 people and a small Danish computer,
               GIER. By mid-1965, it had grown to a staff of 25 with a large-scale computer,
               using the computing facilities at night as a service bureau to pay salaries.
               Training courses were instituted into the established schedule; operations were
               made highly efficient; real-life applications contributed to a non-academic
               appreciation of computers; the computing service was spread all across the
               campus, and many people had a lot of fun.

Key words: University computing, computer management, training, pioneering, GIER

1.   INTRODUCTION

This seminar is about using computers, and we are hearing about an
impressive range of applications that were developed as early as fifty years
ago during the Golden Age of Computers. From the very start there seemed
to be no limit to the ideas that computers spawned – mathematics,
engineering, manufacturing, finance, management and so on. No one was in
charge. No one pontificated on what we should or should not do. Everyone
with an idea was welcome on board; you did not need any formal
qualifications. All you needed to do to get it all going was to make the
computer available, and this is what we tried to do here at Norges Tekniske
Høgskole (NTH) as with all the other organisations represented here these
days.

However, how do you make a computer available? One way might be to open the computer room door and announce to anyone who might be passing, "Roll up folks; here it is. Just come on in and make yourself at home. Last one to finish locks up and drops the key through my front door". That's one way of making computers available. Though often used in those days, it's known as the not terribly brilliant way of running a computing centre, so we tried something different.

This talk is about how we did it, in our own sweet way, as opposed to how anyone else might have done it. The details depended very much on our particular circumstances, the way NTH was organised, the people involved, their academic interests, and so on. Moreover, since I was ultimately responsible for trying to bring the many varied interests together, this talk is inevitably rather personal, starting by stating that I had never been to Trondheim before, could not speak the language, did not know anything about the structure of NTH, its culture, or its members. I knew absolutely nothing and was therefore admirably suited to the job.

2.   THE BEGINNINGS

I arrived in Trondheim on a very cold January day in 1963, straight from Seattle via Los Angeles, without a stitch of warm clothing. The computer was Danish. It had 1 K words of core, a 12,800-word drum, no tape or printer; and it had a wooden door. I thought it was the broom closet. It had an Algol compiler, but I was a FORTRAN man. The staff consisted of a secretary, Sidsel Rom, and a post-graduate, Knut Skog, who was just about to leave. I had only known one Norwegian before my arrival, Ole Hestvik of the Control Engineering Department. It was overall a sobering prospect.

I was on leave of absence from Boeing, and was expected to return by April 1965. By that time, however, Regnesentret had become an establishment of about 25 people, with a giant Univac 1107 on its way (so we thought) from St. Paul, Minnesota, and computing had spread all over Gløshaugen and down into the town. It was an explosive two years!

I don't think, however, that the youngsters of today are a bit interested. Computing today is as available as the air they breathe. It comes as some God-given right and is literally at their fingertips, as it should be. This is indeed what we were striving for right from the start. Nevertheless, I think a great deal of the fun was in getting it that way. I don't think that many people today know what a computer is. Indeed, the irony is that the larger and more complicated the computer, the simpler the things we do with it. A secretary could not have used Cambridge University's 1949 1K EDSAC to type a letter, but it helped discover the shape of DNA. Language facilities and software generally are so powerful today that hardly anyone needs to know the concepts of a bit, a word, an instruction, an exponent, a floating point number, an index register or an overflow indicator—and rightly so. But there goes the fun. On the other hand why should computers be fun? They are too expensive. Nevertheless, the "Golden Age" was fun.

So how do you start? You have something that looks like a broom closet, a secretary and a solitary computer man just about to call in the movers. The whole thing is being organised by an on-campus research institute called SINTEF on behalf of the university because the latter didn't have the structure to do it itself. You have no budget apart from the secretary's salary and half yours. There is no provision for any courses on the schedule. All input is via punched paper tape; that is, every program change means an entire recopying of the tape instead of a one-card insertion. There are seven Flexowriters at which sit seven users making seven times seven errors per minute. The professor of Numerical Analysis is from Germany and his English is hardly better than your Norwegian. There is no printer. Output is by punched tape, to be printed later character by character on the Flexowriters. Something called a carrousel was on order from Denmark consisting of 128 mini-magnetic tapes on a rotating wheel, highly reminiscent of a fairground. Moreover, Algol to you is as a red rag is to a bull.

We have arrived at the fairground. Since you never get a second chance to make a first impression, I create a seven-digit job number system on Day One. (Whenever you are at a loss for something to do, just start a seven-digit job number system. It won't get you a Nobel Prize but it will pay off sooner than you think.) However, there are two glimmers of real hope. The first is that no one actually expects anything, so no matter how much you muck it up no one will ever know. Secondly, here and there in this and that niche were people who had already acquired considerable experience on the computer. If we could bring about a balanced hardware configuration, close the shop and give some courses, in five years we might develop ourselves into a computing centre.

3.   USING THE "GIER" COMPUTER

Among the primeval users of GIER (as the machine was called) were the structural engineers in Professor Holand's institute, Professor Borgen's chemists (who used to sleep on the computer room floor) and Professor Balchen's control engineering boys. Indeed, the latter had been largely responsible for building the machine at Dansk Regnesentral in Copenhagen. Here I would like to pay an especial tribute to Nils Ivar Bech, whose generosity and helpfulness made it possible to acquire the computer. We shall find out that GIER was a far smarter move than I had originally thought, as the vastness of the 32 K of the IBM 7090s that I had left behind at Boeing had blinded me.

The first thing to do seems to be to put the actual hardware in the hands of full-time operators; this is the only way of getting any efficiency out of it. However, efficiency on the computer itself does not mean much at first because so little work is reaching it largely because of the lack of skill of the users at the keys of the Flexowriters. So before that we need to hire some secretaries to operate the Flexowriters. However, you cannot do this because you have no money to pay them. Where on earth do you start?!

A ray of hope, however, was the university's decision to let me use the night shift as a sort of private computer services company. But to do that we needed some staff, a chicken-and-egg catch-22 situation. If you can earn money on night shift, you can hire staff. But, how can you earn money if you don't have any staff in the first place? To prime the pump they let me keep Knut Skog. I remember he was on Kr. 32,000 per annum, but where the money came from I simply don't recall. (Probably Karl Stenstadvold sold a violin.)

Step zero, then, is to bring in some work from the big wide commercial world. But how do you talk to people about their computer problems when they don't know what a computer is? (How do you talk to the blind about colour?) Somehow, we managed it. The roll of honor of those two first years reads somewhat as follows: Sausage Helgesen, The Norwegian Fisheries, The Norwegian Geological Survey, The Institute of Statistics at the University of Uppsala (we went international right from the start), an oil company, a cement factory, a chemical company, a mapping company, a mining company, the farmers' cooperative and several others. Think of it! They actually trusted our computer and us. Nevertheless, we delivered the goods, on time and within budget – we had to. Such on-time performance is a rare occurrence now with its virtually infinite machine capacities and highfalutin languages and data structures! We were probably the only university computing centre in the world in the service bureau business. We were at least as good as any commercial outfit and without those wonderful customers, there would never have been a university computing centre as we knew it. The government did not provide the funding that we needed to make the centre viable. The individual private companies and institutions made it all possible by rewarding hard work performed well into the small hours. (Fortunately, we did not have any government working regulations in those days destroying our enthusiasm and preventing us getting the job done.)

In addition to the income, the commercial work served to teach these fresh graduates, and sometimes their professors, something about the real world. The experience crept into the lectures and often spawned careers.

However, not all this happened over night; hiring people had to go hand in hand with getting jobs. At first, we hired three women to do the keypunching. Immediately a wave of work started hitting the computer and the bottleneck moved to the printer. It was now Easter, so we flew down to see Bech in Copenhagen. What we needed was a high-speed printer, which we could buy with the carrousel money. But, that was not legal; it had to be an official Norwegian government order. OK, so they sent us a printer but billed us for a carrousel. Mission accomplished!

When we got back, there was an outcry. Poor Professor Romberg; he had set his heart on the carrousel. His pockets were bulging with mini tapes. With all those data in the computer and no way of getting it out, it would have been a case of "data constipation" without equal. When the printer arrived (and 20 characters per second became a thousand lines a minute), all doubts were dispelled; the ranks were closed and the government would never know.

4.   CREATING EFFICIENCY

Then we had to start squeezing some efficiency out of the main frame. We trained the women to operate the machine and worked behind closed doors for hours a day. The irony was that *we started making the computer available by closing the door*. No one seemed to complain though. Probably the novelty of actually pressing the wrong buttons yourself had worn off in favour of someone else pressing the right ones. Turn-around time was short. The error rate is down. Why? The keypunch women, with no formal Algol training, even spotted errors in the original coding sheets and correct them while punching.

We started to hire more people. These included (in addition to Knut Skog, today professor at Tromsø) Karl Schjetne from Kjeller, later to take over as director of the centre; Harald Michalsen, later to get his Dr. Techn. on computer-based school timetabling; Nils Høeg from Boeing, later Managing Director of Hydro Data and Fjerndata, and Øivind Solvang also from Boeing, later Managing Director of Guru Papp, now sadly departed; Arnt Otto Østlie, NTH's first candidate to write software for his diploma (and what a fight it was to prise him loose from his NTH institute); Ralph Høibakk, founder of NorData and later Managing Director of Tandberg Data; Tore Bough-Jensen, later to become a senior consultant with Habberstad; Arne Sølvberg, today Professor of Computing at NTH; Olav B.

Brusdal who kept the machine going, later Assistant Professor at NTH, now also sadly departed, and part-time third shift student operator Kristen Rekdal, later Associate Professor with SINTEF. That was a star-studded team to have stacked around the computer itself. In addition, we had a rapidly growing user group typified by people like Johannes Moe, then Professor at the Division of Marine Structures, later Rektor of NTH and Director of SINTEF, and Øivind Bjørke who combined mechanical engineering with control engineering and who is now Professor of Industrial Automation. There were many others. Once we removed the stopper from the computer djinne-bottle, star performers started pouring out. Starting a computing centre is easy if you make it all available.

Another component of Regnesentret's early success was the course offerings, both to NTH and to the outside world. At NTH some of the older members were a little reluctant to dive in, but the students were very adventurous. In the autumn of 1962 Aimar Sørenssen had already given the very first programming course, but he later left for C.E.R.N. in Switzerland. We now needed a replacement teacher, and I'll never forget my first meeting with Jim Tocher, who came limping out of the lift on crutches, his left leg encased in plaster, his face covered in a red beard years before beards ever hit Norway. Three weeks later, both the cast and the beard disappear. He had just finished a post-doctoral year with Professor Holand and was about to return to Berkeley. I promised him a good job at Boeing if he would stay on six months and do the teaching. Teaching that first year was an utter revelation. Then he moved to stay on at Boeing until retirement.

Actually, there was no place in the timetable for teaching programming, so we announced a spare-time course, three times a week for eight weeks. We expected twenty people to show up; 250 came. When that was over, Knut Skog said that that was it; there would be no further interest this year. "Well let's find out, Knut, and see if it's a waste of time. Let's at least offer the course; if twenty show up, we'll run it." Unbelievably, 150 turned up. "That's absolutely it," says Knut eight weeks later. Me: "Come on, let's try once more." Knut: "Look, I know NTH, you're new here." Me: "There's no harm in asking; if twenty show up, we'll run the course." As we approached the lecture room where the initial meeting was to take place a large crowd had assembled outside the door. "Damn it, they've forgotten to open the door." But no, this is the overflow; 450 people had turned up. One thousand people learn to program the computer during its first year at NTH, all in their spare time. One of the professors complained that the students have deserted his lectures for the computing centre. "They don't even drink any more," he said. "GIER is better than beer," observed Karl Stenstadvold.

Two other courses were available from the start. The first was Brusdal's course on hardware, which became the first ever credit course in computing at NTH. The other was a general awareness course which I gave called something like, "How to use the computer" based on years of experience at Boeing. In addition to the internal courses, we started giving courses to practicing engineers, and that became our most successful way of getting new customers.

Another component of availability was the solution to the problem of helping half-trained people write programs while they were learning Algol. Here we experienced a very strange phenomenon indeed. The immediate problem was that soon after we started the first Algol course, Knut Skog found himself inundated with interruptions and could not get anything done. "How do I get out of an infinite loop?", "How can I do complex arithmetic if Algol only deals with real numbers?", "This machine keeps dividing by zero." The usual suspects. We had to hide him, but we also had to answer the questions – we had to make the computer available. Hence, we put together a team of advanced (three-month) users whose job it was to operate a support office during the day. "What shall we call it?" asked Knut. "How about calling it the Oracle service? Keep it going until the summer. That should get it all going."

That was forty years ago, but Oracle still runs today. The most interesting thing is that no one actually runs it. It has been self-perpetuating ever since. Today it consists of some twenty undergraduate and post-grad students; it has no manager and no place in any organisation chart. Whenever people leave, they simply drag in a replacement from around the campus. (Heretical thought: perhaps we only need managers when we wish to perpetuate things that really ought not to be there.) Oracle is very popular amongst its members because they learn far more from other people's mistakes than from their own.

5. THE NEXT STEPS

No one anticipated the explosive growth of computing at NTH SINTEF and the probable intention was to have the GIER computer operational on campus through to the 1970s. However, by the end of 1963, we could see GIER would be getting jugged by 1965, and the long, frustrating process of getting a replacement started already in January, 1964, just a year after we got going. The first step was to get funding from the Department of Education. At first, there was absolutely no question of a new computer for five years. We go down to Oslo loaded with paper and the list of project numbers and titles. Remember, the first thing we ever did in January of 1963 was to set up a seven-digit project number and accounting system. We know very accurately who is doing what on the GIER, and when we open our bag and dump our statistics on the official's desk, the day is won. The only question was - how much?

One of the problems that beset us was that there were already two enormous computers in Norway, a Univac 1107 at Norsk Regnesentral in Oslo, and a CDC 3600 at the Atomic Energy Department in Kjeller. We must be compatible with one or the other. To get an IBM computer and present Norway with three incompatible machines would have been an act of inexcusable folly. So which should we get, a 3600 or an 1107? Two factors helped us make the decision, one was that we managed to talk Univac into an 1107 for half price, and the other was that the Exec II operating system was admirably suited to large numbers of small jobs, which very much characterised NTH computing at that time. So the 1107 selected itself, but not until after a great deal of marketing effort involving half a dozen computing companies, all of whom had seen the desirability of getting their machine in at NTH, where tomorrow's decision makers were developing their computing edge. That is largely the reason Univac grew so strongly in Norway.

As a postscript, and to demonstrate to today's users that computers did not come quite automatically, when I returned to Boeing the First of May 1965, a telegram was awaiting me from Nils Høeg saying that Univac had cancelled the 1107 because it was half price. A new person had taken over the Univac company—General Baker. He was a tough guy with a new broom, and his first action was to sweep away all unprofitable actions that the company had undertaken. Ours was the most unprofitable. Therefore, I had to go New York, halfway back to Trondheim, to rescue our 1107. As I said at the start, computing was not so much fun anymore. The most fun I ever had, though, was rescuing that 1107. It's all very well having learned theories about acquiring computers, but it's what goes on behind the scenes that matters. I would like to pay another tribute, this time to General Baker whose fairness and generosity made it possible for NTH to acquire a large, modern computer.

There must be thousands of anecdotes of those times. However, one that is ever vivid in my memory is the way we put one of the Trondheim banks through the wringer. They hired me as a consultant (but not for long). I did not know anything about banks, so I started to find out. To help the process along, I started signing my cheques Charlie Brown, and so did the rest of The Computing Centre. I do not know how many Charlie Brown cheques were cashed, but not a single one was either refused or caught by the auditor's department. Not all problems are computer problems!

We had our frustrations, of course. One thing that people may not be aware of is that the 1107 at Norsk Regenesentral was a world pioneer in remote computing. At one time, there were four terminals simultaneously coupled to it over telephone lines, one in Sweden, our 1104 in Øivind

Solvang's office, and two others in other parts of Norway. The technical problems were solved, but not the problems Øivind had with the telephone operators! They would listen in suspiciously after two hours of silence, interrupting the data transmission, causing him to start all over again. That brings me to my third debt of gratitude, to Leif Olausen who ran Norsk Regnesentral in those days. His energy, drive, enthusiasm and the tireless way he supported us in Trondheim until we could stand on our own feet deserve our deepest appreciation. He knew how to inspire a bunch of people and get the last ounce of effort out of them. No government working regulation was down there either.

6. CONCLUSION

The seed that initiated the Regnesentret crystal was undoubtedly GIER itself. It had a core memory of only 1K. It was a microcomputer in a broom closet. However, it had two vital properties; it was a highly reliable piece of equipment and it had an excellent compiler-cum-operating system; that is, it was both hardware and software. That was a lesson that the Norwegian computer industry still did not understand a decade later. A computer consists of its software. Had programming been tedious or had productivity been low because of downtime, computing would have got a bad name right from the start. However, Algol is a good language, despite my article in Datamation, January 1963, and, as a result, computing took on like wildfire from the first day. GIER's task was to convince NTH - SINTEF that they needed a computer. No computer that I know of could have achieved that goal more admirably. So by definition, we got the timing right. Had NTH tried starting computing a year earlier, before the compiler was ready, we could not have been able to accomplish anything like such a good start. A software-free computer is no computer.

Those were the good old days, of course. In particular they were noisy – mostly laughter. When you tiptoe around current computing departments, all is solemn silence. I suppose they are far more productive than we were, but I doubt whether they work with more enthusiasm, and I hope I don't hurt anyone's feeling if I opine that we worked far longer hours. At any rate, in those days people put in enormous amounts of time and the reason they did so was that it was tremendously fun. We had an esprit de corps. We had a feeling of being wanted.

I would like to end by paying my fourth and last debt of gratitude. Without the unceasing, total, committed support of Karl Stenstadvold, then Director of SINTEF, Regnesentret, NTH, would never have come about. In theory, Regnesentret was impossible, but Karl Stenstadvold was a man who made the impossible possible.   You can write academic books on management; they aren't worth a row of beans because they aren't written by managers, at least managers of the calibre of Karl.   I have known hundreds in my time, but none like him. He's the best of all my memories of Regnesentret, NTH.   Sadly, he is no longer with us but we who knew him miss him greatly.

Ending on a note for the computer people of today, the whole point of pioneering anything is to provide following generations with something of value.   NTH went from GIER to CRAY in twenty-five years – a factor of 100 million speed-size units in a single human generation - an unimaginable growth.   Silicon Graphics machines with 898 processors and the customary array of PCs now surrounds them.   NTH has inherited something close to a miracle.   I hope they use it well.   I hope it was all worth the effort.   Despite what I said, I hope it will still be great fun!   In the end, we made computing available—the rest was history.

SCIP: A SCANDINAVIAN PROJECT ON SYSTEMS ANALYSIS AND DESIGN
A personal account from a perspective of some 30 years later

Paul Lindgreen [1]

Prof. emeritus, Systems Analysis, Copenhagen Business School; P_lindgreen@hotmail.com

Abstract: Three distinct historic development phases are identified. These phases are based on a review of two years participation together with other Scandinavian colleagues in a very inspiring research group on the development of computer supported analysis and design of computer application systems. These include: 1) Making the computer itself a reliable device, 2) Creating the necessary software and recognizing sound programming principles, and 3) Trying to utilize the provided tools in organizations and business. The paper ends with some reflections on why the two first phases were successfully while the present third phase still is characterized by so many disasters.

Key words: Effective computer usage, co-research, early success versus present failures

1.   BACKGROUND

In June 1969 during the NORDDATA conference that took place in Koncerthuset in Stockholm I presented a paper that partly argued for the need of a formal language enabling to specify the functions of computerized data processing systems, and which also discussed the possibility of constructing a compiler transforming the specifications to programs that could be executed on a computer. The most prominent argument for this intended tool, however, was not the program generation itself, but rather that the well-definedness of the possible requirement statements (supported by an underlying formalism) would force the "systemeers" – a term coined in

---

[1] See author's note at the end of this article.

Scandinavia at that time – really to consider what the data-processing needs were and to be explicit in the specifications thereof.

After the presentation, Professor Börje Langefors from Royal Institute of Technology, Stockholm, contacted me. He commented upon the intentions and ideas I had presented and asked if I would have an interest in joining a group – named SCIP – of researchers from a number of universities and business companies in Scandinavia. He explained that the letters in the word 'SCIP' meant to associate to 'SCandinavian', 'Information', 'Processing', and 'Project' as keywords for some of the main interests and aims behind the work of the group. They had recently and formally established SCIP with economic support from the national research boards in the Scandinavian countries and from an organization named NORDFORSK (Scandinavian Council for Applied Research). Thereby, funds were available during a couple of years for the participation in SCIP by representatives from interested research groups in Scandinavian universities and business companies who were working with theories, principles and tools for proper and effective development of computer application systems – in particular with the design of tools where computers were intended to support the development.

At that time, I was in the employ of the Danish company Regnecentralen, and as a young engineer with no academic background myself other than a master's degree in electronics from the Technical University of Copenhagen, I was, of course, very honored by Langefors' invitation. Knowing that it would be fully in the spirit of Regnecentralen [1] for an employee to take part in such a Scandinavian co-research project, I immediately accepted to join the SCIP group. At that time, I knew Langefors only by name and from reading a few selected parts of his comprehensive textbook: "Theoretical Analysis of Information Systems" from 1966 [2]. He had mentioned to me the names of some of the other SCIP-participants, but I must admit that at that time none of them were known to me, nor were their research projects. However, as I joined the SCIP group I experienced all its members to be inspiring and intellectually open-minded colleagues, and mutual friendships with some of them have lasted since then.

In the preamble of the proceedings [3] from a SCIP-organized conference in Århus, Denmark, that in practice seems to be the last officially recorded act of the SCIP group, Langefors writes about the background for establishing SCIP:

"The present SCIP work may perhaps in retrospect be regarded as having started in 1968 in Trondheim, Norway (SINTEF), when a group headed by Arne Sølvberg started to implement a computerized system for information system analysis and design. About a year later (1969), project CADIS was started at the Department for Information Processing at Stockholm University and the Royal Institute of Technology; and shortly after, at a meeting in Stockholm with people from Denmark, Finland, Norway, and Sweden, it was decided that a Nordic cooperative research (and application) effort was desirable. Thus SCIP was formed with support from ...”

2.   SCIP PROJECTS AND PARTICIPANTS

The only (at least publicly available) documentation about the Scandinavian research projects involved under the SCIP-umbrella appears in the above-mentioned proceedings from the Århus conference [3]. These proceedings are rather unusual as regard the *editorial form*, because each paper includes unusually and extraordinary detailed records of the associated discussions during the conference.

Langefors himself had an introductory paper in the proceedings, but this paper does not describe a proper SCIP project. Rather, it summarizes some aspects more or less common for all the projects. Additionally, it contains some personal comments about issues and concepts that he – at least at that time – regarded as important in system analysis and design. In addition, the discussions on these issues are recorded.

In the following, the “hereby official” SCIP projects appear listed in the order in which they appear in the proceedings with specification of the name of the project and/or a short summary of the aim(s) of the project, with names and affiliation of those of the involved or associated persons who at least once attended a SCIP arrangement:

1. SYSKON – a project concerning System Development
   – Christian Andersen, Institute of Management, University of Århus
   – Fritz Krogh – Jespersen, A/S Regnecentralen, Århus
   – Anders Petersen, Århus Business School

2. Project NO (Apparently an acronym based on the first name of each of the two project members)
   The purpose of project NO is to develop methods for the production of a decision basis for political decisions, the documentation of the decision basis and of the political decisions, and ensuring that the system owner makes political decisions.
   – Ole Øhlenschlæger Madsen
   – Niels Jørgen Relsted
both from Institute of Management, University of Århus

3. DATAMATICS and INFORMATICS

The task is to develop the abstract foundation of datamatics — named *systemology* and *systematics* — and its application to the development of information systems — named *informatics* (or *pragmatic cybernetics*).
　　– Poul Sveistrup, University of Copenhagen

4. Exact Description of DAtamatic Problems (EDDAP)
　　The purpose of EDDAP is to:
- Analyze and describe the conceptual basis for a formal language for specifying the systemic function of datamatic systems, i.e. the function as experienced by the users of the system
- Construct a declarative language based on the realized concept structure
- Design and program a compiler that from an EDDAP description can generate the program that determines the function of the described datamatic system.

(The contribution to the conference was in fact a working paper under the first of these three sub-projects.)
　　– Paul Lindgreen
　　– Flemming Sylvest Pedersen
both from A/S Regnecentralen Copenhagen

5. DIFO – *Design of Information systems, especially File Organization*
　　To develop methods for the design of a file organization that minimizes the sum of the following cost factors: design of files, programming of file manipulation programs, generation of files, maintenance of files, data processing, and required or reserved space.
　　– Pertti Järvinen, Departement of Computer Science, University of Tampere.

6. CASCADE – *The development of tools and methods for the analysis and design of information processing systems*
　　– Per Aanstad
　　– Geir Skylstad
　　– Arne Sølvberg
all from Computing Center, University of Trondheim

7. CADIS – *Computer-Aided Design of Information Systems*
　　The CADIS project proceeds along two strongly interrelated lines. One is to expand and develop the methodology of information systems analysis and design. The other is to develop computer-based tools (man-machine interactive programs) which may aid analysts and designers in their work.
　　– Stig Berild
　　– Janis Bubenko, Jr.

 – Olle Källhammer
 – Eva Lindencrona
all from Dep. of Information Processing, Royal Institute of Technology, Stockholm.

8. The specification of formal information systems for administrative control
 – E. Torsten Lundquist, Departement of Development, KemaData AB, Stockholm.

9. The development of a computerized real-time documentation system applying computer graphics as a means for interaction.
 – Hans E. Andersin
 – Kristel Siro
 – Markku Syrjänen
all from Institutionen för Informationsbehandlingslära, Tekniska Högskolan, Helsinki.

In addition to this list of projects and participants it should be mentioned that in a great part of SCIP's lifetime the extremely friendly and helpful employee from NORDFORSK, fil.cand. Ann-Kristin Wentzel, served as a perfect host for the SCIP-sessions on the various sites in Scandinavia where we joined.

3.   SCIP IN PERSPECTIVE

In the relatively short time around 1970 when SCIP was active and the involved persons could meet two to three times a year, they would discuss and exchange knowledge and experience. In fact, they had a "co-research life" in that period, I believe, and we all sensed that we were at a turning point at the start of a new phase in *datamatics* – a term I coined in the sixties for the discipline of applying electronic computers in society. I do not recall how this shift happened explicitly – neither in SCIP, nor in broader context. But in retrospect the following three *phases of problem-focus* in the area of the electronic computer usage can be clearly distinguished:

1. In the 1960s, research concentrated on *developing reliable hardware* for computers and for data-storage devices in a scale that was enormous compared to the pioneering time in the forties. In Scandinavia, this period ended with the manifestation of computers such as BESK, DASK, and SARA and organizations that could provide access to use of them.

2. In the 1960s, we also saw a decade where the concept "software engineering" emerged. The major research effort was to construct and specify *adequate programming languages* such as FORTRAN, ALGOL, and COBOL to invent *useful compilation principles and techniques,* and actually to develop *compilers for practical use.* In this period, the basic principles for constructing *reliable and maintainable algorithms* became important with principles that later on became known under the term 'structured programming'. With the contemporary construction in Norway of the SIMULA-language [4] also the conceptual basic principles were laid for what later on became known as "the object-oriented approach" – the dogma that from the nineties and on has become an extremely successful paradigm in software engineering and, unfortunately, elsewhere in analysis and design remains a sad conceptual misunderstanding (see the concluding reflections).

3. It was at the end of the 1960s that SCIP was born and from that on had its relatively short life. At that time where the technological foundation for a widespread practical use of computers in society was established, *"the era of datamatics"* was born which we up to now in still increasing scale experience in all parts of society. However, SCIP clearly showed an indication of a change of focus <u>from</u> computers themselves and how to program them <u>to</u> *how to utilize* the available potential of data processing and data storage technology in organizations. That is, *how to do it in a sensible, rational, and resource-effective way.*

But, alas! Despite all the inventions and data-handling and transmission possibilities of datamatics that have appeared nearly continuously since then, and despite that some of them in practice have revolutionized the way we *potentially* can act and cooperate in society – we still are not able to organize projects aiming at utilizing the technical potential in a sensible way. Many development projects have become organizational and/or functional disasters. New projects still do so and most of them far exceed their budgets both as regard costs and as development time. Furthermore, nearly always when a developed system finally is released for use, a long period follows with costly activities to modify the system such that it finally will support effective business procedures instead of prohibiting them.

It is interesting that in strong contrast to the previous two phases this third one aiming at *utilizing* the datamatic potential in a sensible way – *this phase has lasted for more that 30 years.* As I see it, we are still far from reaching a practice where project teams and their employers *honestly* can say: "Our development was rational and resource-effective, because our approach was in accordance with well-recognized principles and based on *a consistent structure of relevant concepts* that support our understanding instead of distorting it".

However, we must admit that to reach such a state was never the official goal of SCIP. The task was not to search for a proper theoretical basis for "systemeering". Since the official intentions of NORDFORSK were to support *applied* research, the primary objective of SCIP was to provide a forum for exchanging research results and provide them for the public to help improving the practical development of datamatic systems. In accordance with this, most of the projects under the SCIP-umbrella were concerned with the construction and implementation of some kind of working approach and/or practical tools to support the work – most often computer-based ones. However, as I remember the extremely vivid, interpreting, and often very exited discussions during the SCIP meetings, they nearly *always* were theoretic and primarily concerned with basic concepts and the conceptual structures that were assumed to be behind the various system design issues in practice. This deviation from the official SCIP intentions can actually be seen in the above mentioned introductory paper of the proceedings from the SCIP conference in Århus,. There Langefors directly regrets the strong focus on (assumed) relevant concepts, which constantly popped up during the discussions of the conference papers.

On the other hand, this deviation from the official NORDFORSK goal was exactly what created the "academic seed" that would grow into a new very active international research forum. Arne Sølvberg and Börje Langefors took the initiative. They (and possibly supported by others as well) carried out a great deal of organizational work. This resulted in the establishment of a new technical committee under IFIP named TC8 (Information Systems) and in the forming of its first working group 8.1 (Design and Evaluation of Information Systems), a group I also later on joined and where I again met many of the former SCIP colleagues. Over the time, TC8 became one of the most active organs of IFIP. Nevertheless, it is interesting that whenever I listened to or took part in the always-stimulating discussions during the various WG 8.1 sessions, I usually experienced a SCIP déjà-vue.

4. SOME REFLECTIONS ON THE THREE HISTORIC PHASES OF PROBLEM FOCUS

When I presented the draft version of this paper in Trondheim, I stated:

> "Although I am not a historian, it is my opinion that any historic record is of little interest, unless we can learn something from it – something that in some respect may help us to behave better in the future".

Up to this point, the paper to my best knowledge is historically correct, although – as mentioned in the preamble – it was not possible to provide the full story of SCIP. The temporal position of SCIP within the three phases of problem focus is also correct. Somebody may object that the description of the last (current) phase might be too negative, taking into account "all the great achievements" we have seen in our professional domain.

Well, future historians must decide how fair the judgment of this phase really is, because my historic point of realization is a quite different one – the obvious question every active computer professional in my opinion should ask and try to answer:

> Why is it that the epoch covering the first two phases was so relatively short, and still – despite the pioneering conditions – extremely successful compared to the current epoch of the third phase: the one characterized by an endless flow of implementation-"catastrophes" and a galore of short-lived buzzwords for fancy new "concepts" and "revolutionary" approaches?

It is far beyond the scope of the present HINC conference to aim at a full answer to that question. However, on the professional and historic background of having been active through all three phases, I have over the years tried to find some *key issues* behind the apparently lasting problems with utilizing the datamatic potential in organizations. On that background I allow myself to conclude with an interpretation of *some important differences* between the two epochs, and also – in the spirit I experienced both at Regnecentralen and in the SCIP project – to give a few hints of what in my opinion basically must be changed in "the datamatic society", if the current epoch shall end with success. (Several much more detailed comments on some of the issues can be found in [5] and [6]).

So what are the most crucial differences between the two epochs? In both phases of *the first epoch*, the focus was on making the computer *a reliable and effective tool*. The epoch was very successful in this respect, and the main reason was that the objects of the problems were *deterministic*. As the outcome of the epoch, the people behind the development projects provided society with:

- *A fast data-processing device* that after the invention of the transistor (and other kinds of electronic components) became *reliable in* practice
- *Useful programming principles and languages*
- *Reliable compilers and operating systems* that permitted a relatively effective and fail-safe utilization of the datamatic tools as such.

Most characteristic for the first epoch compared to the present one is that only *relatively few people* worldwide   –   often in university(-like) environments   –   were involved in the development of the necessary hardware and software. Of course, already at that time, thousands of electronic engineers and software pioneers were active in the development, but probably less than fifty *key-persons* worldwide really made the difference by fostering the right ideas and creating the insight that was the

basis for the success. Important is also that the development in practice mainly took place under conditions where the involved persons freely could:
- Exchange design and research results
- Discuss with each other across national and organizational domains and thereby filter out common *useful* concepts that supported the understanding of the datalogical problems and principles
- Provide techniques for each other that enabled the construction of effective and reliable computers and software for controlling them.

The present epoch, in contrast, is quite different at least in two respects. *First,* the number of people active in datamatic development has increased dramatically, and the whole area is now commercialized. The most prominent result is that the intense and insight-giving communication characteristic for the first epoch has given way to a narrow-sighted clinging to ideologies and dogmas.

Secondly, the problems have moved from the deterministic hardware/software domain into the basically *un-deterministic* realm of *organizations*. Here the datamatic systems were to interact with *human actors*. Well-known expectations are that computers should be able to serve the organization – typically by mediating the communication between people, by acting as an external memory for them, and even to take over some of their former business activities – for example to make useful estimates or to take proper decisions. Moreover, because computers compared to humans are deterministic and extremely faster, they are often supposed to be able perform their tasks in a much better and cheaper way than people can do.

In principle this may be correct, but often it is realized too late in the development process that it is not necessarily so in practice, and then severe problems occur. Ironically, it is the success with computers in the first epoch that is the reason: It has caused a severe blindness as regard two underlying, but generally unrecognized or ignored problems:

1. Exactly because computers are deterministic they lack the important human ability *to improvise* – to deviate from strict rules and to react in a sensible manner also in situations that were not foreseen by the programmers.
2. Even worse – the success in developing an effective data-processing tool caused the widespread misunderstanding that the hardware/software *concepts* useful for solving the problems of that epoch also were those relevant for understanding and solving the present problems with computers as actors in organizations.

From many years of trying "to understand the world", it is my experience that for a notion of something to justify as a *concept* it must be in accordance with the following definition:

A *concept* is a conception of a thing characterized in such a way that exactly thereby it becomes *useful* for understanding other things – in particular for understanding other concepts. However, a set of sensible concepts is not enough: One of the important things I learned from participating in SCIP was that even the most well renowned and generally recognized concepts could be disastrous to base your insight on, *if they do not properly reflect* the phenomena that are relevant in your domain of analysis. That is exactly the sad situation we now have experienced twice in the present epoch:

For many years, the dogma behind the development and implementation of datamatic systems as co-actors in organizations was to use the popular, guru-advocated, but utterly naive Structured-Analysis and Structured-Design approaches. When at the end of the eighties it finally became obvious – even for the most religious adherents – that the approaches were quite unsatisfactory, an alternative ideology had to be found. And what luck; it was there just to pick. In the software-engineering domain, a truly successful development codex had emerged.

Exactly because the so-called *object-oriented approach* has been – and still is – *extremely successful in software design*, we wrongly assume that then it must also be the proper paradigm in an organizational context. That is not so. The reason is that the OOA-paradigm is far from reflecting the concepts that are relevant for understanding and describing organizations. One can model organizations in many ways, but behind the understanding of any organization is a set of *fundamental un-avoidable concepts* of which the most important are:

> Actors, actions, and co-actions, interaction with the environment, operands, goals for the activities, communication between actors, information, and data representing the information.

However, brainwashed by the OOA-paradigm, the OOA-systemeers view an organization just as a complex structure of interacting "objects" of various types.

5.   CONCLUSION

Therefore, what can we learn from the "story" of SCIP viewed in this subjective historic perspective? Well, Piet Hein once expressed it generally as "TTT"; that is, "Things Take Time". I could add, "Getting insight takes much more time".

REFERENCES

[1] Per V. Klüver, Technology Transfer, Modernisation, and Welfare State – Regnecentralen and the Making of Governmental Policy on Computer Technology in Denmark in the 1960s. Procedings of HiNC1.

[2] Börje Langefors: Theoretical Analysis of Information Systems. Studentlitteratur 1966.

[3] Janis Bubenko jr., Börje Langefors, Arne Sølvberg (Eds.): Computer Aided Information Systems Analysis and Design. Studentlitteratur 1971.

[4] Stein Krogdahl: The birth of Simula. Procedings of HiNC1.

[5] Paul Lindgreen: Systemanalyse: Analyse af organisatoriske systemer med henblik på fornuftig edb-anvendelse. Jurist- og Økonomforbundets Forlag, 1990.

[6] Paul Lindgreen: Towards a useful Information concept. In: Brinkkemper, Lindencrona, Sølvberg (Eds.): Information Systems Engineering. Springer 2000.

AUTHOR'S NOTE

I regard the period of participating in the SCIP activities as an extremely vivid and inspiring part of my research career, and as one during which I learned much from Scandinavian colleagues. It was a time when I became conscious of many of the fundamental principles and concepts underlying all kinds of practical use of computers. Despite this, I have been able to dig out only a minor part of the SCIP-history. Many facts about SCIP were apparently never recorded or safely stored, and much knowledge about participants, projects, and about the many discussions of concepts, approaches, issues, positions , etc. that may be relevant from a historic point of view, is now forgotten or is lost in the minds of those SCIP participants who have passed away.

IS SCANDINAVIAN INFORMATION SYSTEMS DEVELOPMENT BECOMING PASSÉ?

Juhani Iivari

Department of Information Processing Science, University of Oulu, 90014 Oulun yliopisto, Finland; Juhani.iivari@oulu.fi

Abstract: This essay discusses possible intellectual contributions of the Scandinavian IS research traditions to the future of IS as a discipline. It suggests that the infological problems identified by Langefors still capture much of the essence of IS as a discipline of computing. The essay also revisits the infological equation, showing its continued relevance in the field. Finally, it discusses some trends in ISD.

Key words: Organizational alignment, user requirement, knowledge, information, data

1.   INTRODUCTION

In their historical review of the "Scandinavian approach" (or more strictly the Nordic approach) to information systems development (ISD), Iivari and Lyytinen (1998) did not attempt to define the "Scandinavian approach" but pointed out that it is a plurality of approaches rather than a monolithic unit. These approaches differ substantially in their explicit or implicit value orientation, distinctive constructs used to clarify the concepts of IS and ISD, and the focus on ISD in terms of process coverage, stakeholders and type of system. Despite these differences, we can regard them as 'Scandinavian' due to their geographical or genealogical origin and due to their orientation. The Scandinavian approaches as whole have the characterization of "grass root" approaches as compared with the North American MIS tradition. They have emphasized IS evolution, user participation, alternative process models and the seeking of varying theoretical foundations for IS and ISD.

More specifically, Iivari and Lyytinen (1998) analysed ten Scandinavian ISD approaches, Infological, Formal, Socio-Technical, Sociocybernetic, Trade Unionist, Language Action, Professional Work Practice, Object-Oriented, Activity Theory and the Structuration Theory, pointing out that the Scandinavian approaches as whole have made a substantial intellectual contribution to information systems as a discipline, whereas the practical contribution is more questionable.

The purpose of this essay is not to update their analysis but to take a personal look at the future of the Scandinavian approaches in view of the likely evolution of IS as a discipline. First, one may question whether there is space for distinctively Scandinavian approaches in the increasingly globalized world partly made possible by information technology. Among the Scandinavian approaches reviewed in Iivari and Lyytinen (1998), the Trade Unionist approach of the 1970's and 1980's is the best example of a distinctively Scandinavian contribution based on the strong trade unions characteristic of the Scandinavian societies (Spinuzzi, 2002). It seems, however, that distinctively Scandinavian approaches to ISD are fading out.

Thus, instead of looking for distinctively Scandinavian approaches, this essay will attempt to assess possible intellectual contributions of the Scandinavian IS research traditions in the foreseeable future. It is structured in terms of three revisits. First, it revisits the infological problems (Langefors, 1977) and demonstrates their continued relevance, suggesting that they largely capture the distinctive ISD competences of IS experts. This brings a normative aspect into the essay: the author's view of areas in which Scandinavian and non-Scandinavian IS researchers should especially invest their efforts. Second, the essay revisits the infological equation (Langefors, 1966; 1980) and illustrates its continued validity as a succinct crystallization of the relationship between data, information and knowledge, interest in which has been revived recently, especially in Knowledge Management (KM). Finally, the essay revisits the ISD process and takes up a couple of recurrent trends in it: the increased use of pre-fabricated software in ISD and the move towards light methods.

2.   INFOLOGICAL PROBLEMS REVISITED

2.1   Background

Langefors (1977) makes a distinction between the infological problem of specifying the service provided and the datalogical problem of designing and realizing the data system that provides the specified service. He further divides the infological problem into three parts:

- Object system analysis and design (organizational change)
- Information analysis and design (user concepts and work)
- Implementation of the new (organizational) system

The application areas of information systems in the 1970's were largely limited to operative and managerial systems. Table 1 shows, however, that the more recent application areas include the same infological problems of understanding the activities to be supported by the information system, specifying the information services provided by the information system, while at the same time taking into consideration the technical possibilities, and the organizational implementability of the system. Table 1 also shows that there are plenty of infological research problems involved with the understanding that information systems support these activities with appropriate information services to support those activities. This is obvious in the context of the more recent application areas, but applies even in the case of operative information systems (e.g. ERP) and managerial information systems. To exemplify the latter, much of the research into Decision Support Systems (DSS) is based on Simon's (1960) model of decision making (intelligence, design, choice), whereas Langley et al. (1995) proposed five alternative models, which to my knowledge have been seriously neglected in DSS research.

As far as the more recent systems/technologies such as Content Management Systems (CMS) and Knowledge Management Systems (KMS) are concerned, Smith and McKeen (2003) point out that no one really knows what Content Management is. It is obvious, however, that if Content Management is not to be used only as a fashionable buzzword, one must pay serious attention to the "content" included in CMSs.[1] Knowledge Management Systems (KMS) encounter similar problems of what are the services (expertise and knowledge) that make them in some sense distinctive. Content Management Systems and Knowledge Management Systems illustrate another infological problem. Neither of them is based on clear ideas of the activities to be automated and/or supported.

Table 1: Infological problems in selected application areas

---

[1] The word "content" has a number of meanings, of which the following, as quoted in the Oxford English Dictionary (second edition 1989) seem most relevant in this context: 2.a. *spec. (pl.)* The things contained or treated of in a writing or document; the various subdivisions of its subject-matter, 2.b. *table of contents (content):* a summary of the matters contained in a book, in the order in which they occur, usually placed at the beginning of the book, 3.a. The sum or substance of what is contained in a document; tenor, purport, 4. The sum of qualities, notions, ideal elements given in or composing a conception; the substance or matter (of cognition, or art, etc.) as opposed to the *form.*

	Systems/ technology	Information services to be provided	Activities to be supported or automated
Operative information systems	TPS (1950) ERP (1990)	Automation	Transaction processing Business Process Reengineering (Hammer and Champy, 1994)
Managerial information systems	MIS (1960) DSS (1970)	Reporting Modelling	Decision making (Simon, 1960, Langley et al., 1995)
Inter-organizational information systems	IOS (1980) EDI (1980) WWW (1990)	eCommerce	Business networks (Powel, 1990; Miles and Snow, 1992) Business models (Weill and Vitale, 2001)
Office and document management information systems	OA (1970) EDMS (1980) WWW (1990) Semantic Web (2000) CMS (2000)	Content services	Clerical work (Document management) (Content management)
Groupware systems	GWS (1980)	Coordination services	Computer supported cooperative work (Schmidt and Bannon, 1992; Schmidt and Simone, 1996; Schmidt, 2002)
Knowledge work support systems	ES (1980) KMS (1990) KWSS (2000)	Expertise Knowledge	(Knowledge management) Knowledge work
Mobile computing	NMT (1980) GSM (1980) ... UMTS (2000)	Content services	Activities to be supported

CMS	= Content Management System	KMS	= Knowledge Management System
EDI	= Electronic Data Interchange	KWSS	= Knowledge Work Support System
EDMS	= Electronic Document Management System	MIS	= Management Information System
GSM	= Global System for Mobile Communications	NMT	= Nordic Mobile Telephone
GWS	= Groupware System	OA	= Office Automation
DSS	= Decision Support System	TPS	= Transaction Processing System
ERP	= Enterprise Resource Planning	UMTS	= Universal Mobile Telephone System
IOS	= Inter-Organizational information System	WWW	= World Wide Web

Content Management and Knowledge Management do not really specify the users or the activities in which the content, expertise, and knowledge services provided by CMSs and KMSs are really used. In the context of KMSs, I would suggest that it is more appropriate to talk about Knowledge Work Support Systems (KWSS). By knowledge work, I refer to work with four characteristics (Iivari and Linger, 1999): (i) it is based on a body of knowledge (BoK), (ii) it entails working on representations (data) of the objects of the work, (iii) it stipulates a deep, theoretical understanding of the objects of work, and (iv) its results entail knowledge as an essential ingredient.

The three infological problems identified by Langefors (1977) correspond closely to the IS experts' distinctive competence areas of information/software systems development proposed by Iivari et al. (2001):

- Organizational alignment
- User requirements construction
- Organizational implementation
- IS evaluation/assessment

Organizational alignment refers to the process in which the information system is aligned with the organizational and social context into which it is embedded.   User requirements construction points to defining the information services to be provided by the system in order to satisfy the needs of its users.[2]   Organizational implementation refers to the institutionalization of the information system in its organizational and social context. By contrast, with the software engineering tradition, it is significant to make a distinction between organizational alignment and requirements construction. One reason is the dilemma between the organizational change and users' capabilities to express their requirements.   Normally full deployment of the potential of IT requires changes in organizational work practices. The more the new work practices differ from the current ones, however, the harder it is for users the figure out the requirements for the new system.

I shall discuss the first two infological problems (competence areas) in more detail in the following, especially from the perspective of Scandinavian IS research. One reason for this is that the Scandinavian contribution to the latter two areas seems to be very limited. With respect to the problem of organizational implementation, it seems that the Scandinavians have been much more interested in the design of systems than in their organizational implementation and acceptance. There is an extensive worldwide literature on IS evaluation, especially concerning user information satisfaction, but much of this research is not clearly integrated into ISD development.[3]

---

[2]   The term "requirements construction" was originally coined by Flynn (1996). Like "requirements engineering", it implies that requirements are not out there to be gathered and analyzed but are socially constructed. I prefer "requirements construction" because it does not imply a specific engineering paradigm.

[3]   To my knowledge, the PSC method (Kerola and Järvinen, 1975) and the PIOCO method (Iivari and Koskela, 1979; 1987) as its successor were the first to include IS evaluation and related quality and choice criteria as integral parts of an ISD method.

2.2   Organizational alignment of information systems

Langefors (1977) saw that an information system and its organizational context can be aligned by conscious object system analysis and design. For a number of reasons, this process has become more of a reciprocal, continuing process of aligning the information system and its organizational context rather than a one-time decision. Organizations have changed from formal-rational structures towards more interactionist forms (cf. Kling and Scacchi, 1980; Kling and Scacchi, 1982), technology has become more flexible, and the relationship between the technology and its organizational context has become socially more complex (Iivari and Hirschheim, 1996). As a result, it is neither possible nor necessary to the same extent as earlier to align the information system and its organizational context by deliberate design. It can be more an evolutionary process in which the technology and the organizational context are gradually aligned with each other. In fact, the process may also be an emergent one in the sense that there is no final "alignment."[4]

There is a rich body of IS literature that addresses the issue of making an information system 'fit' (Iivari, 1992) its organizational and social context. Most of this pervious research has been limited to the initial design and implementation of the system, however, without paying attention to the post-implementation mutual adaptation of the system, its use, and the organizational context. Barley's (1986) study of the adopting of CR scanners in two radiological departments and the case study of Majchrzak *et al.* (2000) describing the dynamics of adopting groupware technology in a virtual team nicely illustrate the dynamics of the alignment process. In view of this neglect, it is not so surprising that Scandinavian IS research has not contributed much to the dynamic process of aligning the information system with its organizational context, although the dissertations of Karsten (2000) and Porra (1996) at least partly address the problem. Karsten's dissertation, like Barley's work, reflects theoretically Gidden's (1984) structuration theory, which seems to provide a useful theoretical lens for viewing this dynamic process. Porra's (1996) dissertation builds on biological colonial systems and evolution in these.

Based on their review of all articles published in the Scandinavian Journal of Information Systems up to 1997, Henfridsson et al. (1997) concluded that Scandinavian IS research has largely neglected organization theory as a reference discipline. This neglect may be explained by the predominance of the Trade Unionist approach in Scandinavian ISD discourse from the late 1980's onwards. After its first phase, informed by

---

[4]   There is a similarity here, of course, to the distinction between deliberate strategy and emergent strategy (Minzberg, 1994).

the class theory view of organizations (Kling and Scacchi, 1980), the Trade Unionist approach adopted a view that the essence of work is tacit (Ehn, 1988). Consequently, it did not pay attention to the articulation of the work supported by information systems but instead adopted a strategy of "computer artifact-oriented design work" rather than "work-oriented design of computer artifacts" (Ehn, 1988). One could interpret this artifact-oriented design of work, using cooperative prototyping for example, as emphasizing the evolutionary process of aligning the information system and its organizational context, but I am not aware of any studies of the post-implementation mutual adaptation of the system and its organizational context.

More recently, the Activity Theory-based approach and the Structuration Theory-based approach have attempted to fill the above void. Kuutti (1990), for example, suggested the concept of activity as an intermediate between individual actions and a larger social system (such as an organization). Activity theory also has the benefit that it does not reflect organizational or inter-organizational contexts of activity, but may also cover any activities in families and society (which we do not normally regard as organizations). On the other hand, at least activity theorists in the IS field have had a tendency to neglect organization theory as a reference discipline, despite the fact that the activities often take place in an organizational context.[5]

2.3   User requirements construction

Despite all the progress made in its methods and techniques, requirements construction (engineering) still continues to be the major problem in information systems and software development. There are a number of explanations for this. Information systems and software products have become more complex and their information requirements more fuzzy (Iivari and Kerola, 1983) in the sense that it is not possible to define absolutely correct (complete and consistent) requirements. One further reason is that methods and techniques for requirements construction are developed without paying proper attention to the nature of the requirements. This has biased the methods and techniques to focus on limited types of requirements.

Iivari and Hirschheim (1996) identify three views of user requirements: *objective*, *subjective* and *intersubjective*.[6] The objective view emphasizes

---

[5]   A review of recent papers in the special issues of Scandinavian Journal of Information Systems (Vol. 12, 2000) and Computer Supported Cooperative Work (Vol. 11, Nos. 1-2, 2002) on Activity Theory clearly confirms this.

[6]   The three views of user requirements bear some similarity to the "agreement" dimension in the three-dimensional framework for requirements engineering proposed by Pohl

the importance of impersonal features such as the organizational position and task of the user as a determinant of his/her information requirements or the objective existence of the slice of reality modeled by the system. The subjective view stresses that the personal characteristics of the user (his frame of reference, cognitive styles, etc.) primarily determine the information requirements. The intersubjective view emphasizes the need to attain intersubjectivity among the community of IS users so that the system can serve their communication needs. Information requirements are socially negotiated and are a matter of social agreement.

The Scandinavian contribution in the area of objectivist requirements construction has been substantial. The infological tradition, especially the ISAC method (Lundeberg et al., 1978; 1981), includes the idea that requirements can be derived from a detailed analysis of users' work (activity studies). Many later methods, of which Contextual Design (1998) is a recent example, have followed this lead. To my knowledge, Bubenko (1980) was the first to propose the idea that requirements could derived from the theory of the application domain (Gustafsson et al., 1982). The Trade Unionist approach is not very explicit in its view of user requirements. User participation, mock-ups, and prototyping may in principle support objectivist, subjectivist, and intersubjectivist views of user requirements. Nevertheless, my general impression is that the Trade Unionist approach places its major emphasis on the objective, although essentially tacit, requirements of work. More recent methods and techniques of requirements construction based on use cases (Jacobson et al., 1992; Booch et al., 1999) and related scenarios mainly reflect the objective view of user requirements.

The subjective view of information requirements genuinely reflects a user-centered approach.[7] Research into DSS has paid most attention to subjective user requirements, but otherwise the subjective view has been largely neglected in research into user requirements. The idea of personification, however (Brusilovsky, 1996), is a new attempt to take users as individual personalities into account in IS development.

Goldkuhl and Lyytinen (1982) were the first to introduce explicitly the idea of intersubjectivity in the context of user requirements. They saw IS development as a formalization of the professional language of the user community. One can also claim that the idea of a canonical conceptual schema includes an implicit idea of intersubjectivity. It is obvious that

---

(1996). This dimension describes the degree of agreement reached on the specification, ranging from a personal view to a common view. Pohl seems to interpret the dimension more as agreement between different stakeholders (systems analysts, manager, user, etc.), while Iivari and Hirschheim (1996) view intersubjectivity solely within the user community.

[7] Many so-called user-centred methods are actually work-oriented rather than user-centred.

intersubjectivity is gaining new relevance in the context of groupware and knowledge management systems. If an information system is to support a community of practice (Wegner, 1998), we should obviously base it on intersubjectively shared user (community) requirements. In the context of CSCW, Carstensein and Schmidt (1999) discuss 'classification schemes' as publicly visible and permanent pointers to items in the field of work. They point out that in large-scale settings actors cannot always ensure a consensus, implying that the classification scheme evolves in a process that is only partially concerted. Thus, they conclude that groupware systems should provide basic structures that one can use for establishing and maintaining conceptual structures, negotiate these, and still be open and flexible to local interpretations. This implies that we should view the user information requirements primarily as emergent, and that they may be only locally consistent.

3. THE INFOLOGICAL EQUATION REVISITED

3.1 Introduction

Every book on KM seems to start with its interpretation of concepts such as data, knowledge, and information. Much of this discussion suffers from very simplistic views, however. For example, Davenport and Prusak (1998) define data as a set of discrete, objective facts about events, Spiegler's (2000) definition of data echoes this view. Hammarberg (1981) discusses similar views, arguing that they are based on a foundationalist thesis that there exist raw, objective records of facts. He shows that this thesis fails. One reason is that we must always express data in a representational language of some kind, which provides the categories in terms of which we view the reality, implying that data are also "cooked" (cf. Hammarberg, 1981).

Tuomi (1999) points out that the generally accepted view in the KM community sees a hierarchy of data, information, and knowledge in which data are a prerequisite for information, and information is a prerequisite for knowledge (cf. also Spiegler, 2000). He criticizes this view and proposes a reversed hierarchy in which data emerge only after we have information, and that information emerges only after we already have knowledge. He points out that the world as an object of human knowing exists only as an interpreted world that is completely infused with meaning. Human cognition cannot see simple facts without these facts being part of its current meaning structure, and even the most elementary perception is already influenced by potential uses, expectations, context, and theoretical constructs.

It is obvious that the above controversy echoes the discussion of the concepts of data, information, and knowledge within the Scandinavian infological tradition more than 20 years ago. The following section outlines how we can define these concepts within that tradition, applying Langefors' famous infological equation (Langefors, 1966; 1980).

First, applying Sundgren (1973), one can define data as follows: A datum is an arrangement of physical symbols according to some language to represent and communicate some idea. The physical symbols cover oral speech, written text, and computer representations. The represented idea may be a simple fact, a rule, or a complex piece of knowledge. It is just a historical "coincidence" that many of the traditional information systems processed data representing simple facts.

By the concept of information, I refer to the idea embedded in or conveyed by the data. The idea may be a simple fact or a complex piece of thought. The proposed definition allows a number of interpretations of the concept of information. Firstly, one can interpret the represented idea by the datum as information (INF_s). A person interpreting the datum may capture the idea with greater or less accuracy, forming his own interpretation of it (INF_{r1}). On the other hand, Mingers (1995) points out, referring to Dretske (1981) that a sign (data) carries all the information implied by the original idea. These consequences can be analytical (i.e. follow by definition), or nomic (based on scientific facts) or they may follow from the logic of the situation. Moreover, they may lead to expanded information on the part of the interpreter (INF_{r2}). Based on his/her pre-knowledge, the interpreter may also uncover hidden information in the datum, something that the original speaker or author really intended to convey, even though perhaps unconsciously (as exemplified by a psychoanalytical interpretation of a patient's stories), or something that (s)he said without intending to do so. These may provide the interpreter with additional information (INF_{r3}). Normally, at least in the case of a complex idea, $INF_{r1} \neq INF_s$. If one takes a traditional transmission view of communication, we can interpret the difference caused by noise. On the other hand, the difference between INF_s and INF_{ri} opens a window for mutual learning and innovation, especially in the case of dialogue between a sender/speaker s and a receiver/reader r.

What is knowledge? As is well known, philosophers have puzzled over this question for centuries without achieving a clear answer. If we confine ourselves to definitions that lie closer to KM, Bell (1976) defines knowledge as "a set of organized statements of facts or ideas, presenting a reasoned judgment or an experimental result transmitted to others through some communication medium or in some systematic form". Stehr (1992) characterizes knowledge as "capacity for action" and Nonaka and Takeuchi (1995) define it as "justified true belief." Based on these definitions a general characterization of knowledge could be: an organized set of reasonably justified ideas that increases one's capacity for action. The first characteristic "organized" implies that a collection of separate simple facts does not form knowledge. The second characteristic "justified" emphasizes that not all ideas constitute knowledge, but in order to be knowledge they must have some validity. For the sake of generality, I do not presuppose truthfulness to be the only criterion for validity. Actually, I interpret the third characteristic, that knowledge increases one's capacity for action, as a general criterion for a justified idea. I assume that action is the ultimate test of the validity of knowledge.

We can now analyze the relationship between knowledge, information, and data using the infological equation proposed by Langefors (1966).

3.2   Articulation of the idea

Langefors used his infological equation to describe the interpretation of data. In the following, I will first adopt the idea to describe the articulation of data (codification of the idea)

$$D(INF_s) = d_s(INF_s, K_s, t).$$

INF_s is the idea to be represented in data by the speaker/sender s. K_s is the knowledge of the speaker/sender, and t is the time available to the speaker/sender for expressing his/her idea. K_s covers all relevant knowledge that affects the speaker's/sender's capability to express his/her idea, such as knowledge of the topic (idea), knowledge of the potential reader(s)/receiver(s), knowledge of the potential use and context of use of the idea, and knowledge of the language and medium used.

3.3   Interpretation of data

We can model the interpretation directly using the infological equation of Langefors (1966; 1980):

$$INF_r = i_r(D(INF_s), K_r, t).$$

This maintains that the information INF_r acquired by the receiver/reader r by interpreting the data $D(INF_s)$, representing an idea INF_s, is a function i_r of the data $D(INF_s)$ to be interpreted, the pre-knowledge K_r of the receiver/reader and the time t available for the interpretation. The pre-knowledge K_r covers all relevant knowledge that affects the receiver's/reader's ability to interpret the data $D(INF_s)$. These include one's pre-knowledge of the idea that the speaker/sender wishes to communicate, knowledge of the potential speaker/sender, knowledge of the situation that articulated the data, including the time available for the articulation, knowledge of the language and medium used, and all the relevant analytical, nomic and social knowledge affecting the interpretation (Mingers, 1995).

3.4   Interpretation and articulation as "hermeneutic" processes

The data (text) we interpret may be complex in terms of the idea INF_s. Its meaning is not necessarily revealed in a one-pass process of interpretation, but each successive reading of the data (text) may provide new insights, in the spirit of the hermeneutical spiral. Langefors (1980) suggests that this spiral can be modelled using the infological equation

$$INF_r' = i_r(D(INF_s),K_r',t),$$

where K_r' is the receiver/reader's knowledge after the first reading of the data $D(INF_s)$, i.e.

$$K_r' = K_r + i_r(D(INF_s),K_r,t).$$

This process can continue as long as each new reading sheds new light on the interpreted data.

As a special case, the speaker/sender may serve as a reader/receiver of his/her earlier data (text). This may trigger revision of the earlier data (text); that is,

$$D(INF_s)' = d_s(INF_s,K_s',t),$$

where K_s' is the sender's knowledge after reading his/her earlier text. That is,

$$K_s' = K_s + i_s(D(INF_s),K_s,t).$$

4.   INFORMATION SYSTEMS DEVELOPMENT REVISITED

We will look in this section at two recurrent trends in IS development:
- From in-house IS development to prefabricated IS development
- From heavy ISD methods to light ISD approaches

These trends are recurrent in the sense that they have popped up a number of times during the history of information systems.

4.1   From in-house to prefabricated information systems development

Adapting Gustafsson et al. (1982), one can interpret an information system as a computer-based system that provides its users with information on specified topics in a certain organizational context. This implies that an information system is specific to the organizational (or inter-organizational) context in which we implement it. Consequently, no prefabricated commercial software product is an information system as such. We cannot buy an information system, only the software (and hardware, and possibly data) to be used in its implementation.

Although much of our IS research has assumed in-house IS development, there have been recurrent instances of academic and business interest in prefabricated IS development under the labels of application packages in the 1980's, ERP in the 1990's and COTS in the 2000's. The Scandinavian contribution to these movements seems to have been surprisingly thin, however,[8] perhaps partly because of the relatively small number of major organizations in Scandinavia that have been interested in ERP. On the other hand, the majority of information systems implemented in Scandinavia have been based on application packages.[9] This has especially been the case in small organizations, but it is nowadays increasingly common in large ones.

It is obvious that the predominance of prefabricated IS development will move the main emphasis of ISD onto the four (infological) problems discussed above.   They are organizational alignment, requirements construction, organizational implementation, and IS evaluation.

4.2   From heavy ISD methods to light ISD approaches

Tensions between conceptualizations of the information systems and the ISD process models have driven our views of ISD.   Function/process-oriented methods such as SA/SD and ISAC dominated in the 1970s, to be replaced in the 1980s by data-oriented methods such as IE and NIAM.   The 1990's saw the emergence of object-oriented methods such as OOA/OOD, OMT, and OOSA.   These conceptualizations have tended to grow quite complex, as exemplified by UML (Booch et al., 1999).   At the same time, lighter ISD process models have been proposed.   Prototyping and evolutionary approaches made their appearance in the late 1970s, spiral models in the mid-1980s, and concurrent development in the 1990s, while agile methods emerged in the 2000s.

Having co-developed one ISD method during the 1980's, I have become more and more skeptical about the usefulness of these methods as such.   It seems to me that they are often too complex as conceptual artifacts to be useful in practice.   Without abstracting their essence, it is impossible to make sense of them.   The concept of an ISD approach characterized by the

---

[8] I know that the acquisition of application packages has been addressed in Finland by Iivari (1990a) and Saarinen and Vepsäläinen (1994), and that at least Nilsson (1991) and von Hellens (1991) have also worked on the topic at a Ph.D. dissertation level.

[9] I do not have any definite statistics on this, but I would estimate that more than 90% of information systems, when measured in terms of the number of systems, are based on prefabricated application software. The often cited "horror" statistics of ISD failures tend to forget this majority of ISD development efforts.

goals, guiding principles, major concepts, and principles of the ISD process (Iivari et al., 1998; 2000) attempts to provide an abstraction of this kind. I believe that ISD approaches are in line with agile "methods" in the sense that they are considerably lighter than specific methods.

One could consider agile "methods" to constitute a systems development approach. Abrahamson et al. (2002) provide a useful review of these, summarizing agility in four characteristics: incremental (small software releases with rapid cycles), cooperative (customer and developers working constantly together in close communication), straightforward (the method itself is easy to learn and modify) and adaptive (open to last moment changes). These features have much in common with the Scandinavian ISD approaches. The first characteristic is largely consistent with prototyping (Iivari, 1982; Bødker and Grønbæk, 1991). More explicitly, the PIOCO/OCIT method also allows fast incremental software development (Iivari, 1982; 1990a; 1990b), even though it does not specifically require it. The Trade Unionist approach has contributed to the cooperative aspects of systems development (Kensing and Munk-Madsen, 1993). Referring to the third characteristic, the PIOCO/OCIT method was explicitly developed with the idea of in-built flexibility so that it can easily be adapted not only to the characteristics of an organization or the specifics of a project but also to the daily contingencies of systems development (Iivari, 1989).

5.   CONCLUSIONS

In summary, this essay proposes four distinctive ISD process knowledge areas for IS experts: organizational alignment, requirements construction, organizational implementation and IS evaluation. These correspond closely to the infological problems identified by Langefors (1977). Furthermore, increased prefabricated IS development will move the main emphasis of ISD towards these infological problems. In addition, to prefabricate IS development, a move may be perceive towards lighter ISD methods/approaches than are represented by current methods such as UML and RUP.

REFERENCES

Abrahamson, P., Salo, O., Ronkainen, J. and Warsta, J., *Agile Software Development Methods, Review and Analysis*, VTT Publications 478, Espoo, 2002

Barley, S.R., Technology as an occasion for structuring: Evidence from observations of CT scanners and the social order of radiology departments, *Administrative Science Quarterly*, 31, 1996, pp. 78-101

Bell, D., *The Coming of Post-Industrial Society: A Venture of Social Forecasting*, Basic Books, New York, Basic Books, New York, 1976 (First published, 1973)

Beyer, H. and Holtzblatt, K., *Contextual Design, Defining Customer-Centered Systems*, Morgan Kaufmann Publishers, Inc. San Fransisco, 1998

Booch, G., Rumbaugh, J. and Jacobson, I., *The Unified Modeling Language User Guide*, Addison Wesley, Reading, MA, 1999

Brusilovsky, P., Methods and techniques of adaptive hypermedia, *User Modeling and User Adapted Interaction*, 6(2-3), 1996, pp. 87-129

Bubenko, J.A. Jr., Information modeling in the context of system development, Lavington, S. (ed.), *Information Processing 80*, North-Holland, Amsterdam, 1980, pp. 395-411

Bødker, S. and Grønbæk, K., Cooperative prototyping studies - users and designers envision a dental case record system. in Bowers, J.M. and Benford, S.D. (eds.). *Studies in Compute Supported Cooperative Work.* Elsevier Science Publishers B.V. (North-Holland), Amsterdam, 1991, 315-332

Carstensen, P.H. and Schmidt, K., Computer supported cooperative work: New challenges to systems design, in Itoh, K. (ed), *Handbook of Human Factors*, Tokyo, 1999

Davenport, T.H. and Prusak, L., *Working Knowledge*, Harward Business School Press, Boston, Massachusetts, 1998

Dretske, F., *Knowledge and the Flow of Information*, Basil Blackwell, Oxford, 1981

Ehn, P., *Work-Oriented Design of Computer Artifacts*, Arbetslivscentrum, Stockholm, 1988

Flynn, D.J. and Jazi, M.D., Constructing user requirements: a social process for a social context, *Information Systems Journal*, 8(1), 1998, pp. 53-82

Goldkuhl, G. and Lyytinen, K., A language action view of information systems, in Ross, C. and Ginzberg, M. (eds.): *Proceedings of the Third Conference on Information Systems*, Ann Arbor, Michigan, 1982, pp. 13-29

Gustafsson, M.R., Karlsson, T. and Bubenko, J. Jr., A declarative approach to conceptual information modeling, in Olle, T.W., Sol, H.G. and Verrijn-Stuart, A.A. (eds.): *Information systems design methodologies: a comparative review*, North-Holland, Amsterdam, 1982, pp. 93-142

Hammarberg, R., The cooked and the raw, *Journal of Information Science*, Vol. 3, No. 6, 1981, pp. 261-267

Hammer, M. and Champy, J., *Reengineering the Corporation, A Manifesto for Business Revolution*, Nichola Brealey, London, 1994

Henfridsson, O., Holmström, J. and Söderholm, A., Why are organizational theories so rarely used in Scandinavian IS research, *Scandinavian Journal of Information Systems*, 9(2), 1997, pp. 53-56

Iivari, J., Taxonomy of the experimental and evolutionary approaches to systemeering, in Hawgood, J. (ed.), *Evolutionary Information Systems*, North-Holland, Amsterdam, 1982, pp. 101-119

Iivari, J., A methodology for IS development as organizational change: A pragmatic contingency approach, in Klein, H.K. and Kumar, K. (eds.), *Systems Development for Human Progress*, North-Holland, Amsterdam, 1989, pp. 197-217

Iivari, J., Implementability of in-house developed vs. application package based information systems, *Data Base*, 21(1), 1990a, pp. 1-10

Iivari J., Hierarchical spiral model for information system and software development, Part 1: theoretical background, *Information and Software Technology*, 32(6), 1990b, pp. 386-399

Iivari J., Hierarchical spiral model for information system and software development, Part 2: design process, *Information and Software Technology*, 32(7), 1990c, pp. 450-458

Iivari, J., The organizational fit of information systems, *Journal of Information Systems*, 2(1), 1992, pp. 3-29

Iivari, J. and Hirschheim, R., Analyzing information systems development: A comparison and analysis of eight IS development approaches, *Information Systems*, 21(7), 1996, pp. 551-575

Iivari, J., Hirschheim, R. and Klein. H.K., A paradigmatic analysis contrasting information systems development approaches and methodologies, *Information Systems Research*, 9(2), 1998, pp. 164-193

Iivari, J., Hirschheim, R. and Klein, H.K., A dynamic framework for classifying information systems development methodologies and approaches, *Journal of Management Information Systems*, Vol. 17, No. 3, 2000-2001 pp. 179-218

Iivari, J., Hirschheim, R. and Klein, H.K., Towards more professional information systems development: ISD as knowledge work, *ECIS'2001*, Bled Slovenia, 2001

Iivari, J. and Kerola, P., A sociocybernetic framework for the feature analysis of information systems design methodologies, in Olle, T.W., Sol, H.G. and Tully, C.J. (eds.), *Information systems design methodologies: a feature analysis*, North-Holland, Amsterdam, 1983, pp. 87-139

Iivari, J. and Koskela, E., Choice and quality criteria for data system selection, in Samet, P.A. (ed.), *Proceedings of EuroIFIP 79, European Conference on Applied Information Technology*, North-Holland, Amsterdam, 1979, pp. 143-150

Iivari, J. and Koskela, E., The PIOCO model for IS design, *MIS Quarterly*, Vol. 11, No. 3, 1987, pp. 401-419

Iivari, J. and Linger, H., Knowledge Work as Collaborative Work: A Situated Activity Theory View, *Proceedings of the 32nd Hawaii International Conference on System Sciences*, 1999

Jacobson, I., Christerson, M., Jonsson, P. and Övergaard, G., *Object-Oriented Software Engineering, A use case driven approach*, Addison Wesley, Wokingham, England, 1992

Karsten, H., *Weaving Tapestry: Collaborative Information Technology and Organisational Change*, Jyväskylä University Press, Jyväskylä, 2000

Kensing. F. and Munk-Madsen, A., PD: Structure in the toolbox, *Communications of the ACM*, 36(4), 1993, pp. 78-85

Kerola, P. and Järvinen, P., *Systemointi II* (Systemeering II), Oy Gaudeamus Ab, Helsinki, 1975

Kling, R and Scacchi, W., Computing as social action: The social dynamics of computing in complex organizations, in Yovits, M.C. (ed.). *Advances in Computers*. 19, 1980, 249-327

Kling, R and Scacchi, W., The web of computing: Computer technology as social organization, in Yovits, M.C. (ed.). *Advances in Computers*. 21, 1982, pp. 1-90

Kuutti, K., Activity theory and its applications in information systems research and design, Nissen, H.-E., Klein, H.K. and Hirschheim, R., (eds.), *Information Systems Research Arena for the 90's*, North-Holland, Amsterdam, 1991, pp. 529-550

Langefors, B., *Theoretical Analysis of Information Systems*, Studentlitteratur, Lund, Sweden, 1966

Langefors, B., Information systems theory, *Information Systems*, 2, 1977, pp. 207-219

Langefors, B., Infological models and information user views, *Information Systems*, 5, 1980, pp. 17-32

Langley, A., Minzberg, H., Pitcher, P., Posada, E. and Saint-Macary, J., Opening up decision making: The view from the black stool, *Organization Science*, 6(3), 1995, pp. 260-279

Lundeberg, M., Goldkuhl, G. and Nilsson, A., *Systemering*, Studentlitteratur, Lund, 1978

Lundeberg, M., Goldkuhl, G. and Nilsson, A., *Information Systems Development: A systematic approach*, Prentice-Hall, Englewood Cliffs, New Jersey, 1981

Majchrzak, A., Rice, R.E., Malhotra, A., King, N. and Ba, S., Technology adaptation: The case of a computer-supported inter-organizational virtual tem, *MIS Quarterly*, 24(4), 2000, pp. 569-600

Miles, R.E. and Snow, C.C., Causes of failures in network organizations, *California Management Review*, 34(4), 1992, pp. 53-72

Mingers, J.C., Information and meaning: foundations for an intersubjective account, *Information Systemes Journal*, 5, 1995, pp. 285-306

Minzberg, H., *The Rise and Fall of Strategic Planning*, Prentice Hall, 1994

Nilsson, A.G., *Anskaffning av standardsystem för att utveckla verksamheter, Utveckling och prövning av SIV-metoden*, Ph.D. Diss., Stockholm Handelshögskolan, Stockholm, 1991

Nonaka, I. and Takeuchi, H., *The Knowledge Creating Company*, Oxford University Press, New York, 1995

Pohl, K., The three dimensions of requirements engineering: A framework and its applications. *Information Systems*. 19(3), 1994, pp. 243-258

Porra, J., *Colonial Systems, Information Colonies and Punctuated Prototyping*, Jyväskylä Studies in Computer Science, Economics and Statistics 33, University of Jyväskylä, Jyväskylä, 1996

Powell, W., Neither market nor hierarchy: network forms of organization, *Research in Organizational Behavior*, 12, 1990, pp. 295-336

Saarinen, T. and Vepsalainen, A.P.J., Procurement strategies for information systems, *Journal of Management Information Systems*, 11(2), 1994, pp. 187-208

Schmidt, K., The problem with "awareness", Introductory remarks on 'awareness in CSCW', *Computer Supported Cooperative Work*, 11, 2002, pp. 285-298

Schmidt, K. and Bannon, L., Taking CSCW seriously: Supporting articulation work, *Computer Supported Cooperative Work*, 1(1-2), 1992, pp. 7-40

Schmidt, K. and Simone, C., Coordination mechanisms: Towards a conceptual foundation of CSCW system design, *Computer Supported Cooperative Work*, 5(2-3), 1996, pp. 155-200

Simon, H., *The New Science of Managerial Decision*, Harper and Row, 1960

Smith, H.A. and McKeen, J.D., Developments in practice VIII: Enterprise content management, *Communications of the Association of Information Systems*, Vol. 11, 2003, pp. 647-659

Spiegler, I., Knowledge Management: A new idea or a recycled concept?, *Communications of the Association for Information Systems*, Vol. 3, Article 14, June 2000

Spinuzzi, C., A Scandinavian challenge, a US response: Methodological assumptions in Scandinavian and US prototyping approaches, *SIGDOC'02*, Toronto, Ontario, Canada, 2002, pp. 208-215

Stehr, N., Experts, counselors and advisers, in Stehr, N. and Ericsson, R.V. (eds.), *The Culture and Power of Knowledge*, Walter de Gruyter, Berlin, 1992, pp. 107-155

Sundgren, B., *An Infological Approach to Data Bases*, Skriftserie utgiven av statistiska centralbyrån, Nummer 7, Statistiska Centralbyrån, Stockholm, 1973

Tuomi, I., Data is more than knowledge, Implications of the reversed knowledge hierarchy for knowledge management and organizational memory, *Journal of Management Information Systems*, 16(3), 2000, pp. 103-117

von Hellens, L.A., *Conditions for Success in the Design and Implementation of Packaged Software. A Study of Accounting Software for Small Companies in the United Kingdom*, Publications of The Turku School of Economics and Business Administration, Series A-3, Turku, 1991.

Weill. P. and Vitale, M.R., *Place to Space: Migrating to eBusiness Models*, Harvard Business School Press, Harvard, MA 2001

Wenger, E., *Communities of Practice: Learning, Meaning and Identity*, Cambridge University
   Press, Cambridge, 1998

SIGNIFICANT APPLICATIONS
Session Summary

Nils Høeg

Session Chair; nils.hoeg@hydro.com

1.   INTRODUCTORY REMARKS

Applications or the *use* of computers is the raison d'être for computers and everything associated with them. We have identified some *significant* applications conceived and developed in Scandinavia; they also had some lasting impact in the Nordic nations. As it happened, we ended up with examples from Norway.

The first two papers are addressing applications in the Maritime and Offshore Industries, which are among the most significant "clusters" in Norwegian industry. The third paper is a significant application of Nordic networking. The two papers on "Applications and Technologies for Maritime and Offshore Industries" are coordinated.

2.   AUTHORS

Trond Vahl worked for more than twenty years in the Veritas Group, one of the world's leading ship classification and design companies. Vahl was a researcher in mathematical modeling, and systems and programming, and later on Managing Director of Computas, and Deputy Managing Director of the Veritas Group.

Trygve Reenskaug is professor emeritus of informatics at the University of Oslo. He has 40 years experience in software engineering research and the development of industrial strength software products. He has extensive teaching and speaking experience including keynotes, talks, and tutorials. The goal of his current research is to understand the nature of the *Information Systems of the 21st Century*.

Rolf Nordhagen is professor emeritus at the University of Oslo Centre for Information Technology Service (USIT). From 1972 to 1988, he was Director of the Oslo University Computer Centre. As a member of steering groups and boards he was active in creating the Norwegian academic network UNINETT, and the Nordic network NORDUnet.

APPLICATIONS AND TECHNOLOGIES FOR MARITIME AND OFFSHORE INDUSTRIES
Industrial Significance of Computer Applications

Trond Vahl

Former Managing director of Computas, Oslo; tvahl@c2i.net

Abstract: This paper gives an overview of the computer applications, hardware and software, that were essential in the rapid development of ship technology during the sixties and seventies and the subsequent development of offshore oil technology.

Key words: Industry computing, maritime technology

1. INTRODUCTION

The maritime industry in Norway, comprising ship owners, brokers, shipyards, consultants, research and education institutions and classification society, experienced a strong growth and considerable changes during the sixties and early seventies. An internationally competitive Norwegian shipping industry, operating one of the world's largest merchant fleets and being in the forefront both commercially and technologically, drove this growth. The rapid technological development that took place, not least in Scandinavia, also contributed to this growth. This technological development, which they could not implement without extensive use of computers, also turned out to be of great importance in the first decade – the seventies - of the Norwegian offshore oil industry.

The very rapid build up of a national offshore oil industry, based on national skills and resources, relied heavily on the maritime technology developed during the sixties and the early seventies. Thus, in fact, the early offshore oil industry was part of the maritime cluster, using i.e. to a large extent the same people, engineering skills and computer software and hardware, the same production facilities and the same investors and financial institutions.

The systems that were developed, mainly using UNIVAC 1107 and 1108, from the beginning of the 1960s were a necessary condition i.e. for the design and construction of large oil tankers (the size grew from 60000 tons to over 300000 tons in a decade), the new spherical gas-tankers, special cargo vessels etc. At the same time, process control computers were installed for automatic engine room control, based on a technology to be used later on as in controlling the movements and position of mobile rigs.

The skills, software, and hardware thus available around 1970 could immediately apply to the offshore oil industry in the design and construction of the huge concrete and other fixed platforms such as the semi-submersible mobile rigs and their control systems. The significant Norwegian seismic industry also grew out of the same nucleus. In addition to benefiting the Norwegian and international maritime and offshore technology, these hardware and software developments resulted in an export oriented hardware and software industry.

In Norway, the oil era began in 1967 with the discovery of the Balder Field and the commercially more interesting Ekofisk Field in 1969, changing the industrial and economic structure of Norway. The oil and gas sector now contributes directly to the Norwegian economy with 23% of the GDP and 45% of the export. Norway is the third largest exporter of oil in the world. The yearly investments in the sector amount to around 60 billion NOK and the yearly oil and gas production is worth about 300 billion NOK. The complexity and size of the systems being designed and installed is illustrated by the fact that the cost of developing the Statfjord field alone amounted to around 90 billion NOK.

The "Norwegian content" of the investments in the first phase rapidly approached 70%, which was the political goal. This was an ambitious target taking into account that the investments in fixed and mobile marine structures, process equipment, operational systems and various services was heavily based on completely new technologies to be applied in the very harsh and demanding environment in the North Sea, on the surface and down to more than 500 meters. They met the target fairly soon, partly because much of the basic skills and infrastructure was already in place in the maritime cluster: In shipyards, shipping companies, research institutes, and Det norske Veritas.

In the following, we will give a survey of the application of computers in the design, construction, and operation in the maritime and offshore sectors in the sixties and seventies, showing by a few examples how software, skills and infrastructure developed for the maritime industry could readily be applied to the development of the offshore industry. The present contribution is not based on the thorough research that the topic deserves, but rather on the author's memory, on manuscript of speeches given at various occasions, and on internal notes. Some information also comes from informal conversations with key people from the period in question.

We do not intend to give the full picture. The examples will provide an illustration of the rapid development of advanced ship technology in the 1960s. They will also show the remarkable development of new technology in the following decade in the offshore oil and gas sector, of the synergy between these sectors, and an illustration of the considerable significance of computer application in these achievements. The topics chosen and the description of the examples are naturally coloured by the author's position in Det norske Veritas and its subsidiary, Computas, during the sixties and seventies and through other mentioned achievements.

2.   EXAMPLES OF APPLICATION OF COMPUTERS IN SHIP DESIGN IN THE SIXTIES

The increasing demand for transportation of oil made it commercially interesting to use larger oil tankers, bringing the size from 60.000 tons dwt around 1960 to more than 300.000 tons ten years later. This rapid development left the ship designers with great challenges. In earlier times, the criterion for the ship's structural strength related to its longitudinal strength, considering the ship as a beam with variable cross sections. With the larger ships, one had to consider also the transversal strength and the strength of its various components such as plates and frames. This called for increasingly complex and theoretically based methods and calculations, which at that time were part of the ship design, hull as well as engine, to enhance the more empirically based methods being used until then. In 1956, Det norske Veritas started using computers for such calculations. At the same time, a number of new, large shipyards were erected in many countries to handle the building of these large tankers. This also called for new computer based systems in design and production.

These more elaborate methods, like the finite element method for structural analysis and the statistically based calculation of impact of waves on the ship, turned out to be necessary to support the development of new ship structures. The development started in 1960 at Det norske Veritas, inspired by work done by Børje Langefors at Saab Aircraft ten years earlier. Later on in the sixties strong groups were established at NTH in Trondheim.

The first programs appeared in 1960 in a very simple assembly language, almost a binary machine language, on the Ferranti Mercury at NDRE, the Norwegian Defence Research Establishment. They used the capacity of this machine to its maximum to solve the up to 200 simultaneous linear equations involved at that time to take into account the 200 degrees of freedom of the model of the physical system. They were able to augment the capability of the programs when the Univac 1107 was in place in 1963 at Norsk Regnesentral. They could now solve up to 5000 linear equations. The productivity in writing new software increased considerably by using the now available high level languages like Fortran and by using remote batch terminals, like Univac 1004. Because interactive terminals were not available at that time (they were introduced to this application around 1975), a large proportion of the programmers were engaged in creating the user interface.

The users themselves made much of the software development. For example, by 1970 many individuals of the technical staff of Det Norske Veritas were skilled Fortran programmers. At this time, therefore, all disciplines involved in ships and machinery design and related areas used computers.

It became obvious later on in the 1960s as the size of the tankers grew and as new problems appeared (when dealing with new types of ships like the LPG and LNG tankers, developed and built by the Kværner group, with spherical tanks, and carrying liquid gas at very low temperatures) that even more elaborate methods had to be used. They had to take into account more complex representations of the structures, fracture mechanics, nonlinear, thermal, and dynamic effects. As the complexity of the calculations increased and as more and more fields needed computerization, the demand for more computer capacity became obvious, and Det norske Veritas decided in 1969 to install a Univac 1108.

Thus, around 1970, we were able to handle up to 500.000 simultaneous linear equations, which was necessary to analyse the LNG Tankers. We should note though, that in order to do this one had to utilize the a priori information one had about the internal pattern of the structures and the matrixes representing them, for instance the bandwidth and the multilevel system of substructures. Using machine code and double precision in the inner loop of the equation solving routine were necessary to maintain accuracy without increasing computer time too much. Nevertheless, it took a whole night to perform a complicated calculation. This was rather exciting when the mean time between system breakdowns was less than 12 hours in the first year of operation of the Univac 1108.

To do such analysis (the finite element analysis being only one out of several other important applications), the introduction in 1963 of Univac 1107 at NR with the remote batch terminals and good Fortran compilers, and later on 1108 in 1969 were just in time and necessary for the development. Another key to the development were the methods and software, named SESAM, developed at NTH during the late sixties and acquired by Det norske Veritas in 1970. This system were used extensively in the coming years by Det norske Veritas who also developed it further and brought it to the world market, an activity that today are still bustling with a staff of 150 in marketing, maintenance and support.

3.   TRANSFERRING SKILLS AND USING THE INFRASTRUCTURE IN THE OFFSHORE DEVELOPMENT

The first achievement of computer application in the offshore development was the design analysis of the Ekofisk Tank, a huge cylindrical structure, built in concrete and steel, 100 meters in diameter and placed on the bottom, 70 meters below the sea surface. To calculate the structure they had to use the most advanced finite element programs together with the newly developed, statistically based methods for assessing the impact from the waves on the structure. To illustrate the transfer of technology, they used the same methods, the same software, even the same people as they were in designing the large LNG tankers. When the Aker Group designed the new generation of mobile platform, the H3, the finite element programs were indispensable tools.

The next technological break-through came with the introduction in 1974 of the huge concrete platform, Condeep, still operating in many waters around the world. Completed in 1995, the largest of these platforms, including their topside processing plants, are up to 450 meters tall (the tallest structure on earth at that point in time), placed in deep water with only its topside above the surface. The Norwegian consultancy firm, Dr. Techn, designed the Condeep platform. Olav Olsen, in cooperation with Norwegian Contractors, a Norwegian construction company, also developed the unique production method. The design required extensive dynamic and non-linear finite element calculations.

Again, it was the same group of people, mostly employed by Computas, a Veritas subsidiary, that did the calculations, using the same methods, the same software, and the same infrastructure. This time one overall analysis of the structure required a mesh of several hundreds of thousands elements, with up to three millions of degrees of freedom. The solution of the resulting several millions of linear equations took up to six days on the 1108 requiring continuous surveillance and complicated logistics to restart if anything went wrong, which sometimes occurred, even if the mean time between system breakdowns on the 1108 at that time (1974) was considerably longer than a few years earlier. The Condeep analysis was, however, so frequent and extensive that they acquired computer time on several 1108's around Europe (in Basel, Oberhausen, and London). Needless to say that this was before Norwegian government introduced the Working Environment Act (Arbeidsmijøloven).

4.   OTHER EXAMPLES

4.1   The Autokon and related systems

The Autokon system for computer-aided design of ships, developed in the sixties by SI (Sentralinstitutt for Industriell Forskning, The Central Institute for Industrial Research) in cooperation with the Aker Group. Trygve Reenskaug covers this in his paper in these Proceedings. This system played an important role in the design and building of the large tankers and other modern ships as did the related systems and equipment for design and manufacturing automation (drafting and cutting equipment, etc.) and the production control software developed in cooperation with the Kongsberg group. All these systems, based on SI's mathematical modelling of 3-D surfaces and their database design were important tools when the large shipyards were converted into offshore yards in the seventies, then building huge mobile and fixed drilling, production and accommodation platforms.

4.2   Process automation

The first Nord computer was used in the Taimyr-project, a joint effort between Institutt for reguleringsteknikk (Institute for Control Engineering) at NTH, SFI (the Norwegian Ship Research Institute), the shipping company Wilh. Wilhelmsen, Det norske Veritas, and Norcontrol. In this project, completed in 1970, they installed a minicomputer for the first time onboard a merchant ship to control the engine room operation. The result of the project was a system that allowed for unmanned engine room, which was a great achievement both when it comes to safety and cost. There were at the same time other efforts to install minicomputers onboard to control the operations, but the Taimyr project was the most successful, bringing Norcontrol in front of the development and the Nord computer to the market. Norcontrol is still a market leader with this application.

The skills that were developed was one of the cornerstones in the later development of many process control systems in the offshore sector, for instance the mobile positioning systems developed and produced by The Kongsberg Group to control the movements and position of the mobile platforms and vessels operating at the offshore oil fields. Also this application, like many other successful developments in computer applications in this period of time, had its roots at Institutt for reguleringsteknikk (Institute for Control Engineering) at NTH.

4.3   Seismic exploration

In 1972, Det norske Veritas established the marine seismic company, Geco (Originally Geoteam-Computas AS), through its subsidiary Computas in cooperation with Geoteam, a consulting firm specializing in geophysics and geology. The basis for the establishment was the geophysical group of Geoteam, having for several years being conducting seismic surveys on land and at sea, and the computer and instrumentation activity at Det norske Veritas, including the Univac 1108.

The marine seismic activity consists basically of two activities. Firstly, seismic data are acquired by a large number of sensors attached to one or more cables of considerable length (i.e. 5 km.), towed after a vessel cruising at low speed, at that time usually a converted trawler or supply ship. By sending signals to the sea floor, the signals penetrating further and reflected by the geological layers beneath, and picking the reflected signals up by the sensors, they were able to collect a huge amount of raw data.

Secondly, they had to process the reflected data to make the data understandable to the geophysicists and geologists. This data processing is advanced signal processing, using various correlation and de-convolution techniques that require the computer to perform a huge number of operations, proportional to the second or even third power of the number of data. With 24 groups of sensors and a sampling rate of 4 milliseconds, which was state of the art in the 1970s, one can imagine computer time that was necessary to process the bulk data (approx. 20 billions of numerical data) each day. It soon turned out that the 1108 was to slow and that dedicated computers with array processors were better suited for this task.

In the first half of the 1980s, Geco had 1500 employees, operated 15 vessels, seven data processing centres around the world, and two manufacturing plants. It made its own electronic equipment, thus being one of the largest and most profitable seismic companies in the world. The geophysical industry in Norway now consists of several companies with total sales of approximately 1 billion dollars and with more than 50% of the world market for marine seismic services. Most of these companies have their roots in Geco.

4.4   Software export services

For most of the software development described in this paper and in the Autokon paper, the objective of the development was in the first place to make the participating industry, like the Aker Group and Det norske Veritas, more competitive. Very soon, it turned out that it was possible to develop profitable business on services based on the software; the potential for exporting it also was present. The first overseas installation of the ESSI-Autokon combination was at the General Dynamics, Quincy Yard, Massachusetts, in 1965. This could be the first major application exported from Europe to America. Major shipyards all over the world eventually adopted Autokon. Three distinct technologies emerged from this project: mathematical modelling, data base technology, and personal information systems. They formed the basis of several systems that came onto the market by a number of companies in the following decades.

Det norske Veritas decided in 1966 to start selling the software programs they developed and the services based on them. This led to the establishment of the subsidiary, Computas in 1968, with the main purpose of selling the software that Det norske Veritas had developed. The Aker group also established a separate subsidiary, Shipping Research Services, to market Autokon and related software.

The finite element programs were the most sold software of the Computas portfolio. It also brought to market a large number of other applications within shipbuilding, offshore industry, mechanical industry, and civil engineering. They sold the programs to almost all industrialized countries in the world in the following decades and they established service centres in most of the major Veritas offices around the globe, mostly in conjunction with the local Veritas office. The economic results of the export activity in Computas were not spectacular in the first years. However, it contributed considerably to the necessary maintenance and further development of the software and its use, and to the success of Det norske Veritas in its worldwide operation. The Sesam system is still operative with some 150 people engaged in marketing, maintenance, and user support after having sold around 300 licenses of the system. However, today they integrated the system with other software into a much more extensive information processing and production environment.

Let me mention one thing as a curiosity. In the late 1980s, the author received an inquiry from Korea about a bug that someone found in the software that he developed in the mid-1960s. That is a long lifetime in the computer business.

5.   CONCLUDING REMARKS

The applications mentioned in this paper were undoubtedly successes. We have omitted the many failures. Success has many fathers; failure is an orphan, as the old saying goes.

Most of the successes were obtained in broad multidisciplinary milieus and in areas with extensive cooperation between business, research institutes and NTH and where all parties (including the users) were operationally involved. This was especially true towards the end of the 1960s and in the 1970s, a substantial number of people switched between the various institutions and companies. It turned out that we achieved the best results in projects where the participants were on equal footing with a common goal, and not where one being regarded the sub-vendor of the other.

A typical feature of the milieus involved was the presence of *basic* technological understanding. This made it possible to apply the skills to the new areas of development. We demonstrated this when we showed the transfer of skills in ship design, production, and operation to the development of the offshore oil and gas industry, or when the skills in mathematical modelling obtained by developing the methods for automatic ship design were transferred to the design of ocean wave power plants. Another typical feature was the lack of distinction between programmers, systems designers, and experts in the subject matter.

Is there anything to learn from the story briefly outlined above? We developed most of the skills and software in an environment where leaders in business and academia allowed creative people with visions to use their energy to realise the visions. The bureaucracy was almost not present. The achievements were not the results of formalized strategic plans and strict control, but the results of visions. There was hardly an accountant around to demand cost-benefit analyses. The people involved were extremely dedicated and had what they considered obvious goals and the necessary authority, and mostly the economic resources to reach them. The successes were not the result of user initiative and *control* (brukerstyring), but end-user *involvement*, also operationally. (Is this just wishful thinking supported by a fading memory? Perhaps not.)

APPLICATIONS AND TECHNOLOGIES FOR MARITIME AND OFFSHORE INDUSTRIES
Technological Significance of Early Norwegian Applications

Trygve Reenskaug

Department of Informatics, University of Oslo; trygver@ifi.uio.no

Abstract: Autokon, a CAD/CAM system for ships, was one of the most important early Norwegian applications. We describe the background for the Autokon project and its results. We will specifically follow three technology threads that we have called *Data-centred Architectures, Mathematical Modelling, and Personal Information Systems*, where the last one includes distribution and component based architectures. An important part of the Autokon background is the history of the earliest computers in Britain and Norway. We therefore start with a brief history of computing

Key words: Computing history; CAD/CAM; system architectures; mathematical modelling; personal information systems

1.   INTRODUCTION

The Second World War was largely a war of science. It was a war of electronic navigation measures and countermeasures: "The early detection and partial frustration of Knickebein - a feat known only to a few - was an early and major British victory in the Battle of Britain." [Jones-98] Even more important was the breaking of the Enigma code used by the German navy, army and air force. This critical work was started by the Poles and completed by the British by means of electro-mechanical computers called Bombes: "Between 1939 and 1945, the most advanced and creative forms of mathematical and technological knowledge were combined to master German communications. British cryptanalysts, Alan Turing at the forefront, changed the course of the Second World War and created the foundation for the modern computer" [Sale]. The code used by the German high command, the Lorenz code, was also broken by the British using the world's first electronic digital computer, the Colossus [Small] [Colossus]. By the end of the war, the British had built ten Colossi machines. This gave them invaluable experience with the design, construction, and operation of digital computers, an experience that gave them a head start over the Americans who only got their single ENIAC operational more than a year after the first Colossus. We give more details of this interesting story in Section 2, introducing the roots of some early Norwegian computers.

In this paper, we take Norway's first computer and the Autokon project as our main starting point. Autokon is a system for the computer aided design and construction of ships. Its vision is a data-centred architecture with a product model in a central information store surrounded by a number of application programs that support various shipbuilding activities. It first went into production at the Stord shipyard in 1963. Most of the world's major shipyards later adopted Autokon. We describe the Autokon project in more detail in Section 3. Three technological threads that grew out of this project are discussed in Sections 4, 5 and 6.

Different milieus grew up around each of the early computers in Norway. We do not claim that Autokon was our most important early application; but it happened to be the one with which we were familiar. This means that we will not go into the important developments that grew up around our second computer, the Ferranti Mercury at Kjeller. Object orientation and Simula[Simula] sprang out of this nucleus. So did the international minicomputer company Norsk Data and the computer-based activities of Kongsberg Våpenfabrikk. Norcontrol was established 1965 for the exploitation of an anti-collision and machine room control system for M/S Taimyr. Kongsberg Maritime Ship Systems, the world's largest supplier of ship automation and control systems, can trace its history to this project. Other early applications proved to be significant in various ways. Most of these were important for a single organisation only, while a few had wider impact. An example is the simulation of waterpower reservoirs with their installations of electrical power generators at the Norwegian Water Resources and Energy Directorate (NVE) that started on the Facit EDB 3 in 1960. Better overviews of early Norwegian computing can be found in the papers by Drude Berntsen[Bernt-03] and Trond Vahl[Vahl-03] at this conference.

2. THE ROOTS OF THE EARLY NORWEGIAN COMPUTERS

2.1 The first British computers

The German High Command used a code nicknamed "Fish" that was more sophisticated than the Enigma code used in routine operations. The British managed to break this code with the aid of *Colossus*, a special purpose parallel computer with more than 1500 valves. Registers were in the form of thyratron rings; main memory was a loop of paper tape continuously read at 5000 characters per second. The Colossus was programmed to a limited degree via its plugboards and switches. The first Colossus went into full operation in January 1944, and by the end of the war, there were ten Colossi in operation at Bletchley Park[Colossus]. Colossus was top secret, known only to a select few in Britain and the U.S.A.[Small].

Another special purpose electronic computer was the American *ENIAC* designed for ballistic and other computations. It was gradually put into operation from June 1944, and was only completed in the fall of 1945, [ENIAC] reference calls it "the world's first electronic digital computer". This is clearly wrong, since ten Colossi preceded it.

Colossus and ENIAC were electronic digital computers programmed via plugboards. The concept of a stored program computer was first suggested by Alan Turing in his seminal paper that appears to have been written while he was at Princeton under von Neuman's eye.[Turing-36] By 1946 the pressing needs of war were over and a number of people on both sides of the Atlantic were ready for the next step. In July and August 1946, there was a series of 48 lectures at the Moore School of Electrical Engineering[Moore-49]. Twenty-eight people attended from the U.S. and Great Britain. Threads from the ENIAC and, indirectly, the Colossus were merged with Alan Turing's complete design of the previous year[O'Connor] and the ideas of von Neuman, Eckert, Mauchly and others. This must have been a memorable event for all participants with a free flow of ideas and much enthusiasm. It must also have been a very frustrating event for the British participants because the Official Secrets Act prevented them from giving the audience the benefit of their deep Colussus experiences. Nevertheless, it appears that all participants went home eager to realise the computer vision.

The Colossus was top secret, yet the accumulated expertise migrated after the war together with its developers to various British research establishments. A highly productive computer community was at the *University of Manchester*. The word's first stored program electronic computer appears to be the *Manchester Small Scale Experimental Machine*—"The Baby"[Baby] that executed its first program as early as on 21st

June 1948. Baby was designed for testing the Williams-Kilburn cathode ray tube high-speed storage device. It was truly minimal computer with an operations repertoire of just seven instructions. Baby lead through several stages to the design of the *Ferranti Mark 1*. The first machine off the production line was delivered to Manchester University in February 1951, allegedly making it the world's first general-purpose commercial computer.

A group at the University of Cambridge started work on the *EDSAC* computer in October 1946 as one of the developments following the Moore School Lectures. EDSAC ran its first program 6 May 1949 when it computed the squares of 0..99. This made it the first complete and fully operational regular electronic digital stored program computer [EDSAC].

2.2   The first Norwegian computers

We now get to Nusse, the first Norwegian computer. There was a committee, *Utvalg for matematikkmaskiner*. There was an instigator, *Henry Viervoll*, who was working with X-ray spectra and needed a computer. And there was an achiever, *Thomas Hysing*, who made it happen. A decisive event was a visit to the committee by Professor D. R. Hartree who was involved with the EDSAC work at Cambridge. He strongly recommended that the committee should go for an electronic stored program computer. The result was that Hysing spent a half-year at the EDSAC laboratory in 1949. A computer on the scale of EDSAC could not be financed in Norway at that time. Through his work with X-ray spectra, Viervoll had contact with Andrew D. Booth at Birkbeck College, London. Booth had plans for the APEXC computer (All Purpose Electronic X-Ray Computer)[APEXC]. These plans were modest and within reach for the Norwegians[Hy-03]. The Norwegians subsequently acquired APEXC(N) in kit form, a kit that proved to be both incomplete and unsound. Hysing and his crew at the *Central institute for industrial research* (SI) got the computer up and running in the spring of 1953 after a number of modifications and extensions[museum]. By 1954, she was sufficiently stable for her operation to be taken over by the *Norwegian Computing Centre* (NCC).

Nusse's main memory was a rotating drum with 512, 32-bit words. Input/output was with five-channel paper tape in addition to a Teletypewriter printer. There were three main registers called *Ar*, *Mr*, and *Or*. Nusse used a 1+1 operation format as follows: Not Used *b* (one bit), Counter: (*n*, seven bits), Data Address: (*x-addr*, ten bits), Operation: (*Op*, 5 bits), address of Next Operation: (*y-addr*, ten bits). The latter was important since it enabled optimisation by making sure that the next operation was under the read/write head when it was needed. There where sixteen basic operations. *Operation 14*, for example, transferred the (32-n) least significant bits from *Ar* to memory in address *x-addr* and fetched the next operation from *y-addr*. Basic operation time was about 1 ms, but could be as high as 16 ms if it had to wait a complete turn of the drum for its data. (*And* 32 ms if it had to wait another turn for its next operation).[AmEvj-53] Nusse was decommissioned in 1961 when her last project, the development of Autokon, was ported to the Swedish *Facit EDB 3* at the Norwegian Meteorological Institute.

Figure 1: Reliability was the key problem with the early computers.

The Swedish government took an early initiative for building computers in Sweden. A committee, *Matematikmaskinnämden*, was established as early as December 1948. Their first electronic computer, *BESK*, was completed in November 1953. Facit developed *Facit EDB 3*; a commercial product based on the BESK. The first Facit machine was completed in 1957. For a short period, Facit EDB was the fastest machine in existence. A Facit EDB 3 was installed at the *Norwegian Meteorological Institute* (NMI) in July 1961, making it the third meteorological institute in the world to get their own computer.

Facit EDB 3 had a core memory of 2048, 40-bit words, or 4196 half words of 20 bits. I/O was paper tape and punched cards; printing was off-line via punched cards. There was a core-based buffer of 4096 40-bit words and a drum secondary store. An operation was held in a half-word with 12-bit address and 8-bit operation code. There were no index registers so indexing had to be done with arithmetic on the instructions. The interesting random access "carousel" tape station ECM 64 had a removable wheel with 64 tape spools; each spool could hold 8192 40-bit words. A read or write operation was in two steps. First position the carousel for the required spool, then read or write the data blocks off that spool[Facit].

The Facit was the engine for the first Autokon production runs. The database for a ship was held on one Facit carousel. Autokon was subsequently ported to FORTRAN on NCC's Univac 1107. This computer was the first large-scale computer in Norway and had an immense impact after its installation in August 1963[Elgsaas].

Another event that proved important to our story was the arrival of an *IBM 650* computer in Bergen in 1958 at AS Emma. This supported a strong computing group at the *Bergen Mekaniske Verksteder* (BMV) shipyard. This group developed original shipbuilding applications that were later integrated into Autokon. AS Emma thrived and had 260 employees in 1985.[Emma]

3.   SHIPBUILDING WITH ESSI AND AUTOKON

We start our main story at SI in 1959. Nusse was in full operation and was used in a number of scientific and technical applications in shipbuilding. These applications were most notable for their influence on future events. One of these events was the invention of *ESSI*, a patented, special-purpose device for numerical control[Kveim-61]. This controller had a curve generator for guiding a tool along straight lines, circular arcs and parabolas. The first installation was for the control of a flame cutter at the *Stord Yard* in the autumn of 1960[RBj-03]. The Stord Yard people were highly attuned to new technology. For example, they computed tank-sounding tables on the Facit EDB in Gothenburg as early as 1959.

Kongsberg Våpenfabrikk later marketed ESSI for the control of flame cutters and other machine tools as well as the *Kingmatic*, a very large and highly accurate flatbed plotter for shipbuilding and many other industries. The ESSI code format is still used in the industry.

By 1958/59, the scene was set for Thomas Hysing to merge the ideas of computers and numerically controlled machine tools into the vision of a digital basis for the design and construction of ships. He presented it at the first IFAC congress in Moscow in 1960[Hy-60]. The vision covered the complete ship design process from owner's specifications to the construction in the yard as shown in Figure 2.

"The most remarkable difference is that in the future digital computers will take over much of the design work which now is carried out by manual means. In the illustration shown it is assumed that manual labour is needed to any great extent only for the first drawing of the ship lines, for the making of ship arrangement, possibly also for classification drawings and for section planning. The rest of the work will eventually, for the greater part, be done by digital computers."[Hy-60]

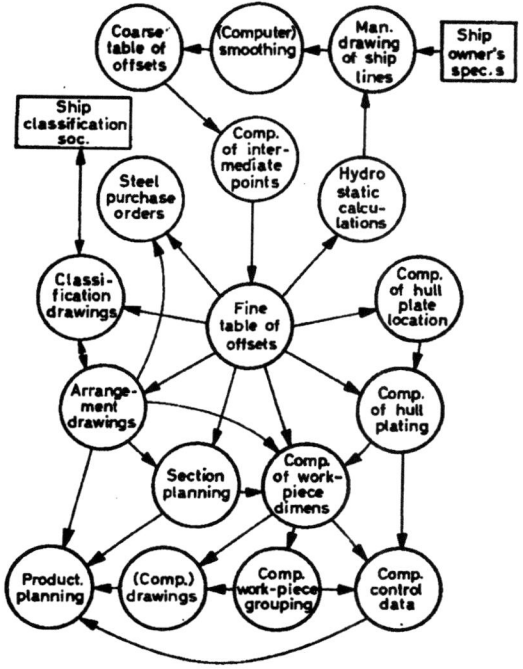

Figure 2: The computerised shipyard

The idea was to begin at the end and produce control tapes for the numerically controlled machine tools before gradually working back towards the early design stages. This was an important decision, because it made it essential to work with a complete and accurate numerical product model from the very beginning. It also forced the developers to understand and include all the small production details and considerations required in generating production data tapes for NC machines.

In 1959, MIT announced the Automatic Programmed Tools[APT] programming language. In 1960 followed Direct Numerical Control (DNC). The ESSI controller, therefore, appears to be among the first DNC controllers in the world. More importantly, APT was a language for specifying cutter location data sets so that its scope was restricted to the interface between a completed design and the machine tool. Contrast this with Hysing's vision that covered the complete design process; probably making it one of the first examples of true Computer Aided Design/Computer Aided Manufacturing (CAD/CAM). Even today, nearly half a century later, many CAD tools are merely automated draftsmen. They are neither integrated with a product model at the conceptual end nor with the machine tools at the physical end.

The Central Institute for Industrial Research (SI) in Oslo submitted a proposal to the Norwegian Council for Scientific and Technical Research (NTNF) 30 November 1959[Proposal]. The proposal was accepted and the Autokon project started August 1960. (Those were the days! Only seven months from proposal to project start.)

The proposal sketched the ship production process from the owner's specification through delivery. It focused on the lofting and detail design activities and the transition to construction (where the ESSI-controlled flame cutters created the ships parts from numerical information). The six main modules in the proposed system were:

1. Fairing of sculptured surfaces.
2. Plate part definition for planar surfaces.
3. Automatic detailing based on end user programming..
4. Nesting plate parts in a raw format and producing numerical control data.
5. Automatic plotting and final checking.
6. The central database system

System design and development started August 1960.[HyRee-63] Autokon went into production at the Aker Stord Yard on the West Coast of Norway in 1963 where it formed the cornerstone in their continuous efficiency improvements for building a stream of supertankers. The programs were run on the Facit, and the public five-channel Telex service was used to transmit Autokon part specifications and computed ESSI tapes between SI in Oslo and Stord Yard on the West Coast. The reliability of this service was excellent and no serious difficulties were recorded during its several years of service. (This was fortunate, because nobody had thought to add redundant checking information to the data tapes).

Figure 3 shows an example of a part. The curved contour is taken automatically from the hull shape. The positions and dimensions of the cutouts for longitudinal frames are determined by the positions and dimensions of the longitudinals. This information is automatically taken out of the database and adjusted for the skew angles between the part and the longitudinals.

The first version of Autokon covered the pre-production stage with detail design and lofting. Work with the previous stage, steel design, started as soon as the first version was up and running. The result was called Autokon II, a system that integrated a large part of the ship design process. Figure 4 illustrates an automatically designed web frame. The figure is taken from the Autokon II project proposal and does not show the rich details of the actual design drawings.

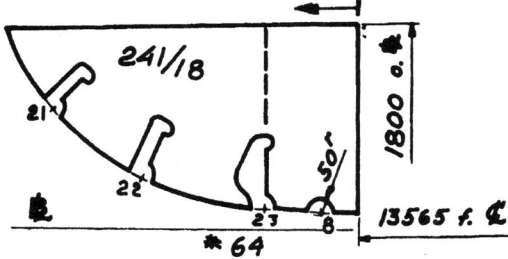

Figure 3: Example part

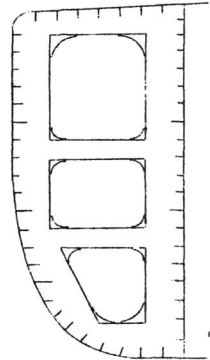

Figure 4: Example of simplified steel design drawing.

The first overseas installation of the ESSI-Autokon combination was at the General Dynamics Quincy Yard, Mass. circa 1966. This could be the first major computer application exported from Europe to America. Autokon was subsequently adopted by major shipyards all over the world. Product functionality was steadily extended over the years. The original architecture still proved viable when the system was converted from workstations to PCs in the early nineties. Autokon is still in production in many shipyards around the world more than forty years after its original design and implementation.

Bergen Mekaniske Verksteder (BMV) was one of the initiators of the *Emma* computer. One of its first projects related to preliminary design computations. This evolved into the *Prelikon* system that was later integrated with Autokon and marketed as part of the product. In 1966, the

LOCOS part programming system developed at BMV was merged with the Autokon Part Program after BMV had become part of the Aker Group.

In the rest of this paper we will follow three significant technology threads that started with the Autokon project. We will present these threads under the headings of *"Data-centred architectures"*, *"Applied Mathematics"*, and *"Personal Information Systems"*. We will study these threads from a Norwegian perspective, but it must be kept in mind that we have at all times been tightly coupled to the world-wide community of computer technologists. We conclude this paper by seeing the Norwegian efforts in the light of international developments in the past and in the future.

4.   DATA-CENTRED ARCHITECTURES

A central part of the Autokon project was the development of a full-fledged database system called *Filemaster*. The sheer draught is the foundation for most of the ship design work. In Autokon, it is a centrally placed *table of offsets* as shown in Figure 2. From the very beginning, this was translated into an Autokon system architecture with the sheer draught stored in a central data store and various programs organized around it. It was quickly found that this central, random access store should be the repository for a numerical model of the ship including the position of decks and frames as well as the shapes of individual parts. It also included user-defined programs for generating the parts (called Autokon *norms*). In the first production version of Autokon, the database for one ship was held on one Facit ECM64 carousel.

Filemaster's access model was based on geometry; it was easy to find a part's record directly from the part's co-ordinates or indirectly by navigating from a part to its spatial neighbours. A part was stored as a dataset with some common information followed by an ordered collection of curve segments describing the part's contour. Each curve segment was stored on canonical form and represented a straight line or a circular or parabolic segment.

The Filemaster system was made into a separate product and commercialised by *ICAN* under the name of *Autobas*. This product evolved into *Tornado*, a knowledge repository.

Another independent and important database product developed at SI was the navigational database system *SIBAS*, a cornerstone of the Nord computer's software library. SIBAS was the kernel of the *Maplis* system for materials management. Stord Yard was the first Maplis user. It has later evolved into a modern material management system and is marketed under the name of *Sireko MIPS* [Sireko].

5. APPLIED MATHEMATICS

A ship is essentially constructed from a number of plane parts that fit within the space bounded by the doubly curved surfaces of the hull (the sheer draught) and the main deck. The first version of Autokon used a very primitive method for the definition of the sheer draught. It was soon replaced by a sophisticated system based on a mathematical model that minimized the deformation energy in splines with varying cross-section. This method corresponded to the earlier manual methods and the generated curves were very well received by expert loftsmen. The algorithms and computer programs were called *KURGLA* (KURve GLAtting).[Mehlum-69] A special feature of KURGLA was that its curves were computed as sequences of straight line and circular segments. They could, therefore, be used directly by the ESSI controller without any further approximation.

KURGLA was commercialised from around 1968 when the Aker Group (ships), Hawker Siddeley (UK, aircraft) and British Leyland (automobiles) co-operated to extend KURGLA for use in the water turbine, aerospace and car industries. The new product was delivered to the users in 1974 and marketing and maintenance was taken over by Shipping Research Services, the Autokon marketing company.

The Group for Applied Mathematics at SI sprang out of the 3D surface definition work in 1961. One of its first projects was to generate synthetic holograms from a computer-based definition of a shape. A simulation program used the differential equations for wave propagation in optics to compute the holographic interference patterns. The physical patterns were created photographically on a Japanese *JEOL* electron microscope that was specially modified for computer control of its electron beam. The result was probably the world's first computer-generated optical holograms. Some spin-offs from this project can be found in modern offshore seismic technology.

Another spin off was a method for the design, construction and testing of holographic lenses in 1977. Lenses were developed for the focusing of ultrasound, infrared light, and water waves. The latter were particularly interesting since such lenses enabled the focusing of ocean wave energy in power stations. A Company, *Norwave,* was established and the first prototype wave-powered generating station was completed in 1985.

6. PERSONAL INFORMATION SYSTEMS

The first version of Autokon consisted of a number of tools designed for the ship designer. One of the applications included a designer's language for the generic specification of plane parts. Autokon II came around 1965 and evolved into Autokon -68 and -71. The user community was now extended to the steel design department, and one of the applications included a ship designer's language for the definition of generic designs.

The long term goal for all Autokon work was to look at the shipyard as a socio-technical system where organisation, individuals, computers and machine tools are equally important: *"The goal is that we shall create a system that optimally combine human insights, experience and imagination with the computer's speed, accuracy and capability for managing large sets of data."*

An important insight was caused by a blunder. The steel design and lofting departments shared a common database. Steel design produced the numerical equivalent of the old 1:50 drawings. A bright lad in lofting recognised that all information was now precisely represented in the database. Presto! Control tapes for the flame cutters could be pulled straight out of the database. They cut more than three hundred tons of steel before discovering the difference between precision and accuracy. Yes, the data in the database had 40-bit precision. No, dimensions were still as approximate as they had been in the 1:50 drawings. Three hundred tons of scrap steel and some angry finger pointing was the result.

The blunder itself was of course easily fixed and never repeated. Many results from steel design could be used as long as they were carefully checked, corrected and augmented in lofting. But the real problem was a deep one. In the manual system, the steel design department had ownership and full control over their information. Similarly, lofting had control of *their* information. And most important, the transfer of information was formal and carefully controlled by both sender and receiver. We believed the required solution to be fundamental and general: *The computer system must mirror the line organisation and the line departments must remain in control of their data and their programs.* The systems should be interlinked in such a way that transfer of information can be computer assisted, but must remain under human control.

The first application according to this paradigm was NIPOL. This was a system for the dispatching and control of production at A/S National Industri, a major Norwegian manufacturer of large power transformers. *"The NIPOL project is a first step towards a new type of systems, systems that build on the individual and his needs, and for use in the daily work."* (Freely translated from[NIPOL]). The system architecture is visualised in Figure 5. The total system had several "owners": the machine tool operators, the foremen, the planners, store room personnel, etc. The application was implemented around 1970 on a Nord-1 and later ported to Kongsberg's SM-3. NIPOL was commercialised by Kongsberg Våpenfabrikk and had some success in Sweden.

Figure 5: Production control in custom manufacturing

The next step along this thread was the vision of a total, distributed information system for the shipyard. The system should reflect the yard's line organisation with tight coupling between local components and loose coupling between organisationally distant ones. The vision was heavily rooted in current organisation theory with self-governing groups etc. and was proposed as a research program under a title that went somewhat like this: *The data systems of the 70-ties. A fundamental proposal.* The vision was later published in the referenced article.[Ree-73]

The vision unites two conflicting requirements. On the one hand, a person needs to see a coherent information space that is structured according to the person's mental models. On the other hand, the enterprise requires that various functions such as planning and control, accounting, design, materials management, etc. are integrated both individually and jointly.

The solution was a structure of communicating components in a matrix as visualised in Figure 6. Each function is decomposed into a number of communicating components. The system architecture is such that each unit in the line organisation owns a group of components. Each user's information space is realised by a user-near component called a *toolset*. The user could here be a person or a department.[Ree-73]

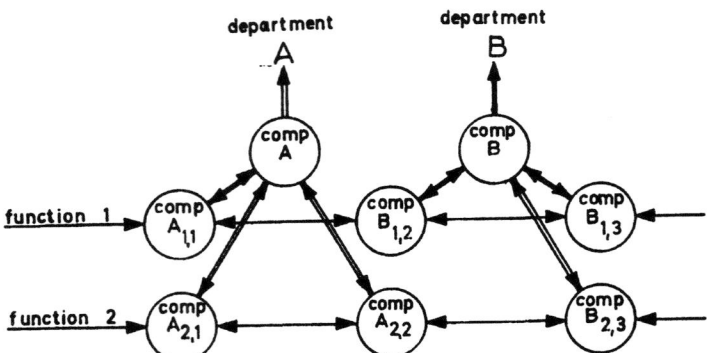

Figure 6: Two decomposed functions. Each component
is controlled by the responsible department

The first project to build on this vision was *Prokon/Plan*, a distributed
system for planning and control in the shipyard. The goal was to loosen up
the centralised and rigid planning system. The idea was to replace the
"dumb" activity and resource records of the standard planning program with
"smart" objects that would be owned by the various users who would control
not only their data but also the way they did their work. So the piping
design department could plan and control differently from the lofting
department, while the panel assembly line could be handled differently
again. The key to success would be to find ways of integrating the plans
from the different departments. It was clear that the overall planning process
had to be transparent and comprehensible. The line not only needed to
understand the process; they must be able to define it and to redefine it
quickly to resolve urgent problems.

The Prokon/Plan project got under way and an experimental application
was implemented. A first version written in Simula was abandoned because
its rigid typing system made it hard to code the interaction of very different
components. A first experimental version was finally written in Fortran with
a pre-processor that made it somewhat object based. Then an acute oil crisis
abruptly removed all funding and the project died. This was probably just as
well; in retrospect the project seems technologically premature. The project
was reported in[Ree-77], two of its diagrams are reproduced in Figure 7. These
diagrams could be the world's first, primitive examples of what in UML is
called *collaboration diagrams* and *message sequence charts*.

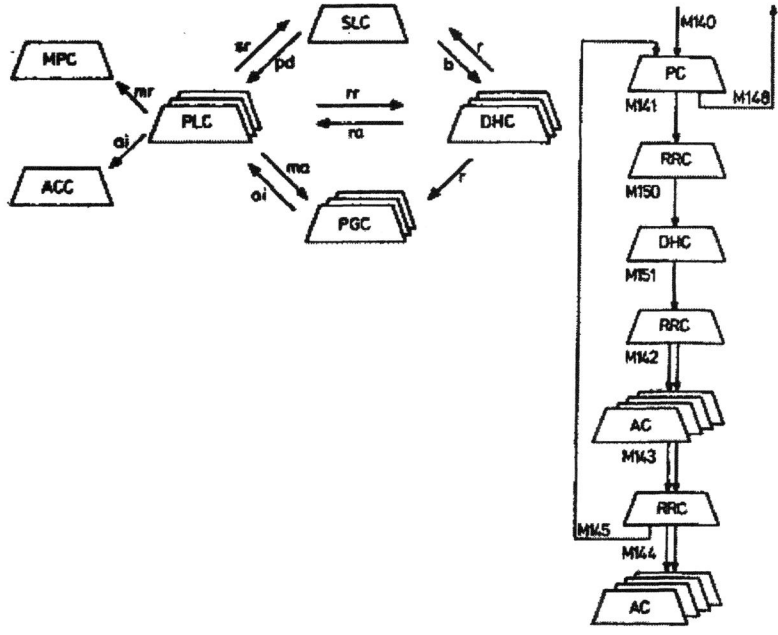

Figure 7: Example component structure and interaction diagrams.

Experiments with user interfaces to a large, distributed and component based plan continued at Xerox PARC in 1978/79. This time the programming was done in Smalltalk, Alan Kay's pure object oriented personal information environment based on Simula with the addition of the human-centric thinking of Douglas Engelbart and the extreme uniformity of Lisp. One result of the work was the *Model-View-Controller* paradigm that is illustrated in Figure 8. Business information is held in background *model* components. The users have task oriented *controllers* (tools) that may appear on a computer screen as a window with one or more panes (panels). Each pane holds a *view* on a certain aspect of a model. The MVC can exist in many variants and is now industry standard. (More information concerning this appears in the referenced article.[Ree-03])

We end this thread in the early eighties. An early, wholly object oriented application, *Tender One*, was demonstrated at the first OOPSLA conference in 1986. The product was a tool for tender preparation that seamlessly mixed text, tables, and drawings with results computed from data in a database. The application failed as a product because it required a special workstation and lacked integration with common text processors such as Word®. Another initiative was the *Eureka Software Factory*; a major

attempt at creating a software development environment based on the above
ideas. The project did not end up in a product because the industrial
partners, two minicomputer manufacturers, faded out of the picture.

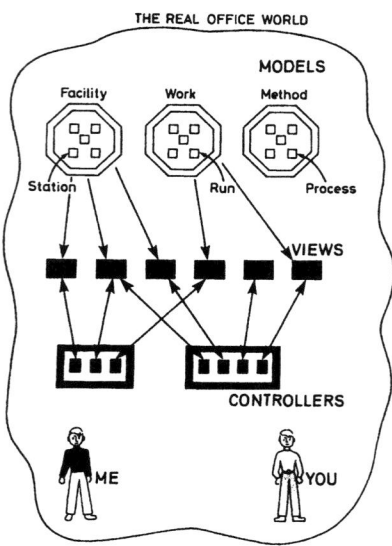

Figure 8: The Model-View-Controller paradigm, an industry
standard that sprang out of Prokon/Plan

7.   WHERE ARE THEY NOW?

Autokon. It was estimated that in the year 2000, there could still be as
many as a dozen Autokon sites around the world, 40 years after its first
production run. It was at its commercial apex in the eighties until the glory
of the YAPs pulled the rug under the marketing company. The Autokon
operation was then acquired by its Swedish competitor, *Kockums Computer
Systems.* Autokon is now merged with Kockums' Steerbear into the *Tribon
system* that currently is the world market leader.

Data-centred architectures became mainstream with the database
systems from the late sixties. The Autokon database system itself was
extended and commercialized by Metis A/S under the trade name of
Tornado. This activity has ended up in *Computas AS* with the software
product Metis® *"Visualising Your Enterprise Knowledge"*. Metis is
marketed internationally with offices in Norway, Sweden, and North
America.

Mathematical modelling evolved into more general mathematical modelling of physical phenomena, in particular wave phenomena The value of general and sound understanding of a scientific field can be illustrated by the diversity of applications from the mathematical modelling group: [math]

The design of lenses for the focusing of sound waves.

Platforms in the North Sea are exposed to extreme wave loads. Calculations of forces from waves hitting the legs of the platform are important to the safety offshore.

Computation of how ocean waves are refracted off the coast. The project *Geosim* demonstrates the use of Geographic Information Technology (GIT) in numerical calculations of natural phenomena.

Scientific visualisation of data from a supercomputer models. A weather map over Europe is generated by the NIMBUS software, which was developed at SI/SINTEF. This was the predecessor of the weather forecast system used on the Norwegian TV2. The program is being further developed by *Weather One* in co-operation with SINTEF Applied Mathematics.

An experimental water wave focusing device was tested in Hakadal near Oslo in the autumn of 1979. This lead to the invention of the "tapered channel" principle for concentrating ocean wave energy. A pilot power plant at Toftestallen in Øygarden outside Bergen utilized this principle. It was finished in 1985 and worked according to theory until 1991, when a contractor accidentally blasted several tons of rock into its focusing channel in conjunction with an experiment. In 1998, a Norwegian team coordinated by *Indonor AS* and including *Norwave AS, Groener AS* and *Oceanor ASA* won a contract to deliver a *Tapchan*® (tapered channel) wave power plant. The site, at Baron on the south coast of Java, utilises a bay with its own natural basin. The 1.1 MW plant was planned to harness power from waves entering the 7-metre wide mouth, flowing down a narrowing channel, being forced over the walls of the basin (reservoir) and being returned to the sea via a conventional low-head turbine.[waves].

Together with the University of Oslo, the mathematical modelling group is now establishing a Centre of Excellence for mathematics for applications

The work with *Personal Information Systems* evolved into object oriented role modelling. The associated modelling tool, *OOram*, did not prove commercially viable, but its conceptual model was fed into the OMG standardisation process[UML-Prop-97]. These concepts are now part of the *Unified Modelling Language (UML)*. The notion of a distributed corporate information architecture mapped onto the organisation structure and controlled by the line remains a vision, 30 years after its conception. It is needed more than ever and the technology exists or could exist. Nevertheless, we have not seen a commercial interest in making it come true.

The idea of using the computer to augment the human intellect is still not main stream in spite of the pioneering work of Douglas Engelbart and others. A part of both Tender One and OOram was an authoring tool. When writing this paper, the author first tried Word® and then FrameMaker®. Both of them are merely automated typists. None of them helped the author in collecting material, organising it and polishing it. In desperation, he ended up using his old OOram tool.

Some people claim that development goes very quickly in the computer field. This is true for hardware, but not for software. The substance of information processing develops only slowly. However, there is a great deal of vendor created noise and developer created complexity. We are still far from the simple, transparent and controllable information environments that we all really need.

8.   CONCLUSION

The success of Autokon was largely due to the five essential preconditions being satisfied; *market, organisation, finance, technical talent,* and *marketing talent.*

Ship construction changed from riveting to welding during WW 2. All major shipyards around the world were busy modernising to exploit the new technology.

The development was done in close and friendly co-operation between the researchers at SI and the end users in the line and on the shop floor at Stord. The Stord Yard in general and particularly key personnel in their lofting department were very open to new ideas and made essential contributions to the final result. (None of the researchers/developers were shipbuilders. It was later said that this was an advantage; they didn't understand that they had embarked on an impossible task).

Available technology was adequate. Computing power was sufficient and the random access secondary stores enabled a database-oriented architecture. The Facit carousel tape station ECM 64 semi-random access store was particularly important as was the large memory drum of the Univac 1107 where Autokon migrated after the Facit era. (The Autokon developers escaped from the endless spooling of magnetic tapes that hindered true progress in so many communities).

The designers/users at Stord Yard and the researchers/developers at SI were embedded in disjoint organisations and independently financed. This firmly put the two groups on an equal footing but joined by a common goal. The Aker Group wanted to become the world's most effective shipbuilders and SI wanted to create a truly great, innovative and commercially successful software product.

The project was securely rooted in the top-level management of the Aker Group; its CEO was an active president of the SIAG steering committee where priorities were set and budgets approved.

Marketing efforts were greatly helped through the Aker group being part of an extensive network of international shipbuilders.

The most important impact of the Nusse computer was probably the high tech milieu that was established around it and its research culture. A culture that was passed on to a stream of University master students who did their research in the Autokon milieu. This was clearly not the least significant result from the work.

From the start, work was highly oriented towards creating value for the end users in the short and long term. The research results were measured by their utility, not their academic acceptance. The focus was on comprehension, abstraction, design, and quality; the goal being to get it right the first time. (*"Any method that prevents the programmer writing code, is a good method"*). It also helped that initially; the same people were system architects, designers, coders, trainers of users, system operators, trouble-shooters, maintainers, and salesmen. The richness and viability of the many Autokon spin-offs illustrate the long-term value of broad, concerted, and goal-directed research efforts.

It is worth noting that the Autokon project could probably not have happened today. The current fashion is to let end users dominate research projects. The nebulous Autokon project could not have survived a head on competition with real and urgent shipyard investment needs. On the other hand, the project could have failed if the research had been permitted to dominate; there were many interesting problems that could have diverted the project from its strictly utilitarian goals. The project achieved a delicate balance between these two forces; the developers focused sharply on the needs of the users, but they took the users' concrete requirements as symptoms of a general classes of problems that needed general solutions.

It is frustrating to observe that the Norwegian government's current research goals are linked to the expenditure on research rather than on its results.

"If you don't know where you want to go, you can't expect to get there".

ACKNOWLEDGEMENTS

Thanks to Anton Landmark, Arve Langseth, Christian Balchen, Even Mehlum, Frank Lillehagen, Rolf Bjerknes, and Thomas Hysing for generous help during in preparation of this paper. Also my sincere thanks to Trond Vahl for his able presentation of the paper when I was unable to attend the conference.

REFERENCES

[ACE] ACE 2000. A conference at the Science Museum of London, 18 may 2000 and the National Physical Laboratory, 19 may 2000. http://www.bshs.org.uk/conf/ace2000.html

[AmEvj-53] Ole Amble, Tor Evjen: Anvendelse av den elektroniske siffermaskin Nusse. Norsk Regnesentral, desember 1953. A copy is archived at The Norwegian Museum of Science and Technology, Autokon archive, Box #1.

[APEXC] http://cvs.mess.org:6502/cgi-bin/viewcvs.cgi/sysinfo.dat.diff?r1=1.16&r2=1.17 &sortby=author History and Trivia.

[APT] Sam Chiappone: Machining Centers, History. Rensselaer Polytechnic Institute. http://aml2.eng.rpi.edu/GMPWeb/Powerpoint/Machining%20Centers.ppt

[Baby] Kulwinder S. Gill: The Manchester Small Scale Experimental Machine—"The Baby" http://www.computer50.org/mark1/new.baby.html

[Bernt-03] Drude Berntsen: The Pioneer Era in Norwegian Scientific Computing (1948-1962). HiNC 2003.

[Colossus] Tony Sale: Lorenz ciphers and the Colossus. http://www.codesandciphers.org.uk /lorenz/index.htm

[EDSAC] University of Cambridge. A brief informal history of the Computer Laboratory http://www.cl.cam.ac.uk/UoCCL/misc/EDSAC99/history.html

[Elgsaas] Knut Elgsaas, Håvard Hegna: The Norwegian Computing Center and the Univac 1107 (1963-70). HiNC 2003

[Emma] See http://www.uib.no/elin/emma/

[ENIAC] Martin H. Weik: The ENIAC Story. Ordnance Ballistic Research Laboratories, Aberdeen Proving Ground, MD, 1961. http://ftp.arl.mil/~mike/comphist/eniac-story.html

[Facit] Facit EDB 3 computer and ECM 64 carousell. Some documents are archived at The Norwegian Museum of Science and Technology, Autokon archive, Box #1.

[Hy-03] Thomas Hysing, private communication March 2003.

[Hy-60] T. Hysing: On the Use of Numerical Methods in the Design and Manufacture of Ships. Proceedings of the First International Congress of the International Federation of Automatic Control. Moscow, 1960. Butterworths, London.

[HyRee-63] Thomas Hysing, Trygve Reenskaug: A system for computer plate preparation. Numerical methods applied to shipbuilding. A NATO Advanced Study Institute organized by Central Institute for Industrial Research and Det norske Veritas. Oslo-Bergen 1963. pp.324ff. A copy of the proceedings is archived at The Norwegian Museum of Science and Technology, Autokon archive, Box #2.

[Jones-98] R. V. Jones: Most Secret War. Wordsworth Editions, Ware, Herts., England 1998.

[Kveim-61] Norwegian patent No. 100916. Application date: 31 August 1961. Inventor: Kjell Kveim

[math] http://www.math.sintef.no/highlights/bolger_e.html

[Mehlum-69] Even Mehlum: Curve and Surface Fitting Based On Variational Criteria for Smoothness. Dr.Philos. Thesis, University of Oslo, 24 December 1969.

[Moore-49] The 1946 Moore School Lectures http://www.computer50.org/mark1 /moore.school/intro.html [museum] anon: Fra NUSSE til internet http://www.museumsnett.no/ntm/no/utstillingene /stroem_lys/inthist.htm

[NIPOL] Odd Hübert: On-line oppfølgingssystem ved A/S National Industri - NIPOL. SI Project Report project 700131/19 June 1970

[O'Connor] J J O'Connor and E F Robertson: Alan Mathison Turing. http://www-gap.dcs.st-and.ac.uk/~history/Mathematicians/Turing.html

[Proposal] Søknad om bidrag på kr. 270.000 for halvåret 1/7-31/12 1960 til arbeid med industriell automatisering. SI, 10 November 1959. (kr. 90.000 var til Autokon) A copy is archived at The Norwegian Museum of Science and Technology, Autokon archive, Box #2.

[RBj-03] Rolf Bjerknes, private communication Dec. 2002.

[Ree-73] Trygve Reenskaug: Administrative Control in the Shipyard. ICCAS Conference, Tokyo, August 1973. A scanned version at http://www.ifi.uio.no/~trygver/ mvc/index.html.

[Ree-77] Trygve Reenskaug: Prokon/Plan—A Modelling Tool for Project Planning and Control. Information Processing 77, B. Gilchrist, Editor. IFIP, North-Holland Publishing Co. (1977)

[Ree-03] Trygve Reenskaug: The Model-View-Controller. Its Past and Present. Talk. JavaZone 2003 and JAOO 2003.

[Sale] Tony Sale: *Codes and Cipher in the Second World War* http://www.codesandciphers.org.uk/

[Simula] Jan Rune Holmevik: The History of Simula. http://java.sun.com/people/jag /SimulaHistory.html

[Sireko] See http://www.sireko.no/

[Small] Albert W. Small: Special Fish Report. http://www.codesandciphers.org.uk /documents/small/smallix.htm The original document is held in The American National Archive (NARA) College Campus Washington: NR 4628 Special Fish Report (Box 1417)

[Turing-36] A. M. Turing: On computable numbers, with an application to the entscheidungsproblem. Proceedings of the London Mathematical Society, ser. 2. vol. 42 (1936-7), pp.230- 265; corrections, Ibid, vol 43 (1937) pp. 544-546. Also at http://www.abelard.org/turpap2/tp2-ie.asp

[UML-Prop-97]Taskon, Reich Technologies, Humans and Technology, Data Access Technologies: The OOram Meta-Model combining role models, interfaces, and classes to support system centric and program centric modelling. OMG document ad/97-01-14. 8 January 1997.

[Vahl-03] Trond Vahl: Applications and Technologies for Maritime and Off-shore Industries. Industrial significance of computer applications. HiNC 2003.

[waves] http://www.worldenergy.org/wec-geis/publications/reports/ser/wave/wave.asp, also http://www.oceanor.no/projects/wave_energy/index.htm

COMMENT FROM NORMAN SANDERS

This paper was one of the most exciting of a very exciting conference. Looking back over fifty years since the first computers were built, it must be admitted now that it was a very risky business committing the computer to the manufacture of anything. Computers were only ten years old. Central memory sizes were one percent and less of today's capacity. Programming languages were only just emerging. A lot of numerical analysis had to be invented. The user interface, if you could call it that, consisted of punched cards or paper tape; it was to be thirty years before we were to get graphical interaction. The associated machinery, drafting machines, flame-cutters, milling machines etc were also in their infancy. Senior management had to swallow hard before allocating the funds and launching their companies on un-chartable voyages of exploration into a new industrial age. To leap from a solitary 1K computer to the panoply of equipment described in this paper in only ten years was an astonishing achievement. Had it not been successful we would not be surrounded today by the CAD systems that permeate industry. The people who did it may now wallow in retirement in the glow of satisfaction of a superb job well done. It was an industrial revolution as radical as its nineteenth century predecessor.

NORDUNET: THE ROOTS OF NORDIC NETWORKING

Rolf Nordhagen

USIT, Centre for Information Technology Services, University of Oslo, Norway; rolf.nordhagen@usit.uio.no

Abstract: NORDUNET began as an informal cooperation between Nordic "networkers" in 1980. With support from the Nordic Council of Ministers, a NORDUNET project for a common Nordic academic network began in 1985. Mats Brunell (Sweden) and Einar Løvdal (Norway) led the work. Originally based on existing interim services of EARN, DECnet and ISO OSI support, lack of services led to complete reorientation in 1987. With bridges running Ethernet over slow lines, a Nordic-wide Ethernet connecting major nodes in the countries linked national Ethernets to a common node at KTH, Stockholm. The major services of the time, X.25, EARN and RSCS, DECnet, and TCP/IP, were connected in through switches, bridges and routers called "the NORDUNET plug". The operational network NORDUnet, a first international multi-protocol network, began services in 1988 and officially opened in 1989. Major links to the US NSFnet and European networks connected to the KTH node. The project had a strong impact on Nordic networking competence that influenced the European move to TCP/IP services in opposition to the prevailing adherence (politically supported) to ISO OSI. Over time, TCP/IP won the "protocol war". The early introduction of TCP/IP gave the Nordic area a head start in internet penetration, still reflected in the countries being in the front of public use of the internet. A major lesson was the success of Nordic cooperation on all levels, through sharing of responsibilities, joint development of competence and creation of enthusiasm. NORDUnet is today owned by the national ministries, run through cooperation by the national networks, and able to supply the Nordic academic internet with exceptionally cost-effective bandwidth to all major international networks such as Startap and Geant.

Key words: Computer communication, Nordic cooperation, internet penetration, multiprotocol networks

1.   INTRODUCTION

The history of NORDUNET, the project, is one of cooperation and friendship. It is also the history of the world's first international, multi-protocol network and on how the NORDUNET team won the "great European protocol war". This version of the story reflects a personal background from the University of Oslo and its approach to computer networking.

1.1   The beginning

The arrival of network projects on the computer scene in the late 60s and beginning 70s fueled our beginning interest. The emergence of powerful standards to construct networks, based on the OSI-model, inspired our technical people. The phrase "Open networks" had the meaning of "An open network is a network following an open, common standard". In addition, after years of dependence on the large mainframe, we escaped from the rigors of batch processing by the affordable minicomputer.

In Oslo, we did remote stations to mainframes, and transferred to timesharing in the mid-70s, spurring interest on terminal networks. Also, after initial study groups, Norwegian universities and research institutes initiated a national academic network project, UNINETT, which by 1978 had established a packet switched service and by 1979 had access to all major university machines, all solidly based on the X.25 protocol. Similar efforts got under way in Sweden where SUNET, established in 1980, created a service also based on connecting the institutions local terminal networks to the public X.25 network. As the service gave international dial up connectivity, we could reach out internationally, also to US and Canadian networks.

1.2   The first ARPANET connection

In 1973, as the first outside the U.S., ARPANET was connected to a seismic array project NORSAR at Kjeller, Norway, by a 2.4 kb/s satellite link. In the Cold War, it was clear that the Norwegian bedrock was a perfect listening station for nuclear arms testing. A terrestrial line soon extended the connection itself to the University College of London.

The later history of how this connection evolved into a full internet service for a few informatics institutes in Norwegian universities is in itself fascinating. In reality, the availability of the TCP/IP suite of protocols under Berkeley UNIX moved the connectivity out of the Kjeller labs. In retrospect, sadly, the activities never became part of the mainstream efforts leading to a national network, mainly due to close dependence on a few enthusiasts with little support from their own institutions. At that time, all official network projects had their foundations on the OSI protocols. Thus, the enthusiasts did not accept them as suitable partners; rather, they viewed them as competitors.

However, by 1983/84 a number of institutes in Norway enjoyed full internet access, but not available nationally or accessible from other countries, in contrast to the by then established but limited X.25 services. This became a general envy and a strong pressure on major projects to supply similar services.

It is an interesting twist of history that when the satellite connection, then part of SATNET, was finally removed in 1987 and the institutes lost their internet connectivity, we were only a few months away from bringing up the identical NORDUnet service properly organized in a common network.

1.3 The early introduction of computer communication

In my opinion, another major inspiration for Nordic networking was the early emergence a powerful communication service, the Stockholm KOM program. The university computer centre in Stockholm, (they called themselves QZ as these letters were used by no one else) installed a timesharing DIGITAL DEC-10 in the early 70s. Jakob Palme, working with the DEC-10, became inspired by the communication ideas of Murray Turoff at the New Jersey Institute of Technology ("The network nation") and wrote what he called a computer conferencing system he named KOM. Today we would class it as a breed between a mail system and a "news"-system, with features that even today were superlative to presently used systems. It was an instant success and over the years, it was reachable by remote login via the growing international X.25 services. It finally became a European meeting place.

In Oslo, we installed a DEC-10 in 1976, running the first timesharing service in Norway. Close cooperation sprung up between the Oslo and Stockholm installations, based on good personal relations between the Swedes and Norwegians involved. In 1978, we were able to install KOM in Oslo, again an instant success, which really brought home to us the qualities of computer communication. Even if was a centralized system, as the remote login services improved in UNINETT, it became an important national service.

2.   INTRODUCING NORDIC COOPERATION

Then enter true Nordic cooperation. To strengthen the bonds between the Nordic countries in the wake of the WW2 disruptions, several councils emerged and as examples, they introduced a Passport Union and a common labor market. A Nordic Council of Ministers, being the responsibility of the Nordic governments, had created an office for coordination in research called Nordforsk. The director, Bjørn Grønlund, caught onto the idea of Nordic cooperation in computer networking. In 1980, he convened a workshop in Tellberg, Dalarne, Sweden, where all major network projects in the Nordic countries were invited. To me, this was an exhilarating experience, to meet many fellow enthusiasts. The various network adherents banded together, dreaming of Nordic-wide DECnets, IBM-nets, and common X.25 access. This workshop continued as meetings under the name of NORDUNET, Nordic University Networks, circulating among the nations, Denmark, Norway, Finland, and back in Göthenburg, Sweden in 1984.

2.1   The EARN network

In 1984, another important part of the play began. The computer firm IBM found that they had a thriving computer network community based on BITNET running among large IBM installations initially on the East coast of the U.S. They saw an opportunity to get a foothold among the less organized European networks, and donated a network, EARN, European Academic Network, based on BITNET and running on international leased lines sponsored by IBM. This offer was very well received and with some of the larger Nordic IBM installations, became an important service.

2.2   And then: The NORDUNET program

By 1983, the NORDUNET meetings, apart from inspiration, had produced no concrete actions. Nevertheless, the time was ripe to go one-step further, actually to apply for Nordic money for network activities. The major network groups agreed to launch a true NORDUNET network project, and a group, led by Arild Jansen, University of Oslo and Jorgen Richter, NEUCC, Denmark received the task to edit together a full project application. The meeting in 1984 approved the application "NORDUNET - a Nordic program of action in data-communication" and later in 1984, NORDFORSK presented the application to the Council of Ministers.

As it turned out, the ground was well prepared. The Council of Ministers found they had extra money due to favorable exchange rates, and wanted ideas on inter-Nordic actions in computing. At one stage, Bjørn Grønlund suggested a supercomputer centre. "How much will that cost," they asked. Bjørn answered, 100 million kroner. Next question: "Can we do anything less expensive?" Yes, we can create a common Nordic computer network at a cost of 10 million kroner. Thus, in May 1985, the Nordic Ministers of Culture and Education granted 9.2 million NOK to a Nordic University Network, NORDUNET, and directed NORDFORSK to act as secretariat for the program. Hence, NORDUNET, the network project was born.

2.3   The initial requirements

1. The program will run for four years and establish a stable, operating computer network, connecting the Nordic Educational and Research institutions (NR&Es) and offering easily accessible communications services.

2. The program shall open for electronic exchange of letters, documents, and data and make a common use of data-resources, programs, and databases available throughout the Nordic area. Users shall be given access to Nordic and international networks and information services.

3. NORDUNET should not establish its own network, but build on existing university networks. Use should be made of the Nordic telecommunication networks, and the network be based on international standards for tele- and data-communication.

4. This will establish a common Nordic infrastructure for the NR&E community by connecting the national nets, and new competence and services will be created for the smaller communities. The same opportunities for collaboration and information exchange as in other European countries and in the North American research communities will be made available.

5. The resources to achieve these goals will in the main have to be found in the national network organizations, with the local, university service providers, charged with the day-to-day .operation of the net.

6. Other important, positive arguments for the decision were the clear cooperative nature of the program and the belief that a computer network would greatly increase bridging the large geographical distances characteristic in the Nordic countries. Thus, opportunities for research in

remote communities would be greatly improved. All arguments we have used since the beginning of networking, and still use.

2.4   The NORDUNET work begins

After the administrative dust settled, a steering group was set up and the work began, in earnest in 1986. Initially Bjørn Grønlund, NORDFORSK, administered the project; later it was transferred to Stocholm QZ and Mats Brunell. A technical coordinator/manager was hired from the University of Oslo, Einar Løvdal. (See Figure 1.) It is largely due to the efforts of these two energetic persons that NORDUNET achieved its results. Actually, two friendly organizations picked their two best people and set them to the task.

Figure 1. Mats Brunell and Einar Løvdal

At the time, people believed that any common service had to be based on the connection oriented OSI protocols. This even became a hot political issue, as the European commission strongly backed OSI as a platform for European networking. As is known in retrospect, this unfortunate involvement killed a European networking hardware industry, as the policy did not survive. Also at the time, a number of European initiatives emerged, RARE, a cooperation similar to NORDUNET, but aimed at unifying European networking, an EARN cooperative body, and COSINE, an effort to coordinate the development of OSI-based services. RARE/COSINE initiated a common network project IXI. Because of the NORDUNET project, we already had a clear benefit by financially being able to join these bodies as joint Nordic members, something most of the countries would have difficulties in doing separately.

Initially the task of creating a common network service seemed chaotic. At that time, a number of networks were in operation, local and private, such as the national network groups ran private X.25 networks, accessed by Telecompany PAD-services. All major institutions also ran Ethernets as isolated, local networks. Coordinate common services seemed a formidable task.

As a start, popular services were selected and made available Nordic-wide. As they had to operate as separate services, the efforts were strategically named "Interim" services, on the way to a common service.

The EARN services joined and accessed the European wide services through UNI-C in Denmark. A joint DECnet effort worked to connect the high-energy physics institutions to HEPNET, originating in CERN. For the X.25 based services, an X.400 based message-handling system, EAN, from University of British Columbia was already part of UNINETT; it became available in the other countries through licensing agreements. The UNINETT group did the coordination. This effort led to the group also got responsibilities for a similar service in Europe.

2.5   The protocol challenges and reorientation

An overall effort to develop further services became a major part of the program. Work began with partners in several major network groups in the countries. The big question of the time was what suite to base the services on. The political pressure as mentioned, as well as the belief of the European technical expertise, was to use the CCIT recommended OSI style connection oriented protocols such as X.25. However, services were slow in development. Additionally, stable standards were not yet available; the work in the ISO standardization in CCIT progressed slowly and continuously as it was close to finalization. This led to a reorientation of original NORDUNET goals. The effort to develop services independently was regarded as unrealistic. The interim solutions with services based on the separate, not yet connected, private network would continue to be supported, but prepared for OSI-migration. Furthermore, services were to be as much as possible based on industry-supported products. Interim solutions to connect to international networks, such as EARN, UUCP, DECnet and INTERNET should be sought. Moreover, to prepare for OSI-migration, pilot services emerged and organized on a Nordic level. NORDUNET should actively work in the European OSI-efforts in RARE and COSINE, to strengthen Nordic competence and coordinate Nordic and European efforts.

Several subprojects began. One was an effort to develop a file-transfer pilot service based on the FTAM protocols. This turned out to be highly resource consuming. One discussion was on choosing the JANET colored book services; other efforts were to use the ISODE suite of programs to run X.25 over IP. Progress was still enthusiastic, but slow. Furthermore, the X.25 pilots showed the service to be far less stable than expected; they were slow and resource consuming. The future for a full, reliable set of standards seemed still to be years off, JANET talked about still ten years, which would mean the NORDUNET project would be in only a pilot phase for the duration of the four-year period.

Since the technical challenges were still formidable, the setbacks were regarded as just that, challenges. The goal of a common network service was still a great source of inspiration. Since they kept project costs at a minimum, the main expenses being part time management and modest coordination support, mostly travel, licensing, and financing the effort was not a severe problem. Therefore, the work went doggedly on.

3.   THE NEW DIRECTION AND BREAKTHROUGH

However, in 1987 a number of major technical and organizational happenings came together to change the networking world for NORDUNET. Firstly, IBM announced that the support of the (expensive) leased lines for the Nordic EARN-network had to be cut, thus putting heavy pressure on the NORDUNET resources for continuation. Secondly a major technical breakthrough occurred, bridges transmitting Ethernet over slow, leased lines became available, the Vitalink bridges. These became an immediate success. The University of Oslo quickly managed to get these bridges for connecting the Ethernet on the main campus with local networks in their institutions spread all over the Oslo area. Prompted by the need to take over a Nordic wide leased line network, at the time linking major nodes in four countries, they quickly understood that such a network suitably supplied with Vitalink bridges in each node, could constitute a Nordic wide Ethernet. Moreover, since just as the local Ethernets supported the protocols that the various private networks required, the Nordic Ethernet, suitable equipped with routers, gateways and bridges also could support the same networks. The meetings in which this understanding first became clear, was I firmly believe, personally my high point in our NORDUNET work. The gate to realizing our original goal had opened.

Things happened quickly. The new project was aptly named X.EARN, a strategic name to underline that we just had an improved and continued effort to replace the EARN network, hiding the perhaps controversial fact that we aimed at supporting other network protocols and even straying away from the orthodox OSI line. A brain trust of prominent networkers from four countries wrote a X.EARN project plan, adopted early in 1988 by the

NORDUNET steering group, and subsequently by the national networks. The report covered a number of important points, as it turned out, all solvable by common efforts.

3.1   The NORDUnet becomes operational

The techniques, of course, are well known today. An Ethernet based on bridges connected national nodes in each country, itself a bridge between the common net and a national Ethernet. Thus, the inter-Nordic nets stayed clean from national connections. On the national Ethernet, again local Ethernets connected the member institutions. Anywhere on the Ethernets, but in practice nationally or institutionally, they could connect routers, bridges, and gateways to the various supported protocols and services.

The concept was formulated by Einar Løvdal with his NORDUNET "plug" (Figure 2) that carried the basic X.25 service, EARN and RSCS, DECnet, and TCP/IP.

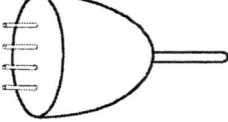

Figure 2. Løvdal's "plug" concept

Note that the challenge was not directly technical; running these services over Ethernets was well in use. The challenge was organizing the strategic placing of the various connecting devices, and coordinating Nordic-wide operation. Management of the various services and the localization of major gateways were awarded by contract to competent groups in the countries. The principle of a distributed service organization was introduced.

Another helpful event coincided with establishing a private Nordic net. The Nordic telecom companies created a joint company providing one-stop shopping for inter-Nordic lines called Scantele. The contracting for the lines between the major Nordic sites (Copenhagen, Helsinki, Stockholm, and Trondheim) became reasonably easy. The network ran on 64 kb/s; Iceland was on a separate connection running originally at 9.2 kb/s. During 1988, the network was established, with the necessary equipment in place, and named NORDUnet (with the lower-case letters) indicating the operational net. The major node on the Nordic Ethernet was located at KTH (Royal Technical Institute) in Stockholm.

3.2   Worldwide connectivity

An important strategy was to create worldwide connectivity for Nordic research through international nets. Excellent contacts with US universities and research groups made it possible to connect via a 56 kb/s satellite line to the supercomputer centre in Princeton, New Jersey, and then onto NSFnet, thus connecting the Nordic academic area into the budding internet and the TCP/IP based services. Furthermore, important European networks were connected in Stockholom, EARN, HEPnet, CERN, and EUnet. The operations centre in KTH, Stockholm was the common connection point, were the concept of peering was introduced. Thus, NORDUnet and EUnet provided backup for their transatlantic connections. Over the years, the KTH group developed the node into an important European interchange, GIX, connecting other countries such as those in the Baltics and Poland.

Thus, the world's first, truly international and multi-protocol network was created. Although services already had been available, the official opening was in October 1989, at a NORDUNET meeting outside Stockholm. Figure 3 illustrates its expansion.

3.3   When TCP/IP took over

The NORDUNET program itself went on, working hard on harmonization of mail and other services. In addition, the strategy of OSI-migration was still followed, with participation in the European IXI effort to create an OSI-based net. Projects on running connectionless over OSI were launched. Remember, that at the time, US standardization bodies were also true believers in OSI. With extensions, the program lasted until 1991.

All this is now history. NORDUnet, the network was arranged to be self sustained, originally run by the national network, today a limited company owned by educational institutions in the countries. It is still based on a small secretariat, with the actual operational work being contracted to the national networks. By joint purchase of bandwidth, the Nordic academic networks can negotiate for very cost effective agreements. The area has some of the heftiest transatlantic connections in Europe.

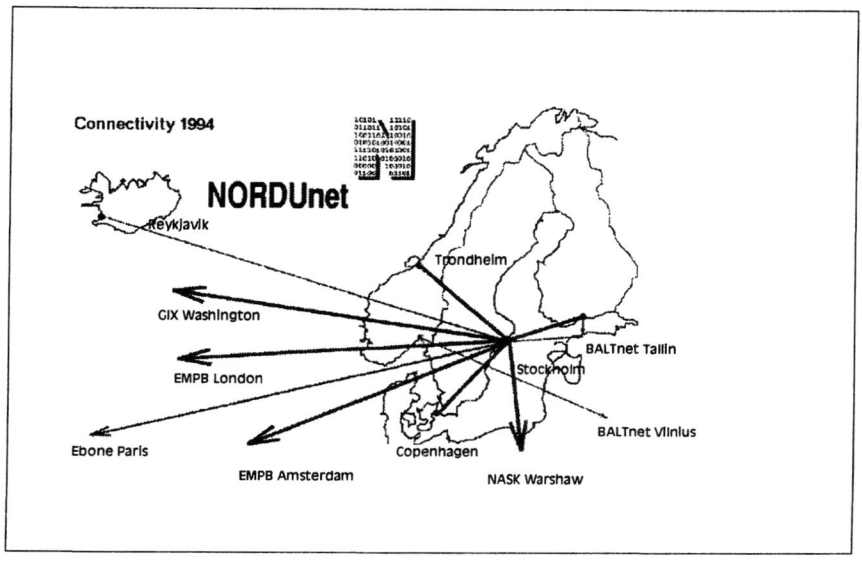

Figure 3. NORDUNET in October 1989

From opening up the network to multiple protocols, a natural migration took place. It became apparent early that the TCP/IP based services were far superior to (almost non-existing) services on other nets. Important cooperation in Europe, working with US and Canadian collaborations, such as the high-energy community, were urging for transition to TCP/IP. Einar Løvdal, while presenting his plug at the RARE meeting in Trieste in 1989, made a plea for European wide introduction of TCP/IP. He received very mixed reactions. The conviction that Europe should forge ahead with OSI-based services was solidly rooted in the then existing largest national networks, JANET in the UK and DFN in Germany.

Again, we know the history. One by one, the other services disappeared. The last to go was X.25, taken down in NORDUnet in 2001. By giving all protocols equal opportunity, we won the protocol war as the best services survived—TCP/IP and the internet.

3.4   Not only a network

NORDUNET created more than a network. The extensive use of inter-Nordic workgroups in network management and protocol development created competence on many levels. This had a catalytic effect on national networks and introduction of services. Teaching network technologies became part of university curricula. All this, further led to an early commercial introduction, first by startups, later by the National Telecom companies.

Joint activities created international recognition and status in international bodies. The first DNS-rootserver outside the US was in Stockholm. Members of the Stockholm team, Mats Brunell and Bernhard Stockman, were central in establishing RIPE as a European internet coordinator. They participated in forming the work of IEPG, and in IETF Operations WG. A number of NORDUNET experts were active in IETF working on MIME. Working in RARE WG8-management, the NORDUNET team received support for an open policy on protocols and services, similar to the NORDUnet policy, opening up for the introduction of TCP/IP while at the same time working on ISO OSI. A policy at the time regarded as highly controversial but important to move Europe on to the internet. Figure 4 shows the phenomenal exponential growth of NORDUnet network links in the US.

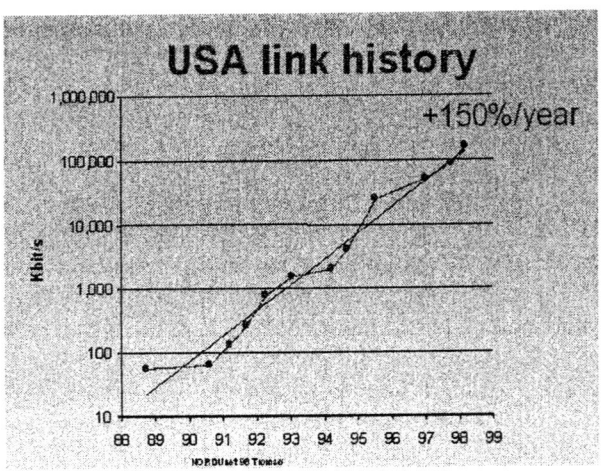

Figure 4. NORDUnet growth in the US

3.5   The roots

Thanks to the early access to the internet, the growth of network nodes in the Nordic area has been spectacular. In October 1991, 14,000 of the 32,000 IP-nodes in Europe were located in the Nordic area. Several major European networks were years behind in providing IP-based services. Even after commercial services has vastly surpassed NORDUnets early introduction of internet access, the head start is still reflected in the statistics, with the Nordic countries for years have been among the ten on top as to internet penetration in their populations, in 1999 actually among the seven with Canada and the US. Truly, NORDUNET and NORDUnet are the roots of Nordic networking.

Table 1. Nordic internet penetration % per capita

	1999		97		1999		97
1	Canada	42,82	7	8	Australia	34,33	5
2	Sweden	41,42	8	9	Singapore	31,08	9
3	Finland	40,80	1	10	N.Zealand	26,49	6
4	U.S.	40,65	4	11	Netherland	25,56	13
5	Iceland	40,35	3	12	Switzerland	24,58	11
6	Denmark	39,60	10	13	United Kingdom	23,64	12
7	Norway	37,96	2				

4. CONCLUSIONS

As a conclusion, here follows a number of statements, comprising what we call the NORDUNET lesson. The challenge became "communication is cooperation". The highlights are:
- Services could not be done by one provider alone
- The necessary level of competence could not be reached on a country by country basis
- Institutional groups too small both in people with interest and knowledge resources and demanding users
- Development cooperation required on all levels
- Cooperation gives weight to international presence

The NORDUNET lesson is as follows.
- Many institutions scattered across several countries worked together by each getting major responsibilities
- Distributed projects created joint enthusiasm and work towards common goals
- Shared responsibilities
- All received benefit from building competence
- Network communication is working together

Hence, we can use the following syllogism.

Networks are communication
Communication is Cooperation
Networks are Cooperation

FINAL REMARK

Moreover, the attitude to know carefully what you aim to do, and to take responsibility for the consequences, is brought out by the NORDUNET slogan:

"Skalat madr rúnar rísta, nema ráda vel kunni"
– Egill Skallagrimsson

Written by the greatest Icelandic poet of the 11th century, a simple translation says, "If man draws runes, he must know what he is doing". However, they tell me the meaning is more subtle in that he must realize the power and meaning of his runes. As we in networking are reminded when we realize what we have unleashed on the world, the internet, the web, and a deluge of content.

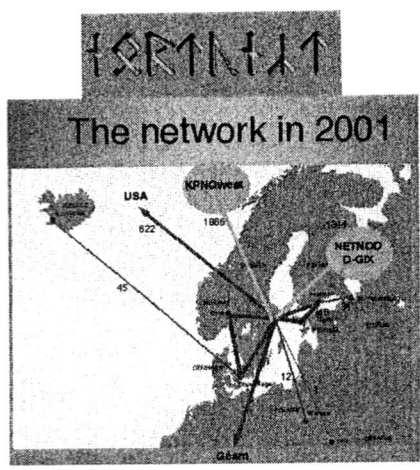

WHERE WERE THE WOMEN?

Eva Lindencrona

Formerly CEO of SISU (Swedish Institute for Systems development), today Director at VINNOVA (Swedish Agency for Innovation Systems); Eva.Lindencrona@vinnova.se

Abstract: There were few women in the early days of computing. Why was this so? Who were the female pioneers in higher education in the area of Information processing? How were women represented in higher education? What was it like to be a female academic student in those days? Has the situation changed?

Key words: Women, higher education, computing, information processing.

1.   WHY A WOMEN INTEREST?

Why is it of interest whether there were more women involved in the early development of Information technology and its applications? Would the technology have looked different? Would females have developed other applications? Would the implementation of IT applications have been different? Would the resources allocated to research, development, and implementation be different if there had been more women involved in the development processes?

When I was studying and teaching Informatics (Informationsbehandling – ADB) in the late 60s and the 70s, there was no such debate. By that time, the technology had not yet reached very far out in society and the topics that we studied and discussed were primarily technological such as programming languages, database technology, and systems design methodologies. When applications were studied or discussed it was often done in order to show that something could be made – a kind of proof of principal – rather than focusing on the effects or impact of application of the technology. New areas of application were very interesting as they introduced new requirements and thereby challenged the existing technologies and influenced the development and improvements in the technology.

In today's information society, most people agree that information technology is a powerful tool changing, developing, and innovating any business, as well as social development in general. With that perspective, it becomes necessary that people share the vision for change and development – that is, among both men and women. It becomes important that women understand the technology and the potential of that technology, and that they are involved in the development, production, and innovation processes where IT is an enabling technology.

Below, comments are given concerning the IT and the gender situation in Sweden. Certain additional material is available concerning the US situation. In Europe, however, Sweden was as an early information society developer. For that reason, the situation in Sweden in the early days can be of interest.

There are different approaches for quantification of the importance of women in businesses. For example, in a recent report *"Jämställdhet och lönsamhet"* published by the Swedish public authority NUTEK in 2002, it addressed gender equality and profitability acquired in 14 000 Swedish companies. One conclusion in the report was that low equality in working groups had negative impact on profitability. Reasons why equality may have positive impact on profitability are, for example, that employees find themselves more motivated, resources are better used, and synergic effects emerge as new views and contacts open.

The Swedish public national IT strategy since 2001, formulated in an IT bill by government, has as a goal that every citizen should have equal possibilities to use IT as a tool for access to increased knowledge, democracy, and civil rights. A prerequisite for this is equal impact on information society, and its development for men and women.

2.   WOMEN IN INFORMATION SOCIETY TODAY

Even today, early in the new century, there are comparatively few women in the IT area, in businesses as well as in higher education. In the year 2000, only 20% of persons working in Swedish IT companies were women. In leading IT positions, there were only 6% women. As the main reason for this situation, company representatives expressed that it was not easy to find and employ women with higher technical education, and specifically IT education. From the women organizations point of view, however, this seemed a contradiction and women argued that there generally are well-educated women available, but that the companies and the recruiters are looking in the wrong places, and are using only traditional networks. However, among the university graduates from electronics, computing and data processing areas the number of women still is less than 30%, and is even decreasing (for example from 26% to 19% during the period form 1990 to 1999).

Access to Internet in Sweden (2003) exceeds 65% of the population, and the differences between men and women here are small. However, concerning specific application services like Internet banking and shopping, the differences in usage between men and women is bigger.

3. FEMALE STUDENTS IN HIGHER EDUCATION IN THE IT AREA 1967 - 1985

In the Information technology field in Swedish universities, the first PhD thesis was presented in 1973, the first licentiate thesis in 1972, and the first master thesis in 1968. In all, for the period from 1966 until 1985, there were 202 masters' theses, 11 licentiate theses, and 19 PhD theses published in the department for Informationsbehandling at Stockholm University/KTH. For the master's theses, there was often more than one author. For the 202 masters theses, there were in all 518 authors; that is, an average of two or more authors per such thesis. Of the 518 authors, there were 388 men and 130 women. This shows that of those students that reached the masters level 74% were men and 26% were women. For licentiate theses during this period there were 11 theseses, of which only one had a female author, i.e. 9% women. For the 19 PhD theses presented at Stockholm University during this period, none had a female author. In summary, 74%, 91%, and 100% of the authors were men!

During this period, I received my PhD degree in Informationsbehandling in 1979 at Chalmers Technical University in Göteborg. This was the first female PhD in Informationsbehandling-ADB in Sweden. The title of the thesis was "A study on conceptual modeling". The examiner was Professor Janis Bubenko, the opponent on the thesis was Professor Arne Sölvberg. During the period mentioned above, there were a few female PhD exams in Lund University and a few in Linköping University (datalogi). In Stockholm University, however, it took many years before there was a female PhD. The first was Terttu Orci who received her PhD in 1997.

4.   WHO WERE THE PIONEERS?

At Stockholm University, in the department for Data och Systemvetenskap (formerly Department for Informationsbehandling-ADB), it has been preserved files of all theses that have been presented since the department started to exist in 1967. These files include information about PhD, licentiate, and master levels. (At that time, the level most comparable to master's level was the "3-betygsuppsatser", corresponding to today's 60-point thesis.) Looking at the female master students for the five first years, we find several of the pioneering females in the IT area.

During spring 1968, the University published the first four master theses. One of these had female authors: Anita Hellberg and Gunhild Sandström. The title of their thesis was "Informationssystem för styrning av Arbetsmarknadsverket – en redovisning av systemarbetets första etapp". It is interesting to notice that Anita Hellberg in 1973 recieved her licentiate degree, and that she is the only female IT licentiate in Stockholm University during the period 1966 to 1985. Gunhild Sanström completed her PhD in Lund University, and later became a professor at Lund University.

During the autumn of 1969, again there were four masters' theses in Stockholm, out of which one had three female authors: Karin Gillström, Eva Samuelson, Louise Yngström. The title of the thesis was "Databaser". Of these authors, Louise Yngström has later received her PhD and has become a professor at Stockholm University.

During 1970, the University published 20 master theses. There were in total 35 authors, out of which eight were female. The authors and the title of their theses were as follows.

- Ann-Catrine Appelquist and Ann von Corswant: " Utformning av programbudgetsystem för en ADB-institution"
- Kerstin Holm (and Tomas Montelius): "Studie av användningsområden för en teckenskärm"
- Madelene Hilding: "Registreringssystem för forskarutbildningen – en förstudie".
- Ann-Marie Lind: "Elementär informationsanalys av praktikfallet KOSAB (tillämpning av en vidareutveckling av grundläggande systemeringsmetodik enligt Langefors)"
- Anna-Stina Eskilson, Ewa Lindström: "Datorprogram för lagring och manipulation av systemstrukturer"
- Eva Lindencrona: "Analys av en bokföringsrutin"

In 1971, there were 27 theses presented, four of which had female authors:
- Beila Engelhardt (and PerDanielson): "Några hardware egenskaper hos processdatorer".

- Britt-Marie Lind (and Corneliu Pitulia):" Time-sharing contra remote batch processing"
- Birgitta Gustafsson (and Bengt Bohlin): "Jämförelse mellan olika databassystem som är aktuella för TAD"
- Katrin Sundling: "Några frågeställningar vid övergång från serieminne till direktminne"

In 1972, there were 31 master theses presented. Among the 46 authors, five were female. They are:

- Marie Cederlund: "Undersökning av trånga sektioner i datorsystemet vid Stockholms Datamaskincentral"
- Inger Georgson, Gunnel Lindquist: "Programmeringsmetodik. Problemlösning, flödesplanteknik och modulprogrammering"
- Lena Axlund (and Inge Beiming): "Vilka kunskaper och vilken utbildning bör en god programerare ha"
- Ann-Margret Svensson:"Några alternativa minidatorbaserade informationssystemarkitekturer lämpliga för IP och institutionen för tiden fram t.o.m. 1975".

It is interesting to see the titles of these early theses. Some of them are very out of date while others could well be relevant also in 2003. It is not easily possible to see any clear tendencies of female students preferring more or less technical problems or choosing more user or people oriented topics.

In summary, this historical review reveals an astonishing gender unbalance. There were so many men, and so few women. Why? No evident answer has been found. Convention and un-reflected tradition seems to have played a roll. Engineers have by tradition initially been men, and computing seems to have been looked on as a topic of that same type.

5. WHAT IS THE SITUATION TODAY? HAS THERE BEEN ANY GENDER BALANCE CHANGES?

Today, in the beginning of the new century, the number of female graduates from Swedish universities in institutions like "ADB and Systemvetenskap" is still less than 50%. The percentage of female graduates is decreasing: For example from about 45% in 1989 to less than 40% in 1999. The number of female graduates from Swedish University education in the "Electronics and data processing" area has decreased from 26% to 19% during the years 1989 to 1990. The number of female students in higher education (forskarstuderande) is also decreasing at present. In 1989, 41% of the students were women. In 1998, the number had decreased to

26%. In IT related areas the number of female students at the change of the century was less than 20%.

Why is that so? There are many different approaches to understanding the situation. One example can be found in the study "IT in schools", a project financed with about 1.5 billion SEK (less than 200 million US dollars) by the public authority KKS, and with the aim of understanding differences in usage of IT among boys and girls.

In 1997, when the University of Umeå realized that the number of female students in the IT area was only 10%, they started to investigate the situation and search for relevant measures to take. An empirical study showed that the students thought that some of the reasons why female students were not attracted were that

- Teachers assumed computer experience that was not official prerequisites for the courses
- Exercises were often adapted to the interests of the male students
- There were few female teachers or patterns

A number of measures to be taken were proposed. Among these were:

- Stress carrier planning for female doctoral students
- Reward the institutions more for female than for male students exams
- Include more "soft" courses into the educational system
- Introduce specific curricula for female students
- Define mentorship programs for female students

The Swedish government has initiated educational programs outside the universities and outside the public schools to increase the number of females in IT related work. A conclusion from these courses was that the female students tended to choose more "application" oriented than "technology" oriented courses and that the teachers frequently used males as the norms for prerequisite knowledge and expected frames of references.

6.   CONCLUSIONS AND COMMENTS

As a young student in Informationsbehandling, I did not personally experience any differences in the areas of interest between my male and female student comrades. The area was new to all of us, and there were no implicit expectance of some gender related knowledge, or any gender differences concerning earlier experience in the area. In general, during these early years, in spite of the gender unbalance, I did not experience much of gender problems, and my impression and feeling is that female and male students at the time were treated as equals. For this, I am grateful to my teachers from that time.

Today, with a long working life experience and more knowledge about gender issues I feel I can find many examples of differences in the prerequisites for male and female university students. After the time that we had received our degrees, often applying for formal positions in the university department, I felt very strongly that the system was not transparent and that decisions were taken on grounds that favored male applicants. In addition, I have a feeling that for the male researchers and teachers, long-term career plans existed – implicit or explicit – but for the females, few such plans existed. If this was true, something had happened during a short period between finishing studies and starting a career. There is reason to analyze this.

Today, thinking back, there is much in this field to discuss with my female colleagues from the early times. This includes:

- Which were your experiences of being female students in the IT area in the 70's? How do you feel today about that time?
- Did you experience the difference in being a student and – having finished studies – and being a competitor for positions?
- In what way do you think that the situation for female students has changed since then?

With my male colleagues, it would be interesting to discuss several questions like:

- Did those of you who later became recognized pioneers in the IT area ever consider gender problems? If so, did you do anything about the situation?
- From your experience, do you think women in general are more interested in the use of technology rather than in the technology itself?
- What would you suggest as the most efficient measures in order to support female students and researchers in the IT area?

Likely, many observers would look forward to answers to gender related questions like these. It is amazing that there is so little documented material concerning this in the Swedish IT field.

REFERENCES

Statistics from Stockholm University, concerning degrees and exams, from 1960+
"Jämställdhet och IT – en kartläggning på uppdrag av JÄMIT. SOU 2000:31.
"Om kvinnors användning av Internet". Håkan Selg, IT Kommissionens rapport 49/2002.
"Women and Computing", inroads, ACM SIGSCE Bulletin, Volume 34, Number 2, June 2002.

WHEN COMPUTERS BECAME OF INTEREST IN POLITICS

Sten Henriksson

Computer Science Department, Lund University, Lund, Sweden; Sten.Henriksson@cs.lth.se

Abstract: Technical progress was for a long time uncontroversial in the Scandinavian left and labor movements. World events like the American war in Vietnam and a new zeitgeist changed this at the end of the sixties and politically aware computer enthusiasts started seeing computers in a new light. Three themes were central in the Swedish discussion: the IBM hegemony, computers, personal privacy, and the threat to democratic development by a changed balance of power. Swedish debate at the time is from a personal point of view.

Key words: Sweden, computers, government, politics

1.   INTRODUCTION

In the first decades following WW II, technical developments like nuclear power and computers were uncontroversial in the pragmatic Scandinavian societies. However, in the 1960s some of us developed a fascination for computers started to look upon them with new eyes. The computer had become a tool for established power, used to register our lives, forcing organizational changes in society and the workplace that we could not accept. One company – IBM – had a monopoly position. In addition, as we could understand from TV every day, computers were central for the efficiency of the bombing fleets killing Vietnamese peasants.

The intention of this paper is to draw a picture of an awakening critical view of computerization and the birth of computer policy. Maybe the time has come to evaluate what we said then: Was it correct, relevant, and fair?

We will concentrate this study to the years around 1970 and we will discuss three main themes.

- Industrial policy. If you considered computers to be the most important contribution to technology during the twentieth century and if you saw the potential of computers in all areas of human life, it was obvious that an advanced industrialized country like Sweden should have an industry for the production of computer hardware and software.
- The threat to privacy. Computers handled personal information storing it in databases. Inspired by the American tradition of respect for individual privacy, we questioned the practices. This theme was the most successful point in our agenda but in an unexpected way.
- Problems of democracy. The advent of computers changed power structure in the workplace and in society. Computers developed in ways determined by the established powers. There were those who said that we could only use computers in this way.

2.   COMPUTER ENTHUSIASM TRANSFORMED

In 1970 a yellow-colored paperback, "Computers and policy" was published by the then leading left-wing publisher in Sweden, Bo Cavefors. There were four authors: Jan Annerstedt (graduate student of political science), Lars Forssberg (journalist), Sten Henriksson, and Kenneth Nilsson (graduate students of computer science). The title was characteristic for its time – I would guess that there were a dozen book titles these years with titles of the type "X and politics."

The book did not raise much publicity – I believe they shredded most copies in the paper mills when the publisher went broke a few years later. Nevertheless, in some circles there was attention: in a review in the Swedish state radio, a journalist[1] called the book factually incorrect, full of infamy against IBM and lacking any value whatsoever. A central person in the government apparatus,[2] known to be close the minister of finance Gunnar Sträng, declared us dangerous radicals. We even began to know that the board of the Swedish IBM company had discussed whether people could sue us for economic slander. Unfortunately this did not came about – it would have been exhilarating to be inflicted a large sum of money in indemnities to one of the world's most successful companies.

At the end of the 1960s, computers and computerization became controversial. The intention here is to describe how this happened. To some

---

[1] Ulf Örnkloo
[2] Åke Pernelid

extent, this will have a strong personal flavor – not because I have the whole truth but because this conference supposedly intends to catch witness accounts while it is still possible.

The first generation of computer people in Sweden consisted of those who constructed and wrote programs for BARK and BESK. I joined the second generation as a student of Carl-Eric Fröberg, theoretical physicist and a member of the group going to the US 1947-48 for computer studies. With the influence of Torsten Gustafsson, professor of theoretical physics at Lund University and principal scientific advisor to the Swedish Prime Minister, Tage Erlander, the computer SMIL developed in Lund. I attended one of Dr. Fröberg's first courses in numerical analysis and programming. In 1958, I wrote my first program, which in its first trial printed the 50 first Fibonacci numbers. Let me immediately add that this smooth functioning was not characteristic of all the programs I wrote when I working as assistant and programmer with SMIL.

The encounter with a computer was for me an important event. A computer could work upon the data it stored and we controlled it by a program stored in the same way. A computer could bite its own tail and hence be self-governing. Consequently, its potential was without limits! (My encounter with Turing's Halting Problem came later!). Therefore, I spent the first half of the 1960s telling everyone about the power of this new machine to strengthen human intellectual capacity.

3. THE COMPUTER INDUSTRY

The computer was mainly an American development even if we were well aware of the German and British pioneers. The USA was where the significant developments had taken place; this was the location of MIT, Berkeley, Rand Corporation, and all the other exciting institutions. However, I became aware of bitterness among many of those active, over the lack of support for the area in Sweden. After all BESK had been of world class a few years in the beginning of the 1950s. Millions of kronor in government grants were going into the area of nuclear physics, while nobody cared about computers with their immense potential. In 1959 came the final blow to early Swedish computer development: the new computer for the Swedish Defense Research Agency (FOA) and the Royal Institute of Technology (KTH) was to be an IBM 7090. Why not develop a promising Swedish machine that was under construction? We did not understand that nuclear weapons ambitions were what mattered. Significantly, government money was later given to computer construction (for Saab jet fighters) only when channeled through military contracts. There was a long fight for a large contract for computers used by regional authorities for the revenue service and citizen registration, where the choice was between the less costly and technically more interesting Saab D22 computers and the commercially proved IBM 1401. Finally, Saab and IBM divided the order equally, a classic Swedish compromise. Nevertheless, the difficulties in getting authorities and politicians to understand the importance of a computer industry bewildered me and I felt a need to dig deeper.

I then started an ambitious work: I contacted and visited a number of the key actors in the history of Swedish computer development, from professor Eklöf to admiral Lagerman and the men behind TRASK. The result was a text I published with a translation into Swedish of Peter Naur's "Computers and society"[3] which I volunteered to translate under the condition that I could add my text. I found the key word for the analysis in a Gramsci-inspired text by the sociologist Göran Therborn.[4] The word was *hegemony*. IBM had systematically worked for and reached hegemony in computer usage in Sweden. IBM terminology and ways of looking upon computers what was mattered, solutions of information processing problems occurred within the IBM framework, the IBM school educated far more people than the meager government system. IBM had an extensive base of contacts from its punched cards business and a cash flow from its rental system that was unassailable. IBM was the norm while everything else was a deviation.

I also acted politically as a member of the social democratic student club in Lund. For the 1969 party conference – the one where Erlander was replaced by Palme as chairperson – I wrote a proposal "Government support and control of computer technology".[5] The local branch of the party accepted it as its own. It demanded

- "that the party conference should demand that the government develops such an industrial policy that a vital Swedish state owned industry gets the possibility to work in the computing area;
- that the party conference should ask the government to turn its attention to the importance of following the development of distributed computer power, i.e. generally available distant connections to computers;
- that the party conference should demand that the governing committee of the party should follow with attention technical developments with increasing computer use and hence in its studies and elsewhere form a policy where technical developments are directed in such a way that societal needs are prioritized before managerial and economical needs."

The party board and the conference received the proposals well. A newly started department for industrial developments would handle some of the

---

[3] Peter Naur, "Datorer och samhälle". Med ett tillägg om svenska förhållanden av Sten Henriksson Studentlitteratur, Lund 1969.

[4] En ny vänster (red.Göran Therborn). Rabén & Sjögren Stockholm, 1966.

[5] Socialdemokraterna: Motioner till partikongressen 28 september-4 oktober 1969, Vol I, Motion D24

proposals and the board itself would be attentive to developments. The government produced a number of reports such as those on the electronics industry. Within the party, a working group on computer policy produced a document[6] "Computers adapted to human needs" for the party conference 1978. Tage Erlander took up the theme in a symposium 1980 with the title "Computers and society."[7]

4. COMPUTERS AND PRIVACY

However, let us return to the end of the 1960s. Another computer related problem came up: the threat to personal privacy. Computers made it easy to store and retrieve masses of data about individuals. The inspiration to this debate came from the US with its strong traditions of individualism and personal freedom. This is in strong contrast to Sweden with our parish registration system since 1686, with a strong central power using a personal identity number with a much wider use than the US social security number. News from the US came mainly through the Communications of the ACM and Datamation, the latter now deceased but at the time an important source of news.

Swedish authorities had computerized at an early stage with population statistics and parish registers as a backbone for all the others. Statistics Sweden (SCB) had a register of the total population with basic personal data such as name, sex, date of birth, marital status, and income. These were certainly not secrets – the principle of public access to information is central for all Swedish authorities and a source of pride for the country. However, what happened now was that SCB marketed the information in its possession. The statistics service of SCB turned to advertising agencies giving examples to what addresses it could sell.[8]

> "Unmarried teenagers of both sexes living in Skärholmen with an own income of at least 25,000 kronor.
> Married retired persons in Skåne and Halland with an income between 20 – 40,000 kronor"

At this time (1969), we were a group of students at the Department of Computer Science in Lund who started an informal group, "The critical group of Information Science". We were influenced by the wave of student

---

[6] Datorer på människans villkor. Program för datapolitiken. Socialdemokraterna, Borås 1978
[7] Datorerna och samhällsutvecklingen. Inlägg vid Tage Erlanders datasymposium 1980,Tiden 1981.
[8] Information från Statistiktjänsten, SCB 1969, s. 5-7

activism that followed 1968.[9]   The word "critical" derived from the
terminology the Frankfurt School of critical theory (Horkheimer, Habermas).

We started to look into the SCB policy and argued that its way of
handling data was in conflict with the intentions of the laws of public access
and I wrote a critical article.[10]   A representative of the SCB[11] answered that
this was not new at all: authorities had always been willing to offer such
data. Against this, I argued that the introduction of computer technology
resulted in a situation where quantitative change turned into qualitative
change:

> "When the speed by which one can put together facts is changed, let us say
> with a factor one million, the whole situation has changed. To be frank: we
> could accept that the parish clerk sold bridal pairs and new-borns at a price of
> ten öre per piece, but it is not so great when the vacuum cleaner salesman in
> the door by his smile indicates that he knows quite a lot about us, even if his
> data is public and honestly bought from the SCB"

To find out about the size of these data sales, who bought materials, and
what they sold, I contact the SCB Statistics Service. Rumors at the time
indicated that intelligence agencies of foreign governments were buying data
under disguise. But now SCB was restrictive in its interpretation of the laws
on public access! It was not willing to tell me whom they sold the data to,
this was a business secret of the SCB Statistics Service. It could not have
been demonstrated more clearly how laws were perverted to serve
commercial interests.

5.   COMPUTERS, DEMOCRACY AND POWER

What became the central and most difficult problem was the impact on
power relations in society. "Knowledge is power" is the old saying and of
course, knowledge depends on information. Hence, those working with the
processing of information were in a position of power.   Information
processing was not just a technical matter but also a political one.

Did computers have some intrinsic properties such that they could only
be used to control and govern from above, by governments and authorities
over citizens, by organization leaders over members, by management over
employees, by producers over consumers etc? In the literature, this was
taken for granted. It showed how management could be more efficient and
organizations more centralized. The distance between the governors and
those governed became greater.

---

[9] We were also inspired by CPP, Computer Professionals for Peace, in the US.
[10] "Missbrukas offentlighetsprincipen?", Svensk Sparbankstidskrift 1969:7, sid 380-82
[11] Byrådirektör Edmund Rapaport

In 1969 the Swedish State Radio started an educational series "Human beings and computer technology" with a textbook with the same title. The view of the management totally dominates a text that is supposed to take into consideration human beings. The book[12] asks:

> "How will it be possible to adapt the employees to the changes which will follow from the installation of EDP equipment? There is a natural resistance to change. Who will get the new jobs? Which ones will have to leave? Which ones can expect training?"

It was quite clear that people should adapt to technology, which presumably was steering its own course not controlled by anyone. Technology determinism is a term often used to characterize Marx's famous words about the hand mill giving us the feudal lord, the steam mill the industrial capitalist. Technology determines society. The ideologies surrounding computerization said that computers would by necessity result in more centralized systems. Against this, we said that technology was useful for control in the other direction. A democratic society not only depends on governance from above but also control from below. Citizens should be able to scrutinize those in possession of power and to do this they need information. Governments should answer to parliaments, parliament's members are responsible to their electors, local populations should inspect their local government's handling of zoning and school administration, and unions should be able to look into company plans. In these entire situations, we can apply computer technology. It is a banal statement today, but in the early 1970s, it seemed utopian. Of course, it was then utopian: computers were expensive. Maybe it was it was not until personal computers and the Internet arrived that the computer became an instrument for democracy.

6.   IN RETROSPECT

6.1   The computer industry

Of course, technical and commercial advances crushed any dreams about national and independent computer industries. Even large countries like Great Britain, Germany, the Soviet Union, and France, which all tried, had to give it up. The size of the US market and the extreme research resources channeled through defense budgets gave the results. In addition, within the US, competition became too tough even for large companies as General Electric, Burroughs, and Univac. IBM kept its position until the introduction of personal computers changed the rules of the game.

---

[12] Sven-Erik Johansson och Bo Wiedenborg "Människan och datatekniken", Sveriges Radios förlag, Kristianstad 1969.

In Sweden Datasaab could continue as long as generous military contracts were forthcoming. Some companies found market niches like the one for the Alfascope terminals. Ericsson's failure with a PC in the early 1980s showed what happens when you just copy, while Luxor's ABC 80 demonstrated the difficulty of going alone.[13] It was possible to construct a unique PC system that was internationally competitive for a year or so. Nevertheless, you could not produce further models taking advantage of the rapid technical change. They later repeated the same process within the software industry: niches were found, but for general software, Microsoft was too powerful. Since then the globalization process had made all hopes for nationally independent hardware or software industries obsolete.[14]

6.2   The threats to privacy

Interestingly enough, the privacy problem was the one area that really gave rise to debate. In 1970, a census took place in Sweden, which became controversial. Debate has since then flared up now and then and all the political parties started to write about computers and privacy in their programs and election platforms. Laws were issued on personal information in digital form, first nationally and later in the EU. Our critique came from an anti-commercial position, while the right wing side of politics issued attacks on "Big Brother" tendencies of the state. In the conflict between public access and personal privacy, the left has rather stressed the needs of public access in an open society.

6.3   Democracy and power

Our critique around 1970 did not contribute much of constructive proposals for action. These came with the breakthrough of the ideas of Kristen Nygaard et al in their work with the Norwegian metalworkers union. Nygaard considered the workplace the main arena. For a change, computer scientists should work with the representatives of labor and not only with management. The result was a series of projects in all the Scandinavian countries, together forming what has become known as "the Scandinavian

---

[13] Magnus Johansson, Smart Fast and Beautiful, On Rhetoric of Technology and Computing Discourse in Sweden 1955-1995. Diss. Linköping 1997.

[14] Were the pioneering efforts then just wasted? No, they left a residue of experience which resulted in early adaptation of computers in Sweden. Hans De Geer, På väg till datasamhället : datekniken i politiken 1946-63. Tekniska Högskolan/FA-rådet 1992.

school".[15] Its original forms are not alive any longer but the ideas are lingering on. The importance attached to user influence within the HCI area is a descendant of these ideas as is the continued interest in so-called participatory design.

Computer technology received much political attention during the 1980s and 1990s.[16] Interestingly enough, in a speech by the conservative Prime Minister, Carl Bildt expressed the most explicit statement on the relations between policy and computer technology. With a tone and a choice of words, which is not very common among Swedish politicians, he stressed science and technology as the driving forces of history. According to Bildt, a fundamental shift has taken place from the industrial society (in which he includes early computers) with its belief in large-scale production and social engineering. Industrial society has now moved on to the information society and government must act:

> "We need a broad national project for the development and use of the new information technologies"

> "Let us set the target that by the year 2010 we should belong to the spearheads of global development in the use of information technology"

> "In my government there is no computer minister or IT minister. In my government every minister is a computer minister and IT minister"

Clearly, such pronouncements are showing an awareness of the relation between computers and politics. They certainly fulfill the ambitions of the 1970 authors of "Computers and politics" if not necessarily from a similar point of view.

7. WHAT WOULD WE SAY TODAY?

What would be the agenda of radical political action within computer politics today? Is it possible to give rise to so much offence today as we did then? I doubt it, but let me try.

---

[15] Jørgen Bansler "Systemudvikling- teori og historie i skandivisk perspektiv". Studentlitteratur, Lund 1987. For a philosophic and academic analysis, Pelle Ehn: "Work-oriented design of computer artifacts" Arbetslivsscentrum/Almqvist&Wiksell 1988

[16] Both the Liberal party and the Center party were active in the area, with Kerstin Anér and Olof Johansson as the main actors. For a review of early computer politics, see Kent Lindkvist, Datateknik och politik (1984). For a follow-up to 1994, see S. Henriksson, "Datapolitikens död och återkomst" in B. Atlestam, Infrastruktur för informationssamhället, NUTEK B 1995:1. For an recent study see Lars Ilshammar, Offentlighetens nya rum – Teknik och politik i Sverige 1969–1999. Diss Örebro 2002.

7.1   The software industry

Software began to replace hardware as the central area.   More specifically, the Microsoft near-monopoly is in parallel to the position of IBM thirty years ago – Microsoft has used business practices that in hindsight makes IBM look benign. As was the case with IBM, Microsoft has enough money and political influence to get out of any antitrust lawsuits fairly unchanged.   The challenges are rather coming from technical developments, for Microsoft from the open source movement, where it produces software of high quality at low cost.   There is no witchcraft involved: the method of production is the same as has been practiced for eight hundred years in the production of new knowledge at universities: maximal openness. The driving force is recognition rather than money. For tools like operating systems and basic applications, it should be self-evident that open source is to be used and supported by all schools and universities, as by government and municipal agencies. In many countries, this practice currently happens simply for the reason that they cannot afford to allow Microsoft to become more profitable. We should do it in Sweden too.

7.2   Public access to the commons

There is a conflict between societal needs for information and the individual's need for privacy. We know from the Swedish debate about the secret police registers how the government spied upon a large part of the population in a way that is not consistent with a free and democratic society. We know from the present debate on the DARPA project "Total Information Awareness" how terrorist threats can be used to justify far-reaching measures like the construction of databases taking full advantage of the digitalization of society.

On the other hand, we can see how EU laws about the publications of names on the Internet give absurd results hindering important public information.   Additionally, the commercial interests of media producing companies hinder public access. Lawrence Lessig in his books[17] has shown the importance of "the commons" for creativity and development in a democracy. Fortunately, there is a counter movement speaking for open access, not only for software but also for general material (Richard Stallman's Copyleft initiative[18]). It is obvious that this movement is worth (critical) support.

---

[17] Lessig, Lawrence, Code and other laws of cyberspace, Basic Books 1999. Lessig, Lawrence, The future of ideas : the fate of the commons in a connected world, Vintage Books 2001.

[18] http://www.gnu.org

7.3   A tool for democracy

Many of the demands raised in the 1970s for user influence are satisfied today. Usability has a close coupling to efficiency and quality: computer systems developed with strong user influence are doing their jobs better. Of course, most things remain unfinished: computer systems are still difficult to use for the hundreds of millions of people who expect to use them. Further, we still have the "digital divide" – we cannot expect large groups of people to use computers for reasons of income, education, or age.

For communication between management and those below, between government agencies and citizens there are now many initiatives and examples. The e-mail in its simplicity is a means of communication in all directions. Computers are no longer tools only for those with power and money. Microelectronics in the form of personal computers and mobile phones are today within the reach of all citizens in the Western industrialized countries and in the future maybe for the whole world. There are many examples of how they used computer communications for emancipatory purposes.[19] Antiglobalization movements like Attac are organized using IT, as were the protests against the war on Iraq. Inexpensive computer technology, spread by globalization, is a prerequisite for the antiglobalization movement and this kind of irony is of course characteristic for the history of technology and politics.

---

[19] Manuel Castells,The Information age, vol II, Blackwell 1996.

DEVELOPMENT IN THE GROWTH BASE OF THE 'OULU PHENOMENON'
The role of systems/software methodologies

Henry Oinas-Kukkonen, Jouni Similä, Pentti Kerola,
Petri Pulli, and Samuli Saukkonen

*1. Oinas-Kukkonen, Department of History, P.O. Box 1000, FIN-90014 University of Oulu,
Finland; Infotech Oulu, Oasis Group, University of Oulu, Finland; Henry.Oinas-
Kukkonen@oulu.fi*
*2. Similä, Department of Information Processing Science, P.O. Box 3000, FIN-90014
University of Oulu, Finland; Jouni.Simila@oulu.fi*
*3. Kerola, Department of Information Processing Science, P.O. Box 3000, FIN-90014
University of Oulu, Finland; Pentti.Kerola@oulu.fi*
*4. Pulli, Department of Information Processing Science, P.O. Box 3000, FIN-90014
University of Oulu, Finland; Petri.Pulli@oulu.fi*
*5. Saukkonen, Department of Information Processing Science, P.O. Box 3000, FIN-90014
University of Oulu, Finland; Samuli.Saukkonen@oulu.fi*

Abstract: Oulu has been a place for business and export industry in Northern Finland. In
the 1970s began a difficult period of recession. Then, declining and
unemployment-ridden Oulu seemed unexpectedly to start to boom. High
technology products were being produced in the city and these products were
sold more and more in international market. The main contribution of the
paper is to provide a more thorough view of the multi-scientific expertise
apparent in the gradual building of the growth base of the 'Oulu phenomenon'.
The analysis shows the crucial role of system-theoretical and software-
oriented expertise and complements earlier views.

Key words: Systems software, Oulu, computing history, Finland

1.   INTRODUCTION

Oulu has a long history as a place for business and export industry in
Northern Finland. In the Middle Ages especially fish, butter, train oil, furs,

and hides found their ways to the European market. Later, important were tar export, shipping, and shipbuilding in the seventeenth and eighteenth centuries, leather industry in the nineteenth century and forest and chemical industries in the first half of the twentieth century. In the 1970s, due to international and domestic reasons, began a difficult period of recession and unemployment.[1]

Then, declining and unemployment-ridden Oulu seemed unexpectedly to start to boom. The city began producing high technology products with embedded software and sold these products more and more in international markets. Local people and authorities seemed to believe again in progress and improvement on their life conditions and economy in the region. This overall change was and is an unanticipated and astonishing "jackpot" — the term Oulu phenomenon (Oulu-ilmiö) soon appeared. This major change was not ignored abroad either. Various kinds of delegations from different parts of the world flocked to estimate the situation in Oulu and to learn from it. Others wanted to have their success story realized, too. Foreign and domestic journalists wrote their wonder stories.[2]

We often view the Oulu phenomenon as a triumph of electronics. However, nobody has unambiguously defined the duration or actual content of the Oulu phenomenon.[3] Here, the first basic idea is that the life span of the Oulu phenomenon has not come to its end. Second, existing high technology products in question such as sophisticated mobile phones need software to function. These products contributed to the development of systems, the software industry, and information processing science in the Oulu region even when we consider the period preceding 1985. Furthermore, the Department of Information Processing Sciences (Tietojenkäsittelyopin laitos, later Tietojenkäsittelytieteiden laitos, TOL) in Oulu University was not a concrete outgrowth of the Oulu phenomenon. Why is this so? Has the department, contrary to the general assumption, actually had essential but more abstract and infrastructural effects on the growth of the Oulu phenomenon?

[1]   Jouko Vahtola, "Oulujokisuun keskusasema 1500-luvulla," Valkean kaupungin vaiheet: Oulun historiaa (Rovaniemi: Pohjois-Suomen historiallinen yhdistys, 1987), pp. 65-70; Eino Siuruainen, "Talouselämä Oulussa," Valkean kaupungin vaiheet: Oulun historiaa, pp. 200-207; Turo Manninen, Oulun kaupungin historia, Volume VI (Oulu: Oulun kaupunki, 1995), p. 79.

[2]   See e.g. Hot Tech Cities. BerliNews, 31. March 2000. http://www.berlinews.de /archiv/928.shtml; Carol J. Williams, "A Wireless Wake-Up Call for Finland; The mobile communications industry has reinvigorated the country, changing the way Finns work, play and see their place in the world." The Los Angeles Times; November 8, 1999.

[3]   Comp. e.g. Mika Kulju, Oulun ihmeen tekijät (Helsinki: Ajatus, 2002), passim; Matti Otala, Uskalla olla viisas (Helsinki: Ajatus kustannusosakeyhtiö, 2001), passim; Manninen, pp. 127-128; Experts trust Oulu: the secret of the "Oulu phenomenon" (City of Oulu, Economic affairs office, 199-?), passim.

To the main question, we seek answers through variety of sources. As a starting point, the major newspaper in the Oulu region, *Kaleva*, has actively taken part in the discussion concerning the Oulu phenomenon. This and the published literature concerning high technology and its research in the large do not solely form the source base. Most of the authors of this paper have experience of different kind of scientific backgrounds, paradigms, and even practical careers in computing. In the following chapters, we first describe the birth of the 'Oulu phenomenon' as portrayed in the *Kaleva* newspaper. Then we present the University of Oulu from the viewpoint of computing and analyze the role of TOL as a source of basic research in information systems (IS). Then we describe and discuss the major relationships and co-efforts with other faculties, the City of Oulu, the Technical Research Centre of Finland (VTT, *Valtion teknillinen tutkimuskeskus*), and local industries. Finally, we make significant conclusions with some lessons learned for the future benefit of Nordic computing.

2. THE BIRTH OF THE 'OULU PHENOMENON' IN KALEVA

In order to provide the background for the analysis of the factors behind the growth of the 'Oulu phenomenon,' we provide here a brief account of the chronological flow of events based on the articles published in the local *Kaleva* newspaper between the years 1969 and 1985. The role and importance of the influence of the Department of Electrical Engineering (later electrical and information engineering) on the growth of the Oulu phenomenon has been recognized repeatedly in the public and is clearly supported by historical evidence. Matti Otala[4] and Seppo Säynäjäkangas[5] as professors and directors of the department publicly spoke and wrote about the importance of electronics research and industry for the future of Oulu and the whole of Northern Finland numerous times during the late 1960s, through the 1970s and early 1980s. In addition, Professor Pentti Lappalainen after his appointment in 1974[6] and later as the director of the department continued the theme. VTT came to support the idea.

[4] "Elektroniikan tutkimustyötä Oulun yliopistossa" (Research work in electronics at the University of Oulu), *Kaleva,* 13.9.1969, p. 4; "Elektroniikan teollisuus on hyvässä myötätuulessa" (Electronics industry in good downwind), *Kaleva,* 10.8.1971, p. 3.

[5] Professor Seppo Säynäjäkangas, "Elektroniikka muuttaa maailmankuvaamme" (Electronics will change our world view), *Kaleva,* 12.6.1976, p. 2.

[5] Professor Pentti Lappalainen, "Helmitaulusta tietokoneeseen" (From an abacus to a computer), *Kaleva,* 12.5.1976, pp. 2, 4.

After the planning[7] and finally the establishment of the Laboratory of Electronics in Oulu in 1974[8], the directors of the Oulu branch came to support the creation of electronics industry in Oulu. Again, we see in the articles the promotion by Otala[9] in his new role as the director of the laboratory and the active role of Martti Karppinen[10] as vice-director as well as Jarmo Karvonen[11]. Later during the 1980s, Samuli Saukkonen[12], in his role as the director of the laboratory (established in 1983), continued the support of computer technology.[13] Additionally, on a general level, the University of Oulu actively supported the promotion of electronics industry in the 1970s and thereafter. The active roles of Rector Markku Mannerkoski[14] (in the context of adp education[15]) and of Olavi Jakkula[16] already emerge from *Kaleva* during mid 1970s. VTT and the University of Oulu established an advisory board led on the university side by Professor Juhani Oksman, who at that time was the dean of the technical faculty and later the rector of the university. The advisory board formed a general cooperation agreement in 1974[17] that was the basis of the common public support for electronics industry. After the polemical public appearances of Antti Piippo in 1979[18] and 1980s[19] as executive director of Aspo Electronics,

[7]   "Tutkimusta lisää Pohjois-Suomeen? VTT:n haaraosasto perusteilla Ouluun" (More research in Northern Finland? VTT's branch office to be established in Oulu), *Kaleva*, 4.2.1972, p. 11.

[8]   "VTT aloittaa Oulussa 1.3" (VTT starts in Oulu 1.3), *Kaleva*, 16.2.1974, p. 1.

[9]   Professor Matti Otala, VTT, "Elektroniikassa kaikki mahdollista" (In electronics everything is possible), *Kaleva*, 15.9.1975, p. 5.

[10] "Tuotekehittelyn merkitys kasvaa" (Importance of product development grows), *Kaleva*, 2.3.1978, p. 13.

[11] "Yritysten syntymistä tuettava tehokkaammin" (Birth of companies should be supported more effectively), *Kaleva*, 25.2.1980, p. 10.

[12] "Elektroniikan ohjelmakehitys keskittymässä Oulun seudulle" (Electronics program development concentrating in Oulu area), *Kaleva*, 19.5.1984, p. 20.

[13] "Tietokonetekniikan laboratorio Ouluun" (Laboratory of computer technology in Oulu), *Kaleva*, 4.3.1983, p. 15.

[14] "Oulun yliopisto avasi ovensa: Mannerkoski uskoo teknologiakylään" (University of Oulu opens its doors: Mannerkoski believes in technology park), *Kaleva*, 2.9.1982, p. 6.

[15] "Lisää atk-opetusta: Automaattinen tietojenkäsittely laajenee nopeammin kuin jähmeä koulutus- ja työllisyyssuunnittelu" (More adp education: Automatic data processing expands faster than sluggish education and employment planning), *Kaleva*, 3.11.1982, p. 2.

[16] "Mallia brittien tukitoimista: Elektroniikka-alan kehittämistä tutkitaan" (Model from Brittish support actions: Investigation of development of electronics industry), *Kaleva*, 6.10.1976, p. 6.

[17] "VTT ja Oulun yliopisto aloittavat yhteistyön" (VTT and University of Oulu start cooperation), *Kaleva*, 31.8.1974, pp. 1, 2.

[18] "Komponenttituotanto tulossa elektroniikkateollisuuteemme" (Component production coming into our electronics industry), *Kaleva*, 15.10.1979, p. 9.

the City of Oulu[20] also actively and massively started to promote the electronics industry, especially the establishment of an electronics park in Oulu that finally came about in 1982.[21] We did not observe a public link regarding the role of TOL to the growth of the Oulu phenomenon and we will investigate that later, largely based on the connections made in the chronological analysis of events in this section.

2.1   Two technological tracks apart

Looking at the historical evidence through the *Kaleva* newspaper articles between the years 1969-1985 there seem to be two parallel but separate technological tracks.   One points to the growth of the electronics industry and includes the starting of the Eurodata company in Kempele in 1973,[22] the establishment and enlargement of the Nokia electronics factory in 1974[23] and the Aspo electronics factory in 1975[24] both in the Rusko area, and the establishment of Polar Electro in Kempele in 1977.[25] The electronics track led finally through several growth years to the establishment of the electronics park initially as a haven in the centre of the city[26] for several small companies in various industrial and service areas and later in the Linnanmaa area in 1986 as a real technology park[27] (called later as Technopolis) for future global telecommunication companies.   Mobira, which was to become Nokia Mobile Phones, started its operations in the

---

[19]   Antti Piippo, Aspo, "Oulu ei oivalla missä mennään" (Antti Piippo: Oulu does not realize where we are going), *Kaleva*, 25.2.1980, p. 10.

[20]   "Elektroniikkakylästä vauhtia" (Momentum from electronics park), *Kaleva*, 25.2.1980, p. 10; Oulusta on päätetty tehdä Suomen elektroniikkateollisuuden keskus (Oulu has been decided to become the centre of electronics industry in Finland), *Kaleva*, 2.2.1981, p. 10.

[21]   "Keskiviikkona perustettu Oulun Teknologiakylä Oy selvä osoitus: Oulun elinkeinopolitiikkaa kehitetään nyt tarmokkaasti" (Oulu Technology Park established on Wednesday a clear sign: Oulu's industrial policy is developed vigorously), *Kaleva*, 1.4.1982, p. 18.

[22]   "Eurodatan elektroniikkatuotanto uusilla urilla" (Eurodata's electronics production in new tracks), *Kaleva*, 10.8.1975, p. 2.

[23]   "Elektroniikkatehdas vihittiin" (Electronics factory inaugurated), *Kaleva*, 4.5.1974, p. 7.

[24]   "Ouluun lisää elektroniikkateollisuutta" (More electronics industry in Oulu), *Kaleva*, 4.7.1975, p. 1.

[25]   "Oulun teknologiakylän toimintaidea palkittiin" (Business idea of Oulu technology park awarded), *Kaleva*, 8.4.1984, p. 7.

[26]   Pekka Siltanen, "Korkean teknologian tyyssijaa synnytetään Oulun keskustaan" (Stronghold of high technology in centre of Oulu), *Kaleva*, 19.10.1982, p. 10.

[27]   "Oulun teknologiakylän osakkeista yleisöanti: Varoilla siirto Linnanmaalle" (Public issue of shares of Oulu technology park: funds used for transfer to Linnanmaa), *Kaleva*, 23.11.1984, p. 3; "Teknologiakylä aloittaa rakentamisen Linnanmaalla" (Technology park starts building in Linnanmaa), *Kaleva*, 26.9.1985, p. 18.

technology park in 1986 and was later followed by globally successful companies though on a clearly lower scale.

The other track follows the 'normal' development of automatic data processing (adp) which the Institute of Information Processing Science (the name Department of Information Processing Science was adopted in 1987) was identified with during the 1970s and early 1980s. This includes the establishment of the yearly Blanko conference series in 1973 and the founding of the first systems and software companies in the late 1970s - among others Dataskill in 1976, Systepo in 1979[28], Modera in 1982[29], and CCC in 1985. Computer manufacturers established also offices in Oulu, for example Nixdorf in 1979[30] and HP in 1981[31]. According to *Kaleva* the Finnish adp industry passed the era of 'quiet life' in 1979[32] and the adp processing association[33] called for more education in all levels at that time. The Adp-82 days in Helsinki[34] repeated this call in 1982 and estimated next year the need of new employees in the industry to be between 1500 and 2000.[35] Even later public calls for increase in adp education[36] were not realized in the yearly student intake of the department which slowly rose from the first 10 in 1972 to the level of 25 in 1985 – later the intake again

---

[28] "Atk palveluyritys käyntiin Oulussa" (Adp service company starts in Oulu), *Kaleva*, 3.3.1979, p. 12.

[29] "Yliopistomiesten atk-yhtiö tarjoaa tietoa yrityksille" (University men's adp company offers know-how to industry), *Kaleva*, 6.11.1982, p. 16.

[30] "Uusi tietokoneyhtiö perustettu Ouluun" (New computer company established in Oulu), *Kaleva*, 4.9.1979, p. 10.

[31] "Atk-ala uskoo kasvun jatkuvan" (Adp industry believes growth to continue), *Kaleva*, 22.10.1981, p. 15.

[32] "Suomen atk-teollisuus ohittanut hiljaiselon" (Finnish adp industry passes era of quiet life), *Kaleva*, 9.1.1979, p. 10.

[33] "Tietojenkäsittelyliitto koolla: Atk-oppia pitäisi lisätä keskiasteella" (Data processing association convenes: Adp education should be increased in middle level), *Kaleva*, 29.3.1979, p. 5.

[34] Robert Brantberg, "ATK-82: Toimistoautomaatio, ATK ja tietoliikenne yhdistyvät" (ADP-82: Office automation, ADP and data communication converge), *Kaleva*, 4.3.1982, p.14.

[35] "Atk-ammattien veto jatkuu voimakkaana" (Pull of adp professions continues strong), *Kaleva*, 19.12.1983, p. 8.

[36] Tuulikki Ukkola, "Tietotekniikkaa: Joko lopultakin saadaan vauhtia tietotekniikan opetukseen?" (Do we finally get into stride in information technology education?), *Kaleva*, 23.3.1985, p. 2; "Tietotekniikan koulutusmäärät eivät juuri nouse" (Level of information technology education does not rise), *Kaleva*, 19.5.1985, p. 7; "Tietotekniikan ammattilaisista yhä suurempi pula" (Even stronger shortage of information technology professionals), *Kaleva*, 24.5.1985, p. 19; "Oulu tarvitsisi lisää teknologian koulutusta" (Oulu needs more technology education), *Kaleva*, 24.8.1985, pp. 3, 4; Rector Markku Mannerkoski, "Tietotekniikan merkitystä aliarvioitiin" (Importance of information technology was underestimated), *Kaleva*, 3.9.1985, p. 2.

slowly increased to 45 by 1996 wherefrom it dramatically expanded to the present 250-300 level in only six years.

Looking at the Blanko conference themes (see footnote)[37], we notice that despite the fact that in the first Blanko conference in 1973[38] both professor Matti Otala from the Department of Electrical Engineering and professor Pentti Kerola from the Institute of Information Processing Science presented their respective education curricula and despite the fact that electronics was one of the main themes in Blanko in 1981[39], the Institute of Information Processing Science as well as the Blanko conference series profiled themselves mainly in basic research of information systems. It emphasized the human and organizational aspects especially through Professor Kerola's articles and presentations[40] in the 1970s and early 1980s. This profile

[37] "Tietojenkäsittelyn käytäntöön perehdytään" (Data processing practices discussed), *Kaleva*, 1.11.1975, p. 5; "Blanko-75 Oulussa – ATK-opetus palvelee käytännön työelämää" (Blanko-75 in Oulu – ADP education serves practical working life), *Kaleva*, 28.11.1975, p. 2; "Oulun Blanko-päivät: Kotimainen tietokone 'täysin mahdollinen'" (Oulu's Blanko days: Domestic computer "fully possible"), *Kaleva*, 29.11.1975, p. 4; "Tietojenkäsittely inhimillisemmäksi" (Data processing more humane), *Kaleva*, 25.11.1977, p. 11; "Tietojenkäsittely tulee yksilölliseksi" (Data processing becomes more individual), *Kaleva*, 3.10.1978, p. 1; Professor Yrjö Neuvo, "Automaatiokeskustelu Suomessa hakoteillä" (Discussion on automation in Finland off the track), *Kaleva*, 2.10.1979, p. 13; "Blanko-päivät tulossa: Atk:n käyttäjä vahvasti esillä" (Blanko days coming: Adp user strongly on view), *Kaleva*, 16.9.1980, p. 14, "Blanko-81: Atk-järjestelmä ei ole valmis ensi yrittämällä" (Blanko-81: Adp system is not ready on first try), *Kaleva*, 17.9.1981, p. 15; "Blanko-81: Käyttäjä oppii systemointia" (Blanko-81: User learns systemeering), *Kaleva*, 18.9.1981, p. 13; "Blanko-81: Nyt atk tulee konttoreihin" (Blanko-81: Now adp comes to office), *Kaleva*, 19.9.1981, p. 6; "Blanko-päivät kansainvälistyvät" (Blanko days becoming more international), *Kaleva*, 2.11.1982, p. 13; "Blanko osoitti jälleen elinvoimaisuutensa" (Blanko shows again its vitality), *Kaleva*, 13.11.1982, p. 18; "Uutta tietotekniikkaa puntaroidaan Oulussa" (New information technology deliberated in Oulu), *Kaleva*, 9.8.1985, p. 14; "Helsingin keskityspyrkimykset torjutaan: Blanko-näyttelyllä vakaa asema tulevaisuudessakin" (Helsinki's centralization efforts countered: Blanko exhibition has a strong status also in the future), *Kaleva*, 27.9.1985, p. 8; "Tietotekniikkapäivät: Suomalaisella tietokonetekniikalla 'ruusuinen tulevaisuus'" (Information technology days: Finnish computer technology has a "rosy future"), *Kaleva*, 28.9.1985, p. 18.

[38] "Blanko -73 kertoo tietojenkäsittelystä Pohjois-Suomessa" (Blanko-73 tells about data processing in Northern Finland), *Kaleva*, 8.10.1973, p. 3.

[39] "Blanko-päivät laajenevat: Elektroniikka-ala mukaan" (Blanko days expand: Electronics industry joining), *Kaleva*, 19.6.1981, p. 14.

[40] Pentti Kerola, "Tietokone ihmisen auttajana" (Computer as man's assistant), *Kaleva*, 18.12.1977, p. 2; Pentti Kerola, "Tietokone on nopea idiootti" (Computer is a fast idiot), *Kaleva*, 19.12.1977, pp. 2, 12; "Atk-suunnittelu kuin arkkitehdin työtä" (Adp design similar to architect's work), *Kaleva*, 30.9.1980, pp. 1, 5; Robert Brantberg, "Ihminen on tärkein tietojenkäsittelyssäkin" (Human is most important also in data processing), *Kaleva*, 12.4.1981, p. 9; "Tietotekniikalle otetaan uutta suuntaa: Ihmiskeskeisyys valttia

emphasized general system-theoretical deep structures in the departmental curriculum as can be seen in a later section.

2.2   A pivotal change

A change came in the early 1980s.[41] VTT opened a new research program in software engineering environments in 1981[42] and cooperation between TOL and especially the local computer technology laboratory was started in 1983 in the form of common research projects especially in embedded software. This led to the establishment of a new software engineering study alternative in the TOL's curriculum in 1986.

The Oulu phenomenon appears to have two faces – the public face is the growth of the electronics and telecommunication industry and the lesser publicized the growth of the software industry. The relevance and importance of the cooperation between VTT and TOL in the transfer of methodological knowledge and expertise to the electronics and telecommunication industry will be analyzed more deeply in two later sections. The role of TOL in the growth of the software industry is more direct.

If we look at the companies operating in the adp industry during the 1970s and 1980s it is noteworthy that the adp companies were mainly established and managed by the graduates from the Institute of Information Processing Science – this is true in the case of Dataskill, Modera and CCC as well as Tietoseppo which was established in Kajaani in 1981[43]. Of these only CCC grew later to a nationally sizable company employing more than 500 persons presently. It seems that most graduates from TOL in the 1970s and early 1980s either worked in these companies, or in adp departments of large industrial companies, or in adp departments in public administration. Quite a few also moved to Southern Finland in search of a job[44]. Very few, it seems, worked in the electronics industry.

We noted earlier that the two tracks were separate. This is not completely true but to a large extent and a bit surprisingly this seems to be true and is evidenced by the *Kaleva* articles as well personal experiences of the authors. There are exceptions and these are worth telling about. The

---

järjestelmäsuunnittelussa" (New direction for information technology: human centredness trump in systems design), *Kaleva*, 30.4.1984, p. 5.

[41] "Ohjelmistoteollisuus kasvamassa Suomessa" (Software industry grows in Finland), *Kaleva*, 3.6.1982, p. 5.

[42] "VTT:lle uusia tutkimusohjelmia" (New research programs in VTT), *Kaleva*, 15.10.1981, p. 15.

[43] "Atk-alan palvelujen kysyntä voimistunut" (Demand for adp services strengthens), *Kaleva*, 31.3.1984, p. 17.

[44] Comp. Manninen, p. 127.

best case is Eurodata, which Kajaani Electronics bought in late 1970s and moved to Kajaani simultaneously, only to open an office in Oulu in 1983 as well as to change its name to Edacom[45]. Nowadays, Fujitsu owns the company and operates it in Oulu mainly in its original application area: service station automation. The first system developed by Eurodata was, in fact, mainly subcontracted in 1977-1978 from Dataskill. Both companies had close ties to TOL. Eurodata's system group was managed by Timo Korhonen, a graduate from TOL, who later managed Edacom's system development activities until 1985 when he together with one of the authors, Jouni Similä and some other persons started the CCC companies. Another interesting fact is that the founding of CCC was based on a project contract and project personnel bought from Tietoseppo where another one of the authors, Pentti Kerola was involved for a brief period as research director at that time. Jouni Similä and Juhani Iivari from TOL were also members of the Dataskill development group. Later Jouni Similä worked on several occasions with Edacom and CCC. The product at that time was called super cash register – a clear case of embedded software. Later another one of the authors, Samuli Saukkonen also worked in Edacom in the late 1980s. One of Insele's[46] chief software designers in the early 1980s was also a graduate from TOL. Undoubtedly, there are other cases, too, but smaller ones.

The gap between electronics and information processing science remained however wide until the 1990s when Nokia in fact became a software house. This naturally led to the merging of the two technological tracks - as an example CCC became one of the most important software technology partners of Nokia even on a global scale. The seeds for the growth and the merging of the two technological tracks were sown in the 1970s and early 1980s and the fruits we are enjoying now.

2.3   Questions of size and focus

One of the reasons why the TOL institute had such a small publicly known effect in the growth of the Oulu phenomenon in the 1970s and the early 1980s is of course a question of sheer size. Seppo Säynäjäkangas reported in 1978 that during the first ten years 251 diploma engineers and 4 doctors had graduated from the Department of Electrical Engineering. Of the graduates, an essential percentage (60-70) majored in electronics[47]. In

---

[45] "Edacomille Ouluun suunnitteluyksikkö" (Edacom's development unit in Oulu), *Kaleva*, 8.12.1983, p. 19.

[46] "Tietokone panee lämpölaskut kuriin" (Computer clamps down on energy bills), *Kaleva*, 6.2.1979, p. 1.

[47] Professor Seppo Säynäjäkangas, "Elektroniikkainsinöörien koulutus Oulun yliopistossa" (Education of electrical engineers in University of Oulu), *Kaleva*, 7.10.1978, p. 2.

the case of TOL, the numbers of the first five years were 32 masters of science degrees and four licentiate degrees. The Department of Electrical Engineering had about 400 students in electronics by 1978; TOL had about 80 students. The trend continued all the way to the late 1990s – only now in 2003, the student admissions are on the equal scale. TOL has been, however, already from the beginning actively involved in the offering of courses as secondary subjects to students in other fields of sciences – the role of TOL in the society can be seen as larger than merely in the number of graduates.

Another reason that was already briefly mentioned was the different focus that the departments/institutes had especially before software engineering became a study alternative in TOL. While it can be argued that the education offered at TOL was a viable one (also for a career in the software development sector in electronics industry and personal experience confirms this), it seems clear that when graduating students were not given contacts through the education to the electronics industry in the same scale as to the adp industry, their primary choice for career was for adp industry. Another argument is that simply there were not as many job opportunities in the electronics industry as in the adp industry for graduates from TOL at that time – electronics and software did mix but not in the scale as now. The late 1990s have changed this completely – one can claim that Nokia is indeed a software house and the mobile phone is 90% software nowadays in terms of R&D effort.

2.4   Early role of Technopolis

The role of Technopolis has perhaps been a bit overplayed by the media throughout the years. Out of the companies mentioned here, only Modera[48] and Mobira were directly connected to the technology park. The case of Mobira[49] and its start-up in 1986 in the technology park[50] is of course an important one as it did lead through the growth of Nokia, to the establishment of numerous companies around Nokia and to the growth of the technology park. This however happened only in the 1990s. If we look at the companies that started in the technology park in 1983 none of them has grown to a nationally sizable company except those involved closely with Nokia in the 1990s. The idea that the technology park would act as a

---

[48] "Oulun seutu voimistuu atk-ohjelmien tuottajana" (Oulu regions grows stronger as adp software producer), *Kaleva*, 30.12.1985, p. 9.

[49] "Mobira hajasijoitti ohjelmistoryhmän Ouluun" (Mobira decentralized software group to Oulu), *Kaleva*, 12.10.1985, p. 20.

[50] "Huipputekniikan yritykset kilpailevat menosta Linnanmaalle" (High technology companies competing about moving to Linnanmaa), *Kaleva*, 23.11.1985, p. 22.

'hatchery' for new companies seems a bit over-reaching. The park has however played a major role in the growth of the Oulu phenomenon, has offered affordable rental office space, and has responded to growth needs in an admirable way.

3. MULTIDISCIPLINARY RESEARCH AND HIGHER EDUCATION OF COMPUTING IN THE OULU UNIVERSITY

3.1 Organizational and research paradigmatic context

Previous analyses agree that the University of Oulu, which was established in 1958, had a significant influence on the growth base of the Oulu phenomenon.[51] The Institute of Information Processing Science was established 1968 and it began to operate as a separate and faculty-independent unit in 1969. It had responsibility for research and education of information processing (computing), and in addition for computer and systems/software services for the whole university. As most students came to TOL from the Faculty of Science, where information processing science could be a major subject, ties to this faculty became close. Education of information processing science was coordinated in the Faculty of Science and professor Pentti Kerola became its member in 1973.[52] In Kerola's leadership research concentrated on philosophies and theories of information systems. This and the special organizational structure that forms the broad arena for information processing science in Oulu should be born in mind, when one examines the topic more closely.

In the Faculty of Science the Department of Mathematics directed by professor Paavo Turakainen was interested in theories of formal automata and languages as one subarea of mathematics. The higher education in mathematics was utilized in the master level curriculum of information processing science, partially as obligatory studies of mathematics and partially the theoretical computing courses were utilized on the voluntary basis of students.[53]

---

[51] *Experts trust Oulu: the secret of the "Oulu phenomenon"* (City of Oulu, Economic affairs office, 199-?), pp.6-7; Manninen, p. 274.

[52] Matti Salo, "Yliopiston kokonaiskehitys," *Oulun yliopiston historia, 1958 – 1993*, pp. 109; Matti Salo, "Luonnontieteellinen tiedekunta," *Oulun yliopiston historia, 1958 – 1993*, pp. 434, 435. Cooperation with the Faculty of Science was continuation to Kerola's cooperation with the Faculty of Philosophy begun already in 1971.

[53] Salo, "Yliopiston kokonaiskehitys, " p. 109; Salo, "Luonnontieteellinen tiedekunta," pp. 428, 430, 435.

In the Faculty of Technology information engineering and telecommunication research and higher education as one subarea of electronics were started in the beginning of 1970s under the direction of professor Pentti Lappalainen. A technology driven curriculum "Information Engineering" was developed for engineering students. They interacted and cooperated with TOL on the same voluntary basis, as did students of mathematics.[54]

3.2   "To better theories for best practice" – A guideline in TOL

During 1970-75 Kerola and professor Pertti Järvinen from the University of Tampere started their regular research co-effort on the basis of their practical experiences in the sixties in Finnish wood and metal industry. The main messages of practical experiences were ambiguity and high variety of successes and failures in the utilization of computing facilities and tools. Deeper awareness and understanding was clearly needed.

Kerola and Järvinen utilized philosophies and theories of prominent system theorists Ackoff and Emery, Churchman, Lange and Mesarovic, and more specifically Swedish professor Börje Langefors' core concepts of information systems[55]. Juhani Iivari and Kalle Lyytinen describe the pioneering research results as follows:

> "... The key contributions of the PSC[56] model[57] were the distinction between pragmatic and semantic level, which refined the infological realm of Langefors into two, and the formulation of a set of complicated process equations which challenged the linear lifecycle of model of IS development (sc. Waterfall model, added by us) by suggesting a dynamic and hierarchical process model for IS. The model argued that different design aspects (or levels of abstraction) such as the infological and the

---

[54] Salo, "Luonnontieteellinen tiedekunta," pp. 435; Matti Salo, "Teknillinen tiedekunta," *Oulun yliopiston historia, 1958 – 1993*, pp. 535-537.

[55] Börje Langefors, *Theoretical Analysis of Information Systems*, (Lund: Studentlitteratur, 1966).

[56] P stands for pragmatic, S semantic and C constructive main points of view or aspects of systems analysis.
These aspects concern the efforts to answer into 'why', 'what' and 'how' questions of the information system/software to be developed and used.

[57] Pentti Kerola and Pertti Järvinen, *Systemeering II—system theoretical and cybernetic model of IS development and use*, in Finnish, (Helsinki: Gaudeamus, 1975); Pentti Kerola and Peter Freeman, "A comparison of life cycle models," *Proceedings, 5th International Conference on Software Engineering, March 9-12, 1981. San Diego, California*, (IEEE Computer Society Press, 1981), pp. 90-99.

datalogical design aspect can and most often do proceed **concurrently**, the process is not closed to one process trajectory but may vary due to local contingencies, and that the process model is **recursive** in nature..."[58] (boldfacing ours)

The fundamental ideas of the PSC model were further elaborated into PIOCO models in Oulu, especially by Professor Juhani Iivari and Erkki Koskela.[59] This gradually extended during eighties and early nineties into the sociocybernetic approach. In it IS design is analyzed as human action, modeling it in terms of the sociocybernetic theory of acts[60]. Also, the model was extended to capture principles of object-oriented analysis and design.[61]

This research has especially influenced on the doctoral education of Information Systems Science, not only nationally in Finland, but also on the Nordic level of cooperation by special IRIS doctoral seminars, established by Järvinen and Kerola in 1978.

3.3 Interaction of theories and practice in curriculum of information systems architects and software engineers

From the early beginning of the seventies different philosophies and theoretical approaches for IS development and use have had influence on the master level education at the University of Oulu. This has been recognized by the international committee, which in the evaluation report about the Finnish research and education of computing says:

---

[58] Juhani Iivari and Kalle Lyytinen, "Information Systems Research in Scandinavia—Unity in Plurality," *Scandinavian Journal of Information Systems,* Vol. 10, No. 1&2, 1998, pp. 135-185.

[59] Juhani Iivari and Erkki Koskela, "The PIOCO model for IS design," *MIS Quarterly,* Vol. 11, No. 3 1987, pp. 401-419. The PIOCO models were developed on the basis of the PSC approach, especially utilizing socio-economic background theories. The PIOCO includes three metamodels of IS/SW, its development (including requirements, specification design, implementation and use) and the choice/quality criteria integrated as a hierarchical and dynamic whole.

[60] Yrjö Aulin-Ahmavaara, "A general theory of acts with application to the distinction between rational and irrational 'social cognition'," *Zeitschrift fur allgemeine Wissenschaftstheorie,* Vol. VIII, No. 2, 1977, pp. 195-220.

[61] Juhani Iivari, "Object-oriented design of information systems: the design process," in *Object oriented approach in information systems,* Proceedings of the IFIP TC8/WG8.1 Working Conference on the Object Oriented Approach in Information Systems, Quebec City, Canada, 28-31 October, 1991, edited by F. van Assche, B. Moulin, C. Rolland. (Amsterdam; New York: North-Holland; New York, N.Y., U.S.A.: Distributors for the U.S. and Canada, Elsevier Science Pub. Co., 1991), pp. 61-87.

"TOL research group has a strong cross-disciplinary approach to information processing covering aspects of social science and computer science.   The group is especially strong in IS methodologies and philosophical issues in relation to IS. It is regarded as one of the leading centres in this respect. Over and above the research topics mentioned above, significant research has taken place during seventies and eighties in the group on IS curriculum[62] ...the ideas emanating from this research have been utilized in the design of the curriculum in Information Processing Science[63]. As far as the Committee could judge, the teaching programme seemed to be a comprehensive, well-balanced IS curriculum, covering theoretical as well as applied subjects."[64]

This essential IS theoretical base has at TOL been merged to the software engineering (SE) curriculum in a balanced and synergetic manner.   One interactive and cooperative subfield of this curriculum has been from the early 1970s in project/team efforts between practice organizations (local industry, communal depts. etc.) and TOL personnel and students.

An essential amount, at least some hundreds, of IS and SE professionals and managers from the late 1970s have been educated into the multiscientific and integrative worldview on computing and its utilization with human, organizational, technical and formal features in the theoretical and practical integration.

4.   SYMBIOSIS OF VTT AND TOL

In 1974, VTT established the Laboratory of Electronics (VTT/ELE) in Oulu. The new laboratory got a full mandate to implement VTT's general

---

[62] Risto Nuutinen, Erkki Koskela, Juhani Iivari and Pentti Kerola, "Design and implementation experiences of a curriculum for the information systems architect (ISA) reflected on the IFIP/BCS curriculum," in R. A. Buckingham, R. A. Hirschheim, F. F. Land and C. J. Tully (eds.), *Information Systems Education —recommendations and implementation*, (British Computer Society—Monographs in Informatics, 1987), pp. 179-203.

[63] Pentti Kerola, Erkki Koskela, Risto Nuutinen and Tuomo Riekki, *Tietojenkäsittelyn perustutkinnon kehittämisestä Oulun Yliopistossa* (On Development of Master Level Curriculum for Information Processing Science (Information Systems Architects), in Finnish), Publications of Institute of Information Processing Science A10, (Oulu: University of Oulu, 1979).

[64] International Committee, "Evaluation of Research and Teaching in Computer Science, Computer Engineering and Information Systems," (Helsinki: Publications of the Academy of Finland, 1990), pp. 31-33.

mission in the whole country – to help industry to develop its competitiveness. This meant that the laboratory had to market its services all over Finland, not only in Northern Finland. VTT/ELE interpreted this mission with the goal of creating new industrial and commercial business by positioning its role between basic research and industrial product development.[65] In the beginning, VTT operated mainly as a product development partner with industrial companies. As the new electronics products increasingly included software parts, VTT/ELE started to pay attention to this technology area as well. With this in mind, VTT hired its first scientist with post-graduate degree, Samuli Saukkonen to develop the laboratory's competence in the field of software engineering.[66]

Internally financed research projects were started with main objectives to develop VTT/ELE's own competence to help companies in developing software components and production as part of electronic products. Basic skills in software engineering were developed by implementing the first post-graduate course in software engineering[67] followed with regular courses in software engineering for electrical engineering students at the University of Oulu. This was a basic seeding of potential growth on software engineering knowledge base with the hope of hiring qualified employees to VTT and industry in the future. As there was wider need for software engineering education for engineers working in industry, many short courses were implemented in Helsinki together with INSKO (Continuing Education Centre for Engineers). National conferences like Blanko and Elkom were participated by giving presentations on software engineering.[68] One aim with these activities was general marketing of VTT as a product development partner in software engineering.

During the 1970s and early 1980s, professor Veikko Palva was the director of VTT's Division of Electrical and Nuclear Technology, where VTT/ELE was one laboratory. Professor Palva advised the laboratory to strengthen its relationships with the University of Oulu in embedded

---

[65] Kulju, pp. 63-69.

[66] Martti Karppinen, Minutes of a telephone call, 21.2.2003.

[67] M. Pietikäinen, H. Hakalahti (eds.), *Ohjelmointitekniikka* (Software engineering, in Finnish), (Oulu: University of Oulu, Department of Electrical Engineering, 1979).

[68] S. Saukkonen, Mikrotietokonesovellusten kehittäminen (Development of microcomputer applications), in Finnish, Blanko '79, 1.10.1979, Oulu, 4 p; S. Saukkonen, "Ohjelmistotekniikka mikrotietokonesovelluksissa," *Mikrotietokoneiden ohjelmointi*, osa 3, ("Software engineering in microcomputer applications", Programming microcomputers, part 3), in Finnish, (Helsinki: Insinööritieto, 1980), pp. 155-80; S. Saukkonen, Ohjelmoinnin apuvälineet (Programming tools), in Finnish, Blanko '81, Oulu, syyskuu 1981, 3 p; S. Saukkonen, Mikrotietokoneiden uudet tehokkaat ohjelmointiympäristöt (New efficient programming environments for microcomputers), in Finnish, ELKOM '81, Helsinki, 12 p; S. Saukkonen, Ohjelmistoinsinöörin työkalut (Software engineer's tools), in Finnish, Elektroniikkapäivät '85, Helsinki 13.-15.3.1985, 7 p.

software related issues.[69]   He had a vision to develop the VTT Oulu competence on embedded software engineering and this was crucial to the growth on software engineering skills in Oulu area. Very soon, this led to an increasing amount of cooperation with TOL.

Cooperation was started with one student project during the spring of 1979, followed with a Tekes (*Teknologian kehittämiskeskus*, the National Technology Development Centre) funded research project focusing on software requirements and specification methods for embedded software and a subproject CONSE on conceptual models of embedded systems describing the fundamental elements of embedded systems and their development from the software point of view.[70]   This forerunning and fundamental project opened the eyes of many technically oriented engineers to see the importance of a wider systems perspective to software development.

The TOL cooperation influenced also the first PhD thesis on software engineering in VTT and the University of Oulu[71] by giving grounds for the development of a design approach for real-time embedded software. International research cooperation was started with the help of Professor Pentti Kerola's widespread networks in research community.   Veikko Seppänen was the first PhD student to be sent abroad to the well-known software engineering research group of Professor Peter Freeman, University of California at Irvine, leading to Seppänen's PhD on software component reuse[72].   From these series of actions, we can conclude that VTT Oulu had found its natural role between basic research and industrial product development by strengthening its role in applied research as software engineering technology transfer partner for electronics industry.   PhD training and implementation of industrial projects with applied research in focus were significant in growing a group of professional PhD level researchers.   Again, TOL had a remarkable role in this evolution.

In the beginning of 1983, the Laboratory of Computer Technology of VTT (VTT/TKO) was established by taking the Computer Technology section out of the VTT/ELE. Samuli Saukkonen was the first director of this laboratory, continuing and deepening the cooperation with TOL in software engineering research.   Large research projects were carried out emphasizing

---

[69]   Martti Karppinen, Minutes of a telephone call, 21.2.2003.

[70]   J. Iivari, E. Koskela, M. Ihme, I. Tervonen, *A Conceptual Model for Embedded Software and its Production*, (University of Oulu, Institute of Information Processing Science, Research papers series A7, 1986, 184 p).

[71]   Samuli Saukkonen, *A Constructive Method for the Architectural Design and Correctness Verification of Real-Time Programs*, (Acta Polytechnica Scandinavica, Ma 40, ISBN 951-666-170-X, 1983, 122 p. PhD thesis).

[72]   Veikko Seppänen, *Acquisition and Reuse of Knowledge for Directing the Construction of Embedded Software*, (Technical research Centre of Finland, Publications 66, Espoo, 1990. 218 p. Ph.D. thesis).

development of new practices and software engineering environments for electronics companies. Major technology transfer projects from the early 1980s were the development of product configuration management practices for Telenokia Oy (later Nokia Networks) and software project planning and management practices for Mobira Oy (later Nokia Mobile Phones)[73]. One of the largest efforts (tens of man-years) was the development of an expert system generating customized software packages for elevators. The goal was to get a system where the sales people just specify the properties of a lift by filling a standard sheet and the expert system then combines the software components and its parameters according to the order. With this system, Kone Oy could dramatically decrease the delivery time of customized elevator software. VTT/TKO's mandate inside the VTT to take responsibility on embedded software engineering research made it possible to grow the critical mass of researchers. This was only possible due to the close cooperation with the University of Oulu and especially with TOL where the culture of internationally respected basic research on information systems was highly developed.

4.1   Software engineering environment research

During 1981-1985 VTT Electronics laboratory launched a research project on developing a general purpose Software Engineering Environment (SEE) for industrial microprocessor software application development. By 1982 the term embedded software was launched to denote microprocessor based applications. Key persons behind the initiative at VTT were Samuli Saukkonen, Pekka Kemppainen and Tuomo Tuomikoski. The project did receive funding from process automation, machine building, and telecommunication companies in Finland. This project effectively collected then a very advanced toolbox of software engineering methodologies supporting the so called "Waterfall" process model[74]. Especially worth mentioning was explicit support for requirements specification[75], version control and configuration management, code size, labor, and schedule effort estimation using Boehm's approach[76], and use of email as communication media in software development projects.

SEE research was influenced by the theoretical research on software development methodology for information processing systems carried out at

---

[73] P. Kemppainen, *Mobira Oy:n ohjelmistotyön käsikirja (Manual for software engineering at Mobira OY)*, in Finnish, V1.1 7.5.1984. 97 p.

[74] W. Royce, "Managing the Development of Large Software Systems: Concepts and Techniques," *Proceedings*, WESCON (1970).

[75] SADT (Structured Analysis and Design Technique).

[76] Barry Boehm, *Software Engineering Economics* (New York, Prentice Hall, 1982).

University of Oulu Department of Information Processing Science. Especially important in retrospect has turned out the thinking in *abstraction layers*, which dates back to the research by Professor Pentti Kerola and Juhani Iivari in the 1970s[77]. The main penetration of abstraction layer thinking was via the CONSE project, which reshaped the traditional Waterfall process model based on sequential tasks and milestones. This novel thinking and interpretation allowed early adoption of Ward & Mellor Structured Analysis for Real-Time Systems (SA/RT) methodology[78] when it was launched in USA in 1984-1985. This methodology was highly superior to earlier specification and design methodologies because it provided explicit support for real-time embedded software development via the mechanism of finite state machines, and precise semantics of modeling language elements[79]. Later research at the department led to a software engineering process model and methodology, Bootstrap[80], which gave increased support to project management and process improvement.

5.   FROM MOBIRA R&D PROJECTS TO NOKIA MOBILE PHONES OULU

Mobira was a new company formed in 1979 on operations based in Salo, southern Finland, as a result, of reorganization of several Finnish companies in telecommunication and television production. Mobira was a joint venture of Nokia Corporation and Hollming shipyards[81]. During late 1980s, Nokia bought Hollming out after some bitter in-house conflicts. Mobira later in the beginning of 1990s changed its name and became Nokia Mobile Phones[82] – birth of a giant[83]. Of course, none of this was seen when Mobira was

---

[77] Juhani Iivari, "Taxonomy of the experimental and evolutionary approaches to systemeering." *Proceedings of the IFIP TC 8 Working Conference on Evolutionary Information Systems.* (Amsterdam, North-Holland, 1981), pp. 261-277.

[78] P.T. Ward & S.J. Mellor, *Structured Development for Real-Time Systems.* Vol. 1-3. (New York: Yourdon Press, 1985).

[79] P.T. Ward "The transaction schema: en extension of the data flow diagram to represent control and timing," *IEEE transactions on Software Engineering* 12, 2,1986, pp. 198-210.

[80] P. Kuvaja, J. Similä, L. Kraznik, A. Bicego, S. Saukkonen &G. Koch, *Software Process Assessment & Improvement – The BOOTSTRAP Approach* (Oxford, Blackwell Publishers, 1994).

[81] History of Hollming. http://www.hollming.fi/history_business.html#.

[82] Suomalaisen sähkö- ja elektroniikkateollisuuden laajentuminen 1980-luvulla (Expansion of Finnish electrical and electronics industries during 1980's) , in Finnish. http://www.info.uta.fi/winsoc/ajankohtaista/hist.htm#9.

[83] Nokia is currently the leader in mobile phone manufacturing and sales in the world measured in global market share.

established. It was just a wobbling company with about 200 employees spun out of a big industry reorganization.

VTT Electronics laboratory had a brilliant hardware designer, Lauri Vatjus-Anttila, who had specialized in design using low-power consuming CMOS[84] logic circuits. He had also become an expert in RCA[85] 1800 Cosmac 8-bit CMOS-processor,[86] which was the only proper general-purpose CMOS processor during early 1980s. In 1983, he started an important project to design the processing and memory unit for new generation NMT[87]/TACS[88]/AMPS[89] cellular car telephone for the then little known Finnish company Mobira. He designed a radical architecture introducing two CMOS processors, Cosmac for the radio unit and Hitachi 4-bit processor[90] for handset user interface. The radio unit was communicating with the handset processor with a serial link, which produced a breakthrough in convenience of use, since the thick parallel signal "bullworker" cable was replaced with thin flexible cable.

Mobira aimed to build the software for the phone themselves but they soon found out that they were not capable of meeting the aggressive schedule they had agreed with the contract of the UK TACS system version ordered by Vodafone UK[91], which was then a little known startup operator[92]. As a desperate move, Mobira ordered the TACS version software development project from VTT Oulu, since they already knew the people from the hardware development. The laboratory was confident that they could tackle and accomplish any software project with the new methodologies they had acquired within the SEE research. The radio unit software project was lead by Jukka Korhonen and later by Erkki Veikkolainen, and Handset unit software project by Petri Pulli. By 1984 the software projects for both processors were completed a few months overtime after typical struggling with software errors and performance optimization. Although the Oulu based TACS part was a little late, all other parts of the Mobira's project were late much more, which brought Oulu in very good light.

---

[84] Complementary Metal-Oxide Silicon.
[85] Radio Corporation of America.
[86] RCA 1802 Processor. http://www3.sk.sympatico.ca/jbayko/cpu2.html#Sec2Part1.
[87] Nordic Mobile Telephone – analog cellular phone system standard in Scandinavian countries.
[88] Total Access Communication System - U.S. analog cellular phone system standard.
[89] Advanced Mobile Phone Service - U.K. analog cellular phone system standard.
[90] HMCS40 Series 4-bit microcontroller able to drive liquid crystal display directly.
[91] Vodafone. http://www.vodafone.com/.
[92] Vodafone started in 1982 as a subsidiary of Racal Electronics bidding for the private sector UK cellular license. Vodaphone is currently world's biggest mobile operator by number of subscribers.

5.1   Birth of Nokia mobile phones Oulu

Veikkolainen was hired by Mobira to set up a software development unit based in Oulu[93]. He effectively hired the first employees from VTT and University of Oulu. Besides software developers, he also hired hardware and integrated circuit designers, where especially one of his major recruitments was Juha Rapeli[94], who had a major role in development of Mobira's first "one piece" cellular phone, the legendary Mobira Cityman 450/900.[95] He then later became one of the key architects for the 2nd generation cellular phone system GSM[96].

The software engineering expertise for this new Nokia software development unit was carried over from VTT in "leather folders", i.e. in the heads of the key persons hired by Veikkolainen. Also included into the role of this new Mobira unit was to supervise R&D projects within University and VTT[97], so the connection between VTT and Mobira stayed very close and trustworthy.

The Mobira Oulu software unit turned out capable of cranking out software projects very reliably and in time, gaining respect and credibility inside Mobira. Consequently, Mobira allocated more project responsibilities to Oulu growing also the hardware and application specific integrated circuit design (ASIC) personnel. Soon Oulu was exporting software engineering know-how also to other Mobira mobile phones sites in Finland and abroad. Mobira later in the beginning of 1990s changed its name. The Oulu Mobira software unit became Nokia Mobile Phones Oulu.

6.   MAIN CONCLUSIONS

Specifically in addition to the electronics and telecommunication expertise offered as the core of the growth base, a more balanced analysis shows also the crucial role of system-theoretical and software-oriented expertise. When sufficient explanations are given to the growth base of the Oulu phenomenon, it is necessary to take into account development of systems and software industry and information processing science in the Oulu region. Then, what kind of major conclusions could we derive from

---

[93] "Mobira hajasijoitti ohjelmistoryhmän Ouluun," (Mobira decentralized a software group into Oulu), *Kaleva,* 12.10.1985, p. 20.

[94] Juha Rapeli. http://www.ee.oulu.fi/~tsuutari/Rapeli_pages/rapeliindex.html.

[95] Mobira Cityman. http://www.rigpix.com/mobphoneana/mobira_cityman.htm.

[96] Global System for Mobile Communications – digital mobile communication standard.

[97] Nokia in Finnish Innovations system.
http://www.etla.fi/english/research/publications/searchengine/pdf/dp/dp811.pdf.

the development of the Oulu phenomenon, and with which kind of reasoning? We have found three different, but interacting, growth sub bases:
- personal educational knowledge base with high individual variety
- team/project/social knowledge base, where early awareness about cooperation has existed
- systems/software methodological knowledge diffusion and transfer

In the young and fast growing university with its cooperating parties, the mental climate locally was empathic and auspicious for a variety of different scientific paradigms and approaches in research and higher education of computing. The intellectual liberalism and open-mindedness was generally prevalent and needed when fundamental theories were searched for the best practices. Of course, individual preferences varied and challenged each other. During the first years those influenced on varied, more individualistic efforts. Rather soon, however, the needs and value of cooperation were recognized.

The mental climate within the university, and its faculties with partially different research cultures, as well as the Oulu region in general showed clear signs of collaborative open teamwork from early on. Partners with different vested interests worked together setting aside their differences.

As the most factual and significant result of this historical analysis we present the systems and software methodological knowledge diffusion and transfer which has happened at Oulu area. This fundamental, as we claim it, was part of the growth base and can be visualized by Figure 1.

The described growth has happened through a value chain where the basic and applied research results from TOL were transferred to other organizations either directly by individual professionals or through the organizational actions with VTT and IS/SW service companies. During the time period being analyzed (1969-1985) the methodology transfer culminated in the case of Mobira and several software companies.

This paper has concerned the birth and early development of computing in the Oulu area. Actually, it was concurrently a start for an "industrial explosion", especially concerning software development and their embedded use during the last twenty years. The software technological 'explosion' will be the next phase and object of a longer historical analysis which is implemented in near future.

Overall, the early experiences of the 'Oulu phenomenon' have shown to us that the potential integration of technological, mathematical, and humanistic competence can be a probable oasis of success, if the liberal and broadminded intellectualism is prevalent. The co-effort between different kind of researchers, research mediators, and professionals and managers of industrial and community organizations is challenging, but not easy co-effort. However, the scientific and professional 'ecumenism' would be necessary. Various aspects on computing differ quite much, but they are also complementary at the same time. In integration, the 'unity in plurality' is sought.

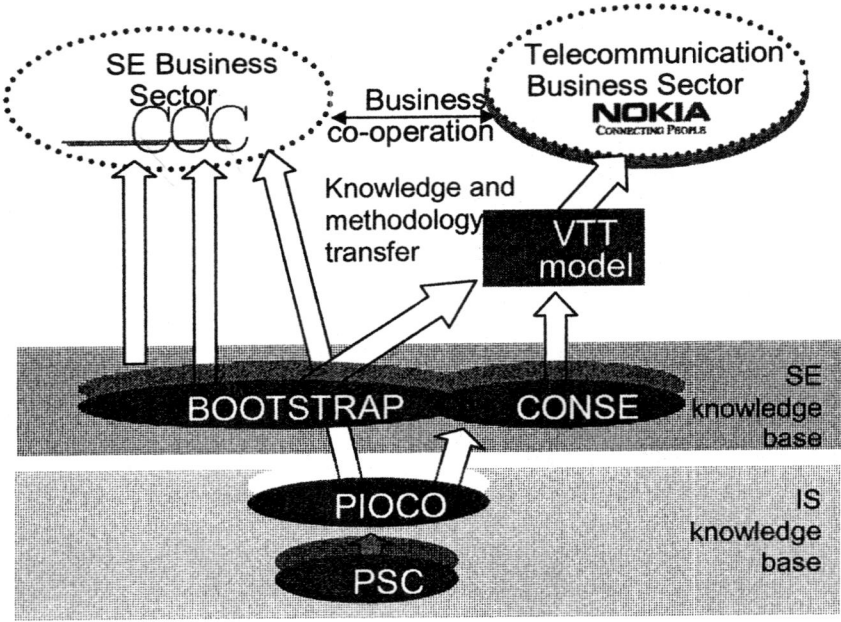

Figure 1. Growth Base of systems and software methodological
knowledge in 'Oulu phenomenon'.

7. DISCUSSION AND COMMENTS FROM THE CONFERENCE

Question 1:   How big is Oulu and University of Oulu and how many high tech jobs there are?

Answer 1:   In the Oulu region there are nearly 200,000 inhabitants, in the University of Oulu there are about 15,000 students and there are more than 10,000 high tech jobs in the region.

Question 2:   What are the total yearly intakes of new students for the curricula of informatics (including information processing science and information technology), and correspondingly the total yearly outputs of master level degrees during the last years?

Answer 2: The student intakes at the Department of Information Processing Science have increased from the level of 45 in the late 1980's and early 1990's (until 1996) to the level of about 300 in the last few years. The acceptance percentage of applicants has remained during these years around 25-30%. Presently, the number of master level degrees is rapidly growing and the expected number for 2003 is more than 50, while it has earlier been between 25-30 students.

The total student intake at the Department of Electrical and Information Engineering has increased likewise but not in the same scale. During the early 1990's until 1995, the student intake was around 150 to rise all the way close to 400 in 2001, during the last two years the student intake is around 320. The acceptance percentage has varied between 40-60% in the early 1990's, and between 70-90% later. The number of master level degrees has been around 60 in the early and mid 1990's and about 85 during the last four years.

Question 3: What kind and how large basic education is given about the development methodologies of embedded systems?

Answer 3: Both the Department of Information Processing Science and the Department of Electrical and Information Engineering have significant amounts of education in this topic of studies. The individual amounts in total are varying because of the distribution between the compulsory and voluntary studies. The embedded system studies usually taken are about 5 study weeks at the Department of Information Processing Sciences and about 20 study weeks at the Department of Electrical and Information Engineering.

ACKNOWLEDGEMENTS

Because of the historical nature of this paper, we have requested 'nonprofessional' comments from many friends and colleagues. We warmly thank Voitto Elomaa, Asla and Ilari Kerola, Sakari Nevalainen, Juhani Paakkola, Varpu Penninkilampi-Kerola, Matti Salo and Tomi Yli-Kyyny about their positive criticism and constructive proposals of change.

THE NORWEGIAN COMPUTING CENTER AND THE UNIVAC 1107 (1963-1970)

Knut Elgsaas and Håvard Hegna

1. Elgsaas, Researcher/Project Director (1963-73), Norwegian Computing Center, elgsaas@c2i.net
2. Hegna, Senior Researcher (1962-), Norwegian Computing Center, havard.hegna@nr.no

Abstract: The Univac 1107 computer installation at The Norwegian Computing Center (NR) from the summer of 1963 was an important asset for Scandinavian research and industry that also set the ground for object-oriented programming. The key to many of the successful computer systems and applications created during the years that followed, was that NR at a very early moment in the history of modern computing, managed to acquire the most suitable computer for these developments and establish a fruitful user community around it. The unwinding of the installation during 1969/70 led to a strong conflict that began as an internal dispute between the employees of NR and its managing director, and ended as an open struggle between NR and the Royal Norwegian Council for Scientific and Industrial Research (NTNF) and to subsequent changes in the research organization of Norway.

Key words: Central computers, research policy, Simula 67, Univac 1107

1.   THE UNIVAC 1107 INSTALLATION AND ITS USE

1.1   Introduction

The Norwegian Computing Center (Norsk Regnesentral, NR), a research institute subordinate to the Royal Norwegian Council for Technical and Industrial Research (NTNF), signed contracts with Remington Rand Univac in 1962/63 that had several important consequences. First, Remington Rand delivered a Univac 1107 computer to NR in August 1963. This delivery gave NR and Norway the largest non-military computer installation in Europe at the time. Secondly, NR was to develop a linear programming package [1] and a simulation language with a corresponding compiler for the Univac computer. The language, Simula I, was the precursor of the Simula 67 language [2, 3] that introduced the concept of object-oriented programming and gave its two inventors Ole-Johan Dahl and Kristen Nygaard the IEEE von Neumann Medal and the ACM Turing Prize 35 years later. However, most important was the intensely creative and productive environment for the development of computer applications, quantitative methods, and computer science research that followed the installation. The principal driving force behind the Univac deal was Kristen Nygaard, Research Director at NR 1960 - 1984.

1.2   Not an easy decision

There were several obstacles to the procurement of the Univac 1107. NR had already signed contracts in 1961 for the delivery of a GIER computer from Danish Regnecentralen (DR) in the spring of 1962. GIER was a wonderful well-constructed middle-sized computer with a good Algol 60 compiler. The compiler was a primary reason for the choice of GIER. Important were also the visions of DR's chief executive, Niels Ivar Bech, for a grand Scandinavian cooperative effort in computer research, education, and industry. DR installed a GIER at the Norwegian Technical University (NTH) in Trondheim in November 1962 [4]. It was part of a double contract where a second GIER should go to NR. The NR decision to go for the Univac solution instead led to Danish-Norwegian intriguing and an internal conflict in NR that ended with the dismissal of several of its employees.

In 1962, the prevalent thinking still distinguished between computers for scientific or for administrative tasks. The Univac 1107 was the first commercial computer to bridge that gap. Nevertheless, it was not obvious that such a tool should come to NR. NR's strongest rival was the Norwegian Defense Research Establishment (FFI) [5]. The leader of FFI lobbied hard for his organization both in NTNF, he was a member of NTNF's working committee, and in the Ministry of Defense, seeing clearly that Norway at the time could not afford, or find use for, two such machines.

In many ways NR was a perfect institution for the double-purpose Univac 1107, being open to research and business both through necessity and by virtue. NR bought the computer through a loan from NTNF that required payments over eight years. NR therefore had to open itself up and act as a service bureau to any interested customer. In all probability, a grant to FFI would instead have placed the computer resources behind military fences, thus keeping it away from most industrial and public use. NR's marketing effort included the design of a logo signifying its dual engagement in digital computing and mathematical-statistical disciplines. Figure 1 is a mosaic rendering of the logo.

Figure 1: NR's Early Logo

1.3   The machine and some problems

The Univac 1107 that was delivered to NR, included 32 K 36-bit words of ferrite memory, 1572 K words of secondary storage on two magnetic drums, 6 magnetic tape stations, a punch card reader (600 cards/min), a line printer (900 lines/min), and a central processing unit with a 4 microseconds instruction cycle. In 1963, it cost 7 million NOK, even at a 50% discount, which today amounts to about 70 million NOK.

This huge and resourceful machine also brought problems. For one thing, NR, even Norway, had very few computer experts in 1963. Remedial actions were necessary. In October 1962, shortly before the final signing of the contract, NR started a one-year intensive course in computer programming and system development. The both theoretical and practical curriculum covered programming languages, algorithms, software engineering, and methods from operations research, statistics, and numeric analysis. One student, a NTH graduate, later said that this year gave him a larger learning return per time-unit than any other education he had followed. Nevertheless, one set of students was far from enough. NR also set out to brain drain Great Britain. A large group of British programmers and computer specialists took the challenge and NR employed them. A side effect was that English rugby was introduced to NR and Oslo, a team was established that later formed the base for the Norwegian Rugby Union [7].

1.4   Putting it to use

NR and its customers used the computer facilities over a wide area of applications. During the Univac years, NR developed Optima (a system for network planning and control of engineering projects [8, 9]), DATSY (a special purpose language and system for describing data and establish economic planning models such as MODIS [10]), and program libraries of routines for statistical and numerical calculations,

VEIVALG (a very advanced tool for city transport planning [10]), PADLP (a linear programming package based on a new non-simplex method discovered at NR [1]), numerous administrative data processing systems, and a wealth of computer simulation models for studies of systems at home and abroad [11]. In addition, of course, it contained the Simula language activities that included exports of ideas and products on a global scale. Among the customers were Norsk Hydro (an international producer of fertilizers and aluminum), Staal Laval of Sweden (a dominant dairy equipment manufacturer), Burmeister & Wain (the largest shipyard of Denmark), Det norske Veritas (DnV) (the Norwegian ship classifier), Akergruppen (a large group of Norwegian shipyards), Kongsberg Weapon Manufacturer, Central Bureau of Statistics, Oslo City Transport Planning, universities, and research institutes. Of particular importance were Autokon (a system for computer aided design and construction of ships developed at the Central Institute for Industrial Research (SI) [12]) and SESAM (a finite element method based structural analysis system developed at NTH and DnV [13]). The work on Autokon and SESAM had started before the arrival of the Univac 1107; they boosted it by the new computer and particularly by the response times made possible by the advanced new drum storage. As early as in 1964, NR together with the Norwegian Teleadministration (Televerket) was able to demonstrate data transmission over the public telephone network. Later that year four distant customers in Sweden, Germany, and two sites in Norway, could communicate over modem and phone to NR simultaneously. NTH, which replaced their GIER computer with a Univac 1107 in May 1965, started their Univac use in 1964 with the installation of a Univac 1004 that communicated with NR [6, 14]. Figure 2 shows some of the important developments that spun from NR and its customers in the sixties and early seventies.

1.5   A success story

Univac wanted NR to be one of their main show windows in Europe. They may not have succeeded in the rest of Europe, but their success in Norway was considerable. Two of the three Norwegian universities at the time, acquired Univac computers, as did several of NR's large customers (Norsk Hydro, Veritas, the Norwegian Teleadministration). Oslo University went for a CDC 3300 [15], but the University was for several years a very strong user of NR facilities. It was too strong, in fact, since the sometimes-inflexible pricing policy of NTNF and NR was too heavy burden on the

University. A payment of more than one million NOK had to be remitted in 1966 after long negotiations. Later, the Institute of Informatics (Ifi) at the University was in many ways born out of the activities and educational efforts of NR. Most of the central personnel of the institute, which the University did not formally establish until 1977, had been part of NR for some time [16]. Ole-Johan Dahl became the first professor of informatics at the University in 1968.

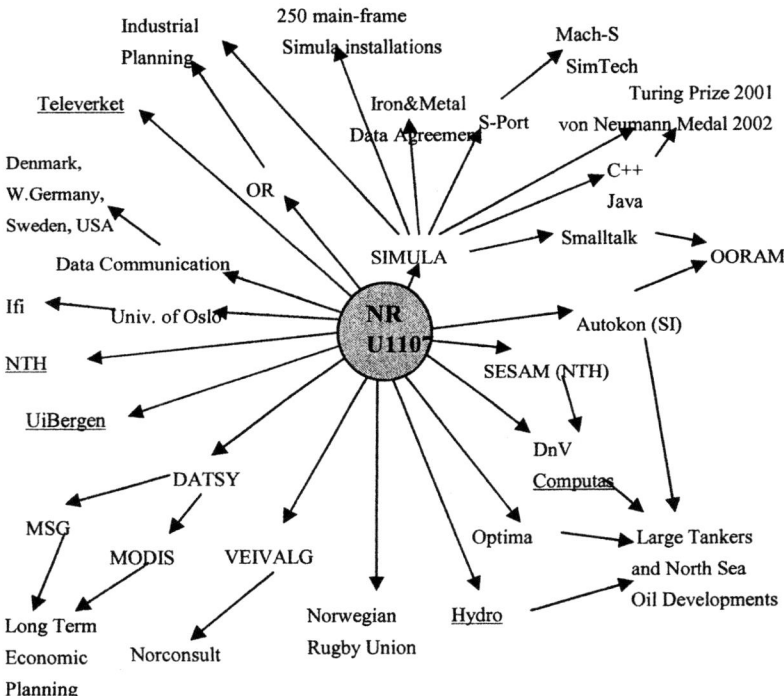

Figure 2: The NR Univac 1107 was at the center of many developments.
(Underlined items refer to large Univac installations in Norway.)

The NR Univac 1107 installation and activities surrounding it in the period 1963-70 were very important for Norwegian industry. The systems that were developed from the beginning of the 1960s, in particular in Akergruppen and Veritas, were a necessary condition for the construction of large oil tankers (the size grew from 30 000 tons to over 400 000 tons in a very short time) as well as for semi-sub oilrigs, spherical gas-tankers, and oil platforms, indeed for the complete technical development of the maritime industry during that period. These developments would not have been possible without the Univac 1107 and the strong integration of industry users and NR. Norway was at the time ahead of the rest of the world in this area, a time that coincided with the start of North Sea oil activities [13].

1.6   An important resource

For NR, the Univac 1107 was a valuable computer resource and source of income at the end of the 1960s. It contributed a yearly net income of about 1.2 million NOK of a total NR turnover of 8-9 million NOK. NR had no problems with settling the loan from NTNF. The income and marginally priced computer power gave important support and freedom to the researchers at the institute. This freedom was a presupposition for the Simula work of Dahl and Nygaard. There was no other available financial support for their far-reaching research. According to the research council and other NR surroundings, both in the 1960s and later, there was no need for another language like Simula; it had been done before, the two initiators were not competent enough, such languages were very short-lived, and language development was not a natural task for the smaller countries [2]. Hardware was considered a more important research theme. It is ironic that the Simula achievements later led to advanced hardware design work and the Mach-S of SimTech/Sim-X that had a Simula-based instruction set and object-oriented addressing [25].

After Computas took over the Univac 1107 in 1970, the developments that started at the NR site advanced further, leading to successful use in application areas such as seismic activities, oilrig construction, engineering control, and building industry. The key to all this was that NR at a very early stage in the history of modern computing managed to acquire the most suitable computer for these developments and establish a fruitful user community around it.

NR had four leaders during the Univac 1107 years. They were Siv. ing. Leif K. Olaussen (1963-66), Cand act. Herdis Thorén Amundsen (1966-67), Siv. oecon. Lars O. Sødahl (1968-69), and Cand. mag. Drude Berntsen (1969-90). In view of the high-tech profile of the institute in this period, and male dominance in computer industry as a whole [17], it is amazing that two of the four leaders of NR at the time were women.

2.   CRISIS AND CONFLICT 1969-70

2.1   Background

During 1969/70 the Norwegian Computing Center (NR) went through a crisis and conflict that reached a magnitude and gave it a public exposure that probably no other Norwegian research institution has ever experienced [18, 19]. The sale of NR's computer Univac 1107 precipitated the conflict. It began as an internal dispute between the employees of NR and its managing director, and ended as an open struggle between NR and the Royal Norwegian Council for Scientific and Industrial Research (NTNF). NR was then a research institute subordinate to NTNF.

Shortly after Univac 1107 became operational in 1963, at that time it was one of the most powerful computers in Europe, NR had many customers from other institutes, the University of Oslo, public agencies, and private business. As mentioned earlier, the operation of Univac 1107 was a scientific and economic success. The computer generated a net profit that made it possible to finance research activities at NR such as the development of the Simula language and compilers.

The market noticed the success of Univac 1107. In 1968, a new company, Computas, a subsidiary of Veritas, planned to acquire a Univac 1108. Computas offered services to its mother organization as well as to other customers of NR at substantially lower prices than the NR level. The director of NR feared the economic problems the Computas competition would create. He therefore proposed to the NR board that they should sell the Univac 1107 with its customers to Computas.

2.2   Start of the conflict

The employees of NR did not know about the sale until after NTNF had received the proposal from the NR board. A majority of the employees were critical of the secret handling of the case. The scientific personnel were also strongly irritated by not being consulted about such a vital matter for NR. The criticism exacerbated when an internal investigation a couple of months later proved that the sales contract between NTNF and Computas was very disadvantageous to NR and NTNF, and even to Computas.

The investigation made it clear that research and development based on the use of computer-time at a marginal cost no longer would be possible. In the future NR therefore would not be able to develop software products like SIMULA or OPTIMA. The operation of Univac 1107 had contributed to a close contact with many public and private organizations and companies. This in turn led to a number of jobs for NR not connected to programming or use of the computer. The staff at NR feared that the sale of the 1107 would reduce the possibilities of such contacts.

The growing criticism caused the establishment of the Union of Employees at NR (FANR) in March 1969. NTNF, in an attempt to answer the criticism from NR, in a letter to FANR in May 1969 stated that they made the decision to sell Univac 1107 with special consideration for the future activities at NR.

The dissatisfaction with the way they handled the sale, led to a vote of no confidence against the director at a FANR meeting in June. Consequently, the director was unable to function as leader of NR. The board of FANR, therefore, advised the board of the NR to engage Drude Berntsen, an NR female employee, as a de facto managing director. During the spring of 1969, an open and good relationship developed between the two boards. The board of the NR acted upon the advice from FANR and appointed Drude Berntsen as deputy director of NR in August. At the same meeting, the board approved a plan for future activities for NR and submitted the plan to NTNF. Berntsen remained in office until 1990.

Robert Major, the managing director of NTNF, did not like the developments at NR. The establishment of a rather militant union was unheard of in the research institutes belonging to NTNF. His displeasure with NR did not decrease when the director, a man handpicked by NTNF to lead NR, was forced to leave.

In October 1969, the chair of the board of NR, Odd Narud (the later General Director of Norsk Hydro) asked for a meeting with Robert Major. He raised the question of appointing a new director of NR. Major stated that they should not announce the position as director until NTNF considered the plan for the future activities for NR. Narud said that the board of NR and the employees felt that the handling of the plan seemed to take too long. Major then informed Narud that he had appointed a 3-man committee to examine the plan. The secretary of the committee was the deputy director of NTNF.

2.3   The report from the three-man committee

On 3 December 1969, the committee presented their report on the plan for NR [20]. The report described the development in data processing and the use of quantitative methods in Norway. The committee members were of the opinion that the data profession in Norway had reached such a high level, quantitative and qualitative, that there was no longer any use for a method-oriented institute like NR. The committee therefore proposed that they should transfer the professional activities at NR to four growth-centers:

- Statistical methods and analysis together with language development to the University of Oslo.
- Research and analysis for the public sector to other institutes belonging to NTNF.
- Work for the building and construction sector to the Institute for Building and Construction (NBI).
- The remainder to the Central Institute for Industrial Research (SI).

The committee's assertion of the high professional level of data competence in Norway was based on a poll made by the secretary. He had called some institutes and firms and asked them how many employees they would describe as qualified systems analysts. The numbers were amazingly high. He had not asked NR of course, but had found out by himself that of 94 employees there were 65 qualified systems analysts. That number was obviously much too high, as was the case with the other institutes and firms. One of the firms, which in the report from the committee was entered with ten systems analysts, declared they had none. The one qualified analyst working for them had quit. In a meeting on 5 December, the secretary admitted the numbers of qualified analysts were somewhat diffuse. When asked for his definition of a qualified systems analyst, he responded: *"I would like to turn the question around. How does one define a qualified systems analyst?"*

2.4   Meeting with NTNF

The report from the three-man committee caused a meeting to take place on 5 December between NTNF, the three-man committee, and the boards of NR and FANR. The report was strongly criticized by members of these boards. At the end of the meeting, the chair of the three-man committee withdrew his support of the report and proposed that they should conclude the meeting with a protocol stating: "We agree on maintaining NR as a method oriented institute on a high [professional] level". The chair of NTNF, the chair of the board of NR, and the chair of the Union of Employees of NR signed a protocol with that statement. A similar protocol had never before been signed in the NTNF-system. It came as a conclusion of a meeting where the chair of NTNF criticized Robert Major and treated the Union of Employees as an equal partner to the boards of NTNF and NR.

Robert Major was not pleased with such a conclusion. A couple of days before Christmas, he was able to get the board of NTNF to approve a drastic reduction of the staff at NR. The reason was the so-called difficult economic situation at NTNF. The board of NR and the board of FANR criticized strongly the proposal from NTNF. The board of NR stated that they could not carry out such a reduction in one year; the earliest would be in two years time. The board of FANR stated they would not accept the proposal.

2.5   The conflict becomes a public issue

The employees of NR felt that this decision was a breach of the protocol entered earlier and the promise given in May by NTNF. At an extraordinary annual meeting of FANR in the beginning of January 1970, they passed a resolution that demanded the withdrawal of the decision of NTNF. They distributed the resolution to all the major newspapers. The next day and the following weeks the headlines in newspapers all over Norway told the story of a serious conflict between NR and NTNF, see Figure 3 and below:

"NR has lost confidence in NTNF". *Aftenposten 13.1.70.*
"Complaints over the reductions at computing center". *Bergens Tidende 13.1.70.*
"Rationalization has created great bitterness at NR". *Fædrelandsvennen 13.1.70.*
"Unrest at NTNF " *Arbeiderbladet 19.1.70.*
"The customers of NR regret the reductions". *Morgenbladet 21.1.70*
"NR to be cut in four. Halvdan Svarte policy"[1]. *Morgenbladet 23.1.70.*
"High political battle on research policy". *Dagbladet 23.1.70.*
"Lack of democracy within NTNF" *Arbeiderbladet 28.1.70.*
"Bring the cards on the table". *Editorial in Arbeiderbladet 30.1.70.*

The press coverage of the conflict continued in February:

"What is going on in NTNF?" *Arbeiderbladet 11.2.70*
"NR holds the knife at NTNF's throat" *Arbeiderbladet 27.2.70*

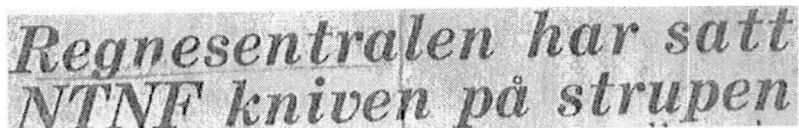

Figure 3: Newspaper headlines 1970, "NR to be cut in four. Halvdan Svarte policy!" and "NR holds the knife at NTNF's throat".

FANR received support from among others, the University, other research institutes, and private business. The conflict caused the leader of

---

[1] Halvdan Svarte, i.e. "Halvdan the Black", was a famous petty king in Norway in the 9th century A.D. Because of his popularity, when he died his body was cut in four parts that were entombed in grave mounds in the four regions of his kingdom.

the Norwegian Labour Party in the Storting (Parliament) to put a formal question before the Prime Minister on 20 January [21] about the organization of research in Norway:

> "Research is an increasingly important factor in the development of modern society. Is the Government of the opinion that we have a satisfactory organization of research [in Norway], or does the Government have plans for organizational, administrative and economic measures to secure a social use of the results of the possibilities of modern research?"

2.6   The end of the conflict

NTNF lost the battle for the public opinion. At a meeting in March, the NTNF council voted unanimously that *"NR shall remain a method-oriented institute at a high professional level"*. FANR had won, and NR is still going strong more than 30 years later.

On 24 March, the council of NTNF in a long article in Aftenposten (the largest and most influential newspaper in Norway) gave their account of the course of events concerning NTNF and NR [23]. The main points were that the staff of NR was unrealistic in their view of the economic future of the institute and that even though the timeframe for decision making about NR was very narrow because of external circumstances, NTNF's decisions were well grounded. On 7 April, the chair of the union of employees of NR, Sverre Spurkland, in an article in the same newspaper documented that the council had misrepresented the facts [24]. He therefore suggested the establishment of a neutral commission with a mandate to collect all written material with relevance to the case. For researchers investigating the decision processes in NTNF such material would be of great value. The council of NTNF did not answer the serious allegations of Spurkland. Nor was a neutral commission established.[1]

The conflict between NR and NTNF appeared to most people to be complicated and difficult to understand. Computers, data processing, and research activities were not common themes in the public debate. What everybody understood, however, was that NTNF had broken its promise in the letter of May 1969. Such a breach of promise was not acceptable, neither in the public opinion nor among politicians.

---

[1] After submitting the first draft, the authors received the following suggestion from the HiNC programme committee: ".... Try also to write the "conflict" part somewhat more impartially - had NTNF written about the conflict, we are sure the text would be somewhat different." Our description of the conflict has not been altered, but we decided to add the above paragraph. Our description has been based on written documentation, letters, minutes, newspaper articles, official documents, etc., see references. NTNF gave its version of the conflict in the Aftenposten article. NTNF never openly challenged the allegations that its presentation misrepresented the facts.

What was the conflict all about? First, it did not concern the continued operation of NR as a seller of raw machine time. Early in 1969, the staff at NR estimated the technical-economical working life of Univac 1107 to last a couple of years until 1971/72. They realized that the period as a vendor of raw computer time soon would end. Nevertheless, the staff was of the opinion that if NTNF and the director of NR had sought their advice, NR would have obtained more favorable terms in the contract with Computas and there would have been a more flexible transition to other computers.

The fundamental cause of the conflict was the organization of NTNF. Many characterized the manner in which Robert Major had run NTNF from its beginning in 1946 as a "one-man show". In central government circles, this was pragmatically accepted. They considered Major as an effective "permanent undersecretary of state" for a successful "ministry of research". However, times were changing.

The conflict initiated a process of reorganization of NTNF and its institutes in the 1970s. In NOU 1981: 30B *"Investigation of public grants to technical and industrial research and development in Norway"* a report from NAVF (Norwegian Research Council for Sciences and Humanities) [22] describes how the conflict influenced the organization and management of NTNF.

> "The conflict with NR caused a wide public debate about the organization of research in Norway and more specifically the organization of NTNF.... Both the question about NR and the later public debate served as parts of the background for the decision of NTNF to make an analysis of their organization in the Habberstad-investigation".

The report from NAVF also points out that the conflict with NR caused a demand for co-determination from other groups of employees within the NTNF-system and more openness around the decisions of NTNF. *"Such demands were earlier almost unheard of within NTNF"*.

2.7   Evaluation of the conflict thirty years later

The employees at NR and most certainly the management of NTNF experienced the conflict as difficult, frustrating, and unpleasant. The conflict was one that they would have liked to avoid. Viewed in retrospect, however, the chair of the board of FANR, Sverre Spurkland, probably was right in saying that the conflict benefited both NTNF and research in Norway. It brought to the light problems and circumstances in NTNF, which later might have caused more trouble than the conflict in 1969-70. The conflict contributed to a greater interest for research and development both among politicians in the Storting and in the public as well. The NTNF also learned a lesson. Later they avoided making the same serious mistakes in relations to their institutes as they did in the case of NR.

The conflict was also beneficial for NR. It forced a thorough analysis of the future tasks of the institute. The conflict strengthened the team spirit between the employees in the difficult process of transition to a situation without a large computer and cheap computer-time. The employees of NR also had the pleasant experience that the victory over NTNF won against all odds, actually strengthened the reputation of NR in the market. That experience contributed significantly to the self-confidence a research institute needs when it goes through an extensive reorganization.

REFERENCES

[1] Spurkland, S.: The Parametric Descent Method of Linear Programming; Norsk Regnesentral 1963
[2] Dahl, O.-J. and Nygaard, K.: The Development of the Simula Languages; in Wexelblat, R.L. (ed): History of Programming Languages; New York: Academic Press 1981
[3] Holmevik, J.R.: Historien om Simula; in NR 1952–2002[1], p. 109–128; Oslo 2002
[4] Stenstadvold, K.: Elektronisk regnemaskin ved NTH; Teknisk Ukeblad, 25 October 1962
[5] Holmevik, J.R.: Educating the Machine; Centre for Technology and Society, Report 22; Trondheim 1994
[6] Olaussen, L.K.: Midt på 1960-tallet; in NR 1952–2002, p. 33–45; Oslo 2002
[7] Edwards, D.Ll.: Hvordan startet rugby i Norge?; in NR 1952–2002, p. 351-354; Oslo 2002
[8] Heier, K.M.: Optima; in NR 1952–2002, p. 191–199; Oslo 2002
[9] Sanders, N.: Project Planning in Norway; Project Manager Today, Great Britain; July 1998
[10] Elgsaas, K. and Hegna, H.: Samfunnsplanlegging; in NR 1952–2002, p. 183-190; Oslo 2002
[11] Hegna, H.; Lund O.J., and Nygaard, K.: User's Experience with the Simula language; Norsk Regnesentral, Oslo, June 1968
[12] Reenskaug, T.: Applications and Technologies for Maritime and Offshore Industries; HiNC-1 <this conference>
[13] Vahl, T.: Industrial significance of computer applications; HiNC-1 <this conference>
[14] Sanders, N.: Kontakten mellom NR og NTH-SINTEF (1963-1965); in NR 1952–2002, p. 307–308; Oslo 2002
[15] Jacobsen, Per H.: IT-historien@UiO; USIT ved UiO; Oslo oktober 2001 (Beta-versjon)
[16] Dahl, O.-J.: Hilsen fra Ifi ved jubileet i 1998; in NR 1952–2002, p. 346–347; Oslo 2002
[17] Lindencrona, E.: An ICT mystery – where were the women?; HiNC-1 <this conference>
[18] Elgsaas, K.: Krise og konflikt (1968-1970); in NR 1952–2002, p. 309–333; Oslo 2002
[19] Sødahl, L.O.; Min tid på Norsk Regnesentral; in NR 1952–2002, p. 334–338; Oslo 2002
[20] NTNF-document K.318: Om Norsk Regnesentrals fremtidige virksomhet (Report on the future activities of Norsk Regnesentral from the 3-man committee appointed by NTNF); (Håkon Sandvold, chair, Erik Brandt Olimb, Tor Evjen, secretary); Oslo December 1969
[21] Stortingstidende (Records of the Norwegian Parliament) 1970, p. 2334-2355

---

[1] Norsk Regnesentral 1952–2002 (The History of the Norwegian Computing Center 1952-2002); Norsk Regnesentral, Oslo, September 2002 (in Norwegian)

[22] Collett, J.P. and Skoie H.: Teknisk-industriell forskningsorganisasjon i Norge 1945-80. Prinsipiell debatt og hovedlinjer i utviklingen; Vedlegg 3 til NOU 1981 30B, Utredning om offentlig støtte til teknisk industriell forskning og utvikling i Norge (Thulin-utvalget); NAVF-utredningsinstitutt Oslo 1981.

[23] NTNF: Om Norsk Regnesentral. Article in Aftenposten, 24 March 1970.

[24] Spurkland, Sverre: Norsk Regnesentral og NTNF. Article in Aftenposten, 7 April 1970.

[25] Syrrist, G. and Piene, J.: SIMULA-historien etter 1980; in NR 1952–2002, p. 134–138; Oslo 2002.

THE WEGEMATIC 1000 COMPUTING CENTRE, 1959-1964
Trans-local cooperation

Jaakko Suominen, Petri Paju, and Aimo Törn

1. Suominen, Department of Digital Culture, School of Cultural Production and Landscape Studies, University of Turku, Pori, Finland; jaakko.suominen@utu.fi, www.tuug.fi/~jaakko/
2. Paju, Department of Cultural History, University of Turku, Turku, Finland; petpaju@utu.fi
3. Törn, Department of Computer Science, Åbo Akademi, Lemminkäinengatan 14, Åbo, Finland; atorn@abo.fi

Abstract: The paper concerns the Alwac and Wegematic computer usage in the Nordic countries focussing on the Southern Finnish town of Turku. This topic has received little academic attention and frequently forgotten. In the paper, we examine the actions that the two universities and involved companies in the Turku region took after they had accepted the donation of a Wegematic 1000 computer. We argue that the Turku Computing Centre, created in 1960, firstly made an effort to combine scientific and educational aspects and commercial service in its activity and, secondly, participated in and benefited from establishing Nordic co-operation among the users of Wegematic computers. Therefore, we conclude that this Wegematic story is important for understanding the early phases of computerisation in Finland, at least outside the capital region of the country. We suggest the same could be true in Sweden and Norway. Further, we suggest that other Wegematic stories might be worth studying to improve our understanding of the Nordic trans-local interaction in early computing. Finally, we suggest applying a comparative method for these future studies.

Key words: Nordic cooperation, regional developments, computing centres, Wegematic 1000

1.   INTRODUCTION

At the end of 1960, a Wegematic 1000 computer[1] became operational in Turku (Åbo), Finland. The two universities in Turku were joint recipients of a computer donated by the Axel Wenner-Gren Centre Foundation. Axel Wenner-Gren (1881-1961) was a famous Swedish and cosmopolitan industrialist and executive as well as being a public figure. In 1952 he had bought a North American company that produced early computers (Alwac computers).[2] The fact that the use of these computers in the Nordic countries is commonly forgotten and frequently left unstudied implies that this element in the history of computing is regarded as being unimportant. It might also be the case that the whole Wegematic story is an unsuccessful venture; a failure that does not seem worth studying. In this paper, we want to challenge these ideas by examining a Finnish computing centre based on a Wegematic computer and the Nordic trans-local[3] co-operation that arose among Alwac and Wegematic users at the beginning of the 1960s.

In Southern Finnish town of Turku, the Wegematic 1000 computer became the heart of a new, local computing centre. At the time, at least in Turku, acquiring an electronic computer involved considerable effort.

---

[1] For a more detailed description of Wegematic technology see Appendix 2.

[2] Axel Wenner-Gren was also an important participant in the Swedish automation debate in the mid-1950s. He aimed to use the computers for planning in another project of his called the Alweg monorail. Wenner-Gren originally made his fortune with the Electrolux Company. He was also a known figure in Finland (cf. Apu 2/1960, 56-57, "Tulevaisuuden rautatie" ["Future Railway"]; Apu 18/1960, 38-41, 68, "Hän ei itsekään tiedä, kuinka rikas on" ["He don't know how rich he is"). See also Wenner-Gren 1937. For more information on Axel Wenner-Gren and the Wenner-Gren Centre Foundation see Wennerholm 2002; Bohman & Dahlberg 1975; Det startet i 1919. Electrolux Konsernets Historie [http://www.electrolux.no /corporate/history/overtheyears.html].

[3] *Trans-local* (or translocal) in cultural studies refers to emigrant and immigrant communities who have transferred their social and cultural practices to new geographical environments or territories. The communities and their origins are interconnected, but at the same time a part of their current multi-cultural context. (see eg. Peleikis 2000, http://www.ceri-sciencespo.com/publica/cemoti/textes30 /peleikis.pdf) One other meaning of trans-local or trans-locality is used within arts and artist networks in the global sphere (see eg Translocation call for proposals, http://www.walkerart.org/gallery9 /jerome/call.cfm). Thus 'trans-local' refers to thematic cultural interaction, which takes into account and nourish the local identity and its specialities and possibilities. In this paper, we use the concept trans-local mostly in a sense of the latter definition. In this case trans-local refers to the interaction and co-operation of the local Wegematic user communities (centres) and their Nordic counterparts. The technological artefact and certain cultural historical context meant that part of the ways of using and seeing the meaning of computing was shared. However, the local context, that is local situations and interactions, also created unique styles of understanding the present day computing and data processing technology and ways of anticipating the future.

Therefore, it is no surprise that the universities existing at that time (the University of Turku and Åbo Akademi University – the Finnish and Swedish speaking universities), several local enterprises and the city of Turku were involved.[4] We should note that this kind of local co-operation was quite new especially for the universities. In this paper, we consider the actions taken and by whom in Turku before and after the Wegematic 1000 arrived. We also examine the possibilities the computer opened up.

We present the history of the Wegematic Centre in Turku in roughly chronological order. The paper contains five sections. After the introduction, we describe the birth and functioning of the collaborative social networks that supported the idea of establishing a computing centre in Turku towards the end of the 1950s. We then sketch the activities in the Wegematic Centre during its early period, 1960-1962. After that, we examine the Centre's attempts to create and solidify Nordic cooperation under an association in the same period. We end by studying briefly the crisis in the late period of the Centre, 1962-1964. We conclude the paper with arguments on the importance of exploring this rather forgotten segment in the Nordic history of computing. We also suggest avenues for further historical investigation of the Alwac-Wegematic Centres.

The primary sources of the paper consist of archival material such as the minutes of the Turku Computing Centre and its administration, letters concerning Nordic dialogue as well as user logs, timetables, and work hour reservations of the Wegematic computer in Turku. We also used newspaper articles and interviews of the people involved.[5]

2. THE NORDIC AND LOCAL ASPECTS INVOLVED IN THE SELECTION OF A WEGEMATIC COMPUTER FOR TURKU

In 1960, Turku, with its population of ca. 112 000, was the second or third largest town in Finland (obviously after Helsinki and almost at the same level as Tampere). Turku is the oldest town in Finland and the former governmental centre of the Finnish province of Sweden (until 1809). The

---

[4] The third university in Turku, School of Economics and Business Administration participated in the project as well, but not that actively.

[5] The paper is partially based on the work conducted for an article in Finnish, "Varsinaissuomalainen linja Suomen tietoteknistymisen alkuvaiheissa 1959-1964. Turun Laskukeskus ja Wegematic 1000 tietojenkäsittelykone" published in Tekniikan Waiheita - Teknik i Tiden 18(2000): 3, 24-46 (see http://www.tuug.fi/~jaakko/tutkimus/wegematic/). The sources are more closely documented there and in the reference section of this paper. See also Törn 2000.

Academy of Turku, the first and for a long time only university of Finland, was established already in 1640. After defeating the Swedes in Finland, the Russians had the Academy transferred to the new capital of the autonomous Duchy of Finland, Helsinki, following the conflagration of Turku in 1827. Roughly a century later, after Finland had gained independence in 1917, two universities, the Finnish speaking Turku University and the Swedish speaking Åbo Akademi University were founded in Turku with the help of donations of individuals, communities, and corporations.   Even for geographical reasons, but of course for language and other reasons too, it was obvious that contacts between Turku and Stockholm had always remained close.

By the end of the 1950s, Turku had developed an extensive industrial base in fields ranging from shipbuilding to food carrying as well as the financial sector in banking and insurance. Major companies had also used accounting machines and punched card installations since the 1920s (the insurance company Sampo first installed punched card machines in 1927) and the 1940s (food carrying Huhtamäki since 1949) onwards. They also participated in the Punched Card Association, a Finnish society for the "punched card men" to teach and to learn from each other. From 1955 onwards, the Punched Card Association discussed the possibilities presented by the new, mostly IBM, electronic data processing machines or computers.[6]

Of course, some of the scientists in the universities of Turku were also interested in the new equipment for scientific calculations. However, these modern machines were quite new for the academia and people perceived them as being financially out of reach for the universities in Finland. Nevertheless, those scientists who knew about the recent developments in Sweden thought and hoped otherwise.

Unsurprisingly, Nordic scientific co-operation in Turku did not begin with the Wegematic 1000 computer in 1960. The contacts that the Physics Professors Kalervo V. Laurikainen (University of Turku) and Karl-Gustaf Fogel (Åbo Akademi) made while studying and doing research in Sweden and Denmark were very important for the Turku Computing Centre's Nordic relations. Actually, these two men had first met in Lund as PhD students in 1948. In the 1950s, Laurikainen also made many professional visits to Stockholm and Copenhagen. It is well known that in all these places,

---

[6] *Reikäkortti* 2/1956 (E. Luhtala: Kokemuksia reikäkorttimenetelmän sovellutuksesta Huhtamäki-yhtymässä [Experiences of punched card applications in Huhtamäki corporation]); Sormunen 1983, 149, 270-271; *Reikäkortti* magazines 1955-1959. See also Vehviläinen 1999 and Paju; this volume.

computers were taken into use very early on.[7] (See Appendix 6—Major Computing Centres and Projects in the Nordic Countries in the late 1950s.)

The departments of nuclear physics and centres like NORDITA (Nordisk Institut för Theoretisk Atomfysik, 1957) in Copenhagen were especially important places for Laurikainen when he was building up contacts across the Nordic countries. The fashionable problems of nuclear physics also required the solution of computing power. For example, Laurikainen had sent his student, Olli Varho, to calculate deuterum models in Paris (the IBM computing centre) in 1956. Laurikainen also had a Finnish colleague (Kalevi Loimaranta) in the Swedish AB Atomenergie company in Stockholm.[8]

In 1959, Professor Laurikainen arranged to teach a course on 'mathematic machines' in Turku. The teacher was the former student of Laurikainen, Olli Varho, who was then working for the National Committee for Mathematical Machines (1954-1960). In 1959, the Committee was still finishing the ESKO, which was earlier supposed to be the first computer used in Finland. Additionally, the Committee also wanted to advance computing education in the country. In Turku, lectures on computing and data processing proved to be very popular. Among the audience were both academic and business people. This wide interest motivated Laurikainen to suggest that it was possible to obtain and locate a computer in Turku. For this purpose, they founded a Mathematical Machine Society in Turku. The society was a joint venture between the local universities, local businesses, the city of Turku, and IBM. Although the business sector was involved, it seems that academic experts were among the most active members in the project.[9]

In the summer of 1959, the Mathematical Machine Society examined the local needs for computing and data processing as well as gathering information on the concepts of existing computer centres. The first information on experiences of establishing a computing centre, were from the EMMA computing centre in Bergen. There they had an IBM 650 computer that was used by both the university and the industries. The IBM 650 set the standards by which they would compare other general-purpose computers. In Finland, one IBM 650 was already in use in Helsinki (in Post-

---

[7] For more on early Nordic computing, see for example De Geer 1992; Heide 1996; Klüver 1999.

[8] Laurikainen 1982, 16-24; Paju 2002, 142.

[9] Turun Matematiikkakoneyhdistys - Abo Matematikförening, Toimintakertomus vuodelta 1959. Turussa 4.3.1960 K. V. Laurikainen, sihteeri, [Annual report of Turku Mathematical Machine Society 1959]; Kokouskutsu. Turun väliaikainen matematiikkakonetoimikunta. Turku 27.5.1959 [Invitation to a meeting of Turku Temporary Mathematical Machine Committee]. Archive of the Turku Computing Centre; Laurikainen 1982, 20-23; Paju 2002, passim. See also Paju; this volume.

Office Bank since the autumn of 1958) and another was on order (Folkpensionsanstalt, installed in the early of spring 1960). Although they explored other possibilities, the main question in the Society in Turku was soon: "IBM or not?"[10]

Soon an alternative solution, a Wegematic computer, arose. It raised an interesting Nordic – or more precisely Swedish – alternative to the IBM domination, as well as offering possibilities for expansion. The local history of Nordic scientific interaction and personal contacts probably contributed to the fact that someone in the Axel Wenner-Gren Foundation had heard of the growing interest in acquiring a computer to be located in Turku. The Foundation planned to donate several computers to Nordic and other universities. Presumably, they did this to get rid of their ageing machines or to penetrate to new markets across Europe—and even in the Soviet Union.[11] A further factor contributing to raising Turku's profile as a possible site for donation was the first NordSAM conference held earlier in 1959 (Nordiskt Symposium över Användningen av Matematikmaskiner) in Karlskrona. Olli Varho had participated in the conference in May 1959. In October, the Wenner-Gren Centre Foundation informed Laurikainen that they could donate a Wegematic 1000 computer to Turku. They already had donated computers for some Swedish universities.[12]

In Turku, they needed more information about the offered Wegematic 1000 computer. Two measures were taken in the beginning of 1960. First, ten men from the Turku universities and firms involved made a trip to see the ADB-Institut in Gothenburg (where a Wegematic 1000/ALWAC was in use). Secondly, Laurikainen visited several computing centres and then reported on them (See Appendix 6). Later that spring, Nils Ivar Bech from Regnecenteralen (Copenhagen) gave a lecture in Turku where he spoke about the Danish experiences. They also arranged a programming course

---

[10] Turun yliopiston konsistorin kokouksen pöytäkirja 1.10.1959. Liite 1. Isännöitsijä H. W. Gullestad: EMMA - suunnitelma Bergenissä. Archive of University of Turku. [Protocol of meeting of Turku University Council. Appendix 1. Emma – a plan in Bergen]. See also IBM - Elektronisten tietojenkäsittelykoneiden käyttöalat. Esite. Liite Turun yliopiston konsistorin kokouksen pöytäkirjaan 1.10.1959. Archive of University of Turku [IBM – Areas of EDP Machines. Appendix of; Protocol of meeting of Turku University Council]. Turun Matematiikkakoneyhdistys - Abo Matematikförening, Toimintakertomus vuodelta 1959. Turussa 4.3.1960 K. V. Laurikainen, [Annual report of Turku Mathematical Machine Society 1959]; Brosveet 1999; Paju 2002, 192-197; Häggman 1997, 121-124.

[11] Paju 2002, 171-173.

[12] Muistio Laskentakeskuksen järjestämisestä Turkuun. Aikaisemmin kertyneen aineiston sekä apulaisprof. K. V. Laurikaisen ja fil. lis. K. Loimarannan kanssa käytyjen neuvottelujen pohjalta laatinut 2.11.1959. Dipl. Ins. A. Rantanen. [Memo of Organising Computing Centre in Turku. Reported by A. Rantanen based on earlier collected material and negations with K. V. Laurikainen and K. Loimaranta]. Archive of Tor-Erik Lassenius. See also *Turun Sanomat* 19.12.1959.

that spring. The teachers were from the ABN Company but paid by the Wenner-Gren Centre Foundation.[13] To the contemporary eye, it must have seemed inspiring that a lively transfer of knowledge was emerging.

All help was of course welcomed in the universities of Turku, which had scant resources for experimenting new and costly ideas or equipment. The society in Turku compared the Wegematic 1000 with the IBM 650 computer, which had become the well-known "standard" for comparison. In their reports, they found the Wegematic computer—with the necessary IBM punched card machines (for input and output of data) —suitable for their needs. Moreover, the magnet tape memory seemed desirable.[14] For the companies in the society, this idea of a computing centre was probably an essentially safe and inexpensive way of studying the new expert area and educating computing specialists of the future.

After the Wenner-Gren Foundation made the offer, IBM made a counteroffer with its 1620 computer, promising all academic discounts, which was typical of IBM's international business strategy at the time. Understandably, however, they chose the Wegematic 1000. The heads of the society in Turku put forward three arguments for this solution. First, the Wegematic 1000 was perceived (and marketed) as a general-purpose computer and it was suitable for both scientific computing and commercial data processing. Second, it was an unconditional donation and was therefore inexpensive. Third, the donator guaranteed the delivery of the computer by the following summer (1960). This was faster than IBM could promise.[15]

---

[13] Ruotsin ja Tanskan laskukeskuksista. Selostuksen laati 8. - 14.1.1960 suoritetun tutustumismatkan perusteella K. V. Laurikainen [On Computing Centres in Sweden and Denmark. Reported by K. Laurikainen]; Raportti 2.10.1959. Kokoajana mahdollisesti A. Rantanen. USA:n ja Kanadan elektroniset laskentakeskukset huhtikuussa 1958. [Report on Computing Centres in USA and Canada in April 1958 by A. Rantanen]. Source *Computers and Automation*, July 1958; Pöytäkirja Turun Matematiikkakoneyhdistyksen kokouksesta 25.3.1960, [Protocol of meeting of the Society's board]; Turun Matematiikkakoneyhdistys - Abo Matematikförening, Toimintakertomus vuodelta 1960. Turussa 23.4.1961 K. V. Laurikainen, sihteeri, [Annual report of Turku Mathematical Machine Society 1960]. Archive of the Turku Computing Centre.

[14] Muistio Laskentakeskuksen järjestämisestä Turkuun. Aikaisemmin kertyneen aineiston sekä apulaisprof. K. V. Laurikaisen ja fil. lis. K. Loimarannan kanssa käytyjen neuvottelujen pohjalta laatinut 2.11.1959. Dipl. Ins. A. Rantanen. [Memo of Organising Computing Centre in Turku. Reported by A. Rantanen based on earlier collected material and negations with K. V. Laurikainen and K. Loimaranta]. Archive of Tor-Erik Lassenius.

[15] Turun Matematiikkakoneyhdistys - Abo Matematikförening, Toimintasuunnitelmaluonnos vuodelle 1960. Turussa 14.12.1959, [Turku Mathematical Machine Society. Plan for the year 1960]. K. V. Laurikainen, sihteeri; Turun Matematiikkakoneyhdistys - Abo Matematikförening, Toimintakertomus vuodelta 1959. Turussa 4.3.1960 K. V. Laurikainen, sihteeri [Annual report of Turku Mathematical Machine Society 1959]; Wegematic 1000 Brochure. Archive of the Turku Computing Centre; Turun yliopisto samt Stiftelsen för Åbo Akademi. Lahjoituskirje Stiftelsen för Wenner-Gren Centeriltä.

3.   THE WEGEMATIC ARRIVES IN TURKU AND
         LOCAL CO-OPERATION TAKES SHAPE

The founding work for the Computer Centre started in 1960. Before the
computer arrived, they engaged and trained employees, they held more
information and programming courses for students and interested groups,
and set up a tentative organisation. (See Appendix 5—The Organisation of
Turku Computing Centre) Office space was also prepared at the University
of Turku. The preparations included negotiating with users (about usage
hour reservation for the computer) and customers as well as taking out bank
loans. Later, the loans become a serious burden on the centre.

To prepare for the use of a computing centre in Turku, the Mathematical
Machine Society transformed into "The Research Foundation for Applied
Mathematics and Data Processing," hereafter referred to as the Foundation.
In September 1960, Laurikainen told the Foundation board that program
exchange had begun. They received some programs from Sweden and
several others in Turku. However, at this point they did not receive the
Wegematic 1000 computer as promised. The shipment of it was delayed
partially because some other universities were placed ahead in the Axel
Wenner-Gren Centre Foundation's donation schedule.[16]

The Wegematic computer finally arrived in November 1960 and
officially became operational on First of December.[17] Consequently, 1961
was the first fully operational year for the centre. Collaborating companies
in the Turku region used and programmed Wegematic and other machines
mostly with the help of Centre's staff, but the most important users
programmed the machines by themselves. The organisations involved had
reserved usage hours in advance. (For a more detailed illustration of the
usage in 1961-1962, see Appendices 3 and 4.)

Stockholm 19.1.1960. Birger Strid, [Donation letter of Wegematic 1000 Computer from
the Wenner-Gren Centre Foundation]. Archive of the Turku Computing Centre.

[16] An another founded new organisation was called to "The Turku Computing Centre's
Supporters' Association". Sovelletun Matematiikan ja Tietojenkäsittelyalan
Tutkimussäätiön hallituksen ensimmäinen kokous 9.5.1960, pöytäkirja. Turun
Laskukeskuksen arkisto [First meeting of the board of The Research Foundation for
Applied Mathematics and Data Processing]. Turun Laskukeskuksen kannatusyhdistyksen
perustamisasiakirjat. Turun Laskukeskuksen arkisto. See also *Turun Sanomat* 6.3.1960;
Wegematic 1000 Memories, an interview with Alfons Ahlnäs
(http://www.abo.fi/~atorn/History/Alfons1.html). For example one installation was
donated to the University of Oslo, Norway during the year 1960 (see *Datahistorien ved
Universitet I Oslo. Fra begynnelsen til ut I syttiårene. Temanummer Fra Usit,* juni 1996.)

[17] Ajopäiväkirja 1.12.1960. Ajopäiväkirja joulukuu 1960-elokuu 1961. Åbo Akademin
laskentakeskuksen arkisto [User logs December 1960 – August 1961].

Picture 1. Professor Kalervo V. Laurikainen and the computer installation in the Turku Computing Centre in 1960 or 1961. *(Courtesy of University of Turku Computing Centre.)*

4.   WORK FOR NORDSAC

The year 1960 was also important for the birth of the Alwac-Wegematic user community in North America. Luckily, this new activity was noticed in the Nordic region. North American Alwac users held a meeting in Oregon, USA. Klaus Appel, from the University of Uppsala, who was temporarily at University of Florida, participated in the meeting. He reported to Sweden on the discussed topics. They included the further development of the Alwac, programming, and program exchange. Firma Teledata, Bo Nymanbolagen supported Appel financially. This support had made his participation in the conference possible.[18]

In early summer of 1961, Bror Stenvik (from Turku) made a tour of Sweden and Norway in order to create closer co-operation and more efficient program exchange between Wegematic and Alwac computer centres in the Nordic countries. Based on these negotiations, one of the many points he suggested (as discussion topics) in the report was founding an association for the Nordic Wegematic and Alwac users, which was later to become known as NordSAC (Nordisk Samarbetsgrupp för Alwac-Wegematic Computers). They discussed this and other topics in two meetings held in Oslo during the NordSAM Congress 18-22.8.[19]

---

[18] 4.6.1960. Rapport Från Alwac Users' Associations Konferens den 9-11 maj 1960 i Oregon [Report from Alwas Users' Association's Conference]. Archive of the Turku Computing Centre.

[19] Bror Stenvik: Studie- och diskussionsresa i Sverige och Norge 29.5. - 9.6.1961 [Report on Educational and Discussion field trip to Sweden and Norway]; Protokollar fört vid Lunch-möten 19.8.1961 och 21.8.1961 i Oslo, [Protocols of two lunch meetings]. NordSACin

In September 1961, the Foundation board in Turku decided that Bror
Stenvik would replace Laurikainen as the head of the computing centre,
because Laurikainen had moved to University of Helsinki.[20] Nevertheless,
Laurikainen reported on the discussions that had taken place in the founding
meeting of NordSAC in Oslo. There, after discussing Wegematic program
exchange, they appointed a Committee to make a proposal concerning the
guidelines for the Nordic co-operation. They also acknowledged a need for
a centre of these operations. The Computing Centre in Turku volunteered
for this task.[21]

At the end of 1961, the co-operation between various users was still
unorganised. The owner of the ABN factory had changed and this caused
the Wegematic users to request that the technical service could continue as
before. Laurikainen had talked to Birger Strid, Wenner-Gren's trusted man
and other persons in Wenner-Gren Centre, but they found no solution.[22]

Several NordSAC meetings had taken place in the autumn of 1961 and
spring of 1962. Important questions included administration aid from the
Wenner-Gren Centre for NordSAC, the creation of a service centre, and
program exchange. In the spring of 1962, a service group began work, with
a Wegematic 1000 computer, in the Royal Institute of Technology in
Stockholm (Kungliga Tekniska Högskola). According to the company's
representative, they had to use the computer for trying out ferrite core
memory and magnetic tape units and for training technical personnel for the
NordSAC members.[23]

---

vuosikertomukset, kokouspöytäkirjat ja kirjeenvaihto. [See also Annual reports, letters and
meeting minutes of NordSAC]. Archive of the Turku Computing Centre.

[20] The Wenner-Gren Foundation donated also an another Wegematic computer into Finland,
probably thanks to Professor Laurikainen. That installation was taken into operation under
the department of nuclear physics, at the University of Helsinki in spring 1961. The two
Finnish Wegematic centres agreed to co-operate but we do not know how true this cooperation became. (Toimintasuunnitelma v:ksi 1961. Hyväksytty säätiön hallituksen
kokouksessa 19.12.1960 [Plan for the year 1961]; Helsingin yliopiston Wegematic 1000 -
koneen huoltosopimus. Turku 11.4.1961, Helsinki 13.5.1961. [Service and Maintenance
contract between Turku and Helsinki Centres]. Archive of the Turku Computing Centre.
See also   Helsingin yliopiston laskentakeskuksen ja fysiikan laskentatoimiston
toimintakertomus vuodelta 1980 [Annual report of the Computer Centre in University of
Helsinki 1980].)

[21] Sovelletun matematiikan ja tietojenkäsittelyalan tutkimussäätiön hallituksen kokouksen
pöytäkirja 8.9.1961, [Protocol of meeting of the Foundation's board]. Archive of the
Turku Computing Centre.

[22] Sovelletun matematiikan ja tietojenkäsittelyalan tutkimussäätiön hallituksen kokouksen
pöytäkirja 15.12.1961, [Protocol of meeting of the Foundation's board]. Archive the of
Turku Computing Centre. Birger Strid was invited to Turku in January 1962.

[23] See for instance Protokoll 28.-29.9.1962, hållet vid NordSAC-möte i Wenner-Gren
Center, Stockholm, den 28/29 september 1962; 5.11.1962 Referat fra styremøte nr 1.;

Finally, in the autumn of 1962, the rules for NordSAC were accepted and Klaus Appel was elected chair. Later that autumn, Mr Wenner-Gren died. Subsequently, the ABN Company proclaimed that it wanted to stop all forms of cooperation that were a financial burden on the company. In the summer of 1963, Appel refused to continue leading the cooperation due to lack of interest among the NordSAC participants.[24]

In Turku, the Foundation then wrote a report in which they summarised how they had benefited from the Nordic co-operation. The points included the following: a) the exchange of programs, b) the receiving of information regarding the computer, c) the supply of spare parts after the producer had gone out of business, d) the creating of a service group (paid by the ABN Company), and e) general benefits of the Nordic cooperation.[25] After NordSAC, Nordic cooperation continued within other organisations (such as NordSAM) and through personal contacts.

5. THE PHASING OUT OF THE CENTRE, 1962-1964

In Turku, Wegematic had seemed to offer an interesting Nordic alternative. For Professor Laurikainen, it even opened up possibilities for gaining a key national position within computing with help of governmental funding. The period from 1961 to early 1962 was central in this respect. During those months Laurikainen, Bror Stenvik, and other people of the Centre negotiated actively with national and international actors in the computing branch. The Research Foundation for Applied Mathematics and Data Processing sponsored new kind of education as well, namely the first system design courses in Finland in 1962. The new Wegematic centre and its computer had a certain image and status value. The computer functioned as a particular, material symbol of progress and modernity transferred in the local sphere.[26]

18.4.1963 NordSAC. Fulcrum Aktiebolag utlägg t.o.m. 31.3.1963. Archive of the Turku Computing Centre.

[24] Klaus Appel: Till medlemmarna i NordSAC, kirje 24.6.1963, [Letter for the members of NordSAC]. Archive of the Turku Computing Centre.

[25] Säätiön hallituksen kokouksen pöytäkirja 6.6.1963, [Protocol of meeting of the Foundation's board]. Archive of the Turku Computing Centre.

[26] K.V. Laurikainen: Säätiön toiminnan laajenemisesta v. 1962. Luultavasti joulukuu 1961. Archive of the Turku Computing Centre. [On Expanding the field of the Foundation. Written by K. V. Laurikainen probably in December 1961]. For more on the symbolical value of computer technology see Suominen 2000, 66-78; Suominen 2003, 64-67.

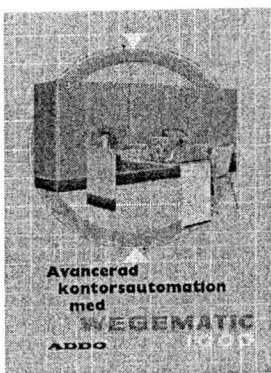

Picture 2. Cover of a Wegematic 1000 brochure in the early 1960s.
Archive of the Turku Computing Centre.

Several interrelated factors led to changes in the situation for the centre. These included: 1) The Wegematic computer was not effective and stable enough for all-purpose usage, so it was less useful than expected. This resulted in less income generation and an inability to pay back the loans. 2) The development of Wegematic computers declined because of the problems the manufacturer faced. Consequently, it never delivered the promised magnetic tape units. The Nordic collaboration within NordSAC was the primary means of resolving these problems. However, there were still some other factors bearing consideration. 3) An important and well-known "primus motor" of the Centre, Professor Laurikainen moved to Helsinki. 4) Manufacturers, like IBM, and user organisations presented new applications and second-generation computers, which confirmed the impression that Wegematic was completely out-dated (not everyone agreed with this in the universities). 5) The Wegematic computer had ceased to be unique on the national level. IBM, and its Finnish competitor Finnish Cable Works,[27] built up their own centres and delivered several machines to customers.[28] One can say that both the technical and symbolical value of the Wegematic computer and the centre decreased quite rapidly during the year 1962.

Already in late 1961, there were discussions about the possibility of purchasing a new mainframe for the centre in Turku. This proved to be financially impossible and the installation expanded only with a tabulating machine. During the winter 1962-1963, a committee for acquiring a new

---

[27] Finnish Cable Works, the predecessor of Nokia Electronics and Computers, imported and used for example Elliott and Siemens and later Bull machineries (see Aaltonen 1993).

[28] Suominen – Paju – Törn 2000, 37-40.

computer was established. Its purpose was to find a solution fulfilling the needs of both the commercial data processing and the scientific computing. The committee comprised mainly Ericsson, IBM, and Finnish Cable Works (they had sponsored the system design course as well). The competition between IBM and Cable Works offered considerable potential for resolving the difficult situation to the benefit of the Turku computing centre.[29]

Finally, in the summer of 1963, IBM decided to build up its own computing centre in Turku. The Wegematic users managed to make a deal with IBM who promised to take care of the unpaid loans and serve the old customers. The IBM service bureau, with an IBM 1401 mainframe, opened in spring 1964 and the Wegematic Centre closed.[30] The two universities used the 1401 computer as well, but soon together purchased their own machines and continued cooperating.

6. CONCLUSION

In this paper, we have argued that the founding and operating of the Turku Computing Centre with the Wegematic 1000 computer needed, and even forced, the actors, that is local municipal, businesses and the universities, to negotiate and co-operate in novel ways. The centre also benefited from Nordic trans-local co-operation with other computing centres, mostly with those using Wegematic computers. The Nordic co-operation was soon organised within the NordSAC user association (1961-1963). Its operation included program exchange, organising joint courses, as well as demanding a shared service centre and other negotiations with the Wegematic manufacturer, the ABN Company in Tyresö, near Stockholm.

[29] Säätiön toimintakertomus vuodelta 1963 [Annual Report of the Foundation 1963]; Säätiön hallituksen kokouksen pöytäkirja 17.12.1963 [Protocol of meeting of the Foundation's board]; Omaisuustase, kevät 1964 [Balance of Capital, spring 1964]; IBM tietojenkäsittelyjärjestelmämainos [Brochure of IBM]; Ehdotus Turun Yliopiston ja Åbo Akademin 1620 tietokoneistoksi 6.5.1963; [Proposal for IBM 1620 installation for the University of Turku and Åbo Akademi] BULL Gamma 30-koneen tarjous 12.-13.2.1963. Bengt Widing, Kurt Wikstedt [Offer for BULL Gamma 30 installation]; Konekomitean kokousten pöytäkirjat ja koneita koskeva vertailumateriaali. Kevät 1963, [Meeting minutes and comparison material of the New Machine Committee]. Archive of the Turku Computing Centre.

[30] Ehdotus Turun Yliopiston ja Åbo Akademin 1620 tietokoneistoksi 6.5.1963 [Proposal for IBM 1620 installation for University of Turku and Åbo Akademi University]; Diskussion den 11.6.1963 med IBM/dir. Dickman [Report on discussions with Director Dickman of IBM in Finland]; Turun Laskukeskuksen toimintakertomus 1.1.1964 - 25.5.1965. [Annual Report of Turku Computing Centre 1.1.1964-25.5.1965]; Sopimusluonnos IBM:n ja Laskukeskuksen välillä [Draft of contract between IBM and Turku Computing Centre]. Archive of the Turku Computing Centre.

Further, we argue that strategic collaboration was prevalent among those players regarded as being economically and symbolically strong at the time. However, it was also emblematic to seek alternatives and counterbalances in the rapidly transforming field of computing and data processing technology. The collaboration between the powerful bodies affected the ways in which they organised work; they also combined technological requirements as well as ways of organising training.

In this paper, we have focused on examining the strategic level of collaboration, planning, and negotiating. This does not mean that we should forget the tactical level, for example the daily work conducted on these computers. Questions that remain unanswered include the following. How did the people in computing centres work on a daily basis? Which way the computer work was perceived by the users and the people in the local community? We propose that researchers should also try answering these kinds of questions, but perhaps with other sources and with other research methods than the ones used in this paper.

We conclude that Turku's Wegematic story is important for understanding the early phases of computerisation in Finland, at least outside the capital region of the country. Leaning on this Finnish case, we suggest that the same could be true for the Wegematic cases in Sweden and Norway. Further, we suggest that the Wegematic stories in Sweden and Norway might be worth studying to improve our understanding of several aspects of the Nordic trans-local interaction in the emerging field of computing. These aspects include education, the start of computing in universities, businesses and local administration and professional development. We think applying a comparative method to these Nordic developments would have particular value. There is plenty of research undone in the Nordic history of computing and there is no reason why the history of the Wegematic could not serve us with good material for studies on many of these questions.

REFERENCES

Archival Material

Tietotekniikan liiton arkisto [Finnish Information Processing Association]
Turun yliopiston arkisto [University of Turku]
Turun yliopiston ATK-keskuksen arkisto [University of Turku, Computing Centre]
Turun Laskukeskuksen arkisto [Archives of the Turku Computing Centre (Collected and saved by Jaakko Suominen & Aimo Törn)]
Turun Sanomat [Local newspaper]
Tor-Erik Lasseniuksen arkisto [Private archive of Tor-Erik Lassenius]
Åbo Akademin arkisto [Åbo Akademi University]
Åbo Akademin laskentakeskuksen arkisto [Åbo Akademi, Computing Centre]

Interviews and Letters

Janis Bubenko Jr.: "Alwac Memories". E-mail to Jaakko Suominen 6th January 2003.
Erik Grannas, phone interview 23.8.2000 (Petri Paju).
Ilkka Junnila, e-mail to Petri Paju in 1999.
Pentti Kaarnisto, phone interview 23.8.2000 (Petri Paju).
Veikko Oula, phone interview 23.8.2000 (Petri Paju).
Aarni Perko, letter to Aimo Törn 13.8.2000.
Wegematic Memories. Collected by Aimo Törn [http://www.abo.fi/~atorn/History/Page31.html].

Websites

The ALWEG Archives [http://www.alweg.com/]. Viewed 1.8.2000.
Electronic Computers Within The Ordnance Corps, Appendix VII -- Approximate Costs [http://ftp.arl.army.mil/~mike/comphist/61ordnance/app7.html]. Viewed 10.9.2000.
Encyclopedia of Computer Science 4th Edition. Timeline of Computing. [http://www.macmillan-reference.co.uk/science/ComputerScienceTimeline12.htm]. Viewed 10.9.2000.
Det startet i 1919. Electrolux Konsernets Historie [http://www.electrolux.no/corporate/history/overtheyears.html]. Viewed 10.9.2000.
Törn, Aimo: Early History of Computing in Turku. [http://www.abo.fi/~atorn/History/Contents.html]. 1999-2003.

Newspapers and Magazines

Apu 1960
Reikäkortti 1956 (Punched Card journal)
Turun Sanomat 1959-1962
Uusi Aura 1960
Åbo Underrättelser 1960

Literature

Aaltonen, Aarre: "Nokian elektroniikkateollisuuden synty: nuorten kokeilijoiden ja keksijöiden pajasta huipputeollisuudeksi. [The Birth of Electronics Industry of Nokia, in Finnish]", in Martti Tienari, ed., *Tietotekniikan alkuvuodet Suomessa*, [The First Years of Information Technology in Finland, in Finnish.] Helsinki 1993, 108-126.
Bohman, Ragnar & Dahlberg, Ingrid: *Dansen kring guldkalven* [Dancing around the golden calf, in Swedish], Askild&Kärnekull. 1975.
Brosveet, Jarle: "IBM Salesman Meets Norwegian Tax Collector: Computer Entrepreneurs in the Making." *IEEE Annals of the History of Computing* 21(1999): 2, 5-13).

Datahistorien ved Universitet 1 Oslo. Fra begynnelsen til ut 1 syttiårene. Temanummer Fra Usit, juni 1996.

De Geer, Hans: *På väg till datasamhället. Datatekniken i politiken 1946-1963.* [On the way to information society. Information Technology in Politics 1946-1963, in Swedish]. Stockholm 1992.

Heide, Lars: Hulkort og EDB i Danmark 1911-1970, [Punched card machines and electronic data processing in Denmark 1911-1970, in Danish]. Århus 1996.

Helsingin yliopiston laskentakeskuksen ja fysiikan laskentatoimiston toimintakertomus vuodelta 1980. [Annual report of the Computer Centre in University of Helsinki 1980, in Finnish.]

Häggman, Kai: *Suurten muutosten Suomessa. Kansaneläkelaitos 1937-1997.* [Finland in Great Changes, Social Insurance Institution 1937-1997, in Finnish.] Helsinki 1997.

Klüver, Per V.: From Research Institute to Computer Company: Regnecentralen 1946-1964. *IEEE Annals of the History of Computing* Vol. 21, No. 2, 1999.

Laurikainen, Kalervo: *Fyysikon tie.* [A Path of a Physician, in Finnish] Helsinki, Hyvinkää 1982.

Lindqvist, Svante: "Forskningens fasader: Wenner-Gren Center som symbol för svensk vetenskap [Façade of the reseach: Wenner-Gren Center as a symbol for Swedish science, in Swedish]," Lychnos 1997.

Paju, Petri: *Ensimmäinen suomalainen tietokone ESKO ja 1950-luvun suunnitelma kansallisesta laskentakeskuksesta,* [The First Finnish Computer ESKO and a 1950's Plan of a National Computing Center, in Finnish]. Licensiate Thesis, Cultural History. University of Turku, Finland 2002.

Peleikis, Anja: "The Emergence of a Translocal Community. The Case of a South Lebanese Village and its Migrant Connections to Ivory Coast." Cahiers d'etudes la Méditerranée orientale et le monde turco-iranien. No 30, juin-décembre 2000. [http://www.ceri-sciencespo.com/publica/cemoti/textes30 /peleikis.pdf].

Sormunen, Tapio: *Keskinäinen Vakuutusyhtiö Sampo osana Suomen vahinkovakuutustoimintaa 1909-1970,* [Insurance Company Sampo as a Part of Indemnity Insurance in Finland 1909-1970, in Finnish]. Licensiate Thesis, Finnish History. University of Turku, Finland 1983.

Suominen, Jaakko – Paju, Petri – Törn, Aimo: "Varsinaissuomalainen linja Suomen tietoteknistymisen alkuvaiheissa. Turun laskukeskus ja Wegematic 1000 tietojenkäsittelykone [Early Computerization in Finland, 1959-1964. A Study of the Beginnings of Computer Center in Turku and Wegematic 1000 Electronic Data Processing Machine, in Finnish]". Tekniikan Waiheita 18(2000): 3, 24-46. [Webified version: http://www.tuug.fi/~jaakko/tutkimus/wegematic/]

Suominen, Jaakko: *Sähköaivo sinuiksi, tietokone tutuksi. Tietotekniikan kulttuurihistoriaa* [Getting Familiar with the Electronic Brain, Getting to Know the Computer, in Finnish]. Publications of the Research Center for Contemporary Culture, No. 67. Jyväskylä 2000.

Suominen, Jaakko: "Koneen kokemus. Tietoteknistyvä kulttuuri modernisoituvassa Suomessa 1920-luvulta 1970-luvulle." [Experiences with machines. Computerised culture in the process of Finnish modernisation from the 1920s to the 1970s, in Finnish], Tampere 2003.

Tienari, Martti (edit.): *Tietotekniikan alkuvuodet Suomessa.* [The First Years of Information Technology in Finland, in Finnish.] Helsinki 1993.

Törn, Aimo: *Early History of Computing in Turku, 1959-1964.* Rapporter från datacentralen vid Åbo Akademi. 1.12.2000.

Vehviläinen, Marja: "Gender and Computing in Retrospect: The Case of Finland." *IEEE Annals of the History of Computing,* Vol, 21, No. 2, 1999, 44-51.

Wenner-Gren, Axel L.: *Vetoomus jokaiseen.* [Appeal for Everyone, in Finnish] Suom. Väinö
J. Vatanen. Helsinki 1937.
Wennerholm, Staffan: "Vetenskapen (och publiken) i framtidens samhälle. Om en
forskningspolitikens konferens i Wenner-Gren Center 1963 [Science (and the public) in
future society. On a conference of research policy in the Wenner-Gren Center 1963, in
Swedish]," *Lychnos* 2002, 196-223.

APPENDIX 1

A Brief Chronology of Wegematic

1952	Axel Wenner-Gren buys Research Logistics (USA). The company starts to construct Alwac computers (Axel Leonard Wenner-Gren Automatic Computers)
1954	The first Alwac III computer is produced and followed by the Alwac III-E model (in 1955)
1958	Research Logistics closes down and is sold
Spring 1959	Information and computer programming course held in Turku
	NordSAM (Nordiskt Symposium över Användningen av Matematikmaskiner) 1959 in May
Autumn 1959	The Turku Mathematical Machine Society comprising of the universities, the city of Turku and ten local enterprises plans the purchasing computer
October 1959	Announcement of the possibility of obtaining a Wegematic 1000 computer to Turku
1959-1960	Bo Nyman Ab begins to build Wegematic 1000 computers, based on Alwac III-E model (produced since 1955)
19th January 1960	The official donation letter of the computer by the Wenner-Gren Centre Foundation
4th May 1960	North American Alwac users meet in Oregon State College, USA
Spring 1960	Preparing office space (130 square metres at the University of Turku) for the Centre
	The first employers are engaged
	The Turku Mathematical Machine Society ends its work
	Turku Computing Centre's Supporters' Association is formed
	The Research Foundation for Applied Mathematics and Data Processing takes control of the computer and the Computing Centre
	Programming and information courses taught in Turku
November 1960	The Wegematic arrives in Turku
1st December 1960	The first official program is operated with the Wegematic at the Turku Wegematic Centre
20th December 1960	The Wegematic computer and the Centre are introduced to local press
20th January 1961	The official opening of Turku Computing Centre

Spring 1961	Another Wegematic Computer is taken into operation at the department of nuclear physics, at the University of Helsinki and the two centres agree to co-operate on use and service
8-22 August 1961	NordSAC (Nordisk samarbetsgrupp för Alwac-Wegematic Computers) is formed in NordSAM 1961 meeting
Autumn 1961	The head of the centre, Professor Laurikainen moves to Helsinki Some early investigations into purchasing a new computer, which is soon learned to be financially impossible The machinery is completed with several accounting machines like tabulator
Winter 1961-1962	The Centre negotiates about co-operation with the Finnish Cable Works and its computer centre
Autumn 1962	The first course for system design near Helsinki and is funded by Foundation and its sponsors
September 1962	The rules of NordSAC are approved and Klaus Appel from Uppsala is elected as the chairman
November 1962	Axel Wenner-Gren dies and the Wegematic manufacturer, ABN (Bo Nyman Ab) goes bankruptcy soon after
Spring 1963	A committee is organized for preparing the purchasing of a new computer to Turku. Consultations takes place with IBM, Cable Works and L. M. Ericsson
Summer 1963	IBM decides to set up its own service centre in Turku
June 1963	NordSAC ends its activities
Autumn 1963	IBM promises to take care of the loans (6 million FIM in the beginning) and the customers of the Wegematic Centre
Spring 1964	IBM opens its local computing centre in Turku with a 1401 mainframe. The Wegematic is shut down and stored.

APPENDIX 2

Wegematic 1000 Technology an a Nutshell

The Swedish businessman Axel Leonard Wenner-Gren's company Logistics Research, Inc in California had built computers since 1952, and the predecessor to Wegematic 1000 the Alwac III-E since 1955. The price for Alvac III-E was $76 950 as compared to $55 000 for IBM 610, and $182 000 for an IBM 650 with tapes [http://ftp.arl.army.mil/~mike/comphist/61ordnance/app7.html]. The Alwac III-E has even been characterized as an early minicomputer   [http://www.macmillan-reference.co.uk/science/ComputerScienceTimeline12.htm]. The first installations were at military units and universities in Canada and the USA. The Alwac III-E was "a first generation" computer (1950-1960). These computers were characterized by the use of vacuum tubes as their switching technology. The most popular memory technique including the prime memory was the rotating drum.

The production of Alwac III-E was shifted to Sweden and under the name Wegematic 1000, it was manufactured by Bo Nyman AB in Bollmora. The processing unit comprised of an operating board and some six meters of racks holding a vertically oriented magnetic drum memory (3 600 rev/min) with 261 channels (tracks), about 10 000 diodes and about 500 electron tubes on laminate circuit boards. The maximum energy consumption was about 15 kW/h. For administrative applications, punched cards were used as a secondary memory. For programs, paper tape was used for input (150 char/s) and output (50 char/s). Correcting program errors was made by cutting out part of the tape and taping in a new part.

The magnetic drum held four registers A-E (part of one channel), the working (prime) memory (four channels) and the main (secondary) memory (256 channels). Each track could store 32 words plus a check word, each word consisting of 32 bits plus a sign bit. The prime memory consisted of four channels with a multiple of read/write heads. The 128 words in the prime memory were addressable half-word wise in hexadecimal from 00 to FF. An addition (subtraction) took 1 ms, a multiplication (division) 16 ms, excluding fetch times. A comparison took 0.5 ms. Fetch times for data and instructions in prime memory were on the average 4 ms and 2 ms respectively, for secondary memory 8 ms. Copying from secondary memory to a prime memory channel and execution of code in another prime memory channel could take place in parallel.

The operating board consisted of a typewriter, paper tape units, and a console containing some arrays of small lights and switches making it possible to view and change the content of a word in the prime memory or in the registers. As an alternative to the normal processing mode, a one-step processing mode could be chosen, which made it possible to check the execution step by step.

Programming was made with a machine code with absolute addresses using hexadecimal representation. There was no floating-point operation; the programmer had to keep track of the exponent for each data stored and explicitly make the shifts necessary for retaining the accuracy in the arithmetic operations. The internal representation was binary and the transformations from decimal to binary on input and from binary to decimal on output had to be included in the program code. A word normally contained two instructions, so for instance 794B 614F means: first, copy to A (79) the content of 4B, and then add to A (61) the content of 4F.

APPENDIX 3

Hours of Real Usage 1960-1962 [363]

Computer Use 1960	Computer Use 1961	Computer Use 1962	Service, repairs, and testing 1961	Service, repairs, and testing 1962
Couple of hours for testing	1094 h 26 min (Univ. 267 h 44 min, others 826 h 42 min)	1841 h 38 min (Univ. 315 h 44 min, others 1525 h 54 min)	793 h	629 h 10 min

[363] Source: Laskukeskuksen toimintakertomukset 1960-1962, [Annual Reports of the Turku Computing Centre].

APPENDIX 4

Computer Users (Other Than Universities) and Reserved Hours [364]

User	Reserved hours 1960 (not used)	Reserved hours 1961	Reserved hours 1962	Reserved hours 1963 (no document about usage)
Huhtamäki Oy Food industry etc., large punched card operations? Decreased usage	312	624	312 (624)	
Paraisten Kalkkivuori Oy – Pargas Kalkberg Ab Mining corporation, decreased usage	200	400	400	240
Wärtsilä Oy. Crichton Vulcan Ship builder, docks measurements of strength and profitability, increased usage	20	50	75	150
The City of Turku The computer was used mainly for billing customers in the electric department, increased usage	20	40	70	320 (office of measuring 100, technical departments 220)
Raision Tehtaat Agriculture, food processing	6	10	2	2
Neste Oy Oil company	5	10	10	10
Verdandi Insurance company	1	1	5	10
Lounais-Suomen Sähkö Electric company, database of 5000 punched cards, billing?	18	30	30	46
Lounais-Suomen Osuusteurastamo Slaughterhouse		5	5	
Oy Juurikassokeri Food industry, sugar manufacturing			30	30
Ky Kumituote Rubber productions			25	
Keskusosuusliike Hankkija Agriculture, wholesale, customer databases, stores, accounting in general?			100	
Professor Laurikainen	1			

[364] Source: Laskukeskuksen toimintakertomukset 1960-1962, [Annual Reports of the Turku Computing Centre].

APPENDIX 5.

The Organisation of the Turku Computing Centre*

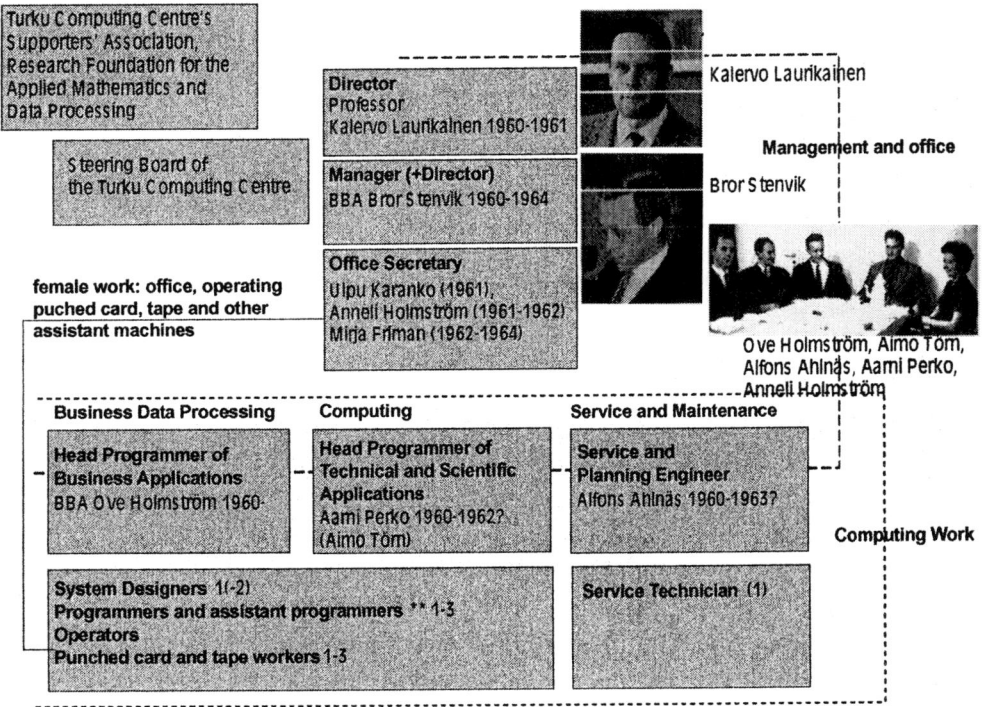

Turku Computing Centre's Supporters' Association, Research Foundation for the Applied Mathematics and Data Processing

Steering Board of the Turku Computing Centre

Director
Professor
Kalervo Laurikainen 1960-1961

Kalervo Laurikainen

Management and office

Manager (+Director)
BBA Bror Stenvik 1960-1964

Bror Stenvik

female work: office, operating puched card, tape and other assistant machines

Office Secretary
Ulpu Karanko (1961),
Anneli Holmström (1961-1962)
Mirja Friman (1962-1964)

Ove Holmström, Aimo Törn, Alfons Ahlnäs, Aarni Perko, Anneli Holmström

Business Data Processing

Head Programmer of Business Applications
BBA Ove Holmström 1960-

Computing

Head Programmer of Technical and Scientific Applications
Aarni Perko 1960-1962?
(Aimo Törn)

Service and Maintenance

Service and Planning Engineer
Alfons Ahlnäs 1960-1963?

Computing Work

System Designers 1(-2)
Programmers and assistant programmers ** 1-3
Operators
Punched card and tape workers 1-3

Service Technician (1)

December 1960: 5 staff members
December 1961: 5-7 staff members (estimation)
December 1962: 9 staff members

* There was no official or stable organization table.
This one is a reconstruction based on the archival material.
** Tasks of system design, programming or operating machines were not strictly separated and neither was the work done in the office and assisting in the operating the machines.

APPENDIX 6.

Major Computing Centres and Projects in the Nordic Countries in the late 1950s Reported by prof. Laurikainen in Turku

Finland
  Committee for Mathematical Machines (1954-1960, ESKO)
  Post-Office Bank, Helsinki (IBM 650 aka ENSI, 1958)

Sweden
  University of Lund (SMIL, a copy of BESK, 1956)
  ADB Institutet, Chalmers University of Technology, Gothenburg
  Ab Atomenergie, Stockholm
  Matematikmaskinnämnden, Stockholm (BESK, Alwac III-E...)
  (IBM Nordic Service Centre)
  University of Uppsala (Alwac III-E?)

Norway
  Bergen (IBM 650 aka EMMA)
  NCC, Oslo (Not mentioned by Laurikainen)

Denmark
  Regnecentralen (DASK), Copenhagen

APPENDIX 7.
Wegematic and ALWAC IIIE Centres in the Nordic Countries

Finland
Turku Computing Centre (ÅB (AB)*)
University of Helsinki (HY)

Sweden
ABN (manufacturer), Bollmora, Tyresö (TO)
Wegematic Service Group, Johanneshov (SG)
Karolinska Institutet, Stockholm (KI)
Kungliga Armétygförv., Stockholm (KA)
Royal University of Technology (KTH), Stockholm (KT)
Kvantkemiska Gruppen, University of Uppsala (KG)
ADB Institutet, Chalmers University of Technology, Gothenburg (AD)
Automatisk Databehandling Ab, Gothenburg (DA)
Malmö?

Norway
University of Oslo (OS)

Other
Gevaert, Belgium (BE)
Weizmann Institute, Israel (IS)
University of British Columbia, Canada (UB)
University of Florida, Gainesville, USA (TR?)

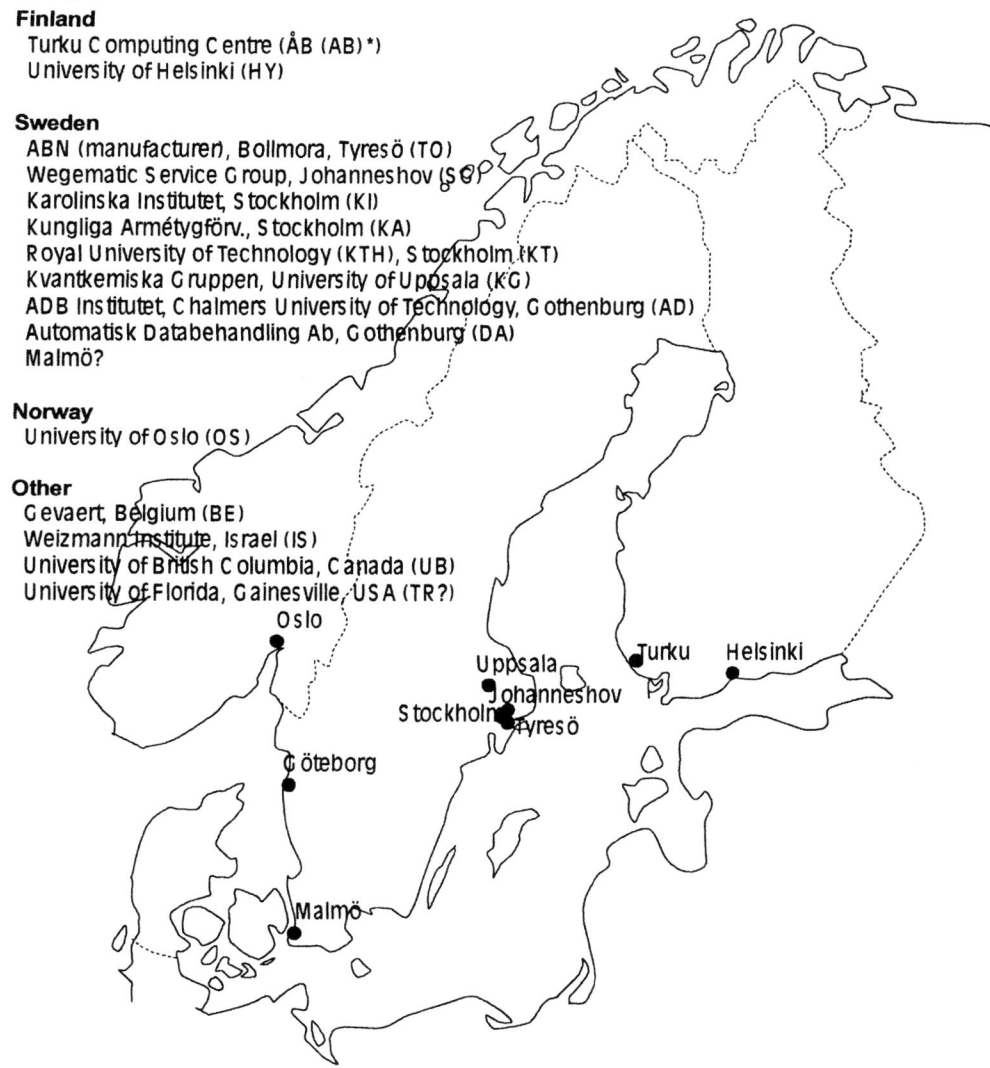

* These acronyms were used in the international co-operation, for instance program exhange, between the computing centres.

CONCLUDING REMARKS

Tomas Ohlin, Lars Heide, Niels Hoeg, Martti Tienari

tomas.ohlin@telo.se, heide.lpf@cbs.dk, nils.hoeg@hydro.com, tienari@cs.Helsinki.fi

Abstract: This is a summary of the First Conference on the History of Nordic
                 Computing. The summary highlights some of the remarks made by panelists
                 and audience participants. Prospects for a second conference on the same
                 theme look promising.

Key words: Nordic computing, history, HiNC1

In a final panel session chaired by Tomas Ohlin at the end of the HINC Conference, concluding remarks came from three different perspectives. The participants (mentioned above) commented from the historic perspective, from the industrial perspective and from the academic perspective, with comments stemming from what participants experienced during the conference.

The comments were brief. It became evident that the broad material and the discussions delivered earlier during the conference sessions could have quite different interpretations. This also did not come as a surprise to the participants. On the contrary, people stressed that history is born from descriptions that emerge from different perspectives.

At the end of the discussion, the audience suggested that the Trondheim HINC conference should be the first in a series of conferences and therefore, followed by other Nordic computing conferences. In this discussion, it was mentioned possible organizational updates concerning invitations, refereeing of contributions, and conference marketing. Future organizers should be mindful of conference economics and the possibilities of external support.

A second HINC conference would naturally concern itself with the development of telecommunications, which the Trondheim HINC did not, since it covered the time up to 1985. A second HINC could also stress historically important applications, education, and information society development to an increased degree. Participants discussed the possible time scope that such a conference would have. Noting the importance of cooperation among all partners with computing history interests, including many US concerns, participants stressed the importance of building active archives, backed by a living website.

The audience was quite active, forming a living dialogue with the panel participants. However, at the time of the Trondheim HINC conference, no plan existed for succeeding conferences. Further organizational efforts would address that issue.